Linguistic Categories, Language Description
and Linguistic Typology

Typological Studies in Language (TSL)
ISSN 0167-7373

A companion series to the journal Studies in Language. Volumes in this series are functionally and typologically oriented, covering specific topics in language by collecting together data from a wide variety of languages and language typologies.

For an overview of all books published in this series, please see benjamins.com/catalog/tsl

Editors

Spike Gildea
University of Oregon

Fernando Zúñiga
University of Bern

Editorial Board

Balthasar Bickel
Zurich

John Haiman
St Paul

Doris L. Payne
Eugene, OR

Bernard Comrie
Santa Barbara

Martin Haspelmath
Jena

Franz Plank
Konstanz

Denis Creissels
Lyon

Bernd Heine
Köln

Dan I. Slobin
Berkeley

William Croft
Albuquerque

Andrej A. Kibrik
Moscow

Sandra A. Thompson
Santa Barbara

Nicholas Evans
Canberra

Marianne Mithun
Santa Barbara

Carol Genetti
Santa Barbara

Volume 132

Linguistic Categories, Language Description and Linguistic Typology
Edited by Luca Alfieri, Giorgio Francesco Arcodia and Paolo Ramat

Linguistic Categories, Language Description and Linguistic Typology

Edited by

Luca Alfieri
University of Studies Guglielmo Marconi

Giorgio Francesco Arcodia
Ca' Foscari University of Venice

Paolo Ramat
University of Pavia

John Benjamins Publishing Company
Amsterdam / Philadelphia

The paper used in this publication meets the minimum requirements of the American National Standard for Information Sciences – Permanence of Paper for Printed Library Materials, ANSI z39.48-1984.

DOI 10.1075/tsl.132

Cataloging-in-Publication Data available from Library of Congress:
LCCN 2021003474 (PRINT) / 2021003475 (E-BOOK)

ISBN 978 90 272 0865 1 (HB)
ISBN 978 90 272 5994 3 (E-BOOK)

© 2021 – John Benjamins B.V.
No part of this book may be reproduced in any form, by print, photoprint, microfilm, or any other means, without written permission from the publisher.

John Benjamins Publishing Company · https://benjamins.com

Table of contents

CHAPTER 1
Linguistic categories, language description and linguistic typology –
An overview   1
   Luca Alfieri, Giorgio Francesco Arcodia & Paolo Ramat

CHAPTER 2
Towards standardization of morphosyntactic terminology for
general linguistics   35
   Martin Haspelmath

CHAPTER 3
Universal underpinnings of language-specific categories:
A useful heuristic for discovering and comparing categories
of grammar and beyond   59
   Martina Wiltschko

CHAPTER 4
Typology of functional domains   101
   Zygmunt Frajzyngier

CHAPTER 5
Theories of language, language comparison, and grammatical
description: Correcting Haspelmath   137
   Hans-Heinrich Lieb

CHAPTER 6
Comparative concepts are *not* a different kind of thing   211
   Tabea Reiner

CHAPTER 7
Essentials of the UNITYP research project: Attempt of an overview   249
   Hansjakob Seiler, Yoshiko Ono & Waldfried Premper

CHAPTER 8
The non-universality of linguistic categories: Evidence from
pluractional constructions   279
   Simone Mattiola

CHAPTER 9
Parts of speech, comparative concepts and Indo-European linguistics   313
    Luca Alfieri

CHAPTER 10
Verbal vs. nominal reflexive constructions: A categorial opposition?   367
    Nicoletta Puddu

CHAPTER 11
The category 'pronoun' in East and Southeast Asian languages,
with a focus on Japanese   389
    Federica Da Milano

Subject index   411

Language index   419

Author index   421

CHAPTER 1

Linguistic categories, language description and linguistic typology – An overview

Luca Alfieri, Giorgio Francesco Arcodia & Paolo Ramat*
University of Studies Guglielmo Marconi / Ca' Foscari University of Venice / University of Pavia

> In this paper we propose a critical discussion of the rationale for this volume. After a short introduction (Section 1), an outline of the long-standing opposition between language particular description and universal grammar in the history of the language sciences is provided (Section 2). This opposition indeed represents the substrate on which our 'comparative concepts debate' is based: a summary of the debate, both in the form it had in the LINGTYP mailing list (January / February 2016) and in the subsequent monographic issue of *Linguistic Typology* 2016, is offered in Section 3 and Section 4. Some critical consideration on the debate and on its relation with the various branches of linguistics are presented in Section 5. An overview of the papers included in the volume closes this introduction (Section 6).

1. Introduction: The rationale for this book

Few issues in the history of the language sciences have been an object of as much debate and controversies as linguistic categories. Although the reflection and discussion on the nature and on the universality of categories is about as old as linguistics, it can hardly be considered a settled issue: quite the contrary, linguistic categories still seem to occupy the center stage in the current theoretical debate. Interestingly, and perhaps surprisingly, there still appear to be profound differences in the understanding of categories not only between scholars in the Chomskyan tradition and those working in the functional-typological framework, but also within the community of typologists.

---

* For academic purposes, Luca Alfieri is responsible for Section 4 and 5, Giorgio F. Arcodia is responsible for Section 1, 3 and 6, Paolo Ramat is responsible for Section 2. Authors' names are listed alphabetically.

While the divergence of opinions between the so-called 'universalist' and 'particularist' fields is hard to miss (see e.g., the overviews in Haspelmath 2014 and Wiltschko 2014), the existence of different, even incompatible views among typologists became especially evident in the stimulating discussion which developed on the LINGTYP mailing list between January and early February 2016.[1] Put very simply, the LINGTYP discussion has shown that even the most 'innocent', so to say, statements as 'the basic word order of Cantonese is SVO' may be understood in significantly different ways by different typologists: namely, as an actual statement about the 'default' order of the constituents Subject (as a syntactic pivot), Verb and Object in a language; as a generalisation about a preferred order of constituents which however are *not* necessarily a Subject and an Object, but possibly an Agent and a Patient; or even as a meaningless association, given that the categories at issue might have no relevance for Cantonese (on the category status of word order, see below, Section 3). Several more fundamental differences involve essential issues in linguistic research, as e.g., the relation between "comparative concepts" (Haspelmath 2010a; this volume) and language-specific categories, the relation between language description and comparative research, and the use of language-specific and/or comparative labels in glossing, inter alia.

As we shall see in the next section, the idea of comparing concepts, or 'comparative concepts', may boast a long history in the philosophical debate on language(s), at least in Western speculation. In this first section of this *Introduction* we limit ourselves to mention the discussions that have impacted on the debate represented in this volume (as can be seen in the references of many chapters): Greenberg 1966 [[1]1963]; Lazard 1975; Comrie 1976, 1978; Dixon 1977, 1979; Keenan & Comrie 1977; Givón 1979; Stassen 1985; Bybee 1985; Croft 2001, among many others, though not using the term "comparative concepts", were well aware of the need for (functional) comparative concepts on the one side and language-specific categories on the other side – a dichotomy that surfaces even in the title of the present volume. The goal of a collection of papers like this one is precisely to reflect the different approaches, without attempting to find nor to create a unifying viewpoint.

However, the debate represented in our volume was not confined to the mailing list mentioned in the Abstract: many of the participants published position papers in a 2016 issue of the journal *Linguistic Typology* (see below, Section 4); a round

---

1. The LINGTYP is a mailing list hosted by the LinguistList which is mostly used by scholars with an interest in functional-typological approaches to the study of language. Interestingly, as we were drafting this article (February 2018), a new 'soul-searching' thread of discussion, entitled "language typology, linguistic typology, comparative linguistics", was initiated on the LINGTYP mailing list.

table on the topic was held at the 49th *Societas Linguistica Europaea* annual meeting in Naples (2016), followed by a workshop at the following meeting in Zurich (2017). In this volume, we collected nine of the papers presented at the Zurich workshop. Moreover, Martina Wiltschko kindly accepted to write a paper in order to broaden the scope of the present book: this is because few (if any) linguists working in a formal/generative framework were part of this debate, and we wanted to include their perspectives on such a central issue in the language sciences.[2]

This introductory paper is organised as follows. In Section 2, we will provide a very concise historical overview of the issue of linguistic categories, showing how this has always been a subject for controversy and deep theoretical reflection. In Section 3, we will summarise the main points of debate, and the different positions, which emerged in the LINGTYP discussion, putting them in the context of recent developments in the field. In Section 4, we will provide an overview of the position papers in the above-mentioned issue of *Linguistic Typology*, showing how the opinions expressed there paint a rather complex picture. Lastly, we shall provide some conclusions, and we shall briefly introduce the contributions to this volume. The presentation of the contributions will show that the topics dealt with do not concern just the discussion 'language-specific vs. universal categories', but that other more specific subjects are present (obviously in the frame of the major discussion: see the papers by Mattiola, Alfieri, Puddu, Da Milano).

2. Language-specific vs. universal categories, description vs. comparison – A long history made short

The discussion about the *differentia linguarum* versus a *grammatica universalis* has a long tradition in Western linguistics. To make a long history short, suffice to mention Gottfried Leibniz as representative of rationalist thought. Leibniz (1646–1716), convinced of the fact that all existing languages derive from a lost original language whose roots are, however, still present in the languages of the world, was looking for a *characteristica universalis*, a kind of algebraic metalanguage for all humans, where every possible thought could be expressed. At the same time, he was convinced that the *differentia linguarum* is not the consequence of the Babel sin, but rather a necessary product of human nature and of its different cultural evolutions. He studied many different languages, including dialects of Saxony, and even organised field research in Russia following the suggestion of the *tsarina* Catherine the Great.

---

[2] We would like to thank Martin Haspelmath for this suggestion.

In a similar vein, Nicolas Beauzée published (1767) a *Grammaire générale ou exposition raisonnée des éléments nécessaires du langage, pour servir de fondement à l'étude des toutes les langues* ('General Grammar or Language Philosophical Explanation, Serving as the Basis for the Study of All Languages'). The title reveals two aspects of 18th-century linguistics. The aim is to arrive at a general, scientific, and speculative (*raisonnée*) theory of language. But to attain this goal, it is necessary to have empirical knowledge of many different languages. In his *Grammaire*, Beauzée mentions not only the three 'holy languages' Greek, Latin, and Hebrew but also Swedish and Lappish, Irish and Welsh, Basque, Quechua, and Chinese (along with Spanish, Italian, German, and English). Even Johann Christoph Adelung's large collection of translations of the 'Pater Noster', published after his death by Johann Severin Vater under the title *Mithridates, oder allgemeine Sprachenkunde mit dem Vater Unser als Sprachprobe in nahe fünfhundert Sprachen und Mundarten* ('Mithridates, or General Language Science with the "Our Father" as Language Specimen in almost Five Hundred Languages or Dialects' [1806–1817]), was an attempt to uncover via the comparison of very different languages the general 'philosophical' principles – that is, the *characteristica universalis* and the '*allgemeine* Sprachenkunde' – and, via the *differentia linguarum*, to recover the evolution of man's faculty of language.

If we transfer Leibniz, Beauzée, and Adelung's approach(es) to language(s) into our modern discussion, we see that '*grammaire générale*' and '*differentia linguarum*' may be compared to 'universal categories' and 'language-specific', respectively. The concept of 'comparison' (*Vergleichung*) of the 18th century referred both to a philosophical comparison of languages (*philosophische Vergleichung*), as in Herder's *Ideen zur Philosophie der Geschichte der Menschheit* ('Ideas about the Philosophy of Humankind's History' [1784–1785]), and to comparative grammar, as in Vater's *Lehrbuch der allgemeinen Grammatick* ('Handbook of General Grammar' [1805]) (see Morpurgo Davies 1994: 93, Ramat 1990: 200). Even in the book which is traditionally considered to mark the beginning of modern linguistics – that is, Franz Bopp's famous 'Conjugation System' (*Über das Conjugationssystem der Sanskritsprache in Vergleichung mit jenem der griechischen, lateinischen, persischen, und germanischen Sprache* [1816]) – we see that 'philosophical', i.e. general reflections on the nature of language are strictly intertwined with a historical approach (as K. J. Windischmann wrote in his Introduction to the *Conjugationssystem*: "das Sprachstudium als ein historisches und philosophisches zu behandeln", 'to treat the study of language both as a historical and philosophical one'). In the *Conjugationssystem* the attempt to demonstrate that verbal conjugation derives from the agglutination of the auxiliary "to be" to verbal roots can be regarded as a typological analysis *ante litteram*.

Unfortunately, for reasons of space, here we cannot illustrate the development of comparativism – necessarily based on the study and description of different languages – and typology in the following times, from Humboldt to Gabelentz, Hjelmslev, Sapir, up until Greenberg (see Ramat 2011; Graffi 2011). It has to be noted that, after Gabelentz, typological studies did not represent the mainstream of linguistic research. Comparison and reconstruction of previous language states gained the forefront in Indo-European, Semitic and Ugro-finnic studies. Typologists of the first decades of the 20th century, such as Finck and Wundt, despite the different approaches, were concerned with problems of language classification without paying much attention to a general theory of language. We have to go back to the above-mentioned *philosophische Vergleichung* in order to find a stricter connection with the problems discussed by typologists in the last decade or so, which are reflected also in the present collection of papers: why and how are languages different if the language faculty is something common to all mankind?

The debate which developed in early 2016 on the LINGTYP mailing list touched on a wide range of topics (see the next section), but one of the key points was the dichotomy (or *non*-dichotomy) between 'typology' and 'documentary linguistics'. *Mutatis mutandis*, this goes back to the question of whether it is possible to combine the study of the *differentia linguarum* and a *grammaire générale* (nowadays considered from the typological perspective): do we need (and, above all, do we *want*) a separation between the description of individual languages and typological comparison (see Haspelmath 2014, among others)? Clearly, the *differentia linguarum* is no longer considered from the psychological viewpoint as in Steinthal's 'ethnopsychology' (*Völkerpsychologie*), let alone the idea of establishing a hierarchy among the languages, still visible in Humboldt's *Sprachverschiedenheit* (linguistic difference). But the current distinction between 'comparative concepts' and 'language specific categories' (Haspelmath 2010a; see below) can be drawn back to the above mentioned two poles of *grammaire générale* and *differentia linguarum*.

Typologists of the 19th century and of the first half of the 20th century were more interested in establishing linguistic families and groups than in defining the universal standards against which crosslinguistic differences could be measured (see Graffi 2011: 39). On the contrary, in Greenbergian linguistic typology the strict connection between typology and the search for language universals occupies center stage (and is already present in Jakobson's 1958 approach). Greenberg's pioneering article 'Some Universals of Grammar with particular reference to the order of meaningful elements' (1963, 1966), in spite of the author's *caveat* about the tentative nature of the conclusions set forth without a much more complete sampling, originated a real 'hunt for universals' (see the overview in Shibatani & Bynon 1995), where description and comparison went hand in hand. Suffice to mention the UNITYP (Universals and Typology) project in Cologne (see Seiler 1995; Seiler, Ono & Premper, this volume), the journal "Sprachtypologie und Universalienforschung" (STUF; Akademie Verlag, later De Gruyter), and books such as Comrie's *Language Universals and Linguistic Typology* (1981) and Croft's *Typology and Universals* (1990; 2nd ed. 2003). In the decades since Greenberg's first article, many of his proposed universals were criticised, and there has been also a 'hunt for counterexamples', parallel to that for universals. Greenberg's 'universals' were actually generalisations drawn from empirical research, but his approach had the great merit of considering implicational relations: if language L1 has property x, with more than chance frequency it will also have property y (see for instance Universal 17: "with overwhelmingly more than chance frequency, languages with dominant order vso have the adjective after the noun"). Typology could thus have predictive value too, much in the sense of Gabelentz, who wished that 'typology' could become, in the future, a science capable of extracting the entire structure of a language from a particular feature.

Since the beginning of the 21st century, a process of reconsideration of the binomial 'Universals and Typology' began. The new generation of linguists was more interested in descriptions of 'exotic', scarcely known or totally unknown languages, and data had to be stored in more and more comprehensive collections: the most influential examples are the *World Atlas of Language Structures* (WALS, Haspelmath et al. 2005; 2nd online edition 2011) and *The Survey of Pidgin and Creole Languages* ed. by S. Michaelis et al. (2013). In these surveys, data of structural (i.e. phonological, grammatical, lexical) properties of languages are gathered without attempting a typological description of the languages themselves. Just to give an example from the WALS: in the section dedicated to 'Nominal Syntax' we find a chapter by David Gil on 'Adjectives without Nouns' (e.g., *I want the red one*), in which a number of languages presenting this construction are quoted, such as Hebrew, Mandarin Chinese, and Kolyma Yukaghir. A world map shows the geographical distribution of such a construction. There is no attempt to tie this particular construct with other syntactic phenomena. Clearly, this approach represents a milestone in the study of very many constructions and phenomena, and also a possibility to have access to much data up to now mostly unknown to the research community. Crucially, however the WALS does not aim at a description of languages: it focuses on specific phenomena such as word order, valence and voice etc., also partly biased by a certain 'eurocentrism' as to the choice of the topics to be dealt with.

This attention to individual linguistic 'facts' rather than to languages considered in their totality has paved the way to the debate which is the subject of this volume. The following two quotes from the LINGTYP debate highlight the points at issue:

> In general, I find it important to recognize that typology works with a heterogeneous class of comparative concepts, which may be defined in a variety of ways (formally, functionally, with respect to discourse, with respect to translation equivalence, etc.). Typology does not (necessarily) work in terms of the descriptive categories that are the most useful in analyzing languages, and it need not define its concepts in a uniform way. (M. Haspelmath, 18.1.2016)

> Let us now consider more closely the [...] case [...] of very different languages, whose respective descriptions will have lots of specific stuff unique to each description, but also some common stuff, shared by both descriptions. Such common stuff would constitute, simultaneously, elements of the respective descriptions of each language, but at the same time also a basis for cross-linguistic comparison, thereby, for cases such as these at least, casting doubt on the necessity for distinguishing between language-specific categories and comparative concepts.
> (D. Gil, 26.1.2016)

The task alluded to by Jan Rijkhoff, namely that "grammatical theorizing and linguistic typologizing must go hand in hand" (25.1.2016) is the heir to the positions alluded to at the beginning of this section and, contrary to Rijkhoff's desire, it is far from accomplished.[3]

3. The LINGTYP debate and its background

The starting point for the LINGTYP discussion was a question from Alan Rumsey (16.1.2016; we follow here the unedited discussion transcript by Plank 2016) on an issue (only) apparently unrelated to the topic of categories: namely, on the relationship between consistency in word order (i.e. being consistently head-initial or head-final) and complexity. The basic suggestion was that structural congruence in the positioning of heads and dependents would make a language 'simpler': this prompted a reaction from Jan Rijkhoff (18.1.2016), who noted that studies on Greenbergian word order correlations, as the VSO & NAdj correlation evoked by Rumsey in his message, are often based on an unclear distinction between 'formal' and 'semantic' categories. In this specific case, in Rijkhoff's view, Adjective, Genitives and Relative Clauses may all be considered part of a semantic category of 'Adjective' – particularly in languages which lack a dedicated class of adjectives, as e.g., Kiribati. According to Rijkhoff, both Hawkins (1983) and Dryer (1992), two major works on word order typology, claim to use semantic defini-

---

[3]. On the connection between typology and grammaticalization, see Bybee et al. (1994), Kuteva et al. (2019).

tions of word classes, but actually employ formal (i.e. identified on the basis of structural/morphosyntactic criteria) categories, distinguishing between adjectives, genitives and relative clauses (e.g., in Hawkins' well-known *Heaviness Serialization Principle*). This, in turn, elicited responses from Randy LaPolla, Martin Haspelmath and William Croft (inter alios), who all expressed different views on the definition of categories; the discussion then broadened, including several more issues and participants, over the space of two (intense) weeks. While here it is simply impossible to do justice to the richness of the debate, in what follows we will try to summarise the main points of the discussion, and the different opinions which emerged, in the context of the current theoretical debate.

The first (and foremost) fundamental point of debate, as hinted at above, was the nature of categories, and their use in comparative research. While it is true that (arguably) most typologists (and even a few generativists; see Wiltschko 2014: 20) adhere to a view of language in which there are no universal, preset categories (see e.g., Croft 2001; Evans & Levinson 2009), they still have to find a way to identify comparable object across languages, lest one wants to give up cross-linguistic research.

In this connection, a proposal which has gained much acceptance in the community, and which was a leitmotiv running through the LINGTYP debate, is the 'comparative concepts' model (Haspelmath 2010a, this volume). In a nutshell, while rejecting universal categories, Haspelmath believes that we may identify both 'descriptive categories', i.e. language-specific categories (as, say, 'the English adjective'), and 'comparative concepts', i.e. "concepts specifically designed for the purpose of comparison that are independent of descriptive categories" (2010a: 664); thus, for instance, while the Russian 'dative' and the Korean 'dative' are not the same, and they are not the instantiation of some crosslinguistic 'dative' category, for the purposes of comparison one may define the comparative concept of 'dative (case)' as (Haspelmath 2010a: 666):

> a morphological marker that has among its functions the coding of the recipient argument of a physical transfer verb (such as 'give', 'lend', 'sell', 'hand'), when this is coded differently from the theme argument.

Thus, for instance, in the Latin double object construction (as *donare aliquem aliquid* 'to give something to someone') the Haspelmathian notion of 'dative' is encoded with an accusative case form (*aliquem* in our example).

The definition of comparative concepts is based on heterogeneous criteria/notions: semantic notions, functional notions, formal criteria, etc.: for some more examples, see Haspelmath (2010a). As pointed out by Haspelmath himself in the LINGTYP discussion, typology "need not define its concepts in a uniform way" (18.1.2016; see above, Section 2). Also, crucially, comparative concepts are just linguists' constructs, and they are, in essence, irrelevant for individual languages (both for users and for grammarians): they are not the 'instantiation' of some putative 'universal' category. This was stated in the clearest possible terms by Haspelmath in the discussion: "[…] we need to give up the hope that the categories that we find in individual languages will in the end converge on something universal" (20.1.2016).

Thus, even one of the most basic parameters for the typological classification of languages, namely, the order of major sentence constituents S, V and O, may have different implications for different typologists (see above, Section 1). While, for instance, Randy LaPolla and Peter Arkadiev have expressed (in different ways) the view that any typological classification must stick to the facts of the language, and hence the label 'S' can be used only if the language does have a category 'subject' (as a syntactic pivot), M. Dryer goes the opposite way in saying that:

> I would have thought it was obvious that classifying languages typologically does not entail that the terms employed in the typological classification correspond to categories in the language […]. I have certainly made that clear in my work that classifying a language as svo makes no claim about the categories in the language, nor that these categories determine word order even if the language has such categories. (19.1.2016)

LaPolla's objection to this is as follows (19.1.2016):

> What does the category 'subject' mean to you such that it would be cross-linguistically useful, to the point of even saying languages that don't have such a category are subject-verb-object languages ? In terms of the correlations you talk about among languages that manifest what is (from my view problematically) subsumed under the vo or svo rubric, my view is that we should look for the reasons why, in terms of information structure, structural pivots, historical development, or whatever, the languages manifest the particular patterns they do. Simply lumping them together under a single rubric does nothing but categorise them, and doesn't explain anything.

In turn, Arkadiev asked in the same crucial way:

> If, as Matthew [Dryer] says, "classifying a language as svo makes no claim about the categories in the language, [….]" what's the point of classifying the given language as svo in the first place? If the categories of a particular language can be totally at variance with those notions which typologists employ for comparative purposes, then the fact that a given language happens to be classified as svo appears to be completely arbitrary and non-informative.

In broad agreement with LaPolla's arguments, D. Everett (19.1.2016) suggested a fitting analogy with the use of the International Phonetic Alphabet (IPA) in the description of the sound system of a language:

> Typological categories, like the phonetic categories of the IPA, are idealisations, though based on data collected from a wide variety of languages. Thus a "p" in the IPA is a voiceless bilabial stop. However, a [p] in Pirahã is a voiceless bilabial

> stop with closure and flattening across the entire length of the lips. It is not the same as the "p" of the IPA. But clearly it is related to it as an individual dog is to the noun "dog."
>
> But we cannot call an alveolar stop a "p" nor a cat a dog. Idealisations do not mean that there is no empirical connection between a specific language and the typological category.
>
> It is possible that we might have something that fails to correspond to any syntactic notion of subject in a particular language. But if the grammar-writer refers to it as a "subject" on semantic grounds this could be the equivalent of calling a "t" a "p" because it is the frontmost voiceless occlusive in a given language. So the grammar-writer would have introduced an error which could potentially be propagated throughout the typological literature. By the same token, calling that language SVO might not only obscure the actual facts of the language, but it would also be a disservice to typology.

Hence, Everett seems to suggest that typological categories are idealisations based on actual language data, and that items of individual languages must (more or less narrowly) correspond to those idealisations, if one wants to use them in cross-linguistic comparison. Again, no language can be classified as SVO if there is nothing like a syntactic notion of 'subject' in that particular language.

But, in yet another reaction to LaPolla's criticism, Dryer (20.1.2016) insists on the significance of using typological variables as constituent order even when the constituents at issue do not correspond to notions relevant for the grammar of some language. He admits he uses labels as 'subject' and 'object' "as they are used in the vast majority of grammatical descriptions produced in the past 100 years", which would "roughly" correspond to the semantic roles 'Agent' and 'Patient'; he argues that, if we rejected this approach, we could miss important correlations. In other words, typological correlations, as e.g., that between VO order and postnominal relatives, could run the risk of not being detected if we "restricted our attention to languages in which the VO order reflected a syntactic rule in the language":

> The fact that languages which are VO in my terms only due to frequency in usage tend to exhibit the word order characteristics associated with VO word order means that we can rule out those lines of explanation that depend crucially on syntactic rules.

This is understood by Dryer as a distinction between 'grammar' (roughly, language-specific rules and categories) and 'usage' (i.e. actual use of constructions), which correlates with the distinction between describing individual languages and doing cross-linguistic comparison. We will get back to this below. In short, besides universalist claims (which did not feature prominently in the discussion – again, because the participants were almost exclusively scholars working in a functional-typological framework), there seems to be a major dividing line: on the one hand, there are those who advocate a 'double standard', namely comparative concepts (or analogous constructs, *tertia comparationis*) for comparison, and/plus language-specific categories for description; on the other hand, there are those who insist on basing comparison on categories which are relevant to the individual languages only. Some sort of compromise, which nevertheless overcomes the need for comparative concepts, came from D. Gil (we repeat this quotation from Section 2 for the sake of convenience):

> Let us now consider more closely the [...] case [...] of very different languages, whose respective descriptions will have lots of specific stuff unique to each description, but also some common stuff, shared by both descriptions. Such common stuff would constitute, simultaneously, elements of the respective descriptions of each language, but at the same time also a basis for cross-linguistic comparison, thereby, for cases such as these at least, casting doubt on the necessity for distinguishing between language-specific categories and comparative concepts.
> (26.1.2016)

This is somehow reminiscent of the use of Swadesh lists in lexical comparison. When one looks at the words for, say, 'hand' or 'red' in different languages, one must keep in mind that the meanings and uses of the corresponding lexemes are very likely to have just a partial overlap: 'hand' may refer not only to the part of the body at the end of the arm, or apply just to humans, and a word which may be translated as 'red' into English often refers to a narrower or broader (or just, for lack of a better word, different) colour spectrum than the English word *red*. This, however, does not prevent us from carrying out comparative research on lexemes and lexica, as long as we can find suitable items.

Moreover, Gil suggests that 'comparative concepts' as S, V and O should have a place in the description of individual languages (as, again, 'Cantonese is a SVO language'), even though each language may be classified in comparative work (as e.g. the *WALS*) as SVO for different reasons: for instance, because there are linearisation/alignment rules that put agents before verbs, and patients after verbs, but no well-defined category of (syntactic) 'subject'. A description of the language at issue should contain both the actual factors conditioning word order, and the broad classificatory statement 'X is an SVO language': one must keep the two levels distinct, but both are useful for the reader (22.1.2016).

A similar line of reasoning was proposed by E. Moravcsik, who believes that there are language-specific categories that may be applied to different languages: for instance, a French adjective and an Italian adjective could be argued to belong to the same category, despite being defined in language-specific terms (for a more articulated exposition of her view, see the next Section). E. König pointed out (22.1.2016) that French adjectives and Italian adjectives differ considerably in their syntax and semantic potential: this gives us a comparative concept 'adjective' and two descriptive categories 'adjectives in Italian', and 'adjectives in French'. In the same line of reasoning B. Bickel noted that, while comparative concepts (or, rather, 'typological variables') and language-specific descriptive categories are in fact different things, the former are also useful for describing a language: "[e]very well-defined typological variable captures or measures something of interest in a language […]. And, yes, saying that Chinese is SVO captures something real in Chinese" (1.2.2016). Consequently, by this kind of statements and by using expressions as "'comparative concepts' – or typological variables, as I prefer to call them", Bickel provides a bridge over the troubled waters between the 'abstract (and often a priori) typological approach' and 'language specific analysis' that characterised the discussion.

From this very brief presentation of a small portion of the debate, it clearly appears that opinions vary considerably, even on very basic issues, and within a relatively compact – in terms of practical aims and theoretical assumptions – community. And, even among those who accept (in one form or another) the idea of comparative concepts – as *tertia comparationis* to be used in comparative studies – opinions on how to define those *tertia*, again, are far from homogeneous. In Haspelmath's (and others') view, comparative concepts constitute an open set, and each concept may be defined according to different parameters (see the quotation in Section 2); in his own words, there are "myriad ways of comparing languages, and thus myriad possible comparative concepts" (20.1.2016). There can be no 'right' or 'wrong' comparative concept, but just more or less useful concepts for comparison (see also Beck, 19.1.2016). But, for instance, P. Ramat believes that some "semantic/functional concepts", his *tertia comparationis*, may indeed be regarded as universal (e.g., the concept 'comparison': 'A is bigger than B'; 'B is older than C'): thus, while you may say that language X has no 'adjectives', all languages must have a strategy to express the function 'attribution of a quality to an X', which may be realised e.g., by an 'adjective', by a 'relative clause', etc.; the latter are obviously language-specific categories (19.1.2016; see Ramat 1999). In Ramat's view, adjectives and relative clauses, as well as NPs formed by Genitive+Noun (or Noun+Genitive) are hyponyms of a hypernym that could be labelled 'property attribution'. This entails that one can (and should) identify prototypical properties for adjectives (e.g., agreement with the head noun, where applicable), and thus one may have items which are "more or less adjectival", in a language-specific sense.

Moreover, while Haspelmath's comparative concepts may be defined in different ways ("formally, functionally, with respect to discourse, with respect to translation equivalence, etc."; 18.1.2016), Ramat's *tertia comparationis* are purely semantic/functional notions (and see also Frajzyngier's 'functions', 24.1.2016, and this volume; Lazard's 'Intuitive Conceptual Framework', 23.1.2016; Lazard 2012). M. Dryer (18.1.2016), in response to Rijkhoff's criticism which 'ignited' the discussion (see the beginning of this section), insists that, in his work, even labels which are commonly used to indicate constructions (i.e. pairings of meaning *and* form), as e.g., 'adjective', 'relative clause', or 'demonstrative', in fact just stand for semantic categories, which may have different formal (syntactic) realisations in languages. However, he suggests, while the variation in formal expression of semantic categories could pose a problem for comparison, in his experience this has proven to be "overall irrelevant: by and large, generalisations over semantic categories apply the same, regardless of the syntactic realisation".

A yet different proposal is the one by W. Croft, who believes that different subtypes of comparative notions, based on different criteria for definition, should be distinguished: one may have purely semantic/functional comparative concepts, but also "constructions", which are hybrid formal-functional concepts (e.g., "adjective construction" as "the construction expressing a property concept used in modification"; Croft 2016: 382), and "strategies", i.e. "constructions that share a relevant cross-linguistically valid formal property" (21.1.2016), as e.g., alignment strategies. We will elaborate on this below (Section 4). Rijkhoff, on the other hand, adopts a somewhat stricter view of what can (and should) be compared across languages: in order to do "responsible cross-linguistic comparison", one should "let go of the idea that we can compare everything in all languages" (22.1.2016). Thus, according to Rijkhoff, the data used in comparison must consist only of units (constructions?) that are "similar enough" in terms of "function, meaning and form"; this entails that, very often, languages and/or constructions will be excluded from a sample precisely because they are just not "similar enough" at all three levels. In Rijkhoff's own example, if one wants to test the hypothesis that "if a language has a dedicated class of (qualifying) adjectives, a modifying adjective will occur next to the head noun in the NP" (i.e. the "Principle of Head Proximity"), one has to delimit, firstly, the domain of inquiry to languages (and, we may add, constructions) in which modifiers of the head noun are found in "simple (non-complex), integral (hierarchically organised) NPs" (22.1.2016). If, for instance, the modifier is expressed as a bound morpheme, or adjectival notions are expressed by phrasal constituents, the data cannot be included (see Rijkhoff 2004). We will get back to Rijkhoff's model for cross-linguistic comparison in the next section.

To sum up, it appears that there are three main points of disagreement as to the 'basics', so to say, of categories:

a. Are comparative concepts (and analogous constructs) a completely different set from descriptive categories? If not, what is the relation between the two?

b. Are comparative concepts just an open list of categories, created by the linguist for the sole purposes of comparison, or are there (also) universal functional concepts that find expression in any language?
c. How should comparative concepts be defined (functionally, formally, hybrid)? Is there just *one* definition for a comparative concept? Can we distinguish between different subtypes of notions to be used in comparison, defined according to different parameters?

The discussion on categories briefly sketched above paved the way for another area of debate (already alluded to): namely, the relationship between language description and 'doing typology'. For instance, if comparative concepts *et similia* have no direct relevance for the description of a language, are we to keep the two enterprises – description and comparison – entirely separate? This seems to be the view expressed by M. Dryer:

> To me, describing or analysing a particular language is a completely different enterprise from classifying the language typologically, except that the former is a necessary prerequisite for the latter. The former should be describing the language entirely in its own terms, rather than trying to fit it into some typology. I am also strongly opposed to questionnaire-based typology, since if one is classifying phenomenon X in a set of languages, one needs to see how phenomenon X in a given language fits into the overall grammatical system of the language.
> (20.1.2016)

Going back to the use of S, V and O in typological research, Dryer suggests that one should distinguish between 'grammar' and 'usage':

> Consider a language which lacks a rule saying the language is ov but where the actual factors conditioning word order result in a higher frequency of ov. Such languages usually have postpositions rather than prepositions. But since the grammar doesn't say the language is ov (it's only ov at the level of usage), the correlation between ov and postpositions is not reflected in the grammar.
> (21.1.2016)

In this view, one can make claims about categories that are not relevant to the grammar of an individual language, as long as they somehow explain facts and correlations which are relevant for typological research, and which would be missed otherwise. This seems to be the fundamental point of opposition between these two aspects of linguistic analysis: "[t]here is a difference between being interested in what different languages have in common and how they differ and being interested in what *grammars* of different languages have in common and how they differ" (21.1.2016; Dryer's italics).

On the other hand, many share the opinion that typology and description "should continue to exist in symbiosis" (M. Haspelmath, 1.2.2016). For instance, W. Croft (21.1.2016) believes that

> Typological research shouldn't end up being as irrelevant to language description as generative syntax has turned out to be. So while I agree that language-specific grammatical categories are just that, I don't believe that what typologists have discovered about languages is irrelevant to language description.

This is in line with Gil's observation (see above) on the relevance of typological parameters, as e.g., basic word order, for the description of individual languages as well. Moreover, Croft rejects the distinction between 'grammar' and 'usage' as proposed by M. Dryer: he believes that 'grammars' do not form a 'system', but, rather, categories are 'construction-specific', and hence vary considerably even among different constructions, calling into question the need for a 'grammar *vs.* usage' distinction.

Lastly, G. Lazard (23.1.2016; quoting from Lazard 2012) suggests that the difference between description and comparison is best explained, in essence, as a distinction between a bottom-up and a top-down procedure: description goes from form to meaning, while typology goes from meaning to form. Thus, again, description is seen as a prerequisite for typology, in a semasiological approach, while typology is seen (in an onomasiological approach) as the search for how a semantic concept or construct is encoded in linguistic form.

The two previous issues have direct bearing on one of the most basic tasks of a linguist in his or her ordinary work: namely, the use and meaning of glosses. When we include language examples in our work, we normally provide not only a translation, but also interlinear glosses; in typological works (and not only), it has become customary to adopt the conventions of the *Leipzig Glossing Rules*,[4] which provide a list of 'abbreviated category labels', as e.g., GEN for 'genitive', IMP for 'imperative', PURP for 'purposive', etc. Even when the *Leipzig* rules are not used, one must still decide which category labels s/he is going to use for the purposes of glossing. Given the existing disagreement on the nature of linguistic categories, it does not come as a surprise that the meaning of glosses was a topic for discussion as well. The issue was raised by Östen Dahl (25.1.2016) in this form: do glosses (particularly *Leipzig* glosses) stand for comparative concepts or descriptive categories? Again, opinions differ to some extent.

---

4. <https://www.eva.mpg.de/lingua/resources/glossing-rules.php> (26 February 2018).

For instance, H. Skirgård (25.1.2016) assumed that glosses stand for language-specific categories (so, e.g., GEN stands for 'genitive' as a case in the language at issue); D. Everett (25.1.2016), on the other hand, remarked that a standardised system of glosses should be based on comparative labels, if not otherwise specified. D. Beck (26.1.2016), following a comment from Skirgård, also believes that glosses stand for language-specific categories, and any attempt at standardisation would mean using comparative labels – not the same as language-specific categories, at least for those who accept the Haspelmathian notion of comparative concepts. In Beck's understanding, then, the Leipzig glosses are not paired to definitions for the proposed labels, but they are rather just a convenient list of shortenings for "common descriptive terms we often use in interlinearizing"; the use of labels from a limited set, even though it may not do justice to the specificities of each language, is anyway necessary, as "it would be a terrible thing if everyone used completely idiosyncratic terms". S. Nordhoff (26.1.2016) seems to support this view: "[a]n author using a Leipzig gloss does, however, not assert any relation between the morpheme being glossed and a comparative concept however defined".

J. Nichols (27.1.2016) believes that glossing labels should be understood in the context of a particular grammar: for instance, one finds the label DAT for 'dative' in the list of abbreviations, but also in the relevant chapter of that grammar, so that one gets exactly what is meant by that label in that specific language. But, on the other hand, she pragmatically suggests that those labels "are usually like terms for the nearest comparative concept, so you don't have to read the grammar to grasp approximately what the category is": in other words, the reader arguably expects that something glossed as DAT roughly corresponds to the notion of 'dative' as commonly understood in the literature (see Haspelmath's definition for the comparative concept 'dative' above). This seems to be in line with Arkadiev's general idea (26.1.2016) that "languages are much more similar to each other than it appears at first sight, and that 'incommensurability' of structures of different languages tends to be considerably overestimated". Actually, also D. Gil (26.1.2016) and M. Haspelmath (27.1.2016) take a more pragmatic position, suitable for the state of art in language analysis and language typology: glosses should both reflect language-specific categories and be informative also for readers who are not familiar with the language being described. Haspelmath further adds that one may choose different glosses depending on the task at hand (context-dependent glossing):

> Language-particular papers and books are more likely to use labels for descriptive categories, while typological works are more likely to use labels corresponding to well-known comparative concepts. But in neither case would it be practical to be rigid.

Dahl's statement against the totally arbitrary nature of comparative concepts goes in a similar direction (see Section 4 below).

The use of somewhat imprecise labels in glossing is justified, in the case of descriptive categories, by the fact that the grammar or a dedicated paper would contain a more detailed explanation of what a glossing label stands for in the context of the language(s) at issue (see Nichols' position above in this section). We may conclude that, in typological work, while the use of comparative concepts is not universally accepted, one however must, for practical reasons, find some sort of compromise between being faithful to the language(s) and - for the sake of readability - use labels which have a widely recognised meaning in the linguistic literature. This is nicely illustrated by Haspelmath himself with this example:

> In Lezgian, there is both a Past tense and an Aorist tense, which [sic!] different meanings and functioning in the tense system, so from a language-specific point of view, the difference is absolutely crucial. But in a typological context, when a Lezgian example is cited for different reasons, it's perfectly OK to ignore the difference, I think.

In this section, we have tried to briefly introduce some of the most relevant issues and positions which were presented in the LINGTYP discussion; these set the stage for the *Linguistic Typology* position papers which will be presented in the next section. Obviously, the divergent opinions found a more articulated expression in the papers, that provide a clearer illustration of the variety of assumptions, practices and methods which may be found in current typological research.

4. Recent insights: The *Linguistic Typology* debate

Just like many other readers, the Editorial Board of *Linguistic Typology* was enthralled by the debate on the LINGTYP mailing list; hence, they asked the participants to write up position papers addressing the points around which the debate revolved, to be published in issue 20.2 of the journal As we have just said, in some cases, the papers presented a more elaborated version of the same ideas sketched in the list messages: hence, the reader will find in this section many issues already dealt with in the previous sections. However, new insights were also presented. On the whole, the anthology represented a substantial contribution for achieving a better understanding of what a *tertium comparationis* can or cannot be.

Almost all scholars agreed that comparative concepts are not of just one type: some are indeed purely functional, arbitrary and totally different from language specific categories, others are not. According to Croft (2016; see above, Section 3), comparative concepts are of three distinct types: (1) 'purely functional' or (2) 'hybrid', which are further divided in (2a) 'constructions' and (2b) 'strategies'.

A purely functional comparative concept is the definition of the ADJECTIVE that is common in word-order typology: e.g., a property concept with no reference to any formal feature (in this context, 'purely functional' covers also 'purely semantic' comparative concepts as defined by Haspelmath 2010a, as well as 'interpersonal', 'communicative' or 'discourse' functions as defined by Rijkhoff 2016). A hybrid comparative concept of the construction type is any pairing of form and meaning coding a given function: e.g., the definition of the ADJECTIVE as a quality modifier (in the following, but differently from what was suggested by Croft 2016: 379, comparative concepts are in small caps). Constructions are universal, although their specific formal coding changes from language to language: in Latin the most typical quality modifier is a simple agreeing stem, while in Garo it is a relative clause. Finally, a strategy is a specific pairing of form and meaning defined further by certain characteristics of grammatical forms: e.g., the ADJECTIVE as a quality modifier construction in integral noun phrases (see Rijkhoff 2016), the case construction, the ergative construction or the middle voice construction. Strategies are not universal, in that only some languages show the formal features referred to in their definition: e.g., not all languages show integral noun phrases, cases, or ergative constructions. Moreover, according to some scholars, hybrid comparative concepts should be defined by a single formal feature: if more features are used, one does not know what to do when they contrast (see Haspelmath 2011 on the notion of 'word').

Different classifications are obviously possible. According to Lander and Arkadiev (2016: 409) comparative concepts are of three types: 1) those based on similarities between languages: e.g., NON-RESTRICTIVE RELATIVE CLAUSE or PERFECT, which are categories relevant to some, though not to all, languages, just as Croft's 'strategies'; 2) those based on differences between languages: e.g., the elementary meanings or functions that constitute the basis of many semantic maps, which resemble somehow Croft's 'purely functional comparative concepts'; 3) those that are not based on descriptive categories at all: e.g., the notion of BASIC WORD ORDER, which is usually considered a universally relevant typological feature, although it may not be a relevant descriptive category for all languages. While type 3 comparative concepts really represent "(to a certain extent) arbitrary boundaries in what is essentially a continuous typological space" in Dryer's opinion (2016: 327), type 1 comparative concepts are based on the similarities that exist in actual languages, thus they are neither entirely functional nor totally arbitrary (Lander & Arkadiev 2016: 404); in Ramat's terms (1999), they are also categories of (some) languages, not only categories of the linguist.

In the same vein, many scholars pointed out that some comparative concepts are actually based on family resemblances or, rather, they are prototypical generalisations abstracted from the categories that are found in one or more (genetically

Chapter 1. Linguistic categories, language description and linguistic typology – An overview   19

and/or areally related) languages. To this purpose, Beck (2016: 396) proposed the notion of *portable terms*, that is, terms that "are suitable both for the description of specific languages and for crosslinguistic comparison", so that they "simultaneously fill the role of comparative concept and of language-particular term": e.g., the notion of BODY PART, CASE or PERFECT. Similarly, LaPolla (2016: 367) distinguishes on the one hand "forms that could be properly labelled with the comparative category label on formal grounds" (e.g., the construction that codes the MIDDLE VOICE in languages in which there is a dedicated middle inflection) and, on the other hand, *strategies* in the proper sense, that is, "forms that seemed to have a similar function as the forms of the relevant category, but did not have a form that could be said to fit the comparative category" (e.g., the construction that codes the MIDDLE VOICE in languages in which there is no dedicated middle voice inflection). Finally, Rijkhoff argues that comparative concepts need not be exclusively functional: rather, if functional criteria are used as the starting point of the research, subsequently formal and semantic criteria are applied to arrive at a morpho-syntactic category whose members are sufficiently similar in terms of function, meaning and form.

Moreover, Dahl (2016: 434) argued against the totally arbitrary nature of comparative concepts saying that "[t]he crucial criterion for a bottom-up typological investigation is that it builds on comparable crosslinguistic datasets based on primary linguistic data". The *tertium comparationis*, in this case, is represented by questionnaires, translational equivalents or experimental data consisting of a reaction to a stimulus. Linguistic expressions (of one or more languages) that have the same functions with respect to the stimulus are grouped together, forming a dataset specific pattern. Sufficiently similar dataset specific patterns form clusters of patterns: when the members of the cluster represent a sufficiently wide sample of languages, there is reason to postulate a *cross-linguistic category type* or a *gram type*, that is, a cross-linguistic category that is not "constructed" by the researcher to compare languages; rather, it is a non-arbitrary "object" that exists *in re* and is "out there to be discovered" (Dahl 2016: 434–435).

The more accurate definition of the different types of comparative concepts makes it possible to pinpoint some theoretical pitfalls of contemporary typological research, namely cases in which the research question is not entirely consistent with the type of comparative concept employed. In addition to the confusion of semantic and formal categories in post-Greenbergian studies (Rijkhoff 2016: 355; see also above, Section 3), Croft (2016: 383, 387) and Dryer (2016: 319, 330) showed that questions as "is category X of language Y an instantiation of the universal category Z ?" or "does language Y have category Z?" have a totally different answer depending on the type of comparative concepts assumed in the research. Asking whether Chamorro has 'adjectives', for instance, is a principled question, if ADJECTIVE is a cross-linguistic category in the generativist sense or if it is a strategy in Croft's sense: it is however a pseudo-question whether ADJECTIVE is a construction or a purely functional comparative concept, since Chamorro necessarily codes the ADJECTIVE somehow, though not in a form comparable to that of Latin (on Chamorro word-class distinction, see issue 38 [2012] of *Theoretical Linguistics*). Similarly, Rijkhoff (2016: 358) and LaPolla (2016: 374) stressed that big-data typology, which uses previous typological research as the starting point for investigation, implicitly assumes that the labels for the comparative concepts used in previous studies cover roughly the same linguistic units. However, this might be the case if the comparative concepts employed in the research are of the strategy type, but it is clearly not the case if constructions or purely functional comparative concepts are used.

A further interesting point of the anthology was a quite widespread criticism of the categorial "particularism" advocated by Dryer, Croft, Haspelmath (as well as others). As Gil said (2016: 434), if language particular categories are unique to each language, or even to each construction, and cannot be exported from a language to similar languages, as the proponents of the comparative concept model seem to believe, there is no logical reason to accept the equation of the categories of two different historical phases of a language, or the categories of two idiolects of the same historical phase, or even the categories of a single idiolect in two different utterances (see also Lander & Arkadiev 2016: 406 and Dahl 2016: 429 for similar claims). In other words, the problem of non-comparability does not stop at typological comparison; it rather concerns any generalizing statement, such as those found in grammatical descriptions of individual languages. Therefore, claiming that language particular categories are strictly construction-dependent may depend on a logical fallacy (Moravcsik 2016: 418) and could lead us to becoming "trapped in the grim world of what Haspelmath (2010) calls 'categorial particularism'" (Beck 2016: 398, see also Newmeyer 2007: 146ff. for a similar view). As Moravcsik pointed out, the criterion for categorisation should not be full identity: "in categorization, things are treated AS IF they were the same, which implies that they are not" (Moravcsik 2016: 418). If we refuse to subsume under a general category CASE the Latin cases, the Sanskrit cases and the Greek cases, since their distribution is not exactly the same in each language, we are acting as if two or more objects could be subsumed under a single category only if all of their properties were just the same, while it is well known that categorisation is based on partial, rather than full identity (that is, on similarity): "shared properties are focused on with the differences backgrounded though not denied" (Moravcsik 2016: 418). Accepting that comparative concepts can also be based on formal similarities among individual languages, therefore, does not necessary lead to inconsistent comparison.

A third crucial point of the anthology was a proposal to overcome the allegedly radical dichotomy between language description and comparison claimed by some of the supporters of the comparative concepts model. The proposal, which significantly enough, the editors published as the last contribution in the LT issue, came from Gil (2016) and was based on Cysouw & Good's (2013) notion of *languoid*. A languoid is a cover term that includes languages, smaller entities such as dialects and registers, but also larger assemblages such as genealogical and areal groupings. Differently from languages,

> languoids [...] exhibit hierarchical nesting, with smaller languoids contained within larger ones. Accordingly any description of any languoid also constitutes a comparison of the smaller languoids contained in it, and thus, the ontological foundation of the distinction between language-specific categories and comparative concepts collapses (Gil 2016: 455)

If the notion of language-particular category is substituted with that of languoid-associated descriptive category, any description of a language is also a comparison (and vice versa), and it can refer to any hierarchical node of the languoid nest, that is, to any level of generality from a single language to LANGUAGE in general. In this case, the alleged dichotomy between language-particular categories and comparative concepts becomes a continuum, with language specific categories and purely functional comparative concepts at its two opposite poles (on this point, see also Beck 2016: 398).

5. Concluding remarks

The 'comparative concept debate', as we may call it, touched upon one of the deepest and most general problem of linguistics: *differentia linguarum* or *grammatica universalis*? (See Dahl 2016: 427–428 for a similar suggestion; see also above, Section 2). To put it simply and at risk of some rude simplification, the domain of linguistics as a discipline can be considered as a surface cut by two lines that divide two different objects of study and two different perspectives of study. The object of study of linguistics can be the individual languages, which are particular and historically determined, or LANGUAGE in general that is, the language faculty.[5] Depending on the approach adopted, the study of LANGUAGE can be identified with a) the study

---

5. Note that Latin, Germanic and Slavic languages have a single term for both concepts (Lat. *lingua*, Engl. *language*, Germ. *Sprache*, Czech and Russ. *jazyk*), but in Romance languages the distinction is lexicalised: It. *lingua* vs. *linguaggio*, Fr. *langue* vs. *langage*, Sp. *lengua* vs. *lenguaje*. Obviously, also in the languages in which the distinction is not lexicalised, the two notions can be distinguished: see the opposition between *Sprachfähigkeit* and *Sprachmaterial* in Gabelentz (Graffi 2001: 43).

of human thought, as in the 17th-18th century *grammaire générale* (see Section 2); b) the study of a Universal Grammar, innate and hardwired in the brain, as in Generative Grammar; c) the study of the language faculty, which has been innatised through cultural development and usage, as in neuro- and psycho-linguistics;[6] d) the description of the sum of the categories, notions and tools needed to compare the whole of the world's languages, as in typology.[7] The research perspective, on the other hand, can be either the study of the functioning, of the change of a single language or of LANGUAGE in general, as was often the case before the 19th century. The two distinctions above divide the architecture of contemporary linguistic knowledge into four different domains. The functioning of individual languages is the domain of *descriptive grammar, individual language grammar* or *particular linguistics* (p-linguistics); the functioning of LANGUAGE in general is the domain of *general linguistics* (g-linguistics), which can be further declined in generative, typological or psycholinguistic terms. The change or the origin(s) of single languages and of language families is the subject of *historical* (or *genetic*) *linguistics* (h-linguistics); the origin or the evolution (rather than the change) of LANGUAGE as a human faculty is the domain of the so-called *evolutionary linguistics* (e-linguistics, in the terms by Hurford 2007, 2012 and Botha 2016).[8] Schematically:[9]

---

6. See, e.g., Tomasello (1999, 2003) and Evans (2013).

7. Scholars working within this framework often retain the label of *Universal Grammar* (UG) to refer to the object of study of general linguistics, but interpret it as a rather empirical notion (Croft 2001: 7-11, Evans & Levinson 2009). However, in this sense the label of *General Grammar* would be preferable: being based on empirical generalisations, such GG may change over time due to the refinement of the categories used to compare languages or to the growth of the amount of data compared. That is, such theory of language can be general, though not really universal.

8. E-linguistics is not a fully empirical research field at present, but it is gaining some success thanks to cross-disciplinary approaches merging neuro-biology, gestural theory, genetic studies, population history and typological universals: see the very recent thread by Haspelmath on the LINGTYP mailing list (20.1.2020) on the relation between typological universals and Proto-World, which is the modern way of labelling the time-honored problem of the origin of LANGUAGE. Moreover, the process of grammaticalization is often understood as an inherently evolutionary (that is, panchronic, ontogenetic) process, or as both an evolutionary and a historical (that is, diachronic, phylogentic) process (e.g., Kuteva et al. 2019; Bybee et al. 1994; Bybee 2010: 116-119, 203).

9. The labels employed in the table follow a widespread convention, but they are not uncontroversial. In a recent post on the LINGTYP mailing list (see above, fn. 1), Haspelmath (28.2.2018) proposed comparative linguistics for "typology (possibly including also historical linguistics)" and/or evolutionary linguistics for "historical linguistics". This is not the place for discussing the adequacy of these labels. However, subsuming under a single label domains with a different positioning on the time axis (see below), as well as using evolution in the sense of "history", may be misleading.

Table 1. Four major domains of linguistics

	Language	LANGUAGE
Functioning	Particular linguistics	General Linguistics
Origin	Historical linguistics	Evolutionary linguistics

Each of the domains above has a different collocation on the time axis: p-linguistics is syn-chronic; g-linguistics is a-chronic, because it aims at establishing general-universal truths independent of space and time, valid in all past, present and future languages; h-linguistics is dia-chronic (in some particular cases phylo-genetic); e-linguistics is pan-chronic or onto-genetic, since it aims at studying any and all aspects of the genesis or the evolution of the human language faculty, from the inarticulate cries of the first *homo loquens* to the actual functioning of all the languages in the world. Schematically:

Table 2. Four major dimensions of linguistics

	Language	LANGUAGE
Functioning	Syn-chrony	A-chrony
Origin	Dia-chrony	Pan-chrony

Saussure clearly identified synchrony and diachrony, and glimpsed the panchronic dimension typical of the study of language origin in the 18th and 19th centuries (Saussure 1922: 134–4), but he did not identify achrony as the specific dimension of g-linguistics, because he considered g-linguistics only as the sum of the categories and the constructs used in the grammars of individual languages or as the domain of evolutionary, universal laws.[10] Therefore, in Europe – or, at least, in many European university departments, especially those concerned with h-linguistics, where Saussure's teaching is particularly alive and well – the label of *synchronic linguistics* usually covers both p-linguistics and g-linguistics, although the general theory of LANGUAGE is a-chronic, rather than syn-chronic, strictly speaking. Besides, from a usage perspective, synchrony should also be seen as dynamic.

---

10. For a critique of Saussure's notions of synchrony/panchrony, see Hjelmslev (1968: 101ff.) and Sommerfelt (1971: 59ff.). The synonymy between synchronic and static in Saussure's work lamented by Belardi (1990) clearly demonstrates that Saussure tended to merge p-linguistics, which is in fact synchronic, and g-linguistics, which is achronic, that is to say really static. On the double nature, achronic and/or panchronic, of language universals, see Plank (2007), Cristofaro (2014) and Haspelmath (2019).

Given this general architecture, the fundamental point around which the comparative concept debate has revolved has been the relation between g-linguistics (in our specific case, Typology, as far as all the discussants considered language comparison as the best way to make generalisations about LANGUAGE) and p-linguistics. Crucially, the discussion centered on the nature of the categories needed for either domain and the inconsistencies that may arise if a single language descriptive category is used to solve a general-typological problem.

Actually, the relation between g-linguistics and p-linguistics has changed many times in the course of history (see above, Section 2), but a particularly fast and deep turn has occurred in the past few years. Most generativists – or, at least, most generativists until recently – conceived the relation between the two levels as one of substantial identity, bar some parameters (see recently, e.g., Newmeyer 2007, 2010). This view prompted the reaction of a group of typologists such as Lazard, Dryer, Croft, Haspelmath, as well as others.[11] In their view, the relation between g-linguistics and p-linguistics is one of radical diversity, almost a dichotomy: the categories needed to compare languages are totally different from the categories needed to describe languages and there are no two categories that are exactly the same across languages. As a reaction to the empirically unfounded universalism of some generativists, such a radical claim was justified and insightful: comparative concepts have become a "necessary component of the typologist's toolkit" (Gil 2016: 456). However, the claim soon appeared to be too radical. By and large, typologists agree that g-linguistics and p-linguistics are conceptually and methodologically two distinct things: many (perhaps most?) comparative concepts are indeed of a functional/semantic nature, thus (to a certain extent) pre-linguistic and independent from descriptive categories that may be needed in order to describe single languages. But, in turn, language particularism may need some rethinking, and to totally deny that comparative concepts can also be based on language-specific categories, with a (partly) formal definition, is not advisable. The general theory of LANGUAGE and the description of individual languages are indeed two different things, but they are very closely and complementarily related. As Lehmann (2018: 35) puts it, taking up Bossong's metaphor (1992):

---

11. See, e.g., Lazard (1992, 1997, 2001a: 365, 2001b: 141, 2004, 2012), Dryer (1997, 2016), Haspelmath (2004, 2007, 2010a, 2010b, 2011, 2012, 2014, 2016, 2018), Croft (2000, 2001, 2005, 2016), Croft & van Lier (2013), van der Auwera & Sahoo (2015). See also Maddieson (2018) with regard to phonology. Obviously, these works were not unprecedented: see section 1 for some of the early Typologists who paved the way for a similar approach.

> Apparently the history of our discipline is doomed to follow the motion of a pendulum: after North American structuralism ("languages could differ from each other without limit and in unpredictable ways" [Martin Joos 1957]), we have had Generative Grammar ("Grammatica una et eadem est secundum substantiam in omnibus linguis, licet accidentaliter varietur" [Roger Bacon 1244]); and apparently it is now time to swing back to Joos ("Language describers have to create language-particular structural categories for their language, rather than being able to "take them off the shelf"." [Haspelmath 2007, section 3]). It seems to be time to halt the pendulum in its middle position.

The challenge, today as yesterday, is to establish where exactly *is* the middle position of the pendulum, that is, which is the right level of granularity and the right type(s) of categories that may allow us to capture significant generalisations. Taken all together, the contributions to this volume represent an attempt to propose some answers to the challenge, following two main lines of research: i) further investigations about the nature of comparative concepts and their collocation in the general theory of LANGUAGE; ii) problems arising in the application of comparative concepts to specific language phenomena.

6. The contributions to this volume

The articles included in this volume tackle the issue of categories from a wide range of perspectives and with different *foci*. While the first six papers deal with general problems, such as the ones discussed above, the following five confront specific issues in the domain of language analysis which pose problems from the point of view of the application of categories.

The article by Martin Haspelmath deals with a most essential issue in relation to categories: the standardisation of nomenclature, i.e. category labels. Haspelmath distinguishes between general cross-linguistic comparative concepts and language-particular categories. Consequently, he advocates a uniform terminology in order to make cross-linguistic comparison possible and understandable. Along with this uniform terminology, particular terms will be needed to account for language-particular phenomena (for instance the German distinction between so-called 'strong' and 'weak' Adjectives). Haspelmath highlights how standardised nomenclature is commonplace in the natural sciences, which deal with natural kinds and entities: the categories of linguistics, on the contrary, do not exist independently of particular cultural contexts or the particular observer's contexts. However, a standardised and widely accepted list of (so to say) 'comparative concepts' exists also for linguists: this is the International Phonetic Alphabet. Thus, while rejecting the idea of 'right' or 'wrong' comparative concepts (see above, Section 3), Haspelmath suggests that, for practical reasons, some standardisation of the names and definition of category labels is desirable: in his paper, he discusses the challenges which are met in the process.

The paper by Martina Wiltschko tries to reconcile the 'classic' Chomskyan idea of the universality of categories (the so-called 'Universal Base Hypothesis') and the opposite view, widespread in the typological literature (but not only therein: see above, Section 3), which she terms 'No Base Hypothesis' (Wiltschko 2014: 19). Elaborating on her previous research (see Wiltschko 2014), Wiltschko argues here that, while the categories we observe are necessarily language-specific, they are built from 'universal building blocks', which she calls the 'Universal Spine', a (hierarchically organised) set of functions. Thus, according to her view, the familiar language-specific grammatical categories are constructed by associating units of language with the blocks in the spine; the spine itself constitutes the *tertium comparationis* for the comparison of language-specific categories across languages. In her paper, Wiltschko applies her proposal to three empirical domains, namely 'typical' grammatical categories (e.g., tense, mood, etc.), categories associated with interaction (interjections, etc.), and categories that express emotions (ideophones, expressives).

Zygmunt Frajzyngier's contribution undertakes a critical reassessment of Haspelmathian comparative concepts, arguing that the use of those concepts in cross-linguistic research may not be suited to reflect the differences and similarities across grammatical systems: in such a view, what is compared are, in essence, arbitrarily chosen comparative notions. As an alternative, Frajzyngier proposes that comparison can be based only on actual categories of languages, understood as 'functional domains', as e.g., tense, aspect, reference systems, and on the functions encoded in those domains; in his paper, this approach is applied to the functional domain of the relationship between the predicate and noun phrases in a 20-language sample.

Comparative concepts are critically re-examined in the light of predicate logic in Hans-Heinrich Lieb's paper. Lieb acknowledges that the distinction between comparative concepts and descriptive categories is not something to be disposed of, but he believes that Haspelmath fails to understand that the notion of comparative concepts is theory-dependent, in that their definition requires a web of notions depending on a theoretical framework. Lieb proposes here a reformulation of the idea of comparative concepts: put very briefly, the grammar of an individual language presupposes a theory of language that may include comparative concepts among its 'constants'. These constants are used in the grammar as part of descriptive expressions that denote linguistic objects of the language: in particular, categories. Lieb's approach has surely the merit of being at the crossroads between different disciplines (philosophy, logic, linguistics) and of proposing a more precise phrasing of many aspects of Haspelmath's theory: it remains to be seen what empirical achievements can be obtained thanks to this increased theoretical precision.

Tabea Reiner provides interesting observations on the nature of the categories used in cross-linguistic comparison. In her paper, she argues against the use of so-called 'pure' comparative concepts, i.e. concepts defined solely on the base of semantics, and proposes that comparison be based not only on (semantically-defined) comparative notions, but also on *formal* comparative categories. Thus, for instance, when comparing two languages, one may ask whether the word forms used for attribution and predication are the same – corresponding to a proposed formal comparative category IDENTITY OF MARKING. By using formal categories as a complement to comparative concepts, we may be able to compare the actual means different languages can use to express a given concept.

Yoshiko Ono and Waldfried Premper devote their paper to a reassessment of the well-known UNITYP project – initiated many years ago by Hansjakob Seiler (see above, Section 2) – on language universals and linguistic typology. The aspects of the UNITYP project which are obviously most relevant for the topic of this volume are methodological: they concern how to identify suitable objects for comparison, and how to group them into categories. The contributors provide a detailed discussion of the evolution of Seiler's approach to the task: the hierarchical model, ranging from 'fundamental functional concepts' (the highest level of abstraction, called by Seiler 'dimensions', such as APPREHENSION, PARTICIPATION etc.) to language-specific expressions, with the highest level of 'observability'; later on, the representation of 'contents of thinking', concretised by 'States of Affairs', in a three-level procedure, including 1) a pragmatic level, 2) a level of strict linguist representation, 3) the level of spoken language. In spite of the specific terminology used in the UNITYP project, the article shows the tight connections between the issues of UNITYP and those dealt with in many other contributions to the present volume – as, for instance, the discussion regarding 'comparative concepts' and cross-linguistic comparison.

Simone Mattiola's contribution is a case study on the so-called 'pluractional constructions'. In this paper, the author's declared aim is to show that linguistic categories are not universal: starting from a definition of pluractionality as the morphological modification of the verb that primarily conveys a plurality of situations or of states of affairs (events/states), through time, space and/or participants, Mattiola shows that pluractional constructions actually encode a wide variety of functions in different languages, as e.g., habituality, continuativity, and reciprocity, which may be expressed with different formal strategies (affixation, reduplication, lexical alternation). Because of this broad range of variation, pluractional constructions may be understood as belonging to domains as aspect, actionality, etc. This is interpreted by Mattiola as evidence of the non-existence of a universal category of 'pluractionality', which is instead a semantically/functionally-defined comparative notion, seen as the only kind of *tertium* that can be used in cross-linguistic investigation. The relations between the notion of 'pluractionality', the marking of plural on nouns and aspectual notions such as iterativity, frequentativity, etc. remain problematic, but the paper brings in a useful array of empirical data supporting the comparative notion of 'pluractionality'.

Luca Alfieri's article adopts and further elaborates on the distinction between comparative concepts and descriptive categories by proposing a partly new definition of parts of speech, and uses that definition to provide a new analysis of two Indo-European languages, Latin and the Sanskrit language of the Ṛg-Veda (RV). Alfieri gathers all the "Adjective" (i.e. Quality Modifier) constructions in a sample of 51 hymns of the RV and shows that, in Latin, three major classes of simple lexical morphemes are found (nouns, adjectives and verbs), while in the RV there are only two major classes (verbal roots and nouns), and the typical "adjective" is a derived stem built on a verbal root and meaning a quality (i.e. a participial-like nominalisation: e.g., *tápas* 'heat', and *tápyate* 'he burns', 'root' *tap-*). The described data are then used to show that text frequency calculations may constitute a useful method to compare word classes across languages, as a complement to Croft's definition of parts of speech (2001), and that a previously neglected typological change at the level of parts of speech occurred between the history and the prehistory of the Indo-European languages (i.e. [N (AV)] → [N, A, V]). Also, Alfieri critically discusses traditional labels such as *noun, adjective, verb, stem, lexeme* and, especially, *root*.

The distinction between nominal and verbal reflexives is the topic of Nicoletta Puddu's contribution. In her paper, Puddu questions whether 'reflexives' may be used in typological research as comparative concepts, and whether the opposition between nominal and verbal reflexives is actually a valid one. With a thorough overview of the relevant literature, Puddu shows that the label 'reflexive' has been used to refer to a wide range of constructions with significantly different properties, sometimes even with a rather limited area of overlap. As to the distinction between nominal and verbal reflexives, she convincingly argues that the criteria employed in the literature are far from consistent. She then proposes that reflexivity be understood as a hybrid (i.e. semantic/formal) comparative concept which can be used as a *tertium comparationis*, and that coreference is not necessarily the central function of a reflexive marker. Also, she highlights that there are probably no universally valid parameters to distinguish nominal and verbal reflexives.

The article by Federica Da Milano is a discussion of the notion of 'pronoun' as applied to East and Southeast Asian languages, with a special focus on Japanese. Since many languages in the East and Southeast Asian area often use nominal items, instead of 'pronouns', to indicate social status, politeness distinctions, etc., it has been proposed that these languages do not possess the category 'personal pronoun' at all. In her article, Da Milano proposes a critical review of the literature on 'pronounhood' and offers a detailed case study of items functioning as personal pronouns in some Southeast Asian languages and in Japanese, both in synchrony and in diachrony. She argues that a prototype definition could best describe the facts of these languages: while personal pronouns e.g., in English might represent the focal instance of the prototype, Japanese would be rather far from the focal area of the definition, but still within its scope.

References

Beck, David. 2016. Some language-particular terms are comparative concepts. *Linguistic Typology* 20(2):995–402. https://doi.org/10.1515/lingty-2016-0013
Belardi, Walter. 1990. Contrasti teorici nella linguistica del Novecento. In *Linguistica, filologia e critica dell'espressione*, Belardi Walter (ed.), 93–154. Roma: Il Calamo.
Bossong, Georg. 1992. Reflections on the history of the study of universals. The case of the *partes orationis*. In *Meaning and Grammar. Cross-linguistic Perspectives* [Belgian Journal of Linguistics 4], Michel Kefer & Johan van der Auwera (eds), 3–16. Amsterdam: John Benjamins. https://doi.org/10.1515/9783110851656.3
Botha, Rudolph. 2016. *Language Evolution*. Cambridge: CUP. https://doi.org/10.1017/CBO9781316471449
Bybee, Joan. 1985. *Morphology. A Study of the Relation between Meaning and Form* [Typological Studies in Language 9]. Amsterdam: John Benjamins. https://doi.org/10.1075/tsl.9
Bybee, Joan. 2010. *Language, Usage and Cognition*. Cambridge: CUP. https://doi.org/10.1017/CBO9780511750526
Bybee, Joan, Perkins, Revere & Pagliuca, William. 1994. *The Evolution of Grammar. Tense, Aspect and Modality in the Languages of the World*. Chicago IL: The University of Chicago Press.
Comrie, Bernard. 1976. *Aspect*. Cambridge: CUP.
Comrie, Bernard. 1978. Ergativity. In *Syntactic Typology: Studies in the Phenomenology of Language*, Winfred P. Lehmann (ed.), 329–394. Austin TX: University of Texas Press.
Comrie, Bernard. 1981[1989]. *Language Universals and Linguistic Typology*. Chicago IL: University of Chicago Press.
Cristofaro, Sonia. 2014. Competing motivation models and diachrony: What evidence for what motivations? In *Competing Motivations in Grammar and Usage*, Brian MacWhinney, Andrej L. Malchukov & Edith A. Moravcsik (eds), 282–298. Oxford: OUP. https://doi.org/10.1093/acprof:oso/9780198709848.003.0017
Croft, William. 1990[2003]. *Typology and Universals*. Cambridge: CUP.
Croft, William. 2000. Parts of speech as language universals and language-particular categories. In *Approaches to the Typology of Word-Classes*, Petra M. Vogel & Bernard Comrie (eds), 65–102. Berlin: Mouton de Gruyter. https://doi.org/10.1515/9783110806120.65
Croft, William. 2001. *Radical Construction Grammar*. Oxford: OUP. https://doi.org/10.1093/acprof:oso/9780198299554.001.0001

Croft, William. 2005. Word-classes, parts of speech and syntactic argumentation. *Linguistic Typology* 9: 431–441.
Croft, William. 2016. Comparative concepts and language-specific categories: Theory and practice. *Linguistic Typology* 20(2): 377–393. https://doi.org/10.1515/lingty-2016-0012
Croft, William & van Lier, Eva. 2012. Language universals without universal categories. *Theoretical Linguistics* 38(1–2): 57–72.
Cysouw, Michael & Good, Jeff. 2000. Languoid, doculect and glossonym: Formalizing the notion 'language'. *Language Documentation and Conservation* 7: 331–359.
Dahl, Östen. 2016. Thoughts on language-specific and cross-linguistic entities. *Linguistic Typology* 20(2): 427–437. https://doi.org/10.1515/lingty-2016-0016
Dixon, Robert M.W. 1977. Where have all adjectives gone? *Studies in Languages* 1: 19–77. (Repr. 1982. Berlin: Mouton De Gruyter).
Dixon, Robert M.W. 1979. Ergativity. *Language* 55: 59–138. https://doi.org/10.2307/412519
Dryer, Matthew S. 1992. The Greenbergian word order correlations. *Language* 68(1): 81–138. https://doi.org/10.1353/lan.1992.0028
Dryer, Matthew S. 1997. Are grammatical relations universal? In *Essays on Language Function and Language Type: Dedicated to T. Givón*, Joan Bybee, John Haiman & Sandra A. Thompson (eds), 115–143. Amsterdam: John Benjamins. https://doi.org/10.1075/z.82.09dry
Dryer, Matthew S. 2016. Cross-linguistic categories, comparative concepts, and the Walman diminutive. *Linguistic Typology* 20(2): 305–331. https://doi.org/10.1515/lingty-2016-0009
Evans, Nicholas. 2013. Language diversity as a resource for understanding cultural evolution. In *Cultural Evolution: Society, Technology, Language, Religion*, Peter J. Richerson & Morten H. Christiansen (eds), 233–268. Cambridge MA: The MIT Press. https://doi.org/10.7551/mitpress/9780262019750.003.0013
Evans, Nicholas & Levinson, Stephen C. 2009. The myth of language universals: Language diversity and its importance for cognitive science. *Behavioral and Brain Sciences* 32: 429–492. https://doi.org/10.1017/S0140525X0999094X
Gil, David. 2016. Describing languoids: When incommensurability meets the language-dialect continuum. *Linguistic Typology* 20(2): 439–462. https://doi.org/10.1515/lingty-2016-0017
Givón, Talmy. 1979. *On Understanding Grammar*. New York NY: Academic Press.
Graffi, Giorgio. 2001. *200 Years of Syntax. A Critical Survey* [Studies in the History of the Language Sciences 98]. Amsterdam: John Benjamins. https://doi.org/10.1075/sihols.98
Graffi, Giorgio. 2011. The pioneers of linguistic typology. In Song (ed), 25–42.
Greenberg, Joseph H. 1966 [1963]. Some universals of grammar with particular reference to the order of meaningful elements. In *Universals of Language*, 2nd edn, Joseph H. Greenberg (ed.), 73–113. Cambridge MA: The MIT Press.
Haspelmath, Martin. 2004. Does linguistic explanation presuppose linguistic description? *Studies in Language* 28(3): 554–579. https://doi.org/10.1075/sl.28.3.06has
Haspelmath, Martin. 2007. Pre-established categories don't exist – Consequence for language description and typology. *Linguistic Typology* 11: 119–132. https://doi.org/10.1515/LINGTY.2007.011
Haspelmath, Martin. 2010a. Comparative concepts and descriptive categories in cross-linguistic studies. *Language* 86: 663–687. https://doi.org/10.1353/lan.2010.0021
Haspelmath, Martin. 2010b. The interplay between comparative concepts and descriptive categories (Reply to Newmeyer). *Language* 86(3): 696–699. https://doi.org/10.1353/lan.2010.0004

Haspelmath, Martin. 2011. The indeterminacy of word segmentation and the nature of morphology and syntax. *Folia Linguistica* 45(1): 31–80. https://doi.org/10.1515/flin.2011.002

Haspelmath, Martin. 2012. How to compare major word classes across languages. In *Theories of Everything in Honor of Edward Keenan* [UCLA Working Papers in Linguistics Volume 17, Article 16], Thomas Graf, Denis Paperno, Anna Szabolcsi & Jos Tellings (eds), 109–130. Los Angeles CA: UCLA. <http://phonetics.linguistics.ucla.edu/wpl/issues/wpl17/wpl17.html> (11 November 2020).

Haspelmath, Martin. 2014. *(Non-)universality of word-classes and words: The mid-20th century shift*. <https://hiphilangsci.net/2014/10/08/non-universality-of-word-classes-and-words-the-mid-20th-century-shift/> (11 November 2020).

Haspelmath, Martin. 2016. The challenge of making language description and comparison mutually beneficial. *Linguistic Typology* 20(2): 299–303. https://doi.org/10.1515/lingty-2016-0008

Haspelmath, Martin. 2018. How comparative concepts and descriptive linguistic categories are different. In *Aspects of Linguistic Variations: Studies in Honour of Johan van der Auwera*, Daniël Van Olmen, Tanja Mortelmans & Frank Brisard (eds), 83–113. Berlin: De Gruyter.

Haspelmath, Martin. 2019. Can cross-linguistic regularities be explained by constraints on change? In *Explanation in Typology: Diachronic Sources, Functional Motivations and the Nature of the Evidence*, Karsten Schmidtke-Bode, Natalia Levshina, Susanne M. Michaelis & Ilja A. Seržant (eds), 1–23. Berlin: Language Science Press.

Haspelmath, Martin, Dryer, Matthew S., Gil, David & Comrie, Bernard (eds). 2005. *The World Atlas of Language Structures*. Oxford: OUP. (On line edition 2013: Haspelmath, Martin & Dryer, Matthew S. (eds). Leipzig: Max Plank Institute for Evolutionary Anthropology).

Hawkins, John A. 1983. *Word Order Universals: Quantitative analyses of linguistic structure*. New York NY: Academic Press.

Hjelmslev, Louis. 1968[1928]. *Principes de grammaire générale*. København: Munsgaard.

Hurford, James R. 2007–2012. *Language in the Light of Evolution*, Vol. 1 (2007), Vol. 2 (2012). Oxford: OUP.

Keenan, Edward L. & Comrie, Bernard. 1977. Noun phrase accessibility and universal grammar. *Linguistic Inquiry* 8: 63–99.

Kuteva, Tania, Heine, Bernd, Hong, Bo, Long, Haiping, Narrog, Heiko & Rhee, Seongha. 2019. *World Lexicon of Grammaticalization*. Cambridge: CUP. https://doi.org/10.1017/9781316479704

Jakobson, Roman. 1958. Typological studies and their contribution to historical comparative linguistics. In *Actes du 8ème Congr. Intern. des Linguistes*, Eva Siversten (ed.), 17–25. Oslo: Oslo University Press.

Lander, Yury & Arkadiev, Peter. 2016. On the right of being a comparative concept. *Linguistic Typology* 20(2): 403–416. https://doi.org/10.1515/lingty-2016-0014

Lazard, Gilbert. 1975. La catégorie de l'éventuel. In *Mélanges linguistiques offerts à Emile Benveniste*, Georges Dumézil, Claude Hagège & Emmanuel Laroche (eds), 347–358. Louvain: Peeters.

Lazard, Gilbert. 1992. Y a-t-il des catégories interlanguagières? In *Texte, Sätze, Wörter und Moneme. Festschrift für Klaus Heger zum 65. Geburtstag*, Susanne R. Anschüz (ed.), 427–434. Heidelberger: Orientverlag.

Lazard, Gilbert. 1997. Pour une terminologie rigoureuse: Quelques principes et propositions. *Mémoires de la Société de Linguistique de Paris (nouvelle série)* 6: 111–133.

Lazard, Gilbert. 2001a. On the grammaticalization of evidentiality. *Journal of Pragmatics* 33: 359–367. https://doi.org/10.1016/S0378-2166(00)00008-4

Lazard, Gilbert. 2001b. Transitivity revisited as an example of a more strict approach in typological research. *Folia Linguistica* 36: 141–200.

Lazard, Gilbert. 2004. On the status of linguistics with particular regards to typology. *The Linguistic Review* 21: 389–411. https://doi.org/10.1515/tlir.2004.21.3-4.389

Lazard, Gilbert. 2012. The case for pure linguistics. *Studies in Language* 36(2): 241–259. https://doi.org/10.1075/sl.36.2.02laz

LaPolla, Randy J. 2016. On categorization: Stick to the facts of the languages. *Linguistic Typology* 20(2): 365–375. https://doi.org/10.1515/lingty-2016-0011

Lehmann, Christian. 2018. Linguistic concepts and categories in language description and comparison. In *Typology, Acquisition, Grammaticalization Studies*, Marina Chini & Pierluigi Cuzzolin (eds.). 27–50. Milano: FrancoAngeli.

Maddieson, Ian. 2018. Is phonological typology possible without (universal) categories? In *Phonological Typology*, Larry M. Hyman & Franz Plank (eds), 107–125. Berlin: De Gruyter. https://doi.org/10.1515/9783110451931-004

Michaelis, Susanne M., Maurer, Philippe, Haspelmath, Martin & Huber, Magnus (eds). 2013. *The Survey of Pidgin and Creole Languages*, 4 Vols. Oxford: OUP.

Moravcisik, Edith A. 2016. On linguistic categories. *Linguistic Typology* 20(2): 417–425.

Morpurgo Davies, Anna. 1994. La linguistica dell'Ottocento. In *Storia della linguistica*, Vol. 3, Giulio C. Lepschy (ed.), 11–399. Bologna: Il Mulino.

Newmeyer, Frederick. 2007. Linguistic typology requires crosslinguistic formal categories. *Linguistic Typology* 11(1): 133–157. https://doi.org/10.1515/LINGTY.2007.012

Newmeyer, Frederick. 2010. On comparative concepts and descriptive categories: A reply to Haspelmath. *Language* 86(3): 688–695. https://doi.org/10.1353/lan.2010.0000

Plank, Frans. 2007. Extent and limit of linguistic diversity as the remit of typology – But through constraints on what is diversity limited? *Linguistic Typology* 11: 43–68. https://doi.org/10.1515/LINGTY.2007.005

Plank, Frans. 2016. Of categories: Language-particular – Comparative – Universal. *Linguistic Typology* 20(2): 297–298.

Ramat, Paolo. 1990. Da Humboldt ai neogrammatici: Continuità e fratture. In *Leibniz, Humboldt, and the Origins of Comparativism*, Tullio De Mauro & Lia Formigari (eds), 199–210. Amsterdam: John Benjamins. https://doi.org/10.1075/sihols.49.13ram

Ramat, Paolo. 1999. Linguistic categories and linguists' categorizations. *Linguistics* 37(1): 157–180. https://doi.org/10.1515/ling.1999.002

Ramat, Paolo. 2011. The (early) history of linguistic typology. In Song (ed.), 9–24.

Rijkhoff, Jan. 2004[2002]. *The Noun Phrase*. Oxford: OUP.

Rijkhoff, Jan. 2016. Crosslinguistic categories in morphosyntactic typology: Problems and prospects. *Linguistic Typology* 20(2): 333–363. https://doi.org/10.1515/lingty-2016-0010

de Saussure, Ferdinand. 1922. *Course de linguistique générale*. Paris: Payot. Italian edn. by De Mauro, Tullio. 1997. *Corso di linguistica generale*. Bari: Laterza.

Seiler, Hansjakob. 1995. Cognitive-conceptual structure and linguistic encoding: Language universals and typology in the UNITYP framework. In Shibatani & Bynon (eds), 273–325.

Shibatani, Masayoshi & Bynon, Theodora (eds). 1995. *Approaches to Language Typology*. Oxford: Clarendon Press.

Sommerfelt, Alf. 1971[1962]. *Diachronic and Synchronic Aspects of Language*. The Hague: Mouton. https://doi.org/10.1515/9783110803624

Song, Jae Jung (ed.). 2011. *The Oxford Handbook of Linguistic Typology*. Oxford: OUP.
Stassen, Leon. 1985. *Comparison and Universal Grammar*. Oxford: Basil Blackwell.
Tomasello, Michael. 1999. *The Cultural Origin of Human Cognition*. Cambridge MA: Harvard University Press.
Tomasello, Michael. 2003. *Constructing a Language: A Usage-Based Theory of Language Acquisition*. Cambridge MA: Harvard University Press.
van der Auwera, Johan & Sahoo, Kalyanamalini. 2015. On comparative concepts and descriptive categories, such as they are. *Acta linguistica Hafniensia* 47(2): 136–173. https://doi.org/10.1080/03740463.2015.1115636
Wiltschko, Martina. 2014. *The Universal Structure of Categories. Towards a Formal Typology*. Oxford: OUP. https://doi.org/10.1017/CBO9781139833899

CHAPTER 2

Towards standardization of morphosyntactic terminology for general linguistics

Martin Haspelmath
MPI-SHH Jena and Leipzig University

This paper proposes that just like phonologists, linguists working on morphosyntax should have a core set of standard terms that are understood in exactly the same way across the discipline. Most of these terms are traditional terms that are given a standard retro-definition, because linguists already behave as if these terms had the same meaning for everyone. The definitions are definitions of general concepts (i.e., comparative concepts, applicable to all languages in exactly the same way), but they are expected to be highly similar to language-particular categories with the same labels. If linguists were close to finding out the true natural-kind categories of Human Language that all grammars consist of, there would be no need for definitions, but since this seems to be a remote goal, research on general linguistics must rely on uniformly defined general terms.

1. Terminological consistency and standardization

Standardization has proved highly beneficial in many domains of technology and trade, and it is impossible to imagine today's world without worldwide standards for basic units of time and space (the International System of Units, the Coordinated Universal Time, and others).

In addition to such practical standards that ensure technological interoperability, there are also standard nomenclatures in many fields of science that affect how scientists talk about their subject domain. Biologists have had generally accepted conventions for naming species since the 18th century, and chemists started to organize terminological standards in the 1860s. Linguists have had a standard for representing general phonetic categories of segments since the 1890s: what is now known as the International Phonetic Alphabet (IPA).

In this paper, I would like to make the case for a morphosyntactic counterpart of the IPA: a standard set of morphosyntactic terms for general linguistics. If such a standard were possible, its advantages should be evident to every linguist who has had more than a few years of experience in the field. Many terms in linguistics are used in a variety of ways that are often confusing, and unless one is a specialist in a particular area, one may be unaware of these ambiguities. As a result, automatic literature search is often problematic or impossible, and unfortunately, there is also quite a bit of incomprehension and talking past each other.

A widespread attitude in the field seems to be that the difficulties of our subject matter – the enormous complexities of the many different language systems that linguists are grappling with – make it impossible to have a standard terminology, at least at the present stage of our knowledge. It is this attitude that I would like to challenge in the present paper. One of the reasons for being more optimistic is that I have observed not only big difficulties, but also quite a bit of sloppy terminological use by linguists. Grammatical terms often change their meanings through a novel use of an existing term that is primarily motivated by the desire to avoid coining a new term. For example, the term *oblique* used to refer to all non-nominative cases (there was the nominative case and the oblique cases). Since the 1970s, however, it has come to be used for all cases apart from the nominative and the accusative, as well as (more generally) for all cases and adpositions that are used for arguments other than the transitive subject and direct object (e.g., Nichols 1984). There was no particular reason for this change, and it would have been easy to coin a new term instead. The confusion generated by the semantic shift of the term *oblique* was thus unrelated to any particular difficulties, and entirely due to the attitude that it does not matter much if an older term is used with a new meaning. And indeed, within a given narrow context, it is often fairly clear what a term means. But from the broader perspective of the entire field of the language sciences, the current level of terminological unclarity and ambiguity is undesirable.

Thus, while there are no doubt many difficulties in the field of general morphosyntax, this need not make it impossible to have a standard terminology. Other fields have difficulties as well (including the phoneticians, who have the IPA), but many fields of science are at least making an effort to have terminological standards. I thus want to argue that the field of general linguistics should have at least a limited set of standard terms (say, a few dozen, comparable to the 107 IPA letters).

It is important to note that my proposal in this paper concerns exclusively terminology for general linguistics, and that I say nothing about language-particular terms here. There are many phenomena that can be talked about only at the level of a particular language, e.g., the French Passé Surcomposé (as in *elle l'a eu vue* 'she had seen her'), or the Genitive Absolute in Ancient Greek, or even the "f-word" in English. There are no counterparts of these phenomena in most other languages, so they are not directly relevant to general linguistics. Terminology of the language-particular kind can perhaps be standardized as well,[1] but in this paper, I will confine myself to terms of general linguistics – in other words, to terms for comparative concepts.

The notion of COMPARATIVE CONCEPTS in grammar has been fairly widely adopted since I first coined the term in 2010 (see Haspelmath 2010, 2018a; Brown & Chumakina 2013; Croft 2016; Dryer 2016), but it seems that many linguists are still not fully clear about it. I will therefore briefly explain the distinction between comparative concepts and language-particular categories in the next section, and contrast both with the notion of (innate) natural-kind categories.

2. Comparative concepts, language-particular categories, and natural kinds

Confusingly, grammatical terms such as *complementizer* or *consonant* are used in three different senses in the literature:

- as (category-like) comparative concepts
- as language-particular categories
- as natural-kind categories

A category-like comparative concept is a term that can be applied to any language and that is identified in all languages by the same criteria.[2] For example, a consonant can be defined as a sound segment that is articulated with at least partial closure of the vocal tract, and a complementizer can be said to be a marker that indicates that the clause in which it occurs is a complement clause. Comparative concepts of this kind are needed for universal claims, e.g., about the position of the complementizer within a complement clause (Dryer 2009). The comparative

---

1. In view of the proliferation of grammatical terminology in different (West) German school textbooks in the 1970s, politicians entrusted some linguistics professors with the task of setting up a standard set of terms for German, English, French and Latin grammar for use in secondary schools. This work has been ongoing for quite a while (see Hennig 2012), showing that grammatical terminology can also be relevant to applied concerns such as teaching of grammar and languages in schools.

2. A comparative concept need not be category-like. A nonverbal stimulus or a text passage in a parallel text can also be a comparative concept (such concepts are called *etic comparative concepts*; Haspelmath 2018a: 87–88). Another type of comparative concept is the standard lexical meaning, as in the *Concepticon* (List et al. 2019). Such comparative concepts are never confused with descriptive categories, probably because of their specific names.

definition of a complementizer merely says that it is a marker (not that it is a word), because many languages have elements that seem to be part of the verbal morphology but function just like the English word *that* or the Italian word *che*. And in fact, English has a marker like this as well: the suffix *-ing*. This is used as a complementizer in cases like *She considered leav-ing*. Thus, from a comparative perspective, English has not only clause-initial complementizer words, but also an affixed complementizer that is postposed to the verb.

Moving now on to language-particular terms, we can talk about English Complementizers and Latin Consonants (with capitalization of unique entities), but these categories are defined differently from the comparative concepts. In English grammar, a Complementizer is generally said to be a word, so that *-ing* is not considered as a Complementizer. And what counts as a word (or rather, an English Word) is determined by English-specific criteria. Likewise, what counts as a Latin Consonant is determined by Latin-specific criteria. Thus, the semivowels [j] and [w] are usually treated as Consonants for the purposes of (Latin-specific) phonotactics, even though by the phonetic criterion, they would not be consonants because there is no closure of the vocal tract.

Language-particular terms are sometimes written with capitalization, in order to distinguish them clearly from comparative terms (Comrie 1976; Haspelmath 2010: Section 5), but most of the time, linguists rely on context to make it clear whether they are talking about concepts of general linguistics or about language-particular categories.

Both comparative concepts and language-particular categories must be defined in a precise way. It is sometimes thought that a prototype definition is sufficient for comparative purposes. For example, Dingemanse (2019: 20) says that "typological definitions generally aim to capture the centre of gravity of a phenomenon rather than providing a list of necessary and sufficient properties", but this is not true. If there were no list of necessary and sufficient properties, it could not be clear whether a phenomenon should be grouped under a comparative concept or not, and it would not be possible to make a cross-linguistic database that records the properties of a sample of languages in terms of the comparative concept.

However, comparative concepts need not be comprehensive, because language comparison is always partial (only language description must ultimately be complete). Languages have many structures that can be compared with similar structures in other languages, but they often have completely unique phenomena that are not amenable to comparison (e.g., German Weak vs. Strong adjectives, or the Latin Attributive Gerundive construction). Thus, it is possible to have definitions of category-like comparative concepts that focus on a shared core, where the corresponding descriptive categories must be extensionally broader (see the discussion in Section 5 below). This may give the wrong impression that the comparative concept is vague or covers only a "prototype" (like the definition of *noun* in (5) below).

In addition to comparative concepts and language-particular categories, many linguists also work with natural-kind categories. These are different from language-particular categories in that they occur not only in a single language but are assumed to be potentially applicable to any language. This is so because they are thought to be innately given (as part of a genetically determined grammar blueprint called "universal grammar"), in advance of language learning (as "pre-established categories", cf. Haspelmath 2007). Thus, it is often claimed that there is a natural-kind category complementizer (often written COMP or simply C), and that different languages instantiate it in different ways (often by zero, and sometimes even by movement of a verb). Similarly, consonants (often written "[+cons]") can be thought of as an innate natural-kind category of phonology, instantiated in different ways (often by zero, as in "CV phonology", Clements & Keyser 1983, or by non-movement in sign languages, Brentari 2002).

Natural-kind categories are very different from comparative concepts and language-particular categories, because they are not instruments for research, but are hypothetical results of research. They have the status of chemical elements in 18th century chemistry, before scientists had figured out what underlies the diversity of chemical compounds (cf. Baker (2001) on the similarities between natural-kind based generative typology and chemistry). Many linguists are skeptical of the natural-kind approach, and even those who assume the basic correctness of the approach admit that the goal of discovering the true natural kinds of the grammar blueprint is still distant. Thus, it would be premature to talk about standardization of natural-kind categories, because we know too little about them, if they exist at all.[3]

In some other fields, the standard terminology concerns natural-kind categories, e.g., in chemistry (whose elements and compounds are natural kinds) and in biology (whose species are also often considered as natural kinds). And still other fields, such as economics or political science, have no natural-kind categories at all, as far as I am aware. Categories such as income, tax, state, and government are

---

3. It seems to me that those linguists who think that standardization of grammatical terminology is too difficult often have natural-kind categories in mind, and if so, I fully agree with them. Many linguists do not distinguish clearly between comparative concepts and natural-kind categories, and this may account for the skeptical attitude toward standardization of grammatical terms.

social categories, and nobody would suggest that they are innate properties of the human mind.[4] Thus, there are three types of disciplines:

i. social sciences, which have culture-specific social categories, but no natural-kind categories;
ii. natural sciences, which have natural-kind categories but no social categories;
iii. sciences at the intersection of social and natural sciences such as linguistics, which have both social categories (such as English Complementizer and Latin Consonant) and natural-kind categories (though the latter are controversial in linguistics).

But importantly, ALL sciences have (observer-made) comparative concepts in addition to the independently existing categories (social or natural) that they encounter in the world.

In the natural and social sciences, comparative concepts are not so easily confused with the independently existing categories, so the distinction is not highlighted frequently. But some well-known nomenclature systems in the natural sciences are systems of conventional comparative concepts, e.g., the Yerkes spectral classification of stars in astronomy,[5] or the International Cloud Atlas Classification of clouds in meteorology.[6] Likewise, the social sciences have some well-known nomenclature systems of conventional comparative concepts, e.g., the Hornbostel-Sachs system of musical instrument classification in the comparative anthropology of music,[7] or the Human Development Index in comparative development economics. These systems of comparative concepts exist alongside culture-specific categories, and there is no danger of confusing them.

3. Examples of possible standard definitions of well-known terms

Before continuing the discussion of issues arising in standardization of terms, let us now look at a few concrete examples of terms and their definitions that I think

---

4. This might be different with kinship categories like 'mother' or 'brother', which might conceivably be innate categories, as they seem to be shared with other mammals that have kinship organization, but nothing like humans' complex culture.

5. <https://en.wikipedia.org/wiki/Stellar_classification#Yerkes_spectral_classification>

6. <https://en.wikipedia.org/wiki/International_Cloud_Atlas>

7. <https://en.wikipedia.org/wiki/Hornbostel%E2%80%93Sachs>

Chapter 2. Towards standardization of morphosyntactic terminology for general linguistics

might be suitable for standardization. Naturally, many of these are taken from my earlier or current work.

(1) sentence[8]
A sentence is a maximal clause, i.e., a clause that is not part of another clause.

(2) clause
A clause is a combination of a predicate (full verb or nonverbal predicate) and its arguments plus modifiers.

(3) morph[9]
A morph is a minimal form, i.e., a form that does not consist of other forms.

(4) root[10]
A root is a morph that denotes a thing, an action or a property.

(5) noun[11]
A noun is a morph (or a root) that denotes a thing, i.e., a physical object or a person.

(6) affix[12]
An affix is a non-promiscuous bound morph that is not a root.

(7) bound form[13]
A bound form is a form that cannot occur on its own.

(8) marker[14]
A marker is a bound form that is not a root.

---

8. <https://dlc.hypotheses.org/1725>
9. Haspelmath (2020).
10. Haspelmath (2012).
11. A colleague has suggested that noun may be better defined as 'a root that can be case-marked', but what does it mean to be case-marked? As seen in (16) and (15) below, 'case-marker' can be defined with reference to 'flag', which is defined with reference to 'nominal'. Maybe the latter term can be defined without reference to 'noun', but I leave this open here.
12. Haspelmath (2021a).
13. Haspelmath (2021a); <https://dlc.hypotheses.org/1779>
14. A reviewer notes that Pollard and Sag (1994: 44–45) provide an exclusively semantic definition of *marker* ("a word whose semantic content is purely logical in nature"), which is perhaps more in line with linguists' intuitions. But I do not think that a free form would be regarded as a marker, and the "non-root" part of my definition amounts to much the same (see (4)), except that it is easier to apply than a vague concept like "purely logical".

(9) A-argument[15]
A-argument is the argument of a two-participant clause that is coded like the 'breaker' or 'killer' argument of 'break/kill', if the other argument (the P-argument) is coded like the 'broken thing'/'killed animal'.

(10) subject[16]
The subject of a clause is its A-argument or its S-argument.

(11) transitive clause (cf. footnote 12)
A transitive clause is a clause that has an A-argument and a P-argument.

(12) ergative construction[17]
An ergative construction is a construction with a transitive verb in which the P-argument is coded like the intransitive S-argument, and the A-argument is coded differently.

(13) argument coding
Argument coding is the marking of an argument's semantic or syntactic role by means of a flag or a person index.

(14) passive construction
A passive construction is a construction (i) which shares the verb root with the transitive construction, (ii) whose S-argument corresponds to the transitive P-argument, and (iii) which requires oblique flagging of the argument corresponding to the transitive A-argument, if it can be expressed at all.

(15) flag[18]
A flag is a bound morph that occurs with a nominal and that expresses its semantic role.

(16) case-marker
A case-marker is a flag that is an affix.

(17) serial verb construction[19]
A serial verb construction is a monoclausal construction consisting of multiple independent verbs with no element linking them and with no predicate–argument relation between the verbs.

---

15. Lazard (2002).
16. Haspelmath (2011).
17. Comrie (1978).
18. Haspelmath (2005, 2019).
19. Haspelmath (2016).

(18) reflexive construction[20]
A reflexive construction is a grammatical construction
  i. that can only be used when two participant positions of a clause are filled by the same participant
  ii. and that contains a special form (a reflexivizer) that signals this coreference.

(19) gender system[21]
A gender system is a nomifier system with up to 20 nomifier classes (= gender classes) whose nomifiers are not restricted to occurring on numerals and possibly other adnominal modifiers, or restricted to occurring on possessors.

(20) nomifier system
A nomifier system is a paradigm of grammatical markers which occur on noun-associated forms and each of which expresses (partly reflects, or partly contributes) a broad property of the selecting noun other than person and number.

Several of these definitions will look strange to experienced readers, and many linguists will find it easy to raise objections. But my proposal here is not that these definitions (which happen to be the ones that I use in my own work) should become standard. And it seems that those colleagues who criticize the definitions generally find it less easy to come up with more appropriate definitions, so I have decided to list them anyway here. The main purpose of this article is to make a general case for standard definitions of terms, and by giving some definitions of some basic terms, I provide a proof of concept how this can be done concretely, even in difficult cases. (More specific terms such as "free relative clause" or "subsective adjective" are presumably easier to define than the basic terms.)

4. Principles for standard morphosyntactic terms

After having seen some concrete examples, let us consider a number of general principles for choosing terms and definitions.

---

20. Haspelmath (2021b).

21. Haspelmath (2018c). I have been asked whether 20 classes is not an arbitrary limit, and indeed it is, but this number is sometimes mentioned in the literature (e.g., Corbett 2007: 242: "the number of genders is not limited to two, nor to three: four is common and twenty is possible"). This arbitrary definition is given here in order to show that some traditional terms cannot be retro-defined in a way that appears natural. But whether a clearly defined concept is "natural" (and what this might mean) is not a question that I address in this paper.

First of all, we would like to have standard definitions of well-known grammatical terms, so many of the definitions in Section 3 concern well-known terms. This is completely analogous to the IPA, which provides standard definitions of the well-known letters of the Latin alphabet. I call such definitions *retro-definitions*, because they assign a precise meaning to an existing term that does not have a widely recognized precise meaning yet. (Some widely known established terms do have a precise meaning, e.g., *interrogative pronoun*, or *concessive clause*; these terms do not need to be retro-defined, because their definition is not in question.)

But this does not imply that widely needed comparative concepts cannot be described by completely novel terms. Just as the IPA includes many novel letters, we need many additional comparative concepts for morphosyntax, and some of the terms in Section 3 are quite novel (*morph, bound form, marker*, and *ergative construction* were added in the 20th century, and *flag* and *nomifier* are even more recent additions). Of course, the list is completely open-ended, and any general linguist who feels the need to use a new concept should feel free to coin a new term. Once a new term has been picked up by a certain number of other linguists, it could be added to the list of standard terms. (This is different from the IPA: phoneticians do not seem to think that the list of possible IPA symbols is completely open-ended.)[22] I do not expect the list of category-like comparative concepts ever to be complete, because the range of morphosyntactic constructions that might be compared across languages is very large and open-ended.

Each of the definitions in Section 3 presupposes a number of other terms, which must either be defined in turn (as comparative concepts), or must be assumed to be generally understood in the same way by everyone. Very basic linguistic concepts such as 'form', 'action', and 'semantic role' can (or must) be left undefined (as primitives), and in addition the definitions may of course contain general nontechnical concepts such as 'not', 'part of', or 'require'. But many technical terms will need to be defined in turn, as in the case of *oblique* in the definition of *passive construction*, or *associated form* in the definition of *nomifier system*.[23] Not all of the sample definitions in Section 3 are thus complete in the sense of being fully comprehensible. Some of them contain terms that are not widely known yet (e.g., *A-argument, flag, nomifier system*), which I decided to include

---

22. However, the actual descriptions of segment inventories in the world's languages contain an extremely wide variety of segment types. The Phoible database (Moran & McCloy 2019) includes over 3,000 different segmental comparative concepts, and for some of them, having a non-compound designation by means of a novel letter might well be useful.

23. Similarly, Corbett (2007: 242) notes that since *gender* is defined in terms of 'agreement', "the definition of agreement itself becomes important".

here in order to show how a number of more familiar terms (*subject, case-marker, gender system*) are defined.

Ultimately, all standard terms must be defined in such a way that their definitions only include primitive concepts or other well-defined concepts. This is not an easy task, of course, so I do not foresee it to be finished within a few years, regardless of whether such proposals will be widely accepted or not.

The examples in Section 3 show that fairly straightforward definitions are possible for frequently used terms, e.g., for *sentence, morph, root* and *marker*. Such terms are not usually defined by linguists, and are typically learned by ostension, like everyday words. For example, Booij's (2005) morphology textbook does not provide a usable definition of *root*: On p 29, we read that "Stems can be either simplex or complex. If they are simplex, they are called roots". This would seem to exclude roots which have no inflection and are therefore not stems (like English *gold* or *solid*). For the stereotypical Indo-European language, this may not be a big problem (because most verbs, nouns and adjectives show inflection), but it does not work for languages in general, because many languages have nouns that cannot be inflected, but we would still call them roots. Moreover, Booij provides no definition of *stem*. There are similar problems with the terms *clause* and *sentence*, which are rarely defined in a way that corresponds to the actual usage of the terms. For example, a well-known online glossary defines a sentence as "a grammatical unit that is composed of one or more clauses",[24] but this is not the way the term is used, because a clause may of course contain another clause (e.g., a relative clause, or a complement clause), and not all such clauses would be called sentences. It is clear that linguists have simply not invested a lot of energy into providing definitions, and that in many cases it is not difficult to improve on the current situation.

But other frequently used terms are harder to define in such a way that their definition broadly corresponds to their current use. For example, *subject* can be defined only through the terms *A-argument* and *S-argument*, which are not easy to define (see (9), and Haspelmath 2011a). And the term *gender system* is particularly difficult to define. Numeral classifiers are very similar to gender markers, and it seems that the main reason they are never included in discussions of gender systems is that they are stereotypically characteristic of East Asian languages, while gender systems are stereotypically characteristic of European (and African) languages.[25] Thus, numeral classifiers have to be specifically excluded, as is done in (19), and a new term (*nomifier*, short for 'nominal classification marker') needs

---

24. <https://glossary.sil.org/term/sentence>

25. Numeral classifiers are very similar to gender markers, cf. Japanese *niwatori san-ba* [chicken three-NUMCL.BA] 'three chickens', Italian *casa nuov-a* [house new-GND.A].

to be introduced as a general term that has numeral classifiers and gender markers as subtypes.

Thus, standardization of grammatical terms has at least two aspects: Retro-definitions of existing widely-used terms (such as *affix, sentence, subject*) and creation of new terms (such as *A-argument, nomifier*) when needed in order to provide retro-definitions.[26]

What are general principles for retro-definitions? A first principle is that an established term should not be defined in such a way that its definition is at variance with traditional use. It should cover the core of the phenomenon designated by the term (as generally understood), it should cover at least 80% of the cases where the term has been applied, and it should not include too many cases which would not be included traditionally. There are some well-known cases where the meaning of existing terms has been changed by prominent linguists (thus leading to much confusion),[27] and this experience should not be repeated. It will often be impossible to find a definition that covers 100% of the traditional usage, because this usage is frequently somewhat inconsistent, but 80% accuracy should be enough to justify continuing the term.

If a traditional term is used so inconsistently that it is not possible to define it in such a way that the definition covers most of its uses, the term should be abandoned. Examples of such terms whose traditional use is not sufficiently coherent are *inflection, (non)finite*, and *clitic*; I do not know how to define them in such a way that their definitions would correspond very largely to traditional usage (see Cristofaro (2007) on *finite*, and Haspelmath (2015) on *clitic*). And even though many people still use *word* in a technical sense, it is not clear either how to define it objectively (Haspelmath 2011b).

The definition of a comparative term should be as simple as possible, even if this means that not all cases that are traditionally subsumed under the term are included. For example, if marker is defined as 'a bound form that is not a root' (see (8) above), this is a simple definition, but it does not fully capture the intuition that a marker expresses a grammatical meaning. Bound forms such as *however* or *basically* are not roots (according to the definition in (4)), but they would not be considered as typical markers. Thus, the criterion of having a simple definition

---

26. But of course, one may also create completely novel terms that may become standard once they prove to be useful and are picked up by many linguists.

27. E.g., *ergative* for 'unaccusative' (e.g., Grewendorf 1989), *government* in Chomsky's (1981) sense (contrasting with the earlier established sense, cf. Lehmann 1983; Kibort 2010), or *anaphor* in Chomsky's (1981) sense (contrasting with the sense in computational linguistics).

may conflict with the criterion of having a good match with traditional usage, and one needs to strike a balance between the two criteria.

These principles will not cover all cases, and there will always be a certain amount of arbitrariness in definitions of comparative concepts. This is as it should be, because comparative concepts are not discoveries, but instruments for research (like units of measurement in physics). If there were no arbitrariness, no standardization would be required. The social implications of this will briefly be discussed in the final section.

Another important aspect of retro-definitions is that they may have a restricted extension in comparison to descriptive categories with the same name, as will be discussed next.

5. Shared-core definitions of comparative concepts

The definition of category-like terms need not correspond very closely to language-particular categories, but may be semantically simpler and merely correspond to the shared core of features of different language-particular categories. This is because it is often clearly meaningful to compare languages with respect to salient "core" concepts, regardless of how exactly the language-particular categories are delimited. For example, it is clearly very useful to compare languages with respect to how they express things (physical objects and persons), e.g., how they form plurals and how they express actions involving persons and things ('the girl took the pens'). We can thus define the term *noun* as a comparative concept as in (5) ('a root that denotes a thing'). Of course, in most or all languages, the class called "noun" goes beyond this core set of possible denotations (e.g., Russian *vojna* 'war', *svoboda* 'freedom'). Thus, the class of Russian Nouns cannot be defined semantically – this is known to all linguists from their syntax textbooks. But language-particular categories are defined by language-particular criteria (e.g., by being combinable with articles, or showing number distinctions, or inflecting for case), and these cannot be applied to all languages. The reason why we call different classes in different languages "nouns" is that they all include roots denoting objects and roots denoting persons, so this is the definition of the comparative concept. The fact that the categories called "noun" in different languages usually include more elements is not relevant to the definition of *noun* is a comparative concept, because the meanings of these other elements play no role in mapping the language-particular classes to the comparative concept.

In a very similar way, Nikolaeva and Spencer (2013: 219–220) mention the example of the term *adjective*, which they propose to define in terms of the concept of 'gradable property'. This decision leaves aside adjectives like 'dead' or 'blue'

(Nikolaeva and Spencer also mention more exotic cases like 'alleged'), but again, everyone seems to agree that gradable-property adjectives do indeed represent the shared core of the various categories in different languages that we call adjectives. If a language had a class of words that does not include any gradable property concepts, it would not be called "adjective".

Another example comes from the domain of gender. Languages with gender classes often have a feminine class, which can be defined semantically as a comparative concept:

> For some values, cross-linguistic comparison is straightforward: feminine gender is the value which includes nouns denoting females, and the interesting typological considerations are what other nouns may be included in this gender value [...] We need to define the core meanings and functions: we call a gender value the feminine if it includes nouns denoting females, whether or not it also includes diminutives. (Corbett 2009: 137)

The German Feminine class and the Arabic Feminine class are quite different in their extension (both contain many inanimates), but they share the common core of female animates, which makes it meaningful to compare them.

Similarly, the English preposition *to* and the Russian Dative suffixes *-u/-e/-am* share the recipient meaning (cf. Haspelmath 2010: 666) and can thus be said to match the comparative concept 'dative', even though they are otherwise quite different (the English preposition also marks spatial goals, and the Russian Dative case suffixes are also governed by some prepositions).[28]

Finally, the term *subject* as a comparative concept is defined in (10) in terms of the A-argument of two-argument clauses expressing a physical effect and patientive single-argument clauses, as discussed in detail in Haspelmath (2011a). By contrast, language-particular descriptions must include all the argument of all the verbs, including atypical two-argument verbs (such as 'to look' or 'to like'), and there is much less cross-linguistic uniformity with these other verbs. The literature is full of discussions of how to use the term "subject" with these more heterogeneous verbs, but there is no doubt about physical-effect verbs and patientive single-argument verbs.[29]

---

28. Corbett (2009: 137) mentions this example, too: "Similarly we call a case value the dative if used for recipients, whether or not it can also be governed by prepositions." (However, Corbett is only concerned with "case features", in which he does not include prepositions.)

29. The need for shared-core comparative concepts is not often mentioned in the literature, but Croft (2016: 378–379) notes something very similar:

> In general, extensionally "large" semantic categories that are given monosemous definitions ... do in fact often fail as comparative concepts. For example, property

It may well be that Dingemanse's formulation in terms of a "centre of gravity" (cited in Section 2 above) refers to what I call "shared core" here. However, what I mean here is not a "core" of a phenomenon that obviates the need for a definition in terms of necessary and sufficient conditions. The definitions must be precise (rather than prototype-based, see Section 6), but the mapping of a language-particular category onto the precisely defined comparative concept is cross-linguistically somewhat variable.

The fact that comparative concepts often refer to a shared core and are extensionally smaller compared to language-particular categories means that not all parts of every language enter the relevant comparison. Inanimate Feminines in German are not part of comparisons of feminine gender classes across languages, and arguments of experiential verbs (which are not typical transitive verbs) are not part of comparisons of subjects across languages. This is not a problem, but it must be kept in mind if one evaluates claims based on such comparative concepts. In order to compare arguments of experiential verbs (such as 'to like'), one needs more fine-grained comparative concepts (cf. the microroles of Hartmann et al. 2014).

6. Stereotypes and prototypes

The literature on grammatical patterns worldwide is full of stereotypes that are widely known, e.g.,

- Latin has free word order, but English has rigid word order
- Italian is a pro-drop language, but English cannot drop its personal pronouns
- Turkish is an agglutinating language, and Chinese is an isolating language
- English is poor in inflection, but richer in derivation
- some North American languages have noun incorporation
- Latin makes much use of nonfinite clauses
- German has many compounds
- the Romance languages have clitic pronouns
- English has gender only in personal pronouns

---

concepts taken as a broad category (stative, unary valency, gradable, inherent) do not serve well as a comparative concept for understanding "adjectives", because semantic subclasses of property concepts – age, dimension, color, value, etc. – exhibit different grammatical behavior in one and the same language […] The usual solution to this problem is to use finer-grained categories, such as the property subclasses, or for core participant roles, the division into A, S, and P.

Linguists almost never ask whether these stereotypes are true, but if they were true, this would be very interesting. We see outside of linguistics that many stereotypes are not true (e.g., most dogs are not called *Fido*), but some stereotypes are true (*Smith* is indeed the most frequent surname in the United Kingdom).[30] Thus, I find it important to know whether the above stereotypes are true (they may or may not be), and in order to assess them, we need objective definitions of these terms.

This should go without saying, but many linguists seem to treat the terms involved in such stereotypes as somehow having an independent existence, regardless of their definition. For example, at the end of their book on clitics, Spencer and Luís (2012: 321) admit that they have not been able to come up with a definition of the term *clitic* that encompasses all and only those phenomena that they discuss in their book. Still, they do not conclude from this that the phenomena they discussed may not be coherent (but united merely by the fact that some people use the same label *clitic* for these phenomena). Similarly, Reuland's (2018) overview paper of "reflexives and reflexivity" contains no definition of "reflexive", and the author is apparently not interested in providing one (because he takes his goal as discovering the relevant aspects of the innate grammar blueprint, not as comparing languages systematically). And even though my (2011b) paper on the definition of "word" has been widely cited, many authors continue to use the term *word*, even in technical contexts, as if the term had a clear meaning (perhaps hoping that such a meaning will be provided by someone eventually). Another example of this nonchalant attitude is Massam's (2017) overview paper on noun incorporation. Massam writes: "There is a lot of disagreement about exactly what constitutes noun incorporation … the field is rich with proposals and counter-proposals as to its true nature" (2017: Section 7), but she provides no definition. She seems to presuppose that noun incorporation has an independent existence, even if we have not found its definition yet. And Lieber and Štekauer (2009: 14) conclude their introduction to a handbook on compounding by saying that "there are (almost) no reliable criteria for distinguishing compounds from phrases or from other sorts of derived words" – but for some reason, they still say that "it's worth looking further", as if finding a definition were a research result (rather than an indispensable methodological prerequisite).

Thus, many linguists have been unable to provide clear definitions of terms, but have nevertheless been unwilling to abandon the traditional terms. While many have been content to simply ignore these problems (hoping that they are not too serious, and/or that someone else will eventually solve them), others have noticed the problem and have reacted by invoking "prototypes". The idea that linguistic categories are (sometimes) based on cognitive prototypes was made famous

---

30. <https://en.wikipedia.org/wiki/List_of_most_common_surnames_in_Europe>

by Lakoff (1987) and was explored in more detail by Taylor (1989). This work was based on mental representations of particular knowledge systems, including grammatical knowledge. But the cognitive notion of a prototype category cannot simply be transferred to cross-linguistic categories, which are not represented in any individual speaker's mind. There was some discussion of cross-linguistic prototypes in the 1980s and 1990s (e.g., Newmeyer 1998: Chapter 4), but this idea has not been pursued systematically in recent decades, as far as I am aware. So, I do not see any basis for a systematic "prototype view" of cross-linguistic categories. Cross-linguistic phenomena often seem to cluster in certain ways, but the extent to which these clusters are real or based on our stereotypes can be assessed only if we have precise ways of measuring differences between languages.

Thus, I see the standardization of well-known terms as one way to help the discipline move beyond the traditional vague stereotypes.

7. Standard comparative terms and language-particular description

Linguists encounter grammatical terminology most often in the context of particular languages, rather than in a comparative context, as most linguists study particular languages most of the time. Thus, the kind of standardization discussed here might seem not to affect most activities of linguists.

But appearances are deceptive. Even when a linguist talks about a particular language, they typically want their findings to be relevant to other linguists studying similar phenomena in other languages. For example, García García (2020) studies causative verbs in Old English (e.g., þwīnan 'dwindle', þwǣnan 'cause to dwindle'), and puts these verbs explicitly in a typological context. Likewise, Nordlinger (2014) studies serial verbs in Wambaya (an Australian language), and she puts these constructions in a typological context. The idea that the study of particular languages has relevance for general linguistics has become almost universal, perhaps because there are nowadays many linguists who study languages outside of an applied context (where languages are studied to facilitate language learning, or understanding of important literary text). And when the research question is theoretical rather than applied, then it is attractive to link one's language-particular insights to larger generalizations.[31]

---

31. The comparative perspective is so deeply engrained in current linguistics that we hardly notice its presence in everyday expressions such as "Turkish has a passive construction", or "Vietnamese has serial verb constructions". Every time when we say that "a language has a category X", we make reference to a category-like comparative concept.

Moreover, even though each language has its own categories (Haspelmath 2007), there are many similarities between the categories of different languages, and we do not want completely different terminologies for different languages. Thus, we call German verb forms like *sind* ('are') Third Person forms, even though they are also used with the polite address form *Sie* ('you') (e.g., *Sind Sie fertig?* 'Are you ready?'). From a language-particular point of view, these verb forms are different from third person forms in, say, French, but it would not serve transparency to give them any other name. Similarly, the Russian Imperative has a use in conditional clauses (E.g., *bud' ja na vašem meste* [be.IMPV I on your place] 'if I were in your place'), so it is different from, say, the Latin Imperative, but it would be strange to give it any other name.

So, from the point of view of terminological transparency, it is best if language-particular categories are given names that correspond closely to comparative-concept names. It is therefore also from a purely descriptive, language-particular perspective that standard terminology is relevant; but because of the fundamental difference between comparative concepts and descriptive categories (Section 2), the standard terms as discussed here are not crucial for language-particular description.

Finally, it should be noted that in practice, IPA characters are used somewhat differently from morphosyntactic comparative concepts as envisaged here, because they are often used for language-particular notation. In fact, linguistics students typically learn IPA characters as a method of transcribing the pronunciation of words in particular languages, and it is only later that they may be confronted with IPA for the purposes of cross-linguistic comparison. But it is a misunderstanding to think of IPA characters as a list of all possible sounds – rather, IPA characters are a list of well-known comparative concepts for comparing sound inventories (Ladd 2011), which happen to work quite well for the practical purposes of transcribing pronunciations. But it should be kept in mind that the IPA, too, arose in a comparative context: English-language teachers in France and French-language teachers in Britain got together in order to create a tool facilitating language learning – which usefully starts with comparing one's original language to the language to be learned. For the purposes of scientifically describing a language (in terms of its own categories), one needs language-particular categories in phonology as well, just as in morphosyntax. The IPA offers a convenient (widely understood) set of symbols, but these are not actually crucial to language-particular description (which must be based on contrasts and phonetic characterizations).

In this connection, a question that sometimes arises concerns the status of gloss abbreviations in interlinear text. There is a standard set of abbreviations in the appendix of the Leipzig Glossing Rules,[32] and this has become very popular (e.g.,

---

32. <https://www.eva.mpg.de/lingua/resources/glossing-rules.php>

ACC for accustive, GEN for genitive, PL for plural, and so on). But some linguists seem to take it as the main aspect of the rules (while in fact, the gloss abbreviations are merely the appendix), and I fear that a few even think that these categories are intended to be universal categories. However, what is standardized here is merely the relation between the abbreviations and the terms (e.g., the use of INS rather than INSTR for the term *instrumental*). The gloss abbreviations say nothing about the meanings of the terms themselves. And since interlinear glossing is typically done from a language-particular point of view, they are normally interpreted as representing language-particular categories. Thus, in the above gloss [be.IMPV] (for Russian *bud'*), the abbreviation IMPV stands for "(Russian) Imperative", not for a comparative concept. However, in context where we compare languages (e.g., in a typological study), it makes good sense to provide "comparative glosses", rather than language-particular glosses. So in a context where word order in conditional clauses in different languages is discussed, it is probably best to gloss the Russian form *bud'* as [be.COND], because the Imperative form serves to indicate a conditional clause in this context. The fact that the actual form is called *Imperative* and is also used for imperative clauses is irrelevant here.

Thus, the technical terms of phonetics/phonology and morphosyntax play a dual role, which helps us understand that some linguists feel that the distinction between comparative concepts and language-particular descriptive categories is somehow problematic or difficult to draw. But it is not a problematic conceptual distinction, and all linguists agree that we should use the same technical terms in both roles (rather than, say, having two completely distinct sets of terms).

8. Concluding remarks

In this paper, I have argued that there should be some standard terminology for morphosyntax, just as there are standards of terminology or notation in other disciplines, including subdisciplines of linguistics such as phonetics. I have given some concrete examples of possible standard definitions of well-known (and novel) terms, and I have addressed some issues and briefly compared the standardization approach with alternative ideas making use of prototypes (or actually stereotypes).

Perhaps the most pressing question that readers have at this point is the question of implementation: What needs to happen so that linguists actually adopt a standard? But this question is outside the scope of the present paper. Adopting a standard is a collective action problem, and there are many different proposals for how to solve such problems. The task that I have set for myself in this paper is merely to address the issue of standardization from a conceptual point of view. The principles discussed in Section 4 should help to make the proposals acceptable to a maximal set of linguists, but there will always be some arbitrariness in any standard.

And as noted in Section 2, many linguists seem to conceive of their grammatical terms as universal mental entities (natural-kind categories of the innate grammar blueprint), though this is not often stated clearly. In order for the standardization programme to make progress, it is crucial to make a clear distinction between hypothetical universal innate categories (as true research results) and universally applicable comparative concepts (as historically arbitrary research instruments which are subject to standardization).

Acknowledgements

I thank the editors for inviting me to submit this paper, and two reviewers (including Eitan Grossman) for helpful comments. I also thank the numerous colleagues who discussed the issues raised in the paper in an Academia.edu session. And I am particularly grateful to Erich Round and Greville Corbett for extensive discussions of some potential problems of my approach, as well as Christian Lehmann, Edith Moravcsik and Andrew Spencer for further discussion.

References

Baker, Mark C. 2001. *The Atoms of Language*. New York NY: Basic Books.
Booij, Geert E. 2005. *The Grammar of Words: An Introduction to Linguistic Morphology*. Oxford: OUP.
Brentari, Diane. 2002. Modality differences in sign language phonology and morphophonemics. In *Modality and Structure in Signed and Spoken Languages*, Richard P. Meier, Kearsy Cormier & David Quinto-Pozos (eds), 35–64. Cambridge: CUP. https://doi.org/10.1017/CBO9780511486777.003
Brown, Dunstan & Chumakina, Marina. 2013. What there might be and what there is: An introduction to Canonical Typology. In *Canonical Morphology and Syntax*, Dunstan Brown, Marina Chumakina & Greville G. Corbett (eds), 1–19. Oxford: OUP.
Chomsky, Noam A. 1981. *Lectures on Government and Binding*. Dordrecht: Foris.
Clements, George N. & Keyser, Samuel Jay. 1985. *CV Phonology: A Generative Theory of the Syllable*. Cambridge MA: The MIT Press.
Comrie, Bernard. 1976. *Aspect: An Introduction to the Study of Verbal Aspect and Related Problems*. Cambridge: CUP.
Comrie, Bernard. 1978. Ergativity. In *Syntactic Typology: Studies in the Phenomenology of Language*, Winfred P. Lehmann (ed.), 329–394. Austin TX: University of Texas Press.
Corbett, Greville G. 2007. Gender and noun classes. In *Language Typology and Syntactic Description, Vol. III: Grammatical Categories and the Lexicon*, Timothy Shopen (ed.), 241–279. Cambridge: CUP. https://doi.org/10.1017/CBO9780511618437.004
Corbett, Greville G. 2009. Universals and features. In *Universals of Language Today*, Sergio Scalise, Elisabetta Magni & Antonietta Bisetto (eds), 129–143. Dordrecht: Springer. https://doi.org/10.1007/978-1-4020-8825-4_7

Cristofaro, Sonia. 2007. Deconstructing categories: Finiteness in a functional-typological perspective. In *Finiteness: Theoretical and Empirical Foundations*, Irina Nikolaeva (ed.), 91–114. Oxford: OUP.

Croft, William. 2016. Comparative concepts and language-specific categories: Theory and practice. *Linguistic Typology* 20(2): 377–393. https://doi.org/10.1515/lingty-2016-0012

Dingemanse, Mark. 2019. 'Ideophone' as a comparative concept. In *Ideophones, Mimetics, and Expressives* [Iconicity in Language and Literature 16], Kimi Akita & Prashant Pardeshi (eds), 13–33. Amsterdam: John Benjamins. https://doi.org/10.1075/ill.16.02din

Dryer, Matthew S. 2009. The branching direction theory of word order correlations revisited. In *Universals of Language Today*, Sergio Scalise, Elisabetta Magni & Antonietta Bisetto (eds), 185–207. Dordrecht: Springer. https://doi.org/10.1007/978-1-4020-8825-4_10

Dryer, Matthew S. 2016. Crosslinguistic categories, comparative concepts, and the Walman diminutive. *Linguistic Typology* 20(2): 305–331.
https://doi.org/10.1515/lingty-2016-0009

García García, Luisa. 2020. The basic valency orientation of Old English and the causative ja-formation: a synchronic and diachronic approach. *English Language & Linguistics*. Cambridge University Press 24(1). 153–177. https://doi.org/10.1017/S1360674318000345

Grewendorf, Günther. 1989. *Ergativity in German* [Studies in Generative Grammar 35]. Dordrecht: Foris. https://doi.org/10.1515/9783110859256

Haspelmath, Martin. 2005. Argument marking in ditransitive alignment types. *Linguistic Discovery* 3(1): 1–21. https://doi.org/10.1349/PS1.1537-0852.A.280

Haspelmath, Martin. 2007. Pre-established categories don't exist: Consequences for language description and typology. *Linguistic Typology* 11(1): 119–132.
https://doi.org/10.1515/LINGTY.2007.011

Haspelmath, Martin. 2010. Comparative concepts and descriptive categories in crosslinguistic studies. *Language* 86(3): 663–687. https://doi.org/10.1353/lan.2010.0021

Haspelmath, Martin. 2011a. On S, A, P, T, and R as comparative concepts for alignment typology. *Linguistic Typology* 15(3): 535–567. https://doi.org/10.1515/LITY.2011.035

Haspelmath, Martin. 2011b. The indeterminacy of word segmentation and the nature of morphology and syntax. *Folia Linguistica* 45(1): 31–80. https://doi.org/10.1515/flin.2011.002

Haspelmath, Martin. 2012. How to compare major word-classes across the world's languages. In *Theories of Everything: In Honor of Edward Keenan* [UCLA Working Papers in Linguistics 17, article 16], Thomas Graf, Denis Paperno, Anna Szabolcsi & Jos Tellings (eds), 109–130. Los Angeles CA: UCLA. <http://phonetics.linguistics.ucla.edu/wpl/issues/wpl17/wpl17.html>.

Haspelmath, Martin. 2013. Argument indexing: A conceptual framework for the syntax of bound person forms. In *Languages across Boundaries: Studies in Memory of Anna Siewierska*, Dik Bakker & Martin Haspelmath (eds), 197–226. Berlin: De Gruyter Mouton. https://doi.org/10.1515/9783110331127.197

Haspelmath, Martin. 2015. Defining vs. diagnosing linguistic categories: A case study of clitic phenomena. In *How Categorical are Categories? New Approaches to the Old Questions of Noun, Verb, and Adjective*, Joanna Błaszczak, Dorota Klimek-Jankowska & Krzysztof Migdalski (eds), 273–304. Berlin: De Gruyter Mouton. https://doi.org/10.1515/9781614514510-009

Haspelmath, Martin. 2016. The serial verb construction: Comparative concept and crosslinguistic generalizations. *Language and Linguistics* 17(3): 291–319.
https://doi.org/10.1177/2397002215626895

Haspelmath, Martin. 2018a. How comparative concepts and descriptive linguistic categories are different. In *Aspects of Linguistic Variation: Studies in Honor of Johan van der Auwera*, Daniël Van Olmen, Tanja Mortelmans & Frank Brisard (eds), 83–113. Berlin: De Gruyter Mouton. http://doi.org/10.5281/zenodo.570000

Haspelmath, Martin. 2018b. The last word on polysynthesis: A review article. *Linguistic Typology* 22(2): 307–326. https://doi.org/10.1515/lingty-2018-0011

Haspelmath, Martin. 2018c. *Toward a new conceptual framework for comparing gender systems and some so-called classifier systems*. Stockholm University talk handout. https://doi.org/10.5281/zenodo.1230569

Haspelmath, Martin. 2019. Indexing and flagging, and head and dependent marking. *Te Reo* 62(1): 93–115. https://doi.org/10.17617/2.3168042

Haspelmath, Martin. 2020. The morph as a minimal linguistic form. *Morphology* 30(2). 117–134. https://doi.org/10.1007/s11525-020-09355-5

Haspelmath, Martin. 2021a. Bound forms, welded forms, and affixes: Basic concepts for morphological comparison. *Voprosy Jazykoznanija* 2021(1). 7–28.

Haspelmath, Martin. 2021b. Comparing reflexive constructions in the world's languages. In Janic, Katarzyna & Puddu, Nicoletta & Haspelmath, Martin (eds.), *Reflexive constructions in the world's languages (to appear)*. Berlin: Language Science Press.

Hennig, Mathilde. 2012. Grammatische Terminologie in der Schule: Einladung zur Diskussion. *Zeitschrift für Germanistische Linguistik* 40(3): 443–450. https://doi.org/10.1515/zgl-2012-0028

Kibort, Anna. 2010. Towards a typology of grammatical features. In *Features: Perspectives on a Key Notion in Linguistics*, Anna Kibort & Greville G. Corbett (eds), 64–106. Oxford: OUP. https://doi.org/10.1093/acprof:oso/9780199577743.003.0004

Ladd, D. Robert. 2011. Phonetics in phonology. In *The Handbook of Phonological Theory*, John A. Goldsmith, Jason Riggle & Alan C.L. Yu (eds), 348–373. Chichester: Wiley-Blackwell. https://doi.org/10.1002/9781444343069.ch11

Lakoff, George. 1987. *Women, Fire, and Dangerous Things: What Categories Reveal about the Mind*. Chicago IL: The University of Chicago Press. https://doi.org/10.7208/chicago/9780226471013.001.0001

Lazard, Gilbert. 2002. Transitivity revisited as an example of a more strict approach in typological research. *Folia Linguistica* 36(3–4): 141–190.

Lehmann, Christian. 1983. Rektion und syntaktische Relationen. *Folia Linguistica* 17(1–4): 339–378.

Lieber, Rochelle & Štekauer, Pavol. 2009. Introduction: Status and definition of compounding. In *The Oxford Handbook of Compounding*, Rochelle Lieber & Pavol Štekauer (eds), 3–18. Oxford: OUP. https://doi.org/10.1093/oxfordhb/9780199695720.013.0001

List, Johann Mattis, Greenhill, Simon, Rzymski, Christoph, Schweikhard, Nathanael & Forkel, Robert (eds). 2019. *Concepticon 2.0*. Jena: Max Planck Institute for the Science of Human History. <https://concepticon.clld.org/>.

Massam, Diane. 2017. Incorporation and pseudo-incorporation in syntax. *Oxford Research Encyclopedia of Linguistics*. https://doi.org/10.1093/acrefore/9780199384655.013.190

Moran, Steven & McCloy, Daniel (eds). 2019. *PHOIBLE 2.0*. Jena: Max Planck Institute for the Science of Human History. <https://phoible.org/>.

Newmeyer, Frederick J. 1998. *Language Form and Language Function*. Cambridge MA: MIT Press.

Nichols, Johanna. 1984. Direct and oblique objects in Chechen-Ingush and Russian. In *Objects*, Frans Plank (ed.), 183–209. London: Academic Press.

Nordlinger, Rachel. 2014. Serial verbs in Wambaya. In *Language Description Informed by Theory* [Studies in Language Companion Series 147], Rob Pensalfini, Myfany Turpin & Diana Guillemin (eds), 263–282. Amsterdam: John Benjamins.
https://doi.org/10.1075/slcs.147.11nor

Reuland, Eric. 2018. Reflexives and reflexivity. *Annual Review of Linguistics* 4(1): 81–107.
https://doi.org/10.1146/annurev-linguistics-011817-045500

Spencer, Andrew & Luís, Ana R. 2012. *Clitics*. Cambridge: CUP.
https://doi.org/10.1017/CBO9781139033763

Taylor, John R. 1989. *Linguistic Categorization: Prototypes in Linguistic Theory*. Oxford: Clarendon Press.

CHAPTER 3

Universal underpinnings of language-specific categories
A useful heuristic for discovering and comparing categories of grammar and beyond

Martina Wiltschko
ICREA, UPF

The goal of this paper is to argue that the assumption that there are universal underpinnings for the construction of language specific categories is a useful, if not necessary assumption for the discovery and comparison of categories. Specifically, I will explore three empirical domains:

i. **grammatical categories** of the familiar kind (e.g., tense, voice, demonstrative, etc.);
ii. categories associated with the **language of interaction** (e.g., sentence final tags, response particles, interjections, etc.); and
iii. categories that express **emotions** (e.g., ideophones, certain types of intonational tunes, expressives, etc.).

The argument will be developed as follows.

I start by introducing the framework for the analysis of grammatical categories I have developed in Wiltschko (2014). This approach seeks to reconcile the tension between the two opposing views which this volume addresses: typologists observe that languages differ in their categorial inventories but some linguists (especially of the generative tradition) assume that there is a core which all languages share, including a set of universal categories. The key to reconciling this tension, I argue, is to assume that the categories we observe are always constructed on a language-specific basis, but that there are some universal building blocks involved in their construction, namely the *universal spine*, a hierarchically organized set of functions which is at the core of constructing sentential meanings. The spine has to be associated with units of language (I use the term unit of language as opposed to morpheme or word because I include – among other things - features as well and intonational tunes in the set of elements that can associate with the spine). Familiar grammatical categories are constructed via this association: that is, units of language *per se* do not form grammatical categories, they do so only in interaction with the spine. It follows that grammatical categories will always be language-specific, since the units of language are language-specific (for traditional morphemes this follows from the Saussurian assumption that the relation between form and meaning is arbitrary – hence must be conventionalized on a language specific basis). What this assumption allows us to do is to compare language-specific categories via a third element (Humboldt's *tertium comparationis*), namely the spine. Comparing language-specific categories directly to each other is typically meaning-based, but categories of similar meaning do not always have the same distribution and hence cannot be classified as universal categories (assuming that the hallmark of units of language of the same category is that they display the same distributional patterns).

I then proceed to show that the same framework can be used for the discovery and comparison of categories which are not typically assumed to be part of grammar proper: interactive and emotive categories. I first show that they, too, display the patterns of grammatical categories: we find classes of UoLs which enter into syntagmatic and paradigmatic relations; and they display patterns of contrast and patterns of multi-functionality.

1. Introduction

Grammatical categories are at the core of much linguistic description and analysis. It is virtually impossible to describe any language without assuming that its units are classified into categories. For example, when we present data, we need to gloss them. And once glosses are provided, grammatical categories are imposed, no matter what the assumption is about the status of these categories. For any description, let alone analysis, to be useful, linguists must generalize over the individual *Units of Language* (henceforth UoL) such as words, morphemes, intonational tunes, features, etc. The necessity to postulate generalizations over individual UoLs is especially evident when comparing languages to each other for the sake of establishing language universals and the range of variation across languages. One cannot compare individual UoLs to each other because all UoLs are necessarily language-specific. This follows from the assumption that the relation between sound and meaning is arbitrary – hence must be conventionalized on a language specific basis. But comparison can only be meaningful if it is clear what is to be compared. Hence it is useful to classify UoLs such that their grammatical properties can be compared across languages. Comparing languages to each other is really the only way in which we can determine universals and variation. Thus, we are facing a conundrum: it seems that we have to identify a set of categories that can be universally applied to all languages; yet linguists still do not agree on what this set of categories might be, and – even more disturbing – there is no consensus as to whether universal categories do indeed exist.

The goal of this paper, is to address this conundrum. Following Wiltschko (2014), I assume that grammatical categories are always language-specific: there is no universal inventory of categories. However, I also assume that there are universal underpinnings for the construction of language specific categories. I show that this is a useful assumption for the discovery and comparison of categories. In fact, I argue that it is a necessary assumption which allows us to understand certain universal patterns of categories. That is, while categories differ across languages, there are also universal patterns that hold across categories and across languages. This suggests that there is a universal mechanism at play that is responsible for these patterns.

The paper is organized as follows. I start by introducing the problem which the need for postulating universal categories for language comparison posits (Section 2). I then introduce the framework for the analysis of grammatical categories I have developed in Wiltschko (2014) (Section 3). I further proceed to show that this view of categorization is not only useful for the discovery and comparison of traditional grammatical categories but it can also be used to describe and analyse UoLs that are used to facilitate ongoing conversations, i.e., categories of interactional language (Section 4). These categories have traditionally neither been part of the empirical domain for theoretical linguists nor for typologists. In Section 5, I conclude.

2. The (non-) universality of categories

2.1 An analytical conundrum

Categories have to be diagnosed based on language-specific criteria which are based on distributional patterns, both syntactic and morphological. This holds for lexical and for grammatical categories. For example, in English, nouns are diagnosed by plural marking, which is restricted to (count) nouns, and determiners, among other diagnostics. However, in languages, where plurality is not marked, or where plural marking is not restricted to nouns, plural marking will not serve as a proper diagnostic for the (lexical) category noun. Similarly, in English, the grammatical category tense can be diagnosed by its syntactic and morphological distribution: tense markers attach to the highest verb (either a main verb or an auxiliary), there is only one tense marker per clause, tense marking is obligatory in finite clauses, etc. But again, this is not universally the case. In some languages, tense marking is optional; or it remains marked on the verb even if there is an auxiliary, or it can be marked on nouns. (Wiltschko 2003; Nordlinger & Sadler 2004; Tonhauser 2007).

But if the diagnostics for a particular category are language-specific, then how can we diagnose universal categories? Take for example tense. If a language allows for the marking of past on nouns, do we classify it as a tense marker or not. If we do, then the distributional restriction we observe in English requires explanation. It would mean that tense has different distributional properties across languages. But this begs the question as to whether we are really dealing with the same category. Categories should be identified via their distributional properties. But if, on the contrary, we decide not to classify past marking on nominals as tense, because its distribution differs, then we run the risk of imposing the distributional patterns of a particular language on a putative universal category or vice versa. And indeed, if we do this, then it appears that hardly any markers of temporality would fit the bill of the grammatical category Tense. Thus, the fact that the criteria that identify categories are language-specific makes it virtually impossible to identify universal categories. Either we have to accept that the same (universal) category has different distributional properties or else we have to accept that not everything that we might think of as belonging to a particular (universal) category is in fact an instance of that category. Neither of these approaches is satisfying because we lose the insight that distributional criteria are the hallmark of categorial identity. But then, if we do not have proper diagnostics to determine whether a given category instantiates a universal category, how do we determine whether there are universal categories? How do we even compare the categories of the languages of the world without comparing apples to oranges? This is a serious conundrum that anyone who is interested in comparative linguistics, language typology, or the properties of universal grammar faces.

It is surprising, however, that this conundrum is not discussed in the generative tradition – though it is addressed in the typological literature. In what follows, I review some conclusions that have been drawn based on the empirical mess we find ourselves in if we do not recognize the conundrum just outlined. And I discuss some attempts to dissolve it.

2.2 A theoretical controversy

Given the analytical conundrum introduced above, it is hardly surprising that the issue surrounding the (non-)universality of categories has sparked a theoretical controversy. Within the generative tradition it is common to assume that there is a set of universal categories, and that language variation reduces to picking among this set. In contrast, within the more functionally oriented typological tradition it is often assumed that universal categories do not exist (Evans & Levinson 2009) and that at the most we can identify some prototypical categories (see Hopper & Thompson 1985; Comrie 1989; Langacker 1991; Corbett 1999, among others) which are however instantiated in different ways across different languages. Here I will briefly review the core assumptions within each tradition (see Wiltschko 2014 for detailed discussion).

2.2.1 *The generativists' take on categories*

Within the generative tradition, there has long been a commitment to the postulation of a *Universal Grammar* (henceforth UG). The arguments for UG have originally derived from considerations of learnability (Chomsky 1965 and subsequent work), which themselves have sparked much controversy, but which do not concern us here. What is important for us is that the assumption of UG has initiated a productive research program, which has led to interesting discoveries about the nature of natural languages, including the range of attested variation. In Chomsky's (1965: 58) terms: *"The real problem is that of developing a hypothesis about initial structure that is sufficiently rich to account for acquisition of language, yet not so rich as to be inconsistent with the known diversity of language."*

While the concept of UG is meant to capture the cognitive underpinnings of our language faculty, it is still at best a theoretical construct and unsurprisingly the assumptions about the nature of UG have changed significantly over the past decades. This perspective makes the goals of generativists quite different from those of the typologists. Generativists are not so much concerned with the discovery of language universals in the Greenbergian sense. Rather, they are concerned with understanding the make-up of UG. Thus, the concerns are more about the architecture of UG and the algorithms that derive well-formed sentences. Interestingly, the inventories of the ingredients of UG, categories and features, are of much less concern within this framework. Typically, the features and categories are assumed, and often based on traditional pre-generativist assumptions.

Perhaps one of the key assumptions relative to categories within the generative tradition concerns so-called functional categories. That is, ever since Chomsky 1986 it is standardly assumed that sentences are hierarchically structured by means of a universal set of ordered functional categories which dominate the lexical core (e.g., CP>TP>*v*P>VP). These categories are of a different nature than the categories assumed in the typological tradition. In particular, they create positions which actual UoLs can occupy. But crucially, because movement plays a major role in the derivation of sentences, these positions can be occupied by UoLs that are not a member of the category of the position they move into.[1] For example, in

---

1. I do not discuss non-transformational versions of the generative enterprise, like HPSG and LFG.

Verb-Second languages the verb is assumed to move into C, but it is not the case that verbs in such languages belong to the set of complementizers (C). Thus, the postulation of functional categories that define the structural architecture of language, i.e., the functional spine, makes available a second notion of grammatical categories, in addition to those categories that define UoLs. Within the generative tradition it is mostly the nature and inventory of these functional categories which receives attention. Furthermore, the categorial status of UoLs is less often discussed. For both types of categories, however, we find different assumptions regarding their universality and their variation.[2]

As for the functional categories of the spine, we find the full spectrum of assumptions logically possible. According to strict minimalist assumptions, there is no spine. This is because of the *inclusiveness condition* according to which no information can be introduced that is not already present in the lexicon. Hence, there cannot be any functional categories that exist independent of the UoLs that build the structure. According to this view structure is built by merging UoLs and not by associating UoLs with a pre-determined spine. At the same time however, the category status of these UoLs is barely discussed.

On the other end of the spectrum, we find *cartography*, a framework which assumes a fine-grained functional architecture which provides sites of association for a plethora of different UoLs (which include words, affixes, as well as features). It is worth noting that many of the categories assumed within the cartographic enterprise are virtually identical to classic categories of the Greenbergian typological tradition (including different subcategories of tense, aspect, and mood, etc.).

In between these two extremes (minimalism and cartography) we find much diversity in the inventory of categories generative linguists assume. The lack of consensus regarding the inventory and the nature of functional categories is striking, given that categories comprise, in some sense, the atoms of language. They are the linguistic objects that syntactic derivations operate over.[3] In fact there is no generally accepted view on the types of categories we might expect. The categories that have been proposed to exist are diverse and include labels that refer to word classes (*complementizer, determiner*), substantive content and or/phi-features

---

2. It is also worth mentioning here that categories like *passive* and the like are considered constructions which have no primitive status and hence are not expected to be universal.

3. One might object that it is not categories, but features that play that role, however, it is not clear what the difference may be between features and categories and much of what I identify here as being problematic for categories equally holds for features. There is no consensus about the universality and variation for features within the generative tradition.

(*tense, number, person*), morphological type (*infl*(*ection*)) or traditional grammatical categories (*mood, aspect*).

Turning now to what has been said about the inventory of categories of UoLs, we find a similar spectrum (though the discussion is much more scarce). On the one hand, we find the assumption that actual UoLs are intrinsically associated with categorial identity, especially those UoLs that would traditionally be classified as belonging to the set of lexical categories. Instead their categorial identity is syntactically conditioned. This is the hallmark assumption of *distributed morphology*. The core evidence for this claim stems from the fact that, in English, roots are frequently multi-categorial, in the sense that the same form can be used as a noun or as a verb or as an adjective, depending on the distribution. An economical way to account for this pattern is to dissociate the categorial label from the lexical entry, which in turn consists of a sound-meaning pairing ($<\pi,\Sigma>$) only, i.e., the exponent. The categorial label is "added" by way of syntactic structure. In the context of the functional category T or *v*, a root becomes a verb; in the context of the functional category D or *n*, a root becomes a noun. This is the essence of category-neutral roots. In the context of functional categories, however, the matter of categorization has received less attention. Category-neutrality is not typically assumed for function words, like it is for roots with substantive content, even though we find similar patterns of multi-functionality. For example, in English, *that* can be used as a complementizer or as a demonstrative determiner, depending on its distribution. This pattern is typically attributed to the process of grammaticalization; synchronic explanations are not usually given despite the fact that patterns of multi-functionality are ubiquitous within and across languages. In turn, this supports the classic assumption that categorial identity (κ) is essential for regulating the distribution not only of words of substance (nouns and verbs) but also of functional elements. It is thus essential to gain a good understanding of the sources and properties of κ. What is universal about κ, and what is the range of variation?

This question is much more widely discussed in the typological tradition to which I now turn.

2.2.2 *The typologists' take on categories*

While there is no consensus on the exact nature of categories in this tradition as well, what unites many typologists is the assumption that universal categories should not be assumed *a priori*. Nevertheless, work in this tradition has to assume a baseline notion of comparison, independent of its cognitive status. This is because otherwise cross-linguistic comparison would not be possible in the first place. That is, in order to really establish whether there are linguistic universals there has to be way to compare languages to each other. Because otherwise one doesn't know whether category X in language 1 is the same as category Y in language 2. But since distributional evidence has to be language-specific these properties cannot universally serve as diagnostics. Language-specific differences in distributional diagnostics make it difficult to determine whether or not two categories are identical. And a conclusion one might draw based on these differences is that there simply are no universal categories and hence every language will have to be described in its own terms (Joos 1957; Dryer 1997; Croft 2001; Haspelmath 2007). Nevertheless, some form of universal categories is still assumed as is evident from the way the World Atlas of Languages (WALS) is designed. To make language comparison possible, the categories and/or features of individual languages are labeled in identical ways. Traditional terms such as PERSON, NUMBER, PLURAL, DEMONSTRATIVE, DEFINITE, PRONOUNS, PAST TENSE, IMPERATIVE, etc. are used in the description of individual languages. It is then possible to ask, for example, whether 3rd person pronouns are the same or different from demonstrative determiners (Bhat 2013). Without a notion of 3rd person, pronoun, and demonstrative, it would not be possible to ask this question. But if we assume such notions, then their universal applicability has to be assumed. The same is true for the glossing conventions that are shared among typologists. The Leipzig glossing rules <https://www.eva.mpg.de/lingua/resources/glossing-rules.php> consist of rules for interlinear glosses which are supposed to cover linguists' needs in glossing texts and which serve as a standard set of conventions. But if such conventions are established, a certain degree of universality has to be assumed. So, this leaves us with an apparent paradox. On the one hand, language comparison requires the assumption of universal categories. On the other hand, there is a common denial of universal categories based on the fact that languages simply differ in the kinds of categories they have and in the distributional differences among categories which – according to some criteria – might be considered identical. The type of criteria usually assumed is based on notions of meaning, or what Haspelmath (2007) refers to as "substance".

The question as to how to deal with this paradox is addressed in various ways in the typological tradition. For example, Haspelmath (2010) proposes a distinction between language-specific *descriptive categories* and *comparative concepts*. Subscribing to the structuralist insight of *categorial particularism*, descriptive categories are necessarily language-specific and have to be described in their own terms (Boas 1911). This makes sense for the purpose of describing an individual language without the goal of language comparison. To respond to the need of having 'universal categories' as a means of comparison, Haspelmath (2010) introduces the notion of a *comparative concept*, which is meant to be universally applicable, hence needs to be defined solely in terms of other comparative concepts. Haspelmath (2010: 665) describes them as follows: They are solely defined for the purpose of comparison; they are not part of a particular language system; they are not psychologically real; they cannot be right or wrong but they can only be more or less useful for cross-linguistic comparison; they are often labelled in the same way as descriptive categories, but stand in a many-to-many relationship with them. Most of these comparative concepts are conceptual-semantic in nature; this is because of the typologists' commitment to the assumption that cross-linguistic comparison of morphosyntactic patterns cannot be based on formal patterns. The latter are simply too diverse (Haspelmath 2010: 665). Note further that there is no claim here that these *comparative concepts* do correspond to universal categories; different researchers can define their universal concepts according to the phenomena they are interested in and hence universal concepts differ depending on the researcher and depending on the occasion. This is a very different conceptualization than that of the universal category within the generative tradition.

There are two typological approaches which still assume some kind of universal patterning and thus provide a basis for comparison: Corbett's *canonical typology* (Corbett 1999, 2009, 2015) and Bickel's *multivariate typology* (Bickel 2010, 2011). What both approaches have in common is that they seek to deconstruct categories into dimensions or variables of variation. Within canonical typology the assumption is that there is a canon, a base which defines a canonical category. But explicit criteria are developed to decide whether something counts as more or less canonical. Within multivariate typology, similarities across languages are taken to reveal identity in some regards but differences in others: thus, categories are to be deconstructed into a set of variables which can vary individually and which allow for comparison across languages. Once the constructions of individual languages are analyzed in this way, this approach will allow for the exploration of recurrent patterns across languages.

2.3 The significance of distributional (formal) patterns

So now we have identified an analytical conundrum. Empirical findings in the typological tradition suggest that universal categories do not exist, yet to meaningfully compare languages to each other some universally applicable notion of a category has to be assumed. This implies, however, that to find universal categories, one has to assume them, running into problems of circularity. Moreover, the types of categories postulated for comparison in the typological tradition (including its generative version, namely cartography) are often characterized by meaning rather than form. But this is problematic because we know that, at least for language-specific categories, it is their formal properties that identifies them as a category. So, in what sense can we really speak of a "universal" category if we cannot identify formal diagnostics? In Wiltschko (2014), I address this problem from a generative perspective, identifying two formal diagnostics for categorical patterning.

2.3.1 Patterns of multi-functionality

Recall from above that at least some UoLs are category-neutral in the sense that the same form can be used with different categorial identities, correlating with their syntactic distribution. This is the case for both words of substance (i.e., lexical categories) as well as for words of grammatical significance only (i.e., functional categories) (see section 2.2.1). What this pattern of multi-functionality suggests is that the sound-meaning pairing $<\pi,\Sigma>$ has to be independent of its categorial identity (κ); nevertheless, κ has to associate with $<\pi,\Sigma>$ at some point so as to regulate the distribution. We can represent this as in (1) where sound and meaning associate with each other before categorial identity is added, creating a complex UoL.

(1) $<<\pi,\Sigma> \kappa>$

This view on categorization sheds immediate light on the problem functionalists have identified with the postulation of universal categories. Languages differ in their formal properties of categories, e.g., for example whether a given concept is realized as a word or an affix, whether it precedes or follows other categories, etc. Given the representation in (1), this is not surprising, because these formal properties are subsumed under π, which determine the idiosyncratic conventionalized properties of individual lexical entries.

In light of the preceding discussion the question we are faced with concerns the nature of κ: What is its status language-internally, cross-linguistically, and universally? We need more than semantic concepts to make claims about categories. But formal properties have to be general enough such that they can go beyond the language-specific properties that make language comparison so difficult. I argue that we have to acknowledge that there are indeed universal properties of categorization, ones that cannot be reduced to functional pressures alone. Specifically, in Wiltschko (2014), I identify two universal patterns that all language-specific categories adhere to: patterns of multi-functionality, and patterns of contrast. These patterns can then be used as universal diagnostics for membership in a category; though they still do not diagnose membership in a particular category. I address the latter question in Section 3 below.

We have already seen the essence behind patterns of multi-functionality (Section 2.2.1 above), which led us to postulate the (partial) independence of categorial identity from sound meaning bundles ($<<\pi,\Sigma> \kappa>$). To the best of my knowledge, there are no cross-linguistic investigations exploring patterns of multi-functionality; hence we cannot assert with certainty that such patterns are indeed universal. But we find patterns of multi-functionality across unrelated languages and I strongly suspect that all languages have them. So let us assume that patterns of multi-functionality are universal. If this is the case, then it would mean that κ is indeed significant in all languages. Specifically, to model the distribution of UoLs, we cannot rely on the sound and meaning of UoLs alone, but instead, there is a third factor (κ), which regulates their distribution independent of their sound and meaning <π,Σ>.[4]

If this is the right way to think about multi-functionality, then we can also learn something about the nature of κ: it has to add a dimension of meaning to a given UoL. This is because the difference in distribution, which is regulated by κ, also correlates with a difference in interpretation of the UoL. Hence, patterns of multi-functionality are a useful heuristic to explore the nature of κ across languages, and thus to deduce its universal properties, if any.

Note that the significance of multi-functionality has been ignored within the generative tradition as a means to explore the logic behind grammatical categories. The phenomenon has been treated almost exclusively in the study of semantic maps (see footnote 4) and *grammaticalization*. That is, patterns of multi-functionality are often treated as indicating the diachronic development of a given UoL from membership in one category to membership in another. Within formal approaches towards grammaticalization (Roberts & Rousseau 2003) it is viewed as the effect of association with syntactic structure in different positions along the functional architecture. Typically, grammaticalization appears to be upward reanalysis, such that a given UoL starts out in a particular structural position and is then re-integrated into the structure in a higher position. However, even if grammaticalization is at play, we still want to have a synchronic model of patterns of multi-functionality. Moreover, the mere existence of systematic changes in category-membership (which often occur in similar ways across unrelated languages) suggests that there is something universal at play. I submit that without assuming κ, neither the process of grammaticalization nor its effects can be understood.

Here I consider patterns of multi-functionality an important hallmark of linguistic categorization. It is found universally and thus suggests that there is a universal mechanism at play that serves to categorize UoLs.

2.3.2 *Patterns of contrast*

Patterns of multi-functionality are not the only signature of κ. In Wiltschko (2014), I argue that patterns of contrast, too, may serve as a universal diagnostic for category membership. To see this, consider the pattern of number marking in English, for example.

---

[4]. Patterns of multi-functionality (or rather polysemy) have been a key fact in the development of semantic maps (Croft 2001; Croft & Poole 2008; Haspelmath 1997). The approach I pursue here is different in nature as it takes the syntactic spine, rather than conceptual space, to be the driving force behind some patterns of multi-functionality (especially multi-functionality in the domain of functional rather than lexical categories).

(2) a. *dog* singular
    b. *dog-s* plural

When the noun *dog* is suffixed with the plural suffix -*s*, it is interpreted as plural (2)b; but in the absence of the plural marker, it is interpreted as singular (2)a. Crucially, there is no overt UoL which corresponds to the marking of singularity. We cannot simply assume that an unmarked noun is interpreted as denoting a singularity. For example, in the context of a compound the unmarked noun is not interpreted as singular; a *dog-leash* is not a leash for a single dog, but instead refers to leashes for any dog. Unmarked nouns are completely unmarked for number and are therefore compatible with a singular or a plural interpretation. It is only in syntactic contexts where nouns could be marked for plural that the absence of overt marking is interpreted as singular. Hence, we have to conclude that the interpretation of the apparently unmarked form is syntactically conditioned: in a well-defined syntactic context, silence is interpreted. This is illustrated in (3).

(3) Lexical entry for the singular UoL (preliminary)
    <<π: ø, Σ: singular> κ: NUMBER >

κ is crucial for recovering the interpretation of the silent form (π: ø). In English, a nominal phrase following a determiner, has to be marked for number. If the noun is not marked for plural, then it has to be interpreted as singular. Formally, we can model this by assuming that, in English, the determiner (D) selects for the category NUMBER, which in turn has two contrasting values: *singular* and *plural*. Plural is the marked form, whereas *singular* is unmarked (silent). But without the assumption that there is an underlying category which is interpreted in a certain way if there is no overt form, silence cannot be interpreted. It is κ, which is responsible for the patterns of contrast, which, just as the patterns of multi-functionality, are ubiquitous in human languages.

Patterns of contrast are not restricted to inflectional paradigms such as number marking in English. For example, in Korean, *ko* is used as a complementizer introducing a finite embedded clause, as in (4).

(4) *ku-uy   mal-i   kecis-i*
    he-GEN   words-NOM lie-NOM

   aniye-ss-ta-ko   *mit-nun-ta.*
   not.be-PST-DECL-COMP believe-PRES-DECL

   'I believe that what he said wasn't a lie (lit. his words were not a lie).'
                                                           Ceong 2019: 131 (127)

But *ko* is not limited to embedded clauses; it can also introduce main clauses no matter their force. This is shown in (5) for declaratives, which are marked by *ta* and in (6) for imperatives, which are marked by *ko*. In this case, *ko* marks the utterance as a reiteration of what the speaker already said. Thus, the speech act is not used to perform an assertion or a command directly (as is the case in the unmarked (a) clauses); rather, it is used to express that the speaker has previously performed said speech act.[5]

(5) a. *na, cha sa-ss-ta* ↓
 1sg car buy-PST-DECL
 'I bought a car.'

 b. *cha sa-ss-ta-ko* ↓
 car buy-PST-DECL-COMP
 '(I SAID) I bought a car!' (didn't you hear what I said?)

 Ceong 2019: 133 (129a/c)

(6) a. *swul sa-la* ↓
 alcohol buy-IMP
 'Buy a drink!'

 b. *swul sa-la-ko* ↓
 alcohol buy-IMP-COMP
 'I'm saying/ I said you should buy a drink!' Ceong 2019: 160 (158)

When it introduces a matrix clause, sentence-final *ko* enters into paradigmatic contrast with other UoLs. In (7)–(10) we witness matrix clauses of different force introduced by *(a)y* which indicates hearsay. Thus, while *ko* marks the utterance as having been performed by the current speaker, *(a)y* marks the utterance as having been performed by someone else and hence that the current speaker has heard about the reported event but has not directly witnessed it.

(7) a. *nayil pi-ka o-n-ta.*
 tomorrow rain-NOM come-IMPERF-DECL
 'It rains tomorrow.'

 b. *nayil pi-ka o-n-t-ay.*
 tomorrow rain-NOM come-IMPERF-DECL-ay
 '(I was told by someone that) It rains tomorrow.'

 Kwon, 2011: 59, cited from Ceong 2019: 138 (138)

(8) a. *cemsim-ul mekess-ni/nya?*
 lunch-ACC ate-INT
 'Did you eat lunch?'

---

5. See Ceong (2019) for detailed discussion, including arguments that this is not an instance of ellipsis, but rather it is genuine instance of a matrix clause introduced by a complementizer.

    b. *cemsim-ul   mekess-nya-y.*
        lunch-ACC ate-INT-HEARSAY
        'pro said, did you eat lunch?'[6]   Ceong 2019: 144 table 4-1

(9) a. *cemsim-ul   meke-la.*
        lunch-ACC eat-IMP
        'Eat lunch!'

    b. *cemsim-ul   meku-la-y.*
        lunch-ACC eat-IMP-HEARSAY
        'pro said, eat lunch!'   Ceong 2019: 144 table 4-1

(10) a. *cemsim-ul   mek-ca.*
        lunch-ACC eat-EXHO
        'Let's eat lunch!'

    b. *cemsim-ul   mek-ca-y.*
        lunch-ACC eat-EXHO-HEARSAY
        'pro said, let's eat lunch.'   Ceong 2019: 144 table 4-1

What is important for our purpose is that in the absence of *ko*, the matrix clause is unmarked. Nevertheless, it is still associated with a specific interpretation, namely it is interpreted as a *first hand* utterance. The speaker is performing the speech act at the time of the utterance. But there is nothing in the sentence itself that marks this aspect of the meaning. Hence, I assume, following Ceong (2019), that the sentence final UoLs *ko* and *(a)y* stand in paradigmatic relation not only to each other but also to a silent UoL, which marks the utterance as a first hand utterance. This establishes that patterns of contrast are not restricted to inflectional categories of the familiar type.

    We have now seen that there are patterns of multi-functionality and patterns of contrast which are the universal hallmarks of categories. My argument here is that the universality of these patterns arises because of the presence of a universally available mechanism for categorization. That is, it is not the categories *per se* that are universal, it is the underlying mechanism that derives these categories. Neither patterns of contrast nor patterns of multi-functionality are logically necessary: as can be gleaned from the fact that not all UoLs behave in this way. That is, some UoLs behave as modifiers and hence simply add information to the phrase they modify. As such they do not enter into patterns of contrast and hence cannot license silence to be interpreted (see Wiltschko 2004, 2014 for detailed discussion).

---

6. *Pro* here indicates that in the Korean example there is no overt constituent. Reference is retrieved contextually.

3. Why do languages categorize their UoLs and how?

In this section, I introduce the framework developed in Wiltschko (2014) which seeks to reconcile the tension between universalist assumptions (there are universal categories) and typological observations (the inventories of grammatical categories across languages differ dramatically). While the diversity of grammatical categories across languages poses a problem for the universalists, the particularists face the problem of comparison: how can we compare categories to each other in the absence of a common denominator.

To resolve this conundrum within a generative tradition, Wiltschko (2014) proposes that grammatical categories are always language-specific, siding with categorial particularism; however, there are universal properties of categories that suggest that there is an underlying mechanism at play, which restricts the making of language-particular categories. In other words, language-specific categories are constructed in a universally restricted way. In particular, in Wiltschko (2014), I propose that there is a universal spine comprised of a hierarchically organized set of functions (reviewed in 3.1) which are associated with particular formal properties that derive the distributional patterns of categories across languages. The ingredients that serve to construct the language-particular categories are summarized in section 3.2.

3.1 The universal spine hypothesis

One of the key assumptions of the generative tradition that has shaped much research over the past few decades is that there are functional categories that define the architecture of sentence-structure. Though, the precise inventory of (universal) functional categories is a matter of debate, as we have seen (see 2.2). In Wiltschko (2014), I argue that the uncertainty in the field regarding the inventory of functional categories results from the failure to recognize the difference between language-particular grammatical categories and the universal basis that underlies the construction of these categories. This is essentially the same argument that Haspelmath (2010) introduces when he distinguishes between language-specific descriptive categories and universally applicable comparative concepts. The difference is that I assume that the universal 'concepts' correspond to core abstract functions that define the architecture of a universal spine. They should not vary among researchers depending on their particular goals; instead I claim that they are indeed universal.

In particular, the universal spine I propose in Wiltschko (2014) is comprised of four layers (as in (11)), which are instantiated in the construction of clauses as well as in the construction of nominal arguments. (i) *classification* serves to classify events and individuals into subcategories (e.g., telic vs. atelic events; mass vs. count nouns, etc.); (ii) the introduction of a *point of view* serves to map the classified event or individual to a particular perspective on it (e.g., viewing it as perfective or imperfective); (iii) *anchoring* serves to map the perspectivized event or individual to the deictic center, and (iv) *linking* serves to map the anchored event or individual to the ongoing discourse (see Wiltschko (2014) for detailed discussion and motivation).

(11)   The universal spine

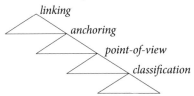

The universal spine serves as the basis for the construction of language-specific categories. Specifically, I propose that language-specific UoLs are used to further substantiate the abstract functions of the spine. For example, TENSE is constructed by associating temporal content (past) with the anchoring category as in (12), where c represents the language-specific category and κ represents the universal categorizer it associates with.

(12)   c:TENSE = κ:*anchoring* + UoL:*past*

Temporal content is well-suited to substantiate the anchoring category because it allows to establish a relation between the reported event and the deictic center. However, it is not the only content that may associate with κ:*anchoring*. Essentially any type of substantive content that allows to establish, in principle, a relation between the reported event and the deictic center can substantiate κ:*anchoring*. In Ritter and Wiltschko (2014), we argue that other categories traditionally classified as *deictic* can serve the same function, namely spatial distinctions (*here* vs. *there*), and person. Temporal content will relate the event to the deictic center via times, location via place, and person via participants. In each case it is asserted whether or not the event coincides with the time, the location or with the participant of the utterance context. This is the essence of anchoring. Note that according to this view, *deixis* is not an intrinsic property of UoLs; rather it comes about when a given UoL is associated with the spine. Thus, the same universal category (κ:*anchoring*) can be instantiated with different substantive content, constructing categories that are superficially very different, yet have the same formal and functional properties. On the other hand, UoLs with similar content may associate with the spine in different ways. For example, UoLs with temporal content do not always associate with κ:*anchoring*. They can, for example also associate with the spine as modifiers resulting in very different formal properties than those that associate with κ:*anchoring*. On this view, language variation arises because the UoLs that associate with the spine are always language-specific and hence the categories that they serve to construct will also be language-specific. However, the construction of these language-specific categories is constrained by the spine and its formal properties, to which we turn next.

3.2 Universal ingredients of categorization

In Wiltschko (2014), I argue that it is not only the functional properties of the spine that are universal, but also the formal properties associated with the spine. In this section, I briefly review these properties, and how they derive the universal formal properties of categories: patterns of contrast and patterns of multi-functionality.

Each layer in the spine consists of a categorizer κ which relates two abstract arguments. One of these arguments occupies a position traditionally known as the specifier position; the other occupies the complement position (or the specifier of the complement position). The arguments (arg) are conceived of as abstract situation arguments which contain times, locations, and participants. Depending on the substantive content of the UoL which associates with κ, different aspects of the situation are related to each other. The relation between these arguments is established via an abstract feature [coin(cidence)] for verbal categories and [ident(ity)] for nominal categories. This feature is intrinsically associated with κ no matter what the functional content of the particular κ is. This is illustrated in (13).

(13)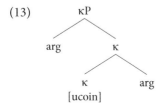

The significance of coincidence for our understanding of categorial identity has already been established in Hale 1986. He conceived of it as a feature that can operate over different domains including aspect, case, complementizers, and tense. It is not uniformly marked morphologically, and it can "be observed in parts of the grammar which are not otherwise intimately related" (Hale 1986: 238).

I argue that [coin] and its nominal counterpart [ident] are in fact the only universal features; it underlies the construction of all grammatical categories and features. In particular, I propose that it is intrinsically unvalued [*u*coin]. In the course of a derivation it is valued to either a positive [+coin] or a negative [−coin] specification. Valuation can proceed via the substantive content of the UoL that associates with κ. If it is valued positively, it specifies the relation between the two arguments as coinciding; if it is valued negatively, it specifies the relation between the two arguments as non-coinciding. For example, the UoL that signifies *pastness* values [*u*coin] as [−coin] thereby ordering the temporal arguments as non-coincidental: the event time does not coincide with the utterance time. The contrasting UoL (silent in English) will value [*u*coin] as [+coin] thereby ordering the temporal arguments as non-coincidental: the event time coincides with the utterance time. But if the content of the valuing UoL is locational, for example, then the coincidence feature will order event location relative to utterance location.

On this view then, UoLs are simple sound meaning bundles, as in (14)a, which receive their grammatical and thus categorical properties via the universal spine. Of course, UoLs are conventionally associated with the information where and how they associate with the spine (as in (14)b but the point is that we can isolate the sound meaning bundle <π, Σ> from the categorical identity that derives from the spine.

(14) Lexical entries for past UoL
    a.   <<π: -ed, Σ: past>
    b.   <<π: -ed, Σ: past> κ: *anchoring*> = c:TENSE

In this way, the USH is conceptualized as a framework that derives language specific grammars and the categories that these grammars make use of. Grammatical categories (*c*) are constructed with UoLs and the universal spine, as in (15).

(15)   c = κ + UoL

The assumption that grammatical categories are constructed as in (15) captures the fact that they are always language-particular since one of the key ingredients of categories, namely UoLs, is always language-specific. However, at the same time we also capture the fact that there are universal patterns associated with all categories. In fact, the other ingredient of grammatical categories, κ, is universal and κ is what is responsible for the universal formal properties of grammatical categories. Patterns of contrast arise because UoLs that associated with κ will be contrastive, while UoLs that associate as modifiers will not. Patterns of multi-functionality arise because for any given UoL, its interpretation will differ depending on where and how it associates with the spine. The functions intrinsically associated with the layers of the spine will affect its interpretation. In this way, syntax not only mediates the relation between sound and meaning for complex expressions but also for simplex ones. Thus, the USH satisfies Haspelmath's (2007: 119) desideratum that "comparison cannot be category-based, but must be substance-based, because substance (unlike categories) is universal". The substance of the spine allows for comparison of categories across languages even when these categories do not share the same formal properties. However, according to the USH, it is not the lexical substance of UoLs that we need to compare. If we were to compare, for example, UoLs with temporal content across languages, we might find that they don't share the same formal properties, giving the impression that there are no universal categories. It is only via the abstract functions that the spine provides that language-comparison can successfully identify the universal underpinnings of categorization.

Thus, the USH sets itself apart from other attempts to define underlying universal patterns of categorization (including cartography in the generative tradition and canonical typology or multivariate typology in the functional tradition) in that it predicts that the substantive content of categories can be quite different even though they instantiate the same functional categories (such as tense and location for example). Thus, based on the USH the apparent absence of a particular category (say tense) would prompt a researcher to look for other categories with a similar abstract function. Hence the USH makes for a novel way to look at typological patterns. Whether or not the predictions of the USH are superior than those of other approaches will have to be determined.

In sum, what the USH allows us to do is to compare language-specific categories via a third element (Humboldt's *tertium comparationis*), namely the spine. In Wiltschko (2014), I emphasized the linguistic reality of the spine, without claiming psychological reality. It was conceived of as a heuristic for discovery and comparison. Its usefulness can be gleaned from how successful it is in allowing for these tasks. One way to do this is of course to study the familiar grammatical categories across the languages of the world and see whether they can indeed be properly compared across languages. Another way is to explore UoLs that are not typically explored, neither in the generative, nor in the typological tradition, namely categories of interaction (but see Evans et al. 2017a, b; Dingemanse 2020). I turn to this in the next section.

4. Beyond grammatical categories: The categories of interaction

When people interact with each other in conversational dialogue, they do this in ways that go beyond formulating sentences of the type traditional grammatical descriptions seek to describe and analyse. On the one hand, utterances in interaction are not always complete sentences; on the other hand, interactional language also differs in that it is filled with UoLs that serve to negotiate the interaction, but which are not typically assumed to be part of grammar. To see this, consider, for example, the exchange in (16).

(16) A: Oh wow, look at that!
      B: Mmmmhmmmmm!
      A: What a great view, eh?
      B: Yeah, I know, eh?

UoLs that are exclusively found in interactional language, and which are not typically considered to be part of grammar, include: *oh, wow, mmmmhmmmmm, eh,* and *yeah.* Without these UoLs, the interaction would have a very different flavor. While these UoLs are certainly not required for the well-formedness of the utterances, they are generally required for successful interaction. Hence, they comprise an important aspect of human language and therefore should be part of linguistic description. There are properties associated with such UoLs which suggest that their form, function, and distribution is systematic in ways that suggest that they, too, should be analyzed as being associated with categorial identities that regulate their distribution. For example, they adhere to constraints just as regular UoLs do. To see this, consider what happens when the order of some of the UoLs in (16) is changed as in (17); the utterances become ill-formed suggesting that there is a grammar that regulates their distribution.

(17) A: *Wow oh, look at that!
      A: *Eh, what a great view?

Moreover, it appears that all languages have UoLs of this sort. For example, Dingemanse et al. 2013 find that *huh* is a *universal word:* it is used with similar form, function, and distribution across a sample of 31 genetically and geographically unrelated languages. This is a striking result especially given that universals of this sort have not been established in the grammatical domain. While we have seen above that we do in fact find universal patterns in the domain of traditional grammatical categories, this universality certainly does not extend to form meaning correspondences.

There are two lessons to be learned from this. First, we have to include interactional language in the domain of investigation of language universals and variation. And second, we have to take seriously sound-meaning correspondences which do not conform to the familiar arbitrariness. Both these empirical domains are usually ignored in both typological and generative traditions. In this section I show that the USH is a framework which allows for the discovery and comparison of categories in these domains as well. It allows us to compare the form, function, and distribution of interactional UoLs across languages for the sake of establishing language universals and the range of variation in this domain as well. I start by introducing a proposal to extend the universal spine to accommodate interactional language (section 4.1). I then explore a few categories of interactional language (section 4.2). Next, I show how the USH allows for a straightforward analysis of instances where the sound meaning relation does not abide to Saussurian arbitrariness, i.e., it provides a novel way capture iconicity (section 4.3). And finally, I present a preliminary analysis of *huh* within using these assumptions (section 4.4).

4.1 The extended universal spine

When we talk, we do not only say things, we do things with what we say. This was the major insight of Austin (1962) which led to the development of speech act theory. It is evident when it comes to performative utterances such as *I promise to go to bed soon* where the utterance is a promise. However, as Ross (1970) points out, it is true also for declarative clauses which do not contain a performative verb. In this case, what we do with the utterance is *telling* it to the addressee. Ross (1970) suggests that what we do is directly encoded in the utterance, even when this encoding is not overtly spelled out. In particular, he proposes that a silent performative predicate (akin to *tell*) dominates the sentence: its subject is the speaker, its direct object is the proposition uttered, and its indirect object is the addressee. In the course of the derivation, this performative clause is deleted. This is illustrated in (18).

(18) $_S[I_{VP} [tell_{NP} [you]_{S'} [that_S[prices\ slumped]]]]$

Ross' performative hypothesis has been dismissed almost immediately after it was proposed (Anderson 1971; Fraser 1974; Leech 1976 and Mittwoch 1976) for various empirical and theoretical reasons, some having to do with the demise of generative semantics. However, there has been a resurrection of the syntacticization of speech acts in the generative tradition. That is, assuming that the clausal architecture consists of a series of hierarchically organized functional categories allows for a reconceptualization of the original speech act structure proposed by Ross. Many of the arguments against the speech act structure disappear when it is analyzed as being comprised of functional architecture (see Wiltschko & Heim 2016; Wiltschko, in print for discussion). One of the seminal papers that re-conceptualized Ross' idea in terms of functional architecture is Speas & Tenny 2003. They propose that there is a recursive functional category that encodes speech act meaning (SAP) and which takes the speech act participants as arguments. This is illustrated in (19).

(19) $_{saP}[Spkr\ [sa\ _{SAP}[_{CP}[UTT\ SA\ [ADR]]]]]$

Many proposals have since put forward that seek to capture the same insight and many phenomena of natural language have been successfully analyzed utilizing this type of speech act structure (Rizzi 1997; Etxepare 1997; Cinque 1999; Ambar 1999; Speas & Tenny 2003; Hill 2007; Coniglio & Zegraen 2010; Haegeman & Hill 2013, 2014; Haegeman 2014; Paul 2014; Zu 2015; Haegeman 2015, a.o.). However, what most of these proposals have in common is that they seek to take Ross' insight at face value and translate it directly into functional architecture. For example, Speas & Tenny's (2003) proposal essentially encodes "I tell you that" in the form of functional speech act structure. However, this research agenda on the syntacticization of speech acts misses years of development within speech act theory ever since Austin's work. Within more recent developments of speech act theory, it is acknowledged that what people do when they say something is first and foremost to *interact*. Moreover, speech acts are not primitives and hence labelling a functional category as SAP misses the complexity of speech acts (see Wiltschko, in print for detailed discussion). Note further that within the functional typological literature the significance of conversational interaction on grammatical form is acknowledged and many grammatical categories are analyzed as resulting from functional pressure of human interaction. However, UoLs that are dedicated to facilitate conversational interaction such as confirmationals and response markers are rarely discussed in these frameworks as well. It is precisely to accommodate these types of UoLs that Wiltschko and Heim (2016) propose an extension of the universal spine. Specifically, they propose that there are two structured layers dominating the spine of propositional structure: *grounding* (GroundP) and *responding* (RespP) (see also Wiltschko 2017, in print) This is illustrated in (20).

(20) the extended universal spine
  $[_{\text{Interactional language}} [_{\text{propositional language}}]]$
  $[_{\text{Responding}} [_{\text{Grounding}} [_{\text{Linking}} [_{\text{Anchoring}} [_{\text{PoV}} [_{\text{classification}}]]]]]]$

The core function of *Grounding* is to encode the attitudes of the interlocutors towards the propositional content of the utterance: whether they believe what is being said or not, how long they may have believed it, or how strong. In other words, *grounding* is about expressing commitment in the sense of Gunlogson (2008) (see also Heim 2019). To capture the interactive nature of GroundP, Wiltschko & Heim (2016) propose that GroundP is articulated and consists of two separate projections: a speaker-oriented GroundP (Ground$_{\text{Spkr}}$P) and an addressee-oriented one (Ground$_{\text{Adr}}$P). This facilitates the negotiation of common ground as it allows for situations in which the interlocutors share a common belief as well as those in which there is an imbalance in belief states. This is, after all, the core goal of a typical conversation: to achieve equilibrium in belief states, a common ground.

The core function of the second layer of structure, RespP is to facilitate the interaction *per se*, i.e., turn-taking. As such, the function of RespP is sensitive to the turn-type of which I assume there are two basic ones: *initiation* and *response* (Wiltschko in print). In the initiation phase, RespP is responsible to encode what the current speaker (the initiator) expects the interlocutor to do with the utterance. In English, for example, rising intonation encodes that the initiator expects the interlocutor to respond and hence to take the next turn. In contrast, in the response phase, RespP is responsible for encoding whether or not the current utterance is in fact a response to the previous turn.

The functional architecture of the extended interactional spine is otherwise identical to the functional architecture of the propositional spine. There is a transitive head (κ) which is intrinsically associated with an unvalued coincidence feature [$u$coin]. It relates two abstract arguments: the propositional content of the utterance occupies the complement position; the interlocutor's ground occupies the specifier position. If the coincidence feature is valued positively, it specifies that the propositional content is in the belief set of the interlocutor (p coincides with Ground), if it is valued negatively, it specifies that the propositional content is not in the interlocutor's ground. This is illustrated in (21).

(21)　[Ground$_{Spkr}$ [+/−coin]$_{Ground}$CP]$_{Ground\text{-spkr}}$

In the RespP, the specifier is occupied by the response set. Depending on the turn-type, the response set is either that of the current turn-holder or that of the other interlocutor. In the initiation phase, [+coin] specifies that the utterance is placed into the other's response-set. It results in what Beyssade & Marandin 2006 refer to as the Call on Addressee; [−coin] specifies that the utterance is not placed in the other interlocutor's response set and thus that the current turn-holder wishes to continue their turn. In contrast, in the response phase, [+coin] specifies that the current utterance is in the response set of the current interlocutor and hence identifies it as a response; [−coin] specifies that the utterance is not in the response set of the current interlocutor and hence that what is being said should not be taken as a response. This is illustrated in (22).

(22)　[Resp-set [+/−coin]$_{Resp}$ GroundP]$_{RespP}$

This proposal does not face the same problems as those that simply translate Ross' performative hypothesis into the functional architecture. It captures the interactive nature of language that goes beyond "I give this utterance to you". This is in line with much recent work on the semantics and pragmatics of speech acts which views assertions as proposals to update the common ground. As such conversational negotiations can be viewed as a combination of expressing commitment to what is being said as well as engagement with the interlocutor (Heim 2019). The proposal also does justice to the fact that speech acts are not primitives and that there are UoLs across unrelated languages that are dedicated to this type of conversational interaction. I turn to a discussion of such UoLs in the next subsection.

4.2 Confirmationals, response markers, and other categories of interactional language

The assumption that there is a layer of structure above the propositional structure dedicated to regulating dialogical interaction predicts that there should be UoLs that associate with these layers. Moreover, it predicts that these UoLs will be linearized at the sentence periphery. This is because the higher in the structure a given UoL associates with the spine, the more peripheral it will be linearized, either sentence-initially or sentence-finally. And this is indeed what we find in many unrelated languages.

Consider again the conversation in (16) repeated below. We observe sentence-initial *oh, wow,* and *yeah*, sentence-final *eh* and stand-alone *mmmmhmmmmm*.

(16)   A: oh wow, look at that!
            B: Mmmmhmmmmm!
            A: What a great view, eh?
            B: yeah, I know, eh?

Let us consider each of these UoLs in turn. The sentence initial *oh* marks change of (mental) state, acknowledging new information (Heritage 1998). In (16), this change of state concerns the belief state of the speaker: *oh* is used to express that the speaker is surprised by what they are seeing right now (the view). The use of *wow* immediately following *oh* reinforces the significance of the change of state by adding emotional evaluation; it marks the speaker's state as one of heightened emotions related to being suprised. The other sentence-initial UoL (*yeah*) in (16) is a response marker; here it marks agreement with the previous utterance.

At the other end of the sentence we find sentence-final *eh* in two utterances. Following the exclamative 'What a great view!' it marks that the initiator A is seeking confirmation from their interlocutor. That is, the propositional content in the exclamative expresses a positive evaluation of the current situation and *eh* is used to elicit confirmation that the interlocutor shares this evaluation. In their response, the responder B also tags their utterance with *eh*. It is also used to elicit confirmation. Note, however, that the function of *eh* differs significantly from regular tag-questions, which typically elicit confirmation that the content of the utterance is true or, as is the case with exclamatives, that it is appropriate (Exclamatives cannot be said to be true or false). Following *I know*, regular tag questions would not be felicitous, at least not in this context. If appropriate at all, it would be interpreted as rude, which is not the case for *eh*.

(23)   I know, don't I.

Rather, *eh* in (16) is used to elicit confirmation that the interlocutor A really knows that the current speaker B agrees with A's assessment. It is precisely these types of UoLs which the extended universal spine is meant to accommodate.

4.2.1 A syntactic analysis of sentence final eh?

Let us consider the sentence final-tag *eh*. Wiltschko and Heim (2016) analyse this tag as associating with Ground$_{Spkr}$ or Ground$_{Adr}$ (see also Wiltschko 2017; Thoma 2016; Wiltschko et al. 2018; Wiltschko in print). It values [*u*coin] positively expressing that the propositional content is in the speaker's ground and, if it also associates with Ground$_{Adr,}$ it also expresses that the propositional content is in the Addressee's ground. While, of course, the speaker cannot be certain about the content of their interlocutor's belief set, they can make some educated guesses about it. What is expressed is thus not what is actually in the addressee's set of beliefs, it is what the current speaker believes to be there. But this does not yet explain the fact that the use of *eh* also indicates a request for confirmation for the speaker's beliefs. The key to understanding this lies in the fact that *eh* is associated with rising intonation. It is this intonational tune which is used to indicate that the current speaker requests a response (Heim et al. 2016). In particular, the final rise on *eh* positively values [*u*coin] in Resp hence indicating that the current speaker places the utterance into their interlocutor's response set: they request a response, which in turn is interpreted as requesting confirmation. Depending on whether *eh* occupies Ground$_{Spkr}$ or Ground$_{Adr}$ the current speaker may either request that their belief about the propositional content is true or appropriate or alternatively that their assessment of the Addressee's belief set is appropriate. This analysis is schematized in (24).

(24) A syntactic analysis of *eh*

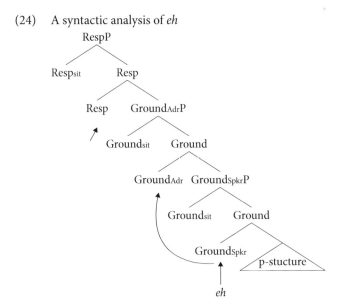

The syntactic analysis within the framework of the extended universal spine hypothesis has several advantages over previous analyses. First, in previous treatments of *eh*, it was analysed as being associated with many different functions (Holmes 1983; Gold & Tremblay 2006) without an explicit account for what accounts for these functions. The present analysis recognizes that there are several factors that contribute to the function of *eh*; it is not only a matter of associating several functions with the UoLs itself (Wiltschko et al. 2018). The contributing factors include the UoL, which in this analysis serves to value the coincidence feature in the grounding layer. In addition, the rising intonation associated with *eh* contributes the request for confirmation and is analysed as a separate UoL. Evidence for this comes from the fact that *eh* can also be used with level intonation in which case, no request for response ensues. This is known as the narrative use of *eh*. Moreover, the content of the spine itself plays an important role in the interpretation of *eh*. That is, the Grounding layers are responsible for encoding that the content is in the speaker's or in the addressee's ground, with the two different functions being associated with different syntactic representations. And the response layer is responsible for expressing that a response is requested. The content of what is to be confirmed depends on the complement of the head with which *eh* associates.

The advantage of decomposing the function of *eh* into several independent components lies in the fact that it allows us to make predictions about universals and variation that we may find in this domain. For example, we predict that we might find sentence-final tags that are only Addressee-oriented. And indeed, this is precisely what sentence final *huh* does in English: it is used to confirm the addressee's belief but does not express that the propositional content is in the speaker's ground. Within the analysis developed here, it is associated with Ground$_{Adr}$ only, as shown in (25).

(25) A syntactic analysis of *huh*.

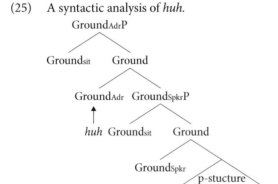

Evidence for this analysis comes from the data in (26). In the context of the conversation in (16), *huh* cannot be used (26a). This is because people usually know if they know something and do not require confirmation. Hence, in this context it would not be appropriate not to specify that the propositional content is in the speaker's ground. In contrast, it is possible to ask for confirmation that the propositional content is in the addressee's ground if it concerns content that the addressee has privileged access to, as in (26b).

(26) a. *Yeah, I know huh.
　　　b. You know everything, huh?

This is one way in which the present analysis can account for the kind of variation we observe in the UoLs that serve this function. Moreover, if indeed there is a grammar that regulates the form, function, and distribution of these interactional UoLs, we expect them to be able to enter paradigmatic relations.

4.2.2 *The paradigmatic organization of sentence final particles. Evidence from Mandarin*

The unvalued coincidence feature in the grounding and the responding layer should in principle be valuable positively or negatively and hence there should be UoLs that instantiate negative values. In what follows I discuss evidence based on Mandarin Chinese which shows that this prediction is indeed borne out.

There are many sentence-final particles in Mandarin, but here I only consider four that enter into the kind of paradigmatic contrasts predicted by the present analysis. *de* and *a* are speaker-oriented particles. *de* is used to convey that what is being said is in the speaker's ground, as illustrated in (27). According to Li, An and Zhang (1998) the function of final *de* is to express certainty. Specifically, by using *de* the speaker conveys that he is not just reporting on an event, but in addition he is expressing his attitude towards this report, namely that he is certain. It is for this reason that in the context in (27), it is obligatory to add *de*.

(27) **Context**: John was told that Mary drives to work. He wonders whether he can catch a ride. But he is not sure whether Mary drives every morning. He runs into Bob, Mary's husband, and wants to know whether it really is true. Bob says:

　　a. *Ta　meitian　　zaoshang　kaiche　shangban　de.*
　　　　She every.day　morning　　drive　　work　　　PRT
　　　　'(I confirm that) she drives to work every morning.'

　　b. **Ta　meitian　　zaoshang　kaiche　shangban.*
　　　　She every.day　morning　　drive　　work
　　　　'She drives to work every morning.'

In contrast, the sentence final particle *a* serves to express that the content of the utterance is new to the speaker. In other words, it conveys that up until now the proposition was not in their ground. This is illustrated in (28).

(28) Student: *Dou wancheng le. Wo xianzai deng zhe biye le*
'Everything is done. Now I am waiting for my graduation.'
Advisor: *Buguo ni hai xuyao fabiao yi pian lunwen.*
But you need to publish one more paper (before you graduate).
Student: *Shenme? Wo hai dei xie yi pian lunwen a*
What? I   still must write one CL thesis PRT
What? I still have a thesis to write (I didn't know that).

The difference between *de* and *a* provides exactly the type of paradigmatic contrast our analysis predicts. *de* conveys that the speaker knows p, whereas *a* conveys that the speaker doesn't know p. Thus, I analyse *de* as valuing [*u*coin] in Ground$_{Spkr}$ positively, and *a* as valuing it negatively.

A similar contrast is found with the addressee-oriented particles *ma* and *bei*. *Ma* is used to convey that (the speaker thinks that) the addressee already knows what is being said whereas the latter is used to convey that (the speaker thinks that) the addressee doesn't already know what is being said. Consider first *ma*. There are two ways in which the speaker might assume that the addressee already knows what they are saying. First, the speaker may have first-hand experience of the addressee witnessing the truth of the proposition as in (29).

(29) Context: Mary gave John a puppy. After a month, John calls Mary to ask which kind of dog food is better for his dog. He says to Mary:
Ni shangci gei wo le tiao gou ma ...
You last.time give me asp CL dog PRT
Wo xiang wen ni nage paizi de gouliang hao.
I want to ask yo which brand of dog food is good.
'Remember you gave me a dog last time.
Now I want to ask which food is good for him.'

With the use of *ma* the speaker reminds the addressee of their common knowledge. Note however that the English translation contains '*remember*' which has no direct correlate in the Mandarin utterance. It simply is an effect of the use of *ma* which conveys that the speaker thinks that the addressee knows what is being said.

A second way in which a speaker can be sure that the addressee already knows what is being said comes about when it is an obvious state of affairs. For example, Wang 2009 argues that *ma* is used to express the obviousness of a fact or state of affairs; and according to Chappell and Peyraube (2016: 323) *ma* is used for *"situations which are viewed as highly evident in nature and which follow logically from the given facts"*. This is shown in (30).

(30) a. *Diqiu weirao taitang zhuan.*
    Earth round sun turn
    The earth goes around the sun.

b. *Diqiu weirao taiyang zhuan **ma**.*
    Earth round sun turn PRT
    '(It's known by all that) the earth goes around the sun.'

Finally, there is also a particle (*bei*), which can be used if the speaker thinks that the addressee does not already know what he is telling her. This is illustrated in (31)

(31) **Context:** Mary knows that John doesn't like cates. But one day, as they are shopping together in the supermarket, Mary observes that John is looking at cat toys, and the following conversation ensues.

Mary: *Ni zenme kan mao de dongxi?*
    Why are you looking at the cat stuff?

John: *Wo erzi jian huilai yi zhi mao **bei***
    (You haven't know that) my son picked up a cat somewhere

    ...*yiding yao yang*
    ...and wants to keep it anyway

We can analyse *ma* and *bei* as UoLs that associate with Ground$_{Adr}$ such that *ma* values [ucoin] positively whereas *bei* does so negatively.

We have now seen that there are four Mandarin sentence final particles which neatly instantiate the paradigmatic contrast expected by the syntactic analysis I have developed. There are particles used to convey speaker-old and -new information, respectively as well as particles that are used to convey addressee-old and -new information, respectively. "This is summarized in Table 1."

Table 1. The paradigm of grounding particles in Mandarin

	Speaker-oriented	Addressee-oriented
old	*de:* Ground$_{Spkr}$[+coin]	*ma:* Ground$_{Adr}$[+coin]
new	*a:* Ground$_{Spkr}$[−coin]	*bei:* Ground$_{Adr}$[−coin]

Finally, another virtue of the syntactic analysis developed here is that it views syntax as mediating between form and meaning. The distribution of UoLs is regulated by the syntactic spine and moreover, by virtue of being associated with the spine in a certain way UoLs are enriched with the spinal functions. In this way, the spine contributes to the interpretation of UoLs and furthermore it functions as a point of comparison for categories across languages. This is significant in that it allows us to compare UoLs with superficially very different properties. The universality of categories is defined via spinal functions, which are universally hierarchically configured and not via the idiosyncratic properties of language-specific UoLs. This allows us, for example, to make sense, in a formal way, of the observation that the functional load of sentence-final particles in languages such as Mandarin or Japanese is carried by intonational contours in English (Wakefield 2010, 2012)) which I turn to next.

4.2.3 The functional equivalence of particles and intonation

While we have seen that English does have some sentence-final particles, its inventory is not nearly as rich as that of East-Asian languages. For example, it lacks a sentence-final particle that would value [*u*coin] in Ground negatively, i.e., there is no particle that would be used to express that the propositional content is not part of the speaker's or the addressee's ground. To convey this meaning, speakers of English can make use of a particular contour, namely the so-called incredulity contour. It is used to express uncertainty and disbelief (Ward & Hirschberg 1985) as shown in (32).

(32) Incredulity contour
A: I'd like you here tomorrow morning at eleven.
B: Eleven in the morning!
    L*+H   L*+H L H%
Ward & Hirschberg 1986: 3 (2)

The response move by B expresses disbelief, and – according to Ward and Hirschberg 1985 – the disbelief is encoded context-independently via the sentence final fall-rise contour. The context-independence of this interpretation is crucial, as it clearly suggests that the contour itself is meaningful, i.e., it functions as a UoL. Consequently, I propose that intonational tunes associate with the spine and may serve to value the coincidence feature associated with spinal heads. In particular, the incredulity contour is syntactically complex: it associates with both $Ground_{Spkr}$ and Resp. [*u*coin] in $Ground_{Spkr}$ is valued negatively thereby encoding that the utterance is not in the speaker's ground. This captures the observation that L*+H L H% conveys disbelief and uncertainty. I further propose that the incredulity contour is also associated with Resp: it positively values the coincidence feature thereby indicating that the speaker requests a response. Specifically, I assume that the complexity of the incredulity contour (a rising accent L*+H and a rising boundary tone L H%) correlates with syntactic complexity: the rising accent negatively values [*u*coin] in $Ground_{Spkr}$ encoding disbelief, whereas the rising boundary tone positively values [*u*coin] in Resp encoding a request for a response. This is illustratd in (33).

(33) Analysing the Incredulity contour

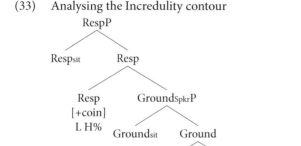

While there are several analyses that have recently been developed that suggest that intonational tunes function like morphemes (Truckenbrodt 2012) and as such are associated with the spine (Davis 2011), the present proposal differs in several ways. In particular, I assume that sound itself is interpreted along the spine. This is the topic of the next subsection.

4.3 How sound is meaning

In the last sub-section we have seen that UoLs with different properties may associate with the same position along the spine: for example particles and intonational tunes may both be associated with the same position along the spine. This accounts for the fact that they carry a similar functional load. Hence the spine serves as a tool for cross-linguistic comparison of categories. Note, however, that intonational tunes constitute a very different type of UoL: unlike other UoLs, which are typically bundles of sound and meaning ($<\pi,\Sigma>$), intonational tunes only have meaning once they associate with the spine. They cannot even be pronounced in isolation. Moreover, many intonational tunes receive virtually identical meanings across different languages. This suggests that the relation between sound and meaning for intonational tunes may not be as arbitrary as is the case for other UoLs. I propose that this property of intonational tunes can be modelled if we assume that it is the sound itself that associates with the spine, rather than a bundle of sound and meaning. This is illustrated in (34).

(34) $<\pi, \kappa>$

The claim here is that sound appears to have meaning by virtue of being associated with the spine. Since the spine is universally associated with the same functions, this results in (near) universal (non-arbitrary) sound-meaning relations. This is at the root of so-called iconicity. That is, particular properties of intonational tunes may serve to value the coincidence feature by virtue of their phonetic properties. In particular, Heim (2019) argues that in English intonational tunes can be decomposed into pitch duration and pitch excursion: pitch duration serves to encode speaker commitment while pitch excursion serves to encode addressee engagement. On the present analysis, commitment is a function of GroundP while engagement is a function of RespP. The precise mechanism with which these phonetic properties are interpreted goes beyond the scope of this paper.

I note, however, that the prosodic properties of intonational tunes are not the only way in which sound may be interpreted along the spine by serving to value the coincidence features of the functional heads. Here I briefly review evidence from Yamato Japanese discussed in Fujimori (2011) to the effect that vowel-quality serves as a perfect predictor for the telicity of verbs. In particular, Fujimori demonstrates that mono-syllabic verbs containing /e/ or /u/ are always telic, and those with /i/ or /o/ are always atelic (verbs with /a/ can be either telic or atelic). This holds for all verbs in Yamato Japanese. In addition, based on experimental evidence, Fujimori (2011) shows that Japanese speakers are sensitive to this distinction even in nonce verbs. This is precisely the type of behavior we may expect from a system where a particular sound serves to value [ucoin]. In particular, within the USH, telicity may be analysed as follows. Within the classification layer of vPs, we identify two abstract arguments: the event situation and the final event situation. Events are interpreted as telic (i.e., as having a natural endpoint) if the final event is specified to coincide with the event situation (i.e., if [ucoin] is positively valued). In contrast, events are interpreted as atelic (i.e., as not having a natural endpoint) if the final event is specified to not coincide with the event situation (i.e., if [ucoin] is negatively valued. This is illustrated in (35).

(35) The sound valuation of telicity

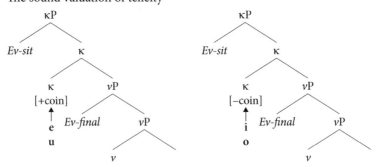

But what aspect of these vowels might be responsible for this pattern? In terms of features that have traditionally served to classify vowels to define natural classes (*low/high* and *front/back*) this pattern is somewhat unexpected. Neither /e/ and u/

nor /i/ and /o/ form a natural class in terms of these features. However, as Fujimori (2011) observes, there is a way in which these sets of vowels form a natural class: /e/ and /u/ are close to the tongue rest position (i.e., ([central]) while /i/ and /o/ are far from the tongue rest position, they are produced at the edges of the vocal tract. In contrast, /a/ is somewhat neutral. I suggest that it is precisely this phonetic property which is interpreted on the spine: it values the coincidence feature iconically. Closeness of the tongue rest position is interpreted as [+coin] while distance is interpreted as [−coin]; and the neutrality of /a/ with respect to this phonetic property is interpreted as neutrality in terms of coincidence as well. Hence /a/ may be interpreted either way and does not correlate with telicity. Again, we see how the assumption that the spine is intrinsically associated with substance (the function and the abstract arguments associated with each layer as well as the coincidence feature) allows us to model iconicity. In particular, the coincidence feature provides the interface between the spine and the language-specific UoLs such that the UoLs serve to value it. Typically, UoLs consist of sound and meaning (<π,Σ>) and typically it is the meaning (Σ) which serves to value [$u$coin]. However, nothing precludes sound (π), as well, to serve this function. In fact, there is no privileged relation between either sound or meaning and the spine. Both belong to different cognitive domains, and both interface with the spine. It is in this way, that syntax (here conceived of as the spine) mediates between sound and meaning. Iconicity arises if it is sound alone that is interpreted by the spine. This is possible by associating sound alone with the spine, as is the case with intonational tunes, which on their own are not associated with a meaning. But it is also possible by associating a regular sound meaning bundle <π,Σ> with the spine. But instead of using its meaning to value [$u$coin], it is the sound which does the job. This is what happens with Yamato Japanese verbs.

This analysis accounts for the iconic properties of this pattern, but it also leaves room for arbitrariness, at least in two ways. First, UoLs differ as to whether they consist of sound alone (like intonational tunes) or whether they also include meaning. Second, UoLs that consist of sound and meaning may differ as to how they interact with the spine: via its meaning or via its sound. And third, if it is the sound that is interpreted, languages may differ as to which phonetic property of the sound is interpreted. For intonational tunes in English, Heim (2019) has shown that it is pitch duration and pitch excursion which are interpreted; for vowels in Yamato Japanese, Fujimori has shown that it is the centrality or periphery of the vowel which is interpreted. However, everything else being equal we might expect systems that use other phonetic properties of vowels to be interpreted (see Dingemanse 2018, for a recent overview of the properties of ideophones).

In sum, the USH provides a new way of dealing with unconventional associations between sound and meaning including ideophones: in particular the assumption that the spine has substance which is interpreted in interaction with UoLs allows for sounds to be interpreted as well. This accounts for certain universal patterns of interpretation precisely because the functions that interface with these UoLs are universal. It differs from previous approaches towards intonational meaning according to which the tunes or tones themselves are viewed as morphemes (see Truckenbrodt 2012 for a recent generative approach, and 2019 for a detailed overview). `

4.4 The category of *huh*

I have now shown how the USH allows for cross-linguistic comparison of grammatical categories. Furthermore, I have shown how we can apply the same framework to compare categories which are not typically taken to be grammatical categories, namely those that characterize interactional language (including discourse markers and intonational tunes). There are two assumptions which I have introduced that make this possible. The first assumption is that the structure which regulates the distribution and function of UoLs includes structure with functions to regulate dialogical interaction (GroundP and RespP). The second assumption is that sound can be interpreted by the spine resulting in what is known as non-arbitrary meaning. Hence there are UoLs that consist solely of sound rather than being sound-meaning bundles where the relation between sound and meaning is arbitrary. Such UoLs reveal the function of the spine because there is no language specific meaning associated with the UoL.

I now suggest that these two assumptions allow us to understand the properties of *huh* discussed above. According to Dingemanse et al. 2013, *huh* is found across many unrelated languages with virtually identical form and function. In terms of its form, it is universally realized as a single syllable with at most a glottal onset consonant, an unrounded low front central vowel, and questioning intonation. In terms of its function, it is universally used as an *open other-initiated repair* strategy. That is, repair of a given turn is initiated not by the speaker but by the other participant. It serves to signal that the interlocutor has problems understanding what was being said, but it leaves open what the problem is. Based on these findings Dingemanse et al. 2013 argue that *huh* is a universal *word*. It is classified as a word because it does not behave like an involuntary grunt. For example, it adheres to phonological constraints of the language at hand, and it displays patterns of acquisition that are akin to words, rather than to involuntary sounds. The universality is striking because it contradicts the Saussurian arbitrariness usually observed with (simplex) words. According to Dingemanse et al. (2013: 7) its universality is the result of "cultural evolution in the adaptive context of its interactional environment." Specifically, they identify its context of use as one where the interlocutor uttering it has to signal that no response can be given and this has to happen fast. The need for speed in turn requires a form with the least amount of effort. It has to be fast due to the rules of turn-taking, which are universally constrained. Typically, the break between turns is no longer than 100–300ms (Stivers et al. 2009; Pomerantz 1984). But this requires that planning an utterance has to happen well-before a turn has come to an end (Levinson & Torreira 2015). If there is a problem understanding a given turn, the interlocutor has to signal this fast and without much effort and it will have to serve as a request to solve the problem (typically by repeating the utterance). According to Dingemanse et al. (2013: 7) "These requirements are met rather precisely in the combination of minimal effort and questioning prosody that characterises the OIR [other initiated repair; MEW] interjection across languages."

In the context of the framework I have developed here, the mechanism that underlies the creation of this universal form follows straightforwardly. Suppose that all that is required in this context is to signal a request for response. If nothing else is added, the previous interlocutor will interpret this to mean that their interlocutor is not able to respond to the turn they just finished. That is, the utterance itself is maximally unmarked; all it is, is a request for response. However, intonational tunes cannot occur without some form of phonological substance and to provide this the maximally unmarked form is used. This is in part universally determined, but in part language specific (as discussed in Dingemanse et al. 2013). Thus, I argue that the phonological properties of *huh* follow from the fact that it merely serves as a host for the intonational melody responsible to request a response. This is typically rising intonation, and indeed in most of the 10 languages investigated in Dingemanse et al. 2013, *huh* is realized with rising intonation. The only two exceptions are Icelandic and Cha'palaa which use falling intonation, and interestingly, in these languages, falling intonation is also used in questions, which are the prototoypical speech acts that require a response.

In as much as the analysis of *huh* developed here is on the right track, we can conclude that the assumptions that define the extended USH are useful ones. That is, under standard assumptions about the way sound-meaning bundles are compared the properties of *huh* are surprising on many levels. Words, are not usually universal. But assuming that all that this particular sound does is provide a host for the intonational tune that is used to request a response its properties fall into place. Like intonational tunes themselves, *huh* can be viewed as pure sound that associates with the spine, with the resulting meaning being purely based on the spinal function. If one accepts the universal spine as a system that derives categories both in the propositional as well as in the interactional structure then, nothing more has to be said about the properties of *huh*. They fall out from the system, no further assumptions are needed.

5. Conclusion: How to do typology

The goal of this paper was to explore the question regarding the universality of categories and their range of variation. We started with an analytical conundrum: how is it possible to compare languages to each other if we do not assume a set of universal categories which we can use as the standard of comparison. But then, if we do that, how can we actually discover universal categories, if we have to presuppose them. Thus, comparative linguistics brings with it an intrinsic problem of circularity. This conundrum, while not often explicitly acknowledged, is at the root of a theoretical controversy that has a long tradition. Generative linguists assume the existence of universal categories based on arguments having to do with the cognitive underpinnigs of natural language, while (functional) typologists deny them based on the seemingly limitless diversity the languages of the world display.

In this paper, I have explored a way to resolve this conundrum and to bridge the gap between the generative and the functional typologists' perspective. While I agree with the core assumption that grammatical categories are not universal, I do not agree with the more general assumption that there is nothing universal about grammatical categories. In particular, I have reviewed, the core tenets of Wiltschko's 2014 Universal Spine Hyothesis (USH), according to which grammatical categories are necessarily language specific because they are always constructed, and hence can be constructed in different ways. Nevertheless, there is a universal core that restricts the construction of these language specific categories, and this core is the universal spine. The universal spine consists of a set of hierarchically organized structures which are intrinsically associated with functions, and which in turn add meaning to the language-specific units of language (UoLs) that associate with the spine. On this view, language variation in the inventory of grammatical category results from the fact that one of the ingredients of grammatical categories is language-specific UoLs. On the other hand, the universality of categorial patterns I identified derives from the fact that the universal spine is implicated in the creation of categories. It derives universal patterns of contrast and universal patterns of multi-functionality. Without the assumption that there is an underlying mechanism that is responsible for categorization, these patterns would be coincidental.

I then showed how these assumptions derive categorial patterns in the familiar domain of grammatical categories. In my own experience, the usefulness of the USH lies in the fact that it allows us to ask new questions. That is, when we observe that a given language appears to lack a category that we may have expected to be universally attested (e.g., TENSE) then the USH leads us to expect that this language will have another category that fulfills the same function (namely *anchoring* in the case of tenselessness).

But I have also applied the same logic to categories that are restricted to interactive language. That is, when we are having conversations, sentences often contain UoLs which are not always considered to be in the scope of grammatical analysis. However, I have argued that we can extend the universal spine to include a layer of structure which is responsible for regulating interactive language. Hence, the universal spine truly serves as a tool for discovery and comparison. In this novel empirical domain, we cannot fall back onto assumptions that derive from traditional grammars, because traditional grammars never compared the categories that belong to the language of interaction.

But this approach towards grammatical categories, including those of interactional language, requires detailed and careful investigation of data that are often not part of typical descriptions. We cannot simply assume that a UoL with a particular meaning will have to be analysed as belonging to the same category as its notional equivalent in the language(s) of comparison. It is for this reason that this type of typological research cannot easily be large-scale. Especially when working on understudied languages, fieldwork has to be conducted to determine the grammatical categories of propositional and of interactional language that this language constructs. But this doesn't make the enterprise less valid. It takes time to get to the core of a language and so too it is not surprising that it takes a long time to get to the core of UG. While descriptions of surface properties are useful to some degree, they run into the danger of leading to false generalizations which takes us further away from the core.

In as much, as the USH with its extension to include interactional language is successful, we can begin to think about the psychological underpinnings of the spine.

References

Ambar, Manuela. 1999. Aspects of focus in Portuguese. In *The Grammar of Focus* [Linguistik Aktuell/Linguistics Today 24], George Rebuschi & Laurie Tuller (eds), 23–53. Amsterdam: John Benjamins. https://doi.org/10.1075/la.24.02amb
Anderson, Stephen 1971. *On the Linguistic Status of the Performative/Constative Distinction*. Bloomington IN: Indiana University Linguistics Club.
Austin, John. 1962. *How to do Things with Words*. Oxford: OUP.
Beyssade, Claire & Marandin, Jean-Marie. 2006. The speech act assignment problem revisited: Disentangling speaker's commitment from speaker's call on addressee. In *Empirical Issues in Syntax and Semantics* 6, Olivier Bonami Patricia & Cabredo Hofherr (eds), 37–68. http://www.cssp.cnrs.fr/eiss6/index_en.html
Bhat, Darbhe Narayana Shankara. 2013. Third person pronouns and demonstratives. In *The World Atlas of Language Structures Online*, Matthew S. Dryer & Martin Haspelmath (eds), Leipzig: Max Planck Institute for Evolutionary Anthropology. <http://wals.info/chapter/43> (30 August 2019).

Bickel, Balthasar. 2010. Capturing particulars and universals in clause linkage: A multivariate analysis. In *Clause Hierarchy and Clause Linking: Syntax and Pragmatics* [Studies in Language Companion Series 121], Isabelle Bril (ed.), 51–101. Amsterdam: John Benjamins. https://doi.org/10.1075/slcs.121.03bic

Bickel, Balthasar. 2011. Multivariate typology and field linguistics: A case study on detransitivization in Kiranti (Sino-Tibetan). In *Proceedings of Conference on Language Documentation and Linguistic Theory 3*, Peter K. Austin, Oliver Bong, Lutz Marten & David Nathan (eds), 3–13. London: School of Oriental and African Studies.

Boas, Franz. 1991. Introduction. In *Handbook of American Indian Languages*, Vol. 1 [Bureau of American Ethnology Bulletin 40–1], Franz Boas (ed.). Washington DC: Government Printing Office

Ceong, Hailey Hyekyeong. 2019. The Morphosyntax of Clause Typing: Single, Double, Periphrastic, and Multifunctional Complementizers in Korean. PhD dissertation, University of Victoria.

Chappell, Hilary & Peyraube, Alain. 2016. Modality and mood in sinitic. In *The Oxford Handbook of Modality and Mood*, Jan Nuyts & Johan van der Auwera (eds), 296–339. Oxford: OUP.

Chomsky, Noam. 1965. *Aspects of the Theory of Syntax*. Cambridge MA: The MIT Press.

Chomsky, Noam. 1986. *Barriers*. Cambridge MA: The MIT Press.

Cinque, Guglielmo. 1999. *Adverbs and Functional Heads*. Oxford: OUP.

Comrie, Bernard. 1989. *Language Universals and Linguistic Typology: Syntax and Morphology*. Oxford: Blackwell.

Coniglio, Marco & Zegrean, Iulia. 2010. Splitting up force evidence from discourse particles. *Linguistics* 20: 7–34.

Corbett, Greville G. 1999. Prototypical inflection: Implications for typology. In *Yearbook of Morphology 1998*, Geert Booij & Jaap van Marle (eds), 1–22. Dordrecht: Springer. https://doi.org/10.1007/978-94-017-3720-3_1

Corbett, Greville G. 2009. Canonical inflectional classes. In *Selected Proceedings of the 6th Décenbrettes: Morphology in Bordeaux*, Fabio Montermini, Gilles Boyé & Jesse Tseng (eds), 1–11. Somerville MA: Cascadilla Proceedings Project.

Corbett, Greville G. 2015. Morphosyntactic complexity: A typology of lexical splits. *Language* 91: 145–193. https://doi.org/10.1353/lan.2015.0003

Corbett, Greville G. & Fedden, Sebastian. 2016. Canonical gender. *Journal of Linguistics* 52: 495–531. https://doi.org/10.1017/S0022226715000195

Croft, William. 2001. *Radical Construction Grammar: Syntactic Theory in Typological Perspective*. Oxford: OUP. https://doi.org/10.1093/acprof:oso/9780198299554.001.0001

Croft, William & Poole, Keith T. 2008. Inferring universals from grammatical variation: Multidimensional scaling for typological analysis. *Theoretical Linguistics* 34(1): 1–38. . https://doi.org/10.1515/THLI.2008.001

Davis, Christopher. 2011. Constraining Interpretation: Sentence Final Particles in Japanese. PhD dissertation, University of Massachusetts, Amherst.

Dingemanse, Mark. 2018. Redrawing the margins of language: Lessons from research on ideophones. *Glossa: A Journal of General Linguistics* 3(1): 4. https://doi.org/10.5334/gjgl.444

Dingemanse, Mark, Torreira, Francisco & Enfield, Nicholas J. 2013. Is 'Huh?' a universal word? Conversational infrastructure and the convergent evolution of linguistic items. *PLOS ONE*, 9(4). https://doi.org/10.1371/journal.pone.0078273

Dingemanse, Mark. 2020. Between sound and speech: Liminal signs in interaction. *Research on Language and Social Interaction* 53(1): 188–196.
https://doi.org/10.1080/08351813.2020.1712967

Dryer, Matthew S. 1997. Are grammatical relations universal ? In *Essays on Language Function and Language Type: Dedicated to T. Givòn*, Joan L. Bybee, John Haiman & Sandra A. Thompson (eds), 115–143. Amsterdam: John Benjamins. https://doi.org/10.1075/z.82.09dry

Etxepare, Ricardo. 1997. The Grammatical Representation of Speech Events. PhD dissertation, University of Maryland.

Evans, Nicholas & Levinson, Stephen C. 2009. The myth of language universals: Language diversity and its importance for cognitive science. *Behavioral and Brain Sciences* 32(5): 429–448.
https://doi.org/10.1017/S0140525X0999094X

Evans, Nicholas, Bergqvist, Henrik & San Roque, Lila. 2017a. The grammar of engagement, I: framework and initial exemplification. *Language and Cognition* 10(1): 1–31

Evans, Nicholas, Bergqvist, Henrik & San Roque, Lila. 2017b. The grammar of engagement II: Typology and diachrony. *Language and Cognition* 10(1): 141–170.
https://doi.org/10.1017/langcog.2017.22

Fraser, Bruce. 1974. An examination of the performative analysis. *Papers in Linguistics* 7: 1–40.
https://doi.org/10.1080/08351817409370360

Fujimori, Atsushi. 2011. The correspondence between vowel quality and verbal telicity in Yamato-Japanese. PhD dissertation, University of British Columbia.

Gold, Elaine & Tremblay, Mireille. 2006. *Eh?* and *hein?* Discourse particles or national icons? *Canadian Journal of Linguistics* 51(2–3): 247–63. https://doi.org/10.1017/S0008413100004096

Haegeman, Liliane. 2014. West flemish verb-based discourse markers and the articulation of the speech act layer. *Studia Linguistica* 68(1): 116–139. https://doi.org/10.1111/stul.12023

Haegeman, Liliane & Hill, Virginia. 2013. The syntacticization of discourse. In *Syntax and its Limits*, Raffaella Folli, Christina Sevdali & Robert Truswell (eds), 370–390. Oxford: OUP.
https://doi.org/10.1093/acprof:oso/9780199683239.003.0018

Haegeman, Liliane & Hill, Virgina. 2014. Vocatives and speech act projections: A case study in West Flemish. In *On Peripheries. Exploring Clause Initial and Clause Final Positions*, Anna Cardinaletti, Guglielmo Cinque & Yoshio Endo (eds), 209–236. Tokyo: Hituzi Syobo.

Haspelmath, Martin. 1997. *Indefinite Pronouns*. Oxford: OUP.

Haspelmath, Martin. 2007. Pre-established categories don't exist: Consequences for language description and typology. *Linguistic Typology* 11(1): 119–132.
https://doi.org/10.1515/LINGTY.2007.011

Haspelmath, Martin. 2010. Comparative concepts and descriptive categories in crosslinguistic studies. *Language* 86: 663–687. https://doi.org/10.1353/lan.2010.0021

Heim, Johannes. 2019 Commitment and Engagement: The Role of Intonation in Deriving Speech Acts. PhD dissertation, University of British Columbia.

Heim, Johannes, Keupdjio, Hermann, Lam, Zoe Wai-Mam, Osa-Gómez, Adriana, Thoma, Sonja & Wiltschko, Martina. Intonation and particles as speech act modifiers: A syntactic analysis. *Studies in Chinese Linguistics* 37(2): 109–129. https://doi.org/10.1515/scl-2016-0005

Heritage, John. 1998. Oh-prefaced responses to inquiry. *Language in Society* 27: 291–334.
https://doi.org/10.1017/S0047404500019990

Hill, Virginia. 2007. Vocatives and the pragmatics–syntax interface. *Lingua* 117: 2077–2105.
https://doi.org/10.1016/j.lingua.2007.01.002

Holmes, Janet. 1983. The functions of tag questions. *English Language Research Journal* 3: 40–65.

Hopper, Paul J. & Thompson, Sandra A. 1985. The iconicity of the universal categories 'noun' and 'verb'. In *Iconicity in Syntax* [Typological Studies in Language 6], John Haiman (ed.), 151–183. Amsterdam: John Benjamins. https://doi.org/10.1075/tsl.6.08hop

Joos, Martin. 1957. *Readings in Linguistics: The Development of Descriptive Linguistics in America since 1925*. Washington DC: American Council of Learned Societies.

Kwon, Iksoo. 2011. Mental spaces in the Korean reportive/quotative evidentiality marker-ay. *Discourse and Cognition* 18(2): 23–50. https://doi.org/10.15718/discog.2011.18.2.23

Langacker, Ronald W. 1991. *Foundations of Cognitive Grammar*, Vol. 2. Stanford CA: Stanford University Press.

Leech, Geoffrey. 1976. Metalanguage, pragmatics and performatives. In *Semantics: Theory and Application*, Cléa Rameh (ed.), 81–98. Washington DC: Georgetown University Press.

Leiss, Elisabeth. 2005. Submorphematische Motiviertheit als Grammatikalisierungsergebnis: Zur Grammatikalisierung von Reflexivpronomen. *Zeitschrift für germanistische Linguistik* 32: 233–244.

Levinson, Stephen C. & Torreira, Francisco. 2015. Timing in turn-taking and its implications for processing models of language. *Frontiers in Psychology* 6: 731. https://doi.org/10.3389/fpsyg.2015.00731

Li, Charles N., Thompson, Sandra A. & Zhang, Bojiang. 1998. Cong huayu jiaodu lunzheng yuqici 'de' (On modal particle 'de' from the perspective of conversation). *Zhongguo Yuwen (Chinese Linguistics)* 2: 93–102

Mittwoch, Anita. 1976. Grammar and illocutionary force. *Lingua* 40: 21–42. https://doi.org/10.1016/0024-3841(76)90030-9

Newmeyer, Frederick J. 2007. Linguistic typology requires crosslinguistic formal categories. *Linguistic Typology* 11: 133–157. https://doi.org/10.1515/LINGTY.2007.012

Nordlinger, R. & Sadler, L. 2004. Nominal tense in crosslinguistic perspective. *Language* 776–806. https://doi.org/10.1353/lan.2004.0219

Paul, Waltraud. 2014. Why particles are not particular: Sentence-final particles in Chinese as heads of a split CP. *Studia Linguistica* 68: 77–115. https://doi.org/10.1111/stul.12020

Pomerantz, Anita. 1984. Agreeing and disagreeing with assessments: Some features of preferred/dispreferred turn shapes. In *Structures of Social Action: Studies in Conversation Analysis*, J. Maxwell Atkinson & John Heritage (eds), 57–107. Cambridge: CUP.

Ritter, Elisabeth & Wiltschko, Martina. 2014. The composition of INFL. An exploration of tense, tenseless languages and tenseless constructions. *Natural Language and Linguistic Theory* 32: 1331–1386. https://doi.org/10.1007/s11049-014-9248-6

Rizzi, Luigi. 1997. The fine structure of the left periphery. In *Elements of Grammar: Handbook of Generative Syntax*, Liliane Haegeman (ed.), 281–337. Dordrecht: Kluwer. https://doi.org/10.1007/978-94-011-5420-8_7

Roberts, Ian G. & Roussou, Anna. 2003. *Syntactic Change: A Minimalist Approach to Grammaticalization*. Cambridge: CUP. https://doi.org/10.1017/CBO9780511486326

Ross, John R. 1970. On declarative sentences. In *Readings in English Transformational Grammar*, Roderick A. Jacobs & Peter S. Rosenbaum (eds), 222–272. Waltham MA: Ginn.

Speas, Peggy & Tenny, Carol. 2003. Configurational properties of point of view roles. *Asymmetry in Grammar*, Vol. 1: *Syntax and Semantics* [Linguistik Aktuell/Linguistics Today 57], Anna Maria Di Sciullo (ed.), 315–45. Amsterdam: John Benjamins. https://doi.org/10.1075/la.57.15spe

Stivers Tania, Enfield, Nicholas J., Brown, Penelope, Englert, Christina, Hayashi, Makoto et al. 2009. Universals and cultural variation in turn-taking in conversation. *Proceedings of the National Academy of Sciences of the United States of America* 106: 10587–10592. https://doi.org/10.1073/pnas.0903616106

Thoma, Sonja C. 2016. Discourse particles and the syntax of discourse-evidence from Miesbach Bavarian. PhD dissertation, University of British Columbia.

Tonhauser, Judith. 2007. Nominal tense? The meaning of Guaraní nominal temporal markers. *Language* 83(4): 831–869. https://doi.org/10.1353/lan.2008.0037

Truckenbrodt, Hubert. 2012. Semantics of intonation. In *Semantics: An International Handbook of Natural Language Meaning*, Vol. 3, Claudia Maienborn, Klaus von Heusinger & Paul Portner (eds), 2039–2069. Berlin: Mouton de Gruyter.

Wakefield, John. 2010. The English Equivalents of Cantonese Sentence-final Particles: A Contrastive Analysis. PhD dissertation, The Hong Kong Polytechnic University.

Wakefield, John. 2012. A floating tone discourse morpheme: The English equivalent of Cantonese *lo1*. *Lingua* 122: 1739–1762. https://doi.org/10.1016/j.lingua.2012.09.008

Wang, Fang. 2009. "'Ma' de yuqi yiyi shuolyue" (A brief introduction of the pragmatic meaning of ma). *Journal of Changchun University of Science and Technology (Higher Education Edition)* 4(11): 90–92.

Ward, Gregory L. & Hirschberg, Julia. 1985. Implicating uncertainty: The pragmatics of fall-rise intonation. *Language* 61: 747–776. https://doi.org/10.2307/414489

Ward, Gregory L. & Hirschberg, Julia. 1986. Reconciling uncertainty with incredulity: A unified account of the L*+H LH% intonational contour. Paper presented at the Annual Meeting of the Linguistic Society of America, New York, 27–30 December.

Wiltschko, Martina. 2003. On the interpretability of tense on D and its consequences for case theory. *Lingua* 113: 659–696. https://doi.org/10.1016/S0024-3841(02)00116-X

Wiltschko, Martina. 2004. On number in Halkomelem Salish or The problem with "*the two man*". In *Proceedings of the Ninth Workshop on the Structure and Constituency of the Americas (WSCLA IX)* [UBC Working Papers in Linguistics 15], Christine Ravinski & Yunhee Chung (eds), 143–158. Vancouver: University of British Columbia.

Wiltschko, Martina. 2014. *The Universal Structure of Categories: Toward a Formal Typology*. Cambridge: CUP. https://doi.org/10.1017/CBO9781139833899

Wiltschko, Martina. 2017. Ergative constellations in the structure of speech acts. In *The Oxford Handbook of Ergativity*, Jessica Coon, Diane Massam & Lisa deMena Travis (eds), 419–446. Oxford: OUP.

Wiltschko, Martina & Heim, Johannes. 2016. The syntax of confirmationals. In *Outside the Clause: Form and Function of Extra-Clausal Constituents* [Studies in Language Companion Series 178], Gunther Kaltenbock, Evelien Keizer & Arne Lohmann (eds), 305–340. Amsterdam: John Benjamins. https://doi.org/10.1075/slcs.178.11wil

Wiltschko, Martina, Denis, Derek & D'Arcy, Alexandra. 2018. Deconstructing variation in pragmatic function: A transdisciplinary case study. *Language in Society* 47: 569–599. https://doi.org/10.1017/S004740451800057X

Wiltschko, Martina. In preparation. *The Grammar of Interactional Language. Towards a typology of discourse markers*. Cambridge: CUP.

Zu, Vera. 2015. A two-tiered theory of the discourse. In *Proceedings of the Poster Session of the 33rd West Coast Conference on Formal Linguistics*, 151–160. Somerville MA: Cascadilla Proceedings Project.

CHAPTER 4

Typology of functional domains

Zygmunt Frajzyngier
University of Colorado

The aim of this study is to advocate one of the aims of linguistic typology, viz. the discovery of how languages are similar or different with respect to the functions they encode and consequently for the development of a typology based solely on the functions encoded in the grammatical systems of individual languages. Such a typology has the advantage of not requiring or depending on aprioristic definitions.[1] Such a typology also has the following additional advantages: it can serve as a tool in explaining the forms of utterances in individual languages and in explaining why certain languages have functions that other languages do not.

1. Aims of typology

Linguistic typology is a tool that can be used to accomplish a wide variety of aims. Some of the current and past work using cross-linguistic data has had the following aims:

- (1) Examination of languages with respect to certain selected phenomena, e.g., gender, number, person, aspect, demonstratives, noun phrases, and a large number of other formal and functional categories, e.g., Comrie's early work

---

1. The work on this study was supported by an Innovative Seed Grant from the University of Colorado. Other participants in the project were Erin Shay, Marielle Butters, and Megan Schwabauer. Erin Shay read the current study and contributed many substantial and editorial comments. I am grateful to the audience at the 50th annual meeting of Societas Linguistica Europaea in Zürich for their questions and comments. I am most grateful to anonymous readers for the comments and questions concerning an earlier version of this study. I have reacted to most of the comments in the current text, reorganized the original study, and added new material while bearing in mind the limitations of space. Some of the comments represented the anonymous readers' theoretical or methodological assumptions at variance with the assumptions and methodology of the present study. A discussion in journals will provide the best way to engage with theoretical or methodological differences.

with respect to aspect and tense (1976, 1985), Cohen 1989 with respect to aspect, Corbett 1991 and 2000 with respect to number and gender, Siewierska 2004 with respect to the category 'person', and numerous studies by Leningrad (now St. Petersburg) school with respect to causatives, resultatives, and reflexives.
- (2) Discovery of correlations among language phenomena, as early as Milewski 1950, 1962 and Greenberg 1963 and Fenk-Oczlon and Fenk's work on several phenomena that, on the face of it, are not expected to be related (e.g., Fenk-Oczlon & Fenk 1989, 2005).
- (3) Discovery of which functions are encoded more often across languages and which functions are encoded less often (see Wohlgemuth & Cysouw (eds.) 2010).
- (4) Cataloging of differences across languages, which can serve as a tool for discovering phenomena that need to be explained (Frajzyngier 2013).
- (5) Explaining why certain functions are coded in some languages and not in others. This is a fundamental question if one wants to explain differences across languages. This line of query has yet to develop its own methodology (but see Frajzyngier and Butters, 2020).
- Providing support for various theoretical claims.
- Serving as a tool for making 'generalizations' about languages. The term 'generalizations' can refer to a wide variety of research questions, e.g., 'how language code subjects' or 'core relations', word orders (cf. numerous studies including Greenberg 1963; Dryer 1991, 1992, 1995; Siewierska 1994, 1998; and Siewierska & Bakker 1996) or whatever function or formal means is being examined across languages. A 'generalization' in and of itself does not guarantee fruitful research results.

Since the present volume is concerned with the functions ('categories') encoded in languages, the rest of this study focuses on a few fundamental issues in the study of functions across languages. Markers of grammatical functions may stem from erstwhile lexical items (Kuteva et al. 2019) or from a variety of other sources (Cuyckens, Davidse & Verstraete (eds) 2010; Heine & Narrog (eds) 2011; Frajzyngier 1996, 2008b, 2010, 2011; Frajzyngier & Butters 2020.

2. Approaches to the study of functional categories

Lazard 2004, 2015 and references therein have pointed out the difficulties in conducting typological studies that focus on forms. He proposed to study functions instead of the forms. The fundamental question that Lazard did not ask or answer is this: Which functions should be taken up in typological studies? Lazard's assumption is summarized by the following claim: 'What is common to languages is precisely the semantic substance, **which basically is supposed to be roughly the same for all humans**' (Lazard 2004: 403 (bolding mine)). This claim would have to remain unsubstantiated until some common 'semantic substance' is proposed and its universal existence is properly documented.

It is commonly and rightly assumed that the direct comparison of two entities, e.g., two languages, is not a good method for discovering the similarities and differences between entities. Therefore, it is often postulated that for comparative studies we need *tertium comparationis*, whereby there exists a standard of comparison which does not have to be present in any of the actually existing languages. Lazard (2004), following Granger (1960), favors establishing 'arbitrary conceptual frameworks' as heuristic devices. Lazard (2004) states that such conceptual frameworks are not hypotheses to be verified or falsified; they are just heuristic devices for comparative purposes. Lazard's approach was taken up by Haspelmath 2010 and 2011, whose term 'comparative concepts' came to be widely used. Corbett, with respect to morphology, uses the term 'canonical morphology', which also does not necessarily rely on forms actually existing in specific languages. Tacit assumptions about the existence of 'common semantic substance' can be found in many typological studies, including those mentioned in Section 1, where some linguists use the terms 'subject', 'causative', 'passive', 'reflexive', and 'ditransitive' and examine how these functions are coded across languages.

3. Problems with conceptual frameworks (comparative concepts)

A major theoretical issue with the conceptual frameworks (comparative concepts) is the lack of grounding in a well-defined linguistic theory. It is not clear what linguistic theory generates these conceptual frameworks, where they come from, and why some conceptual frameworks rather than others merit an investigation. Another issue is methodological: The use of comparative concepts requires their definitions. Definitions, in turn, no matter how well conceived, represent either categories in certain languages with which the linguist happens to be familiar, e.g., the starting point for the discussion of definiteness and indefiniteness in Dryer 2013a and b, or the linguist's attempts to generalize from their knowledge of individual languages which, in the best of cases, is very limited. Most definitions are grounded in very few languages and all are grounded in linguists' theoretical assumptions, which again, in our current state of knowledge, stem from the study of a few, most often Indo-European, languages.

There is a third major issue with the use of comparative concepts in the cross-linguistic study of functions, namely that a typology based on comparative concepts answers questions regarding those concepts but may overlook categories that are coded in the grammatical systems of individual languages. Such a typology does not reflect the differences and similarities across grammatical systems with respect to issues other than those of selected comparative concepts. Consider the concept of transitivity, which is widely assumed to be a fundamental concept in clause formation, and its components S, A, and O, which are widely used in typological studies. A common assumption behind the notion of transitivity is the existence of a 'prototypical action, conceived as volitional discrete action performed by a controlling human agent and actually affecting a well-individuated patient' (Lazard 2004: 407). This definition assumes a connection between non-linguistic phenomena, events, actions, or whatever name one wants to use for physical phenomena in the real or imagined world, and language structure. This assumption cannot have cross-linguistic support for the simple reason that we do not have a non-linguistic apparatus to describe 'events'.

The most important problem with the notion of transitivity is that it does not explain differences across languages even if they are presumed to be explained by this notion. One of the questions pertaining to transitivity is why some languages have means of transitivizing (e.g., 'causative') and intransitivizing (e.g., 'passive', 'reflexive') while other languages do not. Many West and Central Chadic languages do not have any intransitivizing formal means, whether 'passive' or 'reflexive'. Here is an example from Mina, a Central Chadic language spoken in Northern Cameroon that has the categories subject and object and the linear order SVO: The plural verb *hùrók*, glossed below as 'die (about many people or animals dying)' or 'kill (many people)', can occur with one or two arguments without any changes in the form of the verb and without any markers on the arguments. As in other languages that code verbal plurality (Frajzyngier 1985a), the verb codes plurality of the subject of the intransitive verb or plurality of the object of a transitive verb, but not plurality of the agent ('subject') of the transitive event:

(1) à   nkə́   **hùrók**   vəŋ   tòk-yíi
    3SG FUT   kill.PL   family 1PL-PL
    'it's going to massacre our family'

    kwàlàrà   ndí   **hùrók**   hìdíi
    cholera   HABIT   kill.PL   people
    'cholera kills people'

    í   **hùrók**   rà
    3PL   die.PL   PROG
    'they are all dying'   (Frajzyngier & Johnston, field notes)

The notion of transitivity does not explain the clausal syntax of Mina. The clausal structure displayed by examples in (1) is perfectly explainable by the functions actually coded in the grammatical system of Mina (Frajzyngier, Johnston with Edwards 2005). The relevant function here is affectedness of the subject without any implication of control either on the part of the subject or on the part of some other constituent of the clause or some other entity in the event. Verbs whose broad semantic equivalents in Indo-European language are transitive and take the agentive subject, in Wandala take the affected argument as the subject, regardless of whether the subject has or does not have the control of the event (see also Schuh 2017).

While we may assume that 'forgetting' is an event that involves the person who forgets and the entity that is forgotten, such an assumption has no predictable implications for linguistic representation. In Indo-European languages, the unmarked argument ('subject') of the verb corresponding to 'forget' is the person who forgets. Some Indo-European languages indicate the point of view of the subject, as in Spanish *me olvide* 'I forgot', and mark the second argument by a preposition. In Polish, the verb *zapomnieć* 'forget' with the point of view of subject marker *się* means 'lose one's control'. In Hdi (Central Chadic, Frajzyngier with Shay 2002), the unmarked argument of the verb 'forget' is the entity that is forgotten:

(2) zà-p-z-á   kɗíx
      forget-OUT-forget   donkey
      'a donkey was forgotten'

(3) zà-p-z-á   pìtsákw
      forget-OUT-forget   hoe
      'a hoe was forgotten'

The addition of the participant who forgets requires an additional morphological marker, namely the suffix *ná* added to the verb, plus the coding of the person who forgets, either through inflectional marking on the verb or a free noun phrase:

(4) zà-**ná**-p-z-í
      forget-DEM-OUT-forget-1SG
      'I forgot'

(5) zà-**ná**-p-z-í   tá   pìtsákw-á-ghá
      forget-DEM-OUT-forget-1SG   OBJ   hoe-GEN-2SG
      'I forgot your hoe'

The mere addition of the object without the addition of the suffix *ná* to the verb results in an ungrammatical expression:

(6) *zà-p-z-ì   tá   pìtsákw-á-ghá
      forget-OUT-forget-1SG   OBJ   hoe-GEN-2SG
      for 'I forgot your hoe'
                 (Frajzyngier with Shay 2002; glosses as in the reference)

The discovery of functions that are coded in Mina and Hdi explains the forms of the utterances in those languages. Existing comparative concepts—transitivity, in this case—do not provide explanations for these forms. The main point here is that there is no non-linguistic notion of 'event'.

4. Current approaches to the discovery of functions

The most frequent means of describing the meaning of a grammatical form, as found in current linguistic practice, is by listing the constructions in which the form occurs or by describing the situations in which the construction is used, the situations the constructions refers to, or the situations the form invokes, and then possibly drawing some generalizations from the lists. The first method is akin to Wittgenstein's claim that 'For a *large* class of cases–though not for all–in which we employ the word "meaning" it can be defined thus: the meaning of a word is its use in the language' (Wittgenstein 1963, Section 43 of *Philosophical Investigations*). This approach may be used, at best, to describe the referential meaning of words. The use of this approach in the description of meaning is inadequate. The description of meaning as solely determined by the category 'word' ignores all the other coding means that a language may have. A cursory look at any utterance in English demonstrates that words contribute only a part of the meaning of the whole utterance. Consider the following example consisting of five 'words', if we understand 'word' as a stress-bearing unit in English:

(7) He's going to always break out, (COCA)

At least three components of the meaning of the clause in Example (7) are not coded by words. One meaning, namely assertion, is coded by the order Subject Verb. The future tense meaning is marked by the sequence 'be going to', hence three 'words' code a single function. Another meaning is action: 'break out', coded by two words, as opposed to 'break', coded by one word.

The description of the words alone, applying Wittgenstein's approach, results simply in a statement of the distribution of the forms; it does not explain why a given form is used in an utterance or what function it encodes. A list of utterances or constructions in which a form appears is a useful set of data for further research, but it is not a sufficient source of data and, most important, it is not an analysis or description of the meaning.

In contemporary studies, too numerous to list, the meaning of an utterance is often identified with the inference about the real or imagined world that the researchers draw from the utterance. Such an approach is theoretically unjustified and methodologically inadequate because it leaves the interpretation of meaning to the whims of the individual analyst. But even if different analysts draw identical inferences, we still do not know on what basis they have drawn those inferences. The description through implications and entailments is less exposed to the individual interpretations, but it is still based only on the truth conditions of the proposition, while the utterance has many components unrelated to the truth conditions. Moreover, as Hewson and Bubenik 2006 observed, 'If truth function is supposed to determine linguistic meaning, there is a major problem: how can truth function determine meaning, when the meaning of the sentence has to be known before its truth function can be established?' (Hewson & Bubenik 2006: 7).

The evidence that a description of an event cannot be taken as a description of the meaning of the utterance is provided by the well-known fact that the same event or situation (no matter how defined) may be described in different ways in the same language. Those different ways carry different meanings. Hence, the event or situation does not determine, in any way, the meaning of the utterance as illustrated by the following two sentences having the same participants that have the same role in the physical event:

(8) a. John smeared paint on the wall
    b. John smeared the wall with paint

(9) a. John planted peas and corn in his garden
    b. John planted his garden with peas and corn (Fillmore 1968: 49).

(10) Of course, that record was broken by our guest, Cal Ripken, Jr. (COCA)
     Of course, our guest Cal Ripken **broke** that record.

Hence there is a need to find an objective method to discover and describe the meaning of a linguistic form.

5. Theoretical foundations for a non-aprioristic description of functions

Frajzyngier with Shay (2016) proposes that the grammatical system of each language encodes a unique semantic structure. This semantic structure is composed of functional domains, e.g., modality, tense, aspect, point of view, various types of predications, reference system(s), and others, whose existence is confirmed by the formal means that are used to code them. The number of functional domains in a language may be quite large, and at any given time the number of functional domains in a given language is finite. This does not mean that there are no changes with respect to functional domains. For example, a language that did not have a tense system may acquire one (Frajzyngier & Butters 2020, chapter 11). Similarly, a language that did not have the domain of number comprising singular and plural distinction in nouns may acquire one (Frajzyngier 1997). The loss of an entire functional domain is not well documented, but the loss of a function within a domain is a frequent phenomenon, e.g., the loss of indirect object function in English, as described below. The emergence of new domains is, however, a slow process, slow enough to permit a taxonomy of functional domains in a language at any given time.

A functional domain is a domain whose members share a single characteristic (a feature) such as the coding of temporal relation or the coding of some number. This characteristic defines the domain. Hence, there is no need for a definition of functional domain other than the discovery of the meaning shared by each of its members.

Each functional domain may have subdomains. Within a subdomain, all members share one characteristic but differ from other functions in just one characteristic. Thus, in the domain of tense, all functions share the coding of temporal characteristics but may differ in the coding of a specific time with respect to some point of temporal reference.

Languages differ with respect to the domains encoded in the grammatical system and with respect to the internal structure of similar domains. Thus, some languages have the domain of tense and other languages do not. There may be some domains that are universal, but such domains, if any, remain to be discovered. It is likely that the domain of modality is universal. The domain of grammatical relations that comprises the function 'subject' and 'object' has been shown in Mithun (1991) and Mithun & Chafe (1999) not to be universal. Even the domain of relationship between the predicate and noun phrases may not be universal, as documented in Klein & Perdue 1997.

The number and types of functions within a domain are subject to more rapid change than are the number and types of functional domains in the language: New functions emerge, some functions disappear, some functions become broader or narrower. One can observe the emergence of new functions, such as a new aspect, within the speech of one generation. A case in point is the emerging 'change of state' aspect in English that is coded by the auxiliary 'go', as in 'the lights went blue', 'he goes missing', and 'he went crazy'. The rapid rate of change in individual functions is not an obstacle in the description of the semantic structure of a language.

6. Discovery of the function of a linguistic form

6.1 The prerequisites for the discovery of functions

The fundamental prerequisite for the discovery of functions in any language is the discovery of the formal means of coding existing in the language. The existence of a formal means is established by the recurrent patterns occurring in the language.

There is no aprioristic connection between a formal means and the function it may encode. A function or meaning exists only if it is coded by some formal means. Theoretically, the list of formal means that one can encounter in individual languages is open. The following are some of the formal means described so far in many languages:

- Phonological means, including prosodic means. This formal coding means also includes such means as deletion or retention of a part of the underlying form of a lexical item (Frajzyngier 2016). In that large set of formal means, we may also include vowel and consonant harmonies. Phonological means can code a variety of functions within different functional domains, e.g., information structure, relations between predicate and noun phrases, relationships between nouns, relationships between clauses, and relationships between nouns within a noun phrase.
- Lexical categories and derivational means, i.e., means for deriving another lexical category or deriving a new lexical item within the same category. The very existence of the category 'word' in many languages is a coding means that allows the parsing of the utterance.
- Inflectional means on all lexical and sometimes grammatical (e.g., adpositions) categories. Paradigms of various categories are a simple means to discover the inflectional categories.
- Rich verbal inflections. In some languages, verbal inflection codes complex action, such as associated movement and other associated events (Guillaume 2016 and references there). This coding is not simply a matter of coding on the verb certain functions that in other languages are coded by other formal means, such as case, conjunctions, and adpositions. Polysynthesis may be recognized as a formal means, distinct from compounding, derivation, and inflectional coding, if it co-occurs with analytic constructions (Fortescue, Mithun & Evans 2017). As demonstrated in Frajzyngier and Butters (2020), inflectional coding means have different potential with respect to the number of functions they encode than do other formal means such as linear orders and adpositions. Further studies with respect to the potential of various coding means are badly needed in order to understand the similarities and differences across languages.
- Deployment of lexical items as a coding means for grammatical functions. Some examples of such deployment are auxiliary verbs coding tense, aspect, modality; verbs coding inter-clausal and discourse relationships; and nouns coding spatial relations with respect to the deictic center. The relative high frequency of some lexical items as opposed to others is an initial step in the discovery of the grammatical function of lexical items.

- Serial verb constructions coding a wide variety of functions in languages of Asia and Africa.
- Prepositions, postpositions, conjunctions, complementizers, subordinators, and all other kinds of morphemes referred to by the term 'particles'.
- Linear orders of lexical items (see Frajzyngier with Shay 201; Frajzyngier 2011).
- Repetition of a lexical item, a phrase, or a part of a phrase (Frajzyngier 2008a).

These simple formal means can be combined to produce constructions, i.e., recurring coding means consisting of more than one simple form of coding. For example, a construction might consist of a combination of a certain grammatical morpheme with a certain linear order (Frajzyngier 2011; Frajzyngier with Shay 2016); the linear order of certain lexical categories and the use of grammatical markers; or a combination of a certain linear order, inflectional markers, and prepositions. There is no theoretical limit to the number of simple formal means of which a construction may be composed (for a similar approach to the notion of construction, see Kuteva et al. 2019). Within the approach proposed here, one must discover what kinds of constructions exist before one can discover the meanings of these constructions.[2] The discovery of a construction involves observing recurrent patterns of co-occurrence among lexical categories, grammatical morphemes, linear orders, inflectional morphemes, and other formal means.

6.2 Two types of functions in the present approach

Once the formal coding means, including constructions, have been discovered in a language, one must discover the functions of individual forms and constructions. There appear to exist two types of functions: One that allows the listener to parse the utterance into constituents, and one that allows the listener to access the speaker's intentions and what is broadly referred to as the relationship between the speech and non-linguistic reality. We refer to the first as the 'structural function' and the second as 'meaning'. Frajzyngier and Shay (2003) illustrate the notion of the structural function using two examples: The marker -s on third-person singular present-tense verbs in English, whose main function is to indicate which constituent is the verb, and the complementizer że in Polish, whose main function

---

2. Goldberg and van der Auwera (2012) rightly invoke meaning as one means of discovering the existence of a construction. This is in accordance with the Construction Grammar approach, wherein a construction consists of two components: a form and an associated meaning. Construction Grammar does not, however, provide a methodology for the discovery of the meaning of a form, nor does it provide a theoretical base or a methodology to support the proposed meanings of linguistic forms.

is to divide a sentence into two clauses so that noun phrases in each clause are associated with the proper predicate (see also Frajzyngier 1996).

6.2.1 *Relationship between functions as a main discovery tool*

The first step in the discovery of functions coded in the grammatical system of a given language is to establish the functional domain to which a given form belongs. The second step is to establish the differences between the functions belonging to the same functional domain. The basic method for answering the two questions is to examine the distribution of the formal means in the given language.

If two formal means cannot co-occur within the same formal constituent, e.g., phrase or clause, it is more than likely that they belong to the same functional domain and that one contradicts the other. Thus, a past tense marker cannot co-occur with a future tense marker in English:

(11) He will issue his own executive orders when he enters the White House on Friday
*He will issued his own executive orders when he enters the White House on Friday
The marker 'will' cannot co-occur with the marker '-s' on the verb:

(12) *He will issue his own executive orders when he will enters the White House on Friday

Hence, the forms 'will', '-ed' and '-s' are markers in the same functional domain.

If two formal means can co-occur within the same formal unit, one needs to determine whether the two forms code one function or two different functions. The classic example of two forms coding one function is the literary French cooccurrence of the forms *ne* . . . and *pas* coding negation. In contemporary spoken, non-literate French variety, only the form *pas* is used.

The two statements, viz. the domain to which the function belongs and the differences between one function and other functions within a domain, constitute the complete description of a function, without invoking inferences about real or imagined world. A statement of the differences between functions and between functional domains obviates the need for aprioristic or 'prototypical' definitions.

We assume that all speakers have knowledge of the grammatical system of their language and the functions encoded in that system.[3] Based on the knowledge of the functions encoded in the grammatical system and the formal means that code

---

3. This assumption does not preclude the possibility that speakers of the same language may differ with respect to the range of functions they express or even understand. Those inter-speaker differences that can be observed in both literate and non-literate societies do not affect the theoretical or methodological approach advocated in this study.

them, the speaker can detect the presence of functions in individual utterances. Taking into consideration the functions detected and the lexical items deployed in the utterance, speakers make inferences about the real or hypothetical world. This explains the need to shift the description of meaning from the description of individual utterances, be they sentences, clauses, or words, to the description of the meaning encoded in the grammatical system. Having a description of meanings encoded in the grammatical system will make it possible to describe the meaning of individual sentences, clauses, or other utterances by combining functions represented in the given utterance and the lexical items deployed in the utterance.

An analysis of forms and functions in a given language, as opposed to checking if and how categories observed in other languages are coded, allows for the discovery of categories that are encoded in the grammatical system and whose existence explains the form of utterances in the language.

7. The basic questions in the cross-linguistic study of functions

Many linguists agree that languages differ in the types of functions encoded in their grammatical systems. Hence, the first question: Why do some languages code functions that other languages do not? Here are a few examples of questions for which the answer is provided within the present study or has been provided in the previous studies as cited:

a. Why some languages, including English, code the malefactive function and other languages, including some Western Indo-European languages, do not.
b. Why some languages, including some Western Indo-European languages, code the point of view of subject function (marked by reflexive markers) and other languages, including English, do not.
c. Another question is why utterances describing events, actions, and processes in some languages have types of markers that do not occur in the descriptions of the same events, actions, and processes in other languages. For example, why is there a ventive marker coding movement toward the speaker or another deictic center in Hona (Central Chadic) but not in English?[4]

(13)   h-eŋ-dî   bə̀rmá   nù-ná   bà
       buy-3SG-1SG   yam   woman-1SG   VENT
       'I bought yams for my wife'

---

4. An anonymous reader claims that 'why' is not a productive question. Whether the question is or is not 'productive' can be assessed only by the product. If answering the question yields new explanations the question is productive. At least three such explanations are provided in the current study.

(14) hí-dí   bə̀rmá   bà
buy-1SG yam VENT
'I bought a yam'   (Frajzyngier field notes on Hona)

And why is there an allative marker coding movement away from the speaker or another deictic center in Hona (glossed as ALL) but not in English?

(15) h-éŋ-dì   bə̀rmá-ɗ
buy-3SG-1SG yam-ALL
'I sold a yam'

Another, more difficult, question is why the verb in Hona has the marker éŋ in examples (13) and (15) but not in the example (14). Note that examples (14) and (15) appear to refer to different transactions, those of buying and selling, respectively, while examples (13) and (14) refer to the same transaction, namely buying.

The list of such questions in the cross-linguistic study of functions is very large indeed. It is limited only by the number of functions—many thousands—coded in individual languages. So, would the number of comparative concepts be the same as the number of functions coded across languages? Or are some functions to be collapsed? And what would be the basis on which the functions encoded in the grammatical system of one language are collapsed into one or several comparative concepts? Where would the comparative concepts come from? What about all functions encoded in the grammatical system of another language?

Such questions, and many others not listed here, pose a methodological question: how to conduct a cross-linguistic study of functions. This question is addressed below.

8. Proposed object of typology of functions

Recall from the introductory section that typology is merely a tool that can be applied to investigate a variety of questions. Within the present approach, typology can be applied to study the reasons for similarities and differences across languages, not with respect to some individual comparative concepts but rather with respect to the totality of functions encoded in the grammatical systems. Those similarities and difference will in turn contribute to the explanation of why utterances allegedly describing the same situations/events differ across languages. Consequently, one must find:

1. What functional domains are encoded in the grammatical systems across languages;
2. The types and number of functions encoded in each functional domain.

In what follows I illustrate a few functions which are coded in some languages but not in others. The chosen functions all belong to clausal predications. Individual clauses are always composed of several functions from different functional domains.

The term 'clause' in the present study refers to the smallest unit of the language that has a modal value such as assertion, question, command, hedging, or negation, regardless of how this modal value is marked. In many languages, there may exist a modality that is not overtly marked by segmental markers or by prosodic means, but that does not mean that the clause has no modal value. In many languages, the clause with no overt markers of modality carries the assertive modality as a default value (Frajzyngier 1985b, 1987). The proposed criterion for defining the clause is different from criteria that invoke the notion of the predicate and its relations to the arguments (e.g., Dixon 2010–2012 and many other approaches).

In what follows I discuss one functional domain, 'point of view', and four predications belonging to the domain of relations between the predicate and noun phrases: a locative predication; the indirect object predication; the benefactive predication; and the malefactive predication. The purpose of this discussion is not to add to comparative concepts but rather to illustrate that different languages code different functions and that the description of the functions consists of a statement of their relationship within a functional domain rather than their relationship with some pre-established definition. The functions discovered for each language are the base on which the typology of functions should be conducted.

9. Point of view

In some languages, including several Western Indo-European languages, there exists a domain 'point of view'. The functions within this domain instruct the listener to look at the proposition from one of the points of view coded in the grammatical system. In the present study, I focus on the point of view of the subject and the function of goal orientation, but there are languages in which other points of view can be encoded.[5] The coding of this functional domain affects the syntax and morphology of those languages, since the distinctions of the functional domain are what the speakers must attend to.

---

5. Inflectional forms of the verb in Tagalog and other Austronesian languages may well code a variety of points of view (Schachter & Otanes 1972).

9.1 Point of view of the subject as a marked category

The point of view of subject function tells the listener to consider how the event concerns/affects the subject or the state of the subject rather than what the subject does (this is the main hypothesis in Stefanini 1962 with respect to French). In languages in which this function exists, the point of view of the subject may be overtly marked, and it may be an inherent property of some verbs. Romance, Slavic, German, and Dutch use so-called '(short) reflexive' forms to code the point of view of the subject with verbs that do not inherently carry this meaning. These forms can occur with intransitive and transitive verbs, e.g., French: *s'évader* 'escape', *s'évanouir* 'pass out', *s'enfuir* 'flee'. The short reflexive can also occur with a transitive verb, albeit without an object:

(16) il   se   jeta   dans la   rivière
     3M   REFL   throw in   DEF river
     'he threw himself into the river'   (Stefanini 1962)

The following examples are from the Kate Beeching Corpus. The reflexive forms are bolded. Although some of the verbs are transitive, the reflexive forms used in the examples do not code coreferentiality of the subject and object.

Potentially transitive verbs:

(17) je   **me**   plaisais   pas   dans le   dans le   monde
     1SG   1SG.REFL   please.PAST   NEG   in   DEF   in   DEF   world
     du   travail
     GEN   work
     'I didn't feel well in the world of work'

     je   **me**   suis   toujours   battu...
     1SG   1SG.REFL   be.1SG   always   fought
     'I always fought...'

An intransitive verb:

     maintenant je   **me**   balade   en short   et   puis je...
     now   1SG   1G.REFL   walk around   in shorts   and   then 1SG
     'Nowadays, I walk around in shorts and then I...'

The point of view of subject marker can be used with intransitive verbs, as in the following examples from Spanish and Italian:

(18) **me**   voy   Spanish
     1SG.REFL   go.1SG
     'I am going'

     me   ne   vado   Italian
     1SG.REFL   from.here   go.1SG
     'I am going'

In Polish, both transitive and intransitive verbs can co-occur with the so-called reflexive markers *się* or *sobie*, glossed as REFL.DAT. The occurrence with both transitive and intransitive verbs indicates that the function of the reflexive markers is not that of changing the transitivity of the verb. The use of the reflexive marker with intransitive verbs is particularly important as it requires an explanation that will be valid for both transitive and intransitive verbs. In Frajzyngier (1999) it is proposed that the reflexive markers in Polish and some other Indo-European languages indicate that the event should be seen from the point of view of the subject. Such an activity is marked as non-goal oriented.

Intransitive verbs with reflexive dative marker:

(19)   a   ja   tak **idę**   *sobie*   *drogą*   *Niemiłowany*
CONJ 1SG so go.1SG.PRES REFL.DAT road.INSTR unloved.M.SG.NOM
przez nikogo
by nobody
'And me, I am just going on the road, unloved by everybody'
(Brzechwa via NKJP)

ale **stoję**   *sobie*   *spokojnie i myślę:*   *do*
but stand.1SG.PRES REFL.DAT calmly and think.1SG.PRES to
nogi, piesku
leg.GEN dog.DIMIN.VOC
'But I keep standing calmly and think: "heal!, little doggy"'
(S. Mrożek, via NKJP)

Transitive verb with object and the reflexive dative marker:

(20)   *tedy*   *zjadłem*   *sobie*   *pstrążka,*   *ale w*
therefore PRF.eat.PAST.1SG.M REFL.DAT trout.DIMIN.ACC but in
niemiłym humorze
unpleasant mood
'Then I ate a little trout but I still was in an unpleasant mood' (NKJP)

Hence, in several Indo-European languages, the point of view of the subject can be marked by morphosyntactic means when the verb does not inherently code this function. The importance of the point of view of the subject in Romance, Slavic, and Germanic languages is that its marker has been mischaracterized as coding intransitivity. The intransitivizing function, passive function, antipassive, and coreferentiality of arguments of reflexives are all subsumed by the point of view of subject . Such interpretations were prompted by tacit assumptions about the nature of transitivity, more specifically about the expectation that a transitive verb should be followed by an object. The occurrence of reflexive pronouns with intransitive verbs in languages for which de-transitivizing, passive, and antipassive functions of reflexives were postulated indicates that these three or four functions are not the functions of reflexive forms. The intransitive interpretations are a byproduct of the fundamental point of view of the subject function.

The explanatory value of the discovery of functions is that it provides a more general explanation for the effects of the deployment of the form in various syntactic environments. The function point of view of the subject explains the presence of the reflexive form with both transitive and intransitive verbs. Moreover, it demonstrates that the coreferentiality inference is a byproduct of the basic function of the form.

The typological implications are that some languages have the function point of view of the subject and other languages, e.g., English, do not. English does have a reflexive marker, but its function is most probably that of coding coreferentiality of arguments.

9.2 Point of view of the subject as unmarked category

The point of view of the subject can be the unmarked inherent characteristic of the verb. There is a class of verbs in Wandala (Central Chadic, Frajzyngier 2012) which represent the event from the point of view of the affected subject, i.e., how the event affects the subject or how it concerns the subject. Whether the subject does or does not control the event is irrelevant to the point of view of the subject. Subject pronouns in Wandala must occur in the clause regardless of whether the clause has a nominal subject. In the pragmatically neutral clause, i.e., a clause that has no constituent in focus and does not topicalize any noun phrase, subject pronouns precede the verb while all nominal arguments follow the verb:

Unmarked point of view:

(21) à tsà   nábbà
     3SG stop Nabba
     'Nabba stopped'

     à kyà   gàhè
     3SG break pot
     'a pot broke'

Changing the inherent point of view of the subject requires the addition of some morphological markers. To code the point of view of the goal, the goal marker á must be added to the verb:

(22) à ts-á   nábbà
     3SG stop-GO Nabba
     'he stopped Nabba'

     à ky-á   gàhè
     3SG break-GO pot
     'he broke a pot'

To add a pronominal object in the predication that has a goal marker, the third-person object marker -*n* must be added to the verb:

(23) à tsà-*n*-á nábbà
3SG stop-3SG-GO Nabba
'Nabba stopped him'

A similar explanation applies to example (2) from Hdi, presented earlier. The verb *zà* 'forget' in Hdi inherently represents the point of view of the affected entity.

Verbs in Lele, an East Chadic language (Frajzyngier 2001), do not code the point of view of the subject. The language codes two functions that are not intransitivizing, passive, etc., and that do not code coreferentiality. One form, marked by the noun *kusu* 'body' plus a possessive pronoun, codes affectedness of the subject with or without the subject's control:

(24) na-du è go mónge **kusu-ro** úsìnyo pinyà na-du hab kìrè
HYP-3F go REF bend body-3F ground even HYP-3F find way
ɗé lay
NEG also
'When she wants to bend forward, she does not find a way to do so.'
(Garrigues-Cresswell avec la participation de Christophe Weibegué 1981, further abbreviated as G-C & W 1981: 10–11, as cited in Frajzyngier 2001)

dàw-gé **kusi-gè** jèn wàl-gé ɗangá ná kur
gather-3PL body-3PL stay cut-3PL calabash ASSC day
wèlè-ì wèlè-ì.
lie down.VN-3M lie down.VN-3M
'They [women] gather and spend all day lying down and carving calabashes.' (G-C & W 1981: 40–41)

The other form, marked by the noun *cà* 'head' plus a possessive pronoun, codes the movement of the subject:

(25) dà kur go kumno è dàná ná kìn-je **cà-ì** è-je
PREP day REF God go UP ASSC return-VENT head-3M go-VENT
hab kara tòn-gè na
find people ask-3PL HYP
'When God was going up, he returned, found people, and asked them:'
(G-C & W 1981: 7–8)

For a fuller discussion of the issues of coreferentiality in Chadic, see Frajzyngier 2018a.

The explanatory value of the fact that a language has the point of view of the subject as the unmarked value of the verb is that the language does not have overt markers of the point of view of the subject. The importance of this fact for linguistic typology is that it explains why certain markers across language have different distributions, e.g., why markers that appear to have been grammaticalized from the same source code different functions.

9.3 Goal orientation

One of the questions that need to be answered for Polish verbal predications is why some non-subject noun phrases are coded by the accusative case and others by the genitive case. Consider the following pair of examples:

(26) *kupuje   dom*
     buy.3.SG.PRES house.ACC
     'he/she is buying a house'

     nie   kupuje   domu
     NEG   buy.3.SG.PRES house.GEN
     'he/she is not buying a house'

The frequently found statement that objects in Polish negative clauses are marked by the genitive rather than by the accusative case is correct, but it is a mere observation of a fact. It is not a statement of the function of either the accusative or the genitive case. The assignment of the category 'object' to the argument marked by the genitive case is most likely driven by the fact that its equivalent in the affirmative clause is labeled 'object', and by the fact that in so many other languages the second argument in an affirmative or negative clause is categorized as object. But in Polish the second arguments of the verb in affirmative and negative clauses are marked differently. The second argument is also marked by the genitive case in clauses that are formally affirmative but whose predicate contains the negative form *nie-*, which makes the meaning of the clause negative:

(27) *zaniechał   samochodu*
     unwant.PAST.PRF.3M.SG car.GEN
     'He stopped wanting a car' lit. 'he "unwanted" a car'

Compare the affirmative clause, where the second argument is marked by the accusative case:

(28) *szef zrzędził   o   byle co,   widać   żona znów*
     boss grumble.PAST.3M.SG about anything   looks like wife again
     chciała   samochód do kolorze   płaszcza   albo odwrotnie,
     want.PAST.3F.SG car.ACC   to color.GEN coat.GEN   or   opposite
     'The boss grumbled about any small thing. Looks like his wife wanted a car in the color of her coat, or maybe it's the other way around.'

Consider the next two examples in Polish, where the second argument, *brewiarz* 'breviary', is coded by two different case markers, while in English it is marked in the same way by the position following the verb. In the Polish affirmative clause, the second argument *brewiarz* 'breviary' is in the accusative case, while in the clause with inherently negative verb *zaniedbać* 'neglect', the second argument is in the genitive case. Hence, the second arguments in the two clauses in Polish represent different semantic relations. In the affirmative clause the second argument is the goal of the event. In the clause with the negative predicate the second argument is not a goal:

(29) *Antoni szybkim ruchem zgarnął brewiarz i*
Antoni fast.INSTR movement.INSTR sweep.PAST.3M.SG breviary.ACC and
kielichy do kosza,
chalice.PL to basket.GEN
'Antoni with a fast movement swept the breviary and chalices into a basket,'
(NKJP)

tego wieczoru zaniedbał brewiarza.
that.GEN evening.GEN neglected.3M.SG.PRF.PAST breviary.GEN
'That evening he neglected the breviary.' (NKJP)

Another alternation between the second argument coded by the accusative or genitive case obtains when the clause has the so-called short reflexive marker *się*. In a clause with the reflexive marker, the second argument must be in the genitive case:

(30) a. *wypił wodę*
drink.PRF.PAST.3M.SG water.ACC
'he drank up the water'

b. *napił się wody*
drink.PRF.PAST.3M.SG REFL water.GEN
'he drank water'

Analyzing example 30b as indicating partial, as opposed to complete, affectedness would be a result of describing the meaning of a grammatical form through inferences based on the meaning of judiciously selected individual utterances. Evidence that the partitive function of the genitive is a false interpretation of the function of the genitive is provided by clauses where the second argument is still marked by the genitive but the partitive interpretation is ruled out:

(31) *złapał drabinę*
catch.PRF.PAST.3M.SG ladder.ACC
'he caught the ladder'

But:

(32) *złapał   się   drabiny*
    catch.PRF.PAST.3M.SG REFL   ladder.GEN
    'he gripped a ladder' (e.g., to steady himself)

So, the question is: What is it that clauses with the reflexive marker share with negative clauses in Polish, both of which require the second argument to be marked by the genitive case? The answer is provided by the analysis of the function of the short reflexive marker in Polish: It codes the point of view of the subject (Frajzyngier 1999). Since the reflexive marker is incompatible with the accusative marker on the second argument, the accusative marker must be coding a value opposite to that of the reflexive marker. I propose that that function is coding the second argument as the goal. The explanation of the genitive marker coding the second argument in the negative clauses is that these clauses do not have the goal. The transitive verbs, however, do imply a goal, and therefore there is a need to indicate that the nominal argument that occurs in the negative clause is not the goal.[6]

The typological conclusion is that Polish and English code different functions in the domain of the relationship between the predicate and noun phrases.

9.4 Point of view of the subject and goal orientation in Hdi

Hdi (Central Chadic, Frajzyngier with Shay 2002) codes two points of view: Point of view of the subject, marked by the suffix *-u* and glossed as so [subject orientation], and goal orientation, glossed as PVG in Frajzyngier with Shay (2002), marked by the suffix *a*. Some verbs are inherently unmarked for the point of view, and for these verbs, either the point of view of the subject or the goal orientation must be overtly marked.

The point of view of the subject is marked by the suffix/infix *ú*:

(33) *gún-ú-gúná   sígà*
    open-so-open   pot
    'The pot opened.'

---

[6]. An anonymous reader raises the issue of Russian, which also has case inflection and where the genitive case may, but does not have to, be used with the second argument of the negative clauses. This is an issue for the analysis of functions of Russian genitive and accusative cases. The fact that forms in different languages are labeled the same by linguists and may have similar functions in one domain, e.g., relations between nouns, does not provide evidence for other functions those forms may code.

Keeping the same argument as the subject and marking the verb for goal orientation would produce a nonsensical utterance:

(34) ?gún-á-gúná   sígà
    open-PVG-open pot
    'The pot opened [something].' [the clause was judged unacceptable by a native speaker]

The verb *blà* 'break' is also inherently unmarked for the category point of view of the subject. With the goal orientation marker, the subject is controlling and is not affected:

(35) bl-á-blà   tá   xàsú'ù
    break-PVG-break OBJ branch
    'He broke off a branch.'

With the point of view of the subject, the subject is affected:

   bl-ú-blá   xàsú'ù
   break-SO-break branch
   'the branch broke off'

The evidence that the vowel *ú* codes the point of view of the subject is provided by the fact that one cannot add an indirect object that is different from the subject to a clause whose predicate has the point of view of subject marker:

(36) hlr-ú-hlrà   tá   pìtsákw
    forge-PVS-forge OBJ hoe
    'He forged a hoe.' (This implies that he forged a hoe for himself.)

No other beneficiary can be added, hence the ungrammaticality with *ngá-dà* 'for me':

(37) hlr-ú-hlrà   tá   pìtsákw *ngá-dà
    forge-SO-forge OBJ hoe   FOR-1SG
    intended for 'He forged a hoe for me.'

One can add an indirect object phrase to a verb with the goal orientation marker:

(38) hlr-á-f-hlrà   tá   pìtsákw **ngá-dà**
    forge-PVG-UP-forge OBJ hoe   FOR-1SG
    'Forge a hoe for me!'

Hence, to explain why certain expressions are grammatical and others are not in Polish and Hdi, one needs to discover what functions are coded in these languages. It turns out that both Polish and Hdi code the functions point of view of subject and point of view of goal. Neither of these functions is coded in English.

10. Locative predication

Although presumably all languages have some means to indicate the location of an entity in a certain place or movement to or from a certain place, only some languages have locative predication encoded in their grammatical system. The coding of locative predication means that the formal means used to code locative predication are distinct from the formal means used to code any other predication in the language. In a language that codes locative predication, some predicates are inherently locative while others are not, and some complements are inherently locative while others are not (Frajzyngier, Johnston with Edwards 2005). Toponyms in such languages are inherently locative. In Hausa (West Chadic), if the predicate is inherently locative and the complement is a toponym, no preposition precedes the locative complement (data and analysis from Frajzyngier & Munkaila in progress). Because the verb *tàfi* is inherently locative, there is no preposition before the toponym *Kano*:

(39) yaa tàfi Kanòo
3M.COMPL go Kano
'He went to Kano.'

Because the verb *akwai* 'exist' is not inherently locative, the toponym *Kano* must be preceded by the locative predicator *a*, analyzed as 'preposition' in traditional Hausa studies (Newman 2000):

Non-locative predicate:

(40) akwai mutane dà yawa a kano
exist people ASSC many PRED Kano
'There are many people in Kano.'

The predicator *a* must also be used if the complement is not inherently locative:

(41) sun sa/ajiye kaya a akwati
3PL.COMPL put thing PRED box
'They put the goods into the box.'

Omission of the predicator *a* with a non-inherently locative complement would result in an ungrammatical expression if the intended predication is locative:

(42) *sun sa/ajiye kaya akwati
3PL.COMPL put thing box
Intended for 'They put the goods into the box.'
(Frajzyngier & Munkaila in progress)

Note that in the English translation the locative complement must be preceded by a preposition regardless of the nature of the predicate and regardless of the nature of the complement. Locative expressions in English are coded by prepositions only. However, not all prepositions code locative expressions, and consequently locative expressions do not differ formally from non-locative expressions.

In Lele (East Chadic), all locative complements, regardless of directionality, are marked by the preposition *dà*. The inherently non-locative noun must be marked for the locative function by the postposition *nì*:

(43) ŋ   kil-iy   dà   bónú-m   ni
      1SG buy-3M   PREP brother-2M.SG LOC
      'I bought it from your brother.'   (Frajzyngier 2001)

Lele has a small class of inherently locative nouns to which belong all toponyms, the noun *túgú* 'home', and possibly a few other nouns. When one of these nouns serves as a locative complement, it is not followed by the locative postposition:

(44) se   è-gé   dà   túgú pòi kúsíge-ŋ   kè-y
      INCEPT go-3PL PREP home Poi Kusige-DEF GEN-3M
      'They went to the house of Poi Kusige.'   (Lele, Frajzyngier 2001)

The importance of locative predication for the typology of functional domains is that some languages have such a function encoded in the grammatical system and other languages do not. In languages that do have such a function, some verbs and nouns are inherently locative and others are not. Whether or not the language codes locative predication determines the form of the utterances, such as deployment or non-deployment of prepositions before locative complements. If a noun or verb deployed in the locative predication is not inherently locative, some formal means of coding, such as adpositions, must be used to code locative predication. In languages, such as English, in which locative predication is not a function encoded in the grammatical system, there are no classes of inherently locative verbs or nouns whose behavior is different from those of other verbs and nouns.

11. Benefactive, malefactive, and the indirect object

The present section demonstrates that the analysis of functions coded in languages allows for predictions that could not be made if one were to make a typology based on inferences from individual utterances about events. This section demonstrates again that the functions encoded in a language are not determined by the events or situations that the utterances allegedly refer to. The presentation in this section also gives a glimpse of what the typology of functions may look like.

The functions discussed in this study have been referred to by their formal characteristics, such as 'ditransitive constructions', 'indirect object', the sometimes formal and sometimes quasi-semantic term 'dative', or by their semantic characteristics, such as 'benefactive' and 'malefactive' (papers in Zuniga & Kittilä (eds) 2010). In the present section, which takes into consideration only the functions, regardless of what formal means that code them, I demonstrate that (paraphrasing Frajzyngier 2013):

1. Some languages have encoded in their grammatical system a benefactive predication, i.e., a predication indicating that the event is for the benefit of a participant.
2. Some languages have encoded in their grammatical system an indirect object predication, i.e., a predication indicating that an entity is indirectly affected, whether positively, negatively, or in any other way, by the predicate.
3. Some languages have encoded in their grammatical system both a benefactive and an indirect object predication.
4. Some languages have encoded in their grammatical system a malefactive predication along with a benefactive predication.
5. Some languages do not encode in their grammatical system the indirect object predication, the benefactive predication, or the malefactive predication. In those languages, the semantic inferences pertaining to those various meanings can be drawn from the coding of other predications.
6. The admittedly small number of languages examined suggests that if the language does not code the benefactive predication it also does not code the malefactive predication.

11.1 Benefactive function

English is one of the few languages that codes the benefactive predication, a predication indicating that an action is performed for somebody's benefit. This function is coded by the form V NP NP, i.e., a structure in which two noun phrases follow the verb. The evidence that the function is benefactive is provided by the fact that it cannot be deployed with verbs that inherently indicate an adverse effect on the participant:

(45) Sally baked her sister a cake (Goldberg 1995: 141)
vs.
*Sally burned her sister a cake

In Polish, which does not code a benefactive function, any verb that indirectly affects a participant, whether positively, adversely or in some other away, can be used with a noun phrase marked for the dative case:

(46) *Sally ugotowała   swojej   siostrze   obiad*
Sally cook.PRF.PAST.3F.SG POSS.REFL.DAT sister.DAT lunch.ACC
'Sally cooked her sister lunch'

Sally zepsuła swojej siostrze obiad
Sally spoiled PRF.PAST.3F.SG POSS.REFL.DAT sister.DAT lunch.ACC
'Sally spoiled lunch for her sister'

Whether the verb can or cannot be used in each construction in English does not depend solely on the verb, but rather on the totality of the meaning resulting from the deployment of the verb and the specific nouns involved. Thus, the clause:

(47) I burned her a CD

is perfectly grammatical but the following clause is not, unless the burning of the CD player was a favor:

(48) *I burned her a CD player

The last example would be grammatical if 'she' requested the CD player to be burned (Frajzyngier with Shay 2016, chapter 8).

The interesting consequence of coding a benefactive function in English is the emergence of an incipient malefactive function coded by the preposition 'on'. The affected argument of an adverse verb is often marked by the preposition 'on', as already noted by Radetzky and Smith 2010: 115:

(49) I spent months trying to find him, and it took a real toll **on** me.

Use of the preposition 'on' with verbs that do not adversely affect the non-subject arguments produces a malefactive effect:

(50) " You told **on** me, man, " he said, asking Bey
      Had someone told **on** me, yet again?

The claim that the malefactive function is only incipient in English is supported by the fact that the use of the preposition 'on' does not always trigger the malefactive effect:

(51) No one checked **on** me for hours
      For the last two days, she's **checked on me** every fifteen minutes.   (COCA)

Gidar (Central Chadic, Frajzyngier 2008a) has encoded in its grammatical system a benefactive predication and the indirect object predication. The coding of the benefactive predication depends on whether the predicate is inherently benefactive or not. If the verb is inherently benefactive, the benefactive argument follows the verb and the object (e.g., the thing given) follows the benefactive. With verbs that are not inherently benefactive, the direct object follows the verb and the benefactive must be marked by additional means. The verb *psə̀* 'give' is inherently benefactive, and the pronominal benefactive is marked by an object suffix after the verb:

(52) á-psə̀-n/t/m   ɬúà
      IMPER-give-3M/F/1PL meat
      'give him/her/us meat!'

If the verb is not inherently benefactive, the benefactive function of the pronominal argument is coded by the preposition sə̀. The beneficiary phrase, i.e., the preposition and its pronominal complement, is incorporated into the verbal piece, as evidenced by the position of the perfective marker -k after the benefactive phrase. The nominal direct object follows the verbal complex:

(53) à-lbà   sə̀-wə̀/tə̀/nə̀-k   wàłíyà
      3M-buy DAT-1SG/3F/3M-PRF   cow
      'He bought a cow for me/her/him.'

The evidence that the marker sə̀ codes the benefactive argument is provided by the fact that it is used to code the real-world beneficiaries of the event:

(54) mà-m   tə̀-mbát-ək   á   gàgám   əkày   sə̀-m   əzə̀má
      mother-1PL 3F-go-PRF   PREP Gagam   search DAT-1PL to eat
      'our mother went to Gagam to look for something for us to eat '

The beneficiary noun phrase is coded by the marker sə̀- followed by a pronominal suffix coding the gender and number of the beneficiary, which is followed by the noun phrase representing the beneficiary. The direct object does not have to occur:

(55) á-psə̀-n   sə̀-n   də̀fà
      IMPER-give-3M   DAT-3M   man
      'Give (it) to somebody!' (the use of the noun də̀fà 'man' codes an unspecified human referent)

The form sə̀ can code the addition of one entity to another, as shown in the following example, where form sə̀ precedes an inanimate noun, bíinà 'roof':

(56) mə̀ł̀ı   dà   zzá-ŋ   sə̀   wrá   á   zà-n   ná   sómbò-y
      chief D.PROG   return-3M PREP bush   PREP side-3M COMP Sombo-COP
      á   ddə̀f   bíinà   à-dí   sə̀-nə̀-k   óffò   sə̀-n   bíinà
      PREP inside roof   3M-put   DAT-3M-PRF   fire   DAT-3M roof
      'Upon his return from the bush, the chief, thinking that it was Sombo who was in the roof, set the fire to the roof'

Verbs of saying in Gidar do not inherently imply the presence of the indirect object, as evidenced by the fact that the preposition sə̀ precedes the pronoun coding the addressee:

(57) də̀rbágà-nì   wíin   sə̀-t   də̀và-t   má-n   à-tə̀ŋə̀-k
      after-3M   boy   PREP-3F belly-3F mother-3M 3M-start-PRF
      əpél   sə̀-tá
      talk   DAT-3F
      'During his absence, a boy from inside his mother started to talk to her.'

(58) à-ná   sə̀-tə̀-k   ná   ə̀mmá   ní-gíl   də̀   ngáa   dì
     3M-say PREP-3F-PRF   COMP mother 1SG-leave ASSC where SQ
     'He said to her, "Mother, through where should I leave?"'

Gidar is also one of the languages that codes malefactive predication in its grammatical system. The malefactive predication, unlike the benefactive predication, is coded by object suffixes to the verb without the preposition *sə̀*, i.e., the preposition coding the benefactive predication. The addition of these object suffixes does not depend on the inherent properties of the verb. Clauses with such pronominal coding may have nominal objects as well. In the following example, the indirectly affected argument is marked by the pronominal suffix:

(59) à-ḫá-nə̀-nə̀-k   glà   ná-wísnè
     3M-break-3SG-PL-PRF   house   GEN-SOMEONE
     'They burned his house.'

(60) à-nǥù-wə̀-k   ḡèngé   ná-wà
     3M-break-1SG-PRF   stick   GEN-1SG
     'He broke my walking stick (to my detriment).'

Without the first-person object pronoun on the verb, the clause does not imply a malefactive effect:

(61) à-nǥà-nə̀-k   ḡèngé   ná-wà
     3M-break.GO-3M-PRF   stick   GEN-1SG
     'he broke my walking stick'

11.2 Indirectly affected argument

Many Indo-European languages do not code the benefactive predication or the malefactive predication. Many languages, including some Indo-European languages, code an indirectly affected argument predication. In this predication, the argument C is indirectly affected when A acts (on B) and thus affects C. Note that the scheme represents only the semantic relations; it does not represent linear order or other formal means. The relationships A, B, and C are relationships within a proposition, not relationships in some type of external reality. In the scheme above, the direct object B is optional: The coding of indirect affectedness does not have to involve a direct object. Even an intransitive verb may have an indirect object, as illustrated in the present study. Therefore, the construction involved cannot be characterized in any way as representing a three-participant event (Margetts and Austin 2007). The number of participants in the event, and indeed the very notion of the 'event', has no bearing on the issue at hand. The referential scope ('meaning') of 'indirect object' only partially overlaps with the referential scope of the benefactive construction ('ditransitive') in English.

A language has an indirect object predication when it has formal means that code such a function and that distinguish it from all other functions (Frajzyngier and Mycielski 1998). The indirect object predication can be realized through one or more formal means within the same language. If the indirect object predication has been grammaticalized, the set of formal means used to code the indirect object predication will be distinct from the set of formal means used to code any other predications in the language.

11.3 Conclusions

One of the main benefits of a cross-linguistic study of functions is the discovery of correlations between the presence and absence of various functions. The important conclusion for the proposed typology is that whether a language has a benefactive predication or an indirectly affected argument predication allows us to make predictions about the existence of malefactive predication in the language. The discussions in Radetzky & Smith (2010) and in Frajzyngier (2013) indicate that if a language codes benefactive predication in its grammatical system, one can expect the emergence of malefactive predication in the grammatical system. The existence of indirectly affected argument predication does not allow for the prediction of malefactive predication. And indeed, in the small sample of languages examined, the malefactive predication does not exist as a separate predication in languages that code indirect object predication but not benefactive predication. The 'ditransitive construction', which often boils down to structures involving the equivalents of the verb 'to give', does not necessarily represent a function encoded in the grammatical system.

12. Advantages of comparing functions encoded in the grammatical systems

By examining only the functions actually encoded in the languages under study, one can:

a. Establish how the grammatical systems of different languages are similar and how they are different; and
b. Explain why utterances (sentences, clauses, phrases) that have the same referential meanings across languages may have different forms.

The differences and similarities across languages can be reduced to the following:

The similarities consist of encoding the same function.
The differences consist of encoding different functions.

The similarities consist of using the same forms to encode the same functions. The differences consist of using different forms to encode the same functions.

The morphological and syntactic forms (a) realize functions encoded in the grammatical system, and (b) ensure the principle of functional transparency (Frajzyngier 2004b), whereby the role of every element in the utterance must be transparent to the listener. This principle explains the use of prepositions in English for functions that cannot be coded by linear order.

13. What the typology of functional functions will look like

Discovering in what ways languages are similar and in what ways they are different with respect to the functions encoded and the formal means by which similar functions are encoded can help in explaining the forms of the utterances in individual languages. The functions to be listed for each language are those that comprise the functional domains rather than some aprioristic, comparative concepts. Thus, a prerequisite for a typology of languages with respect to functions is a list of functions encoded in every language. Once such lists are available, it will be possible to discover which functions are encoded more often, which functions are encoded less often, and which functions are more likely to co-occur or not co-occur. Such a typology cannot be accomplished now as we do not have such a list for any language. However, such a typology can be implemented gradually with respect to various areas of grammatical systems. Frajzyngier with Shay (2016) is an example of the implementation of such a typology with respect to relations between predicate and noun phrases for a small number of languages. Frajzyngier, Liu, and Ye (2020) is an illustration of a description of functions for one language in one area, namely that of reference. Frajzyngier (2018) is an illustration of typological investigation in the area of reference. A typology of all functions encoded is a long-term project.

It appears that unrelated languages have only a few functional domains in common, such as assertion, questions, some functions involved in given orders, and some ways of coding negation. Other functional domains and other functions are not expected to overlap across unrelated languages and often differ across related languages.

Abbreviations

ALL	Allative	CAUS	Causative
AR.	Arabic	COLL	Collective
ASSC	Associative	COM	Comment marker
ATT	Attributive	COND	Conditional

CONJ	Conjunction	NOM	Nominalizer
COP	Copula	NP	Noun Phrase
D.	Dependent	OBJ	Object
DAT	Dative	OBL	Oblique
DEF	Definite	P	Proximate
DEM	Demonstrative	PART	Partitive
DIMIN	Diminutive	PAST	Past
DU	Dual	PL	Plural
DUB	Dubitative	PREP	Preposition
EP	Epenthetic	PRF	Perfective
EXCL	Exclusive	PRO	Pronoun
F	Feminine	PROG	Progressive
FR.	French	PURP	Purpose
FREQ	Frequentative	Q	Interrogative marker
FUT	Future	QUANT	Quantifier
GEN	Genitive marker	REDUP	Reduplication
GEN:PL	Genitive plural marker	REF	Referential marker
HUM	Unspecified human subject	REL	Relative
HYP	Hypothetical marker and complementizer	S	Sentence
		SG	Singular
IMP	Imperative	SPEC	Spatial specifier
IMPF	Imperfective	SQ	Specific question marker
INCEPT	Inceptive	SUBJ	Subjunctive
INCL	Inclusive	TOT	Totality
INDEF	Indefinite human subject	TQ	Question about the truth
INF	Infinitive	V	Verb
LOC	Locative	VENT	Ventive
M	Masculine	VN	Verbal noun
N	Noun	1	First-person
NEG	Negative marker	2	Second-person
NG.	Ngambay	3	Third-person

References

Beeching, Kate. 1980–1990. *Un corpus d'entretiens spontanés. Enregistrés et transcrits par Kate Beeching.* Southampton: LLAS Centre for Languages, University of Southampton.

COCA: *Corpus of Contemporary American English.*

Cohen, David. 1989. *L'aspect verbal.* Paris: PUF.

Comrie, Bernard. 1976. *Aspect: An Introduction to the Study of Verbal Aspect and Related Problems.* Cambridge: CUP.

Comrie, Bernard. 1985. *Tense.* Cambridge: CUP. https://doi.org/10.1017/CBO9781139165815

Corbett, Greville G. 1991. *Gender.* Cambridge: CUP. https://doi.org/10.1017/CBO9781139166119

Corbett, Greville G. 2000. *Number.* Cambridge: CUP. https://doi.org/10.1017/CBO9781139164344

Cuyckens, Herbert, Davidse, Kristin & Verstraete, Jean-Christophe (eds.). 2010. *Grammaticalization and grammar.* Amsterdam: Benjamins.

Dixon, Robert M.W. 2010. *Basic Linguistic Theory, Vol. 1: Methodology*. Oxford: OUP.
Dixon, Robert M.W. 2010. *Basic Linguistic Theory, Vol. 2: Grammatical Topics*. Oxford: OUP.
Dixon, Robert M.W. 2012. *Basic Linguistic Theory, Vol. 3: Further Grammatical Topics*. Oxford: OUP.
Dryer, Matthew S. 1991. SOV languages and the OV: VO typology. *Journal of Linguistics* 27: 443–482. https://doi.org/10.1017/S0022226700012743
Dryer, Matthew S. 1992. The Greenbergian word order correlations. *Language* 68(1): 81–138. https://doi.org/10.1353/lan.1992.0028
Dryer, Matthew S. 1995. Frequency and pragmatically unmarked word order. In *Word Order in Discourse* [Typological Studies in Language 30], Michael Noonan & Pamela Downing (eds), 105–135. Amsterdam: John Benjamins. https://doi.org/10.1075/tsl.30.06dry
Dryer, Matthew S. 2013a. Definite articles. In *The World Atlas of Language Structures Online*, Matthew S. Dryer & Martin Haspelmath (eds). Leipzig: Max Planck Institute for Evolutionary Anthropology. <http://wals.info/chapter/37> (28 May 2017).
Dryer, Matthew S. 2013b. Indefinite articles. In *The World Atlas of Language Structures Online*, Matthew S. Dryer & Martin Haspelmath (eds). Leipzig: Max Planck Institute for Evolutionary Anthropology. <http://wals.info/chapter/38> (28 May 2017).
Fenk-Oczlon, Gertraud. 1989. Word frequency and word order in freezes. *Linguistics* 27(3): 517–556. https://doi.org/10.1515/ling.1989.27.3.517
Fenk-Oczlon, Gertraud & Fenk, August. 2005. Crosslinguistic correlations between size of syllables, number of cases, and adposition order. In *Sprache und Natürlichkeit: Gedenkband für Willi Mayerthaler*, Gertraud Fenk-Oczlon & Christian Winkler (eds), 75–86. Tübingen: Gunter Narr.
Fillmore, Charles. 1968. The case for case. In *Universals in Linguistic Theory*, Emmon Bach & Richard, Harms (eds), 1–88. New York NY: Holt, Rinehart, and Winston.
Fortescue, Michael, Mithun, Marianne & Evans, Nicholas (eds). 2017. *The Oxford Handbook of Polysynthesis*. Oxford: OUP. https://doi.org/10.1093/oxfordhb/9780199683208.001.0001
Frajzyngier, Zygmunt. 1985a. Ergativity, number, and agreement. In *Proceedings of the Eleventh Annual Meeting of the Berkeley Linguistic Society*, Mary Niepokuj, Mary VanClay, Vassiliki Nikiforidou & Deborah Feder (eds), 96–106. Berkeley CA: BLS.
Frajzyngier, Zygmunt. 1985b. Truth and the indicative sentence. *Studies in Language* 9(2): 243–254. https://doi.org/10.1075/sl.9.2.05fra
Frajzyngier, Zygmunt. 1987. Truth and the compositionality principle: A reply to Palmer. *Studies in Language* 11(1): 211–217. https://doi.org/10.1075/sl.11.1.12fra
Frajzyngier, Zygmunt. 1996. *Grammaticalization of the Complex Sentence: A Case Study in Chadic* [Studies in Language Companion Series 32]. Amsterdam: John Benjamins. https://doi.org/10.1075/slcs.32
Frajzyngier, Zygmunt. 1997. Grammaticalization of number: From demonstratives to nominal and verbal plural. *Linguistic Typology* 1: 193–242. https://doi.org/10.1515/lity.1997.1.2.193
Frajzyngier, Zygmunt. 1999. Domains of point of view and coreferentiality: System interaction approach to the study of reflexives. In *Reflexives: Forms and Functions*, Vol.1 [Typological Studies in Language 40], Zygmunt Frajzyngier & Traci Walker (eds), 125–152. Amsterdam: John Benjamins. https://doi.org/10.1075/tsl.40.06fra
Frajzyngier, Zygmunt. 2001. *A Grammar of Lele* [Stanford Monographs in African Linguistics]. Stanford CA: CSLI.
Frajzyngier, Zygmunt. 2004. Principle of functional transparency in language structure and language change. In *Linguistic Diversity and Language Theories* [Studies in Language Com-

panion Series 72], Zygmunt Frajzyngier, David Rood & Adam Hodges (eds), 259–283. Amsterdam: John Benjamins. https://doi.org/10.1075/slcs.72.13fra

Frajzyngier, Zygmunt. 2008a. *A Grammar of Gidar*. Frankfurt: Peter Lang.

Frajzyngier, Zygmunt. 2008b. Grammaticalization, typology, and semantics: Expanding the agenda. In *Rethinking Grammaticalization: New Perspectives* [Typological Studies in Language 76], Maria Jose Lopez-Couso & Elena Seoane (eds), 61–102. Amsterdam: John Benjamins. https://doi.org/10.1075/tsl.76.06fra

Frajzyngier, Zygmunt. 2010. Grammaticalization within and outside of the domain. In *Formal Evidence in Grammaticalization Research* [Typological Studies in Language 94], An Van linden, Jean-Christophe Verstraete & Kristin Davidse (eds), 43–62. Amsterdam: John Benjamins. https://doi.org/10.1075/tsl.94.03fra

Frajzyngier, Zygmunt. 2011. Grammaticalization of the reference systems. In *The Oxford Handbook of Grammaticalization*, Bernd Heine & Heiko Narrog (eds), 625–635. Oxford: OUP.

Frajzyngier, Zygmunt. 2012. *A Grammar of Wandala*. Berlin: Mouton de Gruyter. https://doi.org/10.1515/9783110218411

Frajzyngier, Zygmunt. 2013. Indirect object and benefactive predications in Chadic: A typological sketch. *Studies in African Linguistics* 42(1): 33–68.

Frajzyngier, Zygmunt. 2016. Inflectional markers of sentential parsing. *Lingua* 183: 1–33. https://doi.org/10.1016/j.lingua.2016.05.004

Frajzyngier, Zygmunt. 2018a. Toward a typology of reference systems. *Languages and Linguistics* 79: 1–44. https://doi.org/10.20865/20187901

Frajzyngier, Zygmunt. 2018b. Coding locative predication in Chadic. In *Afroasiatic: Data and Perspectives* [Current Issues in Linguistic Theory 339], Alessandro Mengozzi & Mauro Tosco (eds), 203–233. Amsterdam: John Benjamins. https://doi.org/10.1075/cilt.339.12fra

Frajzyngier, Zygmunt. 2019. What the grammaticalization of 'head' reveals about the semantic structure of a language. In *Embodiment in Cross-Linguistic Studies: The 'Head'*, Iwona Kraska-Szlenk (ed.), 51–75. Leiden: Brill.

Frajzyngier, Zygmunt & Butters, Marielle. 2020. *The Emergence of Grammatical Functions*. Oxford: OUP.

Frajzyngier, Zygmunt, Johnston, Eric, with Edwards, Adrian. 2005. *A Grammar of Mina*. Berlin: Mouton de Gruyter. https://doi.org/10.1515/9783110893908

Frajzyngier, Zygmunt, Liu, Meichun, Ye, Yingying. 2020. The reference system of Modern Mandarin Chinese. *Australian Journal of Linguistics* 40(1). https://doi.org/10.1080/07268602.2019.1698512

Frajzyngier, Zygmunt & Mycielski, Jan. 1998. On some fundamental problems of mathematical linguistics. In *Mathematical and Computational Analysis of Natural Language* [Studies in Functional and Structural Linguistics 45], Carlos Martin-Vide (ed.), 295–310. Amsterdam: John Benjamins. https://doi.org/10.1075/sfsl.45.27fra

Frajzyngier, Zygmunt with Shay, Erin. 2002. *A Grammar of Hdi*. Berlin: Mouton de Gruyter. https://doi.org/10.1515/9783110885798

Frajzyngier, Zygmunt with Erin Shay. 2003. *Explaining Language Structure through Systems Interaction* [Typological Studies in Language 55]. Amsterdam: John Benjamins. https://doi.org/10.1075/tsl.55

Frajzyngier, Zygmunt with Erin Shay. 2016. *The Role of Functions in Syntax: A Unified Approach to Language Theory, Description, and Typology* [Typological Studies in Language 111]. Amsterdam: John Benjamins. https://doi.org/10.1075/tsl.111

Frajzyngier, Zygmunt & Munkaila, Mohammed. In progress. *Locative predications in Hausa*.

Frajzyngier, Zygmunt. n.d. *Field-notes on Hona*.
Frajzyngier, Zygmunt & Johnston, Eric. n.d. *Field-notes for Mina dictionary*.
Garrigues-Cresswell, Martine with Weibegué, Christophe. 1981. *Livre de Lecture Lélé*. Sarh: Centre D'études Linguistiques.
Goldberg, Adele E. 1995. *Constructions: A Construction Grammar Approach to Argument Structure*. Chicago IL: University of Chicago Press.
Goldberg, Adele E. & van der Auwera, Johan. 2012. This is to count as a construction. *Folia Linguistica* 46(1): 109–132. https://doi.org/10.1515/flin.2012.4
Granger, Gilles Gaston. 1960. *Pensée Formelle et Science de l'Homme*. Paris: Aubier.
Greenberg, Joseph H. 1963. Some universals of grammar with particular reference to the order of meaningful elements. In *Universals of Grammar*, Joseph H. Greenberg (ed.), 73–113. Cambridge MA: The MIT Press.
Guillaume, Antoine. 2016. Associated motion in South America: Typological and areal perspectives. *Linguistic Typology* 20(1): 81–177. https://doi.org/10.1515/lingty-2016-0003
Haspelmath, Martin. 2010. Comparative concepts and descriptive categories in cross-linguistic studies. *Language* 86(3): 663–687. https://doi.org/10.1353/lan.2010.0021
Haspelmath, Martin. 2011. Comparative concepts for alignment typology. *Linguistic Typology* 15(3): 535–556. https://doi.org/10.1515/LITY.2011.035
Klein, Wolfgang & Perdue, Clive. 1997. The Basic Variety (or: Couldn't natural languages be much simpler?). *Second Language Research* 13(4):301–347.
Kuteva, Tania, Heine, Bernd, Hong, Bo, Long, Haiping, Narrog, Heiko & Rhee, Seongha (eds) 2019. *World Lexicon of Grammaticalization*, second, extensively revised and updated edition. Cambridge: CUP. https://doi.org/10.1017/9781316479704
Lazard, Gilbert. 2004. On the status of linguistics with particular regard to typology. *The Linguistic Review* 21: 389–411. https://doi.org/10.1515/tlir.2004.21.3-4.389
Margetts, Anna & Austin, Peter K. 2007. Three-participant events in the languages of the world: Towards a crosslinguistic typology. *Linguistics* 45(3): 393–450. https://doi.org/10.1515/LING.2007.014
Milewski, Tadeusz. 1950. La structure de la phrase dans les langues indigènes de l'Amérique du nord. *Lingua Posnaniensis* 2: 162–207.
Milewski, Tadeusz. 1962. Typological similarities between Caucasian and American Indian languages. *Folia Orientalia* IV: 221–230.
Mithun, Marianne. 1991. Active/agentive case and its motivations. *Language* 67: 510–546. https://doi.org/10.1353/lan.1991.0015
Mithun, Marianne & Chafe, Wallace. 1999. What are S, A, and O? *Studies in Language* 23(3): 579–606. https://doi.org/10.1075/sl.23.3.05mit
Newman, Paul. 2000. *The Hausa Language: An Encyclopedic Reference Grammar*. New Haven CT: Yale University Press.
NKJP: Narodowy Korpus Języka Polskiego-Polish National Corpus.
Radetzky, Paula & Smith, Tomoko. 2010. An areal and cross-linguistic study of benefactive and malefactive constructions. In *Benefactives and Malefactives. Typological Perspectives and Case Studies* [Typological Studies in Language 92], Fernando Zúñiga & Seppo Kittilä (eds), 97–120. Amsterdam: John Benjamins. https://doi.org/10.1075/tsl.92.04rad
Schachter, Paul & Otanes, Fe T. 1972. *Tagalog Reference Grammar*. Berkeley CA: University of California Press.

Schuh, Russell G. 2017. *A Chadic Cornucopia*, Paul Newman (ed.). Oakland CA: California Digital Library. <https://escholarship.org/uc/uclaling_chadic> (12 November 2020).

Siewierska, Anna. 2006. Word order and linearization. In *Encyclopedia of Languages and Linguistics*, Vol. 13, Keith Brown (ed.), 642–649. Oxford: Elsevier. https://doi.org/10.1016/B0-08-044854-2/01995-7

Siewierska, Anna. 1998. Variation in major constituent order: A global and European perspective. In *Constituent Order in the Languages of Europe*, Anna Siewierska (ed.), 475–552. Berlin: Mouton de Gruyter. https://doi.org/10.1515/9783110812206.475

Siewierska, Anna. 2004. *Person*. Cambridge: CUP. https://doi.org/10.1017/CBO9780511812729

Siewierska, Anna & Bakker, Dik. 1996. The distribution of subject and object agreement and word order type. *Studies in Language* 20(1): 115–161. https://doi.org/10.1075/sl.20.1.06sie

Stefanini, Jean. 1962. *La voix pronominale en ancien et en moyen français*. Aix-en-Provence: Ophrys.

Wittgenstein, Ludwig. 1963. *Philosophical Investigations*. Oxford: Blackwell.

Wohlgemuth, Jan & Cysouw, Michael (eds). 2010. *Rara & Rarissima. Documenting the Fringes of Linguistic Diversity*. Berlin: De Gruyter Mouton. https://doi.org/10.1515/9783110228557

CHAPTER 5

Theories of language, language comparison, and grammatical description
Correcting Haspelmath

Hans-Heinrich Lieb
Freie Universität Berlin

This essay is a study of Haspelmath's conception of 'comparative concepts' vs. 'descriptive categories' from a new angle: a study concentrating on questions of logical form and formal explicitness rather than on linguistic adequacy; it is suggested that the inconclusiveness of previous discussion of the conception is mainly due to formal flaws hidden in Haspelmath's account by its informality. Three major flaws of the conception are identified: (i) a failure to explicitly relativize comparative-concept terms to languages: to construe the terms as relational, as denoting relations between linguistic items, or constructions, and languages; (ii) misconstruing empirical statements on descriptive categories as definitions of the category terms; and (iii) a failure to recognize the importance of theories of language in dealing with 'comparative concepts' vs. 'descriptive categories'. There are serious consequences of these flaws, which are pointed out in detail. The conception as such is not rejected: ten revisions are proposed for an improved version. An attempt is made throughout to actually settle matters, which requires going into details rather deeply. The essay proceeds in three steps, using background notions from logic and the philosophy of science: after the introductory Part A (Sections 1 and 2), Haspelmath's definition of "serial verb construction" is carefully analysed in Part B (Sections 3 to 10) as the most elaborate example of how he wishes to deal with comparative concepts; in Part C (Sections 11 to 19), the conception of 'comparative concepts' vs. 'descriptive categories' is modified by introducing the revisions, first with respect to comparative concepts (Sections 11 to 13), then with respect to descriptive categories (Sections 14 to 16), resulting in a different view of their interrelations (Sections 17 and 18) and in a more adequate conception of the relations between general linguistics, comparative linguistics, and descriptive linguistics (Section 19).

A. Introduction and background

1. Introduction

1.1 Motivation: Why this essay, and for whom

How are theories of language, language comparison, and the grammatical description of individual languages related to one another, or rather, how should the relation be conceived?

Most prominent in recent discussion have been partial answers given by Haspelmath, arguing for a distinction between 'comparative concepts' and 'descriptive categories', on a conception that was put forward most explicitly in Haspelmath (2010) and was reasserted in Haspelmath (2018):

> This essay reasserts the fundamental conceptual distinction between language-particular categories of individual languages, defined within particular systems, and comparative concepts at the cross-linguistic level, defined in substantive terms. [2018: 83]

Following his 2010 essay, there has been extensive discussion of Haspelmath's views, partially documented in 2016 in *Linguistic Typology* 20(2) and subsequently continued in Lehmann (2018) and in Lieb (2018). Haspelmath's (2018) essay gives us the latest explicit version of his conception, with an attempt to account for critical objections (Lieb (2018) is not yet considered).

Whenever a conception gives rise to that amount of discussion, then (i) the conception is important, and (ii) we may conclude that it is adequate in some respects but questionable or flawed in others. Haspelmath's conception has been a major influence in typological work; therefore, reconsidering it for problems that have gone unnoticed is worth the effort – even a very detailed one. Attempts are made in the present essay to provide definite solutions, yet to remain convincing also to linguists whose main line of research may normally lie in a different direction.

The essay directly addresses linguists who, from a theoretical or a practical point of view, take an interest in Haspelmath's conception, especially linguists who continue to be dissatisfied with the present state of the Haspelmath debate – general knowledge of the debate and the problems discussed will be largely presupposed. My analyses may lend qualified support to points made informally by others – such as Beck (2016) – but rarely will this be pointed out.

The essay should be of interest more generally, though: by approaching the problems of Haspelmath's conception from an unusual angle; by providing an example of how logic may be helpfully applied in solving conceptual problems in linguistics; by proposing solutions that may be useful for avoiding gaps in linguistics between theoretical and practical work; and, generally, by dealing with fundamental questions raised by the nature and organization of linguistics as a scientific discipline.

Notes. The present essay was finished in December 2019. Its pre-review version, not differing from the printed version in any essential way, was sent to Haspelmath in April 2019, who had not reacted by December; he may or may not have reacted since. – For simplicity's sake, work by Haspelmath will be referred to by dropping the author's name, as in "[2018]" for "Haspelmath (2018)". – Single quotation marks are used for 'scare quotes', double quotation marks for all cases of literal quotation. – Italics are used for emphasis, bold face serves for easy overall orientation in the text; emphasis systems in quotations are retained. – (*Added in print.*) The present essay was finished in December 2019. Its pre-review version, differing from the printed version in minor ways only, was sent to Haspelmath in April 2019, who did not react. Since, Haspelmath has published or pre-published additional papers (in particular [2020], [*to appear*]) that are relevant to the topics discussed in Section 19 (below); they do not refer to the present essay, are quite informal and do not supersede my account.

1.2   Topic and coverage (1): General

In the present essay I will be dealing with certain flaws of Haspelmath's conception of 'comparative concepts' vs. 'descriptive categories' – essential ones I believe, concerning formal and logical aspects that were largely neglected in previous discussion, which may explain its inconclusiveness: when problems have a formal or logical source that is not recognized, solutions are difficult.

The flaws were already pointed out and treated to some extent in Lieb (2018); otherwise, they have been overlooked in the relevant literature, with a few partial exceptions such as Lehmann (2018), with references to Lieb (2018). I will propose revisions of the conception to eliminate the flaws, in this sense 'correcting Haspelmath'. To keep the present essay on centre, I select [2010] and [2018] for Haspelmath's general view, the former as the frame-setting paper and the latter for giving us the latest explicit version of the conception. (Haspelmath (2021) does not go beyond [2018] in the relevant passages.)

In [2018], Haspelmath distinguishes two major types of comparative concepts, 'category-like comparative concepts' and 'etic comparative concepts'; the former type is loosely subdivided into comparative concepts whose terms "were originally used for the description of some particular language and were extended to comparative use only later (they could therefore be called "descriptive-derived terms")" [2018: 86], and comparative concepts "that are not normally used in descriptions"; these are typically "defined more narrowly than the corresponding language-particular categories" [2018: 87].

I will be dealing in this essay with 'category-like comparative concepts', covering both subtypes but concentrating on 'descriptive-derived terms'. As to the etic type of comparative concepts, this will not be considered. Its description in [2018] simply proved too vague for a formal analysis. I do believe that my statements on comparative concepts in general also cover the etic type, but I must leave this question open. – There are some other limitations.

1.3 Topic and coverage (2): Limitations

Haspelmath's term "comparative concept" is unfortunate because the term is traditionally used in the philosophy of science for the distinction between classificatory concepts ('tree', 'sister-of'), comparative concepts ('greater than') and quantitative concepts ('length'), a distinction going back to Rudolf Carnap and Carl G. Hempel. Comparative concepts as envisaged by Haspelmath appear to be classificatory, not comparative. However, the term as used by him is so well established by now that it will have to be retained, despite the ambiguity.

There is no reason why comparative concepts in Haspelmath's sense should be limited to classificatory concepts. In particular, such concepts are known to be insufficient when it comes to dealing with linguistic *clines* (also called "scales" or, somewhat misleadingly, "continua"). There has been a long tradition in typology – prominently represented by Hansjakob Seiler's well-known UNITYP model and also advocated, once again, by Puddu (2021) and Da Milano (2021) – of using clines in linguistic classification to account for gradation.

For a complete analysis of the problems presented by Haspelmath's conceptions, clines should be included as a topic, even though Haspelmath does not consider them. This could indeed be done using Lieb (1992: 186), the only attempt so far, it seems, to formally explicate the notion of a cline as employed in typology, making use of the logic of relations. I will leave this to another time, though, and generally stay with classificatory concepts to keep the present essay more strictly on course.

Another limitation is this: I will not be dealing with questions of methodology such as, what are the methods by which fruitful comparative concepts may be obtained, or descriptive categories or universals may be established? While important, such questions will not be discussed here.

1.4 Method (1): General

Obviously, some logic must be applied. *Let me therefore emphasize*: no knowledge of formal logic is presupposed on the part of the reader who seriously wishes to follow the argumentation. Instead of expressions from formal logic, I will mostly employ semi-formal expressions that have the status of readings of formal ones that are left unspecified and are characterized only indirectly by their readings. The *semi-formal* expressions are sufficient to bring out the logical properties of the *informal* expressions used by Haspelmath that are being analysed. It is hoped that this method will serve to keep readers interested who otherwise may feel inclined to disregard more formal work in or on general linguistics, considering it unnecessary at best. Logic will be used strictly as a tool: the essay studies problems in linguistics not logic.

In addition, Haspelmath's work will be evaluated in the light of basic literature on (i) definitions, (ii) concepts, (iii) properties, (iv) categories, and (v) natural kinds, referring, in particular, to recent high-quality survey articles from the *Stanford Encyclopedia of Philosophy*. (I do not find any reference in Haspelmath's work to such articles, nor to any of the literature reviewed in them.)

1.5 Method (2): Specifics

Theoretical discussions without examples tend to be tedious and may be unconvincing. For this reason, Part B of my essay, which is devoted to the notion of ***comparative concept***, will consist in a thorough-going analysis of an ***example*** that Haspelmath himself has provided as a model for the way he means to deal with comparative concepts: his definition of "serial verb construction" in [2016].

Essential use will be made in Part B of the theory of definitions as developed in logic and the philosophy of science; it is indispensable that readers should have relevant parts at their disposal. For the benefit of readers who are less familiar with the theory, such parts will be characterized. An excellent overview of the theory of definitions is provided by Gupta (2015), whom I will largely follow, adding, in particular, Suppes (1957: Ch. 8), which has remained a classic.

The definition will be analysed strictly for its formal and logical properties; the linguistic adequacy of the definition or of the concept introduced is not my topic. The definition has been seriously questioned with respect to linguistic adequacy by Aikhenvald (2018: 18). Her criticism may or may not be justified; for the purposes of the present essay, I need not take sides.

The concept of serial verb construction introduced by the definition clearly belongs to the 'category-like type of comparative concepts'. Based on the history of the concept of serial verb construction as outlined in [2016: 292] and Aikhenvald (2018: Section 1.7), this concept should be assigned to the 'descriptive-derived' subtype.

The results of Part B will be used for motivating and exemplifying the revisions proposed in Part C for the notion of comparative concept. These, in turn, are essential to a revised view of ***descriptive categories***. The method employed in Part C is an in-depth analysis of [2010] and [2018], making informal use of certain parts of logic.

Revisions will be proposed in Part C concerning both 'comparative concepts' and 'descriptive categories'. The revisions will result in an improved conception of the relation between 'comparative concepts' and 'descriptive categories', leading to a more adequate view of how general linguistics, comparative linguistics, and descriptive linguistics are related.

1.6 Major theses

There are at least two major topics that have remained contentious in the Haspelmath debate, roughly: (i) the relationship between 'comparative concepts' and 'descriptive categories', largely one of mutual independence according to Haspelmath, and (ii) the relationship between 'comparative concepts' and 'general categories', Haspelmath arguing against the latter.

It will be established that Haspelmath's position on (i) is not tenable and on (ii) is ill-founded, due to three formal flaws in his conception of 'comparative concepts' vs. 'descriptive categories', and a serious consequence:

(1.1) On Haspelmath's conception of comparative concepts, terms for such concepts do not reserve a place for entities such as languages openly and explicitly. ('Problem of the hidden variable'.)

(1.2) On Haspelmath's conception of descriptive categories, the empirical identification of descriptive categories is misconstrued as the definition of terms that denote the categories.

(1.3) The importance of theories of language for the conception is not recognized.

There is a serious consequence of these flaws:

(1.4) On Haspelmath's conception the relationship between comparative concepts and descriptive categories is inadequately construed, with consequences for the relationship between general linguistics, comparative linguistics, and descriptive linguistics.

The conception should be revised:

(1.5) Adopting ten revisions, the conception of 'comparative concepts' vs. 'descriptive categories' turns into an acceptable version.

In particular, new basic types of comparative concepts will be distinguished by means of criteria that have become newly available; a treatment of syntactic functions that sets them apart from categories like word classes is outlined. Existing classifications of descriptive categories are reconceived, and improvements on existing terminology are proposed.

1.7 Organization

Part A (Sections 1 and 2) is concluded in Section 2 by characterizing the background in logic and philosophy that is presupposed in the present essay. Section 2, which may simply be skipped at a first reading, is the only Section of the essay to require, for a fuller understanding, some training in logic on part of the reader.

Part B (Sections 3 to 10) is devoted to Haspelmath's definition of "serial verb construction" [2016] as a model example of how he intends to deal with

Chapter 5. Theories of language, language comparison, and grammatical description 143

'comparative concepts'. The analysis will be in two steps, *first*, with respect to *definition type* (Sections 3 to 5), and *second*, with respect to *definition form* (Sections 6 to 8). Both steps are introduced by briefly characterizing relevant parts of the theory of definitions as background (Sections 3 and 6; these may be passed over on a first reading; readers who are *not* sufficiently familiar with the theory of definitions may consult them as need arises; readers who *are* familiar with the theory may skip the two Sections). Based on the results of the first two steps, the concept of serial verb construction (as different from the concept term) is characterized (Section 9) and it is shown (Section 10) how the concept term applies.

Using the results of Part B, **Part C** (Sections 11 to 19) proposes ten revisions of the conception of 'comparative concepts' vs. 'descriptive categories', eight for dealing with comparative concepts (Sections 11 to 13) and two for the treatment of descriptive categories (Sections 14 to 16). On the basis of these revisions, the relationship between comparative concepts and descriptive categories is critically evaluated and reconceived (Sections 17 and 18). Finally, the consequences are outlined for the relationship between theories of language, language comparison and language description, and for the organization of linguistics generally (Section 19).

2. Background

2.1 Logic (1): General

Sections 2.1 to 2.4 – which may be skipped on a first reading of the essay – are to characterize the background in logic that is assumed in the essay. This is meant as orientation for readers with a training in logic; they are primarily addressed in the four Sections. Readers without such a training may still find pointers to places where further information is available. In addition, there will be some notes on terminology.

Logic is used in the present essay as a *tool*: a tool for analysing conceptual problems that have arisen in linguistics. What is required of a tool is its usefulness; this does not mean the tool has to be described in detail. This is also true of the language of logic that is presupposed in the essay; it must be identified, and its usefulness guaranteed, but its structure need not be described.

The language of logic chosen as a basic tool for the analysis of Haspelmath's conception is Language B (with additions from Language C) in Carnap (1960). (Carnap (1960), written in German, includes some improvements on the first edition of the same book, of which Carnap (1958) – reprinted in 2012 – is an English translation; the differences between the 1958 and 1960 versions are mostly irrelevant for the present essay.) The reasons for this choice, which may come as a surprise, are as follows.

To function as a tool for the analysis, the language of logic chosen has to be well developed, comprehensive with respect to logical coverage, and well-proven in applications. These requirements are satisfied best by versions of classic predicate logic, sufficiently comprehensive to include a version of the lambda calculus.

Carnap's Language B is an 'extensional' version – in many ways unsurpassed – of classic higher-order predicate logic, including a version of type theory and allowing for (typed) lambda expressions; 'state-descriptions', the precursor of 'possible worlds', are still employed in semantics. Details of Language B need not concern us here (the original motivation for type theories and developments in this area up to the present are characterized in Coquand (2018)), with one exception: some remarks on Carnap's version of the lambda calculus are in order.

2.2 Logic (2): Lambda expressions

An up-to-date characterization of the (untyped) lambda calculus, including a brief history, is given in Alama & Korbmacher (2019). In a standard form, "The λ-calculus is an elegant notation for working with *applications* of *functions* to *arguments*." (2019: 2).

There is an alternative, though, to this strictly *functional* conception, an alternative in which the following is true (Alama & Korbmacher 2019: 32):

> For any formula ϕ and any finite sequence $x_1, \ldots, x_n$ of variables, the expression '$\lambda x_1 \ldots x_n [\phi]$' is a predicate symbol of arity n.

(Note "*predicate* symbol", not "*function* symbol"; "formula" means "sentential formula", not "term"; n ≥ 1.) Carnap, in the first, 1947 edition of Carnap (1956), is mentioned as the originator of this approach, which is shown to have been adopted, once again, by the most recent work on theories of properties (Alama & Korbmacher 2019: 32–33). (Carnap also provided the starting-point for the use made by Montague and his followers of the lambda calculus in linguistic semantics.)

In his Language B, Carnap allows for both: lambda expressions that are n-ary function expressions and lambda expressions that are predicate expressions; for function expressions, ϕ must be not a sentential formula but an expression of the type system (an individual expression or a predicate or function expression – these are expressions of different types of the type system).

Carnap's treatment of lambda expressions makes his Language B (with additions from Language C) particularly useful as a basic tool for the analyses in the present essay, and this provides an additional reason for choosing the language: allowing lambda expressions that are predicate expressions agrees with the role of lambda expressions in current property conceptions, which are important in construing comparative concepts as a specific kind of concepts; lambda expressions are also relevant to our analysis of how to obtain terms that denote 'descriptive categories'.

Terminological note. I use the expression "term" (i) informally in the sense of, roughly, "technical expression", (ii) formally for any individual expression, predicate expression or function expression (which need not be constants) – this excludes sentential formulas.

2.3 Logic (3): Intensions

Carnap's Language B has one feature that has to be changed before the language achieves its full usefulness as a tool for the purposes of the essay: the language is 'extensional', that is, equivalence of properties implies identity, and only extensions (sets and their elements) not intensions (properties and propositions) are considered in the semantic system.

It has turned out that a purely extensional language is too weak a tool for analysing Haspelmath's conceptions: he informally uses a notion of concept that is hard to reconstruct without taking intensions seriously. Therefore, I am adopting an *intensional version of Language B*, essentially obtained from Language B by dropping from its syntactic system the transformation rule for extensionality and using intensions not extensions as values in the semantic system.

This raises the question of the nature of intensions. It is answered in *intensional logic*, on whose development Carnap had a vast influence (Fitting 2015: 8):

> Carnap's fundamental idea is that intensions, for whatever entities are being considered, can be given a precise mathematical embodiment as functions on states, while extensions are relative to a single state. This has been further developed by subsequent researchers, of course with modern possible world semantics added to the mix.

For details, the reader is referred to Fitting (2015), also for a propositional modal logic as an example.

Generally, intensions may be understood here as in intensional logic, where Carnap's 'fundamental idea' has been used as a basis. At least in the case of *closed predicate and function terms*, intensions may be identified with *properties*. (There are well-known problems with the intensional interpretation of terms that are individual expressions, but the argumentation in the present essay does not depend on their interpretation.)

Orilia and Swoyer (2017) provide an up-to-date overview of notions of property in philosophy. Following their example, we generalize the notion of property by using a concept of ***n*-place property** such that one-place properties are properties in the usual sense and n-place properties, for n > 1, are properties of n-tuples. This applies to properties as the intensions of predicate expressions but may be extended to the intensions of n-place function expressions by construing their intensions as properties of (n+1)-tuples such that for each tuple that has such a property the following is true: there is no other tuple that has the property and has the same first n components as the given tuple but differs in its last component. (Compare the function of addition and the (2+1)-tuple whose first two components are the numbers 3 and 4 and whose last component is the number 7.)

To obtain names for properties, use of lambda-expressions "is followed in the most recent versions of property theory" (Orilia & Swoyer 2017: 49; 49–52).

For an alternative conception of intensions – intensions as algorithms, in an abstract sense of "algorithm" – see Fitting (2015: Section 4); and similarly, Alama & Korbmacher (2019: Section 1.2) on intensionality as typically conceived in lambda calculus work on the foundations of mathematics ('functions as rules').

2.4   Logic (4): The language

In summary, then, what is used as a logical tool in the present essay is **an intensional version of Carnap's Language B**, essentially obtained by removing the basis for extensionality from the syntactic system and using intensions, not extensions, for the interpretation of expressions in the semantic system. An n-place property conception is adopted for the intensions of terms (problems with the intensions of individual terms remain undiscussed as irrelevant to subsequent argumentation). On a possible-worlds account, extensions of terms would turn out to be extensions in the 'actual world'.

Terminological note. Following Carnap (1956: Section 5), the expressions "equivalent" and "logically equivalent", important in later discussion and primarily applied to *expressions*, will also be transferred to the *intensions* of expressions that are equivalent or logically equivalent.

2.5   Notions of category (1): General

The meanings of the term "category" as used in linguistics are related to but different from the meanings of such terms in philosophy, where they have been in use for more than two thousand years.

The notions of category that have prevailed in philosophy are surveyed in Thomasson (2018). They all share a major orientation: they are primarily about *ultimate* or *most general* distinctions rather than about the sub-distinctions that can be based on them, and they are primarily *intensional*, in some sense, rather than extensional. Categories are then construed – possibly by the same philosopher – either in an *ontological* sense (as something 'in the world', say, categories as properties) or in an *epistemological* sense (as something 'in the mind', say, categories as concepts that organize human understanding); with language being involved in various ways.

The conceptions of categories that have come to prevail in linguistics are mostly ontological and extensional not intensional; compare van der Auwera & Gast (2010: Section 1), who trace their origins back to von der Gabelentz, Jespersen and Bloomfield, remarking (2010: 169):

> The use of the word 'category' for formal and/or basic [least general, H.L.] sets is a relatively recent phenomenon that is often lamented in philosophy as being inflationary and even down-right wrong.

Most of van der Auwera & Gast (2010) consists in a critical overview of how notions from *prototype theories* of concepts – rather than from 'classical' theories where concept terms are defined by necessary-and-sufficient conditions – have been applied in linguistics in dealing with categories; the authors conclude that while "prototype theory cannot account for all the problems of categorization, it certainly has its place in contemporary linguistics" (2010: 188).

An up-to-date general evaluation of the two types of concept theories may be found in Margolis and Laurence (2014). Independently, proposing prototype theories as an *alternative* to classical ones when dealing with categories in linguistics, extensionally understood, is inadequate for two reasons: *first*, classical theories are frequently applied without making use of their full potential (typically, there is a neglect of cross-classifications); *second*, it was already shown in Lieb (1980) how to formally reduce prototype theories to classical ones via a specific notion of similarity concept, satisfying the motivation for prototype concepts also in a classical framework; this approach continues to apply. I consider the question as settled in principle (quantitative approaches to categories as concept extensions would have to be more carefully considered, though), and will therefore continue to use a classical framework.

2.6 Notions of category (2): Descriptive categories

Use of the term "category" in the discussion of 'comparative concepts' vs. 'descriptive categories' is characterized by two features: it is less general rather than most general categories that tend to be considered, and a clear distinction between intensional conceptions and extensional conceptions of categories may be missing.

In the case of Haspelmath, there is a corresponding inconsistency. On the one hand, the claim that different categories arise when different criteria are used for the definition of category terms makes sense only on a conception that identifies the categories with *properties* that are the intensions of category terms, on an intensional interpretation of the language of the definition.

On the other hand, the only explicit statement in [2010] and [2018] on what descriptive categories ('language-particular categories') are to be is the following from Croft (2016: 7), as quoted and adopted by Haspelmath in [2018: 95]:

> Language-specific categories are classes of words, morphemes, or larger grammatical units that are defined distributionally, that is, by their occurrence in roles in constructions of the language.

(In a footnote, Haspelmath assigns "the same status" to "phonemes and other phonological categories, as well as language-specific meanings" – the extension to phonemes is dubious, and so is the extension to meanings even if a distributional semantics were to be presupposed: not every distributionally determined class of language-specific entities should be construed as a language-specific *category*.) This is clearly an *extensional* conception: descriptive categories are to be *classes* – not properties – of entities, are to be the *extensions* of category terms.

You can't have it both ways: classes or sets are not properties, and adopting an intensional language of logic, as appears to be necessary for analysing Haspelmath's conceptions, the difference between classes and properties cannot be neglected. – I will assume an extensional view of descriptive categories in discussing Haspelmath, which on the whole appears to be his preferred option.

B. Determining a comparative concept: The definition of "serial verb construction"

3. Background: Definition types

3.1 A basic ambiguity: 'Real' vs. 'nominal' definitions

There are two major aspects of definitions, definition type and definition form. I begin by considering definition type, providing background to Sections 4 and 5 where the definition of "serial verb construction" will be analysed for its type.

Informal discussion of definitions is fraught with ambiguities, especially in regard of *what* is being defined (Gupta 2015: 2):

> Ordinary discourse recognizes several different kinds of things as possible objects of definition […]

Most major dictionaries of English testify to a basic ambiguity of "definition" in English: as referring *either* to words or phrases and their meanings, *or else* to objects that words or phrases may apply to. For example, two basic meanings are given, with examples, in the *Cambridge Advanced Learner's Dictionary* for "definition" in (UK) English: "a statement that explains the meaning of a word or phrase" and "a description of the features and limits of something".

A similar ambiguity, vague but of long standing, also exists for "definition" (and corresponding terms in other languages) in philosophy. "Definition" may be used either for so-called **nominal definitions** or for so-called **real definitions**. As characterized by Gupta (2015: 3), nominal definitions but not real definitions "explain the meaning of a term", and:

> Perhaps it is helpful to indicate the distinction between real and nominal definitions thus: to discover the real definition of a term X one needs to investigate the thing or things denoted by X; to discover the nominal definition, one needs to investigate the meaning and use of X.

("The real definition of a term" should be understood as short for "the real definition connected with a term".) Like Gupta, I will be concerned with nominal definitions rather than 'real' ones (for some literature concerning 'real' definitions, see Gupta (2015: 3)).

3.2 Types of nominal definitions (1): Stipulative definitions

Following Gupta (2015: Sections 1.2 to 1.6), *five types* of nominal definitions may be distinguished: *dictionary definitions, stipulative definitions, descriptive definitions, explicative definitions,* and *ostensive definitions*. Of these, dictionary definitions and ostensive definitions are of marginal interest in the present context and will be left undiscussed here. This is also true of descriptive definitions, which "like stipulative ones, spell out meaning, but they also aim to be adequate to existing usage" (Gupta 2015: 5). – Stipulative definitions are characterized in Gupta (2015: 4) as follows:

> A stipulative definition imparts a meaning to the defined term, and involves no commitment that the assigned meaning agrees with prior uses (if any) of the term.

It is not quite clear to me if not involving commitments to prior uses is meant by Gupta as a necessary condition for stipulative definitions. Independently, I will understand "*stipulative*" as "imparts a meaning to the defined term", and will distinguish between (i) definitions that are *all stipulative* by imparting a meaning *without* a commitment that it 'agrees' with prior uses (if any) of the defined term, which must not be the explicatum in a process of explication ("agrees" should be replaced by a weaker term such as "is positively related to", and "explicatum" is to be understood as below, Section 3.3), and (ii) definitions that are *part stipulative* by imparting a meaning *with* such a commitment or by being the explicatum in a process of explication.

It should be noted that a stipulative definition cannot be an empirical hypothesis; it simply takes a term and lays down a meaning for it; no claim is made on anything.

3.3 Types of nominal definitions (2): Explicative definitions

This type – of special importance to our discussion below – is informally introduced by Gupta (2015: 6) as follows:

> Sometimes a definition is offered neither descriptively nor stipulatively but as, what Rudolf Carnap (1956, Section 2) called, an *explication*. An explication aims to respect some central uses of a term but is stipulative on others.

> What is important for explication is not antecedent meaning but function. So long as the latter is preserved the former can be let go.

The decisive condition is "aims to respect some central uses of a term". A standard example of an explication, also discussed by Gupta (2015: 6), is the explication – going back to W. V. O. Quine – of "ordered pair" in set theory, where "the pair ⟨x, y⟩ is defined as the set {{x}, {x, y}}" (2015: 6), paying attention just to the condition that two pairs should be identical if and only if their corresponding components are. As shown by this example, "respect some central uses of a term" is compatible with impacting a meaning to the term.

Unfortunately, the term "explicative definition" as used by Gupta ("Viewed as an explication, this definition [...]", 2015: 6) is a misnomer: *explications are not definitions*. This appears from the passage in Carnap (1956: pp. 7–8), referred to by Gupta:

> The task of making more exact a vague or not quite exact concept used in everyday life or in an earlier stage of scientific or logical development, or rather of replacing it by a newly constructed, more exact concept, belongs among the most important tasks of logical analysis and logical construction. We call this the task of explicating, or of giving an **explication** for, the earlier concept; this earlier concept, or sometimes the term used for it, is called the **explicandum**; and the new concept, or its term, is called an **explicatum** of the old one.

I will understand "*explicative definition*" as "definition of the explicatum of an explication", employing "explicandum" and "explicatum" only for terms not concepts. As used by Carnap, the term "*concept*" is (1956: 21)

> a common designation for properties, relations, and similar entities (including individual concepts [...] and functions, but not propositions) [...] it is not to be understood in a mental sense, that is, as referring to a process of imagining, thinking, conceiving, or the like, but rather to something objective that is found in nature and that is expressed in language by a designator of nonsentential form.

3.4   Explications and the status of explicative definitions

Understanding explicanda and explicata as terms not concepts, an *explication* can be characterized roughly as consisting of:

i.   the determination of the explicandum or the explicanda and a clarification of their uses,
ii. the determination of the uses that are to be reconstructed,
iii. the introduction of the explicatum and determination of its uses, possibly by a definition, on the basis of (i) and (ii),
iv. checking (iii) for its relation to (ii) and evaluating (iii) with respect to precision, fruitfulness, and, possibly, simplicity.

An excellent recent survey article on conceptions of explication is Cordes & Siegwart (n. y.), which also contains a historical outline, characterizing Carnap (1950: Ch. 1) as "the seminal text on the topic" (n. y.: 4) and considering work up to and including 2017.

While not formulated in exactly this way in the literature, points (i) to (iv) represent the most essential features that are typically assigned to explications. I will not go into details here but simply add a few remarks.

The explicatum and its uses require a larger context for their determination: this is at least a language to which the explicatum belongs and in which it can be used as determined – the *explicatum language*. The explicatum, understood as a term, may but need not be given by a *proper definition*. Such definitions are relative to theories (see Suppes 1957: Ch. 8); therefore, if a proper definition is used for introducing the explicatum, this must be a term of a theory formulated within the explicatum language: a term of the *explicatum theory*.

A definition of the explicatum is *stipulative*; on Carnap's conception (see Section 3.3, above), the explicatum is, or involves as a meaning, a concept that is "newly constructed". More precisely, an explicative definition should indeed be taken to be *part stipulative*: because of step (iii) in the explication, the definition of the explicatum is related to certain uses of the explicandum (a term that may or may not differ from the explicatum).

Haspelmath's example of a definition of "serial verb construction" can now be considered, and placed within the general framework for definition types, distinguishing the basic type of the definition (nominal, Section 4) from its subtype (explicative, Section 5).

4. Basic type of the definition

4.1 The definition

The following proposal is made in [2016: 296]:

(11) Serial verb construction: a definition
A serial verb construction is a monoclausal construction consisting of multiple independent verbs with no element linking them and with no predicate-argument relation between the verbs.

This is immediately followed by:

(12) Key components of the definition
    a. construction
    b. monoclausal
    c. independent verbs

>   d. no linking element
>   e. no predicate-argument relation between the verbs

To avoid confusion with my own numbering, I will refer to the two passages quoted here as "(H 11)" and "(H 12)".

Presupposing (H 12) and referring to relevant passages in [2016], I am going to analyse the definition (H 11): not for the adequacy of its intended linguistic content but for its definition type. This requires first dealing with an ambiguity in Haspelmath's text.

4.2 The objects of the definition: A threefold ambiguity

There is a basic ambiguity in [2016] when "define" and "definition" are used in conjunction with "serial verb construction": between definition of a term, definition of a concept (as different from a term), and definition of an object language entity; compare [2016: 292 and 293] (italics added):

> With each extension of the term ["serial verb construction" as applied to individual languages, H. L.] to a new language, there is a danger that the meaning of the *term* may change, because the *defining properties* that were applicable in the original languages have no relevance in the new language.

> Thus, what we need is not a *definition* of a *cross-linguistic category* of serial verb construction (such a cross-linguistic category does not exist), but a comparative concept of serial verb construction (Haspelmath 2010). *Comparative concepts* are not DISCOVERED in the way natural phenomena are discovered, but are DEFINED by comparative linguists in order to allow comparison of languages.

According to the first quote, we are dealing with a term and its definition, according to the second, with the 'definition' of concepts and, *ex negativo*, with the 'definition' of a cross-linguistic category.

The two quotes together exemplify the ambiguity between nominal definitions and real definitions that was explained above (Section 3.1), adding concepts as new items that enter into the ambiguity – there is a ***threefold ambiguity*** here with respect to what a definition may be a definition of: a term, a concept, or a linguistic entity such as a category; the ambiguity is typical also of "definition" and "define" in [2010] and [2018].

4.3 The ambiguity resolved

There are a few passages in [2016] that indicate how the ambiguity might be resolved in a way that may agree with Haspelmath's intentions, such as [2016: 312]:

Chapter 5. Theories of language, language comparison, and grammatical description 153

> We have seen in this article that although serial verb constructions are quite diverse in the world's languages, it is possible to define the term *serial verb constructions* [note the plural, H. L.] (or in other words, to create a comparative concept 'serial verb construction') in such a way that a substantial number of interesting and testable generalizations can be formulated about them.

And, talking about his own definition:

> [...] while I admit that it is (of course) arbitrary (in the sense that I could have chosen a different concept to attach to the label *serial verb construction*), it is motivated by two goals: that of preserving the continuity of the research tradition, and that of identifying universal properties of human languages.

The following resolution of the ambiguity may therefore correspond to Haspelmath's intentions, notwithstanding many of his formulations.

In (H 11), we are dealing with a *concept* that is **introduced** for the **term** "serial verb construction" through a ***definition of the term*** formulated by Haspelmath, a definition that is to allow the formulation of "interesting and testable generalizations" about ***the referents of the term***; these jointly form ***the extension of the term***, which is identical to the ***extension of the concept***, that is, to the set of entities that are covered by the concept; the term may be said to ***denote*** its extension. (Note the double use of the term "extension".)

We may then speak of (i) "serial verb construction": ***the concept term*** (double quotation marks, no plural), (ii) serial verb construction: ***the concept of serial verb construction*** (no quotation marks, only singular, articles not possible), and (iii) serial verb constructions: (***components of***) ***the referents of the concept term*** (no quotation marks, singular or plural, articles possible – it will turn out that serial verb constructions are not themselves referents but only *components* of referents).

4.4 The definition as a nominal definition

We may now consider (H 11) as a nominal definition of the term "serial verb construction".

It is the term that is being defined, not the *concept*. Obviously, the concept is of primary importance, and is somehow 'given' through the part of (H 11) that follows "is" in (H 11) and is further analysed in (H 12). The details very much depend on how "concept" is to be understood. I will return to this question below, in Sections 9 and 11.3.

Again, it is the term not its *referents* or its *extension* that are defined in (H 11). Applying the term "definition" to the concept or to the referents or to the extension of the term takes us back into the area of real definitions (above, Section 3.1), contrary to Haspelmath's insistence on the 'arbitrariness' of his definition. – If (H 11) is a nominal definition, what kind of nominal definition is it?

5. Subtype of the definition

5.1 The definition as an explicative definition

The following passage [2016: 293], partly quoted in Section 4.2, above, clearly shows that the definition is meant to be *stipulative*:

> Thus, what we need is not a definition of a cross-linguistic category of serial verb construction (such a cross-linguistic category does not exist), but a comparative concept of serial verb construction (Haspelmath 2010). Comparative concepts are not DISCOVERED in the way natural phenomena are discovered, but are DEFINED by comparative linguists in order to allow comparison of languages. Thus, instead of lamenting the lack of agreement, linguists should feel free to simply advance a definition and then work with it. If the resulting work turns out to be interesting and productive, then the definition has proved useful.

It appears from passages such as the comments immediately following (H 11) and (H 12) that (H 11) is *explicative*, by defining a term that figures as the explicatum of an explication [2016: 296] (also compare the second quote in Section 4.3, above):

> It should be noted that this definition is considerably narrower than definitions used by most other authors; I know of no other definition that is narrower than this. This means that a number of phenomena that have been called SVCs are excluded by the definition, but it also means that the definition is more practical than some of the other, broader definitions, and that the generalizations that are based on it are more readily testable.

Being explicative, definition (H 11) is only *part stipulative*.

5.2 The explication

The explication that leads up to the definition is informal and is presented in a way that does not strictly follow the order of parts (i) to (iv) listed in Section 3.4, above, but still contains them in a recognizable way.

(i) *Determination of the explicanda and clarification of their uses.* – The explicanda are the terms "Serial Verb Construction", "SVC", and orthographic variants, with uses as found in language descriptions and in the typological literature, where Aikhenvald (2006) receives special attention. The uses are clarified in [2016] in two ways: *first,* in [Section 1.2], by "examples of SVCs from a range of diverse languages" [2016: 293], examples that precede the definition (H 11) and characterize

Chapter 5. Theories of language, language comparison, and grammatical description   155

the usage of the explicanda, and *second,* in [Sections 2.2–2.5], by a number of remarks that are distributed over the explanations and follow the definition.

(ii) *Determination of the uses that are to be reconstructed.* – These are specified as part of the explanations that follow the definition [Sections 2.2–2.5].

(iii) *Introduction by a definition of the explicatum and determination of its uses, on the basis of (i) and (ii).* – The explicatum is "serial verb construction" (no capitals!) as defined in (H 11) (the abbreviation "SVC" continues to be allowed). The uses of the explicatum are specified further in [Sections 2.2–2.5].

(iv) *Checking (iii) for its relation to (ii) and evaluating (iii) with respect to precision, fruitfulness, and, possibly, simplicity.* – Some checking is done in the explanations of the definition [Sections 2.2–2.5], but the major argument for the *fruitfulness* of the definition is a list of ten 'generalizations' in [Section 4], introduced as follows [2016: 307]:

> I will now list and discuss some generalizations about SCVs as defined in Section 2. These are claimed to hold across all languages with SVCs and all SVCs in them, so they are really intended as hypothesized universals.

Both the generalizations and the explanations concerning (H 11) and (H 12) make use of fragments of an informal theory, the explicatum theory (Section 3.4, above), expanded by including the definition.

5.3 The explicatum theory

Haspelmath appears to be unaware of the explicative nature of his definition, consequently, there is no statement in [2016] to the effect that he is assuming a theory in defining "serial verb construction", adding his definition to this theory and its language (a certain fragment of technical English).

The theory used is informal but is still a theory; it is part of a version of Construction Grammar, as appears from the very first explanation on (H 12), an explanation concerning the term "construction" used in the definition (H 11) [2016: 293]:

> To fall within my definition, a serial verb construction must be a productive schematic CONSTRUCTION such that the meaning of a concrete construct can be determined on the basis of the meanings of its parts and the construction meaning.

Such statements are sufficient to identify the type of theory we are dealing with – the explicatum theory is an (informal, partial) *theory of language* that is part of a version of Construction Grammar: constructs 'belong to' languages, and clarifying the nature of constructions, constructs and the relation between them cannot be achieved independently of a theory dealing with languages in general, regardless of how constructions are conceived, as belonging or not belonging themselves to languages.

The nature of the explicatum theory as a theory of language also appears from the 'generalizations' on serial verb constructions (the term understood as in (H 11)) – the generalizations are "intended as hypothesized universals" (see the quote in Section 5.2, above); for example [2016: 307]:

> Generalization 1
> In all SVCs, the verbs have the same tense value.

On a customary understanding of "universal", universals are properties shared by all languages. Clearly, there is only one natural place for statements on universals – even more so when these are "hypothesized" – and that is as part of a theory of language: a theory whose domain is the set of all languages.

In summary, Haspelmath's definition of "serial verb construction" turns out to be an addition to a *general theory of language* that is part of a version of Construction Grammar. This is not acknowledged by Haspelmath.

I next turn to the definition of "serial verb construction" from the point of view not of definition *type* but of definition *form*, starting again by providing background from the theory of definitions.

6. Background: Definition form

6.1 Informal and formal definitions

Informal definitions are distinguished from formal ones by a classification that is independent of definition type.

An ***informal definition*** is formulated in a variety of some natural language: a variety, mostly written, that is characterized by some technical vocabulary but uses the normal syntax of the language, possibly with some minor adjustments.

Formal definitions *either* are ***semi-formal***: are formulated in a written language variety that is characterized by its technical vocabulary but also uses a regimented syntax, a syntax that allows us to render explicit the logical properties of sentences; *or else*, are ***truly formal***: use a formal language of logic for logical explicitness and adopt a specific format. In either case, a proof system and, mostly, a semantic system for the language must be available in some form.

There is nothing wrong *per se* with using informal definitions; there are even standard forms for them. Informal definitions have an inherent problem, though: they are not explicit with respect to logical properties, and this may lead to misconceptions when they are applied in a theoretical context, and to misuse in a practical one. Stipulative definitions are especially sensitive in this respect, which will prove important in relation to Haspelmath's definition of "serial verb construction", a definition that is both informal and stipulative.

6.2 Requirements on stipulative definitions

Such definitions, even informal ones, must satisfy two major requirements (Gupta 2015: 11):

> First, a stipulative definition should not enable us to establish essentially new claims – call this the *Conservativeness* criterion. We should not be able to establish, by means of a mere stipulation, new things about, for example, the moon.
>
> Second, the definition should fix the use of the defined expression X – call this the *Use* criterion.

Making the Use criterion more precise is hard for informal definitions; this is one reason for translating them into more strictly regulated formal languages (Gupta 2015: 11–12):

> Let us confine ourselves to ground languages that possess a clearly determined logical structure (e.g., a first-order language) and that contain no occurrences of the defined term X. And let us confine ourselves to definitions that place no restrictions on legitimate occurrences of X. The Use criterion now dictates then that the definition should fix the use of all expressions in the expanded language in which X occurs.
>
> A variant formulation of the Use criterion is this: the definition must fix the meaning of the definiendum. The new formulation is less determinate and [12] more contentious, for it relies on "meaning", an ambiguous and theoretically contentious notion.

(The ground language is the language to which the definition is to be added, the expanded language is the ground language plus the definition.)

On a traditional account of stipulative definitions, a strong version of the Use criterion is employed, the *Eliminability* criterion (Gupta 2015: 12):

> the definition must reduce each formula containing the defined term to a formula in the ground language, i.e., one free of the defined term.

If the ground language has a "precise proof system of the familiar sort", syntactic formulations can be given for both the Conservativeness criterion and the Eliminability criterion; if a semantics is also available for the language, semantic formulations are possible (for details, see Gupta 2015: Section 2.3).

Obviously, informal stipulative definitions, such as Haspelmath's definition of "serial verb construction", can be properly evaluated with respect to these basic criteria only indirectly, by matching them with formal versions; in particular, matching them with 'definitions in normal form' (Gupta 2015: 14):

> Since definitions in normal form meet the demands of Conservativeness and Eliminability, the traditional account implies that we lose nothing essential if we require definitions to be in normal form.

'Definitions in normal form' correspond to one type of *proper definitions* in the sense of Suppes (1957: Ch. 8). To this day, this has remained a classic text on the theory of definitions; I am going to follow it, rather than Gupta (2015: Section 2.4), because it makes for easier formulations in the present context. (The two accounts are compatible, and I will not comment here on the differences or on what motivates them.)

6.3 Proper definitions (1): Equivalences

Proper definitions in the sense of Suppes (1957: Ch. 8) are definitions *in a theory*. This is more restrictive than Gupta's account, where only a 'ground language' is presupposed. A theory becomes necessary as soon as we consider an application context for the ground language.

Proper definitions are formulas of the language of the theory that are either *equivalences* (corresponding to normal-form definitions in Gupta 2015: Section 2.4) or *identities*.

The terms that can be defined are *constants*: unanalysable symbols (which, in a semi-formal theory, may be of arbitrary linguistic complexity but are still treated as unanalysable), symbols that are either *individual constants* ('names'), *n-place predicates*, or *n-place function terms* ($n \geq 1$); when interpreted, they denote individuals, n-place relations (sets of ordered n-tuples), or n-place functions construed as (n +1)-place relations of a certain kind (see Section 2.3).

Definitions of individual constants are not relevant in relation to Haspelmath's definition of "serial verb construction" and need not be characterized here.

Predicate definitions that are *equivalences* will prove directly important, though. They have the form in (6.1) (compare Suppes 1957: 156):

(6.1) $P(v_1, ..., v_n) \leftrightarrow S$; informally: "$(v_1, ..., v_n)$ is P if and only if S"

P in (6.1) is an *n-place predicate* newly introduced into the given theory by its definition; $v_1, ..., v_n$ are distinct variables; S is a sentential formula with free variables whose free variables are (exactly or at most) $v_1, ..., v_n$, and the only non-logical constants in S are primitive symbols or previously defined symbols of the theory.

The part of (6.1) left of the equivalence sign is called the *definiendum* of the definition, P is *the defined term* (note the difference between definiendum and defined term); the right-hand side is the *definiens*.

6.4 Proper definitions (2): Identities

Suppes (1957: 158) characterizes definitions of function symbols that, again, are equivalences. More important for us is an alternative (Suppes 1957: Section 8.6), definitions of function symbols that are identities of the following form:

(6.2) $f(v_1, ..., v_n) = t$; informally: "f of $(v_1, ..., v_n)$ is identical to t" f is an *n-place function symbol* newly introduced into the theory by the definition, and the following conditions are satisfied: $v_1, \ldots, v_n$ are distinct variables, and t is a *term* (not: a sentential formula) with free variables whose free variables are $v_1, \ldots, v_n$, and the only non-logical constants in t are primitive symbols or previously defined symbols of the theory. The terminology of *definiendum, defined term*, and *definiens* applies in the same way as before.

Given a language that contains *lambda expressions* (Section 2.2, above), definitions as in (6.2) could be further simplified to identities of the form "f = t", where the definiendum coincides with the defined term and t is a closed term (containing no free variables) introduced by a lambda operator. Actually, given lambda expressions, all proper definitions can be re-formulated as identities where the definiendum is identical to the defined term and the definiens t is a term that is a closed lambda expression (as already explained in Carnap (1960: Sections 21e, 33c, 33d)).

We are in a position now to consider Haspelmath's definition of "serial verb construction" for its logical form.

7. The definition of "serial verb construction": Logical form (1)

7.1 Introduction

For ease of reference, the quotes from [2016: 296] are repeated here as follows, with a new numbering – (7.1) = (H 11) and (7.2) = (H 12):

(7.1) Serial verb construction: a definition
A serial verb construction is a monoclausal construction consisting of multiple independent verbs with no element linking them and with no predicate-argument relation between the verbs.

(7.2) Key components of the definition
a. construction
b. monoclausal
c. independent verbs
d. no linking element
e. no predicate-argument relation between the verbs

Modification
"Construction" in (7.2) is explained in [2016: 296]: "[…] a serial verb construction must be a productive schematic CONSTRUCTION […]", for which there are "concrete constructs". At the same time, "independent verb" in (7.2) is defined in [2016: 303] so as to refer to *forms*. This is inconsistent: schematic constructions cannot consist of forms, as required in definition (7.1), while this is certainly true of their *concrete constructs*; these are forms in individual languages. Therefore, the defining part of (7.1) will be reformulated to read:

(7.3)   a monoclausal construction whose constructs consist of multiple independent verbs with no element linking them and with no predicate-argument relation between the verbs.

(For a definition of "construct", see (10.4), below.) This is the version on which I will proceed.

Terminology
We still need a way of relating informal definitions to formal ones. By a *logical form of an informal definition* I will understand the logical form of any definition that belongs to a formal language of logic and may count as a translation of the informal definition; analogously, for *parts* of an informal definition; *the logical status of the defined term* in the informal definition will be considered to be the same as the logical status of the defined term in the translation of the definition. – What, then, is a logical form of (7.1), given (7.2) and taking the modification into account?

7.2   Formal rendering of the definition: The translation D1

As the language of logic presupposed for translations of informal definitions, I am using Carnap's Language B as explained above, in Sections 2.1 to 2.4, employing readings of the translations as semi-formal English-language versions of the definitions. Translations of informal definitions will not be formulated explicitly; instead, the translations will be characterized in general terms only or indirectly by their semi-formal readings, to the extent that a characterization is necessary.

The translation closest to (7.1) is a *proper definition* D1 that is *an equivalence* as characterized in (6.1), defining an n-place predicate:

(6.1) $P(v_1, ..., v_n) \leftrightarrow S$

Following traditional informal translation rules for translating natural-language sentences into predicate-logic expressions, an equivalence defining an n-place predicate is suggested by the syntactic structure of (7.1) and (7.3) ("*a* serial verb construction is", not "serial verb construction is", which would require an identity formula; similarly, "*a* monoclausal construction"). – D1 will be specified only to the extent that this is required for the discussion; it will not be formulated in full.

Assuming that **D1** is an expression of form (6.1), an initial characterization of its form may be given as follows:

(7.4)   serial verb construction $(v_1, ..., v_n) \leftrightarrow S^*$,

where "serial verb construction" (equivalently, "SVC") is *the defined term* of D1; $v_1, ..., v_n$ are appropriate variables, whose number and types remain to be established; "serial verb construction ($v_1, \ldots, v_n$)" corresponds to *the definiendum*; and S*, *the definiens* of **D1**, is a formal rendering of (7.3).

So far, **D1** appears unproblematic as a translation of the informal definition (7.1). We must still consider, though, the variables $v_1, \ldots, v_n$ and the definiens S*.

7.3 "serial verb construction": Logical status as a 1-place predicate

By a basic requirement on proper definitions (Section 6.3, above), the variables $v_1, \ldots, v_n$ in (7.4) must be such that each variable that is free in the definiens S* is one of them; actually, we may assume here that the variables $v_1, \ldots, v_n$ are exactly the ones that are free in S*. What, then, are these variables?

The definiens S* of **D1** is to be a sentential formula that is a translation of (7.3), the corrected version of the defining part in (7.1), repeated here as:

(7.5) a monoclausal construction whose constructs consist of multiple independent verbs with no element linking them and with no predicate-argument relation between the verbs

As a *first proposal*, the following paraphrase of (7.5) may be suggested as a semi-formal reading of the definiens S* of **D1**:

(7.6) x is a construction, and *any* construct of x is monoclausal and consists of multiple independent verbs, and for *any* number of these verbs the following is true: it is not the case that *there is* an element linking them and it is not the case that *there is* a predicate-argument relation between them.

"x" stands for entities of the type of 'productive schematic constructions' as they are assumed in the presupposed Construction Grammar version; the nature of entities x may vary with the version. – For the definiens S* of **D1**, paraphrase (7.6) appears to imply:

(7.7) a. there is at least one variable v_1, $v_1 =$ "x", that is free at the two places in the definiens of **D1** that correspond to the two "x" occurrences in the semi-formal version (7.6), and

b. there is no other variable that is free in the definiens of **D1**: any other variable occurring in the definiens will be bound either by universal quantifiers that render "any" in (7.6) or by existential quantifiers that render "there is".

Following (7.7), "serial verb construction" as defined in **D1** would be a *one-place predicate*, which would therefore also be the logical status of "serial verb construction" as informally defined in (7.1). There is, however, a major problem with this: (7.6) as a reading of S* is partly inadequate.

8. The definition of "serial verb construction": Logical form (2)

8.1 The same-language requirement: The problem of the hidden variable

Construing **D1** as a definition of a predicate that is *one*-place turns out to be untenable, due to what may be called *the problem of the hidden variable*: in addition to v_1 = "x", we need a variable v_2 in the definiens S* of **D1** that represents entities such as languages, language varieties, idiolects, or their systems, and this variable must be free in the definiens to avoid serious problems.

Put differently, (7.7b) is wrong, and "serial verb construction" cannot have the logical status of a predicate that is *one*-place, which is obscured by the informality of Haspelmath's definition.

The need for *another variable* in S* as the definiens of **D1** appears as follows. Consider the informal formulation in (7.5), with its paraphrase in (7.6). For the paraphrase to make sense, the verbs, the linking elements, and the predicate-argument relations must satisfy *the same-language requirement*: they must all belong, in some sense, to the same language.

According to Haspelmath's informal definition (7.1), the construction mentioned in its definiens must actually *consist* of the verbs mentioned there, which is sufficient to demonstrate that we are meant to be dealing with a 'productive schematic construction' *in a language*. On any sensible conception, a construction *in a language* must belong to the same language as its constructs; therefore, the same-language requirement for (7.6) must also include the construction x. – How, then, are we to account for the same-language requirement?

8.2 Dealing with the requirement

It may be suggested that we simply use a predicate such as "belongs to the same language as", not specifying the language to which the linguistic entities in the definiens are to belong. This, however, will not work; for example, it does not yet exclude in (7.6) the case of two verbs 1 and 2 belonging to the same language and two verbs 3 and 4 belonging to the same language but the two languages being different. What we need, then, is *a variable "L"* for languages (or language varieties) to specify a single language to which all linguistic entities in (7.6) belong.

The need is for a language-related variable independently of the logical type to which it may belong – individual, predicate, or function variable: the type, to be specified only when Haspelmath's definition is formally reconstructed as part of a theory (not *our* task here), is immaterial to our argument. Similarly, argumentation in the present essay would be strictly analogous if "L" were to be understood as a variable for *systems* of languages or language varieties, or for idiolects or idiolect systems. Haspelmath appears to prefer languages, and I will stay with this.

Note that we are using "L" only for languages and their varieties. If "L" were to be used for '*entities such as* languages and their varieties', "L is a language or language variety" would have to be added in formulations using "L".

Given "L", two ways of formulating the same-language requirement may be proposed (using "y" for entities such as constructs of constructions):

i. We introduce a term such as "has" and then reformulate (7.6) on the pattern of "x is a construction and L has x", "y is monoclausal and L has y", etc.
ii. We simply introduce two-place predicates on the pattern of "x is a construction in L", "y is monoclausal in L", etc.

A "has"-relation as in (i) is envisaged in [2018: 89] for relating linguistic entities to individual languages. In Lieb (2018: Sections 6.4 and 6.5), its converse – "y belongs to L" – is discussed for items y, and is compared with the two-place predicate solution in (ii); it was concluded that the two-place predicate solution is superior to the "belongs" solution. Therefore, (ii) will be adopted here, yielding the following reformulation of (7.6):

(8.1) x is a construction in L, and *any* construct of x in L is monoclausal in L and consists of multiple independent verbs of L, and for *any* number of these verbs the following is true: it is not the case that *there is* an element of L linking them and it is not the case that *there is* a predicate-argument relation of L between them.

The following argument is, however, independent of having chosen (ii) rather than (i): both require a variable for languages.

Formulation (8.1) might qualify as a reading of the definiens S* of the definition D1 of "serial verb construction". However, for this the variable "L" must be *free*, not bound, in the definiens. I argue as follows for "L" being free.

8.3 Status of the hidden variable: Bound or free?

Let us see if the variable can be bound. There appear to be just two possibilities.

First, we may propose to bind "L" in (8.1) by means of an existential quantifier, assuming a logical form as in:

(8.2) *for some L:* [continued as in (8.1)]

As a reading of the definiens of **D1**, this is inadequate in view of Haspelmath's informal definition (7.1), for the following reason. The concept of serial verb construction is to be a comparative concept, and "Comparative concepts [concept terms, H.L.] must be defined in such a way that the definition is equally applicable to all languages" [2016: 299]. This requirement certainly implies that the definiens of any such definition must specify a condition on arbitrary languages. The definiens of Haspelmath's informal definition in (7.1) and the formal and semi-formal reconstructions of the definiens must therefore be understood in this way. This is excluded, though, for (8.2): due to the binding of the variable "L" for languages by an *existential* quantifier, (8.2) no longer specifies a condition on *arbitrary* languages; hence, (8.2) does not qualify as a reading of the definiens of **D1**, and does not qualify as a reconstruction of the definiens of Haspelmath's informal definition.

In summary, "L" must not be bound by an existential quantifier in the definiens of **D1** if we wish to keep to Haspelmath's conditions on comparative concepts. (There are problems with "equally applicable to all languages", but their solution, too, excludes existential quantification as in (8.2); see Section 13, below.)

Second, we may propose to use a universal quantifier "for all L" instead of the existential quantifier, obtaining:

(8.3)   *for all L:* [continued as in (8.1)]

This, however, is too strong: if "serial verb construction" is defined in this way, then the definition implies that any serial verb construction x is a construction in every language: "For all x, if x is a serial verb construction, then for all L, x is a construction in L" (compare (8.3) as completed by (8.1)). This is clearly unacceptable. Once again, "L" must remain free in the definiens of definition **D1**. – It now follows that (8.1) qualifies as a reading of S*: qualifies as a reading of the definiens of **D1**.

In summary, Haspelmath's informal definition of "serial verb construction" does not properly account for the same-language requirement, which must be met by introducing a free variable for languages in the definiens of a formal definition that translates Haspelmath's informal one. The need for such a variable is hidden by the informality of Haspelmath's definition, and appears not to be recognized.

8.4   "serial verb construction": Logical status as a 2-place predicate

There are two variables now, v_1 = "x" and v_2 = "L", that are free in (8.1) and free in the definiens S* of **D1** of which (8.1) is to be a reading. Obviously, no other free variables are needed in S*. It is a **basic requirement** on proper definitions that all free variables in the definiens of a proper definition must appear free in the definiendum (Section 6.3, above). Therefore, the **definiendum of D1** turns out now to have the form "serial verb construction (x, L)", not the form "serial verb construction (x)".

This means that – contrary to what is suggested by Haspelmath's informal definition – the term "serial verb construction" as defined by him should have the logical status of a **2-place predicate**, denoting the set of pairs ⟨x, L⟩ that satisfy (8.1), where L is a language or language variety and x is of the type of 'constructions'. ("x" may have to be replaced by n distinct variables, accounting for a more complex structure of 'constructions'; "serial verb construction" would then be an (n+1)-place predicate. This is irrelevant, though, for our argument.)

Definition D1 may now be assumed to have a semi-formal reading as follows:

(8.4) x is a *serial verb construction* in L if and only if x is a construction in L and for any y, if y is a construct for x in L, then y is monoclausal in L and y consists of multiple independent verbs of L and for any number of these verbs the following is true: it is not the case that there is an element of L linking them and it is not the case that there is a predicate-argument relation of L between them.

This is itself a semi-formal definition, representing a correction and partial explication of Haspelmath's informal version (7.1), whose place it can take – as it will in our discussion.

Note that (8.4) can be trivially used to introduce an additional *one-place* predicate:

(8.5) x is a *serial verb construction'* iff for some L, x is a serial verb construction in L.

Such a definition of a one-place predicate was rejected in our discussion of (8.2), not on any logical grounds but for not corresponding closely enough to requirements made by Haspelmath; anyway, the one-place predicate in (8.5) presupposes the two-place predicate in (8.4).

8.5 An alternative: "serial verb construction" as a one-place function-term

There is an alternative to the construction of "serial verb construction" as a two-place predicate, an alternative that also retains "L" as a free variable: we might have chosen a *proper definition D2* that is an identity of the form:

(6.2) $f(v_1, ..., v_n) = t$

See Section 6.4, above, for details on such identities. In definition D2, $v_1 = v_n = $ "L", and term t would be a lambda expression of the form (λx) S* whose only free variable is "L": an expression whose intension is the property of being an x that satisfies S*, where S* is semi-formally read as in (8.1).

The expression "serial verb construction" (corresponding to "f" in (6.2)) is now construed as a *one-place function-term*, as a term that denotes a function (in the set theoretic sense, a 'function extension' in the sense of Carnap (1960: Section 25a)); this function assigns to any L the *set* – possibly empty – *of all x* such that x and L satisfy (8.1) or, more formally, satisfy S*, understood as before.

This is farther removed from the way Haspelmath's definition is formulated, and will not be followed through here. The two definitions of "serial verb construction" introduce two different but closely related concepts that are equivalent as far as practical consequences go. Only the first concept will be considered.

8.6 A basic inconsistency

It has turned out now that there is just a single way of satisfying the same-language requirement for the linguistic entities mentioned in the definiens of Haspelmath's definition and its semi-formal and formal reconstructions: introducing a free variable for languages in the reconstructions of the definiens, preferably by providing all relevant expressions in the reconstructions with a place for such a variable; and understanding the definiens of the informal definition accordingly.

There is an important consequence: since the variable for languages must be free in the reconstructions of the definiens, it must reappear in the definiendum, by a basic condition on proper definitions, and the defined term must have a place for such a variable.

However, in [2016] Haspelmath consistently uses the defined term, "serial verb construction", as a term denoting a set of constructions rather than a set of construction/language pairs, that is, uses the term without assuming for it a place for a variable that represents a variable.

This creates a basic inconsistency between (i) the definiens of Haspelmath's definition, understood on the basis of the reconstructions, where the defined term is a two-place predicate providing a place for languages, and (ii) the logical status of the defined term as implicitly assumed by Haspelmath, as a one-place predicate not providing for such a place.

Haspelmath's definition of "serial verb construction" is meant as a model for definitions of comparative-concept terms. It may be expected, then, that the inconsistency carries over to all definitions envisaged by Haspelmath for comparative-concept terms. And indeed it does, requiring a revision of Haspelmath's framework (see Section 11.2, below).

The inconsistency has consequences: as it will appear from Part C, the inconsistency in its general form is one reason for Haspelmath ending up with an artificial break between comparative concepts and descriptive categories, and between general linguistics and descriptive linguistics. – We next consider the question of what kind of entity the *concept* of serial verb construction might be, turning, once again, to the definition.

9. The concept of serial verb construction

9.1 Basis for the concept

A distinction was drawn in Section 4.3 between the concept term, the concept, and the extension of the concept, identical to the extension of the concept term. The concept – what is it? This is a question that remains to be answered;

Chapter 5. Theories of language, language comparison, and grammatical description **167**

answering it we go beyond Haspelmath, who simply uses "concept" without further explanations.

Consider, once again, the formal definition **D1** of the term "serial verb construction" as partially characterized in Section 8.4: the definiendum is "serial verb construction (x, L)", and the definiens is the sentential formula S* that has "x" and "L" as its free variables. **D1** has (8.4) as a semi-formal reading, with the part following "if and only if" as a semi-formal reading of S*.

Let us now *close the definiens* S* by a lambda-operator not with "x", as in Section 8.5, but with "x" and "L", which binds the two free variables, using lambda notation as available in our presupposed language of logic, Carnap's Language B in an intensional version (Section 2.4, above):

(9.1)   (λxL) S*

Whereas S* is a sentential formula, (9.1) is a closed predicate expression (not containing any free variables), to be read as: "the two-place property of any ⟨x, L⟩ such that S*" (compare Section 2.2, above).

In our presupposed language of logic, a closed n-place predicate expression, n > 0, has an *intension*, construed as an n-place property, and an *extension*, which is the set of entities (n-tuples, for n > 1) in the 'actual world' that have the n-place property; the expression **designates** its intension and **denotes** its extension. The property that is the intension of the term in (9.1), and is its interpretation, is semi-formally given in (9.2), its extension is given in (9.3):

(9.2)   the two-place property of any ⟨x, L⟩ such that [continued as in (8.4), following "if and only if"]

(9.3)   the set of ordered pairs ⟨x, L⟩ such that [continued as before]

It is property (9.2) not the set in (9.3) that will be used as a basis for construing the concept of serial verb construction as a *concept*.

9.2   Two ways of construing the concept

There are two different ways in which property (9.2) can be used for the concept of serial verb construction – either the concept itself is equated with property (9.2), or else the intension of the concept is equated with this property:

(9.4)   a.   The concept of serial verb construction = (λxL) S*.
         b.   The intension of the concept of serial verb construction = (λxL) S*.

"Intension" in (b) has been used not in relation to terms but to concepts, presupposing a conception by which concepts, too, have an intension. The two possibilities in (9.4) spell out as follows.

First construction of the concept
A complete reading for (9.4a) is this:

(9.5) The concept of serial verb construction = the two-place property of any ⟨x, L⟩ such that: x is a construction in L and for any y, if y is a construct for x in L, then y is monoclausal in L and y consists of multiple independent verbs of L and for any number of these verbs the following is true: it is not the case that there is an element of L linking them and it is not the case that there is a predicate-argument relation of L between them.

On this conception, the concept of serial verb construction is a non-mental entity, in agreement with Carnap's understanding of "concept" – also adopted for Language B – as "a common designation for properties, relations, and similar entities (including individual concepts [...] and functions, but not propositions)" (Carnap (1956: 21), quoted more fully in Section 3.3).

Second construction of the concept
A complete reading for (9.4b) is this:

(9.6) The intension of the concept of serial verb construction = the two-place property of any ⟨x, L⟩ such that: [continued as in (9.5)].

On this construction, the *concept* of serial verb construction may still be a mental entity – a concept may be 'mental' even if its *intension* is not.

9.3 Comparison

There is an **advantage of the first construction of the concept**: the concept of serial verb construction introduced by the definition is what the concept term *designates* – is an intension or meaning of the concept term. This appears more clearly once definition D1, an equivalence, is replaced by an equivalent identity (see above, Section 6.4):

(9.7) D1'. serial verb construction = (λxL) S*.

For a reading of "(λxL) S*", see the part of (9.5) following the identity sign.

On the other hand, there is an **advantage of the second construction of the concept**: it does allow for a conception by which the concept of serial verb construction introduced by the definition is a *mental* entity, in some sense, which may be more in line with Haspelmath's use of the term "concept".

Note that we have been using "intension" twice: for the intension of a concept *term* in Section 9.1 – 'intension$_1$' – and the intension of a *concept* in (9.6) – 'intension$_2$'. If (9.6) is adopted, intension$_2$, being identical to intension$_1$, is non-mental while the concept itself may still be mental.

The question of concepts as mental entities has been discussed in the past few decades mainly under the heading of 'concepts as mental representations'

(Margolis and Laurence 2014: Section 1.1), ill-fitting a more traditional account that starts from conceptions and perceptions as mental states or mental events, which is more in line with recent approaches to the study of the human brain. Lieb (1983: Ch. 13) is an exception from the general trend, presenting a more precise version of the traditional account, a version that adopts 'the classical theory' for the structure of concepts while offering solutions to the problems of the classical theory (Margolis and Laurence 2014: Section 2) and, in particular, reconstructing 'prototype theories' in a 'classical' way (see above, Section 2.5).

The theory of concepts outlined in Lieb (1983: Ch. 13) could be used, with a few modifications, to clarify the sense in which the concept of serial verb construction – and concepts in general – can be mental while concept intensions are not.

9.4 Adopting the first construction of the concept

On both constructions of the concept of serial verb construction, the concept term "serial verb construction" has the same extension: the set of all pairs ⟨x′, L′⟩ such that ⟨x′, L′⟩ has the two-place property of any ⟨x, L⟩ such that … [continued as in (9.5), after "such that"]. The extension is not the set of serial verb constructions x′ but is *the set of pairs* ⟨x′, L′⟩ where, informally, x′ is a serial verb construction in L′ (L′ being a language or language variety).

Adopting a view of concepts such as the one in Lieb (1983), any 'non-mental' concept uniquely determines a 'mental' concept, and conversely, and the first construction of the concept is simpler than the second. Therefore, I am going to stay here with the simpler, Carnapian view of concepts; these are conceived as n-place properties as assumed in Orilia and Swoyer (2017). Using the framework for concepts in Lieb (1983: Ch. 13), a more complex, 'mental' conception is automatically covered.

Given this view of the concept of serial verb construction, how does the concept *term* apply? (For 'term application' as different from 'concept applicability' and for Haspelmath's 'universal applicability' of comparative concepts, see Section 13, below.)

10. Applying the concept term

10.1 Universality statements

Such statements, using "serial verb construction", are envisaged in [2016: Section 4] and are exemplified, among others, by:

> **Generalization 1**
> In all SVCs, the verbs have the same tense value.

The generalization is intended as a 'hypothesized universal' [2016: 307]. Accounting for the logical status of "serial verb construction" in its corrected form, this universality statement can be rendered now semi-formally as:

(10.1)   For all L and x, if x is a serial verb construction in L, then for any construct y of x in L it is true that the verbs of L in y have the same tense value in L.

Sentence (10.1) assigns to any (language or language variety) L *the one-place property of being an* L′ such that *for all x*, if x is a serial verb construction in L′, then for any construct y of x in L′ it is true that the verbs of L′ in y have the same tense value in L′. This property is a putative *language universal*, understood in a traditional sense as a general property of languages.

Note that (10.1) does not imply that for every L, *there are* serial verb constructions x in L. Nor is (10.1) restricted to languages L that actually *have* serial verb constructions, a restriction that is implicit in most of the 'generalizations' formulated in [2010]; on strictly logical grounds, (10.1) also covers the case of any L such that "x is a serial verb construction in L" is false for every x.

Equivalently, (10.1) assigns to any x (entity of the type of 'constructions') *the one-place property of being an x′* such that *for all L*, if x′ is a serial verb construction in L, then for any construct y of x′ in L it is true that the verbs of L in y have the same tense value in L. This is no property of languages, therefore, no language universal.

10.2   Comparative statements

Sentence (10.1) is not now a comparative statement – there is no comparison. Comparative statements may now have – among others – a form as in the following example, semi-formal again:

(10.2)   For all x_1 and x_2: if x_1 is a serial verb construction in Edo and x_2 is a serial verb construction in Lao, then for any construct y_1 of x_1 in Edo and any construct y_2 of x_2 in Lao it is true that y_1 is agent-sharing in Edo and y_2 is patient-sharing in Lao.

(Based on [2016: (2a) and (9b)].) The statement may or may not be true; what counts here, is its form. Two language names are used, "Edo" and "Lao", plus four predicates: "serial verb construction", on its corrected definition; "construct"; and "agent-sharing" and "patient-sharing", to be understood as explained by Haspelmath.

By (10.2), *serial verb constructions in two different languages are being compared* for their relationship to agent-sharing and patient-sharing constructs. A statement on *language types* could easily be based on this – we are in comparative linguistics here, more specifically, in language typology.

10.3 Simple descriptive statements

Two statements on Edo and Lao, respectively, are directly obtained from (10.2):

(10.3) a. For all x_1: if x_1 is a serial verb construction in Edo, then for any construct y_1 of x_1 in Edo it is true that y_1 is agent-sharing in Edo.
   b. For all x_2: if x_2 is a serial verb construction in Lao, then for any construct y_2 of x_2 in Edo it is true that y_2 is patient-sharing in Lao.

These are *descriptive statements on individual languages* using the same comparative-concept term "serial verb construction" that was defined in the presupposed theory of language and was then used for the universality and comparative statements in (10.1) and (10.2).

It is, however, descriptive statements of a different kind that are of special interest in relation to Haspelmath's conception of 'comparative concepts' vs. 'descriptive categories': statements that directly identify sets of constructs, understood as linguistic forms.

10.4 Identification statements

Let us formulate here the definition for "construct" that so far has been simply assumed to be available in the presupposed theory of language. Using "y" as before, as a variable for linguistic forms, we *define*:

(10.4) y is a *construct* for x in L if and only if x is a construction in L and y satisfies x in L.

(Any version of Construction Grammar must allow for a valid sentence like (10.4), the concept of *satisfaction* being explained in a version-specific way.)

Let us now consider a *descriptive statement* such as the following:

(10.5) For all y: there is an x such that x is a serial verb construction in Lao and y is a construct for x in Lao, if and only if $t^*(y)$,

where "Lao" replaces "L" as used in (10.4); equivalently, employing lambda notation:

(10.6) (λy) (for some x, serial verb construction (x, Lao) and construct (y, x, Lao)) $\equiv t^*$, which may be read as:

(10.7) the one-place property of being a y such that for some x, x is a serial verb construction in Lao and y is a construct for x in Lao, is equivalent to [*has the same extension as*] the property designated by t^*,

where t^* – left unspecified here – is a certain closed one-place predicate expression designating a property of entities y and denoting a corresponding set. Note that "serial verb construction (x, Lao)" is logically equivalent to:

(10.8) serial verb construction (-, Lao) (x),

using the hyphen notation introduced by Carnap (1960: Section 33d); the expression "serial verb construction (-, Lao)" denotes *the set of serial verb constructions of Lao*. This is not yet a 'descriptive category' in a Haspelmathian sense, such categories have to be sets of linguistic items such as word forms, not sets of constructions.

Once t* in (10.5) and (10.6) has been specified – which I am not going to attempt here, not being a specialist on Lao – the two statements may be said to identify the same set of linguistic forms of Lao (compare (10.7)), they are *empirical set-identification statements*. They are neither definitions nor implied by definitions, which would make them logically true, hence, non-empirical. (The discussion of identification statements will be taken up in a more general way in Section 15, below.)

We are now in a position to characterize comparative concepts from a more general point of view, using Part B as a basis for exemplification, and to properly relate comparative concepts to descriptive categories.

C. 'Comparative concepts' vs. 'descriptive categories': Revising the conception

11. Comparative concepts (1): Basics – Revisions One to Four

11.1 First Revision: Ambiguities resolved

In our discussion of the concept of serial verb construction it proved necessary to resolve a threefold ambiguity in Haspelmath's text by clearly distinguishing between (i) the concept term ("serial verb construction"), (ii) the concept (the concept of serial verb construction), (iii) the *extension* of the concept, identical to the *extension* of the concept term: the set of the entities covered by the concept, the set denoted by the concept term. (For details, see Sections 4.2 and 4.3.)

The presupposed language of logic (Sections 2.1 to 2.4, above) allows us to assign an *intension* and an *extension* to any predicate expression or function expression that is closed (does not contain any free variables – this includes but is not restricted to constants): the expression *designates* its intension, which is an n-place property, and *denotes* its extension, the set (possibly empty) of entities in the 'actual world' that have the property that is the intension.

As for definitions and comparative concepts, it is the concept terms not the concepts that are defined (Section 4.3).

The *First Revision* consists in adopting this terminology and the underlying conceptions; both will be presupposed in the discussion of [2010] and [2018] that is to follow.

11.2 Second Revision: Reference to languages made explicit

My analysis in Part B of Haspelmath's informal definition of "serial verb construction" in [2016] has paid special attention to the logical form of the definition and to the logical status of the defined term.

A basic inconsistency was identified: there is just one way of treating the same-language requirement as satisfied in relation to the definiens of Haspelmath's definition; this way requires that the defined term must be assumed with a place for a variable that represents languages, making it a term that denotes a set of construction/language pairs ⟨x, L⟩, not a set of constructions x; satisfying this requirement is not compatible with Haspelmath's use of the defined term (see Section 8.6, above): the hidden variable is not recognized and is not accounted for.

I have checked this result against the definitions of comparative-concept terms formulated or presupposed in [2010] and [2018], and the use of the defined terms. Allowing for a few doubtful cases, the inconsistency carries over to the definitions and to the use of such terms, in agreement with the model character of the definition of "serial verb construction".

Therefore, Haspelmath's framework must be revised at this point: comparative-concept terms must be construed as explicitly including a place for a variable representing languages (as already argued in Lieb (2018: Section 6.6)). This is the *Second Revision*.

Note. The problem of the hidden variable appears to be typical, too, of the grammatical terms used in the well-known Leipzig glossing rules; a place for a variable that represents languages or language varieties should therefore be assumed in interpreting such terms in isolation (outside an actual glossing context). – For the same problem in formal grammar approaches, see Lieb (2018: 97–104).

11.3 Third Revision: The nature of concepts clarified

I do not know of any place where Haspelmath explains what he means by "concept" (nowhere is there a reference to overview articles such as Margolis and Laurence (2014)).

Comparative concepts are to be concepts, which may be 'mental' or 'non-mental'. A mental conception is suggested by Haspelmath's insistence on comparative concepts being "created by comparative linguists", as in [2010: 665], despite a continuation that is somewhat puzzling:

> Comparative concepts are concepts created by comparative linguists for the specific purpose of crosslinguistic comparison. […] They are not psychologically real, and they cannot be right or wrong.

I take it, though, that the continuation is meant to refer to the minds of the speakers, not of the linguists.

It was argued in Section 9, above, that the concept of serial verb construction should be identified with the *intension of the concept term*. The argument can obviously be generalized; hence, comparative concepts will be identified now with the intensions of the comparative-concept terms, that is, with certain properties.

It was also argued in Section 9 that a 'mental' conception of comparative concept terms can be related to a non-mental one by which concepts are properties: the *intension* of a 'mental' concept may be identified with the property that is the intension of the concept term. Moreover, we may assume that a 'mental' concept is determined by its intension, which allows us to stay with concepts as properties even when dealing with 'mental' concepts (for details, see Sections 9.2 and 9.3, above).

The ***Third Revision*** consists in adopting a non-mental view of comparative concepts as the intensions of concept-terms, a view that is compatible with a mental one.

Because of this revision, an intensional logic must be assumed, explicitly or implicitly, whenever a comparative concept term is used. This also holds when such a term, taken over from a theory of language, is employed in a grammar as explained below in Section 16, where the Tenth Revision is introduced: not only the language in which the theory of language is written, but also the language of the grammar itself can no longer be purely extensional. This may appear as an undesirable consequence, but it can hardly be avoided if comparative concepts are to be assigned a clear ontological status on an approach that is roughly along Haspelmath's lines.

11.4   Fourth Revision: Concept types based on definition types

There is a general emphasis all through [2010] and [2018] that comparative concepts can and should be 'defined'. Therefore, a *first major classification system* (a non-empty set of classifications whose classes may overlap) *for comparative concepts* may be based on properties of the relevant definitions, which, on our account, are definitions not of concepts but of concept *terms*. This is ***the definition-based system of concept types***. The *source* of the system is the set of comparative concepts that correspond to Haspelmath's 'category-like comparative concepts'.

Allowing for comparative concepts whose terms are *not* defined (as we should), we assume a single classification on the source, called "**definitional status**", that contains just two sets: the *definition-based concept type* (consisting of comparative concepts with terms that are defined), and the *primitive concept type* (consisting of comparative concepts with terms that are not defined).

A second classification, called "**stipulation type**", takes the set of definition-based concepts as its base and subdivides it into the *all-stipulative concept type* (consisting of comparative concepts with terms defined by all-stipulative definitions) and the *part-stipulative concept type* (consisting of comparative concepts with terms defined by part-stipulative definitions).

Finally, a third classification, called "**explication type**", on the part-stipulative concept type, subdivides it into the *explicative concept type* (consisting of concepts with terms defined by explicative definitions) and the *non-explicative concept type* (consisting of concepts with terms defined by non-explicative definitions).

By the analyses in Part B, the concept of serial verb construction belongs to the explicative concept type; its term is 'description-derived' (see Section 1.2, above). And indeed, comparative concepts whose terms are 'description-derived' may be assigned to the explicative concept type, typically when the terms belong to the terminology traditionally used in descriptive linguistics [2018: 86]:

> All these terms [listed in a table, H.L.] were originally used for the description of some particular language and were extended to comparative use only later […].

True, the underlying explications may be sketchy for such terms, and frequently hard to tie down to a specific author.

The *Fourth Revision* consists in adopting the definition-based system of concept types.

12. Comparative concepts (2): Intension-based concept types – Revisions Five to Seven

12.1 Fifth Revision: Comparative concepts as properties of construction/language pairs

Assuming the results obtained in Part B, a *first kind of comparative concept* is a *two-place property of pairs* $\langle x, L \rangle$ – a two-place 'intensional relation' between entities x and L – where L is a language or language variety and x is a construction in L. The precise nature of x depends on the Construction Grammar version that is presupposed; the concept is more than two-place if "x" must be replaced by a *tuple* of variables. – *Example*: the concept of serial verb construction as identified in (9.5), above.

As an *alternative*, a comparative concept may be construed as a *one-place function* (two-place property of pairs $\langle L, X \rangle$) whose extension is a function in the set theoretic sense that assigns to each L a set X, possibly empty, of entities x. (See Section 8.5, above.)

On either approach, comparative concepts are easily related to constructions in specific languages (see Sections 8.5 and 8.4, above). The *Fifth Revision* consists in adopting such a conception for a first kind of comparative concepts.

The new conception, in either version, represents a correction of Haspelmath's account of comparative concepts as in [2016], on which such concepts are not explicitly relativized to languages (for details, see Sections 8.1 and 8.2). On the first version, the one to be adopted here, the *extension* of the concept – identical to the *extension* of the concept term – is not a set of constructions; it is a set of construction/language pairs, equivalently, is a two-place relation in the set theoretic sense between constructions and languages or language varieties.

12.2 Sixth Revision: Comparative concepts as properties of item/language pairs

The comparative concepts considered in [2010] are not of the construction/language type. Compare, for example [2010: 670]:

> Comparative part-of-speech concepts such as 'adjective' are necessary for stating the well-known Greenbergian generalizations [...].

This is followed [670] by an informal *definition*, much quoted by now, referring to what would be constructs not constructions in a Construction Grammar framework:

> [...] An adjective is a lexeme that denotes a descriptive property and that can be used to narrow the reference of a noun.

An explanation is added [670]:

> This definition makes use of the comparative concept 'lexeme' and the conceptual-semantic concepts 'property' and 'narrow the reference' [...]

Still, the discussion of the concept of serial verb construction in Part B carries over to this non-construction case, and so do its results. Consider, in this respect, the formulation of a 'generalization' in [2010: 665]:

> In all languages with a dative and an accusative case, the dative case marker is at least as long as the accusative case marker.

Obviously, a variable representing languages is hidden here for "dative case" and "accusative case" in the two prepositions "in" and "with": we are dealing with a dative case and an accusative case *in* or *of* a language. However, "dative case" as a comparative-concept term is then *defined* for 'morphological markers' [2010: 666] without any reference to languages.

We have a second possibility here for comparative concepts: a comparative concept of this kind is a ***two-place property of pairs*** $\langle i, L \rangle$ where L is a language or language variety and i is a linguistic item of L, e.g.:

(12.1)   i is an adjective of L

Chapter 5. Theories of language, language comparison, and grammatical description 177

For comparative concepts of this kind, the precise nature of i depends on what the presupposed theory of language would allow as linguistic items – 'lexemes' at least, in the case of Haspelmath's example.

Again, the *extension* of the concept is not a set of linguistic items but is a set of item/language pairs: is a *relation in the set theoretic sense* between linguistic items on the one hand and languages or language varieties on the other.

The **Sixth Revision** consists in admitting a second type of comparative concepts, properties of item/language pairs.

Here, too, there is the **alternative** of construing a comparative concept as a *one-place function* that allows us, via its extension, to assign to each L a set, possibly empty, of entities i; again, comparative concepts are easily related to items in specific languages on either conception.

Whereas the alternative may but need not be used, there is a case where a comparative concept must actually be construed as a function in the logical sense: the case of concepts that are meant to represent non-semantic 'linguistic functions', such as, in syntax, 'subject' or 'subject in Latin'.

12.3 The problem of dealing with linguistic functions

It appears from [2018: 96] that terms like "subject", when applied to an individual language, are to denote a 'category':

> Subjects can have various kinds of semantic roles [...] but these do not define the category. The category [in Latin and German, H.L] is defined by case and agreement.

The notion of category adopted in [2018: 95] is the *class* notion proposed by Croft (above, Section 2.6). While this may account for the 'subject constituents' in the sentences of a language, say Latin, it does not clearly cover syntactic functions like *the subject function in Latin*, which must not be confused with the set of subject constituents (as it apparently is in the above quote.)

12.4 Seventh Revision: Comparative concepts as properties of language/function pairs

Consider the following statement on Latin and its more formal rendering:

(12.2) a. *nomen* is a (the) subject of *est* in "Nomen est omen." in Latin.
       b. subject (Latin) "Nomen est omen." ≡ {⟨*nomen, est*⟩}.

("≡" means: "is equivalent with", that is, "has the same extension as"; see Section 2.4 above, Terminological Note.) On the more formal account in (b), the term "subject (Latin)" denotes a function in the set theoretic sense, formally, a certain set that involves only items of Latin and happens to be non-empty. This does allow us to consider this set, too, as a language-specific category of Latin, in the sense of "category" adopted in Section 2.6, above.

The conception of subject as a comparative concept can be characterized as follows. The term "subject" *designates* a function that is a two-place property (compare Section 2.3, above) of pairs consisting of a language and a function in the set theoretic sense; for each language there is exactly one such function with which it forms one of the pairs. The functions in the pairs – *denoted* by terms such as "subject (Latin)", "subject-in-Latin", "the subject function in Latin" – take sentences of the given language as arguments – such as "Nomen est omen." for Latin – and assign to each sentence 'the subject relation for the sentence in the language': assign to the sentence a two-place relation between constituents of the sentence, or set (possibly empty) of pairs of such constituents – such as the set {⟨*nomen, est*⟩}.

Somewhat more formally, and extensionally formulated: the term "subject" *denotes* the one-place function (in the set theoretic sense) that assigns to any L the one-place function (in the set-theoretic sense) subject(L) that assigns to any [sentence] s of L the two-place relation (in the set theoretic sense) subject(L)s between any [constituents] f_1 and f_2 [of s] such that: f_1 and f_2 satisfy condition φ with respect to s and L.

φ is left unspecified here; its determination may well make use of meanings, countering Haspelmath's objections to a general notion of subject made in [2018: 96].

It should be noted that for a given language L, the function subject(L) might assign the empty set to every sentence s of L; in this case, 'there are no subjects (subject constituents) in the sentences of L', hence, 'no subjects (subject constituents) in L'.

The two-place property subject is an example of a concept of the language/function type. The **Seventh Revision** consists in adopting such concepts as a ***third type of comparative concepts.***

Terms for concepts of this type can be defined, as might be exemplified by a definition of the term "subject". A definition could have one of two equivalent forms ("L" for languages; "s" for sentences of languages; "f_1" and "f_2" for proper or improper parts of the word sequence of sentences):

(12.3) a.   *subject* (L) = (λs) [(λ$f_1 f_2$) φ(f_1, f_2, s, L)]
        b.   *subject* = (λL) [(λs) [(λ$f_1 f_2$) φ(f_1, f_2, s, L)]]

Definition (a) follows Suppes (1957), see Section 6.4, above; definition (b) makes use of Carnap (1960), see Sections 2.1 to 2.4, above. The expression in brackets in (a) is a *predicate expression* because the operand "φ(f_1, f_2, s, L)" of the operator "(λ$f_1 f_2$)" is a sentential formula. The complete right-hand side of the identity (a)

Chapter 5. Theories of language, language comparison, and grammatical description 179

is, however, a *function expression* because the operand of "(λs)", the expression in brackets, is not a sentential formula any longer but is a predicate expression, an expression of the type system; similarly, for the right-hand side of identity (b). (Compare Section 2.2, above.)

12.5 The intension-based system of concept types

Revisions 5 to 7 amount to adopting a *second major classification system for comparative concepts*, sharing its source with the definition-based system of concept types (Section 11.4, above), whose source is the set of comparative concepts that correspond to Haspelmath's 'category-like comparative concepts'. This is **the intension-based system of concept types**, consisting of a single classification, **the property-type classification**, with three elements: *the construction/language type, the item/language type*, and *the language/function type*, the sets of comparative concepts with a term whose intension is a property of, respectively, construction/language pairs, item/language pairs, and language/function pairs. (Further types may have to be included when clines are considered, see Section 1.3, above.)

13. Comparative concepts (3): 'Universal applicability' – Revision Eight

13.1 'Universal applicability' of comparative concepts: A problematic conception

Haspelmath's most important statement on the 'universal applicability' of comparative concepts is the following quote (2010: 681):

> These comparative concepts [created by comparative linguists, H.L.] must be universally applicable; that is, they must be based exclusively on more primitive universally applicable concepts: universal conceptual-semantic concepts, general formal concepts, and other comparative concepts (or on extralinguistic situations).

The essential condition imposed here on comparative concepts – a necessary condition – is formulated in the part following "that is". A logical analysis of the quote will lead to the result that the condition is unfounded but may be replaced by similar conditions suitable for increasing the degree of generality of comparative concepts while not requiring universality.

13.2 Analysis

Let us consider the quote for its logical structure. There are three preliminaries P1 to P3 to an appropriate formulation and its discussion.

P1. "universally applicable" will be interpreted as "applicable to every language", as it is normally understood in linguistics (Haspelmath: "potentially applicable to any human language" [2010: 681]), whatever the interpretation of "applicable".

P2. "L" will be used as a variable for languages; "e" as a variable for entities in languages (constructions x, items i, and functions in languages); and "C" as a variable for properties of n-tuples, for some n, that consist of entities e and a language L, in some order.

P3. The explanatory part of the quote (following "that is") will be understood as identifying a property ϕ^* of concepts C:

(13.1) ϕ^* = the property of being a concept based exclusively on universal conceptual-semantic concepts, general formal concepts, and other comparative concepts (or on extralinguistic situations).

The *logical structure* of the above quote can now be identified with the following syllogism (consisting of three universal implications, "for every C" to be added in front of (a), in front of (b), and in front of (c)):

(13.2) a. If C is a comparative concept, then C is applicable to every language, and
b. if C is applicable to every language, then C has ϕ^*,
implies:
c. if C is a comparative concept, then C has ϕ^*.

(13.2) in its entirety is *logically true* (it is a case of 'modus barbara'). "Implies" stands for 'material implication'. According to standard propositional logic, a sentence of the form 'p implies q' is true unless p is true and q is false. In particular, such a sentence is true if p is false, regardless of the truth value of q; q may be true but may also be false. Therefore, if p is false, q is **unfounded** given p. In our case, p = (a)-and-(b), and q = (c); (c) may be considered as the ***essential claim*** of the quote. For (a)-and-(b) to be false it is of course sufficient for (a) to be false or for (b) to be false; hence, this is also sufficient for the essential claim to be unfounded. I will argue that it is.

13.3 Interpreting "applicable"

Truth of the major and minor premises (a) and (b) turns out to be doubtful once we ask for a proper interpretation of "applicable".

Nowhere does Haspelmath explain how he would understand "applicable" (or "potentially applicable", see P1, above). Two interpretations can be considered in the present context; neither is available in Haspelmath's unrevised framework, where comparative concepts and their terms are not relativized to languages.

The first interpretation is based on a notion of *applying* that may be used for concept terms not concepts and is a strictly logical notion. It will be explained here only by way of examples (the notion could be made more precise using the presupposed language of logic, see Section 2.4, above).

Consider the following two sentences: "there is an e such that e is an article of English" and "there is no e such that e is an article of Russian". The term "article" occurs here with two different *argument expressions*: "e, English" and "e, Russian", formally: "article (e, English)" and "article (e, Russian)". The argument expressions contain the constant "English" denoting the English language, and the constant "Russian" denoting the Russian language. Because these argument expressions are allowed by the predicate "article", we may say that the predicate (a term) **applies** to both the English language (where there are articles) and to the Russian language (where there are none).

Term application is the basis for the first interpretation of "applicable" when used for concepts. Term application does not imply claims on the existence of any linguistic entities e (understood as above in P2); therefore, this is also true of concept applicability in the first sense (a), as opposed to concept applicability in the second sense (b):

(13.3)   a.   "C is applicable to L" means "there is a term t that designates C and applies to L".

          b.   "C is applicable to L" means "C is *represented in* L" understood as: "there is an n-tuple consisting of linguistic entities e of L and L itself such that C is a property of the n-tuple".

(Interpretation (b) corresponds to proposals made to me by Edith Moravcsik, personal communication.)

Both interpretations of "applicable" are useful for linguistics. To avoid ambiguity, a different term may be chosen for one of them. I will eventually use "***represented in***" instead of "applicable to" in its second sense; this is justified by (13.3b).

13.4   Unfoundedness of the essential claim

We now consider the syllogism (13.2), using one of the interpretations of "applicable".

Assume interpretation (a). On this interpretation of "applicable", *premise (b)* of the syllogism is demonstrably false. Counterexamples to (b) are easily constructed (assuming languages for which there are names); for example, '*him*-word': the property C of being a pair ⟨e, L⟩ such that e is a form of a lexical word of L and e = *him* (applicable to every language, but not having φ*). Therefore, on this interpretation of "applicable", the essential claim (c) is unfounded.

Assume interpretation (b). On this interpretation of "applicable", it is *premise (a)* of the syllogism that is (empirically) false: on a traditional analysis, there is no e such that the concept of *article* (which *must* be a comparative concept, assuming definition (16.1), below, and must be a two-place property) is a property of the pair ⟨e, Russian⟩, equivalently: is a property of e in Russian; similarly for the comparative concept of *serial verb construction* and English (comparative concepts, but not applicable to every language). Again, the essential claim (c) is unfounded.

In summary, the essential claim that every comparative concept has property ϕ* is unfounded when based on claims of universal applicability, whatever the interpretation of "applicable". I have not found any passage in Haspelmath's work to relativize this result. How are we to react?

13.5 Eighth Revision: Rejecting universal applicability, accepting degrees of generality

Haspelmath's essential claim for comparative concepts, which is not supported by the universal applicability of concepts when this is linked to property ϕ*, is still not irrelevant. Its relevance appears from its relation to *concept generality*, understood as follows:

(13.4)   *the generality of C* = the number of languages L such that C is represented in L.

("Represented" used here instead of "applicable" in its second sense.)

Suppose that a certain comparative concept has property ϕ*. This may increase the concept's generality; it may also increase its suitability to function as the meaning of an axiomatic constant in a theory of language. However, maximal generality – equivalent to universal applicability – should not be imposed on comparative concepts as a general requirement, to avoid undue restrictions for assuming such concepts.

The *Eighth Revision* consists in (i) distinguishing term application from concept applicability; (ii) distinguishing two concepts of concept applicability, one based on term application, the other on entity existence in a language; (iii) retaining the term "applicable to" for the first concept and using "represented in" for the second; (iv) introducing a quantitative concept of concept generality; (v) understanding Haspelmath's 'universal applicability' as maximal generality and rejecting it as a general requirement to be satisfied by comparative concepts; (vi) identifying properties that increase the generality of comparative concepts, properties similar to the one postulated by Haspelmath in characterizing 'universal applicability'.

This concludes our revision of Haspelmath's notion of comparative concept. We next turn to his conception of 'descriptive categories'.

14. Descriptive categories (1): The nature of descriptive categories – Revision Nine

14.1 The problem

As explained in Section 2.6, above, Haspelmath adopts a view by which descriptive categories are classes of linguistic items. Such a view may also cover functions in a set theoretic sense, such as syntactic functions (Section 12.4, above). The position taken in [2018] on descriptive categories goes beyond this, though [2018: 91]:

> But what about the descriptive categories that authors of grammars of individual languages set up for their descriptions?
>
> I will argue that language-particular categories are social categories, not natural kinds or observer-made concepts [...]

Social categories are characterized as follows [same page]:

> What they share with natural kinds is that they are pre-established and there is a causal connection between their members and the category.

There is a contradiction between "set up for their descriptions" in the first quote and "pre-established" in the second, with an attempt at resolving it made in [2018: 92–93]:

> Van der Auwera and Sahoo (2015: 2) are right when they observe that not only comparative concepts but also descriptive categories are "made by linguists" but the difference is that linguistic categories must exist for productive language use to be possible, independently of linguists. Different speakers may use different categories, just as different linguists may prefer different categories, but categories of some kind must exist. (In [93] contrast, comparative concepts do not exist in the absence of comparative linguists.)

The quote brings out clearly that – philosophically speaking – we are dealing here with questions of metaphysics ("must exist") that may be answered in different ways. The framework used by Haspelmath for answering them is inconsistent, though.

14.2 Ninth Revision: Adopting a form of weak constructivism throughout

A major topic of discussion in [2018] is the question of how descriptive categories are related to so-called natural kinds. There is an excellent survey article on natural kinds (Bird & Tobin 2018) that is relevant here, characterizing different positions that can be taken on natural kinds, in particular (Bird & Tobin 2018: 3):

> A common view concerning our so-called natural kind classifications is that there are genuinely *natural* ways of classifying things.

This view is called *naturalism* (*weak realism*) by the authors, who go on to list six "often suggested criteria or characteristics of a natural kind classification" [4–5]. *Strong realism* is "the stronger, ontological, claim that the natural divisions between kinds reflect the boundaries between real entities [...]". [9]

A second position is "*conventionalism* (also called *constructivism* or *constructionism*)" [5]. "The chief claim made by all varieties of conventionalism is that facts about the world are in some sense dependent on human beings, their concepts and their activities in society" [7]; and "Weak conventionalism asserts that our actual classifications are not, or are very unlikely to be, natural." [6]

In discussing natural kinds in [2018], Haspelmath takes a *strong realist position*, finding natural kinds in sciences such as chemistry, medicine, and biology but not in linguistics (compare the table [2018: 100]). Linguistic categories are to be 'social categories', on a *weak constructionist conception*, see the last quote in Section 14.1, above.

In linguistics, a view combining features of weak realism and weak constructionism has been worked out over the years in complete detail by Lieb; it is now known as *Modified Realism* (Lieb 2018); similarly, 'Mixed Realism' in Nefdt (2018).

Haspelmath's opposition between categories as natural kinds in the natural sciences and social categories in linguistics, among others, is an exaggeration, given the arguments for constructivism as also applying in the natural sciences; the exaggeration is largely due to taking a naturalist stance when discussing categories in the natural sciences but a constructivist stance when discussing linguistic categories, artificially inflating the differences between categories in the two areas. A more adequate picture would evolve from adopting weak constructivism throughout in a somewhat modified form as discussed in Bird & Tobin (2018: 6–7) with respect to Hacking (1999). Strong versions of the thesis that 'linguistic categories are innate' (still upheld by whom?) would then be automatically rejected.

Note that I have been concerned here exclusively with the adequacy of Haspelmath's conceptions, not of metaphysical views held more generally in linguistics.

The *Ninth Revision* then consists in adopting a modified version of weak constructivism throughout when comparing linguistic and non-linguistic categories, avoiding an implausibly strict opposition.

15. Descriptive categories (2): How not to define category terms

15.1 Background

Talking about "the notion of subject" [2018: 96], Haspelmath remarks:

> From a comparative perspective, it seems best to use the term "subject" as the conjunction of the S argument (the single argument of a verb like 'fall') and the A argument (the agent argument of a verb like 'kill' […]) because, in this way, we can ensure the biggest overlap with the existing literature. However, in particular languages, definitions [sic] of syntactic roles are necessarily rather different. They do not make any reference [sic] to S, A and P but rather to constructions such as case-marking, person indexing and passivization.

Chapter 5. Theories of language, language comparison, and grammatical description **185**

Referring to "the label 'Subject'" in relation to some sentences of English [2018: 96], Haspelmath concludes [2018: 97]:

> that agreement is no longer relevant to the definition of Subject in English [...]. In Icelandic [...] not even case is thought to be relevant for the definition of Subject.
>
> This well-known example nicely illustrates that, in different languages, different criteria are used to identify [*sic*] categories that are rather similar semantically [...]. But since the categories are not defined [*sic*] by their meanings, their nature is different and they are incommensurable.
>
> In such cases of incommensurable definitions [*sic*], it is nonsensical to use the term "subject" as a general term [...]. There is no Subject concept that would work as a descriptive category in diverse languages.

Initial upper case, as in "Subject", is meant to indicate that we are dealing with 'language-particular categories' [2010: 674]. – Similarly, [2018: 109]: "Language-particular categories are defined system-internally, by other language-particular categories [...]."

Obviously, "definition" is used in these quotes ambiguously, and definition is not clearly distinguished from factual identification; also, I would not assume Subject *categories* as sets of constituents (compare Section 12.3, above), as Subject categories are apparently conceived in the first quote; nor would I require that a 'subject concept' must apply non-vacuously in arbitrary languages (Section 12.4, above).

I have been unable to find less ambiguous passages than the ones quoted above in either [2010] or [2018]. Still, what appears to be claimed here, is this:

(15.1) a. The criteria by which the descriptive categories of a language may be identified are specific to that language, in particular, their formulations do not use comparative-concept terms, either directly or indirectly.
 b. Terms for descriptive categories of a language are to be defined, and are to be defined exclusively on the basis of criteria that are as in (a).
 c. Because of (a), definitions according to (b) are, or may be, incommensurable, just as the categories denoted by the defined terms.

Given the ambiguity of "definition" and "define" in Haspelmath's texts, a weaker version of (15.1b) could also be considered:

(15.1b′) Terms for descriptive categories of a language are to be obtained exclusively on the basis of criteria that are as in (a).

(In (15.1c), "the meanings of terms" would then replace "definitions", and "defined" would be dropped.) I will use the stronger version (15.1b) but the following discussion could be adjusted to the weaker one, too.

15.2 The problem of comparability

The *problem* with Haspelmath's position appears in (15.1c): this is highly questionable because it implies that no comparison, or no useful comparison, is possible between categories of different languages. Indeed, according to Haspelmath, the opposite position is a general fallacy whose disproval is a major point of his essay [2018: 84]:

> General category fallacy
> We do not learn anything about particular languages merely by observing that category A in language 1 is similar to category B in language 2 or by putting both into the same general category C [...].

On a stricter formulation, (15.1c) may well be a consequence of (15.1a) and (15.1b). Assume that (a) is accepted. What about (b)?

Obviously, (b) is not implied by (a), that is, we may subscribe to (a) and still not accept (b): condition (b) is a requirement that must be justified independently. There is no such justification, though, in either [2010] or [2018].

While (15.1a) might be acceptable, (15.1b) will turn out to be unacceptable, which removes the basis for (15.1c). *Generally, claims on the 'incommensurability' of category-term definitions or of corresponding categories turn out to depend on an unacceptable requirement that is arbitrarily imposed on category terms in grammars.*

An example will provide a better understanding of what is involved. Since language-specific categories are not clearly specified in either [2010] or [2018], I will choose an example from Lieb (2018), adjusting it to Haspelmath's framework.

15.3 Identification vs. definition: Example

A grammar G of Standard British English might well contain the following sentence:

(15.2) Article of English = the set of lexical words of English whose forms include one of the following: *the, a, sòme, àny, nò.*

(The accent sign on the last three forms is to indicate inherent secondary word stress.)

There are two ways of understanding such a sentence: either as a *factual statement* on a certain category of English, denoted by the expression "Article of English" – understanding the sentence as an *empirical identification sentence*; or else, understanding it as a *definition* of the expression "Article of English".

Suppose that (15.2) is understood as a *factual statement* on the category Article of English. The *identifying criterion* is this: being a lexical word of English that has one of the above forms. This is certainly a criterion specific to English as required in (15.1a). The statement may be false – as it is if *sòme, àny,* or *nò* turn out to be wrongly included. For the sentence to make sense as a factual statement, it must be possible, though, to understand the expression "Article of English" independently of the sentence; this is the only remaining requirement.

Now suppose that (15.2) is taken to be a *definition* of the term "Article of English". This requires construing the term as a *constant* of grammar G, as a term that is logically simple despite being complex from the point of view of English syntax. (It will eventually turn out, in Section 16.2 below, that "Article of English" can indeed be construed as a constant.) The *defining criterion* would be the same as the identifying criterion that was used before: being a lexical word of English that has one of the above forms; this is in conformity to (15.1b).

Given the background as discussed in Section 15.1, a sentence like (15.2) must be understood as a *definition* in Haspelmath's framework, *stipulative* not *descriptive* [2018: 92]:

> Van der Auwera and Sahoo (2015: 2) are right when they observe that not only comparative concepts but also descriptive categories are "made by linguists" [...]

Taking a sentence like (15.2) as a stipulative definition is unacceptable, though.

15.4 Rejection as a definition

There are the following consequences of construing (15.2) as a stipulative definition:

(15.3) a. An empirical statement on a grammatical category of English, which can be false, is turned into a sentence that is non-empirical, is true by definitional fiat.

b. Since the definiendum is an unanalysable constant and the definiens does not involve the comparative concept of article, the category denoted by the defined term "Article of English" cannot – on the basis of the definition – be related to the concept designated by "article", except for a partial similarity between category term and concept term.

c. Since the definiendum is an unanalysable constant and the definiens involves only English (as the language some of whose forms are enumerated), the category denoted by the defined term "Article of English" cannot – on the basis of the definition – be related to categories denoted by analogous terms of grammars of other languages, such as "Article of German", except for a partial similarity between the category terms.

(15.3a) alone is sufficient to exclude an interpretation of (15.2) as a stipulative definition: (15.2) must surely count as a claim newly introduced into grammar G; however: "a stipulative definition should not enable us to establish essentially new claims – call this the Conservativeness criterion" (Gupta 2015: 11; see Section 6.2, above).

In addition, (15.3b) prevents us from establishing a relation between the category Article of English and the comparative concept of article other than, irrelevantly, a purely formal one: the concept term "article" used with an upper-case initial is a part of the category term "Article of English", where it cannot be interpreted separately since it is part of a constant, of a logically simple term.

A relation between the category and the comparative concept that relates the category as a set to the concept as a property and does not involve term form is clearly needed. It cannot be established on the basis of the definition; so it must be established in addition to it. And indeed, Haspelmath uses "match" for such a relation [2018: 104, fn. 19]:

> […] I have used the verbs "correspond to" and "match" for the relation between descriptive categories and comparative concepts rather than "be" or "instantiate".

Unfortunately, there never is an explanation, in either [2010] or [2018], of what is meant by "match" or what the correspondence is to consist in; so this is vacuous.

Finally, consider (15.3c). Again, there is only a formal relationship between the two categories, consisting in having "Article" as a shared part of their names. Nothing follows from this for a relation directly between the categories – not even a 'matching' relation can be established between them: they are artificially *made* 'incommensurable' by the way their names are defined.

In summary, interpreting (15.2) as a stipulative definition must be rejected, we are dealing with a factual statement instead. – This leaves us with the task of making sense of the expression "Article of English" in (15.2).

16. Descriptive categories (3): The proper treatment of category terms – Revision Ten

16.1 Category terms based on comparative concept terms (1): Lambda expressions

Category terms like "Article in English" may be based on comparative-concept terms such as "article": this is the basic idea for making sense of them when they are used in a factual statement like (15.2). For implementation, we make use of lambda expressions. The logical background continues to be an intensional version of Carnap's Language B (see Section 2.4, above, Section 2.2 for lambda expressions), but again, knowledge of this background will not be presupposed; mostly, I will be working with semi-formal readings of formal-language expressions.

A definition of the concept term "article" is given in Lieb (2018: 118); this, too, will not be discussed here for its linguistic adequacy (which I consider as high) or

Chapter 5. Theories of language, language comparison, and grammatical description 189

the precise meanings of the linguistic terms used in its definiens (which could be given); it will be discussed for its form. Adjusted to the present context, the definition may be rendered as:

(16.1) W is an *article* of L if and only if W is a lexical word of L with an empty lexical meaning whose forms may be used in L as the auxiliary parts of noun forms of L.

Replacing "L" by "English" in the definiendum and using a lambda operator, we directly obtain a term that is a closed lambda expression, equivalent to a hyphenated expression (Carnap 1960: Section 33d):

(16.2) (λW) (W is an article of English),

(more formally:) (λW) article (W, English),

(logically equivalent to:) article (-, English),

(with a reading as:) the property of being a W such that W is an article of English.

The lambda expression *designates* the property, which is the intension of the expression, and *denotes* the corresponding set, which is the extension of both the lambda expression and of the property it designates. This set should certainly be admitted as a *category of English*; therefore, the lambda expression in (16.2) is a *category term for English*, based on the comparative-concept term "article".

Suppose that our grammar G of English is formulated in a language with a logical part as required (the logic must be intensional, see Section 11.3, above). Using "(λW) (W is an article of English)" instead of "Article of English", we may then understand (15.2) as in:

(16.3) (λW) (W is an article of English) ≡ (λW) (W is a lexical word of English whose forms include one of the following: *the, a, sòme, àny, nò*),

where "≡" reads: "is equivalent to", that is, "has the same extension as" (said primarily of expressions but transferred here to the properties designated by expressions that are equivalent, see Section 2.4, Terminological Remark). (16.3) is *excluded* as a proper definition by the fact that the left-hand side is not a constant but is a logically complex term. This term is not defined at all; its meaning is given by the rules for lambda expressions. (16.3), a semi-formal rendering of the informal (15.2), can only be a factual statement, as it should be. (We are not dealing with *logical* equivalence, both the expressions and the designated properties are equivalent on factual, not on logical grounds.)

The comparative concept of article is a property of *item/language* pairs. Category terms based on terms for *construction/language* concepts are obtained in an analogous way, with an adjustment made to account for the fact that categories are sets of constructs not of constructions; for example (see above, (10.6) and (10.7); "y" for linguistic forms):

(16.4)   (λy) (for some x, x is a serial verb construction in Lao and y is a construct for x in Lao)

16.2   Category terms based on comparative-concept terms (2): Constants

Given a lambda expression like "(λW) (W is an article of English)", it is possible to actually *define* an expression like "Article of English":

(16.5)   *Article of English* = (λW) (W is an article of English).

(Note the upper-case "Article" in the defined term but the lower-case "article" in the definiens.)

The expression "Article of English" is complex from the point of view of English but is treated in (16.5) as logically simple, as a single, unanalysable constant. The definiens is directly based on the comparative-concept term "article". Therefore, the constant "Article of English" is also *based on this term*, if indirectly so. The definition does *not* use the right-hand side of (16.3) as a definiens; thus, the three problems in (15.3) no longer arise when "Article of English" is defined as in (16.5).

Given definition (16.5) in a grammar of English and understanding "Article of English" as defined, (15.2) can be replaced by the following, more adequate formulation (with which it would be logically equivalent only if the logic of our grammar G were extensional):

(16.6)   Article of English $\equiv$ (λW) (W is a lexical word of English whose forms include one of the following: *the, a, sòme, àny, nò*).

The status as a factual statement remains unaffected. Again, the two terms that are the left-hand and right-hand sides of (16.6) are equivalent (have the same extensions), but they are not *logically* equivalent: "Article of English" is *logically* equivalent with "(λW) (W is an article of English)", by definition (16.5); similarly, for the properties designated.

Sentence (16.3) can be derived now from the definition and the factual statement (16.6): we substitute the definiens of (16.5) for "Article of English" in (16.6) to obtain (16.3).

The expression "Article of English" has been treated here as a constant that is a derived category term based on the comparative-concept term "article". It is such a construction that appears to be closest to the status and actual usage of descriptive-category terms in linguistics.

The concept of article on whose term "Article of English" is based is of the item/language type. For a concept of the construction/language type an analogous category term is introduced in:

(16.7) *Serial Verb of Lao* = (λy) (for some x, x is a serial verb construction in Lao and y is a construct for x in Lao)

16.3 Function category terms

In Section 12.4, the following definition was schematically introduced for "subject" as a comparative-concept term:

(12.3a) *subject* (L) = (λs) [(λf$_1$f$_2$) φ(f$_1$, f$_2$, s, L)]

This definition is analogous to (16.1), though formally different. Given the definition, we may specify *function category terms* (terms denoting categories that are functions) that are analogous to terms in (16.2):

(16.8) subject (Latin)

(logically equivalent to:) (λs) [(λf$_1$f$_2$) φ(f$_1$, f$_2$, s, Latin)]

(whose extension is – "function" and "relation" as in set theory:)

the function that assigns to any s the relation between any f$_1$ and f$_2$ such that f$_1$ and f$_2$ satisfy φ with respect to s and Latin

A category term "Subject in Latin", as a constant analogous to "Article of English", can be defined simply as:

(16.9) *Subject in Latin* = subject (Latin).

What has been evolving by now, is a further revision of Haspelmath's conception of 'comparative concepts' vs. 'descriptive categories', arguably the most important one.

16.4 Tenth Revision: Category terms as standard category terms, basic and derived

The conception of category terms that are based on comparative-concept terms can be summarized by means of the following semi-formal definitions.

A *category term of a grammar of L* is simply any expression of the language of the grammar (in which the grammar is written) that denotes a category of L.

A *standard category term of a grammar of L* is a category term of the grammar such that: in the language of the grammar *or in a more formal or a more detailed version of the language*, the term is *logically equivalent to* a lambda expression that is *properly related to* a comparative-concept term.

The qualification "or in a more formal or a more detailed version of the language" accounts for cases where the grammar's language does not yet contain lambda expressions.

Equivalence of terms as in (16.3) is not enough, it must be *logical* equivalence, as it holds between "Article of English" and "(λW) (W is an article of English)" due to definition (16.5). "Properly related" means: being related as exemplified in (16.2), (16.4), or (16.8). However, further cases may have to be allowed; in this respect, the definiens should be considered as incomplete.

Logical equivalence is reflexive; therefore, lambda expressions that are properly related to a comparative-concept term are covered as standard category terms.

A *basic standard category term of a grammar of L* is a standard category term of the grammar that either is not defined in the language of the grammar or in a more formal or more detailed version of the language, or else is defined in it independently of any other standard category term of the grammar.

A *derived standard category term of a grammar of L* is a standard category term of the grammar that is not basic. – Here are some examples:

i. *Basic*: all lambda and hyphen expressions in (16.2) and (16.8).
ii. *Derived*: "Article of English" in (16.5), "Serial Verb of Lao" in (16.7), "Subject in Latin" in (16.9).
iii. *Basic*: "(λy) (for some x, x is a serial verb construction in Lao and y is a construct for x in Lao)" in (16.4).
iv. *Non-standard*: "(λW) (W is a lexical word of English and *the, a, sòme, àny*, or *nò* is a form of W)".
v. *No category term*: "(λW) (W is an article of Russian)".

Examples (i) are instances of category terms based on terms for comparative concepts of the item/language type or based on terms for concepts of the language/function type; category terms (ii) are similarly related to concept terms of all three types; (iii) exemplifies terms based on terms for comparative concepts of the construction/language type.

Term (iv) is equivalent, by (16.3), with a lambda expression of the kind required for standard category terms, therefore, denotes a category of English; but it is not *logically* equivalent to such an expression; therefore, term (iv), though a category term by denoting a category, is non-standard (assuming that the definiens of the above definition of "standard category term" may be considered as complete).

Term (v), though meaningful, does not denote a category of Russian, or of any language at all: it happens to denote the empty set; allowing the empty set as a syntactic category of any language would be a dubious move indeed.

Haspelmath's conception of descriptive categories is now revised as follows:

(16.10) *Tenth Revision.* Typical category terms of a grammar of a language are *standard category terms* of the grammar.

Note. As for the grammatical terms used in the Leipzig glossing rules, the Tenth Revision should also provide an interpretation for their occurrences in actual glosses (compare Section 11.2, Note, above).

16.5 Non-standard category terms

"Typical" in (16.10) allows for category terms that are non-standard by not being related to comparative-concept terms in the right way, as in example (iv). Such terms are indeed required for empirical identification statements, but otherwise their occurrence is not typical.

Even non-standard category terms of a grammar of a language may be introduced by definitions: by definitions that implicitly or explicitly restrict their use to the language in question. Compare the following term in Leech & Svartvik (1975: 267): "PLURAL IN-*en*"; the term is defined, rather than the category identified, by giving a set of three forms: *children, oxen, brethren*.

Disregarding empirical identification statements, non-standard category terms may occur in language descriptions that require new terminology (compare Beck (2016) for discussion), but they are hard to find in grammatical traditions [*note the plural*]. The terms in [2018: 104] do not belong here, since the classification criterion "Some concepts that do not seem to work for all languages" is not relevant on the revised conception of comparative concepts (see Section 13, above).

Assuming the ten revisions, what are the ***consequences*** for the relation between comparative concepts and descriptive categories?

17. Relating comparative concepts and descriptive categories. Concept types

17.1 Comparative concepts and descriptive categories: The ontological relationship

Comparative concepts and descriptive categories are ontologically different. This is a major claim in [2018: 84]:

> Ontological difference
> Comparative concepts are a different kind of entity than descriptive categories (cf. Section 5).

However, the difference as it is then explained in [2018: Section 5] is methodological not ontological (unless we inconsistently change over here to an intensional conception of categories, see above, Section 2.6): in contrast to descriptive categories, comparative concepts "are defined in a way that is independent of distributions within particular systems" [2018: 95]. Ontology remains in the dark, be it only for not providing a clear answer to the question of what kind of entity a comparative concept is to be; the *ontological* relationship between comparative concepts and descriptive categories is not clearly established, while it is in the revised framework.

Let us understand by a *standard descriptive category of L*, or *standard category of L* for short, any category of L that can be denoted by a standard category term of a grammar of L. Only such categories need be considered for their relationship to *comparative concepts*.

Suppose that K is a standard category of L, t is a standard category term of a grammar of L that denotes K, and C is a (the) comparative concept on whose term t is based. Then three cases must be distinguished.

a. C is of the *item/language type*, and K is the set of items i of L such that C is a property of ⟨i, L⟩. – Example: L = English, C = article, K = the set in (15.2).
b. C is of the *construction/language type*, and K is the set of items i of L such that for some x, C is a property of ⟨x, L⟩ and i is a construct for x in L. – Example: L = Lao, C = serial verb construction, K = the set denoted by t* in (10.7).
c. C is of the *language/function type*, and K is the (set theoretic) function that is assigned to L by the (set theoretic) function that is the extension of C. – Example: L = Latin, C = subject, K = the (set theoretic) function assigned to Latin by the (set theoretic) function that is the extension of subject – in other words, K is the function denoted by "subject (Latin)"; compare Sections 12.4 and 16.3.

Assuming these ontological relationships between standard categories and comparative concepts, *four problematic points* of Haspelmath's conceptions can now be clarified. The first three concern terminology (Sections 17.2 to 17.4); the fourth is Haspelmath's rejection of 'general categories', which is reconsidered in Section 18.

17.2 A notational convention

In [2010], and right through to [2018], Haspelmath adopts a convention for naming descriptive categories vs. comparative concepts that he traces back to typologists since the 1980s and characterizes as follows [2010: 674]:

> [...] grammatical labels with an initial capital refer to language-particular descriptive categories (e.g., 'the Russian Perfective aspect', 'the Spanish Imperfect tense'), while ordinary lower-case spelling is used for comparative concepts. This makes sense because [terms for, H.L.] descriptive categories are akin to proper names in that they refer to unique entities (one can never say that a category is 'an Imperfect', just as one can never say that a city is 'a Warsaw'). Croft (2001: 50) proposes to extend this convention to syntactic categories (e.g., 'the Kutenai Verb') and constructions (e.g., 'the Tagalog Actor Focus', 'the English Relative Clause'), which are just as language-particular as the tense and aspect forms discussed by Comrie, Bybee, and Dahl.

I have respected this notational convention but given it a twist in Section 16 that is very different from Haspelmath's interpretation: the 'grammatical labels with an initial capital' are construed as constants that are defined by means of corresponding comparative-concept terms, using lambda expressions in the transition from the concept terms to the 'labels'. (The notational convention could be formulated as a convention for definitions of category terms.) The 'grammatical labels' may then be used in the grammar in factual statements on the language-particular categories, statements that are misinterpreted in Haspelmath's framework as definitions of the 'grammatical labels'.

17.3 The problem of 'portable terms'

In Beck (2016), a conception of 'portable terms' is introduced (Beck 2016: 399):

> [...] there are portable terms that can be applied in the description of specific languages that are not entirely language-particular and which do (or could potentially if we hammer out good definitions) have the same meaning when applied to the description of different languages.

This is discussed inconclusively in [2018: Section 8].

The terminology of "portable term" is misleading, though, and should be given up. On our account, 'portable terms' – say, "article" used in a grammar of English to denote the set of articles of English – are category terms that may figure as explicanda in explications whose explicata, identical to the explicanda, are comparative-concept terms (see Section 5, above, on explications). However, *any* category term of a grammar that has the status of a constant is 'portable' in this sense. True, no useful comparative-concept terms may result from some explications; also, the explications of some category terms may lead to terms for comparative concepts that are more fruitful than the concepts resulting from other explications, but this is a matter of degree.

Conversely, it is a *defensible hypothesis* that, whatever the tradition, most category terms traditionally used in grammars of different languages are standard category terms (in the sense of Section 16.4, above) based on comparative-concept terms that may well have originated as such from category terms of individual grammars through explications, frequently implicit and hard to pin down to an originator.

We may certainly collect and study traditional grammatical terms for questions of use and meaning, but this is a historical enterprise; it may still be helpful in avoiding terminological misunderstandings. Independently, there will always be a need for terminological dictionaries, and individual authors may well be required to specify how they are using traditional terms, but trying to *prescribe*, rather than *propose*, their future use and meaning as comparative-concept terms would, in my view, be equivalent to putting a straitjacket on linguistics. – Haspelmath worries [2018: 103]:

> How does one distinguish between portable and non-portable category labels? I do not know any simple answer to this question.

An answer is not needed – this is a pseudo-problem.

17.4 Comparative concepts: Orientation types and origin types

Apparently due to criticism such as the one formulated by Beck (2016), two types of 'category-like comparative concepts' are distinguished in [2018]: those which are "known by terms that are not derived from grammars of particular languages", and those known by terms that are so derived: known by 'descriptive-derived terms' (compare Section 1.2, above).

The subdivision is questionable: the second type of comparative concepts (known by 'descriptive-derived terms') is not covered by the general characterization in [2010: 665]: "Comparative concepts are concepts created by comparative linguists for the specific purpose of crosslinguistic comparison". There have been enough cases in the history of linguistics of concepts that, on the one hand, were 'created' specifically in view of grammar writing (for individual languages) rather than created "for the specific purpose of crosslinguistic comparison" (let alone, created by comparative linguists) but which, on the other hand, should still be included among the comparative concepts: the concept terms were, in fact, meant to be used as a basis for standard category terms. (Arguably, this can be claimed already for most of the terminology in Dionysios Thrax, despite the absence of a notion of standard category term; compare Lieb (2005: Section 2.6).)

I therefore propose a *third classification system* on the set of comparative concepts that correspond to 'category-like comparative concepts': *the orientation/origin system of concept types*. There is a first classification in this system, directly on the system's source, **type orientation**, which has two elements: the **grammar-oriented concept type**, consisting of comparative concepts having terms for which there are, or are meant to be, standard category terms of grammars of languages that can be based on the concept terms; and the **free concept type**, consisting of comparative concepts having terms that do not satisfy this condition. There is a second classification, directly on the grammar-oriented concept type, **type origin**, again with two elements: the **grammar-derived concept type**, consisting of grammar-oriented comparative concepts having terms that were originally introduced in grammars (or other descriptions) of individual languages as constants denoting categories; and the **grammar-deriving concept type**, consisting of grammar-oriented comparative concepts having terms that were originally introduced to obtain standard category terms of grammars (or of other descriptions) of individual languages.

Free concepts are exemplified by concepts introduced in typology independently of grammar writing (compare [2018: 86–87] for examples). The concept of serial verb construction as introduced in [2016] and analysed in Part B of the present essay appears to be grammar-derived, but on closer inspection of its origins it might still turn out to be grammar-deriving; this remains to be established.

Generally, Haspelmath's comparative concepts 'known by descriptive-derived terms', though mostly grammar-derived, may in some cases turn out to be grammar-deriving or free when historically investigated; Haspelmath's criterion does not appear to determine a sufficiently natural class and is no longer needed when the orientation/origin system of concept types is adopted.

17.5 Standard comparative concepts and the overall system of types

It appears from the ten revisions that the term "category-like comparative concept" is inadequate; it is a misnomer already in the unrevised framework where 'language-specific categories' are to be *classes* of linguistic items (above, Section 2.6) as opposed to comparative concepts, which are excluded as such. On the revised conception, comparative concepts are *properties* of item/language pairs, construction/language pairs, or language/function pairs, so the concepts cannot be 'category-like', both on formal and on ontological grounds – whatever the relation between concepts and categories may be from a *methodological* point of view.

'Category-like comparative concepts' are the standard case of comparative concepts. I therefore propose to use the term "***standard comparative concept***" to denote such concepts in their revised form, doing away with the term "category-like comparative concept".

Three classification systems have been assumed for standard comparative concepts, each with the set of standard comparative concepts as its source: the definition-based system of concept types (Section 11.4), the intension-based system of concept types (Section 12.5), and the orientation/origin system of concept types (Section 17.4). Having the same source, the three classification systems can be united into a single system with cross-classifications, to be called ***the overall system of types for standard comparative concepts***.

Returning to Haspelmath's unrevised framework, we now consider the second major point that has remained contentious in previous discussion (see Section 1.6, above): the rejection of 'general categories' due to a rejection of type-token relationships between comparative concepts and descriptive categories.

18. The problem of type-token relations

18.1 The non-existence claim

Great care is taken in [2018: Section 5] to demonstrate "why there is no type-token relation between comparative concepts and [elements of, H.L.] descriptive categories" (heading of Section 5), arguing against positions taken in Moravcsik (2016) and in Lehmann (2018), also adopted now by Reiner (2021).

A critical overview and discussion of type-token conceptions is given by Wetzel (2018), who also refers to the "universal and largely unscrutinised reliance of linguistics on the type-token relationship and related distinctions [...]" as "the subject of Hutton's cautionary book (1990)" (Wetzel 2018: 3). A major problem consists in answering the question of "what is a type" (Wetzel: 2018: Section 4).

Of the three basic possibilities mentioned by Wetzel (types as sets, kinds or laws), the set conception appears to fit best in relation to [2018]: in certain cases, "it is possible to see the comparative concepts as categories or classes" [2018: 103], a conception ultimately rejected for comparative concepts by Haspelmath but implying a set-conception of *types*. I will adopt such a conception here, despite its well-known problems as a general type conception.

'Tokens' are usually construed as "spatio-temporal particulars" (Wetzel 2018: 13); this requirement is obviously given up by Haspelmath. (Also, category *elements* rather than categories should be construed as tokens; this appears to agree with Haspelmath's view, some of his formulations notwithstanding.)

I will deal with type-token relations by considering their converse, token-type relations, which makes for easier formulation. On a set-conception of types, token-type relations are subcases of the *element relation*.

Consider, then, the non-existence claim. In Haspelmath's framework, the claim is *trivially true* – it follows from two meta-theoretical decisions: (i) sets are excluded as comparative concepts; (ii) token-type relations are to be subcases of the element relation. Hence, (iii) elements of descriptive categories are not tokens of comparative concepts. Being a consequence of meta-theoretical decisions, the non-existence claim is non-empirical.

On the revised conception of descriptive categories and comparative concepts, the non-existence claim continues to be trivially true, for the same reasons as before, and its status continues to be non-empirical.

Since comparative concepts are not sets in either framework, they are, in particular, excluded as 'general categories' (certain *sets* of linguistic items of arbitrary languages) as these are typically assumed in comparative linguistics, especially in typology.

18.2 The problem of general categories

To do justice to linguistic practice, then, a place must be assigned to 'general categories'. This is not possible in Haspelmath's framework: only comparative concepts are considered as candidates but they are rejected as sets, therefore, as general categories. As the framework itself excludes general categories, making the exclusion non-empirical, linguists who want to retain them on empirical grounds will have to reject Haspelmath's unrevised framework, as Reiner does explicitly (2021).

The situation is different though for the revised framework, as we shall see. Here, sets are allowed that qualify as general categories *and are determined by comparative concepts*, which continue to be properties. Such sets are possible in the revised framework because on the revised conception, comparative-concept terms have a separate place for directly representing languages; in Haspelmath's framework, concept terms are not construed in this way, which prevents him from recognizing the sets.

In the revised framework, the elements of descriptive categories turn out to be elements of general categories, hence, tokens of the general categories when these are understood as types. The non-existence claim for type-token relations must therefore be qualified for the revised framework: the claim continues to hold in relation to comparative concepts and descriptive categories, but does *not* hold when certain sets are chosen as types, sets that qualify as general categories and are determined by comparative concepts. Consider the details.

18.3   General categories as types: Qualifying the non-existence claim

Three kinds of comparative concepts have been distinguished (Section 12.5, above): concepts of the construction/language type, the item/language type, and the language/function type. Concepts of each kind determine sets that qualify as general categories such that the elements of descriptive categories are *tokens of* these sets as types; since the sets are determined by the concepts, this also establishes a *token-based* relation between the elements of a descriptive category and the comparative concept that determines a general category of which the elements of the descriptive category are tokens. In the revised framework, this relation may be considered as a *matching relation* between elements of the category and the comparative concept. The sets that qualify as general categories are obtained as follows.

a.   Comparative concepts of the construction/language type

Let C be such a concept. By the **construct-set for C** we may then understand *the set of all y* such that for *some L* and some x, C is a property of ⟨x, L⟩ and y is a construct for x in L. (This differs from (b) in Section 17.1, where individual languages L are considered.) The construct-set for C can be a *general category* by obviously satisfying traditional demands on such categories.

As an example, consider *the construct-set for serial verb construction*: the set of all y such that *for some L* and some x, x is a serial verb construction in L and y is a construct for x in L. – Now consider a *specific* language L, say, Lao, and the category denoted by the category term "**Serial Verb in Lao**". By definition (16.7) this is the set of all y such that for some x, x is a serial verb construction in Lao and y is a construct for x in Lao.

Obviously, the category is a subset of the construct-set, therefore, each element of the category *is a token of* this set as a type.

b. Comparative concepts of the item/language type

An analogous result is obtained even more directly when C is a comparative concept of the item/language type, such as **article**. Instead of a construct set we then consider the **domain** (the set of first-place members) of the relation that is the extension of C: consider the set of all i such that *for some L*, $\langle i, L \rangle$ is an element of the extension of C. This, again, qualifies as a *general category*.

Consider a specific language, say, English, and the category denoted by "*Article of English*", assuming definition (16.5) for this term. The category is the set of all i such that i is an article of English. This implies that i is an element of the *domain* of the two-place relation that is the extension of the comparative concept of article. It follows that each element of the category *is a token of* the domain as a type.

c. Comparative concepts of the language/function type

Let C be a concept of this type. As exemplified in Section 12.4 by the concept of subject, with a definition of the term as in (12.3b), the extension of C is a function that assigns to any L another function that assigns to any sentence s of L a certain relation between constituents of s ("function" and "relation" understood in a set theoretic sense). It is *the functions assigned to the L's* that have been considered as descriptive categories; the set of these categories is the *range* (set of values) of the function that is the extension of C.

Now consider the **union of the range**: this is another set of the same type as the individual categories; any element of any of the individual categories – the element being a pair of a sentence s of a certain L and a relation between constituents of s – is also an element of the union. Admit the union as a *general category*, as we well may; just as the individual categories, it is determined by the extension of C, hence, by C. Any element of an individual category is an element then also of the general category determined by C.

Consider, for example, the category denoted by "*Subject in Latin*", with a definition of the term as in (16.9). The category is the function assigned to Latin by the function that is denoted by the comparative-concept term "subject". Each pair consisting of a Latin sentence and 'the subject relation' for this sentence is an element of the category Subject in Latin, therefore, of the union of the range of the function that is the extension of subject; hence, the pair is *a token of* the union construed as a general category that is a type determined by the concept of subject.

18.4 General categories and systems of categories

A conception of general categories as just outlined appears to vindicate approaches followed, or argued for, by authors such as Moravcsik (2016), Lehmann (2018) and Reiner (2021), *on three conditions*: first, comparative concepts – under this or another name – must be explicitly recognized; second, comparative concepts must be openly relativized to languages (or language varieties or idiolects, or to corresponding systems: compare Lieb (2018: Sections 6.4 and 6.5)); third, 'general categories' must be construed not *as* comparative concepts but as *sets determined by* comparative concepts.

In typology, and in comparative linguistics generally, classification systems for categories – containing both sub- and cross-classifications – are useful and tend to be established. On the conception of comparative concepts vs. descriptive categories in its revised form, such systems are unproblematic; establishing them is compatible with the revised conception. They may well start with categories that are quite general, in agreement with the classical approach to 'categories' in philosophy (Thomasson 2018), ending with standard descriptive categories and their subcategories.

19. Theories of language, language comparison, and grammatical description

19.1 Theories of language

Very roughly, a theory of language is to be an empirical theory that has as its *domain* the set of all languages, past, present, and future, and as its *subject matter* a certain set of properties of languages, properties that are of different types and may be assumed differently in different theories of language but must include system-related properties. Some or all properties constituting the subject matter of a theory of language are assumed to be universal, but for any given property, this remains a hypothesis because the domain of a theory of language is never available in its entirety to any researcher.

Some properties in the subject matter of an empirical theory will be due to its *conceptual core*, consisting of the theory's logic and the assumptions and definitions meant to be given up or modified last when the theory is confronted with conflicting evidence; changes in the core lead to a substantially different theory. Developing the conceptual core of an empirical theory can hardly be reduced to applying inductive methodology to data, however vast the data set, nor can it be reduced to a purely terminological task: *conceptual decisions* are required to begin with, so far by humans rather than by artificial neural networks however well trained. How to arrive at a core for optimal theories in a given field is a major topic of methodology, but is not a topic of the present essay.

Ontologically, languages as envisaged here are to be 'external', closely related to speech (oral, written, or signed); they are not to be 'brain-internal' entities, whatever the level of abstraction. This excludes Universal Grammar (UG), in any of its versions, as a theory of language; compare Roberts (2017: 9 and 7):

> UG is the general theory of I-languages, taken to be constituted by a subset of the set of possible generative grammars, and as such characterizes the genetically determined aspect of the human capacity for grammatical knowledge.

> *I-language.* This notion, which refers to the intensional, internal, individual knowledge of language […], is largely coextensive with the earlier notion of competence […].

Apparently, the term "theory of language" is never used in the entire handbook edited by Roberts (*ed.* 2017), understandably so, its place is taken by "Universal Grammar".

Haspelmath, a severe critic of generative grammar, obviously shares an 'external' conception of languages. Even so, there is no mention of theories of language in either [2010], [2016], or [2018], and again, the very term "theory of language" does not occur. While I can only speculate on the reasons, I suspect that Haspelmath has been misled by generative grammar to equate theories of language with versions of Universal Grammar; he may also share the typologist's distrust of generalizations that are not derived from vast language comparison. Such distrust, while understandable, fails to recognize the nature and importance of conceptual work as part of the cooperation that is required in general linguistics and in comparative linguistics to arrive at optimal general theories of language as empirical theories. (An example of what conceptual work may mean in this context is provided by the two thousand pages of Lieb *ed.* (2017).)

19.2 Comparative concepts and theories of language

Neglect of theories of language is entirely unwarranted when comparative concepts are considered, even on a strictly Haspelmath conception, as appears from the key passage in [2010: 681] discussed in Section 13, above, which is not superseded by anything in [2018]:

> Comparative linguists create comparative concepts against which the descriptive categories of particular languages can be matched. These comparative concepts must be universally applicable; that is, they must be based exclusively on more primitive universally applicable concepts: universal conceptual-semantic concepts, general formal concepts, and other comparative concepts (or on extralinguistic situations).

The passage characterizes the nature of comparative concepts and their role in relation to language description as Haspelmath sees them. I have argued that his view has to be corrected in important respects, in particular, in relation to the content of this quote. Independently, Haspelmath's requirements on comparative concepts as formulated in the quote after "that is" characterize the concepts in a way that would apply equally well to fruitful concepts designated by constants of a general theory of language (Section 13.5, above). Put differently: comparative concepts are characterized *as* such concepts, and yet, theories of language are skirted.

This inconsistency in theory does not survive in practice, as demonstrated by the analysis in Part B, above, of Haspelmath's definition of "serial verb construction": the definition uses a Construction Grammar version to supply a language-theory background.

Generally, given the revisions introduced in this essay, we may safely assume:

(19.1)   Any comparative concept must be understood in the context of a theory; the theory may be implicit or partial; the concept term is one of its constants; and typically, the theory is a theory of language.

The "lack of grounding in a well-defined linguistic theory" of comparative-concept frameworks is noted by Frajzyngier (2021: Section 3), who goes on to outline what amounts to essential points of a specific theory of language as a basis for typology. (19.1) is more general, though, stating a need for *some* theory of language but allowing for competing theories (whose existence, it would seem, imposes limits on terminological standardization as argued for by Haspelmath (2021)).

19.3   Comparative concepts and language comparison

Language comparison is, in a way, intermediate between theories of language and descriptions of individual languages. It may lead to 'comparative grammars' as theories in their own right; such grammars are briefly characterized in Lieb (1993: Section 21.5).

It is in language comparison – especially in typology – that free comparative concepts (see Section 17.4, above) are most likely to occur. While the status of a comparative concept as grammar-oriented or free does not yet determine its usefulness for language comparison, its status and its usefulness are not unrelated.

Consider a comparative concept whose concept term is a constant of a theory of language. The term may be such that standard category terms in grammars of many different languages can be based on it, of languages that share important properties which set them apart from other languages. In this case, the comparative concept is useful for language comparison that aims at establishing language types.

Or else, the term is such that it may rightly be considered for the formulation of hypotheses on language universals. The comparative concept is then useful for language comparison that aims at establishing such universals.

Either case provides arguments for presupposing a theory of language in language comparison. Generally, given the revised conception of comparative concepts vs. descriptive categories, especially the use of concept terms with variables for languages, we may safely assume:

(19.2)   As a rule, language comparison requires presupposing a theory of language, however partial or implicit, some of whose constants are used as comparative-concept terms in comparative statements, guaranteeing comparability of the languages under study.

Not recognizing or acknowledging this artificially separates comparative linguistics from general linguistics.

19.4   Comparative concepts and grammatical description

It is essential for progress in linguistics that grammatical descriptions of different languages can be written in a way that interrelates them semantically. In [2018: Section 9], Haspelmath worries about the "commensurable description of different languages" (title) – rightly so, on his approach empirical statements identifying categories of languages are misrepresented as grammar-specific definitions of category terms, and semantic ties between grammars of different languages are cut in the key area of grammatical categories.

On Haspelmath's conception, there is no direct semantic relationship between comparative-concept terms and descriptive-category terms as they occur in a grammar. I have argued in Sections 15 and 16 that this is untenable, and is due to a failure to recognize the importance of expressions that are lambda expressions or corresponding readings. Rather than being separated semantically from comparative-concept terms, category terms in a grammar may be *standard* category terms in the sense of Section 16.4, based on comparative-concept terms; from a systematic point of view, such comparative-concept terms are constants of a theory of language – partial or implicit – that is presupposed by the grammar.

Examples are given in Section 16 for the revised conception of category terms in grammars. The comparative-concept term "serial verb construction", on its revised definition in Part B, may serve as a basis for standard category terms; these would turn out to be compatible with some previous uses of "serial verb construction" for obtaining category terms.

Assuming comparative-concept terms as constants of a theory of language is essential to solving the comparability problem in grammar writing. Suppose that the same theory of language is presupposed in two grammars of different languages – using the same descriptive format – and there is a comparative-concept term t that is a constant of the theory of language, designating the concept C. Suppose now that in one grammar a standard category term t_1 is based on t, and in the other, a category term t_2 is based on t in the same way. In this case, the two category terms are *comparable* by their relationship to t, and the two categories denoted by t_1 and t_2 are *comparable* by being related to C in one of the three ways specified in Section 18.2, above: via the construct set for C, or through the domain or the range of the extension of C. Both categories may be empirically *identified* in each language by means of language-specific criteria, and may even be completely different, but this is irrelevant to their comparability.

There is no 'commensurability' problem anymore for different descriptions of the same language or of different languages *if the descriptions presuppose the same theory of language and use the same descriptive format* (possibly specified by a theory of grammars). Such a problem is artificially created by two major flaws of Haspelmath's conception: not relativizing terms for comparative concepts to languages explicitly, and misconstruing empirical identification sentences for descriptive categories as definitions of the category terms – generally, created by failing to recognize *standard category terms*.

A 'commensurability' problem does remain for different descriptions of the same language or of different languages *that presuppose different theories of language or do not use the same descriptive format*. The problem has been receiving increasing attention in recent attempts in computational linguistics to deal with *comparative* grammar-writing ("multilingual and cross-framework grammar engineering" is mentioned by Duchier and Parmentier (2015: 10) as one of the current challenges in grammar engineering). There is no easy solution to this second commensurability problem. Imposing a single theory of language and a single grammatical framework all through linguistics would be utterly unfeasible, nor would it be desirable (as amply proven by the recent history of linguistics). A number of paths will have to be followed simultaneously to achieve a solution; one of them may be comparing empirical consequences – both observational and theoretical – of relevant parts of different grammars when the grammars are construed as empirical theories that do have observational consequences (having them, for example, in the way outlined in Lieb (2018: Section 11)).

Still, given the revised conception of descriptive-category terms and of their relationship to comparative-concept terms, we may safely assume:

(19.3)   As a rule, grammatical description requires that a theory of language, however partial or implicit, be presupposed in a grammar such that some constants of the theory of language are used as a basis for standard category terms of the grammar, guaranteeing comparability of analogous category terms in grammars of different languages, and of the categories themselves, for grammars presupposing the same theory of language and using the same descriptive format.

19.5 General linguistics, comparative linguistics, and descriptive linguistics

On a traditional account, the major aim of *general linguistics* is the development of theories of language specifying language universals as properties shared by all languages; to the extent that *comparative linguistics* is typology, its major aim is the partial comparative characterization of languages to obtain language types as 'relevant' classes of languages, where different interpretations of "relevant" must be allowed; and to the extent that *descriptive linguistics* is grammar writing or grammar-oriented, its major aim is the grammatical description of individual languages.

Let us adopt a traditional account. What, then, follows from our analyses for the relationship between the three fields? The following claim is supported:

(19.4) On the revised conception of comparative concepts vs. descriptive categories, general linguistics, comparative linguistics, and descriptive linguistics are interrelated in the following way:

  a. Theories of language contain constants that designate comparative concepts.
  b. When a theory of language (which may be partial or implicit) is presupposed in a grammar of a language, such constants may be used in the grammar, with the meanings or uses they have in the theory of language, to obtain category terms of the grammar (standard category terms) that can be used in empirical statements on categories of the language.
  c. When the same theory of language and the same descriptive format is used for two grammars of different languages, two analogous category terms – obtained by using the same comparative-concept term – and the categories they denote are comparable via the comparative-concept term and the concept it designates.
  d. Comparative descriptions of languages that aim at establishing language types can be construed as extensions of theories of language (which may be partial or implicit), extensions obtained by introducing new constants of the comparative-concept kind.
  e. (b) and (c) apply in relation to such extended theories and to the new constants.
  f. Because of (e), a grammar that presupposes an extended theory as in (d) uses terms and concepts from general linguistics, comparative linguistics and descriptive linguistics in a unified way.

This complex claim (characterizing some but not all interrelations between the three fields) is not yet supported by Haspelmath's conception of comparative concepts vs. descriptive categories. On the contrary, his conception creates a gap between general and comparative work on the one hand and descriptive work on the other and, shying away from theories of language, fails to clearly interrelate comparative and general work. The conception of comparative concepts vs. descriptive categories should therefore be adopted in its revised form only.

Acknowledgements

Many thanks are due to the discussants of my lecture read at the 50th Annual Meeting of the Societas Linguistica Europea, held in Zurich in 2017, from which the present essay has developed; to Sebastian Drude, Volker Gast, Edith A. Moravcsik, and Frank Richter for their helpful comments on earlier versions of the essay; and to two anonymous reviewers, whose comments made me sharpen a number of points.

References

Aikhenvald, Alexandra Y. 2006. Serial verb constructions in typological perspective. In Aikhenvald & Dixon (eds), 1–68.
Aikhenvald, Alexandra Y. 2018. *Serial Verbs*. [Oxford Studies in Typology and Linguistic Theory]. Oxford: OUP. https://doi.org/10.1093/oso/9780198791263.001.0001
Aikhenvald, Alexandra Y. & Dixon, Robert M.W. (eds). 2006. *Serial Verb Construction: A Crosslinguistic Typology*. Oxford: OUP.
Alama, Jesse & Korbmacher, Johannes. 2019. The lambda calculus. In *The Stanford Encyclopedia of Philosophy* (Spring 2019 edn), Edward N. Zalta (ed.). <https://plato.stanford.edu/archives/spr2019/entries/lambda-calculus/> (12 November 2020).
van der Auwera, Johan & Gast, Volker. 2010. Categories and prototypes. In *The Oxford Handbook of Linguistic Typology*, Jae Jung Song (ed.), 165–189. Oxford: OUP. (Online edn 2012).
van der Auwera, Johan & Sahoo, Kalyanamalini. 2015. On comparative concepts and descriptive categories, such as they are. *Acta Linguistica Hafniensia* 47(2): 136–173. https://doi.org/10.1080/03740463.2015.1115636
Beck, David. 2016. Some language-particular terms are comparative concepts. *Linguistic Typology* 20(2): 395–402. https://doi.org/10.1515/lingty-2016-0013
Behme, Christina & Neef, Martin (eds). 2018. *Essays on Linguistic Realism* [Studies in Language Companion Series 196]. Amsterdam: John Benjamins. https://doi.org/10.1075/slcs.196
Bird, Alexander & Tobin, Emma. 2018. Natural kinds. In *The Stanford Encyclopedia of Philosophy* (Spring 2018 edn), Edward N. Zalta (ed.). <https://plato.stanford.edu/entries/natural-kinds/> (12 November 2020).
Cambridge Advanced Learner's Dictionary, 4th edn. 2013. Cambridge: CUP.
Carnap, Rudolf. 1950. *Logical Foundations of Probability*. Chicago IL: The University of Chicago Press.
Carnap, Rudolf. 1956. *Meaning and Necessity. A Study in Semantics and Modal Logic*. Chicago IL: The University of Chicago Press.
Carnap, Rudolf. 1958[2012]. *Introduction to Symbolic Logic and its Applications*. New York NY: Dover Publications. (Reprinted in 2012 by Courier Corp. North Chelmsford MA).

Carnap, Rudolf. 1960. *Einführung in die symbolische Logik mit besonderer Berücksichtigung ihrer Anwendungen*. Zweite, neubearbeitete und erweiterte Auflage (2nd edn, revised and enlarged). Vienna: Springer. https://doi.org/10.1007/978-3-7091-3590-7

Chini, Marina & Cuzzolin, Pierluigi (eds). 2018. *Typology, Acquisition, Grammaticalization Studies*. Milano: Franco Angeli.

Coquand, Thierry. 2018. Type theory. In *The Stanford Encyclopedia of Philosophy* (Fall 2018 edn), Edward N. Zalta (ed.). <https://plato.stanford.edu/archives/fall2018/entries/type-theory/> (12 November 2020).

Cordes, Moritz & Siegwart, Geo. No year. Explication. In *The Internet Encyclopedia of Philosophy*. <https://www.iep.utm.edu/explicat/> (8 April 2019).

Croft, William. 2016. Comparative concepts and language-specific categories: Theory and practice. *Linguistic Typology* 20(2): 377–393. https://doi.org/10.1515/lingty-2016-0012

Cruse, D. Alan, Hundsnurscher, Franz, Job, Michael & Lutzeier, Peter Rolf (eds). 2005. *Lexikologie. Lexicology. Ein internationales Handbuch zur Natur und Struktur von Wörtern und Wortschätzen. An International Handbook on the Nature and Structure of Words and Vocabularies*, 2. Halbband / Volume 2. Berlin: Walter de Gruyter.

Da Milano, Federica. 2021. The category 'pronoun' in East and Southeast Asian languages, with a focus on Japanese. In *Linguistic Categories, Language Description and Linguistic Typology* [Typological Studies in Language 132]. Amsterdam: John Benjamins. (This volume) https://doi.org/10.1075/tsl.132.11dam

Duchier, Denys & Parmentier, Yanick. 2015. High-level methodologies for grammar engineering. Introduction to the special issue of *Journal of Language Modelling* 3(1): 5–19. https://doi.org/10.15398/jlm.v3i1.117

Fitting, Melvin. 2015. Intensional logic. In *The Stanford Encyclopedia of Philosophy* (Summer 2015 edn), Edward N. Zalta (ed.). <https://plato.stanford.edu/archives/sum2015/entries/logic-intensional/> (12 November 2020).

Frajzyngier, Zygmunt. 2021. Typology of functional domains. In *Linguistic Categories, Language Description and Linguistic Typology* [Typological Studies in Language 132]. Amsterdam: John Benjamins. (This volume) https://doi.org/10.1075/tsl.132.04fra

Gupta, Anil. 2015. Definitions. In *The Stanford Encyclopedia of Philosophy* (Summer 2015 edn), Edward N. Zalta (ed.). <https://plato.stanford.edu/archives/sum2015/entries/definitions/> (12 November 2020).

Hacking, Ian. 1999. *The Social Construction of What?* Cambridge MA: Harvard University Press. (Quoted from Bird & Tobin 2018).

Haspelmath, Martin. 2010. Comparative concepts and descriptive categories in crosslinguistic studies. *Language* 86(3): 663–687. https://doi.org/10.1353/lan.2010.0021

Haspelmath, Martin. 2016. The serial verb construction: Comparative concept and cross-linguistic generalizations. *Language & Linguistics* 17(3): 291–319.

Haspelmath, Martin. 2018. How comparative concepts and descriptive linguistic categories are different. In *Aspects of Linguistic Variation*, Daniël Van Olmen, Tanja Mortelmans & Frank Brisard (eds), 83–114. Berlin: De Gruyter Mouton.

Haspelmath, Martin. 2020. The structural uniqueness of languages and the value of comparison for language description. *Asian Languages and Linguistics* 1(2): 346–366.

Haspelmath, Martin. 2021. Towards standardization of morphosyntactic terminology for general linguistics. In *Linguistic Categories, Language Description and Linguistic Typology* [Typological Studies in Language 132]. Amsterdam: John Benjamins. (This volume) https://doi.org/10.1075/tsl.132.02has

Haspelmath, Martin. To appear. General linguistics must be based on universals (or nonconventional aspects of language). [Preprint]. Academia.edu. (To appear in *Theoretical Linguistics*)

Hutton, Christopher. 1990. *Abstraction and Instance: The Type-token Relationship in Linguistic Theory*. Oxford: Pergamon Press. (Quoted from Wetzel 2018).

Leech, Geoffrey & Svartvik, Jan. 1975. *A Communicative Grammar of English. Based on A Grammar of Contemporary English* by Randolph Quirk, Sidney Greenbaum, Geoffrey Leech and Jan Svartvik. London: Longman.

Lehmann, Christian. 2018. Linguistic concepts and categories in language description and comparison. In *Typology, Acquisition, Grammaticalization Studies*, Marina Chini & Pierluigi Cuzzolin (eds), 27–50. Milano: Franco Angeli.

Lieb, Hans-Heinrich. 1980. Wortbedeutung: Argumente für eine psychologische Konzeption. *Lingua* 52: 132. https://doi.org/10.1016/0024-3841(80)90015-7

Lieb, Hans-Heinrich. 1983. *Integrational Linguistics, Vol. I: General Outline* [Current Issues in Linguistic Theory 17]. Amsterdam: John Benjamins. https://doi.org/10.1075/cilt.17

Lieb, Hans-Heinrich. 1992. Die Polyfunktionalität des deutschen Vorgangspassivs. *Zeitschrift für Sprachwissenschaft, Phonetik und Kommunikationsforschung* 45(2): 178–188.

Lieb, Hans-Heinrich. 1993. *Linguistic Variables: Towards a Unified Theory of Linguistic Variation* [Current Issues in Linguistic Theory 108]. Amsterdam: John Benjamins. https://doi.org/10.1075/cilt.108

Lieb, Hans-Heinrich. 2005. Notions of paradigm in grammar. In *Lexikologie. Lexicology. Ein internationales Handbuch zur Natur und Struktur von Wörtern und Wortschätzen. An International Handbook on the Nature and Structure of Words and Vocabularies*, 2. Halbband / Vol. 2, D. Alan Cruse, Franz Hundsnurscher, Michael Job & Peter Rolf Lutzeier (eds), 1613–1646. Berlin: Walter de Gruyter.

Lieb, Hans-Heinrich. 2018. Describing linguistic objects in a realist way. In *Essays on Linguistic Realism* [Studies in Language Companion Series 196], Christina Behme & Martin Neef (eds), 79–138. Amsterdam: John Benjamins. https://doi.org/10.1075/slcs.196.05lie

Lieb, Hans-Heinrich (ed.). 2017. *Linguistic Research in Progress: Proceedings of the Berlin Research Colloquium on Integrational Linguistics 1992-2003 (Parts I to XXII) / Berliner Forschungskolloquium Integrative Sprachwissenschaft 1992-2003. Protokolle (Teil I bis XXII)*. Berlin: Freie Universität Berlin. <http://edocs.fu-berlin.de/docs/receive/FUDOCS_series_000000000782> (12 November 2020).

Margolis, Eric & Laurence, Stephen. 2014. Concepts. In *The Stanford Encyclopedia of Philosophy* (Spring 2014 edn), Edward N. Zalta (ed.). <https://plato.stanford.edu/archives/spr2014/entries/concepts/> (12 November 2020).

Moravcsik, Edith A. 2016. On linguistic categories. *Linguistic Typology* 20(2): 417–425. https://doi.org/10.1515/lingty-2016-0015

Nefdt, Ryan M. 2018. Languages and other abstract structures. In *Essays on Linguistic Realism* [Studies in Language Companion Series 196], Christina Behme & Martin Neef (eds), 193–184. Amsterdam: John Benjamins. https://doi.org/10.1075/slcs.196.06nef

Van Olmen, Daniël, Mortelmans, Tanja & Brisard, Frank (eds). 2018. *Aspects of Linguistic Variation*. Berlin: De Gruyter Mouton.

Orilia, Francesco & Swoyer, Chris. 2017. Properties. In *The Stanford Encyclopedia of Philosophy* (Winter 2017 edn), Edward N. Zalta (ed.). <https://plato.stanford.edu/archives/win2017/entries/properties/> (12 November 2020).

Puddu, Nicoletta. 2021. Verbal vs. nominal reflexive constructions: a categorial opposition? In *Linguistic Categories, Language Description and Linguistic Typology* [Typological Studies in Language 132]. Amsterdam: John Benjamins. (This volume) https://doi.org/10.1075/tsl.132.10pud

Reiner, Tabea. 2021. Comparative concepts are *not* a different kind of thing. In *Linguistic Categories, Language Description and Linguistic Typology* [Typological Studies in Language 132]. Amsterdam: John Benjamins. (This volume) https://doi.org/10.1075/tsl.132.06rei

Roberts, Ian (ed.). 2017. *The Oxford Handbook of Universal Grammar*. Oxford: OUP.

Roberts, Ian. 2017. Introduction. In Roberts (ed.), 1–34.

Suppes, Patrick. 1957[1999]. *Introduction to Logic* [The University Series in Undergraduate Mathematics]. Princeton NJ: Van Nostrand. (Reprinted in 1999, Dover Books in Mathematics. New York NY: Dover Publications).

Thomasson, Amie. 2018. Categories. In *The Stanford Encyclopedia of Philosophy* (Spring 2018 edn), Edward N. Zalta (ed.). <https://plato.stanford.edu/archives/spr2018/entries/categories/> (12 November 2020).

Wetzel, Linda. 2018. Types and tokens. In *The Stanford Encyclopedia of Philosophy* (Fall 2018 edn), Edward N. Zalta (ed.). <https://plato.stanford.edu/archives/fall2018/entries/types-tokens/> (12 November 2020).

CHAPTER 6

Comparative concepts are *not* a different kind of thing

Tabea Reiner
University of Munich

This contribution challenges the by now established notion of comparative concepts; in particular, it can be read as a (delayed) response to Haspelmath (2010a). Like Haspelmath's original paper, the present one is theoretical in essence, with examples used primarily for illustration. My main point is that Haspelmath's comparative concepts are, despite his claims to the contrary, simply crosslinguistic categories. This point has been made before; however, I offer two new ingredients to the argument: first, an explicit definition of the crucial term *instantiation*, allowing, among other things, a reaction to Haspelmath's (2019) newest defence of comparative concepts, and second, an alternative approach involving multiple monotonic inheritance. The contribution as a whole, though being theoretical, strives to argue as framework-neutrally as possible; in particular I remain agnostic about the existence and nature of Universal Grammar in any sense.

1. Introduction

Since Haspelmath's seminal paper *Comparative concepts and descriptive categories in crosslinguistic studies* (2010a), the explicit use of comparative concepts has become a standard in typology (cf. volume 20(2) of *Linguistic Typology* = LT). At the same time, however, many researchers have expressed discomfort with Haspelmath's radical idea that comparative concepts are completely detached from descriptive categories for individual languages (e.g., Newmeyer 2010; van der Auwera & Sahoo 2015; articles in LT 20 like Dahl 2016 or Rijkhoff 2016: 338; Maddieson 2018). The present contribution sets out to argue that Haspelmath's idea is too radical indeed and suggests a reconceptualization of comparative concepts as highly abstract descriptive categories. In more detail, Section 2 showcases what appears to be the main problem with Haspelmath's idea: if comparative concepts are truly independent from descriptive categories designed for individual languages, then

https://doi.org/10.1075/tsl.132.06rei
© 2021 John Benjamins Publishing Company

how can they reasonably serve to compare those languages? Section 3 then goes on to demonstrate that they can, provided we conceptualize them in a new way: as high or even the highest nodes in a network of inheritance hierarchies, where each hierarchy allows for multiple but monotonic inheritance. A key issue here is ensuring that all nodes are related by instantiation, which requires an explicit notion of that relation. Furthermore, this section broadens the scope of the paper since the last subsection takes up Haspelmath's later idea of a so called Grammaticon. Section 4, finally, sums up the results of the contribution and considers future empirical applications.

2. A critical close reading of Haspelmath (2010a)

The present section serves two goals. First (Section 2.1), I summarize Haspelmath's paper in order to lay the ground for the objections that follow. Readers who are thoroughly familiar with the original paper can skip this part. Second (Section 2.2), Haspelmath's proposal is discussed in detail, my main point of criticism being that, contrary to his claim, comparative concepts are intimately tied to descriptive categories.

2.1 Short summary of Haspelmath (2010a)

In a nutshell, Haspelmath (2010a) argues that

1. crosslinguistic (let alone universal) categories are out of reach;
2. instead linguists are well-advised to use COMPARATIVE CONCEPTS, i.e., notions that are designed specifically for the purpose of language comparison and do *not* relate to categories meant for the description of any individual language (descriptive categories);
3. in practice, many linguists have been using comparative concepts successfully for quite some time, but unconsciously so.

As to 1, Haspelmath bases his claim on two lines of argument, one practical and one theoretical. On the practical side, he draws attention to what might be called the "typologists' everyday problem": a given category, which has proven to be perfectly adequate for the description of a certain language, cannot be readily transferred to the description of another language (pp. 667–669). To give a simple example, if one is used to define 'subject' as 'constituent that controls agreement', one will have a hard time using this category for the description of a language that does not appear to have anything like agreement (or maybe even constituents). On the theoretical side, Haspelmath cites an insight by Culicover (1999, ch. 2) and also Croft (2001: 78–83): there does not seem to be a lower bound on the specificity of potential crosslinguistic or universal categories (pp. 669, 676).[1] In particular, Culicover (1999: 40–41) argues that any universal set of categories would have to provide for any (sub-)category that might be needed in the description of some language, even if the need will arise only once. For example, if you know that 'size/importance' is an inflectional feature in Weining Ahmao (Gerner & Bisang 2010: 75), then your universal grammar will need that inflectional feature too.

As to 2, this is what Haspelmath concludes from the situation sketched above: if reasonable crosslinguistic categories are virtually out of reach, then we should restrict the use of categories proper to the description of single languages and devise something different for the aim of language comparison, i.e., comparative concepts. An example for a draft of a comparative concept is given below:

> A DATIVE CASE is a morphological marker that has among its functions the coding of the recipient argument of a physical transfer verb (such as 'give', 'lend', 'sell', 'hand'), when this is coded differently from the theme argument.
> (Haspelmath 2010a: 666, small caps T.R.)

Please note that single language descriptive categories may match this concept while having additional properties. For example, the respective form in Turkish also has among its functions the marking of the causee (Kornfilt 1997: 212–213). Furthermore, the concept, although containing semantic as well as formal aspects, does not refer to formal properties of individual languages like suffixing (at least not obviously so). More generally, Haspelmath (2010a) stresses throughout that comparative concepts are completely independent from descriptive categories of which kind whatsoever. According to him, the latter do *not* instantiate the former and he is serious about this, as witnessed by the following quotation.

> I make a terminological distinction between comparative CONCEPTS and descriptive CATEGORIES in order to emphasize that there is **no taxonomic relationship** between them.　　　　　　　　　　　　　　　　　　　　　　(p. 680, boldface T.R.)

As to 3, the use of comparative concepts as best practice, Haspelmath gives general examples from morphosyntax and two more hands-on examples, one from phonetics/phonology and one from lexical semantics (p. 668). Regarding phonetics/phonology, he argues that in practice the IPA symbols have long been used as comparative concepts: each IPA symbol represents a certain bundle of articulatory properties, which may be shared by the realizations of two phonemes from different languages although otherwise these realizations might be quite different.

---

1. Culicover's and Croft's perspectives differ in important respects, which will be discussed in Section 2.2.1 below.

For example, the realization of Dutch /s/ differs from the realization of German /s/ at least in that the former realization is rather laminal while the latter is rather apical – still both match the articulatory properties represented by [s].

Regarding lexical semantics, Haspelmath argues that the "somewhat arbitrarily chosen set of standardized lexical meanings" (p. 668), which is generally needed in lexical comparison, likewise has to consist of comparative concepts: each of these standardized lexical meanings combines notions that, in an individual language, might be distributed over several lexemes or make up only one part of a lexeme's meaning. For example, a standardized lexical meaning 'time of the day that includes noon' captures both, Dutch 'middag' and German 'Mittag', although the former but not the latter includes the afternoon.

The reader might be wondering why I am, again, adducing an example from these two closely related languages. The reason is simple: I intend to make it perfectly clear that the methodological considerations leading Haspelmath to introduce comparative concepts are by no means exclusive to large scale comparisons of widely differing languages – they can crop up as soon as one takes into account more than one language.

Concluding my short summary of Haspelmath (2010a), the core arguments for the explicit use of comparative concepts have been reported, however without going into the details of concrete comparative concepts. The only one I mentioned was the DATIVE CASE, which in the original paper serves as an introductory illustration (p. 666). Beyond that, Haspelmath suggests seven concrete comparative concepts in his central section (pp. 670–674), which I save for the discussion below.

2.2 Discussion of Haspelmath (2010a)

The present section first discusses the three core arguments reported above and then comments on a selection of Haspelmath's seven suggestions for concrete comparative concepts.

2.2.1 The core arguments

1. *Crosslinguistic categories are out of reach.* As to the practical part of this argument: it is hard to deny, at least from a theory-neutral perspective. So long as one's theory does not universally postulate things like subjects or case, everyone has trouble defining and identifying these throughout a balanced sample of languages (e.g., Schachter 1996 on subjects in Tagalog, or Spencer 2008 on case in Hungarian). As to the theoretical part of the argument, however, I have serious concerns, both about Croft's and Culicover's version. To be fair, Haspelmath does not cite Croft explicitly here (in stark contrast to the rest of the paper). This might be because Croft's version of the argument is restricted to parts of speech in single

languages – or because it is fairly easy to counter. Croft (2001) shows that, distributionally, the adjective class of Lango splits into two subclasses (pp. 78–80) and the potential adjective, noun, and nominal-adjective classes of Japanese split into six subclasses, not even taking into account idiolectal splits or issues of graded acceptability (pp. 81–83). From these analyses Croft concludes that there is no principled rationale where to stop splitting (p. 83). Yet there is: you stop splitting when every class arrived at shows uniform distributional properties (also cf. Rijkhoff 2016: 339 et passim). For example, a class may comprise all items that for a certain speaker are acceptable in construction x, excluded in construction y, and doubtful in construction z. These classes might be very small indeed and, here I agree with Croft, they won't look anything like traditional parts of speech. I expect them to include more than one member each due to a simple numerical estimation: imagine each and every item in a language was distributed in its own special way – for how many items could that be true at the same time? Thus, within single language descriptions there is, in fact, a lower bound on the specificity of categories.

What does this mean for the availability of crosslinguistic categories? This is where Culicover's version of the argument – cited by Haspelmath – comes into play. Culicover (1999: 40), too, sees the need for rather specific categories in single language descriptions. However, for a category to be available in a single language, it has to be represented by universal grammar, according to classical generative thinking (pp. 40–41). So universal grammar would be populated with a multitude of specific categories *from* and *for* every language (ibid.). I agree with Culicover that this is not what universal grammar is meant to be. However, I fail to see the inevitability of promoting every single language category, including subcategories, to universal grammar. True, classical generative thinking requires any lexical or functional category to fall within the bounds of some rather broad universal lexical or functional category (Culicover 1999: 36–37), for example within the bounds of the lexical category adjective (in the sense of [+N, +V]). This requirement is motivated by reasons of learnability (ibid.). But as far as I am aware, nobody has ever argued that the language learner needs anything beyond this fairly coarse orientation. For example, if an item can be identified as falling within the bounds of the universal category adjective, it does not matter whether it is preposed or postposed. Thus, if the language learner does not need fine-grained prewiring, then there is no motivation for overpopulating universal grammar with such highly specific categories. So the UG-argument Haspelmath refers to does not appear to be conclusive.

As a side note, Haspelmath (2010a) cites Culicover as "coming from a generative background" (p. 669). This is correct, as witnessed by the preceding paragraph; however, it might invite the implicature that Culicover represents mainstream Generative Grammar and, accordingly, that "even those generativists have lost faith in universalism". This impression, however, would be misguided. In the first chapter of his 1999 book cited above, Culicover explicitly commits to central statements from a competing paradigm, i.e., Construction Grammar: idioms are anything but peripheral (p. 32) and there is a lexicon-grammar continuum (pp. 33–35). Needless to say that Culicover is perfectly aware of the connection (p. 15). In sum, he does not make a very good crown witness for mainstream Generative Grammar (if there is anything like that at all).

To conclude the discussion of Haspelmath's (2010a) first core argument (= crosslinguistic categories are out of reach), I agree that there are practical problems with crosslinguistic categories but I doubt that the problems go back to a fundamental unavailability of such categories.

2. Comparative concepts are better because they are independent from descriptive categories. This is Haspelmath's own conclusion from his first core argument (= crosslinguistic categories are out of reach). Above I argued against this argument's theoretical part but had to accept its practical part i.e., "typologists' everyday problem". So my task here is to show that the practical part alone does not warrant the conclusion. To this end, I will discuss the dative example and generalize my objections in the process.

Recall Haspelmath's draft for a comparative concept DATIVE CASE:

> A DATIVE CASE is a morphological marker that has among its functions the coding of the recipient argument of a physical transfer verb (such as 'give', 'lend', 'sell', 'hand'), when this is coded differently from the theme argument.
>
> (Haspelmath 2010a: 666, small caps T.R.)

I will not discuss the premises involved here like having a definition of morphology or a sufficient set of semantic roles since Haspelmath is well aware of these premises (p. 666) and especially the issue of semantic roles has received intensive treatment in Newmeyer's (2010: 689–690) reply as well as in Haspelmath's (2010b: 696–697) reaction to it. Let's suppose that the premises are justified. Then Haspelmath (2010a: 665–666) is happy to note that certain forms from Finnish, Korean, Russian, and Turkish all match the concept despite having additional properties. Thus, the comparative concept DATIVE CASE can be applied to forms in all four (and presumably more) languages without requiring them to show completely identical properties. Up to this point, I fully agree with Haspelmath that the comparative concept under scrutiny is extremely useful. However, I fail to follow him when he writes:

> Note that we can**not** say that the Russian Dative and the Finnish Allative 'instantiate' the 'dative case' concept, because these categories have many **more** properties than are contained in the definition […].
>
> (Haspelmath 2010a: 666, boldface T.R.)

Thus, Haspelmath seems to imply that the sole way for a category to instantiate a concept is to be fully identical to it, copying each and every property from it (cf. also Dahl 2016: 429, 431). Whether this implication is warranted can only be checked by applying explicit definitions of the terms *instantiation, category*, and *concept* to the quotation. Alas, the definitions remain largely implicit in Haspelmath's paper. To be sure, he does define explicitly the complex terms **descriptive** *category* and **comparative** *concept*; however in the lines quoted above he uses the nouns alone and we do not know if the original terms are compositional. In fact, it is not easy to come up with convenient notions of all three terms: neither 'category' nor 'concept' appears to be distinguished routinely and consistently in any discipline, while 'instantiation' is a primitive in Philosophy (McGinn 2012: 167)[2] and rarely fully defined in Information science. When it is (e.g., Stock & Stock 2013: 557–558), the definition appears too narrow for current purposes in allowing as instances only individual items, here: fragments of real speech events. Note, however, that these authors explain 'instantiating a concept' as being an element to which the concept applies, independently of the difference between hyponymy and meronymy (557) and, notably, with instances being capable of having more than one hyponym (558). Against this background I propose the following working definitions:

- category = concept: set of at least one property
- instantiation: a certain relation between categories (or between a category and a particular), namely the relation of sharing at least one property; the *relatum* with more properties is said to instantiate the other.

Some comments are in order. Equating category with concept might seem like begging the question. However, the original motivation for keeping them apart seems to be distinguishing natural kinds from man-made groupings (cf. also Haspelmath 2010a: 665, 678–680). And I take it that *all* classes are created by humans from the continuous stream of consciousness (cf. also van der Auwera & Sahoo 2015: 137; Moravcsik 2016: 418; Rijkhoff 2016: 342 citing Locke).[3] To put it bluntly: it is the observer's decision to see, for example, a cat and a fox or, instead, two bird predators (or two mammals, for that matter). If, however, all classes are artificial, then it is pointless to single out the more artificial ones, as Haspelmath (2010a: 665, 678–680) tries to do by introducing comparative concepts. Moreover, even for that

---

2. To be sure, philosophers do discuss, from quite disparate perspectives, what it fundamentally means for particulars to have properties (cf. the rest of the McGinn chapter or Armstrong 2004), but consensus seems to be far away.

3. A reviewer remarks that this alone "is another reason there can't be universally applicable cross-linguistic categories". As far as I can see, this is a *non-sequitur*.

enterprise the term comparative *concepts* might have been a misnomer from the beginning, since the denoted entities are explicitly *not* meant to be psychologically real (665). So when I equate concept with category here I maintain Haspelmath's terminological usage, even if it is infelicitous.

As to the notion of instantiation proposed here, it does not require full identity between the relata (cf. also van der Auwera & Sahoo 2015: 138–139; Moravcsik 2016: 418, 420; Lehmann 2018: 4) and both the relata may be categories. This flexibility allows for multiple layers of instantiation on different levels of generality, for which examples will follow, e.g., Figure 3. On a side note, I take *instantiation* to be synonymous with *taxonomic relationship*, another term used by Haspelmath as well as in the present paper. A taxonomy is then a given network of such relationships.

With these definitions in mind, it appears that certain forms from Russian and Finnish *instantiate* the concept DATIVE CASE: they share all the properties bundled in the DATIVE CASE concept in spite of having other properties as well, that is: in spite of instantiating other concepts as well, cf. Figure 1.

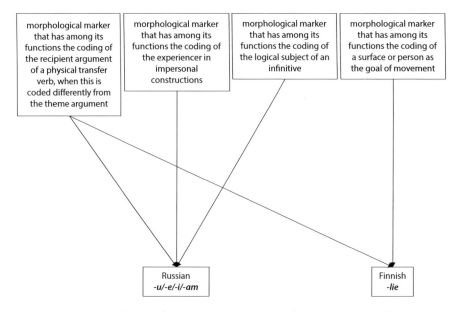

Figure 1. Instantiation (sources for Russian: Brown & Hippisley 2012: 30–33, Wade 1992: 86,100–103; source for Finnish: Karlsson 2015: 119, 143–144)[4]

---

4. Please note that the forms at hand might instantiate further categories, notably less general ones outside of the verbal domain, e.g.: "morphological marker for complements of the preposition *k*" with an arrow to the Russian forms (Wade 1992: 417).

More importantly, all text boxes above the bottom level are quasi-citations from Haspelmath (2010a); the same holds for the two following figures.

The same goes for certain forms in Korean and Turkish, i.e., the two other languages that Haspelmath mentions with respect to the comparative concept DATIVE CASE, cf. Figure 2.

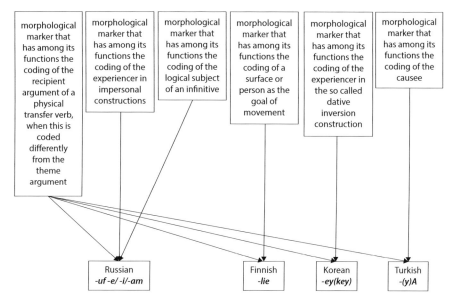

Figure 2. Instantiation, more languages (sources for Russian and Finnish: cf. Figure 1, sources for Korean: Kim 2016: 47–49, 72; Lee 1997: 25, source for Turkish: Kornfilt 1997: 212–213)

The crucial point is that the (comparative) concept does not exclude additional properties. In the example at hand, i.e., DATIVE CASE, it does so without being more general than the additional properties. However, being more general than other properties is a very convenient way of not excluding them. In the preceding figures, for example, one could add a further level at the top, consisting of a comparative concept 'morphological marker that has among its function the coding of event participants'. This is done in Figure 3.

Here it becomes particularly clear that the comparative concept is nothing more than a special category: it is a category since it is a set of at least one property (cf. the definition above), and it is special since it is the one category that happens to get instantiated in *all* lower classes under scrutiny, i.e., in all descriptive categories under scrutiny. So the comparative concept is not only a category but it is also applicable to more than one language – in other words: it is a crosslinguistic category.[5] Crosslinguistic categories in this sense – examples beyond DATIVE CASE

---

5. The relation between 'crosslinguistic' and 'universal' will be addressed briefly in Section 3.3.1 (last paragraph).

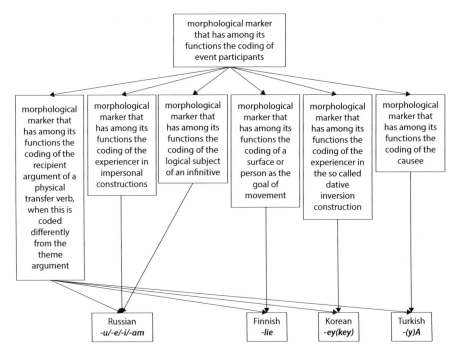

Figure 3. Figure 2 with one more level

can easily be imagined – are simply abstractions from descriptive categories. To be sure, as such they are less rich in properties than the original categories.

Please note that even when re-conceptualized as crosslinguistic categories, comparative concepts keep their well-known benefits: picking out a common property like "[…] coding of the recipient […]" does not depend on language-specific criteria and anyone is free to look for common properties in order to check their usability as a comparative concept/crosslinguistic category. Most importantly, re-conceptualizing comparative concepts as crosslinguistic categories solves the most pressing problem associated with Haspelmath's (2010a) comparative concepts, i.e., how to compare phenomena in two or more languages if the *tertium comparationis* hardly relates to these languages (cf. also Lander & Arkadiev 2016: 404–406; Moravscik 2016: 419 (iii); Alfieri this volume; Lieb this volume). Thanks to instantiation, comparison can simply be pictured as a trip through diagrams like Figure 3: you go all the way up from a phenomenon in one language to a property shared with at least one other language and then all the way down to a phenomenon in that language.

Certainly, in actual fact matters can become more complicated than in the DATIVE CASE example and I will deal with the complications in Section 3.3. My general point here is this: we cannot escape instantiation. And pretending that we could does not save us from serious decisions, as I will demonstrate below with respect to Haspelmath's suggestion for a comparative concept ERGATIVE CASE. Before, however, Haspelmath's third core argument has to be addressed.

3. The use of comparative concepts is de facto best practice. As support for this argument, Haspelmath (2010a: 666–668) claims that many researchers have been using comparative concepts successfully for quite some time, as it were *avant la lettre*. His most hands-on examples appear to be the use of IPA symbols and the use of standardized lexical meanings. I will address both examples in turn and try to show that they offer merely weak evidence for claiming that comparative concepts have a latent basis in academic history.

With respect to the IPA symbols, frankly speaking, I do not know which unconscious notion(s) of their true nature might have been hidden in the minds of phoneticians and phonologists for the last few decades – and admittedly Haspelmath's (2010a: 668) quotations suggest that for some of them the introduction of comparative concepts is indeed a welcome reification of their previously unconscious ideas. However, I will argue that, in fact, comparative concepts in Haspelmath's sense are not at stake here, since, again, there is a relationship of instantiation, this time between what is represented by an IPA symbol and the sound types from single languages. Moreover, I will argue that even if the IPA symbols (more precisely: their contents) could be conceived of as comparative concepts in Haspelmath's sense, nothing would be gained by this shift in perspective.

Consider the example mentioned in Section 2.1: laminal realization of Dutch /s/ vs. apical realization of German /s/. Stating that [s] is merely a comparative concept, which is "matched" by the two realizations, amounts to stating that [s] is not instantiated by them. However, it most obviously is: being an [s], i.e., being a voiceless alveolar fricative, is their common property while they differ in the value of an additional feature, which could be called "part of the tongue". The relationships are depicted in Figure 4.[6]

Please note that the difference (laminal vs. apical) is still accounted for but judged irrelevant to the question of instantiating the category [s]. Crucially, this does not mean that the difference is irrelevant in *all* respects – to use an example from another domain: there are certainly relevant differences between Chomsky (1957) and Croft (2001), still for library purposes both instantiate the category 'linguistic monograph'.

---

[6]. For the sake of simplicity I only depict the values, not the features; the latter can be added at an additional level of abstraction, cf. Figure 11 and, indirectly, Halle et al. (2000: 389).

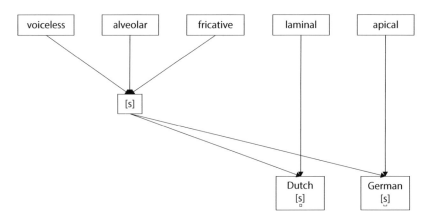

Figure 4. Phonetic instantiation

Thus, if Haspelmath intends to claim that certain shortcomings of the IPA alphabet (like representing the laminal vs. apical distinction by diacritics only) can be overcome by conceiving of the symbols' contents as comparative categories then I do not see why the same goal could not be met by using categories and instantiation.

To be sure, I do not intend to defend those shortcomings. A more general issue that the IPA alphabet has been criticized for is upholding and at the same time blurring the line between phonetics and phonology: on the one hand, the alphabet is declared "phonetic", on the other hand, there seems to be a tendency that a given bundle of phonetic feature values gets its own symbol only if it aligns with a phoneme in some languages (which ones is another issue, to be discussed below). For example, voiceless, dental plosives do not have a separate symbol. Whatever one's stance might be on this problem, it will not be solved by calling the old categories by a new name. The only benefit I can imagine is increased awareness for the fact that categories, concepts, and classes of all kind are man-made, lacking default psychological reality (see references above, p. 217). In order to tackle the phonetics/phonology issue, I suggest, again, simply using categories and instantiation. For example, Figure 5 depicts the situation in English vs. Maori, where *all* alveolar plosives are voiceless (Biggs 1961: 9).[7] As can be seen, there is just no need for any IPA symbol on the right hand side, that is: no need for what Haspelmath regards as a comparative concept.

---

7. If I understand Biggs correctly, they approximate but do not equal dentals.

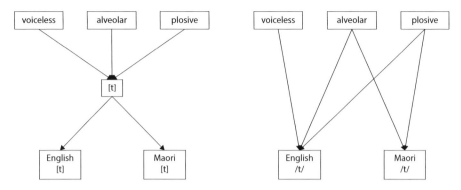

Figure 5. Phones vs. phonemes (source for Maori: <https://phoible.org/inventories/view/42#tipa>)

Something else the IPA alphabet has been criticized for is a certain amount of eurocentrism, connected with the phonetics/phonology issue: if English had a phonological contrast between dental, alveolar and postalveolar plosives, then presumably there would be three symbols (or six with voice contrasts).[8] In fact, pre-stopped nasals, which are phonemic in the Australian Pama-Nyungan language Kaytetye (Koch 2006: 170) do not appear at all in the IPA alphabet's latest version (2018). And they vanish all the same when the alphabet is conceived of as a set of comparative concepts in Haspelmath's sense. Again, thinking in terms of categories and instantiations instead prompts us to pose the relevant questions: are we happy just knowing that the category of nasals, which is visible in the IPA alphabet, has an instantiation that is not visible there but appears crucial in a certain language? Or should we revise the alphabet?

Incidentally, there is a parallel to the UG argument by Culicover discussed above: working with rather coarse categories is often sufficient but does not require anyone to leave it at that. For instantiation is virtually unbounded towards the lower end and only stops at individual sounds in a speech event.

---

8. Voice is another famous topic in discussions on the representation of phonetics vs. phonology in the IPA alphabet. I assume here that [+ voice] is a genuinely phonetic feature value indeed, no matter if the vibration of the vocal folds holds for the full length of a realization and no matter where it comes from. So, for example the initial sound of English *bowl* would be considered [b] here, although the vibration of the vocal folds is merely the result of an early VOT (voice onset time) of the following vowel.

Following the usage of IPA symbols, Haspelmath's second hands-on example for the use of comparative concepts as best practice is employing standardized meanings in lexical semantics research. Recall the Dutch vs. German example adduced above: 'time of the day that includes noon' would make a good comparative concept, matched by both, Dutch 'middag [12–6 p.m.]' and German 'Mittag [12–3 p.m.]'. However, again, merely assessing a "match" misses the fact that both notions are instantiations of the more general one, cf. Figure 6.

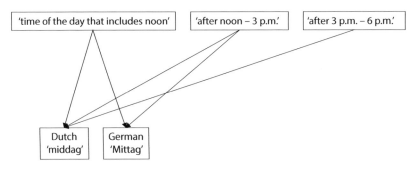

Figure 6. Lexical instantiation

To be sure, if one is not interested in the two additional general categories visualized at the top on the right then it is not necessary to depict them and, more importantly, instead of the general category 'time of the day that includes noon' any other common property could be chosen as well, e.g., 'times of the day that are culturally associated with breaks' or 'times of the day that are culturally associated with eating', possibly each with different subcategories. Thus, reconceptualizing comparative concepts as categories with instantiations preserves their flexibility.

To take an example from large scale typological research, the WALS chapter *Hand and arm* (Brown 2013) distinguishes the following types of languages:

- identity: there is a single word in the language that denotes both 'hand' and 'arm' (whether or not there are specialized words too);
- differentiation: one word in the language denotes 'hand' and another, different word denotes 'arm' (there is no comprehensive word).

In the running text of the chapter, Brown gives various examples from languages around the world and assigns each language to one of the two values:

- identity
  - Czech: *ruka* 'hand', 'arm'

- Gurma (Niger-Congo, Burkina Faso):[9] *nu* 'hand', 'arm'
- Lonwolwol (Oceanic, Vanuatu): *va:* 'hand', 'arm'
- Kadazan (Austronesian, Borneo): *hongon* 'hand', 'forearm', 'arm'
- Bambara (Mande, Mali):
  - *bolo* 'hand', 'arm'
  - *tègè* 'hand', 'palm', 'foot'
- Jicarilla Apache (Athabaskan, New Mexico):
  - *gan* 'hand', 'arm'
  - *l-lá* 'hand'
  - *gani* 'arm'
- Semai (Mon-Khmer, Malay Peninsula):
  - *tek* 'hand', 'arm'
  - *kengrit* 'arm'

– differentiation
- English:
  - *hand*
  - *arm*
- Ngawun (Pama-Nyungan, Australia):
  - *marl* 'hand'
  - *palkal* 'arm'
- Chai (Nilo-Saharan, Ethiopia):
  - *síyó* 'hand'
  - *múní* 'forearm'
  - *yíró* 'upper arm'
- Indonesian:
  - *tangan* 'hand', 'forearm'
  - *lengan* 'arm'

Let's try to picture these examples as instantiations of the two values, viewing the latter as categories (Brown himself uses neither of the terms *category* or *concept*). Please note the additional complication that this means grouping not only phenomena, but also languages. The result can be found in Figure 7. It is worth mentioning that the top-level categories on the left are *not* categories lexicalized in English, so I am not imposing English lexical categories onto other languages.

---

9. I was not able to verify this piece of language information, since the WALS gives as ISO code 639-3 grm, which cannot be found on <https://glottolog.org/>.

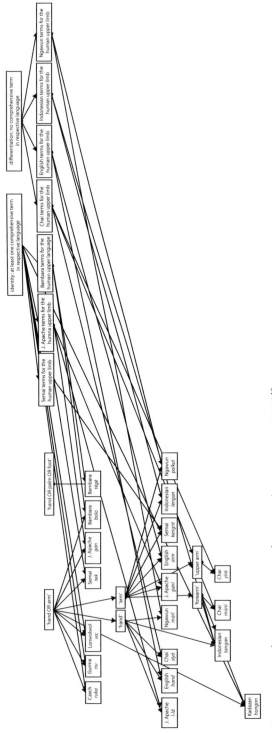

Figure 7. Lexical instantiation, more languages (source: Brown 2013).[10]

10. In contrast to the preceding figures, here the beginnings of arrows are marked by dots in order to indicate whether a given arrow starts at a box or just happens to run through it.

Thus, even seemingly messy lexical data may be captured by categories and instantiation. In particular, the aim of the WALS to group languages and not just phenomena actually calls for a combination of broad categories and successive refinements – free-floating comparative concepts just won't do.

As a side note, the preceding remarks on lexical semantics might be brought closer to the paragraphs on phonetics/phonology by adopting an approach based on feature-like universal semantic building blocks, i.e., Natural Semantic Metalanguage (e.g., Goddard & Wierzbicka 2002, for a critique cf. Riemer 2006).

To sum up my review of Haspelmath's third core argument, the use of comparative concepts as best practice: if this is best practice indeed, it is so unjustifiably. This concludes the discussion of Haspelmath's core arguments, none of which was able to convince me. Next is an investigation of his suggestions for concrete comparative concepts.

2.2.2 *Haspelmath's suggestions for concrete comparative concepts*

Of Haspelmath's seven suggestions for concrete comparative concepts I would like to discuss three: ADJECTIVE, FUTURE TENSE, and ERGATIVE CASE.

1. ADJECTIVE. As a definition of the term *adjective*, Haspelmath suggests the following comparative concept:

> An adjective is a lexeme that denotes a descriptive property and that can be used to narrow the reference of a noun. (Haspelmath 2010a: 670)

The design of this concept is motivated by the well-known observation that lexemes denoting properties and capable of narrowing down a noun's reference (rather, denotation) are an interesting set for typological generalizations but do not cohere as a distributional class in every language. One of the clearest examples appears to be Eastern Ojibwa (Algonquian, Eastern Canada/United States), which Haspelmath (2010a: 670) alludes to via a reference to Dryer (2005) (≙ Dryer 2013):

(1) n-ginooz   (Dryer 2013)[11]
    1SG-tall
    'I am tall.'

(2) n-nagam   (Dryer 2013)
    1SG-sing
    'I am singing.'

---

[11]. Abbreviations in the present paper that were adopted from WALS glosses: NOM = nominative, REL = relative, SG = singular. Furthermore, Dryer treats *ginooz* in (1) and *gnoozi* in (3) as identical, so I assume that the difference is merely phonological.

(3) nini   e-gnoozi-d   (Dryer 2013)
    man   REL-tall-3SG
    'a tall man'

(4) nini   e-ngamo-d   (Dryer 2013)
    man   REL-sing-3SG
    'a man who is singing'

Thus, *ginooz/gnoozi* matches the comparative concept ADJECTIVE without being any different from verbs on the level of single language distributional patterns. Please note that this match is only possible because the comparative concept does not require the lexeme to accomplish the noun-modifying function all by itself (cf. the relativizer in (3)). Thus, strictly speaking, the English lexeme *exceed* likewise matches the comparative concept ADJECTIVE, although it is classified as a verb within the system of English – an outcome that certainly would not surprise Haspelmath. Coming back to Eastern Ojibwa and taking stock: the language does not have adjectives and yet it does have elements like *ginooz/gnoozi* that match the comparative concept ADJECTIVE. Both assertions can be true at the same time (always provided that we can indeed tell what the basic meaning of an element is as well as its function in context, recall Quine's 1960 *gavagai* example). All of that said, however, I do not see why "matches the comparative concept" is any better than "instantiates the category": the double classification of *ginooz/gnoozi* or *exceed* can be captured in both ways (cf. Figure 11).

Moreover, there is a more specific problem. As argued above, the Eastern Ojibwa example works out only thanks to a quite liberal interpretation of the comparative concept's wording: the lexeme under scrutiny is allowed to require extra measures for fulfilling the noun-modifying function. This move is in line with the WALS chapter Haspelmath refers to:

> […]: a word is treated as an adjective, regardless of its word class in the language, as long as it denotes a descriptive property. The map also ignores the question of whether the adjectives are modifying nouns directly or whether they are the predicate of a relative clause which is modifying the noun.
> (Dryer 2005: 354–355, same in Dryer 2013).

Such a move, however, has unwelcome consequences: if we allow relativization as an extra measure, we have to allow other extra measures as well (assuming that there are no good reasons to privilege relativization). For example, also English *beauty* – which Haspelmath (2010a: 670) wants to exclude – matches the comparative concept ADJECTIVE for the simple reason that together with *of* it can modify a noun (*women of beauty*). So this is the slippery slope that Hengeveld (e.g., 1992: 58) has at least implicitly been warning against for a long time. To be fair, the problem specifically concerns Haspelmath's wording of the comparative concept ADJECTIVE, not comparative concepts as such.

2. *FUTURE TENSE*. As a definition of the term *future tense*, Haspelmath suggests the following comparative concept:

> A future tense is a grammatical marker associated with the verb that has future time reference as one prominent meaning. (Haspelmath 2010a: 671)

And he writes further:

> [...], the Spanish Future tense [...] is also used to express probability, but not habituality [...], while the Lezgian Future tense [...] is also used to express habituality, but not probability [...]. [...] **they cannot be 'the same category' in any sense.** (ibid., boldface T.R.)

This wording is revealing and I take the opportunity to repeat my main point: most certainly there is a sense in which they are the same category, viz. both instantiate the abstract category encompassed by the comparative concept, cf. Figure 8.

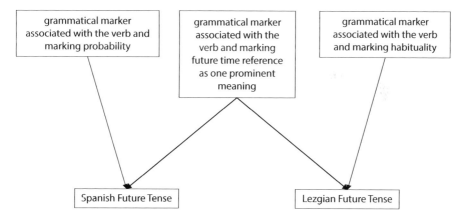

Figure 8. Instantiation, future tenses[12]

The relations might become even clearer when another kind of visualization is used; cf. the intersecting sets in Figure 9.

---

12. I adopt the convention of capitalizing the names of single language categories in this figure in order adhere to Haspelmath's example as closely as possible.

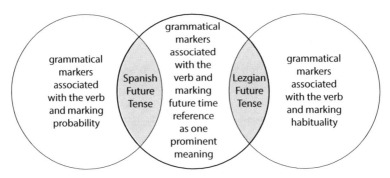

Figure 9. Instantiations, visualized as intersections

Please note that Figure 8 and Figure 9 are equivalent: the fact that two sets share one property is enough for saying that they instantiate this property (among other things) according to the definitions introduced in Section 2.2.1 (p. 217).

3. ERGATIVE CASE. As a definition of the term *ergative case*, Haspelmath suggests the following comparative concept:

> An ergative case is a morphological marker that has among its functions the coding of the agent of typical transitive clauses, when this is coded differently from the single argument of intransitive clauses. (Haspelmath 2010a: 673)

And he writes further:

> [...] the definition [is] neutral with respect to the competing analyses of split ergative systems: Dixon's, according to which languages like Dyirbal have an ergative-absolutive case system coexisting with a nominative-absolutive case system (in the 1st and 2nd person pronouns), and Goddard's (1982), according to which such languages have a tripartite ('ergative-accusative-nominative') system. On the latter analysis, 'Ergative' has a different meaning as a descriptive category, but the comparative concept [is] not affected. (ibid.)

True, the comparative concept is not affected. Yet at the same time it is far from neutral with respect to the two analyses, as I intend to show in the rest of this section. Let's have a closer look at the meaning of the term *ergative* as a descriptive category on the latter analysis, i.e., Goddard's (1982). Goddard writes:

> [...] for most of them [= Australian languages] we should recognise three core cases – a case of the transitive subject (A), a case of the transitive object (O), and a case of the intransitive subject (S) or citation – and I propose to call these cases respectively ergative, accusative and nominative. (Goddard 1981: 169)

Crucially, Goddard adduces two criteria for the nominative without taking into account that these may yield different extensions of the nominative and, indirectly, also of the ergative. For example, this is the case in the Yankunytjatjara dialect of Western Desert, which Goddard discusses extensively. Consider the system of Yankunytjatjara case endings in Table 1.

Table 1. Yankunytjatjara case endings, vowel final stems (Goddard 1982: 179, shading T.R.)[13]

	common nouns	proper nouns, kin names	pronouns, anaphoric
A	-ngku	-lu	ø
S	ø	-nya	ø
O	ø	-nya	-nya

If the criterion for nominative is being a marker of S, then the dark shaded cell hosts a nominative and accordingly the light shaded cell hosts an ergative (the criterion of marking A is fulfilled). Applying this criterion is consistent with the gloss in Goddard's (1982: 181) example (26), although there the gloss is chosen for reasons of agreement. The example is rendered below as (5) with emphasis added.

(5) Wati-ngku/**tjana**   ngulu-ngku pu-ngu.
    man-ERG/**3PL**(-ERG) afraid-ERG hit-PAST[14]
    'The man/**They** hit (it) in fear.'

The descriptive category ergative in this sense does not match the comparative concept ERGATIVE CASE, since the former is the same for the single argument of intransitive clauses as regards anaphoric pronouns (cf. Table 1).

If, however, the criterion for nominative is being in citation form (which I take to be the zero-marked form), then both, the dark and the light shaded cells in Table 1 must host a nominative. Applying this criterion is consistent with the gloss in Goddard's (1982: 181) example (27), although, again, there the gloss is chosen for reasons of agreement. The example is rendered below as (6) with emphasis added.

(6) Wati/**tjana**   ngulu   wala-ri-ngu.
    man(-NOM)/**3PL**(-NOM) afraid(-NOM)   run.away-INCHO-PAST
    'The man/**they** ran away in fear.'

In this case, there is no descriptive category ergative that could match the comparative concept ERGATIVE CASE. The descriptive category nominative does not

---

13. For a more comprehensive account of Yankunytjatjara case endings cf. Goddard (1985: 25).

14. Abbreviations in the present paper that were adopted from Goddard (1982): ERG = ergative, INCHO = inchoative, NOM = nominative, PL = plural.

match either (which, in principle, it could), since it codes both, the agent of transitive clauses and the single argument of intransitive clauses.

Thus, on both versions of Goddard's analysis, Yankunytjatjara A-/S-markings for anaphoric pronouns do not stand a chance of matching the comparative concept ERGATIVE CASE. Yankunytjatjara A-/S-markings for common nouns, though, do match it (cf. Table 1). This overall situation might be considered desirable by many; however it shows that the comparative concept draws exactly the same line as Dixon's well-known analysis does. So, contra Haspelmath's claim (2010a: 673), it is *not* neutral, hence fares no better than the crosslinguistic category it is supposed to replace. Please note that in order to make this point I did not even have to refer to instantiation.

To conclude, Haspelmath's suggestions for concrete comparative concepts reveal difficulties too. That is, on the whole, neither these nor the core arguments have convinced me of using comparative concepts as special tools, different from crosslinguistic categories. What are the alternatives?

Excursus

Before presenting any alternative, however, I would like to add a comment on Haspelmath (2019), which is to date his newest contribution to the discussion about comparative concepts (apart from Haspelmath this volume). Here he gives some new arguments in favour of using comparative concepts as special tools. If I understood the essence of his article correctly, the new arguments can be rendered by the following simile: the relation between a comparative concept and a given phenomenon is like the relation between a yardstick and the object being measured – the two things are qualitatively different from each other and the former has been invented only to show a property of the latter (cf. especially p. 88, also cf. Haspelmath this volume). However, recall a comparative concept like DATIVE CASE: "a morphological marker that has among its functions the coding of the recipient argument of a physical transfer verb […], when this is coded differently from the theme argument" (Haspelmath 2010a: 666, small caps T.R.). As far as I can see, this is less like the yardstick and much more like the property. To be sure, being a dative (i.e., instantiating DATIVE CASE) in Russian is different from being a dative in Turkish – like being an entity of 100 m height in the mountains is different from being an entity of 100 m height in the lowlands. Still, both are datives and both are entities of 100 m height. And we will not get an idea of height variation in the world by generalizing about yardsticks.

A more vital new argument, however, is hidden in this general picture and revealed in a core section of the paper (Haspelmath 2019: 94–97). Every descriptive category is defined distributionally, while no comparative concept can be defined in this way. Rather, a comparative concept is defined by its substantive properties.

Thus, descriptive categories and comparative concepts may happen to overlap *extensionally* but they can never be the same *intensionally* – they are ontologically different, as Haspelmath has emphasized more than once. Does this finally convince Moravcsik, Lehmann, and many others, including the author of the present paper? I think, it does not and I will show why in the rest of this excursus.

Things get a bit complicated here, since in actual practice, language-specific descriptive categories are rarely pure distributional classes. It is well known that they often have an additional substantive component, especially when we are dealing with part of speech categories. Let's take as a purer example three potential classes of Hawaiian expressions: those that in actual use more often follow the element *ua* than they follow the element *ka*, those with the opposite preference, and those with no preference (Elbert & Pukui 1979; Weber 2019). If, for example, the members of the *ua*-class can independently be shown to denote events and, at the same time, denoting (non-reified) events is what defines our comparative concept VERB, then the *ua*-class and the comparative concept *share a property* – regardless of how the two sets have come into being. Importantly, the comparative concept does not have any other properties besides the shared one whereas the *ua*-class does have such properties. So the former is instantiated by the latter according to the definitions introduced above (Section 2.2.1, p. 217). More generally, and independently from any peculiarities of the Hawaiian example:[15] ontologically different objects can share properties and thus entertain a relationship of instantiation. As Lieb (this volume) aptly puts it: "the difference […] is methodological not ontological".

3. An alternative: Monotonic, multiple inheritance

3.1 Background

Strictly speaking, the preceding figures already embody an alternative to the use of comparative concepts, and to be fair, this alternative has been anticipated by Haspelmath:

> Every linguistic category would instantiate a multiplicity of more abstract 'comparative categories', and a 'comparative category' could be instantiated multiple times in a single language. With such rampant many-to-many relationships, a taxonomic conceptualization, while logically possible, only obscures matters. Comparative concepts are simply a different kind of general notion from linguistic categories. (Haspelmath 2010a: 680)

---

15. E.g., does the premise "If […] the members of the *ua*-class can independently be shown to denote events" hold?

Against this background and recalling that the quotation's last sentence was shown to be false in Section 2.2.1, p. 219, my task here is to show that, generally, a taxonomic conceptualization does not obscure matters. In fact, it is apt for neat formalization.

3.2 Blueprint

The knowledgeable reader might have noticed that the preceding figures display not just any kind of instantiation, but monotonic, multiple inheritance (Daelemans et al. 1992: 208). Inheritance is a certain kind of structure, which can best be described by one of the ways to create it (Daelemans et al. 1992; Kaplan 2003: 88): from different categories (and particulars, if any) sets of common properties are extracted and represented as categories in their own right; if the new categories, too, share some properties, these are again extracted, yielding a new layer etc. Thus a hierarchy unfolds in which every category is a node – called *daughter* in relation to any node where its non-exclusive properties have been stored and *mother* in relation to any node whose properties (at least one of them) it stores. The metaphor is that properties are "inherited" as traits from mothers to daughters and accordingly the hierarchies are usually drawn in such a way that properties are transferred in downward direction. Particulars, finally, can be daughters, but not mothers and the highest mother is called *root*. Now that inheritance has been defined, also the two qualifications – monotonic and multiple – require a brief definition. *Monotonic* means: feature values are passed down from mother nodes to daughter nodes without the possibility of overwriting; *multiple* means: a daughter node may have more than one mother node (and it is not excluded that there is more than one root). I chose this combination for the following reason: only in the case of monotonic inheritance it seems to be clear that one can speak of instantiation; but then, without overwriting, the only way to map diversity appears to be multiple inheritance (cf., for instance, the dative example in Figure 3). There are two problems with this choice. First, any particular hierarchy has to be designed in such a way that it will not involve any conflict of feature values. To take a simple example, once more going back to Figure 3, it would not be a good idea to let a daughter node inherit from both, one mother node "morphological marker that has among its functions the coding of the recipient [...] but not the coding of the causee" and another one "morphological marker that has among its functions the coding of the causee". This is different when overwriting is an option, since in that case one of the feature values may be cancelled (although there are different ways to decide which one, cf. Daelemans et al. 1992: 209 et passim). Second, diagrams can become quite large, cf. the lexical example in Figure 7. I embrace both problems, assuming that these are merely matters of practical diligence.

Inheritance hierarchies of various kinds have been used for decades in both computational linguistics and general linguistics, e.g., in HPSG (Kaplan 2003: 88) or, in a sense, also in phonological feature geometry (Clements 1985), which in turn inspired applications to pronominal features (Harley & Ritter 2002). A relatively recent example is Network Morphology (NM, Brown & Hippisley 2012). The authors employ *non*-monotonic, multiple inheritance and I borrow their introductory example from Russian noun morphology as a blueprint for designing hierarchies. In fact, the blueprint has already been applied implicitly in the preceding figures (except Figure 9) and will be applied in a more general way in Section 3.3. Please note that the original example had to be modified in order to involve monotonic inheritance only.

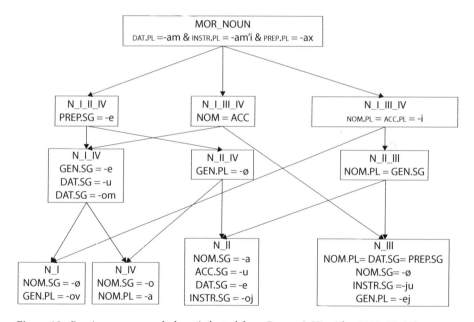

Figure 10. Russian noun morphology (adapted from Brown & Hippisley 2012: 30–33)

This hierarchy is meant to capture the forms given in Table 2.

Table 2. Russian noun morphology (source: Brown & Hippisley 2012: 30) = forms to be captured by Figure 10

	class I	class II	class III	class IV
singular				
NOMINATIVE	zakon	kart-a	rukop´is´	bolot-o
ACCUSATIVE	zakon	kart-u	rukop´is´	bolot-o
GENITIVE	zakon-a	kart-i	rukop´is´-i	bolot-a
DATIVE	zakon-u	kart-e	rukop´is´-i	bolot-u
INSTRUMENTAL	zakon-om	kart-oj	rukop´is´-ju	bolot-om
PREPOSITIONAL	zakon-e	kart-e	rukop´is´-i	bolot-e
plural				
NOMINATIVE	zakon-i	kart-i	rukop´is´-i	bolot-a
ACCUSATIVE	zakon-i	kart-i	rukop´is´-i	bolot-a
GENITIVE	zakon-ov	kart	rukop´is´-ej	bolot
DATIVE	zakon-am	kart-am	rukop´is´-am	bolot-am
INSTRUMENTAL	zakon-am´i	kart-am´i	rukop´is´-am´i	bolot-am´i
PREPOSITIONAL	zakon-ax	kart-ax	rukop´is´-ax	bolot-ax

I conceive of Figure 10 as a blueprint for designing hierarchies because it embodies all the important characteristics of monotonic, multiple inheritance very clearly (despite involving just one language):

- Common properties are combined into classes so that they do not have to be stated more often than necessary. Accordingly, only the lowest level is fully specified.
- A given item on the lowest level may share some properties with one sister node and others with another sister node. For example, N_I shares the genitive, dative, and instrumental singular with N_IV, but the nominative and accusative plural with N_II and N_III.
- All of the nodes instantiate the top-most category: they are all nominal inflections ("MOR_NOUN" in NM-style). This even holds for quite abstract categories like NOM = ACC (read: all nominal inflections that are the same in both cases).
- The hierarchy would look different if we were not interested in inflectional classes but in, e.g., overt vs. covert marking, syncretisms as such, or exclusively cases.

These are exactly the characteristics we saw in Figure 1 to Figure 8 (Section 2.2), i.e., from datives to futures, and we will see them again within a broader context in

Section 3.3. To be sure, the original purpose of Figure 10 is capturing the information in Table 2. If one wishes to check whether this purpose is fulfilled, the easiest way is to play a game: try to reproduce the table by using only and all the boxes in the figure. Please note that it is not even necessary to employ the combined headlines (e.g., N_I_II_IV), since these are merely mnemonic, repeating information from the branching structure. For example, the category of nominal inflections with the prepositional singular in -*e* eventually splits in three classes with certain additional properties and the category of nominal inflections with nominative-accusative syncretism also eventually splits in three classes, two of which are identical to two of the aforementioned classes. Put differently: for each category at the bottom, one can follow the arrows in the opposite direction and "collect" the category's properties. Besides, if in the process one starts wondering how the category "GEN.PL = ø" can possibly inherit from the category "PREP.SG = -e", the answer is simple: the category of nominal inflections that has a zero-marked genitive plural is a subset of the category of nominal inflections that has a prepositional singular in -*e*.

Incidentally, branching structures like in Figure 10 are one way to motivate the name *Network* Morphology. Another one is orthogonality, which I will address briefly in the following Section (3.3). The primary function of that section, however, is going one step beyond the blueprint's previous use in the present paper (Figure 1 to Figure 8 in Section 2.2): I intend to exploit it for a more general framework of categories and relate these to patterns or rules. In the process we will meet again two of the crosslinguistic examples discussed in Section 2.2, i.e., the role of IPA symbols and the term *adjective*.

3.3 Implementation

Anyone who criticizes an established notion and suggests an alternative is obliged to show that the alternative does not only do better in some respect but also preserves the advantages of the original. I attempted to do so in the preceding paragraphs; however, there is a (planned) implementation of Haspelmath's comparative concepts, which I have been ignoring up to now: a huge "Grammaticon" compiled from comparative concepts (Haspelmath 2018a, last sentence). Such a framework could be used as a general reference for language comparison; thus it would be extremely valuable for typologists. Is something similar conceivable for crosslinguistic categories, using the blueprint from Network Morphology?

I claim that it is; Figure 11 presents a first draft, which will be explained in detail below. Please note that of the examples discussed in Section 2.2.2 (dative case, adjective, future, and ergative case) only adjective could be included for reasons laid out in Section 3.3.2. However, I added one of the examples addressed in Section 2.2.1: the use of IPA symbols.

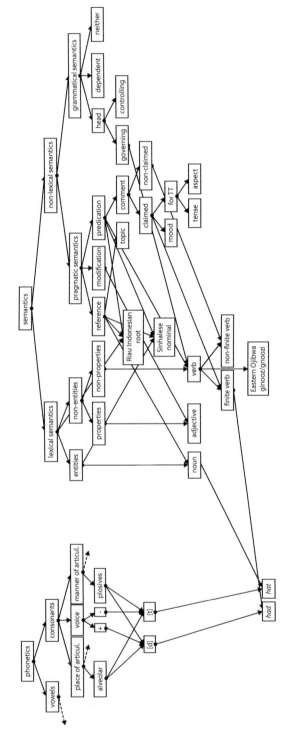

Figure 11. Crosslinguistic categories in an inheritance hierarchy (with monotonic, multiple inheritance)[16]

16. The manner of presentation is the same as in Figure 7 (cf. footnote 10). As to the voicing of plosives in English: in word-final position, too, vocal fold vibration is restricted; however, for present purposes it is only required that there is some of it (cf. footnote 8). Abbreviations: TT = topic time in the sense of Klein 1994.

3.3.1 *A guided tour through Figure 11*

At the top, there are two roots, phonetics and semantics, which is plausible if we think that language is about relating sounds and meaning (it will be addressed in Section 3.3.2 where phonology, morphology, and syntax are). The phonetics node immediately splits into the categories of the IPA alphabet, some of which are plotted here. Generally, not all necessary branches have been depicted in the diagram for reasons of space. Where it seemed reasonable, their absence was indicated by a dashed arrow.

It is via individual items like the minimal pair *had* vs. *hat*, which is given here as an example, that the phonetics tree is connected to the semantics tree. The semantics root at the top splits into lexical and non-lexical semantics. Obviously this only works for those linguists who believe in such a split. I do (Reiner 2014) and, perhaps surprisingly, Haspelmath at the very least does not embrace continuous categories/concepts either:

> In order to express universal claims in an explicit and readily testable way, one needs **discrete** comparative concepts [...]. Appeal to gradience or prototypicality often has a useful heuristic role, [...], but in the end, the big picture has to be dissolved into fine-grained **discrete** comparative concepts.
> (Haspelmath 2010a: 697, boldface T.R., also cf. Haspelmath this volume)

Lexical semantics, in turn, splits into two kinds of lexical concepts, i.e., entities and non-entities with the latter being divided in properties and non-properties. So the last node reads 'category of non-entities that are at the same time non-properties', also known as events.[17] Certainly, the precise structure depends on one's favourite ontology in this domain (cf., e.g., Zaefferer 2007: 204–205) and I am not committed to the one chosen here.

The different kinds of lexical concepts hand down their properties to three part of speech categories (noun, adjective, verb); however the latter also inherit from the other subtree of semantics, i.e., from non-lexical semantics. Non-lexical semantics splits into pragmatic and grammatical semantics – again a division that not everybody would subscribe to. I presuppose it here.

Pragmatic semantics is divided into reference, modification, and predication, more precisely: *potential for* reference, modification, and predication. The respective properties are then transferred to the part of speech categories, which we first met on our tour down the lexical semantics branch. For example, according to Figure 11 a noun is something that expresses an entity concept and has the potential for referring (without further measures being taken, cf. Hengeveld 1992: 58).

---

17. In the broad sense including states, which are different from properties in that they concern *having* a property.

In principle, this could be a string of sounds as well as a gesture or a pictogram. Only when there is a connection to the phonetics tree via individual items (cf. *hat* above) it has to be a string of sounds. Furthermore, I suggest splitting predication in a way that is explained in detail in Reiner (2019: 303–307). The interested reader is referred to that publication, whereas here it seems sufficient to note that the node "(comment) claimed" is used to characterize a subcategory of verb, i.e., finite verb.

Before treating the more concrete examples (Riau Indonesian root, Sinhalese Noun, and Eastern Ojibwa *ginooz/gnoozi*), the rightmost subtree, i.e., grammatical semantics, has to be addressed briefly. It splits into several well-known categories, i.e., head vs. dependent, with the former in turn splitting into government and control. These categories are considered semantic here, since they involve abstract meanings instead of material units and their arrangement (very much in line with classical Cognitive Linguistics thinking). Crucially, the only part of speech category that inherits from this subtree is verb: it is here defined as something that *always* governs (not excluding that additionally it *is* governed), while nouns and adjectives are permitted more flexibility.

What is also flexible is the integration of single languages' part-of-speech categories into the hierarchy, as will be shown in the following paragraphs. In principle even a full Hengeveldian approach (e.g., Hengeveld 2013: 32–37) could be translated into inheritance hierarchies with multiple, monotonic inheritance. One of the reasons I refrain from doing so here is an issue with adverbs to be addressed in Section 3.3.2.

The part of speech categories in Figure 11 give the impression of being rather narrow. So how can we accommodate broader part of speech classes? Certainly, the most famous (potential) example for a language without even a noun-verb distinction is Riau Indonesian (Gil 2013 and much previous work by the same author). Assuming that Gil is right, the Riau Indonesian root can be integrated into the hierarchy quite easily: the respective node is *not* a daughter of any part of speech category but inherits directly from lexical semantics as well as from reference and predication. Note that inheriting from entities as well as from events (*non*-entities & non-properties) is not an option, since this would generate a contradiction and overwriting is not possible given monotonic inheritance. In any case, there is no contradiction involved in inheriting from both the nodes "reference" and "predication", since the two terms are, as mentioned earlier, meant as short forms of *potential for reference* and *potential for predication*. Presumably, also a line from "modification" could be drawn; however for the time being it does not appear in the figure since I am not an expert in Riau Indonesian and the pertaining literature concentrates heavily on the noun-verb distinction (which makes sense considering the hierarchy in Hengeveld 2013: 35).

In this sense, the Riau Indonesian root is precategorial in the sense of van Lier & Rijkhoff (2013: 5–6). There is much more to say about this line of research, rooted in the tradition of Hengeveld (1992), and one issue appears to be particularly important in the context of the present paper. Approaches such as Hengeveld's (1992) – or more recently Rijkhoff's (2016) – that start from pragmatic categories like reference, modification, and predication have been famously criticized for ignoring shifts in root meaning (Croft 2001: 67–75). According to Croft, the meaning of a root in context and the pragmatic function it has in that context do not combine freely: entity meaning in reference function, property meaning in modification function, and event meaning in predication function.[18] If this is right, then, admittedly, the correlation is not shown in Figure 11. A way to integrate it would be the following: remove the arrow from "governing" to "verb", so that the three part of speech categories represent exactly the correlation that Croft has in mind; then move the node "Riau Indonesian root" (deleting all arrows pointing to it originally) below the part of speech categories and let it inherit from all of *them* at the same time.

One reason for doubting Croft's correlation, however, is the existence of so called zero copula constructions, i.e., entity expressions independently functioning as predications. An example from Sinhalese (Indo-Aryan, Sri Lanka) is given in (7).

(7) unnæhee **huṅgak prəsidə kene-k**[19]
    he   very   famous person-NOM
    'He is/was a very famous person.'   (Gair 1970: 45)

It seems hard to believe that the nominal as such does not mean 'famous person' (entitiy) in the context at hand but 'being a famous person' (non-entity). Ultimately, though, the identification of meanings and speech act potentials without the help of overt linguistic markers remains a matter of careful empirical work; so I do not take a stance on this issue here. In any case, (7) provides another example for what can be modelled by monotonic, multiple inheritance: if the meaning does not shift, the node "Sinhalese nominal" inherits from the nodes "entity" and "predication"; if it does shift, the node "Sinhalese nominal" inherits from

---

18. When, elsewhere, Croft (2005: 438) speaks of a merely prototypical mapping he takes into account the fact that there are in total three dimensions: root meanings in the lexicon map onto root meanings in context prototypically, while the absolute relation is between the latter and pragmatic functions. Schematically:

root meanings in the lexicon - - - root meanings in context — pragmatic functions

19. Glossing and translation from Stassen (2013).

"(non-entities &) non-properties" (= events) and "predication". The former version is shown in Figure 11 (in addition to an arrow from "reference").

Conversely, there seems to be no reason to suspect that Eastern Ojibwa *ginooz/gnoozi*, as discussed in Section 2.2.2, undergoes a shift in meaning. The data snippet presented there is consistent with the (presumably most simple) assumption that *ginooz/gnoozi* just means 'being tall'. That is, the lexeme as such denotes a state, not a property. So it does not inherit from "properties" in Figure 11, but only from "verbs" (assuming that it always governs). This classification is at variance with the one implied by Haspelmath (cf. Section 2.2.2), although his comparative concept ADJECTIVE seems equivalent to the crosslinguistic category adjective according to Figure 11: something that expresses a property concept and has the potential for modifying. How can that be? The reason is that the equivalence is only superficial: I do not adopt the liberal reading according to which the element under scrutiny may qualify as a match/instance by help of another element. Thus, Eastern Ojibwa verbs stay verbs in the approach advocated here. That is: in this case, using crosslinguistic categories and instantiation appears to involve less "levelling down" of language diversity than using comparative concepts and matching. However, this is not due to the nature of comparative concepts but just to Haspelmath's way of dealing with one specific comparative concept.

Considering all the nodes in Figure 11, they are abstractions from their daughter nodes (mostly *not* shown in the figure) and in this sense they represent categories that are applicable to their daughters, e.g.: noun is applicable to English *hat*. Roughly speaking, the higher a node, the greater the plausibility that the category is universally applicable (e.g., place of articulation, entity meaning, or headhood if the latter is considered sufficiently general). Whether it is indeed, remains an empirical question: the hierarchy as a tool neither tags any level as universal nor does it prevent us from splitting categories until they are particulars. What it does is providing the possibility of membership in a category without the members having to share all their properties – thus solving the classical problem presented by Gross (1979: 859–860). When tackling the empirical question of universal applicability, anyone has to decide for themselves if trivial applicability (where applying a category c to a language L might come down to stating that L *does not have* c) is enough or not. Crucially, universally applicable nodes in both senses would qualify as comparative concepts à la Haspelmath (2010a), except that they are now nicely integrated into a hierarchy.

3.3.2 Beyond Figure 11

The hierarchy in Figure 11 provides an inventory of categories. Presumably, however, every linguist wants to have further categories at his/her disposal and some of them are hard to capture in the hierarchy. For example, if adverb is defined differently from adjective as 'dependent of verb with a non-entity meaning and modifying potential' then there is a problem in depicting the dependent-of relation within the hierarchy. Certainly, the node "dependent" could split into various "dependent-of" daughters, among them "dependent of verb". But, strictly speaking, at this position the information on what constitutes a verb is not available. Thus, some categories have to be derived from the hierarchy as a whole and in this sense they are second order categories. Another, more complex example would be: 'dependent of [dependent of verb with entity-meaning and referring potential], specifying the entity as carrier of semantic role x'[20] = case (in a broad sense including particles). In the long run, even more complex categories could be designed in this way, for example a version of Role and Reference Grammar's general notion 'privileged syntactic argument' (Van Valin & LaPolla 1997: 274–285; Van Valin 2005: 94–101), which seems to be a good candidate for replacing 'subject' but figures only rarely in pertinent discussions (e.g., Haspelmath 2019: 96–97).

So there is phonetics and semantics, providing first order categories and in addition there are second order categories. But what about phonology, morphology, and syntax? Not even pragmatics proper is covered by Figure 11, since only speech act *potentials* are involved. In fact, all of these missing levels of description have something in common: they are not mere inventories of categories but they comprise *things to do with categories*. For example, phonology takes as input minimal pairs from the hierarchy and extracts phonemes from them, which may then form morae, syllables, and foots. Syntax, understood as a superset of ordering restrictions, arranges categories from the inventories (or instances of those categories). Like different phonemes, certain ordering differences cause a change in meaning without actually carrying meaning. Morphology is more difficult to accommodate since its traditional definition hinges on a universal notion of word, which has proven much more elusive than the notions discussed in the present paper (Haspelmath 2011). It seems to me that nowadays theorists, in particular proponents of autonomous morphology, understand morphology as the totality of phenomena that can only be reasonably described by reference to paradigms, for example the so-called L- and N-patterns in Romance (see Maiden 2009). In this view, morphology is about relating categories and subcategories, i.e., features and their values, to one another. These relations might differ from language to language, e.g.:

---

20. Semantic roles could be included in Figure 11 somewhere below the entities node. So they would be part of lexical semantics, which might seem odd but is in accordance with the definitions of lexical and non-lexical semantics adopted in this paper.

tense	– past/present/future
	– past/non-past
	– ...
case	– nominative/accusative/dative
	– absolutive/ergative/dative
	...

Thus, morphology, too, belongs to those levels of description that capture things to do with categories. The same is true, and more obviously so, for pragmatics proper: it describes how speakers (inter-)act by using nouns, verbs and so on.

As an interim summary, monotonic, multiple inheritance directly or indirectly supplies the categories within phonetics and semantics, while all other levels of description (phonology, syntax, morphology, pragmatics) account for what can be done with those categories. This is similar to but different from the solution adopted in Network Morphology, i.e., orthogonality. Orthogonality means that every level of description (lexicon, morphology, syntax) receives its own hierarchy and the hierarchies are connected by default associations (Brown & Hippisley 2012: 36–37). Nodes, at least morphological ones, can be conceived of as rules (p. 34). A full comparison of the two approaches is beyond the scope of this paper; however their relationship had to be mentioned.

With respect to my approach as a whole, two questions remain to be answered. First, is this pretty? Second, are description and explanation kept apart? The first question is more serious than it appears to be since I set out to show that monotonic, multiple inheritance does not obscure matters. Still, what appears to be lucid remains, to a certain extent, a matter of personal taste and intended applications. Consider, for example, intricate HPSG analyses or gigantic WordNets, both of which may look cluttered to the human eye but are perfectly machine-readable. The second question, however, is as serious as it sounds. In particular, Haspelmath has repeatedly emphasized that description and explanation have to be kept apart (e.g., 2008: 93). I respond: in a strict sense, they *cannot* be kept apart. Every (crosslinguistic) category and every (comparative) concept comprises not only its instances/matches that have been witnessed so far but also all its other possible instances/matches (this is why we create them). Hence, every category that is integrated into a taxonomy and also every concept that entertains any relation with other concepts comes with an inbuilt prediction: all its instances/matches that have not been witnessed so far can occupy the same position in the taxonomy or entertain the same relations with other concepts, respectively. As far as prediction counts as explanation (to be sure, boring top-down explanation), there is explanation in any description using crosslinguistic categories or comparative concepts.

4. Conclusion and outlook

The present contribution scrutinized Haspelmath's notion of comparative concepts and offered an alternative view. In a nutshell: on closer consideration, comparative concepts in Haspelmath's sense do not exist. Rather what have been called comparative concepts *are* crosslinguistic categories, participating in taxonomies just like any other category.

The taxonomies presented here were inheritance hierarchies with multiple, monotonic inheritance. So the next step would be using this tool to model the whole range of variation found within one category in a given language sample.

Acknowledgments

I thank Guido Seiler's Munich *Oberseminar* for discussing the first draft of this paper with me as well as two anonymous reviewers for their detailed comments on the second version. I would also like to thank Martin Haspelmath for bringing Haspelmath (2019) to my attention.

References

Alfieri, Luca. 2021. Parts of speech, comparative concepts and Indo-European linguistics. In *Linguistic Categories, Language Description and Linguistic Typology* [Typological Studies in Language 132]. Amsterdam: John Benjamins. (This volume) https://doi.org/10.1075/tsl.132.09alf

Armstrong, David M. 2004. How do particulars stand to universals? In *Oxford Studies in Metaphysics 1*, Dean W. Zimmerman (ed.), 139–154. Oxford: Clarendon Press.

Biggs, Bruce. 1961. The structure of New Zealand Maaori. *Anthropological Linguistics* 3(3): 1–54.

Brown, Cecil H. 2013. Hand and arm. In *The World Atlas of Language Structures Online*, Matthew S. Dryer & Martin Haspelmath (eds). Leipzig: MPI for Evolutionary Anthropology. <http://wals.info/chapter/129> (18 December 2018).

Brown, Dunstan & Hippisley, Andrew. 2012. *Network Morphology. A Defaults-based Theory of Word Structure* [Cambridge Studies in Linguistics 133]. Cambridge: CUP. https://doi.org/10.1017/CBO9780511794346

Chomsky, Noam. 1957. *Syntactic Structures* [Janua Linguarum 4]. The Hague: Mouton. https://doi.org/10.1515/9783112316009

Clements, George N. 1985. The geometry of phonological features. *Phonology Yearbook* 2: 225–252. https://doi.org/10.1017/S0952675700000440

Croft, William. 2001. *Radical Construction Grammar. Syntactic Theory in Typological Perspective*. Oxford: OUP. https://doi.org/10.1093/acprof:oso/9780198299554.001.0001

Croft, William. 2005. Word classes, parts of speech, and syntactic argumentation. *Linguistic Typology* 9(3): 431–441.

Culicover, Peter W. 1999. *Syntactic Nuts. Hard Cases, Syntactic Theory, and Language Acquisition* [Foundations of Syntax 1]. Oxford: OUP.

Daelemans, Walter, Gerald, Gazdar & De Smedt, Koenraad. 1992. Inheritance in natural language processing. *Computational Linguistics* 18(2): 205–218.

Dahl, Östen. 2016. Thoughts on language-specific and crosslinguistic entities. *Linguistic Typology* 20(2): 427–437. https://doi.org/10.1515/lingty-2016-0016

Dryer, Matthew S. 2005. Order of adjective and noun. In *The World Atlas of Language Structures*, Martin Haspelmath, Matthew S. Dryer, David Gil & Bernard Comrie (eds), 354–357. Oxford: OUP.

Dryer, Matthew S. 2013. Order of adjective and noun. In *The World Atlas of Language Structures Online*, Matthew S. Dryer & Martin Haspelmath (eds). Leipzig: MPI for Evolutionary Anthropology. <http://wals.info/chapter/87> (16 January 2019).

Elbert, Samuel H. & Pukui, Mary Kawena. 1979. *Hawaiian Grammar*. Honolulu HI: The University Press of Hawaii.

Gair, James W. 1970. *Colloquial Sinhalese Clause Structures* [Janua Linguarum; Series Practica 83]. The Hague: Mouton. https://doi.org/10.1515/9783110873207

Gerner, Matthias & Bisang, Walter. 2010. Social-deixis classifiers in Weining Ahmao. In *Rara & Rarissima. Documenting the Fringes of Linguistic Diversity* [Empirical Approaches to Language Typology 46], Jan Wohlgemuth & Michael Cysouw (eds), 75–94. Berlin: De Gruyter. https://doi.org/10.1515/9783110228557.75

Gil, David. 2013. Riau Indonesian. A language without nouns and verbs. In *Flexible Word Classes. Typological Studies of Underspecified Parts of Speech*, Jan Rijkhoff & Eva van Lier (eds), 89–130. Oxford: OUP. https://doi.org/10.1093/acprof:oso/9780199668441.003.0004

Glottolog. <https://glottolog.org/> (18 December 2018).

Goddard, Cliff. 1982. Case systems and case marking in Australian languages. A new interpretation. *Australian Journal of Linguistics* 2(2): 167–196. https://doi.org/10.1080/07268608208599290

Goddard, Cliff. 1985. *A Grammar of Yankunytjatjara*. Alice Springs: Institute for Aboriginal Development.

Goddard, Cliff & Wierzbicka, Anna (eds). 2002. *Meaning and Universal Grammar, 1: Theory and Empirical Findings* [Studies in Language Companion Series 60]. Amsterdam: John Benjamins. https://doi.org/10.1075/slcs.60

Gross, Maurice. 1989. On the failure of Generative Grammar. *Language* 55(4): 859–885. https://doi.org/10.2307/412748

Halle, Morris, Vaux, Bert & Wolfe, Andrew. 2000. On feature spreading and the representation of place of articulation. *Linguistic Inquiry* 31(3): 387–444. https://doi.org/10.1162/002438900554398

Harley, Heidi & Ritter, Elizabeth. 2002. Structuring the bundle. A universal morphosyntactic feature geometry. In *Pronouns. Grammar and Representation* [Linguistik Aktuell/Linguistics Today 52], Horst J. Simon & Heike Wiese (eds), 23–39. Amsterdam: John Benjamins. https://doi.org/10.1075/la.52.05har

Haspelmath, Martin. 2008. Parametric versus functional explanations of syntactic universals. In *The Limits of Syntactic Variation* [Linguistik Aktuell/Linguistics Today 132], Theresa Biberauer (ed.), 75–107. Amsterdam: John Benjamins. https://doi.org/10.1075/la.132.04has

Haspelmath, Martin. 2010a. Comparative concepts and descriptive categories in crosslinguistic studies. *Language* 86(3): 663–687. https://doi.org/10.1353/lan.2010.0021

Haspelmath, Martin. 2010b. The interplay between comparative concepts and descriptive categories (Reply to Newmeyer). *Language* 86(3): 696–699. https://doi.org/10.1353/lan.2010.0004

Haspelmath, Martin. 2011. The indeterminacy of word segmentation and the nature of morphology and syntax. *Folia Linguistica* 45(1): 31–80. https://doi.org/10.1515/flin.2011.002

Haspelmath, Martin. 2018a. Facing the challenge of general linguistics when nature doesn't help us. *Diversity Linguistics Comment of 18 February*. <https://dlc.hypotheses.org/1012> (7 February 2019).

Haspelmath, Martin. 2019. How comparative concepts and descriptive linguistic categories are different. In *Aspects of Linguistic Variation*, Daniël Van Olmen, Tanja Mortelmans & Frank Brisard (eds), 83–114. Berlin: De Gruyter.

Haspelmath, Martin. 2021. Towards standardization of morphosyntactic terminology for general linguistics. In *Linguistic Categories, Language Description and Linguistic Typology* [Typological Studies in Language 132]. Amsterdam: John Benjamins. (This volume) https://doi.org/10.1075/tsl.132.02has

Hengeveld, Kees. 1992. *Non-verbal Predication. Theory, Typology, Diachrony* [Functional Grammar Series 15]. Berlin: De Gruyter. https://doi.org/10.1515/9783110883282

Hengeveld, Kees. 2013. Parts-of-speech systems as a basic typological determinant. In *Flexible Word Classes. Typological Studies of Underspecified Parts of Speech*, Jan Rijkhoff & Eva van Lier (eds), 31–55. Oxford: OUP. https://doi.org/10.1093/acprof:oso/9780199668441.003.0002

Kaplan, Ronald M. 2003. Syntax. In *The Oxford Handbook of Computational Linguistics*, Ruslan Mitkov (ed.), 70–90. Oxford: OUP.

Karlsson, Fred. 2015. *Finnish. An Essential Grammar* [Routledge Essential Grammars], 3rd edn. London: Routledge.

Kim, Jong-Bok. 2016. *The Syntactic Structures of Korean. A Construction Grammar Perspective*. Cambridge: CUP. https://doi.org/10.1017/CBO9781316217405

Klein, Wolfgang. 1994. *Time in Language* [Germanic Linguistics]. London: Routledge.

Koch, Harold. 2006. Kaytetye. In *Encyclopedia of Language and Linguistics*, 2nd edn, Keith Brown (ed.), 170–172. Amsterdam: Elsevier. https://doi.org/10.1016/B0-08-044854-2/05104-X

Kornfilt, Jaklin. 1997. *Turkish* [Descriptive Grammars]. London: Routledge.

Lander, Yuri & Arkadiev, Peter. 2016. On the right of being a comparative concept. *Linguistic Typology* 20(2): 403–416. https://doi.org/10.1515/lingty-2016-0014

Lee, Que. 1997. Dative Constructions and Case Theory in Korean. PhD dissertation, Simon Fraser University.

Lehmann, Christian. 2018. Linguistic concepts and categories in language description and comparison. In *Typology, Acquisition, Grammaticalization Studies* [Materiali Linguistici 79], Marin Chini & Pierluigi Cuzzolin (eds), 27–50. Milano: Franco Angeli. <http://www.christianlehmann.eu/publ/lehmann_ling_concepts_categories.pdf> (9 May 2019).

Lieb, Hans-Heinrich. 2021. Theories of language, language comparison, and grammatical description. Correcting Haspelmath. In *Linguistic Categories, Language Description and Linguistic Typology* [Typological Studies in Language 132]. Amsterdam: John Benjamins. (This volume) https://doi.org/10.1075/tsl.132.05lie

Maddieson, Ian. 2018. Is phonological typology possible without (universal) categories? In *Phonological Typology* [Phonology and Phonetics 23], Larry M. Hyman & Frans Plank (eds), 107–125. Berlin: De Gruyter. https://doi.org/10.1515/9783110451931-004

Maiden, Martin. 2009. From pure phonology to pure morphology. The reshaping of the Romance verb. *Recherches Linguistiques de Vincennes* 38: 45–82. https://doi.org/10.4000/rlv.1765

McGinn, Colin. 2012. *Truth by Analysis*. Oxford: OUP.

Moravcsik, Edith A. 2016. On linguistic categories. In *Linguistic Typology* 20(2): 417–425. https://doi.org/10.1515/lingty-2016-0015

Newmeyer, Frederick J. 2010. On comparative concepts and descriptive categories: A reply to Haspelmath. *Language* 86(3): 688–695. https://doi.org/10.1353/lan.2010.0000

Quine, Willard van Orman. 1960. *Word and Object* [Series in Communication]. Cambridge MA: The MIT Press.

Reiner, Tabea. 2014. Lexical and grammatical meaning. Revisited. In *Semantics and Beyond. Philosophical and Linguistic Investigations* [Philosophical Analysis 57], Piotr Stalmaszczyk (ed), 231–240. Berlin: De Gruyter.

Reiner, Tabea. 2019. Variation in non-finiteness and temporality from a canonical perspective. In *Morphological Variation. Theoretical and Empirical Perspectives* [Studies in Language Companion Series 207], Antje Dammel & Oliver Schallert (eds), 283–310. Amsterdam: John Benjamins. https://doi.org/10.1075/slcs.207.10rei

Riemer, Nick. 2006. Reductive paraphrase and meaning. A critique of Wierzbickian semantics. *Linguistics and Philosophy* 29(3): 347–379. https://doi.org/10.1007/s10988-006-0001-4

Rijkhoff, Jan. 2016. Crosslinguistic categories in morphosyntactic typology. Problems and prospects. In *Linguistic Typology* 20(2): 333–363. https://doi.org/10.1515/lingty-2016-0010

Schachter, Paul. 1996. *The Subject in Tagalog. Still None of the Above* [UCLA Occasional Papers in Linguistics 15]. Los Angeles: UCLA.

Spencer, Andrew. 2008. Does Hungarian have a case system? In *Case and Grammatical Relations. Studies in Honour of Bernard Comrie* [Typological Studies in Language 81], Greville G. Corbett & Michael Noonan (eds), 35–56. Amsterdam: John Benjamins. https://doi.org/10.1075/tsl.81.02doe

Stassen, Leon. 2013. Zero copula for predicate nominals. In *The World Atlas of Language Structures Online*, Matthew S. Dryer & Martin Haspelmath (eds). Leipzig: MPI for Evolutionary Anthropology. <http://wals.info/chapter/120> (17 January 2019).

Stock, Wolfgang G. & Mechthild Stock. 2013. *Handbook of Information Science*. Berlin: De Gruyter.

van der Auwera, Johan & Sahoo, Kalyanamalini. 2015. On comparative concepts and descriptive categories, *such* as they are. *Acta Linguistica Hafniensia* 47(2): 136–173. https://doi.org/10.1080/03740463.2015.1115636

van Lier, Eva & Rijkhoff, Jan. 2013. Flexible word classes in linguistic typology and grammatical theory. In *Flexible Word Classes. Typological Studies of Underspecified Parts of Speech*, Jan Rijkhoff & Eva van Lier (eds), 1–30. Oxford: OUP. https://doi.org/10.1093/acprof:oso/9780199668441.003.0001

Van Valin Jr., Robert D. 2005. *Exploring the Syntax-semantics Interface*. Cambridge: CUP. https://doi.org/10.1017/CBO9780511610578

Van Valin Jr., Robert D. & LaPolla, Randy. 1997. *Syntax. Structure, Meaning and Function* [Cambridge Textbooks in Linguistics]. Cambridge: CUP. https://doi.org/10.1017/CBO9781139166799

Wade, Terence. 1992. *A Comprehensive Russian Grammar*. Oxford: Blackwell.

Weber, Benjamin. 2019. Eine korpuslinguistische Analyse der Wortarten im Hawai'i (A corpus-linguistic analysis of word classes in Hawaiian). Presentation, Munich, 12 July.

Zaefferer, Dietmar. 2007. Language as mind sharing device. Mental and linguistic concepts in a general ontology of everyday life. In *Ontolinguistics. How Ontological Status Shapes the Linguistic Coding of Concepts* [Trends in Linguistics; Studies and Monographs 176], Andrea C. Schalley & Dietmar Zaefferer (eds), 193–227. Berlin: De Gruyter.

CHAPTER 7

Essentials of the UNITYP research project

Attempt of an overview

Hansjakob Seiler (†), Yoshiko Ono & Waldfried Premper
University of Zurich / University of Cologne

> This contribution surveys the insights of 'UNITYP' (Language Universals and Typology), a research project initiated and led by Hansjakob Seiler from 1973 until 1992 and further developed by him until 2017. First, an overview of essential concepts and the architecture of the UNITYP model is given. Of central importance are three levels of research: cognitive-conceptual, general comparative grammar, and individual languages. Then the conceptual and methodological implications are demonstrated by selected analyses. These comprise a summary of Seiler's latest 'works in progress' concerning Identification as well as an application of the crucial abductive method in cross-linguistic investigation, exemplified by the object relation and number.

0. Preliminary remarks

This contribution is based on our presentation at the SLE conference 2017 in Zurich. The first three parts of the present paper were presented there in 2017 in agreement with Hansjakob Seiler after a personal discussion among the three of us. Section 4 was written by Y. Ono after H. Seiler's death on August 13th 2018 as 'in memoriam': some theoretical and methodological aspects are here outlined and discussed as thematically relevant. They could not be mentioned at the conference due to time constraints.

1. Introduction

UNITYP is a shortcut to denote a research project devoted to 'language universals research and linguistic typology' initiated and led by Hansjakob Seiler at the University of Cologne since 1973 and funded by the Deutsche Forschungsgemeinschaft

(DFG) until 1992. The official project title contained the specification "with particular reference to functional aspects". The main characteristics of the UNITYP approach consists in establishing continua of techniques (such as those of identification), which are arrayed according to the functional principles of indicativity and predicativity. Indicativity means global capturing and pointing at (reference) while predicativity corresponds to the act of explicit ascribing properties and predication (content). All techniques exhibit both principles in a different degree.

In this contribution, we take the opportunity to, first, have a look back and trace some central concepts in the development of the UNITYP approach, and then to present aspects of research being continued primarily by Hansjakob Seiler himself until nearly his last days (see the obituary by Christian Lehmann 2019).

2. Some essential concepts of UNITYP

2.1 Driving force

The following can be seen as a *general leit-motif* of UNITYP research: to investigate, in the domain of language, the relationship or interplay between sameness (*invariance*, constance) and difference (*variation*) (see e.g., Seiler & François 2001: 9). A basic assumption is expressed by the statement: "A number of structural phenomena in any given language, although differing in both form and meaning, can be grouped together under a single common functional denominator" (Seiler 2000: 14). An example would be the 'identification of an object or item', which subsumes strategies such as relative clauses, genitives, and demonstratives (see Section 3 below).

2.2 Premise (functional setting)

Language is fundamentally understood as a '*problem-solving activity*' ("problem solving system", Seiler 1973: 11; see Seiler 1983: 458; Langacker 2006: 45; Lehmann 2017: 1). This is the most general common denominator of language, i.e., what ultimately represents the invariant. The concepts of problem solving and of activity presuppose the commitment to language as a dynamic, purposive, and creative mental process beyond its static structure, a premise which reminds one of Wilhelm von Humboldt's concept of *enérgeia* (as opposed to *érgon*). "Sprachen können betrachtet werden als Lösungen von sich permanent in der Kommunikation stellenden Aufgaben" ('languages can be considered to be solutions to tasks that permanently arise in communication'; transl. WP; Seiler 1973: 11, cited after Daneš 1987: 9).

Solving problems by language does not only refer to behavior in the 'world' but it starts with the notoriously close relationship between linguistic and conceptual entities: "It is important to realize that translating a concept into language represents a constant problem to be solved" (Seiler 1985: 5, see 9; see also Premper 2020).

2.3 Function

The notions of task orientation and of function(alism) are tightly connected, see e.g., Daneš (1987: 7) who states that "… the property 'to have a function *f*' appears as identical with the property 'to serve as a means for the end (purpose) *F*'". In the UNITYP frame Seiler defines 'function' as follows:

> For us, 'function' involves three components that can be distinguished, but not separated, from one another: 1. a purposive component as featured in our catch word *repraesentandum*: "(Something) *has to be represented*"; 2. a component 'what?' in the sense of "*that which* (has to be represented)"; and a component 'how'? in the sense of "*how* (is it to be represented)?" Both 2 and 3 can be said to relate to one another as the invariant to its appropriate variants, or, in other words, the relation between a *repraesentandum* and its *repraesentantia*. It is in this, and only in this, sense that we may be said to be functionalists.
>
> (Seiler 2000: 21; his emphasis)

A brief version of the definition is given ibidem, p. 177: "[Function …] is the generalized form of the relation between an […] invariant and corresponding […] variants."

So-called *functional principles* are considered essential for organizing the mentioned relation: *Indicativity* vs. *Predicativity*. These are (ibid.: 181):

- "[…] principles of linguistic encoding"
- "[…] basically motivated by discourse-pragmatic exigencies"
- "[…] to be understood as principles of […] *mental movements* and corresponding […] *operations* […]
 [They …] constitute the basic schema which underlies all continua on all levels."

The concepts of continua, the functional principles, and variants and invariants, are illustrated below.

2.4 Continua/dimensions

By comparison, linguistic operations are ordered in and generalized to functional *dimensions*. Internally, dimensions are structured by the linguistic realization in varying degrees of the (functional) principles of *indicativity* (linguistic implicitness, more reference to the context, pragmaticity) vs. *predicativity* (linguistic explicitness, larger appearance of lexical and morpho-syntactic machinery, semanticity) (see Seiler 2008c: 149). Externally, continua are hierarchical in the sense that a dimension can function as a sub-dimension (technique) as part of a higher dimension.

- "The [...] *continuum*; served as our 'pole star'" (Seiler 2000: 189). A continuum is a metalinguistic construct, but it also "portrays what speakers do" (ibid. p. 178) and it is assumed to be "psychologically real" (Seiler 2008b: 27).
- Part of the concept of the continuum is the idea of functional dynamics: The language user chooses from the techniques available in a dimension.

2.5 Three areas of research (hierarchical levels)

From the point of view of methodology, three areas or levels of research are to be distinguished (see Seiler 1983, 2000):

a. language universals (research) (LUR) or cognitive-conceptual level
b. language typology (LTYP) or level of general comparative grammar (GCG)
c. individual grammar writing (GRW) or level of the individual languages.

The universals are concepts. They "feature the ultimate invariant" (Seiler 2008b: 10). They cannot be determined inductively. The inquiry starts with intuition (Seiler 2008b: 10), namely by "intuitive insights" (Seiler 2008c: 54). This represents the deductive, 'top-down' perspective. Later on, after having done the inductive work at the GCG level ('bottom-up' perspective), the research task consists in an abductive mapping between the spectrum of techniques and the dimension as common denominator, which can then interpreted as a "mental map" (Seiler 2008b: 28).

The typological statements (think of Skalička's "bevorzugte Zusammenhänge" ('preferred connections')) are arrived at by induction (generalization) from the phenomena of the individual languages.

The following citation highlights the status of the notion of universals as mental invariants vis-à-vis the linguistic variants:

> Gedankliche Konzepte sind invariant und in allen Sprachen vorhanden, d.h. universal. Sprachliche Techniken dagegen sind variabel und können von Sprache zu Sprache unterschiedlich sein. ('Mental concepts are invariant and present in all languages, i.e., universal. Whereas linguistic techniques are variable and can vary from language to language'; Seiler 2016ff.a; transl. WP)[1]

---

[1]. It is interesting to compare this with the similar functional tenet of Mathesius (1936: 95; cited after Daneš 1987: 30, fn. 10): "... the only way of approach to different languages as strictly comparable systems is the functional point of view, since

Accordingly, LTYP/GCG can be viewed as a mediating instance between GRW and LUR: 'Die Beziehung zwischen Varianten und der Invariante ist dabei aber keine direkte Relation." ('The relationship between variants and the invariant, however, is not a direct one'.) (Seiler 2016ff.a; transl. WP)

2.6 The three levels and the question of descriptive and comparative categories

As an experienced structuralist, Seiler states that the categories of an individual language are not strictly congruent to those of another language (see level (b) above). As a functionalist, he states that the *tertium comparationis* for cross-linguistic comparison must be the conceptual *exprimenda* (level (a)). A fundamental assumption for research is that (a) can never be arrived at by induction. And of course (c) can never be arrived at by deduction. But level (b) 'mediates' between (a) and (c) (Seiler 2000: 189). The categories at level (b) (generalizations and invariants) are arrived at by the complementary approaches of induction (from level (c)) and deduction (from level (a)). This is the reason why LTYP and LUR are distinct but necessarily cooperative research activities.[2] The universal concepts of level (a) and the invariants of level (b) "can and must be matched with one another" (Seiler 1986: 13). "The conceptual apparatus can either be intuitively posited or represented by a formal theory" (ibid.).

Thus, what is essential at the 'middle' level (b) of GCG are (1) linguistic categories at different levels of abstraction, and (2) functional principles, dimensions and continua. These last three concepts can be considered universal aspects or components of level (b) (see Seiler 2000: 194–197).

3. UNITYP in progress: New aspects and notions

In a further development of UNITYP, Seiler (2015, 2016ff.) adopts an even more comprehensive view and tries to make the difference between the three levels more clearly defined, as a response to some critiques that state that in the UNITYP

---

general needs of expression and communication, common to all mankind are the only common denominators to which means of expression and communication, varying from language to language, can reasonably be brought."

2. "Language typology and language universals are complementary activities corresponding to complementary perspectives in the sense that one is unthinkable without the other one" (Seiler 2000: 28).

model the distinction between the means of individual languages and the cross-linguistic or conceptualized techniques is rather arbitrary with reference to (see above, Section 2.5):

a. the level of language-specific facts
b. the level of General Comparative Grammar (see Lehmann 1989: 133ff.), i.e., 'Dimension' in the terminology of UNITYP
c. the conceptual level

Seiler (2016ff.b) explains these levels with examples of techniques and concepts of IDENTIFICATION, referring to his book (Seiler 2000) where he elaborated this dimension. The level of language-specific facts is exemplified by articles in German with the notion of field in addition to that of continuum:

Scheme 1. The field of *der* vs. *ein* in German³ (Seiler 2000: 153, 2016ff.b)

generic							
1 Ein	Mensch	ist	kein Computer.	1' Der	Mensch	ist	kein Computer.
a	human.being	be.3SG.PRES	no computer	the	human.being	be.3SG.PRES	no computer
2 Ein	Mann	der	Tat	2' Der	Mann	des	Tag-es
a	man	the.F.SG.GEN	action.SG.GEN	the	man	the.M.SG.GEN	day-SG.GEN
3 Ein	Mann	steh-t	draussen.	3' Der	Mann	soll	hereinkomm-en.
a	man	stand-3SG.PRES	outside	the	man	shall.3SG.PRES	come.in-INF

specific divisible (composite), introducing; linking, global

By 'linking', Seiler (2000: 153ff) means the anaphoric or kataphoric functions. On the basis of this Scheme 1, a continuum as in Scheme 2 is obtained:

In Scheme 2, the lines connect topologically analogous points: 'generic' in 1 and 1', 'specific' in 3 and 3', with 2 and 2' as continuous transitions. In the middle of the continuum, equidistant from the topologically analogous points, the turning point of the continuum is assumed. Due to this continuum, *ein* and *der* are claimed to belong to the same category, for which the term ('address') *article* is regarded as justified.⁴ This statement by Seiler suggests that even the existence of

---

3. The first element of each example, *ein* and *der*, is both in the form of masculine singular nominative; similarly, *kein* in 1 and 1' is in the masculine singular nominative form. The interlinear glossing is added by Y. Ono. The meaning of 1 and 1' is obvious, and the other examples may be translated as follows: 2 "a man of action", 2' "the man of the day", 3 "A man is standing outside", 3' "The man should come in".

4. "Das Kontinuum erweist die Zusammengehörigkeit von ein und der und die Berechtigung der Adresse Artikel." (Seiler 2016ff.b, his emphasis) No analogous

Scheme 2. The continuum of the articles in German (Seiler 2016ff.b, see 2000: 153)

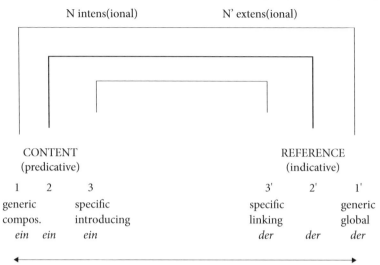

a language-specific category cannot be claimed straightforwardly but demands an accurate analysis, and its category label needs much consideration likewise.

Now, the articles in German exemplify the technique ARTICLE of the Functional Dimension of IDENTIFICATION on the level of General Comparative Grammar. At this level, ARTICLE is regarded as a subtechnique of DEIXIS, which is arrayed in a continuum together with other techniques[5] such as QUANTIFICATION. The continuum is bidirectional according to the principles of Predicativity and Indicativity as in Scheme 3:

Below Scheme 3, Seiler's (2016ff.c) examples for the techniques (functional roles) are given, where [pred] refers to 'predicative' and [ind] to 'indicative':[6]

---

statement is found in Seiler 2000, where *der* and *ein* are referred to as definite and indefinite article (p. 153).

5. In Seiler 2016ff.c, the term *Funktionsrollen* "functional roles" is used instead of *techniques* (*Techniken* in German) for the direct components of a continuum such as DEIXIS, QUANTIFICATION, etc.

6. The interlinear glossing is added by Y. Ono. Example (1) is from Mark 14: 44 and (2) is from Pacuvius fr. 92; for these source references we are grateful to the reviewer of our preliminary version. Moreover, the reviewer addressed a couple of critical comments to some examples and some passages of explication, to which we must remain without any reaction, since the examples and their interpretation as well as the explanations of the scheme and the model are H. Seiler's and we are uncertain as to how he would have answered the questions.

Scheme 3. The Dimension of IDENTIFICATION (see Seiler 2000: 149, 2004: 8; 2016ff.b/c)

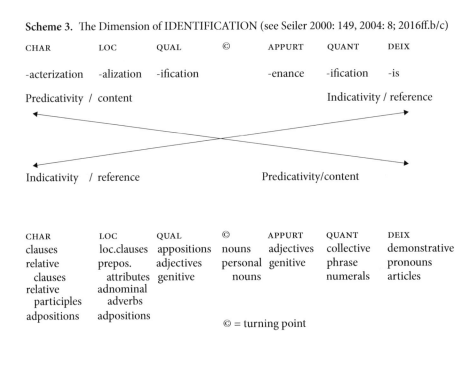

CHAR	LOC	QUAL	©	APPURT	QUANT	DEIX
-acterization	-alization	-ification		-enance	-ification	-is

Predicativity / content ← → Indicativity / reference

Indicativity / reference ← → Predicativity/content

CHAR	LOC	QUAL	©	APPURT	QUANT	DEIX
clauses	loc.clauses	appositions		nouns	collective	demonstrative
relative	prepos.	adjectives		personal	genitive	pronouns
clauses	attributes	genitive		nouns	phrase	articles
relative	adnominal				numerals	
participles	adverbs					
adpositions	adpositions					

© = turning point

(1) CHARACTERIZATION (CHAR)
   Welchen   ich   küss-en   werde   [pred],
   who.M.SG.ACC 1.NOM   kiss-INF   FUT.1.SG.PRES
   der   ist's   [ind].
   that.M.SG.NOM   be.3SG.PRES   it.NOM
   (Rel.Pron.)

(2) LOCALIZATION (LOC)
   Ubi   bene [pred], ibi   patria   [ind].
   where   well   there home.country.SG.NOM

(3) QUALIFICATION (QUAL)
   Er   hat [ind] eine   Narbe   auf der
   he.NOM   has   a.FEM.SG.ACC scar.SG.ACC   on   the.F.SG.DAT
   Stirn   [pred].
   forehead.SG.DAT

(4) Nominal © = turning point
(4i) Hansjakob [pred] Seiler [ind]
(4ii) Seiler [ind] Hansjakob [pred]
   (a given name can be chosen and is therefore predicative)

(5) APPURTENANCE (APPURT)
    der   [ind]   mit   der   Zipfelmütze [pred]
    that.M.SG.NOM   with   the.F.SG.DAT pointed.cap.SG.DAT
    (Instigator: 'Welcher   ist   es (unter   mehreren)?')
                 who.M.SG.NOM be.3SG.PRES   it (under   many.people)
    'which one (among many) is he?'

(6) QUANTIFICATION (QUANT)
    (6i) die   heilig-en [pred] drei [ind/pred] König-e
          the.PL.NOM   holy-PL.NOM   three   king-PL.NOM
          (= marked word order for 'three-ness' essential for ID of *Könige* 'kings', see
          Seiler 2000: 46) 'the holy three kings'

    (6ii) die   drei [ind]   heilig-en [pred] König-e
          the.PL.NOM   three   holy-PL.NOM   king-PL.NOM
          (= normal word order for determination) 'the three holy kings'

(7) DEIXIS (DEIX)
    Wer   da? —   ich   / der   Wildhüter.
    who.NOM   there   I.NOM   / the.M.SG.NOM   gamekeeper

(8) DEIXIS-Amalgam
    (8i) díeser   [ind/pred]   Láfontaine
          this.M.SG.NOM

    (8ii) dieser   [ind]   Lafontaine
          this.M.SG.NOM
          (without stress = determination for contrast: this vs. that)

As shown in the examples, the functional principles of Predicativity and Indicativity are both present at every instance but in different degrees. Depending on their degrees, the techniques ("functional roles") such as CHARACTERIZATION, LOCALIZATION etc. are arrayed horizontally in Scheme 3, whereas the techniques of each horizontal instance are arrayed in a vertical continuum: the greater the degree of predicativity, the higher their position. The number of segmental "subtechniques" of a technique ("functional role") decreases in accordance with the decrease of the degree of Predicativity, but the more indicative a technique ("functional role"), the more the number of pragmatic non-segmental techniques such as stress increases.

A continuum of the 3rd level, e.g., that of the techniques of ARTICLE as a subtechnique of DEIXIS, is shown in Scheme 2. In the last book publication of 2015, Seiler demonstrates this hierarchical model as in Scheme 4 (2015: 7ff.):

The hierarchy can be followed up top-down or bottom-up, from the underlying fundamental functional concept (high level of conceptuality, and at the same time low level of observability) to the language-specific expression (low level of

Scheme 4. Hierarchical processing of concepts and continua assigned to (Seiler 2015: 8)

Conceptuality	DIMENSION		Observability
	fundamental concepts: APPREHENSION POSSESSION IDENTIFICATION etc.		
high ↑	a concept: e.g. IDENTIFICATION	invar.	low
	a continuum of techniques of IDENT$_1$	var.	
	a technique out of $_1$: e.g. DEIXIS$_2$	invar.	
	a continuum of techniques of DEIXIS	var.	
	a technique out of $_2$: e.g. ARTICLE$_3$	invar.	↓
	a continuum of techniques of ARTICLE	var.	
low	language-specific expression, e.g. [+gener., –specif.]		high

conceptuality, high level of observability), or conversely. For Seiler, a central aspect of language activity is the representation of contents of thinking (*Denkinhalte*) as concretized by States of Affairs (*Sachverhalte*).

In his online publication "Vom Denkinhalt: Vom Denkinhalt via UNITYP zur Einzelsprache" ('From content of thinking via UNITYP to individual languages', 2016ff.c), Seiler assumes that it is possible to capture the states of affairs in life as structured contents of thinking, which contrasts with the Saussurean position: "Prise en elle-même, la pensée est comme une nébuleuse où rien n'est nécessairement délimité" (Saussure 1916/1931: 155). Incidentally, it is interesting to compare this new position with Seiler's earlier view connected with the analytic-semasiological, inductive way and the synthetic-onomasiological, deductive approach to grammar à la Georg von der Gabelentz (Seiler 2002: 16). Quoting the same passage from Saussure, Seiler (2002) wonders whether the contents of thinking are given in such a way that they can be captured scientifically: if this were the case, the synthetic-onomasiological approach would have already been applied as intensively as the analytic method going from form to content. One of the aims of the UNITYP model is to even out this asymmetry, not via pure deduction but abductively, i.e., by the cyclical addition of deduction and induction, also in the so-called 'hermeneutic circle', through which the contents of thinking become accessible (see e.g., Seiler 1986: 16, 1996: 40, 2000: 41, 137, 143ff., 176, 189ff.; Ono 2002: 43ff.). In his last online publication, Seiler (2016ff.c) states that interpersonal communication begins with a transfer of the contents of thinking into a semiotic system, maintaining the abductive method as a necessary procedure (pers. comm.).

4. Categories and concepts: *In memoriam* Hansjakob Seiler

4.1 Object relation: Bottom-up procedures and abduction

As an example of the abductive procedure of linguistic analysis, we may take the object relation, which was treated in H. Seiler's last book publication *Das Konzept der Objekt relation und das Kontinuum ihrer Varianten: Ein muttersprachlicher Zugang* ('The concept of object relation and the continuum of its variants: A native-speakers' approach', edited by Seiler, 2015). He decided to publish it, like his last online publications (Seiler 2016ff.), in his native language, German (which is not very popular any more among typological-comparative linguists). Therefore, its main points shall be outlined here and compared mainly with the approach of the Leipzig Valency Classes Project (*ValPaL*, see Malchukov & Comrie (eds) 2015).[7]

As the title of the book suggests, the authors of the chapters were only dealing with their own mother tongues. This was the source of many intense discussions, because we sometimes had different views on what may belong to the object relation and what not, and hence what can or cannot be regarded as an object, partly depending on the properties of our mother tongues. This was reflected in the last clause of the book abstract: "we were lead to consider borderline cases between object- and non-object relations" (Seiler 2015: 2). Seiler states (2015: 3) that 'object relation' can be, pre-theoretically, conceived of as the 'affecting'[8] of an entity. At the descriptive level, we are confronted with the problem of whether a particular overt marker which is a means to express an affected entity may, or even should, be divided into an object and, if it is also used for a relation beyond affecting, a non-object marking. If this is viewed as necessary from the comparative perspective, what might be the criterion which defines a certain cut-off line and justifies this line for each individual language without violating the coherence of its marking system?

For example, in Japanese the same postnominal marking (flagging) by *o* is used not only for an affected thing with a verb such as 'break'[9] or an effected,

---

7. The *ValPaL*'s volumes were published almost at the same time as the book edited by Seiler, so that we could not refer to *ValPaL*'s studies in our publication.

8. In German "BETREFFEN" (p. 3, 19f.) or "Betreffen" (p. 12), which is translated with "influence" in the English abstract (p. 2).

9. Compare: "[a] verb is considered transitive if it contains an A and a P argument. A and P are defined as the arguments of a verb with at least two arguments that are coded like the 'breaker' and the 'broken thing' micro-roles of the 'break' verb"; "we can compare the different types of languages by looking at the coding of an exemplary verb like the 'break' verb. All the verbs that have two arguments (A and P) that use the same

produced thing with a verb like 'produce (build, make, etc.)', but also for a place connected to motion such as a path or a source:

(9) kōen o {a) aruk-u /   b) ik-u /   c) toor-u /
      park   walk-NONPST /   go-NONPST /   pass-NONPST /

      d) watar-u /   e) de-ru /   f) tsukur-u}
         cross-NONPST /   go.out-NONPST /   make-NONPST

'to {a) walk / b) go} in a /the park'
'to {c) pass (= go through) / d) pass/cross / e) leave (= go out of) / f) make} a /the park'
(compare German *einen/den Park begehen* with the accusative *einen / den*)

In (9), verbs for an affecting activity such as *arasu* 'damage, ravage' or *tsukau* 'use' may occur paradigmatically with the verbs a-f). And a place is coded in the same way independently of whether it represents a path or a source or a prototypical P such as an affected (e.g., 'broken, destroyed, damaged') or an effected ('made/built') thing. If we apply the same criteria of valency and coding properties for this pattern as in English or German (see e.g., Comrie et al. 2015: 3, 10f.; Haspelmath 2015: 315f.; see footnote 9), we may state that these examples demonstrate transitivity prominence in Japanese, since the expressions of less affective activities like motions show the same coding pattern as the affective prototype and the effecting action, i.e., the transitive pattern is extended to the expressions of less affective situations. Can the *o*-marked noun, then, be regarded as an object in each case?

The verbs in 9c) and d) are bivalent (= two-place), hence the path must be regarded as an argument, so that the object interpretation seems less problematic. 9e) is a somewhat different case and the valency of the verb is not so clear, despite the translatability by an English transitive (semantically, it is rather tri- than

---

encoding are regarded as transitive verbs"; "[t]his method thus allows us to define transitive encoding as a comparative concept without the need to assume universal or cross-linguistic categories or features (cf. Haspelmath 2010). Concepts such as 'nominative', 'ergative', 'dative', 'actor', 'undergoer', which have proven indispensable at the language-specific (descriptive) level but are difficult to apply cross-linguistically, are thus not necessary for our comparative approach" (Haspelmath 2015: 135f.). See Kishimoto et al. (2015: 802f.) for the verbs for 'break' and other verbs with the same argument marking in Japanese. In Ono (2015), not a verb for 'break' but the verb *yak-u* "burn, broil/grill, bake" was taken as the transitive prototype because of its semantic width allowing both an effective and an affective usage (i.e., with an effected as well as an affected object).

bivalent).[10] Nevertheless, the place representing a source is marked in the same way as P. In other words: individual verbs determine which role may be marked by *o*, and *o* cannot be used as the marker of the path independently of the identity of each verb. That is, a noun marked by *o* must be an argument of the verb in each case. In fact, the verbs c), d) and e), as well as b), reject the replacement of *o* by the locative marker *de* for the place of motion. *De* is, however, acceptable for *aruku* in a):

(10) kōen <u>de</u>   {a) aruk-u /   b) *ik-u /   c) *toor-u /
     park LOC   walk-NONPST /   go-NONPST /   pass-NONPST /

     d) *watar-u /   e) *de-ru (/   f) tsukur-u)}
     cross-NONPST /   go.out-NONPST /   make-NONPST

     a) 'to walk in a /the park'

Tsukuru in (10f) is highly elliptical and presupposes an omitted object marked by *o*, e.g., a pond, a path etc. In an analogous manner, all the other verbs in (10) become acceptable if a noun marked by *o* such as *michi* 'path' appears in the clause:

(11) kōen <u>de</u> michi <u>o</u>   {a) aruk-u /   b) ik-u /   c) toor-u /
     park   path   walk-NONPST /   go-NONPST /   pass-NONPST /

     d) watar-u /   e) de-ru /   f) tsukur-u}
     cross-NONPST /   go.out-NONPST /   make-NONPST

     'to {a) walk / b) go} on a/the path in a /the park'
     'to {c) go through / d) cross / e) leave (= go out of) / f) make} a/the path in a /the park'

Observing these coding patterns, we should regard all those verbs as transitive, among which *aruku* 'walk' represents a special class because it allows the marking pattern *de* in (10). Furthermore, *aruku* specifies the manner of motion ('on foot') and can be used as a monovalent (= one-place) intransitive without any further noun such as *kōen* 'park' (+ *o*, *de* etc.).[11] Nevertheless, it is better to acknowledge its

---

10. With the verb *deru* "go out", the source (starting point) must be marked by *kara* "from, out of" instead of *o* if the goal or the direction of the movement is expressed (marked by *ni* or *e*, and never by *o*) in the same clause. The marking *kara*, on the other hand, may replace *o* in any case with *deru* "go out". See Kishimoto et al. (2015: 790) for the interpretation of "source-argument alternation", assuming a focus condition for the argument status of the source marked by *o*.

11. This type includes manner of motion verbs, such as *hashiru* "run" and *tobu* "fly", which are non-telic and form the progressive with the auxiliary *iru* "be", e.g., *aruite iru* "be walking", in contrast to telic verbs as *iku* "go" and *deru* "go out", which allow only

transitive usage in a way parallel to the other bivalent motion verbs, instead of classifying the verbs categorially into transitives like *tsukuru* 'make' and intransitives like *aruku* 'walk', as is customary in traditional Japanese grammar.[12] Incidentally, Japanese grammarians and lexicologists traditionally consider all motion verbs like (9a-e) and (11a-e) to be intransitive, neglecting their valency properties.[13] It must be stressed again that the usage of *o* is never independent from the identity of the verb: for example, it cannot be used for marking a place noun with verbs such as *odoru* 'dance' or *asobu* 'play' (see Ono 2015: 58ff.).[14] Due to this dependence on verbs, *o* belongs to their valency frame and can hardly be regarded as an adjunct marker. Thus, *o* should be recognized as an argument marker in any case, and an argument coded in the same way as P may be viewed as representing an object, also in cases like (9a-e) and, (11a-e). We do not have observable evidence which is strong enough against the uniform treatment of *o*; if we were to treat nouns with *o* in a non-uniform manner, we would find a cut-off point between a) *aruku* 'walk' and the rest, and neither between the motion verbs a-e) and the affective/effective

---

a resultative reading with the same auxiliary, e.g., *dete iru* "have gone/come out". See Ono (2020: 72f.) for a discussion of this topic in more detail.

12. Miyagawa (1989: 4 and passim), who seems to follow the traditional Japanese categorization of verbs, consequently divides the same marker *o* into two categories: an 'affixed case marker' for an object argument in cases such as (9f) or (11f), and a 'postposition' for an adjunct in usages such as (9a) or (11a) (Miyagawa's view on cases like (9), (11b/c/d/e) is not clear because he gives only *aruku* "walk" as an example). Also Kishimoto et al. (2015) support this standpoint and state as follows: "The argument/adjunct distinction is not tightly correlated with particular forms because all the basic markers are polysemous or homonymous and, therefore, one and the same marker may mark both an argument and an adjunct" (p. 767) and "The same coding frame [= <NOM, ACC>, ACC = *o*, Y. Ono] is superficially associated with intransitive verbs of locomotion such as … *aruku* 'walk' …, where the accusative marker denotes a traversal path" (p. 772), adding: "It is controversial whether the traversal path in the accusative is an argument or an adjunct" (p. 772).

13. One of the crucial factors for this traditional verb classification is, besides semantics, the existence of a transitive, causative-like counterpart which shares the same verb root, e.g., *toosu* "let pass/go through, pass (something) through" for *tooru* "pass", *watasu* "let go across, hand over" for *wataru* "cross" and *dasu* "let (go/come) out, take out" for *deru* "go out". See Ono 2014, 2015: 69 and passim; 2020: 70.

14. Since *o* may never appear more than once in a simple clause, the marking of a place by *o* is not possible if some other noun occurs with *o* in the same clause, e.g., *kōen de/o sanpo suru* "take a walk in a/the park" (with *sanpo su-ru* as the verb) vs. *kōen de / *o sanpo o su-ru* "take a walk in a/the park" (with *sanpo* "a walk" as the object noun of the verb *suru* "do, make"), see Ono 2015: 56ff.

verbs such as *tsukuru* 'make' in f) - as commonly assumed -, nor between a-b) and the rest as suggested by the corresponding English expressions.[15]

An analogous problem to solve for Japanese is the treatment of *ni*, which is used to mark the goal of an action, among other things. The goal of *iku* 'go' in (9b) and (11b) may be marked by *ni* in the same way as a recipient (= the so-called

---

15. A comparable problem is observed with regard to the status of an accusative NP and, accordingly, to the transitivity estimation in German (this topic is not mentioned in Seiler 2015). Ono (2020) discusses whether a noun in the accusative is to be regarded as an object, as an adverbial, or as a nominal part of an object-incorporating verb, particularly if it represents a path, a route, or an amount of distance, e.g.:

(E.a) Ich   bin   diese   Straße schon   oft   gefahren.
       I.NOM   am   this.F.SG.ACC   street already often   drive-PST.PTCP
       'I have often driven this route'

(E.b) Ich   fahr-e   lieber   Autobahn.
       I.NOM   drive-1.SG.PRES   preferably   highway
       'I prefer driving on a highway'

(Example a and b from *Duden Deutsches Universalwörterbuch*, digital version 2017)

(E.c) die   Treppe   hinauflauf-en
       the.F.SG.ACC   stairs.SG.ACC   up.run-INF
       'run up the stairs'

(Example c from *Duden-Grammatik*, 2016 (9th ed.): 476, Berlin: Dudenverlag)

(E.d) 10 km geh-en
              go-INF
       'walk 10 km'

(E.e) i) *die 800 m* /   ii) *einig-e*   *Runde-en*   / iii) *sechs*   *Rennen*   *lauf-en*
       the.PL.ACC /   some-PL.ACC   lap-PL.ACC   six   race.PL.ACC   run-INF
       'run i) the 800 m. / ii) a few laps / iii) [in] six races'

(Example d and e from *Oxford DUDEN GERMAN Dictionary*, digital version 2005)

The *Oxford DUDEN* treats all the verb usages with an accusative NP as transitive, making no distinction between e.g., (E.d: *10 km gehen*) and (E.e.i: *die 800 m laufen*), while the *Duden Deutsches Universalwörterbuch* gives no transitivity specification at all. On the other hand, the *Duden-Grammatik* (2016: 827f. and passim) considers such cases as (E.c: *hinauflaufen*) and (E.d: *gehen*) to be intransitive verbs with an adverbial. Dowty (1991: 567f.) refers to *a mile* in *run a mile* as 'holistic theme', parallel to *drink a glass of beer*, suggesting an argument status of the noun that represents a distance. Hence, it seems adequate to regard (E.e.i: die 800 m *laufen*) as a transitive usage of the verb with the distance as the object, whereas (E.d) is rather a case of an intransitive usage with a distance adverbial. Definiteness and referentiality play a crucial role to evaluate the status of an NP. Thus, (E.b: *Autobahn fahren*) seems to represent a case of incorporation.

'indirect object') or an entity affected by actions designated by two-place verbs such as *katsu* 'defeat'. Moreover, *ni* may, depending on verbs, also mark an agent, as in (16):

(12) {a) *Nihon* / b) *Hanako no tokoro*} *ni ik-u*
    Japan   of place   go-NONPST
    'go to {a) Japan / b) Hanako}'

(13) *Hanako (no tokoro) ni meeru o kak-u*
            of place   mail write-NONPST
    'write an e-mail to Hanako'

(14) *Hanako ni purezento o* {a) *su-ru* /   b) *age-ru*}
                present   do-NONPST   give-NONPST
    'give a present to Hanako'

(15) *Hanako ni* {a) *a-u* /   b) *kats-u*}
              meet-NONPST   defeat-NONPST
    '{a) meet / b) defeat} Hanako'

(16) *Hanako ni* {a) *make-ru*   / b) *purezento o mora-u*}
              be.defeated-NONPST   present   get-NONPST
    '{a) be defeated by / b) receive a present from} Hanako'

A noun for an entity affected by an action as in (15b: *katsu*) should be recognized as an object and, hence, *ni* as one of the means to mark an object, though it differs from the marking of a 'broken thing' of the verb for 'break'. If one accepts only the latter pattern as transitive, as Haspelmath does (2015: 131, with the examples *helfen* 'help' and *folgen* 'follow' in German, which govern a dative, as intransitive verbs), verbs for an affecting action as in (15) would, consequently, have to be conceived of as 'intransitive' verbs with an object.

Now, may all the nouns marked by *ni* in (12)–(16) be regarded as objects? Or should they be divided into objects and non-objects? As far as the semantic criterion of affectedness is concerned, an agent as *Hanako* in (16) can hardly be seen as an object.[16] This case, however, suggests that the meaning of *ni* is not constant, but depends completely from individual verbs; *ni*, thus, belongs to the verbal valency frame, and a noun marked by *ni* must be acknowledged as a verbal argument.

Can we, on the other hand, treat the *ni*-marked nouns which express a goal as objects? The affectedness condition seems to apply for them to a different degree.

---

16. In (16b), *ni* may be replaced by *kara* for a source (see note 11 above), but not in (16a). An agent is marked by *ni* also in causative and passive constructions as well as in constructions with *morau* 'get' as an auxiliary (a kind of 'get'-causative-passive), where *kara* may replace *ni* under certain conditions, i.e., not in every case.

A conceivable criterion for assessing their objecthood is the necessity to express the goal as a place, with *tokoro* 'place' as in (12b).[17] If a person (or an animate being) is the goal of a motion, it is not possible to express it without *tokoro* (i.e., **Hanako ni ik-u* '(lit.) go to Hanako'). If it is the goal of an action as in (13), the locational coding with *tokoro* is optional. This coding is, however, not adequate in (14),[18] though the fact that the object of the action should reach the goal is shared by (13) and (14), and their *ni*-marked constituents are commonly treated as 'indirect objects' in linguistic studies. Here, we observe a gradience of the coding of a goal as a place and as a person.

A further test is to replace *ni* by a locational maker such as *e* '(direction) to, for' or *made* '(up) to', which are possible for (12) and (13) but not for (14) and (15).[19] Here again, the cut-off point does not correspond directly to the borderline between an ('indirect') object as usually defined and a directional NP (or 'PP'). Instead, we observe a scalar increase of objecthood and, at the same time, a decrease of interpretability as a direction. On the other hand, it is not possible to mark a goal or a direction by *ni* (nor by *e*) with e.g., *aruku* 'walk':

(17) kōen <u>ni/e</u> {a)*aruk-u /   b) ik-u /   c) *toor-u /
      park   walk-NONPST /   go-NONPST /   pass-NONPST /

   d) watar-u /   e) de-ru /   f) *tsukur-u}
      cross-NONPST /   go.out-NONPST /   make-NONPST

   '{b) go / d) cross (something) over / e) come (out)} to a/the park'

(18) kōen {a) *<u>ni/e</u>/ b) made} aruk-u
      'walk to a/the park'

These examples show that the goal or the direction marked by *ni/e* is not an adjunct which may occur freely, independently from the nature of the verbs. Furthermore, *iku* 'go' is a telic verb which implies (or presupposes) a goal. In contrast to *wataru* 'cross', which may express a goal/direction in addition to the *o*-marked path, *iku* 'go' rejects the co-occurrence of both. *Iku* is, thus, a bivalent (= two-place) verb which contains the goal marked by *ni/e* as its argument in its valency frame.[20]

---

17. Formally, the noun for the person (e.g., *Hanako*) is the *no*-marked attribute of *tokoro* 'place', therefore, literally, 'Hanako's place; where Hanako is'.

18. The addition of *tokoro* "place" is not possible for (14b), and it changes the meaning of the recipient from individual to collective: "Hanako's home/family" in (14a).

19. In the colloquial language of Tokyo region, *e* is possible instead of *ni* in (14), but not in (15).

20. For this reason, Kishimoto et al. (2015: 769) assign the term 'semi-intransitive' to the verb class to which *iku* 'go' or *tsuku* 'arrive (at)' belong.

The possibility to mark a noun with *ni* is never independent from the meaning of the verb, analogously to *o*-marking (see Ono 2002: 199f., 266ff. for detailed discussions). While *o* may be considered as a marker for an object-argument in a uniform manner, allowing to promote an adjunct to argument status in cases such as (9a) and (10a), it seems unavoidable for a subset of nouns marked by *ni* to be viewed as non-objects, even though *ni*-marked nouns should all be recognized as arguments. However, we cannot draw a clear-cut line between objects and non-objects, and we have to observe a gradience between them, as discussed above.

Also some dative constructions in German illustrate borderline cases, e.g., in a possessor-patient construction:

(19) Karl trat   dem   Fritz auf den   Fuß.
     step.3.SG.PRES the.M.SG.DAT on the.M.SG.ACC foot.SG.ACC
     'Karl stepped on Fritz' foot'   (Seiler 2015: 24)

Objecthood of a dative noun is much less obvious if it is not directly connected with a particular verb, as in the case of the *dativus ethicus* and the *dativus judicantis* (Seiler 2015: 24ff.),[21] e.g.:

(20) Der   Organist spiel-t   den   Hörern
     the.M.SG.NOM organist play-3.SG.PRES the.PL.DAT hearer.PL.DAT
     zu   leise.
     too faint
     'The organist does not play loud enough for the hearers' (Seiler 2015: 25)

Moreover, the dative can be replaced by a prepositional phrase such as *für die Hörer* 'for the hearers <for the.PL.ACC hearer.PL.ACC>' (p. 24f.). An extreme case is represented by the expression of an addressee without any explicit verb (p. 14ff.),[22] e.g.:

(21a) Dem   Finanzamt Düsseldorf
      the.N.SG.DAT tax.office
      'To the tax office Düsseldorf'   (Seiler 2015: 22)

The dative in (21a) may be substituted by a prepositional phrase:

(21b) An das   Finanzamt Düsseldorf
      to the.N.SG.ACC
      'To the tax office Düsseldorf'   (Seiler 2015: 22)

---

21. Seiler considers the *dativus ethicus* to be a *dativus judicantis* applied to the 1st or 2nd person. In the dative usages of this type, the verbs do not show semantic influence: "Semantisch findet keine Einwirkung des Verbs (ACTOR) mehr statt" (Seiler 2015: 25).

22. Seiler himself did not regard this type as a borderline case, because it represents one of the two fundamental two poles of his model.

In usual linguistic discussions, prepositional phrases such as (21b) would be excluded from the object domain. For Seiler, however, this type was of particular importance, because he postulated it as one of the poles of the object relation in his model:

> 'Object' is captured in this work as a relation between two equipollent poles: Pole$_1$ (= verb) as an instance of an action influencing Pole$_2$ (= noun), which is an instance of 'sovereignty' and detachment from the verb's influence. A bidirectional continuum spans between the two poles: in one direction, the influential force of the verb (Pole$_1$) is gradually weakened as we move from Pole$_1$ to Pole$_2$. In the other direction, 'sovereignty' and detachment are strongest at Pole$_2$, and are gradually weakened as we move toward Pole$_1$.
>
> [...] This view stands in contradistinction to current theorizing for which 'Object' is considered to be a dependent of the valency of the verb. [...] Our continuum extends beyond the reach of the traditional direct or indirect object relation. It includes such cases where valency and corresponding tests are no longer decisive, but where the regularities of the continuum still are in force. (Seiler 2015: 2)

Seiler (2015: 6 ff.) states that in individual languages 'object' does not appear as a monolith but has different possibilities for appearance, which may differ from language to language. The basic hypothesis is that different shapes of appearance, in individual languages for the first step, can be arrayed in a continuous order between the two poles, and this makes it possible to regard them as variants of the object relation. He sums up: "Gradience in the two opposite directions is observable and is confirmed by the native speakers of the three languages under study" (2015: 2). Findings from individual languages and their comparison may enable us to capture a common denominator with a conceptual status[23] and to come

---

23. We must mention that Seiler never used 'semantics' as the starting point for cross-linguistic studies. He was, in accordance with Coseriu (e.g., 1969; also Coseriu 1996: 19ff., Seiler 1996: 45, among others), very conscious and cautious with regard to the term 'semantic' (even though we indeed have a consensus about what is meant by 'semantic' e.g., in 'semantic role' in cross-linguistic studies):

> We fully agree in making a sharp distinction between semantics and a superordinated level of content, which ... we shall call 'conceptual'. Semantics is concerned with the meanings of the lexical, grammatical, and syntactic expressions of an individual language. It should not be extended to content arrived at by generalization or 'logical reflection' beyond an individual language. (Seiler 2000: 22)

According to *ValPaL*, in typological studies "[...] the phenomena to be investigated have to be defined in semantic terms to make a comparison possible" (Comrie et al. 2015: 4). Haspelmath's (2010: 665 and passim) expression "universal conceptual-semantic concepts" seems to try to clarify the difference. For discussions of the distinction between a semantic and a conceptual level in more detail, see Premper 2001: e.g., 478, 483ff., Ono 2002: 51ff. Incidentally,

closer to the postulated universality of the notion of object relation (p. 3, 6). Seiler mentions that this bottom-up procedure contrasts with the predominantly conceptual nature of the matter in most UNITYP researches of the past (p. 9).

As quoted above, the object relation is described by a dynamic relation between the two poles with complementary properties, and the prominence between the two is decisive for the positions on the continuum (Seiler 2015: 3, 12, 16). The two parameters are represented by the names for the poles: that of AFFECTING ("BETREFFEN") and that of sovereign/superordinated ENTITY ("abgehobene Entität" p. 12).[24] The pole of ENTITY is the instance that is affected ("betroffen") in a certain way (p. 1). At the pole with the maximum prominence of the sovereign/superordinated entity (and the minimum of affecting), affecting is reflected by no more than 'concern(ing)' (German *Betreff*)[25] (p. 12). At the opposite pole with the maximum prominence of affecting (and with the minimum of the sovereignty of the entity), the verbs are agentive and the process ("Vorgang") is presented as actualized (p. 19). In borderline cases such as the dative usages in German (19 and 20), the dynamics is uni- instead of bidirectional (p. 23ff.). Or, like in Japanese, the continuum extends from the canonical situation (object relation), expanding or exceeding the poles in both directions (Ono 2015: 137).[26]

It is worth remarking that Seiler (18f.) draws a distinction between Object$_1$ and Object$_2$, and at the pole of maximum affecting, Object$_2$ is absent, while the opposite pole of minimum affecting (and of the maximum sovereignty of the entity)

---

the so-called 'semantic role' was referred to in UNITYP publications by the term 'participant role' (among other terms, but never by 'thematic role').

24. Compared to the dimensional model of UNITYP such as PARTICIPATION published so far (see e.g., Seiler 1988, 2000: 170ff.; Premper 1991), it is new (and unique) that the functional parameters of the continuum are not predicativity and indicativity, although the object relation is one of the conceptual techniques within the concept ROLE ASSIGNMENT, which belongs to the fundamental concept (= "dimension", in the terminology of the earlier, canonical UNITYP model) of PARTICIPATION (Seiler 2015: 9f.). In the canonical UNITYP model, all techniques are ordered in a continuum at each level according to the parameters indicativity/predicativity. Furthermore, Affecting (German: *Betreffen*) as one of the two poles of the object relation is represented by predicates (verbs) and what they imply, so that it would conform to the predicativity parameter.

25. Compare further *betr.* = *betreffend* 're (subject)' in English. Seiler (2015: 18f.) uses the term "CONCERNED" for the role of an object which is conventionally referred to as "theme" (i.e., what is given, said etc.) or for addressee/direction.

26. One of the two directions is described above with regard to the place nouns marked by *o* or *ni*. The other direction pertains to object-incorporation, where the object is not an independent nominal element but part of a verb.

lacks Object$_1$. At the turning point in the middle, where the prominence relation exhibits equilibrium, both Object$_1$ and Object$_2$ are present, i.e., they are objects of a ditransitive verb. Therefore, the continuum of OBJECT RELATION subsumes both mono- and ditransitives, and integrates also verbs containing a dative[27] or a prepositional object without a direct object (in accusative). One of the criteria of the ordering is that adjacent positions share a common linguistic coding, e.g., for German (p. 14ff.):

(22) VO – VOO – VOiO/PO – ViO – ViO/PO – VPO – iO/PO
(iO = indirect object, PO = prepositional object)

Moreover, language-specific continua gained in this way (e.g., Seiler & Berthould-Papandropoulou 2015: 37; Ono 2015: 137) are quite comparable (see Seiler 2015: 146).

These continua resemble, despite the fundamental differences in the terms and the parametric notions, the semantic maps of transitivity presented by *ValPaL* (e.g., Comrie et al. 2015: 7ff.; Malchukov 2015: 83; see the above quote from Seiler 2015: 2 against valency-centered approaches).[28] The non-disparate results of the studies suggest that different approaches should be appreciated as mutually relevant in order to gain deeper insights.

4.2 Number and quantification: Abductive methodology and hermeneutic circle

In his insightful book *Apprehension: Language, object, and order. Part III: The universal dimension of Apprehension* (1986) H. Seiler showed how quantification correlates with language properties pertaining to "the ways in which we objectify things – through the medium of language" (1986: 6),[29] which include, among others, classificatory means such as numeral classification and gender (including nominal class systems).[30] Furthermore, he formulated a typological regularity:

---

27. In Seiler's formulation "Verb nur mit indirektem Objekt" ('verb with an indirect object only'; 2015: 14), presumably in correlation with his assumption of Object$_1$, which seems to correspond to direct object, and Object$_2$ for a non-direct object.

28. During the discussion of our articles for the book, Seiler addressed critiques of the same kind to Ono because of her valency-oriented standpoint close to the approach of *ValPaL*. Nevertheless, he accepted her contribution as it was and interpreted it from his viewpoint, as he remarked in an additional chapter (Seiler 2015: 142f.).

29. "APPREHENSION is the dimension that corresponds to the cognitive-conceptual domain of the object, the 'thing', and to the mental operation of construing the notion of 'thing'" (Seiler 1995: 297).

30. "[G]ender […] represents the generalizing, and number […] represents the individualizing" (Seiler 1986: 114).

> If a language exhibits NUMERAL CLASSIFICATION, it does not show AGREEMENT in GENDER and NUMBER – and vice versa. (Seiler 1986: 159).

Above all, Seiler tried to distinguish between language-specific means or categories such as numeral classification in Chinese, Japanese etc., and techniques as problem-solving programmes on a higher level, which he wrote in capital letters:[31]

> [...] the UNITYP framework, which avoids reduction of the phenomena to a single morpho-syntactic category: "*the* numeral classifier", and tries, instead, to take into consideration a maximum range of morpho-syntactic and semantic factors as headed by a common functional denominator: this then constitutes the technique of NUMERAL CLASSIFICATION. (Seiler 1986: 96)

As for the notion of concept and linguistic methodology, Seiler states:

> Universal concepts are necessary prerequisites for all language activity. They are the *tertium comparationis* necessary for the comparison of languages, for translation; necessary also for assembling linguistic data. Ultimately, they constitute the *exprimendum* or *repraesentandum*, that which is to be transposed into language or expressed by means of language. [...] The posited *tertia comparationis* will enable us to assemble the relevant data. (1986: 13f.; see also 1983: 456).

Hence, it is a neat methodology to clearly separate a comparative concept and a language-specific category, as suggested by Haspelmath (e.g., 2010). No doubt that a linguist may make an inquiry as to how number or plurality are expressed in languages. However, it seems to be inappropriate to assume a number distinction for nouns in numeral-classifying languages,[32] since plural reference depends on the quantification expression mediated by a numeral classifier, as, e.g., in Chinese:

(23) {a) *yī-běn* /   b) *sān-běn*}   *shū*
      one-CLF   three-CLF   book
      '{a) one (/a) book / b) three books}'

---

31. "The capitalized terms are related to, but not identical with, categorial notions. ... In contradistinction to the categorial terms, the capitalized terms do not stand for categories but for **techniques**" (Seiler 1986: 20). "*Sub-dimension/Technique* ... 'sub-dimension' underlines the hierarchical relationship to 'dimension'; 'technique' stresses the procedural aspect" (Seiler 1995: 307). In Seiler 2000 (p. 182 and passim) 'techniques' are conceived of as being at the level of General Comparative Grammar between universality and language specificity, see 2.5 above.

32. This consideration is prompted by Haspelmath 2017, where *shū* "book(s)" in Chinese is analyzed as *shū* [SG] : *shū* [PL] in the same paradigm as *vivlí-o* [SG] : *vivlí-a* [PL] in Modern Greek. Haspelmath does this in order to show the inefficiency of symmetric marking patterns, which deviate from the efficient "universal coding asymmetries" where an overt marking is to be found only in the less frequent term of a category such as plural in the category of number, while its unmarked term remains without an overt marking due to its higher frequency.

Even if a linguist might be free in choosing terms for interlinear glossing and even though "interlinear glosses are not abbreviations of deep analyses, but reading aids to the reader" (Haspelmath 2016: 301), it appears to be improper, or ad hoc, to interpret nouns like *shū* as "Plural" when they have plural reference as in (23b), possibly glossed as [book.PL]. This treatment parallels that of e.g., *sheep* in English, which is placed in the same paradigm as *goat* : *goats*, and the derived nouns in *-er* in German (e.g., *Arbeiter* 'worker(s)'), which systematically have, as isolated nouns, the same form for singular and plural (except for the dative). They are in the same paradigm as their number-differentiated nouns, e.g., their feminine counterparts with *-er-in* (SG) vs. *-er-in-nen* (PL) (see Seiler 1986: 121) as well as, e.g., *Mann* 'man' (SG) vs. *Männer* 'men' (PL). In Chinese, however, like in other languages with numeral classification, number is not a formal nominal category.

Even in a language with number as an inflectional category, singular forms may have plural reference as in Hungarian, where the presence of a quantifying expression such as an interrogative like *hány* 'how many' or a numeral requires the noun in its singular form, e.g., *nagynéni* '(an) aunt' : *nagynéni-k* 'aunts' : *öt nagynéni* 'five aunts'. If we proceed in a straightforward way, we would, because of their complementary distribution, identify two variants for the expression of the comparative concept of plurality, one with and one without the suffix which occurs to mark plural reference only when a quantifying modifier is absent. The noun form without overt marking for plurality would then obtain an interlinear glossing like *öt nagynéni* [five aunt.PL] (or even *öt nagynéni-Ø* [five aunt- PL]), if the predicate would not show a singular form as in the following example, in which nouns are not yet glossed with regard to number:

(24) (*Az*) *öt* *nagynéni* *sör-t* *isz-{ik* / **nak}*.
      (DEF) five aunt.NOM beer-ACC drink-{SG / PL}
      '(The) five aunts drink beer' (from Sybesma 2017)

Should we, now, gloss *nagynéni* as [aunt.SG.NOM]?

Analogously, in those numeral classifier languages "showing an opposition between a transnumeral form of the noun and a form marked for number"[33]

---

33. "Most classifier languages do not show grammatical number distinctions. Some others, however, do; but, these so-called optional plurals refer to collectivity rather than plurality, and they are incompatible with counting and thus with the classifier construction" (Seiler 1986: 97). Seiler mentions that "numeral classifier languages can be divided into two groups", of which the one is the type quoted here and the other consisting of "languages which do not show grammatical number marking on the noun – nor on the verb. The noun is strictly transnumeral." (p. 105)

(Seiler 1986: 105), a plural marker (mostly human) and a classifier construction are in principle mutually excluded,[34] e.g., in Chinese:

(25) a. {i) yī-ge / ii) wǔshí-ge} rén (-ge = numeral classifier)
   i) 'one person' / ii) '50 persons'
   b. rén-_men_ 'persons, people' / c. *50-ge rén-men

In contrast to Hungarian, numeral classifier languages of East and Southeast Asia like Chinese do not have number marking on predicates, so we cannot justify the assignment of a noun such as rén 'person' in (25a.ii) either to plural or to singular. Neither the existence of a plurality expression as men in (25b) justifies the assignment of rén 'person' in (25a.ii) to singular, as long as the complementarity between it and (25b) is maintained, excluding (25c). In this respect Seiler (1986) writes as follows:[35]

> Unclassified nouns, i.e., nouns appearing outside of numerical or related contexts, are transnumeral, i.e., neutral with regard to distinctions between singular, dual, and plural. […] Unclassified nouns […] indicate the concept rather than the object qua specimen of such and such a species. (p. 97)
>
> […] nouns do not directly refer to objects, […] they are, on the contrary, purely conceptual labels. In contrast, the notion of counting does not relate to the level of concepts; it is always related to individual objects. This is then what gives rise to the separate category of classifiers (p. 104)

---

34. In Japanese, however, a numeral classifier construction and a plurality marker on a noun may, or even must, co-occur depending on definiteness, pronominal reference and the position of the noun and of the quantifier in a clause (see Ono 2002: 15, 2019: 342f.).

35. "This essential property of the unclassified noun constitutes the reason for the impossibility in these languages of any direct collocation of Q – N." (p. 97); further, "the operational character of classification is one of subsuming an object under the concept X. What matters, then, is not the class in its thing-like aspect but the result of this very operation and the purpose which this serves, viz. to represent an individualized object that is eligible to be counted." (p. 102) "Gender assignment of nouns is a lexical property, but gender marking is necessarily relegated to the agreeing terms and forms a (morphological) constituent with them. This feature of constituent structure may serve to distinguish our technique from that of NUMERAL CLASSIFICATION, where the numeral classifier is never a direct co-constituent of the classified noun." (p. 113); "agreement signals the constancy of an object, […] anaphoric relation is at the basis of all agreement, […] This function of constancy is closely related to the function of reference […] This close relationship between the two functions is probably responsible for the fact that in gender languages a noun virtually and normally refers to a specific object. This is vastly different from the situation in numeral classifier languages where the (unclassified) noun does not refer to an object at all." (p. 123f.)

This view supports us in regarding Chin. *shū* not as Plural even if it has plural reference, at least when it is not accompanied by a numeral classifier. And if a noun co-occurs with a counting expression as in (23) or (25a) we have two options: either to maintain transnumerality as the essential property of nouns in numeral classifier languages, lacking the category of number; or to assume the existence of the nominal category of number consisting of, say, Singular and Plural (but why precisely these two?), whose forms are, however, never different, i.e., systematically indifferent. The first option seems to be adequate, and by no means it resists answering the query how plurality is, or can be, expressed.[36]

And in the case of Hungarian? Should we retain the number category of Singular/Plural or, rather, try to account for its marking system in terms of "transnumerus"[37] or "numerus absolutus" (see Biermann 1982: 237) because Hungarian behaves in a manner analogous to that of numeral-classifying systems, despite the fundamental difference in the existence of a formal category pertaining to number? If a non-marked noun form without any quantifying modifier like *nagynéni* in (24) can be understood only as 'an aunt', and if the 'singular' form of a predicate implies a single unit of the subject referent under the condition that no nominal element appears in the same clause nor is reconstructable from the context, it seems adequate to assume a number system containing Plural. It remains, however, a theoretical matter to discuss whether the non-marked form should be accounted for as Singular or Transnumerus (or *numerus absolutus*) that has, for lack of numeral information, singular reference by virtue of its unmarked nature (for a discussion in more detail, see Ono 2019).

With the above example of number marking, we tried to demonstrate the abductive methodology and the hermeneutic circle.[38]

---

36. The alternative option is comparable to the approaches criticized by Haspelmath (2010: 663ff. and passim): either an aprioristic-universalist one or a straightforward application/extension of Latin or Standard Average European or English categories.

37. For the notion and discussions on transnumerus/transnumerality, see e.g., Greenberg 1972/74: 28f.; Biermann 1982: 230ff.; Seiler 1995: 312; Unterbeck 1996: 149, 1999: xxiv; Ono: 2002: 13, 2019; Löbel 2004.

38. "Function is the central concept of our universals research that allows invariant and universal concepts to be brought together, because function has two aspects: One pertains to the inductive perspective and represents the invariant common denominator of the continua […]. The other pertains to the deductive perspective and represents the *repraesentandum*. Invariant and variant are correlative notions: Under the common denominator of function, variegated structures as correlated with each other in the continua can be considered as the corresponding variants." (Seiler 1986: 14). "Do we know what an 'object' or 'thing' is? It appears that we have some knowledge, some intuition about it, […] conceptualizations have status in

Cross-linguistic studies must always consider how every linguistic means, found in a sample of data, functions in the language system in which it is embedded. And H. Seiler left many deeply insightful works worth to be studied also in the future.[39]

References

Biermann, Anna. 1982. Die grammatische Kategorie des Numerus. In *Apprehension: Das sprachliche Erfassen von Gegenständen, Teil I: Bereich und Ordnung der Phänomene*. [Language Universals Series (LUS) 1/1], Hansjakob Seiler & Christian Lehmann (eds), 229–243. Tübingen: Narr.

Comrie, Bernard, Hartmann, Iren, Haspelmath, Martin, Malchukov, Andrej & Wichmann, Søren. 2015. Introduction. In Malchukov & Comrie (eds), Vol.1: 3–26.

Coseriu, Eugenio. 1969/70. Semantik, innere Sprachform und Tiefenstruktur. In *Sprache, Strukturen und Funktionen* [Tübinger Beiträge zur Linguistik (TBL) 2], Eugenio Coseriu, 213–224. Tübingen: Gunter Narr.

Coseriu, Eugenio. 1996. Die gegenwärtige Lage in der Sprachforschung. In Coseriu, Ezawa & Kürschner (eds), 3–34.

Coseriu, Eugenio, Ezawa, Kennosuke & Kürschner, Wilfried (eds). 1996. *Sprachwissenschaftsgeschichte und Sprachforschung: Ost-West-Kolloquium Berlin 1995*. Tübingen: Niemeyer.

Daneš, František. 1987. On Prague School functionalism in linguistics. In *Functionalism in Linguistics* [Linguistic & Literary Studies in Eastern Europe 20], René Dirven & Vilém Fried (eds), 5–38. Amsterdam: John Benjamins. https://doi.org/10.1075/llsee.20.03dan

Dowty, David. 1991. Thematic proto-roles and argument selection. *Language* 67: 547–619. https://doi.org/10.1353/lan.1991.0021

Durand, Marie-Laure, Lefèvre, Michel & Öhl, Peter (eds). 2020. *Tradition und Erneuerung: Sprachen, Sprachvermittlung, Sprachwissenschaft. Akten der 26. Fachtagung der Gesellschaft für Sprache und Sprachen GeSuS e.V. in Montpellier, 5.-7. April 2018*. Hamburg: Kovač.

---

a deductive, but not in an inductive perspective: They are posited at the outset, but are not in any direct way derived from inductive research. […] no matter which science is dealing with objects, at the beginning there always is and must be some sort of a priori conceptualization of what an object could be. In a way, such conceptualization stands both at the outset and at the end of the respective investigations; the conceptualization must be such that it can accommodate – and not contradict – the findings of each discipline. […] In this sense, our language universals research, although it presupposes conceptualizations of objects, can at the same time be expected to contribute to a better understanding of these very conceptualizations. We are moving in a hermeneutic circle." (Seiler 1986: 16). "[…] our approach [means] a permanent shift from inspection of the data to model building and back to the data, and so forth" (Seiler 1986: 5).

39. For Seiler's biography, main traits of his linguistic approach and claims, see Lehmann 2019. See also <http://ifl.phil-fak.uni-koeln.de/seiler_biographie.html>.

Foley, William A. & Van Valin Jr., Robert D. 1984. *Functional Syntax and Universal Grammar*. Cambridge: CUP.

von der Gabelentz, Georg. 1891[1984]. *Die Sprachwissenschaft*. Tübingen: Gunter Narr.

Greenberg, Joseph H. 1972/74. Numeral classifiers and substantival number: Problems in the genesis of a linguistic type. *Working Papers in Language Universals* 9: 1–39. Also in Luigi Heilmann (ed.). 1974. *Proceedings of the 11th International Congress of Linguists*, 17–37. Bologna: il Mulino.

Haspelmath, Martin. 2010. Comparative concepts and descriptive categories in crosslinguistic studies. *Language* 86: 663–687. https://doi.org/10.1353/lan.2010.0021

Haspelmath, Martin. 2015. Transitivity prominence. In Malchukov & Comrie (eds), Vol.1, 131–147.

Haspelmath, Martin. 2016. The challenge of making language description and comparison mutually beneficial. *Linguistic Typology* 20: 299–303. https://doi.org/10.1515/lingty-2016-0008

Haspelmath, Martin. 2017. On the scope of the form-frequency correspondence principle. E-Handout of his presentation for Jahrestagung der Deutschen Gesellschaft für Sprachwissenschaft, March 8–10, 2017, Saarbrücken.

Kishimoto, Hideki, Kageyama, Taro & Sasaki, Kan. 2015. Valency classes in Japanese. In Malchukov & Comrie (eds), Vol.1, 765–805.

Langacker, Ronald W. 2006. Chapter 1, Cognitive Grammar: Introduction to *Concept, image, and symbol*. In *Cognitive Linguistics: Basic Readings*, Dirk Geeraerts (ed.), 29–68. Berlin: De Gruyter. https://doi.org/10.1515/9783110199901.29

Lehmann, Christian. 1989. Language description and general comparative grammar. 11th International Congress of Linguists, 13 August 1987, Berlin. In *Reference Grammars and Modern Linguistic Theory* [Linguistische Arbeiten 226], Gottfried Graustein & Gerhard Leitner (eds), 133–162. Tübingen: Niemeyer. Also available via <https://www.christianlehmann.eu/publ/lg_descr_gcg.pdf> (last modification: 14 December 2012) (24 February 2020).

Lehmann, Christian. 2017. Linguistic concepts and categories in language description and comparison. In *Typology, Acquisition, Grammaticalization Studies*, Marina Chini & Pierluigi Cuzzolin (eds), 27–50. Milano: Franco Angeli.

Lehmann, Christian. 2019. Obituary: Hansjakob Seiler (1920–2018). *Linguistic Typology* 23: 115–118. https://doi.org/10.1515/lingty-2019-0003

Löbel, Elisabeth. 2004. Transnumeralität und Numerusopposition im Vietnamesischen: Ein Beitrag zur Dimension der Apprehension. In Premper (ed.), 57–71.

Malchukov, Andrej. 2015. Valency classes and alternations: Parameters of variation. In Malchukov & Comrie (eds), Vol.1, 73–130.

Malchukov, Andrej & Comrie, Bernard (eds). 2015. *Valency classes in the world's languages*, 2 Vols. Berlin: De Gruyter Mouton.

Mathesius, V. 1936. On some problems of the systematic analysis of grammar. *TCLP* 6: 95–107. Reprinted in Vachek (ed.), 1964, 306–319.

Miyagawa, Shigeru. 1989. *Structure and case marking in japanese*. San Diego CA: Academic Press. https://doi.org/10.1163/9789004373259

Ono, Yoshiko. 2002. *Typologische Züge des Japanischen* [Linguistische Arbeiten 453]. Tübingen: Niemeyer. https://doi.org/10.1515/9783110924794

Ono, Yoshiko. 2014. Wie wirklich ist Japanisch eine BECOME-Sprache? In *Schriften der Gesellschaft für Japanforschung*, 39–72. <http://www.gjf.de/netzpublikationen/SGJF_Bd1_Ono-Premper.pdf> or <http://d-nb.info/1062629914/34> (14 November 2020)

Ono, Yoshiko. 2015. Kontinuum der Objektvarianten im Japanischen. In Seiler (ed.), 45–141.

Ono, Yoshiko. 2019. Effizienz-Begriff und Systembezogenheit der sprachlichen Formen am Beispiel der Numerus-Markierung. In *Sprachen, Literaturen und Kulturen im Kontakt: Beiträge der 25. Linguistik- und Literaturtage, Miskolc/Ungarn, 2017 (der Gesellschaft für Sprache und Sprachen GeSuS e.V.)*, Erika Kegyes, Renata Kriston & Manuela Schönenberger (eds), 337–344. Hamburg: Kovač.

Ono, Yoshiko. 2020. Fragen von *Sein* oder *Nicht-Sein*: Perfektauxiliar, Status nominaler Elemente, Transitivität. In Durand, Lefèvre & Öhl (eds), 61–75.

Premper, Waldfried. 1991. Introduction. In Seiler & Premper (eds), 3–12.

Premper, Waldfried. 2001. Universals of the linguistic representation of situations ('participation'). In *Language typology and language universals: an international handbook* [Handbücher zur Sprach- und Kommunikationswissenschaft (HSK), 20.2], Martin Haspelmath, Ekkehard König, Wulf Oesterreicher & Wolfgang Raible (eds), 477–495. Berlin: De Gruyter

Premper, Waldfried. 2020. Kognition und Semantik. In Durand, Lefèvre & Öhl (eds), 171–180.

Premper, Waldfried (ed.). 2004. *Dimensionen und Kontinua: Beiträge zu Hansjakob Seilers Universalienforschung* [Diversitas Linguarum 4]. Bochum: Brockmeyer.

Sadakane, Kumi & Koizumi, Masatoshi. 1995. On the nature of the 'dative' particle *ni* in Japanese. *Linguistics* 33: 5–33. https://doi.org/10.1515/ling.1995.33.1.5

de Saussure, Ferdinand. 1916/1931. *Cours de linguistique générale*. Publié par Charles Bally et Albert Sechehaye, 3ᵉ édition. Paris: Payot.

Seiler, Hansjakob. 1973. Das Universalienkonzept. In *Linguistic workshop I*, Hansjakob Seiler (ed.), 6–19. München: Fink.

Seiler, Hansjakob. 1983. Universals of language. In *16. Weltkongress für Philosophie 1978. Eröffnungs- und Schlusssitzung, Plenarsitzungen, Abendvorträge*, Alwin Diemer (ed), 455–465. Frankfurt: Peter Lang.

Seiler, Hansjakob. 1985. Diversity, unity, and their connection. In *Language Invariants and Mental Operations: International Interdisciplinary Conference Held at Gummersbach/Cologne, Germany, September 18–23, 1983* [Language Universals Series (LUS), 5], Hansjakob Seiler & Gunter Brettschneider (eds), 4–10. Tübingen: Gunter Narr.

Seiler, Hansjakob. 1986. *Apprehension: Language, object, and order, part iii: the universal dimension of Apprehension* [Language Universals Series (LUS) 1/III]. Tübingen: Gunter Narr.

Seiler, Hansjakob. 1988. *The dimension of PARTICIPATION. Funcion No. 7*. Universidad de Guadalajara.

Seiler, Hansjakob. 1995. Cognitive-conceptual structure and linguistic encoding: Language universals and typology in the UNITYP framework. In *Approaches to language typology*, Masayoshi Shibatani & Theodora Bynon (eds), 273–325. Oxford: Clarendon Press.

Seiler, Hansjakob. 1996. Zum heutigen Stand der Universalienforschung. In Coseriu, Ezawa & Kürschner (eds), 145–167.

Seiler, Hansjakob. 2000. *Language universals research: A synthesis* [Language Universals Series (LUS) 8]. Tübingen: Gunter Narr.

Seiler, Hansjakob. 2002. Universelles, Generelles, Typisches in der Sprachverwendung. In *Linguistik jenseits des Strukturalismus: Akten des II. Ost-West-Kolloquiums*, Kennosuke Ezawa, Wilfried Kürschner, Karl H. Rensch & Manfred Ringmacher (eds), 15–20. Tübingen: Gunter Narr.

Seiler, Hansjakob. 2004. Über das Verhältnis von Sprachuniversalienforschung und Sprachtypologie: Rückblick und Ausblick. In Premper (ed.), 1–16.

Seiler, Hansjakob. 2008a. *Universality in language beyond grammar: Selected writings 1990–2007*, Thomas Stolz (ed.). Bochum: Universitätsverlag Dr. N. Brockmeyer.

Seiler, Hansjakob. 2008b. POSSESSION: Variation and invariants. In Seiler 2008a, 7–36.
Seiler, Hansjakob. 2008c. Object, language, and communication. In Seiler 2008a, 53–73.
Seiler, Hansjakob. 2008d. Zum Erklärungspotential kontinuierlicher Ordnungen. In Seiler 2008a, 149–162. French version in *Hansjakob Seiler. Notice bio-bibliographique suivie d'un entretien entre Hansjakob Seiler et Jacques François, et de deux exposés de synthèse de Hansjakob Seiler*... [Biobibliographies et exposés, Novelle série 9], Jaques François & Pierre Swiggers (eds), 2008, 125–142. Leuven: Centre Internationale de Dialectologie Générale.
Seiler, Hansjakob. 2015. Vorwort (p. 1), Abstract (English p. 2 and German p. 3), Theoretische Einleitung (pp. 6–13), Das Kontinuum der Varianten der Objektrelation im Deutschen (pp. 14–28), Nachwort (pp. 142–145) and Schlussbemerkung (p. 146) in Seiler (ed.) 2015.
Seiler, Hansjakob. 2016ff.a. *UNITYP*. <http://ifl.phil-fak.uni-koeln.de/seiler_unityp.html> (30 September 2019).
Seiler, Hansjakob. 2016ff.b. *UNITYP weiter*. <http://ifl.phil-fak.uni-koeln.de/seiler_unityp_weiter.html> (30 September 2019).
Seiler, Hansjakob. 2016ff.c. *Vom Denkinhalt*. <http://ifl.phil-fak.uni-koeln.de/seiler_vom_denkinhalt.html> (30 September 2019).
Seiler, Hansjakob & Berthould-Papandropoulou, Ioanna. 2015. Das Kontinuum der Varianten der Objektrelation im Neugriechischen. In Seiler (ed.), 29–44.
Seiler, Hansjakob & François, Jacques. 2001. *Gespräche über Hansjakob Seilers Universalienforschung* [Cahier du CRISCO n° 3A]. Université de Caen: CRISCO (Centre de Recherches Interlangues sur la Signification en Contexte).
Seiler, Hansjakob (ed.). 2015. *Das Konzept der Objektrelation und das Kontinuum ihrer Varianten: Ein muttersprachlicher Zugang*. München: Lincom.
Seiler, Hansjakob & Premper, Waldfried (eds). 1991. *Partizipation: Das sprachliche Erfassen von Sachverhalten* [Language Universals Series (LUS) 6]. Tübingen: Gunter Narr.
Sybesma, Rint. 2017. Classifiers and countability. Handout of his presentation for ECLL Chinese Linguistic Day, April 7, 2017, University of Zurich.
Unterbeck, Barbara. 1996. Numerus aus der Sicht des Koreanischen. In Coseriu, Ezawa & Kürschner (eds), 145–167.
Unterbeck, Barbara. 1999. Gender: New light on an old category. An Introduction. In *Gender in Grammar and Cognition*, Barbara Unterbeck & Matti Rissanen (eds), xv–xlvi. Berlin: De Gruyter.

CHAPTER 8

The non-universality of linguistic categories
Evidence from pluractional constructions

Simone Mattiola
University of Insubria

This paper aims at giving a typological overview of pluractionality in order to show how grammatical categories, in cross-linguistic perspective, cannot be considered as universally valid entities. After having defined the phenomenon, I will present the main functions and some formal characteristics that pluractional markers have in the languages of the world. Then, I will describe the diachronic sources from which pluractional markers come from. Finally, I will discuss the grammatical status that pluractionality has in cross linguistic perspective in the light of the broad variety it shows in the languages of the world and also taking into consideration data from specific languages.

1. Introduction[1]

In the last three decades, the typological community has often focused its attention on an interesting debate: how to conceptualize grammatical categories and relations in cross-linguistic perspective. In other words, the question is whether grammatical categories can be considered as universally valid entities or rather as language-specific phenomena. This issue is not a novelty. Considerations on the differences among languages for what concerns their grammatical organization are known at least by the first modern descriptive works carried out by Franz Boas and his school:

---

[1] I would like to thank: the convenors and the participants of the workshop at SLE2017 in Zürich for the fruitful discussion; two anonymous reviewers for the suggestions and criticism; Sonia Cristofaro for several discussions we had on the topic of the paper; and Doris Payne, Martine Vanhove, and Spike Gildea for having shared with me their data respectively on Maa (Nilotic), Beja (Afroasiatic), and Akawaio (Cariban). Usual disclaimers apply.

> In accordance with the general views expressed in the introductory chapters, the method of treatment has been throughout an analytical one. *No attempt has been made to compare the forms of the Indian grammars with the grammars of English, Latin, or even among themselves; but in each case the psychological groupings which are given depend entirely upon the inner form of each language*
>
> (Boas 1911: 81, italics is mine)

However, it is only in the last twenty-five years that the problem has been discussed at length in the literature (e.g., Dryer 1997; Croft 2001; Haspelmath 2007, 2010; Cristofaro 2009; the debate on the LingTyp mailing list on early 2016 that was partly published in a special issue of Linguistic Typology, Vol. 20(2); and the papers of the present edited volume). We can identify at least three different positions related to this topic (cf. Cristofaro 2009 for a detailed analysis of these positions). First, in some formal approaches to language, it is assumed that categories do exist and can be applied to different languages since they are expressions of the speakers' mental grammar. Thus, while categories of the languages of the world differ from each other for what concerns some properties and parameters, they do have the same grammatical representation within speakers' minds (i.e., Universal Grammar).

A second approach consists in accounting for cross-linguistic phenomena in terms of prototypes. In other words, categories are different from language to language, but they still share some specific fundamental properties. Members of a category can or cannot have all the properties defining the prototype since they have different status inside the category (prototypical *vs.* non-prototypical members). Also, in this case, these fundamental properties reflect some sort of mental representation.

The third position considers grammatical categories as language- and construction-specific entities. Since categories are defined on a distributional basis in single languages, and distributional patterns are by definition language-specific because they refer to morphosyntactic 'positions' within discourse, categories are valid only for the language in which these distributional patterns are found. Of course, it is possible to find similarities among constructions ("any grammatical context that defines a morphosyntactic slot that can be filled by particular linguistic elements" Cristofaro 2009: 445) in the languages of the world, but this does not mean that they are expression of a common category reflecting speakers' mental representation. Rather we can explain these form-function cross-linguistic recurring patterns referring to some functional principles that languages have as a communicative tool. Despite the substantial differences of these positions, the literature seems to agree at least on that fact that the languages of the world exhibit a remarkable linguistic variety.

The aim of this paper is to provide a relevant piece of evidence of the non-universality and the language-specificity of grammatical categories through the cross-linguistic investigation of the phenomenon known as pluractionality. From this comprehensive overview, it will be shown that pluractional markers display a very broad variety in the languages of the world. The differences that pluractional markers present at any level of analysis do not let us presume the existence of a unique cross-linguistic valid category, but rather suggest to conceive the term pluractionality as a comparative concept (Haspelmath 2010). The choice of investigating pluractionality is not random. There are at least two reasons for which pluractionality represents strong evidence for the non-universality of linguistic categories. First, as already noted, pluractional markers show a broad variety in the languages of the world and this variety can hardly be accounted for through a single category. Second, pluractionality is not a phenomenon inherited by the grammatical tradition of ancient Indo-European languages. It is not common in the Indo-European languages of Europe and, thus, it remained an undescribed phenomenon until quite recent years. This means that only a few attempts aiming at classifying it in a pre-established category have been made and that the grammatical status that pluractional markers (henceforth PMs) have in the languages of the world is not biased by any pre-established assumption.

The paper is organized as follows. In Section 2, I introduce and define pluractionality describing the methodological bases on which this paper is grounded. Section 3 and Section 4 give a comprehensive overview of the synchronic characteristics that PMs have in the languages of the world. Firstly, I present the functions these markers express and I give an explanation of the pluractional functional domain through semantic maps. Secondly, I describe the marking strategies languages adopt to express pluractional functions and then I discuss some interesting peculiarities connected to them. In Section 5, I illustrate the few diachronic sources I was able to find within my language sample. Finally, in Section 6, I discuss at length the grammatical status that PMs have in cross-linguistic perspective in light of the characteristics described in the previous sections and analyzing a bit more in detail the pluractional systems of three typologically distant languages.

2. Theoretical and methodological preliminaries

The term *pluractionality* was coined to better describe the functions of the *intensive* verbal derivation of Chadic languages (cf. Newman 1980: 13, fn. 23). It was defined as verbal forms expressing "plurality or multiplicity of the verb's action" (Newman 1990: 54). For example, the only difference between the two sentences of Konso (Afroasiatic, Cushitic) in (1) is the presence of a partial initial reduplication of the verb in (1b). This reduplication – glossed as plural (PL) – expresses the fact that the agent performs the action more than once.

(1) Konso (Afroasiatic, Cushitic)
   a. ʔiʃa-ʔ   ʔinanta-siʔ   ʔi=tuɠɠuur-ay
      3SGM.PRO-NOM   girl-DEF.F/M   3=push[SG]-PFV[3M]
      'He pushed the girl.'   (Orkaydo 2013: 263)
   b. ʔiʃa-ʔ   ʔinanta-siʔ   ʔi=tu~tuɠɠuur-ay
      3SG.M.PRO-NOM   girl-DEF.F/M   3=PL~push[SG]-PFV[3M]
      'He pushed the girl more than once.'   (Orkaydo 2013: 263)

However, in the literature, the term pluractionality is usually used with a more specific connotation. Following the proposals of Cabredo-Hofherr & Laca (2012: 1), pluractionality encodes event-plurality through a modification of the verb form (e.g., affixation, reduplication, suppletive patterns, phonological modification of the verb stem, and so on), while the more comprehensive notion of *verbal number* expresses the same function through any marking strategies (thus including adverbial phrases, adnominal markers, etc.). Consequently, a more precise definition of pluractionality, that I adopt in the present paper, is as follows (Mattiola 2019: 164):

> Pluractionality is defined by a morphological modification of the verb (or a pair of semantically related verbs) that primarily conveys a plurality of situations that involves a repetition through time, space and/or participants.

In the next sections, I will illustrate the main cross-linguistic characteristics of PMs. This paper is based on the cross-linguistic comparison of a variety sample of languages composed of 248 languages (cf. Appendix). The language sample is designed merging the 200-language sample available on the website of the WALS project (cf. http://wals.info/languoid/samples/200; Dryer & Haspelmath 2013) and the 194-language sample adopted by Ljuba Veselinova for her chapter "Verbal Number and Suppletion" within the WALS (cf. Veselinova 2013). I added and modified some languages for convenience (e.g. the actual possibility of reaching a grammatical description for a specific language) and for adjusting the relative representativeness.

For what concerns the terminology, I adopt the widespread practice of using labels with the initial capital letter for language-specific phenomena and labels without a capital letter when referring to cross-linguistic terms (that is, to any particular language) (cf. Comrie 1976: 10). In the glosses, I preferred to maintain the original interlinear glosses used in the bibliographic reference as often as possible. This is because, also in this case, they refer to language-specific phenomena. However, I conformed some of them to the Leipzig Glossing Rules in order to avoid the uncontrolled proliferation of abbreviations and also to make the paper more consistent and the reading smoother.

Finally, for what concerns language classification and names, I decided to adopt the genealogic classification proposed in the Glottolog project (cf. Hammarström et al. 2018), but I preferred to maintain the names used in the bibliographic references.

3. Functional characteristics of pluractional markers

In the languages of the world, a PM is identifiable as a modification of the verb expressing a plurality of situations. This means that every strategy marking event plurality directly on the verb can be described as a PM. However, it is often the case that the same strategy can express several different meanings. For this reason, a specific device can be called a PM only if event plurality is a relevant (in the sense of frequency) meaning.

PMs are extremely multifunctional in the languages of my sample. However, I identified some frequent functions that PMs express. I classified these functions in two main groups: core and additional functions.

3.1 Core functions

Core functions are those functions that directly fall under the definition of pluractionality I gave in the previous section, that is, devices encoding the plurality of situations on the verb. We can recognize different types of core functions depending on which element of the occasion is pluralized. An occasion is usually composed of four elements: (i) the situation (an event or a state) occurring in (ii) a specific (or not) time frame in (iii) a determined or undetermined space involving (iv) single or plural participants (agents, patients, experiencers, etc.). Therefore, the plurality of situations can be spread over time, space or participants.

When the plurality of situations involves time, we have what I call *pluractionals stricto sensu*. In this case, we can identify two different sub-functions: (i) iterativity, when the plurality is limited to a relatively short time frame identified as a single occasion (cf. (2)); and (ii) frequentativity, when the plurality is extended to a long time frame that is identified as composed of different occasions (cf. (3)).

(2) Skwxwú7mesh[2] (Salishan, Central Salish)
    a. *chen   kwelesh-t   ta   sxwi7shn*
       1SBJ.SG shoot-TR DET deer
       'I shot a deer.'   (Bar-el 2008: 34)

---

2. The symbol '7' is traditionally used in Skwxwú7mesh (also known as Squamish) and, more in general, in Salishan studies to represent a glottal stop.

b. *chen* **kwel~kwelesh-t** *ta sxwi7shn*
1SBJ.SG PLAC~shoot-TR DET deer
'I shot a deer several times/continuously.' (Bar-el 2008: 34)

(3) Khwe (Khoe-Kwadi, Khoe)
tí à bɛ̀-ɛ̀-xú-t-a-tè!
1SG OBJ be.too.heavy-II-COMP-FREQ-I-PRS
'It is often too heavy for me!' (Kilian-Hatz 2008: 146)

The plurality of the situations can involve different locations, that is, the situation takes place in different places and is widespread over space. In this case, we have *spatial distributivity* (cf. (4)).

(4) Barasano (Tucanoan, Eastern Tucanoan)
*gahe-rũbũ bota-ri kea-**kudi**-ka-bã idã*
other-day post-PL chop-ITER-RM.PST-3PL 3PL
'The next day they went from place to place chopping down posts (for the new house).' (Jones & Jones 1991: 101)

When the plurality of situations involves several participants, we have *participant plurality* (cf. (5)).

(5) ǂHoan (Kxa)
a. *ya* ǁ*'ai* *'a*
3SG hang.SG PFV
'It is hanging.' (a thing hanging on a wall) (Collins 1998: 56)

b. *tsi* !*ga* *'a*
3PL hang.PL PFV
'They are hanging.' (several things hanging on different walls) (Collins 1998: 56)

Usually, the participant involved in the pluralization is the entity whose state is mostly affected by the situation. In syntactic terms, the most affected argument tends to be the direct object of transitive sentences and the subject of intransitive sentences. From a semantic point of view, the most affected semantic role tends to be the patient.

A specific strategy can be regarded as pluractional only if it has among its main functions at least one of the functions exemplified in the present section.

3.2 Additional functions

Additional functions are those functions that do not directly fall under the definition of pluractionality, but that PMs very often express in addition to at least one of the core functions. I classified these recurrent functions in different semantic clusters according to the kind of relationship they have with the notion of plurality.

The first cluster is *non-prototypical plurality*. The functions of this cluster express a meaning that goes beyond the basic distinction between singularity and plurality.

We have *event-internal plurality* when the plurality does not involve the situation, but it is internal to it. In other words, in this case, the situation is externally singular, but it is composed of several repetitive phases or sub-events making it internally complex (cf. (6)).[3]

(6) Sandawe (Isolate, Africa)
    a. Iterative or frequentative reading (depending on the context) of the Iterative morpheme -*ìmé* ITER.
        gélé-áá |-*ìmé*
        Gele-SFOC come.SG-**ITER**
        'Gele came repeatedly.'   (Steeman 2012: 143)
    b. Event-internal plural reading of the Iterative morpheme -*ìmé* ITER.
        tsháá=sà   xàd-*ímé*-é
        pot=3F.SG scrape_out-**ITER**-3OBJ
        'She scraped out a pot.'   (Steeman 2012: 141)

We have *continuativity* when the situation is singular, but it is prolonged (therefore not repeated) during a period of time (cf. (7)).

(7) Chechen (Nakh-Daghestanian, Nakh)
    a. Unmarked form of the verb stem.
        so   tykana   **vedira**
        1SG.ABS store.DAT **run.WP**
        'I ran to the store'   (Wood 2007: 224)
    b. Frequentative reading of the pluractional verb stem.
        hoora wyyrana so   tykana   **ydu**
        every morning 1SG.ABS store.DAT **run.PLAC.PRS**
        'Every morning I run to the store repeatedly (more than once per day)'
                (Wood 2007: 225)
    c. Continuative reading of the pluractional verb stem.
        so   cwana   sahwtiahw   **idira**
        1SG.ABS one.OBL hour.LOC **run.PLAC.WP**
        'I ran (went running) for one hour'   (Wood 2007: 224)

We have *habituality* when a situation is repeated over different occasions, but, at the same time, it is understood as regular and typical of that specific time frame (cf. (8)). This function is quite similar to frequentativity, the difference lies in the regularity and typicality of the situation, while for frequentativity the repetitions of the situation are more random.

---

3. In the examples of this section, I show in (a) the core pluractional reading of the marking strategy under investigation and in (b) the additional reading of the same marker.

(8) Sandawe (Isolate, Africa)
    a. Frequentative reading of the morpheme *-wǎ* PL.
        nì-ŋ   hík'-wǎ-ŋ   phàkhé-ŋ |èé-ì
        CNJ-CL   go.SG-PL-L   inspect-L   look_at-3.IRR
        'And he will often go, inspect and have a look at it' (Steeman 2012: 242)
    b. Habitual reading of the morpheme *-wǎ* PL.
        mindà-tà-nà=sį̀   hík'į̊-wà
        field-in-to=1SG   go.SG-PL
        'I go to the field.'   (Steeman 2012: 188)

We have *generic imperfectivity* when a situation occurs always like a property or a quality of an entity or a gnomic truth (cf. (9)).

(9) Mapuche/Mapudungun (Araucanian)[4]
    a. Frequentative reading of the morpheme *-ke* CF.
        *tüfa-mew   pe-**ke**-e-y-u   kuyfí*
        this-INST   see-CF-IDO-IND-1NSG-DU-DS   formerly
        'I used to meet you here'   (Smeets 2008: 252)
    b. Generic imperfective reading of the morpheme *-ke* CF.
        *umañ-pa-**ke**-la-y   ta   witran   ta*
        stay-HH-CF-NEG-IND-3   the   visitor   the
        'a visitor does not stay here'   (Smeets 2008: 252)

The second semantic cluster is *degree*. In this case, the functions show a modification of the degree of the situation compared to the prototypical development of the same situation. We have *intensity* when a situation is done with more effort or when we have a situation whose result is augmented with respect to its usual happening (cf. (10)).

(10) Yimas (Lower Sepik-Ramu, Lower Sepik)
    a. Iterative or frequentative (depending on the context) reading of Yimas verbal reduplication.
        *ya-n-**ark~ark**-wampaki-pra-k*
        PL.OBJ-3SG.A-**break~PLAC**-throw-VEN-IRR
        'He repeatedly broke them and threw them as he came'
                                                          (Foley 1991: 319)
    b. Intensive reading of Yimas verbal reduplication.
        *ya-mpu-nanaŋ-**ta~cay**-ckam-tuk-mpun*
        PL.OBJ-3PL.A-DUR-**see~PLAC**-show-RM.PST-3PL.DAT
        'They were showing those to them very well (and they stared at those)'
                                                          (Foley 1991: 319)

---

4. Smeets (2008) glosses these two examples as I reported here giving a not fully consistent morpheme-by-morpheme correspondence.

We have completeness when a situation is performed in its entirety or completely (cf. (11)).

(11) Turkana (Nilotic, Eastern Nilotic)
 a. Pluractional reading of verbal reduplication.
 -poc 'pinch' → a-poc~o-poc' 'pinch repeatedly'
 -ilug 'twist' → a-k-ilug~u-lug 'twist repeatedly'
 (Dimmendaal 1983: 106)
 b. Complete reading of verbal reduplication.
 -ɲrl 'crumble' → a-ɲrl~r-ɲrl' 'crumble completely'
 -ikic 'bone out' → a-k-ikic~i-kic 'bone out completely'
 (Dimmendaal 1983: 106)

We have *emphasis* when a situation is performed with a particular emphasis or affectedness (cf. (12)).

(12) Karo Batak (Austronesian, Malayo-Polynesian)
 a. Iterative or frequentative (depending on the context) reading of Karo Batak verbal reduplication.
 sapu~sapuna kucing é.
 PLAC~stroke.3SG.F cat that
 'She stroked the cat again and again.' (Woollams 1996: 96)
 b. Emphatic reading of Karo Batak verbal reduplication.
 peturah~turah sitik ukurndu
 CAUS.grow~PLAC SOF mind.your
 'Grow up a bit! (i.e., Act like an adult!)' (Woollams 1996: 98)

The last semantic cluster I identified is *reciprocity* and is composed of only one function. In this case, we have reciprocity when at least two different participants perform the same situation reciprocally (cf. (13)).

(13) Jóola Karon (Atlantic-Congo, North Atlantic)
 a. Iterative reading of Jóola Karon Pluractional/Reciprocal marker -*ool* PLAC/RECP.
 *Lopeel a-muus-**ool**-a*
 Robert 3SG-pass-PLAC-ACC
 'Robert went and came back.' (adapted from Sambou 2014: 150)
 b. Reciprocal reading of Jóola Karon Pluractional/Reciprocal marker -*ool* PLAC/RECP.
 *Sana ni Faatu ka-cuk-**ool**-a*
 Sana and Fatou 3PL-see-RECP-ACC
 'Sana and Fatou saw each other.' (Sambou 2014: 149)

3.3 Rare functions

In addition to core and additional functions, PMs can express several other functions that are not very frequent in the languages of my sample. In what follows I exemplify some of these rare functions.

In Karo Batak (Austronesian, Malayo-Polynesian), verbal reduplication can express both core and additional pluractional functions (cf. (12)). Woollams (1996: 101) notes that this strategy can also add "a sense of indefiniteness, 'diffuseness' (Rosen 1977: 4), or a lack of specific orientation or goal; this meaning tends to overlap with the notions of repetition and plurality" (cf. (14)).

(14) Karo Batak (Austronesian, Malayo-Polynesian)
sëh   i   Lau Kawar, déba   ia   ridi~ridi,   déba ngerakit ...é
reach   at Lau Kawar some they bathe~PLAC   some ACT.raft and
maka kundul~kundul ia   kerina i   tepi dano é.
then   sit~PLAC   they   all   at   side lake that
'Arriving at Lau Kawar, some went swimming, others played on rafts and then they all sat around the edge of the lake.'   (Woollams 1996: 101)

In Beja (Afroasiatic, Cushitic), we can identify three pluractional marking strategies: partial reduplication, full reduplication, and the internal modification of the verb stem (cf. Vanhove 2017). These strategies encode several pluractional functions (e.g., iterative, frequentative, participant plurality, habituality, etc.; cf. Mattiola 2019: 111-125). However, the internal modification of the verb (the Intensive derivation) can also express what is generally called *successive events*, that is, the presence of different (not of the same type) consecutive situations (cf. (15)).

(15) Beja (Afro-Asiatic, Cushitic)
j=hankʷil-a=jaː   dhaːj   jhak-i=t
DEF.M=youth-PL=POSS.3PL.NOM   DIR   get_up-AOR.3SG.M=CNJ
i=ḍeːfa   dhaːj   i-naːgil-na
DEF.M=door   DIR   3-open\INT.IPFV-PL
'Ses jeunes messagers se sont levés vers lui et lui ont ouvert les portes successivement' (literal translation: 'His young messenger people got up towards him and opened the door for him' [SM])
(Vanhove 2017: 73)

In Cilubà (Atlantic-Congo, Volta-Congo), the suffix *-angan* (glossed as PR – plurality of relations – by Dom, Segerer & Bostoen 2015) has as its core meaning antipassivity and reciprocity (cf. (16a) and (16b) respectively).

(16) Cilubà (Atlantic-Congo, Volta-Congo)
    a. *mu-ntu   ù-vwa   mu-ship-**angan**-a,*[5] *bà-vwa   bà-mu-ship-a*
       CL-person SBJ-PST CL-kill-**PR**-FV   SBJ-PST SBJ-OBJ-kill-FV
       pà-èndè,   nànasha yêye mu-àna-ènù.
       PRP-POSS   even.if   PRO   CL-brother-POSS.PL

       'The person that has killed (someone), we should kill him as well, even if he is your brother.'   (Dom, Segerer & Bostoen 2015: 355)

    b. *ba-ntu   ba-ònso   bà-di   ànu bà-amb-**angan**-a.*
       CL-human PRP-every SBJ-PRS just SBJ-say-**PR**-FV
       'Everybody just teases each other'   (Dom, Segerer & Bostoen 2015: 355)

However, this suffix can also express sociativity/collectiveness (cf. (17)) and iterativity (cf. (18)) (Dom, Segerer & Bostoen 2015: 355).

(17) Cilubà (Atlantic-Congo, Volta-Congo)
    *m-bowà   nè   N-gandù   bà-vwa ba-eeò-èsh-**àngàn**-e*
    CL-buffalo and CL-crocodile CL-PST CL-throw-CAUS-**PR**-FV
    'The buffalo and the crocodile were having a discussion'
                                              (Dom, Segerer & Bostoen 2015: 370)

(18) Cilubà (Atlantic-Congo, Volta-Congo)
    *mu-lùme ù-di   ù-pòòl-**angan**-a   àmu   ku-pòòl-**angan**-a.*
    CL-man SBJ-PRS SBJ-pluck-**PR**-FV just CL-pluck-**PR**-FV
    'The man is just constantly plucking'   (Dom, Segerer & Bostoen 2015: 374)

Another interesting rare function is *iterative coincidence* (cf. Jacques 2014: 295). In Japhug (Sino-Tibetan, Burmo-Qiangic), verbal reduplication can be used to express pluractional meanings (cf. (19a)). However, when a reduplicated verb (in the perfective) is in a conditional construction, specifically in the protatis, and an imperfective verb is in the apodosis followed by the auxiliary *ŋu* 'be' the resulting construction expresses the situation in which "whenever the event depicted in the protatis is fulfilled, the one of the apodosis necessarily always occurs, and that this has taken place several times in the past" (Jacques 2014: 295) (cf. (19b)).

(19) Japhug (Sino-Tibetan, Burmo-Qiangic)
    a. Pluractional reading of Japhug verbal reduplication.
       tɯ~tu-ɤcqʰe   zo   ɲɯ-ŋu
       RED~IPFV:3SG:cough EM TESTIM-be
       'Il tousse de plus en plus souvent.' (lit. tr. He coughs more and more often [SM])   (adapted from Jacques 2004: 395)

---

5. "This is a nominalized form of the verb with the verbal stem taking a nominal prefix. In combination with an auxiliary it expresses perfect aspect." (Dom, Segerer & Bostoen 2015: 355, fn 2).

b. Iterative coincident reading of the conditional construction with verbal reduplication in Japhug.

cʰa   ɕu~ɕ-kɤ-tsʰi-t-a
alcohol COND~TRANSLOC-PFV-drink-PST:TR-1SG

(zo)   lu-βzi-a   ŋu
EM   IPFV-be_drunk-1SG   be:FACT

'Each time I drink alcohol, I get intoxicated.'   (Jacques 2014: 296)

Finally, in Khwe (Khoe-Kwadi, Khoe) verbal reduplication can encode both pluractional functions and causativity (cf. (20)).

(20)   Khwe (Khoe-Kwadi, Khoe)
   a.   Pluractional reading of Khwe verbal reduplication.
   cii   'proceed'   →   cii~ci   'go continually'
   xòá   'split'   →   xòá~xoa   'reduce to small pieces'
   gyaó   'look/keep the eyes open'   →   gyaó~gyao   'look in all directions'
                                                              (Kilian-Hatz 2008: 147)
   b.   Causative reading of Khwe verbal reduplication.
   |xʼóɛ̀   'be full'   → |xʼóɛ~|xʼoɛ   'fill' (make sth. full)
   ǁxó   'be dry, dry out'   →   ǁxó~ǁxo   'dry sth.'
   kyérí 'be hard/difficult' →   kyérí~kyeri   'make it harder/more difficult'
                                                              (Kilian-Hatz 2008: 161)

3.4 The pluractional conceptual space

In order to better comprehend this broad multifunctionality of PMs in the languages of my sample, I propose to account for the pluractional functional domain through semantic maps. A node is displayed in a conceptual space (the network of functions claimed to be universal, while a semantic map is the language-specific realization of a conceptual space) only if there exists at least one language with a dedicated marking strategy, and two nodes are connected only if there exists at least one language expressing them through the same strategy (cf. Croft 2001; Haspelmath 2003; and Georgakopoulos & Polis 2018).

The pluractional conceptual space resulted from the cross-linguistic comparison of the languages of my sample is showed in Figure 1.

We can recognize three different areas in the space.[6] On the left side, we find the singular areas composed of singulactionality,[7] the functions of the degree

---

6. For reasons of space, I cannot discuss at length the pluractional conceptual space and the notations used therein. For a detailed discussion see Mattiola (2017, 2019).

7. The relationship between singulactionality and the other functions in the space is mediated by others not directly addressed by this work. In addition, since this kind of function

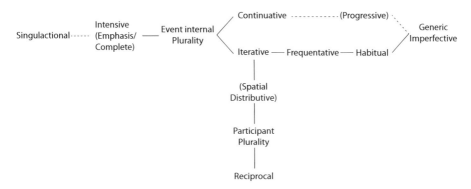

Figure 1. Pluractional conceptual space.

cluster, and at least partially event-internal plurality and continuativity. In the center of the space, we have the core area composed of the core functions (iterativity, frequentativity, spatial distributivity, and participant plurality). The third area is composed of the non-prototypical cluster (event-internal plurality, continuativity, habituality, and generic imperfectivity) and reciprocity.

It is interesting to note here that the functions in the space seem to follow a particular disposition. The functions on the left have a quite specific meaning, while the functions on the right have a more general meaning. This semantic generalization seems to follow two different semantic realizations: the prolongation of the situation over time (from event-internal plurality to generic imperfectivity, through continuativity) or the distribution of the repetitions over time (from even-internal plurality to generic imperfectivity, through iterativity, frequentativity, and habituality). Finally, the vertical area signals the presence of the parameter of distributivity (over space or participants).

4. Formal properties of pluractional markers

The languages of the world display several different marking strategies to express pluractional functions. However, also in this case, we can identify three strategies

---

expresses singular situations, it does not pertain to my investigation. A similar situation involves progressivity for which I found only one occurrence in my data, and this is not sufficient to place this function in the space. However, in the literature, we find the proposal of a diachronic path for reduplication that does include progressivity and that is basically identical to the area on the up-right side of my space (Bybee, Perkins & Pagliuca 1994: 172). I thus decided to put this function in the space to make it the most inclusive as possible, but with a particular status (connected through dotted lines).

that are much more common than others: affixation, reduplication, and lexical alternation.

The most common strategy is affixation. We can find the use of all kinds of affixes in every geographic area of the world.

(21) Prefixation: Kuot (Isolate, Papunesia)
u-me   da-karət=oŋ   [i-sik   kapuna]
3M.SG-HAB PLAC-bite=3M.SG   3M-DEM   dog(M)
'that dog bites a lot'   (Lindström 2002: 7)

(22) Infixation: Koasati (Muskogean, Alabaman-Koasati)
SINGULAR   PLURAL   GLOSS
aká:non   akásnon   'to be hungry'
akopí:lin akopíslin 'to knock something over'
apí:lin   apíslin   'to throw something away'
anó:lin   anóslin   'to devour something'
maká:lin   makáslin 'to open the eyes'   (Kimball 1991: 327)

(23) Suffixation: Huallaga Huanuco Quechua (Quechuan, Central Quechuan I)
Chay-pita paka-ykacha-y+lla+pa   qeshpi-ku-rqa-:.
that-ABL   hide-ITER-ADV   escape-REFL-PST-1
'After that I escaped, hiding here and there'   (Weber 1989: 150)

The second very common strategy is reduplication (both partial and total, and also triplication)[8] which is particularly frequent in African languages.

(24) Partial reduplication: Hausa (Afro-Asiatic, Chadic)
Taa   tat~tàbà   hancìntà
3SG.F.PF RED~touch   nose.her
'She tapped her nose/touched her nose repeatedly'   (Součková 2011: 106)

(25) Total reduplication: Burushaski (Isolate, Asia)
e:gićumane~e:gićumane
e:gićumane~red
sow.PFV-while~RED
'(while) sowing continuously'   (adapted from Munshi 2006: 226)

(26) Triplication: Stau (Sino-Tibetan, Burmo-Qiangic)
a. *ŋæji ɮã*
   1PL   come.1PL
b. *ŋæji ɮə~ɮã*
   1PL   1PL~come.1PL

---

8. Triplication usually expresses many repetitions or a big number of participants involved, as in the example of Stau (Sino-Tibetan, Burmo-Qiangic) in (26).

c. ŋæji ƙə~ƙə~ƙā
   1PL 1PL~1PL~come.1PL
   'We arrived.' (Gates 2017: 19)

Finally, the last very frequent strategy is lexical alternation (sometimes called *stem alternation* or *suppletion* in the literature). In this case, we have two completely different verbs (i.e., different lexical items)[9] that express the same situation but while one verb is singular, the second verb is plural.

(27) Wari' (Chapacuran, Wari')
   a. ***Xin***   *na-in*
      throw.SG   3SG.RP/P-3N
      'He throws it away'   (Everett & Kern 1997: 337)
   b. ***Wixicao'*** *na-in*
      throw.PL   3SG.RP/P-3N
      'He throws them away'   (Everett & Kern 1997: 338)

This strategy can be found in several geographic areas, but it is by far most common in Native North American languages (cf. Durie 1986; Mithun 1988; Fitzgerald 2016: 691-693; among others). There are at least two interesting aspects concerning lexical alternation that deserve mention. First, the verbs alternating for number are not always two, in several native North America languages we find three verbs (e.g., singular *vs.* dual *vs.* plural in Creek and Chickasaw, cf. Fitzgerald 2016: 691-692). Second, there is not a perfect parallelism between nominal number values and verbal number values: for example, in Mojave (Cochimi-Yuman, Yuman) there are two values of nominal number (singular *vs.* plural) and three of verbal number (singular *vs.* paucal *vs.* plural) (cf. Munro 1974: 15, 38).

In addition to these devices, languages adopt several other less common strategies to express pluractional functions. In the next few examples, I exemplify some of these strategies.

(28) Tonal change: Krongo (Kadugli-Krongo, Central-Western Kadugli-Krongo)

BASIC FORM		FREQUENTATIVE FORM	
à-byáanì àlàkà	→	a-byàanì àlàkà	'to spit'
ò-kídò-ònò	→	ò-kìdòonò	'to cut off'
ò-kírò-ònò	→	ò-kìròonò	'to move out'
à-sá-ánà	→	à-sàanà	'to sow, scatter' (Reh 1985: 206)

---

9. This is the reason why I prefer to talk about *lexical alternation* rather than stem alternation, that makes reference to different stems of the same lexeme, or suppletion, that makes reference to an inflectional/morphological alternation of forms within the same paradigm.

(29) Vowel lengthening: Tima (Katla-Tima)

BASIC FORM			PLURACTIONAL	
ŋʌʌl	'smell it'	→	ŋʌl-í	'smell several times'
dááh	'say sth.'	→	dàh-í	'say sth. repeatedly'
múúr	'pick it up'	→	mùr-í	'pick up several times'
lɔ́ɔ́h	'mix it'	→	lɔ̀h-í	'mix several times' (Alamin 2012: 105)

(30) Quasi-auxiliary: Eton (Atlantic-Congo, Volta-Congo)
|à-ŋgá-bɛ   L-**diŋ**-Lgì   L-tìl   H bɔ́ kálàdà|
I-RM.PST-IPFV INF-**HAB**-G INF-write LT PL letter
'He usually wrote letters' (Van de Velde 2008: 235)

A couple of particular facts deserve to be mentioned here. First, interestingly, the marking strategies do not seem to have any kind of specialization. In other words, none of the marking strategy exemplified above recurrently express a particular function. The only tendency we can identify is between lexical alternation and participant plurality.

In addition, several different strategies can co-exist in the same group of languages and also in the same language. If we consider the situation of the Chadic languages of my sample for what concerns marking strategies, the resulting picture is shown in Table 1.

Table 1. Marking strategies of the Chadic languages of my sample.

Languages	Strategies of marking			
	Affixation	Reduplication	Lexical alternation	Others
Hausa (Newman 2000, Jaggar 2001)	==	partial (initial/internal)	==	==
Lele (Frajzyngier 2001)	-wì	==	==	devoicing of initial consonant
Masa (Melis 1999)	NO DEDICATED PLURACTIONAL MARKERS			
Mupun (Frajzyngier 1993)	-a-, -r-, -e, -ep, -wat, -k-	==	yes	==
Wandala (Frajzyngier 2012)	-a-	partial	yes	==

These two facts confirm that, in the languages of the world, PMs are particularly varied also at the formal level.

5. Diachronic sources of pluractional markers

In the languages of my sample, I was able to find only a few data for what concerns the diachronic sources of PMs. Nonetheless, the variety is again remarkable.

The first diachronic path is suggested by Frajzyngier (1997) who identifies demonstratives (in the wide sense of deictic, anaphoric, definite, etc. markers; cf. Frajzyngier 1997: 194) as the source for nominal and verbal number affixes in Chadic languages. This statement is primarily supported by syntactic and phonetic similarities between demonstratives and number affixes. In particular, he proposes several paths of grammaticalization demonstratives underwent to become plural markers. Each of these paths includes an anaphoric stage, and also some other optional stages in which these grammatical elements were cataphoric markers and/or markers of definiteness (cf. (31)).

(31) Chains of grammaticalization of Chadic number markers
  (Frajzyngier 1997: 217)
  i. DEMONSTRATIVE → OBJECT ANAPHOR → PLURAL OBJECT
  ii. DEMONSTRATIVE → OBJECT ANAPHOR → CATAPHORIC MARKER OF DETERMINED OBJECT → PLURAL OBJECT
  iii. DEMONSTRATIVE → OBJECT ANAPHOR → CATAPHORIC MARKER OF DETERMINED OBJECT → MARKER CODING DEFINITENESS OF THE OBJECT → PLURAL OBJECT
  iv. DEMONSTRATIVE → OBJECT ANAPHOR → PLURAL SUBJECT OF THE INTRANSITIVE VERB
  v. DEMONSTRATIVE → OBJECT ANAPHOR → PLURAL SUBJECT OF TRANSITIVE
  vi. DEMONSTRATIVE → OBJECT ANAPHOR → PLURAL SUBJECT OF TRANSITIVE → PLURALITY OF EVENTS

Another possible source for PMs can be verbs of feelings, and, more specifically, verbs meaning 'love/like'. In Eton (Atlantic-Congo, Volta-Congo), the verb *dìŋ* can have two different functions. The first is the independent lexical function as a verb meaning 'love/like' (cf. (32)).

(32) Eton (Atlantic-Congo, Volta-Congo)
  a. *à-Ltɛ L-bùl H L-**dìŋ** H k͡ppɛ̀m*
    I-PRS INF-do_most LT INF-**love** LT [9]cassava.leaves
    'She likes cassava leaves a lot.' (Van de Velde 2008: 340)
  b. *də ù-Ltɛ L-**dìŋ** H ndɔ́gà*
    Q 2SG-PRS INF-**like** LT [10]mango
    'Do you like mangoes?' (Van de Velde 2008: 326)

The second function is grammatical. It can be used as a quasi-auxiliary to express iterative and frequentative readings followed by the infinitive form of a verb giving the lexical value (cf. (33)).

(33) Eton (Atlantic-Congo, Volta-Congo)
    a.   à-ŋgá-bɛ   L-**dìŋ**-Lgì   L-tìl   H   bɔ̀   kálâdà
        I-RM.PST-IPFV   INF-**HAB**-G   INF-write   LT   PL   letter
        'He usually wrote letters.'   (Van de Velde 2008: 235)
    b.   à-mɛ   L-**dìŋ**-gì   L-kɔ́zì
        I-YIMPF   INF-**HAB**-G   INF-cough
        'He coughed often.'   (Van de Velde 2008: 332)

In the languages of my sample, I found other two types of verbs that can be sources for PMs: (i) posture or positional verbs, and (ii) andative verbs.

In Lango (Nilotic, Western Nilotic), the verb *bèdò* 'sit/stay/be' (cf. (34)) becomes an auxiliary expressing pluractional functions, mainly iterativity and frequentativity, when it is followed by another verb which gives the lexical value (cf. (35)).

(34) Lango (Nilotic, Western Nilotic)
     àjanà   ò-**bedò**   ì   kòm   lócɔ
     cat   3SG-**sit**.PFV   on   body   man
     'The cat sat on the man'   (Noonan 1992: 160)

(35) Lango (Nilotic, Western Nilotic)
     à-**bédò**   lwòŋ-ŋò   lócɔɔ
     1SG.SBJ-**stay**.PFV   call-INF   man
     'I kept on calling the man'   (Noonan 1992: 140)

We find a similar situation in Khwe (Khoe-Kwadi, Khoe). We already saw how the suffix *-t(i)* covers pluractional functions in this language (cf. (3) in Section 3.1). Kilian-Hatz (2008) identifies the verb *tīī* 'stay' as the probable source for the Frequentative suffix:

> The origin of this suffix is unclear, but it is noteworthy to add that Khwe has an adverb, *tī* ('often'), which is placed clause initially, and two other adverbs, *-tī-tá* and *-tī-yá* ('often'), which are most likely frozen finite verb forms of the verb *tīī* ('stay').   (Kilian-Hatz 2008: 146)

I found the andative verb 'go' as a source of PMs in at least two different languages. In Rapanui (Austronesian, Malayo-Polynesian) the verb *oho* 'go' can serve as an auxiliary to express pluractional functions.

(36) Rapanui (Austronesian, Malayo-Polynesian)
     e,   koroiti~koroiti   I   kai   I   **oho**   mai   ai.
     EXC   slow~ADV   PST   eat   PST   **go**   TOW   PHO
     'Well they went on eating it and slowly they got used to it.'
                                                                               (Du Feu 1996: 162)

In Ute (Uto-Aztecan, Northern Uto-Aztecan), the suffix -*mi* has frequentative and habitual functions.

(37) Ute (Uto-Aztecan, Northern Uto-Aztecan)
navutigi-mi   súuva-tu-mu-aa-ni   'uni-kya-na,
imitate-HAB other-NOM-PL-OBJ-like do-PL-REL
'he used to imitate what others did'   (Givón 2011: 145)

From a diachronic point of view, Givón (2011) notes that:

> The verbal source of the suffix -*mi*, the verb *miya-* 'walk about', 'go', is sufficiently transparent, given that one may still find it in text as the full form of the habitual aspect, especially when followed by another suffix.   (Givón 2011: 132)

An interesting diachronic source for PMs is given by Japhug (Sino-Tibetan, Burmo-Qiangic). In this language, the prefix *nɯ-* can have three main functions: spontaneous (38a), autobenefactive (38b), and permansive (prolongation of an already begun situation, 38c).

(38) Japhug (Sino-Tibetan, Burmo-Qiangic)
    a. *aʑo ʑo   z-ɲɯ-**nɯ**-ru-a   ɲɯ-nts^{h}i*
        1SG EM TRANSLOC-IPFV-**AUTO**-look-1SG SENS-have.to
        'I have to go to have a look by myself.'   (Jacques 2015: 282)
    b. *ɯʑo kɯ   ɯ-sroʁ   ko-**nɯ**-ri   ɲɯ-ŋu*
        3SG ERG 3SG.POSS-life IFR-**AUTO**-save SENS-be
        'He saved his own life.'   (Jacques 2015: 279)
    c. *tɕʰeme nɯ   ɲɤ-nukʰɤda ri,   mɯ-pjɤ-pʰɤn,   tɕʰeme nɯ*
        girl   DEM IFR-convince LNK NEG-IFR-be.efficient girl   DEM
        *pjɤ-**nɯ**-ɣɤwu   ɕti,*
        EVD.IPFV-**AUTO**-cry be.affirm:FACT
        'She (tried to) comfort the girl, but it was for nothing, the girl was still crying.'   (Jacques 2015: 283)

Jacques (2015) suggests to consider the following diachronic path: autobenefactive > spontaneous > permansive. The semantic evolution has probably followed a pathway composed of four different stages: (i) "Do X for oneself (AUTOBENEFACTIVE)" > (ii) "Do X on one's own" > (iii) "Do X on one's own, disregarding external considtions" > (iv) "Continue to do X, despite (adverse) external factors. (PERMANSIVE)" (Jacques 2015: 284).

Finally, it is interesting to note that in some languages PMs seem to be sources for other kinds of phenomena. In some North America languages, PMs can also be applied to other lexical categories. This is the case, for example, of Cayuga (Iroquoian, Northern Iroquoian) in which a pluractional marker (cf. (39a)) applies to nouns too (cf. (39b-c)):

(39) Cayuga (Iroquoian, Northern Iroquoian) (Mithun 1988: 228-229)
a. ęhsyę:thoʔ → ęhsyęthwahsǫ;ʔ
   'you will plant'   'you will plant a lot of different things'
b. eksá:ʔah → kaeksʔashǫ: ʔǫh
   'child, girl'   'children'
c. hakę́htsih → haekę̨htsíhshǫʔ
   'old man'   'old people'

However, we cannot undoubtedly say that PMs are sources for nominal markers of plurality for these languages mainly because of the ambiguous connotation that the notion of *noun* has in several Native North American languages. In these languages, nouns are often morphological verbs functioning as nouns (cf. Mithun 2000).

We find a similar situation in Chukchi (Chukotko-Kamchatkan, Chukotian) in which the Iterative suffix *-tku* when applied to nouns gives a collective reading (Dunn 1999: 261):

(40) Chukchi (Chukotko-Kamchatkan, Chukotian)
ənqorə ŋan tʔe-ce yiwi-kine-k=ʔm / ŋəra-ca yiwi-kine-k /
then DEICT some-ADV year-REL-LOC=EM four-ADV year-RELT-LOC

emelke ləyen=ʔm cawcəwa-tko-n
probably really=EM reindeer_herder-COLL-3SG.ABS

yənu-lʔ-ə-n itək-ewən
remain-PTCP-EP-3SG.ABS SO-INTS

n-ə-mk-ə-qin ye-ɣnu-lin=ʔm
ADJ-EP-many-3SG PF-remain-3SG=EM

'Then after several years, four years or so, the reindeer folk remaining, quite a few remained'   (Dunn 1999: 156)

6. The grammatical status of pluractional markers in cross-linguistic perspective

In the previous sections, I illustrated the main characteristics that PMs have in the languages of my sample. What clearly emerges from this overview is that pluractionality shows a remarkable variety in cross-linguistic perspective.

In the literature, we find some proposals trying to capture the grammatical nature of these constructions. Giving some examples, on the one hand, both Dressler (1968) and Cusic (1981) describe verbal plurality as pertaining to the domain of actionality/*Aktionsart*. On the other, if we consider in particular the center-right part of the pluractional conceptual space (frequentativity, habituality, and generic imperfectivity), we find several authors describing these functions as belonging to grammatical aspect (cf. Comrie 1976; Bybee, Perkins & Pagliuca 1994; Tatevosov 2002 among others). These two positions reflect the different importance authors gave to some relevant characteristics of PMs. The situation is not straightforward, and this is made even more evident if we look at the difficulties and doubts raised by Corbett (2000). He recognizes some characteristics of PMs as affecting both aspect and number categories at the same time, and asks himself how to treat these markers from a grammatical point of view:

> Given a language which, in terms of number, had only the verbal opposition [...], would we say it had the category of number? Many would say rather that it had aspect: repeated versus non-repeated action is a classic aspectual distinction. Why then should event number be considered here [i.e., in a monograph on number] at all if it may be a type of verbal aspect? First because it is worth noting the parallelism between number for the noun (number of entities) and aspect for the verb (number of events). Second, because the way in which number of this type is marked on the verb may also serve other purposes, which may be harder to distinguish from other types of number, in particular it may mark verbal number of the participant type [...]. And third, because for certain language families there is a tradition of using the term 'plural verb' in such instances and so this usage should be discussed. However, 'event number' may reasonably be taken as a type of verbal aspect. (Corbett 2000: 246–247)

Corbett (2000) does not really answer the question on the grammatical status of PMs, but he acknowledges the problem and decides not to take any particular position.

The problem of the grammatical status of PMs arises from a mis-conceptualization of grammatical categories in cross-linguistic perspective. In other words, it is nearly impossible to classify linguistic phenomena under a unique (often pre-established) category thought to be valid in different languages or to be the speakers' mental representation of grammar.

Let's now briefly consider a bit closer the PMs of three typologically distant and genealogically unrelated languages: Akawaio (Cariban, Venezuelan), Beja (Afro-Asiatic, Cushitic), and Maa (Nilotic, Eastern Nilotic).

In Akawaio, the suffix *-pödï* (and its several allomorphs) expresses pluractional functions. The functions covered are mainly those on the right side of the pluractional conceptual space, in particular, frequentativity and habituality, but also iterativity and generic imperfectivity (cf. Mattiola & Gildea Under review).

(41) Akawaio (Cariban, Venezuelan)
      *möröbang yau tok eji iwang pe wenai tö-**bödï***
      thereafter LOC 3PL be hunger like because go-ITER
      'So, because they are hungry, I keep going to Venezuela several times'
      (RA Personal Narrative 168 <593.426>)

Since *-pödï* covers functions typically described as aspectual and represents a productive and highly grammaticalized device (stable and general semantics, derivational nature, applicable to different types of verbs, etc.), it would appear natural to classify it within the aspectual system of Akawaio. However, this suffix can co-exist with other actual aspectual suffixes, specifically with both imperfective (e.g., the Progressive *-bök*, cf. (42)) and perfective (e.g., Perfect *-zak*, cf. (43)) values. This makes it difficult to consider *-pödï* as aspectual:

(42) Akawaio (Cariban, Venezuelan)
kamoro yebï-zak eji-'pï mörö kaza ta tok ya i-'che bra
3PL.AN come-PF be-PST that like say 3PL ERG 3-DES NEG

t-eji   pök   ning kïrö-rö   eji-'pï mörö mïgï
3.REFL-be occupied_with EM   3SG.AN-EM be-PST AI   HES

sungwa a'chini'ta tau   kaza tok ene-bödï-bök   y-eji-'pï
far_away bushes   within like 3PL see-ITER-PROG 3-be-PST

'Because he did not want the people to say, "those people came here",
he stood far away in the bushes **looking** on'   (EW Kanaimö 133)

(43) Akawaio (Cariban, Venezuelan)
kamoro yak ji tok ewomï-bödï-zak turonnö
3PL.AN into EM 3PL enter-ITER-PF   another
'They had entered into those things'   (EW Kanaimö 161)

As already noted in Section 3.3, Beja displays two verbal derivations expressing pluractional functions, that is, Intensive (internal modification, cf. (44)) and Pluractional (total and partial reduplication, cf. (45)).

(44) Beja (Afro-Asiatic, Cushitic)
 a. *ʔawi=b   jhak-s-an=t   a-**gid**.*
    stone=INDF.M.ACC get_up-CAUS-PFV.1SG=CNJ 1SG-**throw**\PFV
    'I took a stone and threw it'   (BEJ_MV_NARR_05_eritrea_389)
 b. *ti=takat   digiː-ti*
    DEF.F=woman turn_back-CVB.CSL

    hoːsoː geːd-ti=jeːb=ka
    3SG.ABL **throw**\INT-AOR.3SG.F=REL.M=DISTR
    'the woman was throwing stones at it away from her'
                                            (BEJ_MV_NARR_05_eritrea_130)

(45) Beja (Afro-Asiatic, Cushitic)
 a. *naː=t   bi=t-**katiːm**   mhiːn*
    thing=INDF.F   NEG.OPT=3SG.F-**arrive**\OPT place
    '(The donkey stopped) in a place where nothing can arrive,
    (in the cliffs)'   (BEJ_MV_NARR_05_eritrea_183)

b. *i=magʷal*   *hoːg-aː=b=u=it*
    DEF.M=reservoir descend-CVB.MNR=INDF.M.ACC=COP.3SG=CSL
    *ki=i-t-**kat~tam***
    NEG.IPFV=3SG.M-MID-**arrive~PLAC**.PFV
    'since the reservoir was deep, it cannot be reached'
    (BEJ_MV_NARR_05_eritrea_083)

These two derivations cover all the core functions (cf. (44) and (45)), but they also extend to some additional functions, like intensity in (46), and also successive events in (15) in Section 3.3 (Mattiola 2019: 111-125).

(46) Beja (Afro-Asiatic, Cushitic)
     haːj ***gab~gab**-eːti*   *i-niːn*   *eː-d-na*   *eːn*
     COM   **PLAC~be_rich**-CVB.CSL 3SG.M-take\IPFV 3-say\IPFV-PL say\PFV.3PL
     'he becomes over wealthy with it, they say, they said'
     (BEJ_MV_NARR_09_jewel_64)

From a grammatical point of view, Intensive and Pluractional are considered as two independent and productive verbal derivations in Beja (cf. Vanhove 2017).

Finally, in Maa we find an intricate situation. We can recognize at least three different PMs. The first is lexical alternation. This strategy expresses only participant plurality and involves a single pair of verbs: *lo(t)* 'go.SG' and *puo(n)* 'go.PL'.

(47) Maa (Nilotic, Eastern Nilotic)
     *ore peê [L]-í-**lo(t)***   *ɔ-ra*   *ɔl=mʉrráni*
     when   TEMP-2-**go.SG** M.SG.REL.ACC-be M.SG=warrior.ACC
     'when you go as a warrior' (enkiama.002a)

(48) Maa (Nilotic, Eastern Nilotic)
     *n-è-**puo(n)**-í*   *áa₁-ya-ʉ(n)*   *ilɔ́*   *rinká*
     CN1-3-**go.PL**-PL   INF.PL-take-VEN   that.M.SG.ACC   club.ACC
     'They went to bring that club' (arinkoi.041a)

The second strategy is the total reduplication of the verb stem. This kind of reduplication does not seem to be fully productive: half of the occurrences identified and analyzed in Mattiola (2019: 126-142) are lexicalized (without a non-reduplicated counterpart), while the few occurrences still encoding pluractional functions express only core functions.

(49) Maa (Nilotic, Eastern Nilotic)
     *k[H]=è-**ɲurr-i₂~ɲurr***   *kʉlɔ́*
     CN2-3-**cut_crudely-EP~cut_crudely** these.M.ACC
     tuɲaná   *ɛn=kirɔ́rɔ́tɔ́*
     people.NOM F.SG=conversation.ACC
     'these people keep on cutting the conversation'   (camus2.127)

However, a new pluractional marker seems to be emerging in Maa. The andative marker -áa 'AWAY', in addition to its directional functions (real motion or figurative direction away, cf. (50)), in some circumstances can express a plurality of situations (cf. (51)) (cf. Payne 2013).

(50) Maa (Nilotic, Eastern Nilotic)
 n-ɛ-ibuŋ-i   ɛnk-áiná   áa-yiat-aa.
 CN1-3-hold-PASS   F.SG-arm.ACC   INF.PL-stretch-AWAY
 'The hand is held to pull them (=the fingers) to stretch them out'
 (Payne 2013: 269)

(51) Maa (Nilotic, Eastern Nilotic)
 n[HL]-ɛ̀-man-áa   taá   tɛ   ɔl=cháni
 CN1-3-surround-AWAY   FOC.EXCL OBL   M.SG=tree.NOM
 'He [the warrior advising the hero] kept moving (from one end to the other addressing the audience) in the meeting.' (arinkoi.056a)

These three languages display PMs that are hardly classifiable under the same grammatical category. We have an aspect-like suffix in Akawaio, two independent verbal derivations that can be considered the expression of an independent category *pluractionality* in Beja, and three very different strategies in Maa. This situation can be explained only if we take into consideration the hypothesis that grammatical categories are not universally valid entities. One might say that the three languages taken into consideration above are genealogically completely unrelated and, thus, it is normal to have different systems. Even though it is partly true, this fact is further evidence that we are dealing with something that is substantially different. In addition, we do find remarkable differences even within languages that are strictly related. For example, if we look at what happens in Konso, a Cushitic language spoken in Ethiopia and, thus, not only the same language family of Beja (Afro-Asiatic) but also the same branch (Cushitic), we have a sensibly different situation from the one of Beja itself. While in Beja we have two optional strategies, Intensive and Pluractional are derivational in nature, in Konso the gemination/reduplicative patterns expressing verbal number (for both singularity and plurality, singulactional *vs.* pluractional) is mandatory and, from a morphological perspective, it rather represents an inflectional category (cf. Orkaydo & Mous 2017). Further, we do also find cases in which it is almost impossible to treat PMs in terms of a unique category in single languages. Let us again consider the situation of the PMs in Maa. We have three different strategies with different functional and formal characteristics, and different degree of productivity. We have lexical alternation that relates two totally different lexical items connected by their lexical semantics, and, from a grammatical point of view, this makes them more similar to the phenomenon of classificatory verbs found in other languages (like in several

Native North American languages). We have reduplication that is not frequent in texts and that cross-linguistically represents a typical iconic device to express the notion of plurality. But we also have a directional suffix that is probably extending its functional domain towards plurality of situations. These three strategies have different grammatical status *within* the same single language.

So now, the questions to be answered are: how can we classify all these patterns under a single category? How can we consider PMs as elements sharing specific formal and functional properties if, in the end, they do not share much? We can account for this situation only if we consider grammatical categories as language- (like in Beja) and construction-specific (like in Maa). It makes no sense asking to which category PMs belong in cross-linguistic perspective. This is because the different constructions that cross-linguistically fall under the definition of pluractionality I gave in Section 2 are defined through the distributional analysis of constructions within texts of single languages. Pluractionality, as defined in the present paper, must be understood as a comparative concept (Haspelmath 2010), that is, a concept defined only for comparative purposes and that allows to compare constructions that differ at various levels (functional, formal, diachronic) but that share the common semantic trait of encoding a plurality of situations. Even though comparative concepts do not necessarily exist in real languages, they are not senseless because they help us in understanding and explaining (e.g., through semantic maps) recurrent constructional patterns found cross-linguistically.

7. Conclusion

In the present paper, I gave a cross-linguistic overview of the phenomenon known as pluractionality in the languages of the world. Pluractionality is generally defined as morphological verbal devices expressing a plurality of situations. First, I showed how multifunctional PMs can be in typological perspective. They can encode functions directly expressing event plurality (core functions), but also several other additional functions that are semantically connected to their functional core. At the formal level, I illustrated the three most recurrent marking strategies that languages adopt to convey a plurality of situations. Then, I presented the diachronic sources that PMs have in the languages of my sample. The picture that has emerged from this overview reveals that pluractionality is far from being a homogeneous phenomenon. Taking into consideration data both from cross-linguistic and intralinguistic analyses, I demonstrated how we can account for the grammatical status of pluractionality only if we consider grammatical categories and relations as language- and construction-specific entities, not universal. This led us to conclude that cross-linguistic comparison cannot be category-based but must be conducted through comparative concepts.

Abbreviations (cf. Leipzig Glossing Rules)

1	1st person	DISTR	Distributive
2	2nd person	DS	Dative subject
3	3rd person	DU	Dual
I	Agreement prefix of agreement pattern one (Eton)	DUR	Durative
		EM	Emphasis
I	Active for non-past	EP	Epenthetic
II	Active for past	ERG	Ergative
+	Affirmative polarity series	EVD	Evidential
A	Subject of transitive verb	EXC	Exclamation
ABL	Ablative	EXCL	Exclusive
ABS	Absolutive case	F	Feminine
ACC	Accusative	FACT	Factual
ACT	Active	FOC	Focus
ADJ	Adjective	FREQ	Frequentative
ADV	Adverb	FV	Final vowel
AI	Addressee involvement	G	Suffix or infix that occurs in several TAM-forms (Eton)
AN	Animate		
AOR	Aorist	HAB	Habitual
AUTO	Autobenefactive-spontaneous	HES	Hesitation
AWAY	Andative	HH	Hither
BEN	Benefactive	IDO	Internal direct object
CAUS	Causative	IFR	Inferential evidential
CF	Constant feature	IND	Indicative
CL	Coordinating linker	INDF	Indefinite
CN (1/2)	Connective (1/2)	INF	Infinitive
CNJ	Coordinating conjunction	INST	Instrumental object
COLL	Collective	INT	Intensive
COM	Comitative	INTR	Intransitive
COMP	Completive	INTS	Intensifier
COND	Conditional	IPFV	Imperfective
CONS	Consecutive	IRR	Irrealis
COP	Copula	ITER	Iterative
CSL	Cislative	L	Linker (Enumeration)
CVB	Converb	LNK	Linker
CVB.MNR	Manner converb	LOC	Locative case
D	Dative of ditransitive verb	LT	Low tone
DAT	Dative case	M	Masculine
DEF	Definite	MID	Middle
DEF.F/M	Definite Feminine/Masculine (gender)	N	Neuter/Non-eywitness
		NEG	Negative
DEICT	Deictic particle	NOM	Nominative
DES	Desiderative	NR	Non-realis (subject-modality clitic)
DET	Determiner		
DIR	Directional	PASS	Passive

NSG	Non-singular	REPEAT	V repeatedly
OBL	Oblique case	RP/P	Realis past/present
OBJ	Object	SBJ	Subject
OPT	Optative	SENS	Sensory evidential
PF	Perfect	SFOC	Subject focus
PFV	Perfective	SG	Singular
PHO	Phoric	SOF	Softener
PL	Plural	ST	Stative series
PLAC	Pluractional	(SV.)	Subject-verb relation
POSS	Possessive		(downstep not audible)
PR	Plurality of relations	TEMP	Temporal mode
PRO	Pronoun	TESTIM	Testimonial
PROG	Progressive	TOW	Towards subject
PRP	Pronominal prefix	TR	Transitive
PRS	Present	TRANSLOC	Translocative
(RM.)PST	(Remote) Past	V	Gender agreement marker;
PTCP	Participial		gender class (marker is /v/)
RECP	Reciprocal	V	Verb
RED	Reduplication	VEN	Ventive
REFL	Reflexive	VBLZ	Verbalizer
REL	Relator/relative marker	WP	Witnessed past tense
RELT	Relational		

References

Alamin, Suzan. 2012. *The Nominal and Verbal Morphology of Tima: A Niger-Congo Language Spoken in the Nuba Mountains.* Cologne: Rüdiger Köppe.

Bar-el, Leonora. 2008. Verbal number and aspect in Skwx̱wú7mush. *Recherches Linguistiques de Vincennes* 37: 31–54. https://doi.org/10.4000/rlv.1695

Boas, Franz. 1911. Introduction. In *Handbook of North American Languages*, Part 1, Franz Boas (ed.), 1–83. Washington DC: Smithsonian, Institution, Government Printing Office.

Bybee, Joan, Perkins, Revere & Pagliuca, William. 1994. *The Evolution of Grammar. Tense, Aspect, and Modality in the Languages of the World.* Chicago IL: The University of Chicago Press.

Cabredo-Hofherr, Patricia & Laca, Brenda. 2012. Introduction – Event plurality, verbal plurality and distributivity. In *Verbal Plurality and Distributivity*, Patricia Cabredo Hofherr & Brenda Laca (eds), 1–24. Berlin: Mouton de Gruyter. https://doi.org/10.1515/9783110293500.1

Collins, Chris. 1998. *Plurality in ǂHoan.* Cologne: Khoisan-Forum at the Institut für Afrikanistik, University of Cologne.

Comrie, Bernard. 1976. *Aspect.* Cambridge: CUP.

Corbett, Greville. 2000. *Number.* Cambridge: CUP. https://doi.org/10.1017/CBO9781139164344

Cristofaro, Sonia. 2009. Grammatical categories and relations: Universality vs. language-specificity and construction-specificity. *Language and Linguistics Compass* 3(1): 441–479. https://doi.org/10.1111/j.1749-818X.2008.00111.x

Croft, William. 2001. *Radical Construction Grammar. Syntactic Theory in Typological Perspective.* Oxford: OUP. https://doi.org/10.1093/acprof:oso/9780198299554.001.0001

Cusic, David. 1981. Verbal Plurality and Aspect. PhD dissertation, University of Stanford.
Dimmendaal, Gerrit. 1983. *The Turkana Language*. Dordrecht: Foris. https://doi.org/10.1515/9783110869149
Dom, Sebastian, Segerer, Guillaume & Bostoen, Koen. 2015. Antipassive/associative polysemy in Cilubà (Bantu, L31a). *Studies in Language* 39(2): 354–385. https://doi.org/10.1075/sl.39.2.03dom
Dressler, Wolfgang. 1968. *Studien sur verbalen Pluralität: Iterativum, Distributivum, Durativum, Intensivum in der allgemeinen Grammatik, in Lateinischen und Hethitischen*. Vienna: Hermann Böhlaus Nachf.
Dryer, Matthew S. 1997. Are grammatical relations universal? In *Essays in Language Function and Language Type*, Joan Bybee, John Haiman & Sandra A. Thompson (eds), 115–143. Amsterdam: John Benjamins. https://doi.org/10.1075/z.82.09dry
Dryer, Matthew S. & Haspelmath, Martin (eds). 2013. *The World Atlas of Language Structures Online*. Leipzig: Max Planck Institute for Evolutionary Anthropology. <http://wals.info/chapter/110> (5 May 2019).
Du Feu, Veronica. 1996. *Rapanui*. London: Routledge.
Dunn, Michael J. 1999. A Grammar of Chukchi. PhD dissertation, Australian National University.
Durie, Mark. 1986. The grammaticization of number as a verbal category. In *Proceedings of the Twelfth Annual Meeting of the Berkeley Linguistics Society: February 15–17, 1986, Berkeley*, Vassiliki Nikiforidou, Mary VanClay, Mary Niepokuj & Deborah Feder (eds), 355–370. Berkeley CA: BLS.
Everett, Daniel Leonard & Kern, Barbara. 1997. *Wari'*. London: Routledge.
Fitzgerald, Colleen M. 2016. Morphology in the Muskogean languages. *Language and Linguistics Compass* 10: 681–700. https://doi.org/10.1111/lnc3.12227
Foley, William A. 1991. *The Yimas Language of New Guinea*. Stanford CA: Stanford University Press.
Frajzyngier, Zygmunt. 1993. *A Grammar of Mupun*. Berlin: Dietrich Reimer.
Frajzyngier, Zygmunt. 1997. Grammaticalization of number: From demonstratives to nominal and verbal plural. *Linguistic Typology* 1(2): 193–242. https://doi.org/10.1515/lity.1997.1.2.193
Frajzyngier, Zygmunt. 2001. *A Grammar of Lele*. Stanford CA: CSLI.
Frajzyngier, Zygmunt. 2012. *A Grammar of Wandala*. Berlin: Mouton de Gruyter. https://doi.org/10.1515/9783110218411
Gates, Jesse P. 2017. Verbal triplication morphology in Stau (Mazi dialect). *Transactions of the Philological Society* 115(1): 14–26. https://doi.org/10.1111/1467-968X.12083
Georgakopoulos, Thanasis & Polis, Stéphane. 2018. The semantic map model: State of the art and future avenues for linguistic research. *Language and Linguistics Compass* 12: e12270. https://doi.org/10.1111/lnc3.12270
Givón, Tom. 2011. *Ute Reference Grammar* [Culture and Language Use 3]. Amsterdam: John Benjamins. https://doi.org/10.1075/clu.3
Hammarström, Harald, Bank, Sebastian, Forkel, Robert & Haspelmath, Martin. 2018. *Glottolog 3.2*. Jena: Max Planck Institute for the Science of Human History. <http://glottolog.org> (24 September 2018).
Haspelmath, Martin. 2003. The geometry of grammatical meaning: Semantic maps and cross-linguistic comparison. In *The New Psychology of Language*, Vol. 2, Michael Tomasello (ed.), 217–242. Mahwah NJ: Lawrence Erlbaum Associates.

Haspelmath, Martin. 2007. Pre-established categories don't exist: Consequences for language description and typology. *Linguistic Typology* 11(1): 119–132.
https://doi.org/10.1515/LINGTY.2007.011

Haspelmath, Martin. 2010. Comparative concepts and descriptive categories in crosslinguistic studies. *Language* 86(3): 663–687. https://doi.org/10.1353/lan.2010.0021

Jacques, Guillaume. 2004. Phonologie et morphologie du Japhug (rGyalrong). PhD dissertation, Université Paris-Diderot – Paris VII.

Jacques, Guillaume. 2014. Clause linking in Japhug. *Linguistics of the Tibeto-Burman Area* 37(2): 264–328. https://doi.org/10.1075/ltba.37.2.05jac

Jacques, Guillaume. 2015. The spontaneous-autobenefactive prefix in Japhug Rgyalrong. *Linguistics of the Tibeto-Burman Area* 38(2): 271–291. https://doi.org/10.1075/ltba.38.2.08jac

Jaggar, Philip. 2001. *Hausa* [London Oriental and African Language Library 7]. Amsterdam: John Benjamins. https://doi.org/10.1075/loall.7

Jones, Wendell & Jones, Paula. 1991. *Barasano Syntax*. Dallas TX: SIL & University of Texas at Arlington.

Kilian-Hatz, Christa. 2008. *A Grammar of Modern Khwe (Central Khoisan)*. Cologne: Rüdiger Köppe.

Kimball, Geoffrey D. 1991. *Koasati Grammar*. Lincoln NE: University of Nebraska Press.

Lindström, Eva. 2002. Topics in the Grammar of Kuot. A Non-Austronesian Language of New Ireland, Papua New Guinea. PhD dissertation, University of Stockholm.

Mattiola, Simone. 2017. The conceptual space of pluractional constructions. *Lingue e Linguaggio* 16(1): 119–146.

Mattiola, Simone. 2019. *Typology of Pluractional Constructions in the Languages of the World* [Typological Studies in Language 125]. Amsterdam: John Benjamins.
https://doi.org/10.1075/tsl.125

Mattiola, Simone & Gildea, Spike. Under review. The pluractional marker *-pödï* of Akawaio (Cariban) and beyond.

Melis, Antonino. 1999. Description du Masa (Tchad): Phonologie, sintaxe et dictionnaire encyclopédique. PhD dissertation, University of Tours.

Mithun, Marianne. 1988. Lexical category and the evolution of number marking. In *Theoretical Morphology: Approaches in Modern Linguistics*, Michael Hammond & Michael Noonan (eds), 211–234. San Diego CA: Academic Press.

Mithun, Marianne. 2000. Noun and verb in Iroquoian languages: Multicategorization from multiple criteria. In *Approaches to the typology of word classes*, Petra M. Vogel & Bernard Comrie (eds), 397–420. Berlin: Mouton de Gruyter. https://doi.org/10.1515/9783110806120.397

Munro, Pamela. 1974. Topics in Mojave Syntax. PhD dissertation, University of California San Diego.

Munshi, Sadaf. 2006. Jammu and Kashmir Burushaski. Language, Language Contact, and Change. PhD dissertation, University of Texas at Austin.

Newman, Paul. 1980. *The Classification of Chadic within Afroasiatic*. Leiden: Universitaire Pers.

Newman, Paul. 1990. *Nominal and Verbal Plurality in Chadic*. Berlin: Mouton de Gruyter.
https://doi.org/10.1515/9783110874211

Newman, Paul. 2000. *The Hausa Language. An Encyclopedic Reference Grammar*. New Haven CT: Yale University Press.

Noonan, Michael. 1992. *A Grammar of Lango*. Berlin: Mouton de Gruyter.
https://doi.org/10.1515/9783110850512

Orkaydo, Ongaye Oda. 2013. The category of number in Konso. In *Sounds and Words through the Ages: Afroasiatic Studies from Turin*, Alessandro Mengozzi & Mauro Tosco (eds), 253–266. Alessandria: Edizioni dell'Orso.

Orkaydo, Ongaye Oda & Mous, Maarten. 2017. The semantics of pluractionals and punctuals in Konso (Cushitic, Ethiopia). *Journal of African Languages and Linguistics* 38(2): 223–263. https://doi.org/10.1515/jall-2017-0009

Payne, Doris L. 2013. The challenge of Maa 'Away'. In *Functional-Historical Approaches to Explanation: In Honor of Scott DeLancey* [Typological Studies in Language 103], Tim Thornes, Erik Andvik, Gwendolyn Hyslop & Joana Jansen (eds), 260–282. Amsterdam: John Benjamins. https://doi.org/10.1075/tsl.103.13pay

Reh, Mechthild. 1985. *Die Krongo-Sprache (Nìinò Mó-Dì)*. Berlin: Dietrich Reimer.

Rosen, Joan. 1977. The functions of reduplication in Indonesian. In *Miscellaneous Studies in Indonesian and Languages of Indonesia, Part IV*, Ignatius Suharno (ed.). *NUSA* 5: 1–9.

Sambou, Pierre. 2014. Relations entre les rôles syntaxiques et les rôles sémantiques dans les langues jóola. PhD dissertation, Université Cheikh Anta Diop de Dakar.

Smeets, Ineke. 2008. *A Grammar of Mapuche*. Berlin: Mouton de Gruyter. https://doi.org/10.1515/9783110211795

Součková, Kateřina. 2011. Pluractionality in Hausa. PhD dissertation, Leiden University.

Steeman, Sander. 2012. A Grammar of Sandawe. A Khoisan Language of Tanzania. PhD dissertation, Leiden University.

Tatevosov, Sergej. 2002. The parameter of actionality. *Linguistic Typology* 6(3): 317–401.

Van de Velde, Mark. 2008. *A Grammar of Eton*. Berlin: Mouton de Gruyter. https://doi.org/10.1515/9783110207859

Vanhove, Martine. 2017. *Le Bedja*. Leuven: Peeters.

Veselinova, Ljuba N. 2013. Verbal number and suppletion. In *The World Atlas of Language Structures Online*, Matthew S. Dryer & Martin Haspelmath (eds). Leipzig: Max Planck Institute for Evolutionary Anthropology. <http://wals.info/chapter/80> (4 May 2019).

Weber, David J. 1989. *A Grammar Huallaga (Huánuco) Quechua*. Berkeley CA: University of California Press.

Wood, Esther. 2007. The Semantic Typology of Pluractionality. PhD dissertation, University of California Berkeley.

Woollams, Geoff. 1996. *A Grammar of Karo Batak, Sumatra*. Canberra: Pacific Linguistics, Research School of Pacific and Asian Studies, Australian National University.

Appendix. Language sample[10]

Family	Languages
Abkhaz-Adyge	Abkhaz (Abkhazian)
Afro-Asiatic	Tamasheq, Hausa, Lele, Masa (Masana), Mupun (Mwaghavul), Pero, Wandala, Beja, Harar Oromo (Eastern Oromo), Iraqw, Amharic, Egyptian Arabic, Modern Hebrew, Maltese
Ainu	(Hokkaido) Ainu
Algic	Yurok, Maliseet-Passamaquoddy (Malecite-Passamaquoddy), Plains Cree
Angan	Kapau (Hamtai)
Araucanian	Mapuche/Mapudungun
Arawakan	Warekena (Baniva de Maroa), Apurinã
Arawan	Jarawara (Madi)
Athabaskan-Eyak-Tlingit	Tlingit, Hupa, Navajo/Navaho, Sarcee (Sarsi), Slave (North Slavey)
Atlantic-Congo	Bijogo (Kangaki-Kagbaaga Kajoko Bidyogo), Jóola Karon (Karon), Wolof, Dadjriwalé (Godié), Eton (Eton-Mengisa), Ewe, Ha, Igbo, Kisikongo (South-Central Kikongo), Koromfe (Koromfé), Lunda, Makonde, Mambay (Mambai), Mono, Sango, Supyire (Supyire Senoufo), Swahili, Yoruba
Austro-Asiatic	Semelai, Khasi, Cambodian/Khmer (Central Khmer), Khmu, Mundari, Vietnamese
Austronesian	Paiwan, Boumaa Fijian (Fijian), Chamorro, Dehu/Drehu, Kiribatese (Gilbertese), Indonesian, Karo Batak (Batak Karo), Kilivila/Kiriwina, Maori, Mokilese, Paamese (Paama), Rapanui/Rapa Nui, Sakalava (Antankarana Malagasy), Samoan, Taba (East Makian), Tagalog, Tukang Besi (Tukang Besi North)
Aymaran	Aymara (Central Aymara)
Barbacoan	Awa Pit (Awa-Cuaiquer)
Border	Imonda
Bunaban	Bunuba (Bunaba), Gooniyandi
Caddoan	Caddo, Wichita
Cariban	Carib (Galibi Carib), Hixkaryana, Macushi, Panare
Central Sudanic	Ngiti, Mbay
Chapacuran	Wari'
Chibchan	Bribri, Ika (Arhuaco)
Chonan	Selknam (Selk'nam)

(*Continued*)

---

10. The classification follows the one proposed by Hammarström et al. (2018), while the names of the languages follow the terms used in the bibliographic references.

Appendix. Language sample (*Continued*)

Family	Languages
Chukotko-Kamchatkan	Chukchi
Cochimi-Yuman	Maricopa, Mojave (Mohave)
Coosan	Coos (Hanis)
Dagan	Daga
Dogon	Jamsay (Jamsay Dogon)
Dravidian	Brahui, Kannada
Eskimo-Aleut	Central Alaskan Yupik, West Greenlandic (Kalaallisut)
East Bird's Head	Meyah
Furan	Fur
Gumuz	Gumuz, Northern/Southern
Gunwinyguan	Nunggubuyu (Wubuy)
Haida	Haida, Northern/Southern
Heibanic	Koalib (Koalib-Rere)
Hmong-Mien	Hmong Njua
Huitotoan	Huitoto (Minica Huitoto)
Indo-European	Modern Eastern Armenian, Latvian, Russian, Serbian(-Croatian-Bosnian), Irish, German, English, Modern Greek, Bengali, Hindi, Pashto (Northern Pashto), Persian (Western Farsi), French, Spanish
Iroquoian	Oneida, Seneca
Iwaidjan Proper	Maung (Mawng)
Japonic	Japanese
Kartvelian	Georgian
Kadugli-Krongo	Krongo
Katla-Tima	Tima
Kawesqar	Qawasqar/Kawésqar
Keresan	Acoma (Western Keres)
Khoe-Kwadi	Khwe (Kxoe)
Kiowa-Tanoan	Kiowa
Koreanic	Korean
Kxa	ǂHoan (Amkoe)
Lower Sepik-Ramu	Yimas
Maban	Masalit
Mande	Beng, Jalonke (Yalunka)
Mangarrayi-Maran	Mangarayi (Mangarrayi), Mara (Marra)

Appendix. Language sample (*Continued*)

Family	Languages
Matacoan	Wichí (Wichí Lhmatés Nocten)
Mayan	Jacaltec (Popti')
Miwok-Costanoan	Lake Miwok
Mixe-Zoque	San Miguel Chimalapa Zoque (Chimalapa Zoque)
Mongolic	Mongolian (Halh Mongolian)
Muskogean	Creek, Koasati, Chickasaw
Nakh-Daghestanian	Hunzib, Icari Dargwa (Southwestern Dargwa), Lezgian, Chechen, Ingush
Nilotic	Turkana, Lango
Nuclear Macro-Je	Canela-Krahó
Nuclear Torricelli	Bukiyip
Nuclear Trans New Guinea	Asmat (Central Asmat), Western Dani, Kewa (East/West)/Kewapi, Suena, Amele, Kobon, Usan, Una
Otomanguean	Chalcatongo Mixtec (San Miguel El Grande Mixtec), Otomí (Mezquital Otomi)
Pama-Nyungan	Pitjantjatjara, Arabana/Wangkangurru (Arabana/Wangganguru), Kugu Nganhcara (Kuku-Uwanh), Ngiyamba (Ngiyambaa), Martuthunira, Djabugay (Dyaabugay), Yidiɲ (Yidiñ), Djapu/Dhuwal
Pano-Tacanan	Shipibo-Konibo (Shipibo-Conibo), Araona
Peba-Yagua	Yagua
Pomoan	Eastern Pomo
Quechuan	Huallaga Huánuco Quechua
Sahaptian	Nez Perce
Saharan	Beria, Kanuri (Central Kanuri)
Salishan	Bella Coola, Skwxwú7mesh (Squamish), Nxaʔamxcin/Moses-Columbian (Columbia-Wenatchi)
Sentanic	Sentani
Sepik	Alamblak
Sino-Tibetan	Ladakhi (Leh-Kenhat), Garo, Burmese, Japhug, Stau, Lepcha, Eastern Kayah Li (Eastern Kayah), Bawm (Bawm Chin), Meithei (Manipuri), Cantonese (Yue Chinese), Mandarin Chinese
Siouan	Lakhota (Lakota)
Songhay	Koyra Chiini (Koyra Chiini Songhay)
South Omotic	Dime

(*Continued*)

Appendix. Language sample (*Continued*)

Family	Languages
Surmic	Murle
Tai-Kadai	Thai
Ta-Ne-Omotic	Wolaytta
Tangkic	Kayardild
Tsimshian	Nisgha/Nass Tsimshian (Nisga'a), Coast Tsimshian (Southern-Coastal Tsimshian)
Tucanoan	Barasano (Barasana-Eduria)
Tungusic	Evenki
Tupian	Kokama-Kokamilla (Cocama-Cocamilla), Guaraní (Paraguayan Guaraní)
Turkic	Turkish
Uralic	Hungarian, Finnish, Tundra Nenets
Uto-Aztecan	Cahuilla, Comanche, Hopi, Ute (Ute-Southern Paiute), Huichol, Northern Tepehuan, Sonora Yaqui (Yaqui)
Wakashan	Southern Wakashan/Nootkan (Nuu-chah-nulth)
Western Daly	Maranungku (Maranunggu)
Worrorran	Ungarinjin (Ngarinyin)
Yangmanic	Wardaman
Yanomamic	Sanuma (Sanumá)
Yeniseian	Ket
Yukaghir	Kolyma Yukaghir (Southern Yukaghir)
Isolate	Kunama, Sandawe, Burushaski, Nivkh, Tiwi, Basque, Coahuilteco, Euchee (Yuchi), Karok, Klamath (Klamath-Modoc), Kutenai, Tunica, Zuni, Kuot, Lavukaleve, Maybrat (Maybrat-Karon), Cayuvava (Cayubaba), Pirahã, Trumai, Warao

CHAPTER 9

Parts of speech, comparative concepts and Indo-European linguistics

Luca Alfieri
University of Studies Guglielmo Marconi

The paper adopts and further elaborates on the distinction between comparative concepts (CC) and descriptive categories (DC) by proposing a partly new definition of the parts of speech (PoS), and uses that definition to provide a new analysis of PoS in Latin and RV Sanskrit. More, specifically, the paper shows that in Latin three major classes of morphemes are found (nouns, adjectives and verbs), whereas in the RV only two major classes are found (verbal roots and nouns) and the typical "adjective" is a derived stem built on a verbal root meaning a quality (i.e., roughly a nominalization). The data described are then used to contribute to the CC debate in the field of PoS, by showing its relation with historical Indo-European linguistics, by critically analysing traditional labels such as noun, adjective, verb, root, stem and lexeme, and by questioning the alleged incommensurability between CCs and DCs.

1. Introduction

It is well known – at least for a large part of the scholars interested in typology – that comparative concepts (CC) and descriptive categories (DC) are two structurally different types of classes from a logical and methodological point of view. Still, in the most radical formulations, the logical difference between the two types of categories was understood as if they represented two totally unrelated and almost incommunicable sets of classes (see the Introduction to this volume).[1] Three consequences derive from such a radical dichotomy between DCs and CCs: i) there is no principled way to pass from CCs to DCs in single languages; ii) CCs may serve as a tool for comparing languages, but they cannot be used to describe single language grammar; iii) two sets of unrelated technical terms will be developed, one for either set of classes.

---

1. See Lazard (1992, 1997, 2001a: 365, 2001b: 141), Dryer (1997, 2016), Haspelmath (2007, 2010, 2012), Croft (2000, 2001, 2005, 2016), Croft & van Lier (2013).

Points i)-iii) have already been questioned in *Linguistic Typology* 2016, where many scholars pointed out that "logically independent" does not necessarily mean "unrelated" (see Introduction). However, none of the papers in LT addressed parts of speech (PoS) research specifically. The present work aims to fill the gap. It adopts and further elaborates on the distinction between CCs and DCs by proposing a partly new comparative definition of PoS, and employs that definition to provide a new analysis of the PoS in two ancient Indo-European (IE) languages, Latin and the Sanskrit language of the Ṛg-Veda Saṃhitā (RV) – often termed as "Early Vedic" (Dahl 2010: 2) – the oldest literary monument of the Indo-Aryan family.

The data described in the paper will be used to make a possibly novel contribution to both (a) the study of IE linguistics and (b) the CC debate. As for the first point, the paper will show that: (a.i) in Latin 3 major classes of lexical morphemes are found (nouns, adjectives and verbs), while in the RV only 2 major classes are found (verbal roots and nouns) and the typical "adjective" is a derived stem built on a verbal root meaning a quality (roughly a nominalization or a participial-like construction);[2] (a.ii) the difference between the PoS system in Latin and in RV Sanskrit is the result of a previously neglected (or not fully understood) typological change, the change from a PoS system with only two major classes of simple lexical units, verbal roots and nouns, to a PoS system with three major classes of simple lexical units, nouns, verbs and adjectives: schematically [N (AV)] → [N, A, V];[3] (a.iii) that the minimum verbal unit of the Sanskrit language, the root (Skt. $d^h\bar{a}tu$-), is a unit of language analysis that is radically different from the Latin simple verb stem from a functional and categorical point of view.[4] As for the

---

2. Simple lexical units (or *items*, as American Structuralists called them) can also be termed as *lexical morph(eme)s, lexemes* or *lexical roots*. Each term has its own problems. See Mugdan (1986, 2015), Blevins (2016: 19ff.) and Haspelmath (forth.) on the term *morph(eme)*; Aronoff (1994: 16ff.), Touratier (2009) and Mugdan (2015: 253ff.) on the term *lexeme*; Alfieri (2016) and below fn. 4 and Section 7.2 on the term *root*. In the following, the term *root* is avoided, while *lexical morph(eme)* and *lexeme* are used as synonyms, even if *lexeme* means 'simple lexical unit' only in some authors (e.g., Martinet 1980: 16), while it refers to the dictionary word, which can be simple or derived, in others (e.g., Lyons 1977: 19).

3. On the schemas [N, A, V] and [N (AV)], see Beck (2002: 6ff.) and below Sections 5–6.

4. As for claims a.i)-a.iii), see also Alfieri (2009, 2013, 2016, 2018, 2020); as for claim a.i)-a.ii), see also Bozzone (2016), though she projected the lexical structure [N (AV)] to Pre-Proto-IE, rather than viewing it a "synchronic" stage of RV Sanskrit. Moreover, note that the term *root* has both a synchronic and a diachronic meaning. The antecedent of a set of genetically related forms is a diachronic root (i.e., a unit of the linguist): PIE *b^her-oh_2 'to bring' > Lat. *fer-o*, Gk. φέρ-ω, Skt. *b^hár-ā-mi*, but the simple lexical morpheme used as input for productive word-formation rules is a synchronic root (i.e., a unit of the speaker): Skt. *tap-* → *tápyate* 'he burns', *tápas* 'heat'. In the following, the term *root* is used only in its synchronic meaning unless

second point, the paper will show that none of the consequences i)-iii) implicit in the idea of a radical dichotomy between CCs and DCs is fully acceptable. Specifically, it will show that: (b.i) CCs are not only a tool for comparing languages, but also a tool for clarifying some aspects of the synchronic grammar of single languages (in this case: Latin and Sanskrit), as well as the diachrony of the IE family; (b.ii) the CCs of the PoS can be used to explain the traditional terms that refer to PoS, rather than to produce a new set of terms that have no relation with the canonical labels of *noun, verb, adjective* and *root*; (b.iii) CCs and DCs can be more profitably seen as the two poles of a continuum, rather than as two totally unrelated sets of classes.

2. The comparative concept debate in the field of the PoS

As shown in the Introduction, the participants in the CC debate shared the idea that typology is the study of the general theory of LANGUAGE (that is, "general linguistics") and that the categories needed to describe the functioning of LANGUAGE – or to compare languages, which is the same – are structurally different from the categories needed to describe the individual languages. The debate, therefore, revolved around how the categories needed to describe the functioning of LANGUAGE should be designed, how they differ from the categories needed to describe single languages and what kind of inconsistencies arise when the two types of categories are confused and a descriptive-like category is used to solve a general-typological problem.

Apart from the idea that CCs are basically function-based concepts, while DCs are primarily form-based categories, all the participants in the debate agreed that CCs can be of different types and a full list of all types of CCs employable in cross-linguistic research is not yet available. However, many scholars agreed that different CCs point to different levels of generality in the continuum that goes from LANGUAGE to single languages, and CCs can be divided into at least three types in terms of their level of generality (Croft 2016), namely "pure" CCs and "hybrid" CCs, which are further divided into "constructions" and "strategies" (or "portable" CC, in Beck's terms, 2016).[5]

---

otherwise specified (clearly, in the sense of "old-time synchrony" defined by Janda & Joseph 2003: 21).

5. The list above was developed by Croft (2016) with the aim of being a consensus view, but it does not cover exactly the type of CCs described by Dahl (2016) and Lander & Arkadiev (2016). On the idea of a continuum between LANGUAGE and single languages, see Gil (2016).

Pure CCs are the most general type of CCs. They do not represent linguistic categories in the strict sense; rather, they are the zones of universal-cognitive space arbitrarily designed by the researcher to describe some kind of cross-linguistic variation (thus, they are not "true" or "false", nor do they "exist" outside the research for which they are designed, see Haspelmath 2007, 2010). Pure CCs are typically (though not only) designed on conceptual maps – that is, maps of universal-cognitive space – which can be purely semantic or "hybrid", if they include a discourse-pragmatic (or, more generically, syntactic) component.[6] CCs are universal in the sense of Coseriu's "universals of the theory" (2001), since all languages can be classified on how they code the zones of universal cognitive space defined on a map. Pure CCs, in other words, are found in all languages with the same form, because strictly speaking they are formless – that is, they are purely functional concepts that exclude any reference to linguistic forms in their definition. Paramount pure CCs are the notions of BASIC WORD ORDER, ALIGNMENT or the definition of the ADJECTIVE that is common in word-order typology (that is, a property concept with no reference to any formal feature). These notions do not refer to the grammar of any individual language in their completeness, but can be applied to all languages: a language can be SVO or SOV, it can be ergative or accusative, it can code property concepts in one way or in another, but no single language grammar needs the super-ordinate notions of "alignment", "basic word order" or "property concept".

Hybrid CCs aim at a lower level of generality than pure CCs and embrace some reference to linguistic form in their definition. Constructions are form-meaning pairings: any form-meaning pair used to code a specific function or a specific zone of cognitive space defined on a conceptual map is a construction. Both pure CCs and constructions are universal, though in a different sense. Pure CCs are found in all languages with the same form, since they are not linguistic categories in the strict sense. Constructions are already linguistic categories, but they are underspecified categories: they are found in all languages, since each language

---

6. On semantic maps, see Haspelmath (2014) and *Linguistic Discovery* 8.1 (2010). Discourse-based pragmatic categories (or functions) can be seen as interpersonal or communicative functions (Rijkhoff 2016), or at least as syntactic categories, if syntax is considered a universal language-external layer, as in Croft (1991: 61). The term *hybrid* is common, though it is ambiguous with reference to conceptual maps: purely conceptual maps are based only on extra-linguistic factors, while hybrid maps already include a linguistic component. However, discourse-pragmatic notions are extra-linguistic just as semantic-conceptual notions, and the same holds true for syntactic notions, if syntax is meant roughly as "discourse". The map, therefore, is really hybrid only if it has some reference to linguistic forms – that is, if it is semantic-syntactic and syntax is meant as grammatical (thus also formal) processing.

codes the space on conceptual maps in one way or another, but the specific way whereby each language codes the zone of cognitive space arbitrarily identified in the research is language-particular, either for markers that define the construction, for the overall space on the conceptual map occupied by it (that is, its function), or for the level of language structure at which the construction is fixed (e.g., the simple stem, the derived stem, the phrase, the clause, etc.). Paramount constructions are the definition of the ADJECTIVE as a quality modifier proposed by Alfieri (2014a), or the QUALITY PREDICATE studied by Wetzer (1996) and Stassen (1997). While pure CCs are found in all languages with the same form, constructions are found in all languages but have a different form in each language: all languages show a quality modifier construction or an adjectival predicate, but the most typical quality modifier is a simple stem in Latin, while it is a relative clause in Garo, and the most typical quality predicate is noun-like in Latin, but verb-like in Lao.

Finally, strategies (or portable CCs) are the most specific type of CCs. They are usually induced via generalization (that is, abstracted) from a specific category of a single language or group of languages. They embrace some reference to a specific linguistic form in their definition; thus they cannot be applied to all languages but are confined to the languages that display some formal and functional similarity to the language from which the portable CC in question was first abstracted. Paramount portable CCs are CASE or MIDDLE, that is to say categories that can be used to compare the languages in which something similar to the Latin case or the Greek middle is found, but cannot be used to compare languages in which nothing similar to such categories exists (e.g., not all languages display case inflection, perfect tense or middle voice), and also in the languages in which such categories are found, they are not defined through exactly the same function (e.g., the Greek genitive also codes the agent if joined with *hypó*, while the same function is coded by the ablative with *a* or *ab* in Latin, etc.).[7]

Each type of CC is legitimate and can lead to interesting generalizations, if used consistently. Still, not all research questions can be addressed with each type of CC with equal validity; rather some very general typological problems seem to be structurally insoluble if portable CCs or, more generally, descriptive-like CCs are employed. The PoS may easily represent a case of this type, since all languages divide the minimum lexical units into classes, although the classes defined differ,

---

7. Clearly, the notions of MIDDLE and CASE can be defined in purely functional terms, transforming a portable CC into a construction or a pure CC: if we say that in English the ABLATIVE is coded through the preposition *from* (*from the house*), as many Generativists do, we are implicitly defining CASE as a purely functional CC. However, this definition can easily be misleading: if it is accepted, several CASE constructions can be found in Greek, some of which are coded by case endings (e.g., the GENITIVE), others by prepositional phrases (e.g., the ABLATIVE).

sometimes substantially, from one language to another.[8] In fact, if a DC or a portable CC is employed to compare the PoS in two languages – no matter how similar or genetically related – the well-known paradox of the so-called *controversial category assignment* cannot be avoided (that is, the case in which on the basis of the same empirical data, the same language is claimed to show or to lack a given PoS by different researchers).[9] In the following pages this problem will be discussed, reviewing the former analysis of the PoS in Latin and Sanskrit.

3. The PoS in Latin and in Sanskrit: State of the art

The PoS system in Latin is almost uncontroversial, at least in its most superficial features. In Latin three major word classes are found: nouns, adjectives and verbs.[10] These classes are defined through well-known inflectional features: case, number and gender for the noun (*virtus*, Example 1); person, tense, mood and diathesis for the verb (*habetur*, Example 1); agreement and comparison for the adjective (*clara* and *aeterna*, Example 1):

(1)   *virtus*   *clara*
      virtue(F).NOM.SG   splendid.F.NOM.SG

      aeterna=que   *habe-tur*
      lasting.F.NOM.SG=and   have-PRS.3SG.PSS

      'mental excellence is a splendid and lasting possession'   (Sall., *Cat.* 1.4)

---

8. This is, more or less, the position claimed by Dryer (1997: 116ff.), Croft (2000, 2001: 29ff., 63ff., 2005), Croft & van Lier (2012), Haspelmath (2012) and Cristofaro (2009).

9. This problem has a long history in PoS research. See the debate on the PoS in Salish (Demirdache & Matthewson 1995; Croft 2001: 76ff.; Beck 2002, 2013), Mundari (*Linguistic Typology* 9.3, 2005), Iroquoian (Sasse 1993a vs. Mithun 2000), Tagalog (*Theoretical Linguistics* 35(1), 2009), Chamorro (*Theoretical Linguistics* 38(1–2), 2012), only to quote the most famous cases (see Stassen 1997: 31ff., Haspelmath 2007, Shachter & Shopen 2007: 18ff. and Cristofaro 2009 for further examples). A similar problem affects Dixon's adjectival theory as a whole: on the basis of similar evidence, Dixon (1982 [1977[1]]) claimed that most languages lack adjectives and merge quality concepts with nouns or verbs, but Dixon (2004) also said that the adjective is a universal class that is always distinguished from nouns and verbs.

10. The categorization of stems is more specific than the categorization of the word-forms built on those stems, but it is not structurally different: the word-form *amā-mus* 'we love' and the stem *amā-* 'to love' are defined through the same features, though they show different values in each feature: no specified value for *amā-* vs. 1pl.pres.act. for *amāmus* (Ramat 1999, 2014). Therefore, in the following the labels "stem classes" and "word classes" are used as synonyms.

The adjective might seem to be a sub-class of the noun rather than an independent PoS, and in fact it was conceived as such up to the Speculative Grammar in the Middle Ages.[11] However, this view is misleading. In Latin adjectives and nouns show almost the same endings from a formal point of view (although adjectival stems in *-u-* and diphthong are excluded), they do not have a rigidly fixed word order in the phrase, and adjectives can be used as nouns without any overt marking, only by being settled in the appropriate syntactic slot: e.g., *antiqui dixerunt* 'the elders said'.[12] However, comparison and agreement clearly divide nouns and adjectives in Latin. Bar some exceptions (see below), comparison is excluded with nouns and, if used as modifiers or as predicates, adjectives agree, but nouns cannot: Lat. *malae puellae veniunt* 'evil(f.pl.) girls(f.pl.) come' vs. *puellae, donum diaboli, veniunt* 'girls (f.pl.), devil's gift (nt.sg.), come', but not *puellae **donae diaboli*. Therefore, adjectives are noun-like in Latin, but they differ from nouns, since only nouns are already marked for gender in the lexicon (Lat. *angui-* 'snake(M)', *virtus* 'virtue(F)'), and so cannot be used as modifiers if not overtly trans-categorized, while adjectives are gender-neutral in the lexicon (*clara-* 'splendid', *nigru-* 'black'), but have to agree, so can be used both as referents and as modifiers without being overtly trans-categorized.[13]

However, quite a few problems arise if the traditional notion of PoS is looked at more closely.[14] From a technical point of view, a PoS is an unweighted bundle of features, that is to say a bundle composed of a different number of features in which the relative value (the weight) of each feature is not fixed. Therefore, even if semantics is left aside, each PoS is defined by different features: in Latin, the adjective is defined by agreement and comparison, but also by the presence of quite a few adjectival-forming affixes (e.g., *-oso-*, which converts nouns into adjectives: *negotium* 'business' → *negotiosus* 'active') and adjectival-selecting affixes (e.g., *-tat-*,

---

11. The idea that Latin has three PoS can be traced to the Middle Ages (rather than to the 18th century, as said by Rijkhoff & van Lier 2013: 1 fn. 1), but is not shared by Latin grammarians (see Alfieri 2014b).

12. This construction is often defined 'substantivized adjective' in classical grammars and 'syntactic conversion' or 'zero marked trans-categorization' in typological works (Rijkhoff & van Lier 2013: 21ff.).

13. In Aronoff's terms, the endings of the noun are *morphomic* (1994: 22, 45), since they depend on a formal feature that is independent of both syntax and semantics, while the endings of the adjective are not *morphomic* at all, since they depend on a semantic-syntactic feature (i.e., agreement). See also Corbett (2006: 126ff.) on the topic.

14. See Robins (1964: 225ff.), Crystal (1967: 24), Matthews (1967: 155), Lyons (1979: 49ff.) and Gross (1979).

which converts adjectives into nouns: *gravis* 'heavy' → *gravitas* 'seriousness').[15] However, the various features, or more precisely, the various construction that define the adjective do not describe exactly the same group of items: agreement defines adjectives, but not-agreeing adjectives (that is, adjectives that do not mark agreement overtly) are found (*sapiens* 'wise', *audax* 'bold'), and also agreeing nouns, though rare, are possible (*lupus* 'wolf' → *lupa* 'she wolf' and *magister* 'teacher' → *magistra* in *historia [...] magistra vitae* 'history is life's teacher', Cic., *De or.* II.36). In the same vein, comparison defines adjectives, but not-comparable adjectives are found (*sinister* 'left', *dexter* 'right'), just as nouns or pronouns that in specific circumstances can be compared (*amicissimus* 'very friend' in Plaut. *Most.* 340, or *ipsissimus* 'he in very person' from the pronoun *ipse* 'he in person' in Plaut. *Trin.* 988). In sum, the group of items defined by agreement do not coincide with the group of items defined by comparison and neither group coincides with the group of items defined by adjectival-selecting or adjectival-producing affixes. Nonetheless, if the various features that usually define the adjective are gathered together to form a bundle, the bundle can be used to delimit a class of items that is descriptively useful for illustrating the functioning of Latin grammar (and especially inflection), although the margins of the class are fuzzy on cases and one does not exactly know what to do when the various features that compose the bundle are in contrast.

3.1 The former (Western) classifications of Sanskrit

When Sanskrit entered the horizon of western scholars in the beginning of the 19th century, by and large it was described using the traditional DCs elaborated by Latin grammarians, partly because the similarity between the two languages seemed to allow such an operation with relatively minor problems.[16]

At present, it is broadly agreed that, bar a few marginal facts, the PoS systems in Latin and Sanskrit are almost identical, the two languages being related genetically. In both cases, three major word classes are found and these classes are defined through grossly the same inflectional features: case, number and gender

---

15. The constraints that define each suffix can change diachronically: *-no-* attaches to verbal roots in PIE (Lat. *plē-nus* 'full' from PIE *$pelh_1$-* 'to fill'), but it attaches only to nouns in Latin (*pater-nus* 'paternal' from *pater* 'father').

16. More precisely, the native tradition of Indian grammar influenced the earliest Western grammars of Sanskrit, especially those published between Roth (1660–68) and Bopp (1827). However, during the 19th century, in German universities a Western standard of Sanskrit grammar was developed using Latin DCs and this standard is at the basis of any modern grammar of Sanskrit (Law 1993). Clearly, influxes of Sanskrit indigenous grammar are not excluded in the Western standard (especially regarding the notions of root and word-formation, see Alfieri 2013b, 2014c), but the bulk of the standard is clearly rooted in the Latin-based tradition.

for the noun; person, tense, aspect and diathesis for the verb; agreement and comparison for the adjective. Also in this case, adjectives may resemble a sub-class of nouns, since adjectives show almost the same endings as nouns (if minor differences are excluded),[17] have a free position in the phrase and can be used as nouns only by being settled in the appropriate syntactic slot (Example 2):

(2) āmā́su   cid   da-dʰi-ṣe   pak-vá-m   antáḥ
    raw.F.LOC.PL   indeed   RED-put-PF.2SG   cook-NM-NT.ACC.SG   inside
    '[Indra] you placed the cooked (milk) inside the raw (cows)'   (1.62.9ᶜ)

However, in this case too agreement clearly singles out nouns and adjectives, since adjectives agree, while nouns cannot, since they are gender-marked in the lexicon. Agreement mismatches are thus possible with nouns used as modifiers or as predicates, though not with adjectives (Example 3):[18]

(3) strī́   hí   brahmā́   ba~bʰūvi-tʰa
    woman(F).NOM.SG then   brahman(M).NOM.SG   PF~be-PF.2SG
    "for you, brahmin(NOM.M.SG), have turned into a woman(NOM.F.SG)!"
                                                                                    (8.33.19ᵈ)

Beneath the surface, however, things get complicated. While the definition of the noun and the verb are (or at least seem to be) similar (see Section 6), the definition of the adjective differs in the two languages. Agreement divides adjectives and nouns also in Sanskrit, but most of the items subject to agreement in Sanskrit are derived adjectives built from verbal roots, rather than simple adjectives, as in Latin (see Alfieri 2016, 2018 and Example 4):

(4) agní-s   tig-ménā   śoc-í-ā
    Agni(M)-NOM.SG   be_sharp-NM.INS.NT.SG   burn-NM.NT-INS.SG
    yā́s-a-d   víśva-m   ní   atrí-am
    drive-SBJ-3SG   every-M.ACC.SG   into   Atri(M)-ACC.SG
    "with a sharp flame, Agni will attack every Atri [a daemon]"   (6.16.28ᵃᵇ)

---

17. In Sanskrit, adjectival stems in diphthong are not found, while adjectives in -u- are found (tapú- 'hot'). Moreover, in RV Sanskrit (not in the classical language) adjectives tend to show the instr.pl. ending -ebʰis (from the ending of the PIE consonant stems *-bʰi), while nouns more readily show -āis (from the ending of the PIE pronouns *-ois), see Lazzeroni (2008).

18. See also pāpā́ḥ kanī́yā gaccʰanti 'evil(f.pl.) girls(f.pl.) come' vs. kanī́yās, dānám ásurasya, gacchanti 'girl(f.pl.), daemon's gift(nt.sg.), come', but not **kanī́yās, dānā (f.pl.) ásurasya, gac-cʰanti. Note that in Sanskrit the final consonant of each word is always subject to sandhi: that is the nom.pl. ending is -ās both in pāpā́ḥ and kanī́yā, but -ās before a voiceless stop becomes -āḥ, while it becomes -ā before a voiced stop or a vowel.

Moreover, the group of agreeing nouns (that is, the nouns that regularly join to the feminine suffix -ī- and agree) is far larger in Sanskrit, including not only specific names of deities and animals as in Latin (devá- 'God' → devī́- 'Goddess', vŕ̥ka- 'wolf' → vr̥kī́- 'she-wolf'), but also a large number – probably the majority – of derived nouns, such as the agent nouns in -tar- → -trī́-. See Example 5:

(5) úd u   stómāso   aśvín-or   a-bud^h-rañ
    up now   hymn(M).NOM.PL   aśvín(M)-GEN.DU   PST-wake_up-AOR.3PL
    jāmí   bráhmāi   uás-aś
    related.NT.NOM.PL   prayer(NT)-NOM.PL   dawn(F)-NOM.PL
    ca   dev-ī́-ḥ
    and   God-F-NOM.PL
    'The praise songs of the Aśvins have awakened, also our family
    formulations, and the Dawns, the Goddesses"   (7.72.3^{ab})

In the same vein, adjectival-forming or adjectival-selecting affixes are not a diagnostic criterion for distinguishing nouns and adjectives in Sanskrit. Indian native grammarians divide Sanskrit suffixes into two groups. Primary suffixes (usually called kr̥t) attach only to roots and build derived nominal stems, while secondary suffixes (usually called tadd^{h}ita) attach to simple or derived nominal stems and build secondarily derived nominal stems. Some affixes are more likely to build nouns (especially with root accent), but others more readily build adjectives (especially with suffix accent), but there is no clear-cut distinction between the two cases. E.g., the kr̥t suffix -as- often builds nouns with root accent, but it can also build adjectives with suffix accent: máh-as- 'greatness' and mah-ás- 'big' from mah- 'be big'. The tadd^{h}ita suffix -ya- usually builds adjectives of relation from nouns, but it also builds nouns from other nouns: pítr-ya- 'paternal' from pitár- 'father' and vīr-yá- 'manliness, strength' from vīrá- 'hero'.[19]

Comparative and superlative affixes show the same distribution as all other suffixes in Sanskrit, so they cannot be used to define adjectives. The primary comparative-superlative suffixes -īyāṃs- and -iṣṭha- attach only to verbal roots: see náy-iṣṭ^{h}a- 'who conducts in the best way' from nī- 'to conduct'; jáv-īyāṃs- 'faster' from jū- 'move fast'. See Example 6:

(6) yó   véd-iṣṭ^{h}o   a-vyat^h-íṣu
    who.M.NOM.SG know-SUP.M.NOM.SG   not-waver-M.LOC.PL

---

19. This interpretation of the kr̥t and tadd^{h}ita suffixes is quite traditional in Sanskrit grammars; for discussion see Alfieri (2009: 34 fn. 62). Also in this case, diachronic changes may determine the passage of a suffix from one class to the other (see Burrow 1955: 119ff.).

áśvā-vant-aṃ   jari-tṛ̊-bʰyaḥ   vājaṃ
horse-ADJ-M.NOM.PL sing-NM-M.DAT.PL prize(M)-ACC.SG

'[Indra] who among the unwavering is the best in finding the prize that
brings horses for the singers'   (8.2.24[ab])

The secondary comparative-superlative suffixes *-tara-* and *-tama-* attach to adjectives, to nouns, pronouns, prepositions and numerals without distinction: *tavástara-* 'stronger' from *tavás-* 'strong' (a secondary adjective derived from the verbal root *tū-* 'be strong'); *vīrá-tara-* 'more man', *vīrá-tama-* 'the most man' from *vīrá-* 'man'; *ka-tará-* 'which among two', *ka-tamá-* 'which among many' from *ká-* 'which'; *ut-tara-* 'higher', *ut-tama-* 'highest' from *úd-* 'up' and *śata-tama-* 'hundredth' from *śatam* '100'.[20] See Example 7:

(7) *ámbi-tam-e   nádī-tam-e*
     mother(F)-SUP-VOC.SG   river(F)-SUP-VOC.SG

     dév-i-tam-e   sárasvati
     God-F-SUP-VOC.SG   Sarasvati(F).VOC.SG

     'Best mother, best river, best Goddess, Sarasvati'   (2.41.6[a])

Looking at these data, Sanskrit philologists usually conclude that the PoS system in Latin and in Sanskrit are *almost* identical, though in Sanskrit the adjective is not as sharply distinguished from the noun as in Latin, since only some of the criteria that are used to define the adjective in Latin give a positive answer in Sanskrit.[21] But this conclusion, possible as it may be in practice, is highly problematic from a theoretical point of view. To the extent that there is no objective criterion to weight the various features that define the "adjective" in Latin, it is logically impossible to establish what to do when two or more features are in contrast or when one of these features gives only a partly positive answer. In other words, Sanskrit philologists are perfectly able to describe Sanskrit data and their differences with respect to Latin, but they have no objective criterion to decide whether these differences are more adequate to claim that both languages show the "same" adjectival category, despite minor differences, or that Sanskrit has no adjective class at all, despite

---

20. This distribution of comparative-superlative suffixes is a conservative feature of Sanskrit: Av. *gaotəma-* 'a proper name', lit. 'big cow', Gk. βασιλεύτερος 'big king'; Av. *uštama-*, Gk. ὕστερος parallel to Skt. *uttama-*, etc. For discussion, see Lazzeroni (2005, 2013) and Alfieri (2009: 14).

21. See, e.g., Whitney (2000 [1879[1]]: 111), Delbrück (1888: 188f.), Wakernagel (1905: 1), MacDonell (1975 [1910[1]]: 178), Renou (1952: 338, 1965: 231) and Morgenroth (1977: 65).

some similarities with Latin.[22] Again, this is not a serious problem for Sanskrit philologists, who usually also know Latin, so they can use the Latin DC "adjective" as a reference and detail the differences in practice. Nonetheless, a similar strategy paves the way to misunderstandings and ambiguities when it is transferred from language-individual grammar to cross-linguistic research.

3.1.1 Joshi (1967) and Bhat (1994, 2000)

Sanskrit philologists often claim that the PoS systems in Latin and Sanskrit are *almost* identical, but more radical formulations can be found. As Speijer puts it (1974 [1896[1]]: 2): "Während Nomen und Pronomen im Indischen einen merkbaren Unterschied der Flexion aufweisen, werden die beiden Kategorien des Nomens, Substantiv und Adjectiv, im Flexion, Composition, Derivation fast unterschiedlos behandelt". Speijer's view is based on the same data discussed above and reported in any Sanskrit manual, but his conclusions are more radical in comparison to the common view (see fn. 21) and also compared to what he claimed elsewhere (e.g., Speijer 1998 [1886[1]]: 179), where the noun and the adjective are said to be *almost* identical, rather than *almost completely* identical. The reasons underlying Speijer's radical formulation are hard to fathom: his claim may be a shortcut used for the sake of brevity in a (relatively short) manual; it may be a tribute to Indian native grammar, which does not recognize the adjective as a relevant category;[23] or it may be the result of a complex reasoning in which Speijer evaluated the empirical data discussed so far and concluded that, despite the vulgate, Sanskrit has no adjectives, but quality nouns. Be that as it may, an objective criterion to establish whether the Sanskrit data support or discourage the employment of the category "adjective"

---

22. One of the main inconsistencies of contemporary PoS theory is the impossibility of distinguishing major and minor classes, that is to say of establishing when a given group of items represent an independent PoS or a sub-class of a different PoS. On this point, see Sasse (1993b), Stassen (1997: 31ff.), Croft (2000, 2001: 78ff., 84, 2005), Shachter & Shopen (2007: 4) and Haspelmath (2012: 111ff.).

23. Sanskrit grammarians recognize the existence of quality nouns (*guṇavacana* 'indicator [*vacana*] of a quality [*guṇa*]'), of gender-marked nouns (*liṅgavacana* 'indicator of gender [*liṅga*]'), of nouns commonly employed as appositions (*sāmāyavacana* 'indicator of a general class [*sāmāya*]') and of a class of exocentric words which are usually compounds (*anyapadārtʰa* 'exocentric, which takes its meaning [*artʰa*] from a different [*anya*] word [*pada*]'). Moreover, in the analysis of compounds and phrases, they acknowledge that two nouns can be co-referential (*samānādʰikaraṇas* 'referred to the same substrate') and either noun is the head of the substrate (*viśeṣya* 'qualified') and either is the modifier (*viśeṣyaṇa* 'qualifier'). However, they do not accept a true "adjective" class comparable to that defined by grammarians. See Cardona (1997a, 1997b) and Radicchi (1973–74) for Indian PoS theory, and Pontillo & Candotti (2011) for the terms above.

cannot be found if the Sanskrit data are described simply by transferring the Latin-based DC "adjective" to the cross-linguistic level.

As confirmation, Joshi (1967), followed by Bhat (1994, 2000), took up a part of the evidence discussed so far (namely, the ability of adjectives to head a NP and the lack of a fixed position in the NP), radicalized Speijer's view and claimed Sanskrit as a typical language "without" adjectives or with "true" noun-like adjectives (that is, adjectives that are indistinguishable from nouns). Obviously, this view can be criticized from a "splitter" point of view (or from the point of view of single language description, which is almost the same), saying that gender agreement is solidly established in Sanskrit (see Example 3) and it clearly singles out nouns and adjectives, although for the most part gender-agreeing stems are derivatives from verbal roots (see below).[24] But even this position is weak from a theoretical point of view. The point is that there is no principled way to establish whether the existence of an agreement system mainly limited to derived stems is or is not a sufficient criterion to say that Sanskrit has "adjectives", inasmuch as the category "adjective" is defined as an unweighted bundle of features, since the weight of the single features that compose the bundle cannot be determined objectively.

3.1.2 *Works following Dixon's approach (2004)*

As a confirmation, a few years after Bhat's publication, Dixon (2004) took up his previous work on adjectival typology (Dixon 1982 [1979[1]]) and proposed a different definition of the "adjective". He accepted the idea that PoS are simple lexemes and that simple lexeme classes can be defined also as unweighted bundle of features, but enlarged the bundle so as to include any possible difference between simple lexical units meaning qualities, objects and actions in any language. In other words, Dixon tried to pass from the mere transfer of a Latin-based DC on the cross-linguistic level, as the Sanskrit philologists usually did, to the building of a portable CC based on an open-ended list of possible diagnostic features (e.g., occurrence as verbal or non-verbal predicates, occurrence of head or modifier of a NP, different possibility in the predicate slot, different possibility in transitivity, comparative constructions or in forming adverbs, see Dixon 2004: 14ff.). However, following a partly similar claim in Stassen (1997: 359ff.), Alfieri (2009)

---

24. The terms "splitters" and "lumpers" have been current in PoS research since Croft (2001: 63ff.). Splitters are the scholars who tend to use all the available criteria in all languages to define the PoS, with the results of having a different group of items for each criterion (that is, for each construction), splitting each PoS into a myriad of sub-classes. Lumpers are those who tend to ignore arbitrarily (i.e., without an explicit and cross-linguistically constant criterion) some of the criteria that can be used to distinguish two or more classes of lexemes, and so lump these classes into a single PoS.

applied Dixon's criteria to RV Sanskrit and claimed that Sanskrit displays a small class of noun-like adjectives (that is, of primary lexical units meaning qualities divided from primary lexical units meaning objects by means of agreement), but it also shows a large number of verb-like adjectives, that is to say lexical units meaning roughly a quality that can be predicated verbally, as in Example 8–11:[25]

(8) yā-bʰiḥ   sómo   mód-a-te
    who(F).INS.PL soma(M).NOM.SG   enjoy-PRS1-3SG.MD
    harṣ-a-te   ca
    be_excited-PRS1-3SG.MD   and
    'thanks to which [sc. the Waters] Soma is delighted and becomes excited'
    (10.30.5ᵃ)

(9) ayáṃ   ha   túbʰyam
    3SG.M.NOM   indeed you.DAT.SG
    váruṇo   hr̥-ṇí-te
    Varuṇa(M).NOM.SG be_angry-PRS9-3SG.MD
    'Varuṇa now is angry with you'
    (7.86.3ᵈ)

(10) jāyā   tap-ya-te   kitavá-sya
     wife(F).NOM.SG be/make_hot-PRS4-3SG.MD   gambler(M)-GEN.SG
     'the wife of the gambler is grieved [lit. 'is hot, burns (with pain)']'
     (10.34.10ᵃ)

(11) ná   sváp-nâya   spr̥h-aya-nti
     not sleep-NM.M.DAT.SG   be_eager-PRS10-3PL
     'They [sc. the Gods] are not eager for sleep'
     (8.2.18ᵇ)

Also in this case, Alfieri's conclusion is neither true nor false, it simply is the product of a specific definition of the "adjective". However, this definition – like that employed by Bhat – is based on an unweighted bundle of features and the

---

25. Sanskrit roots range from stative-unaccusative meanings (śubʰ- 'be beautiful', tr̥ṣ- 'be thirsty', śī- 'to lie'), to unergative meanings (i- 'to go', bʰā- 'to shine'), to true transitive-causative meanings (han- 'kill', bʰid- 'split'), not to mention roots that are compatible with a wide array of meanings that go from the stative to the transitive (svād- 'be, become, or make tasty', br̥h- 'be, become or make big, thick or strong', tap- 'become hot, heat'). Therefore, only a limited number of roots are listed in dictionaries with an exclusive quality meaning, but the absence of a quality meaning among the translational equivalents of a Sanskrit root in a dictionary does not preclude such a root being able to code a quality if inflected in the appropriate form. Sanskrit philologists acknowledge the high frequency of verb-like adjectival predicates indirectly. Gren-Eklund showed that nominal sentences with adjectival meanings are rarer in Sanskrit than they are in the modern European languages (1978: 34): but noun-like adjectival predicates are rare precisely because adjectival predicates are often coded verbally.

Chapter 9. Parts of speech, comparative concepts and Indo-European linguistics 327

classifications based on unweighted bundles of features arrive at family resemblances, but forbid any consistent typology. In other words, if the "adjective" is defined through an open-ended list of features whose relative weight cannot be determined, one can identify one "adjectival" category for each of the (possibly infinite) features included in the list, but there is no principled way to establish which of the classes so identified is a major PoS, which is a minor class, how many adjective classes can be accepted in a language, and so on.

In sum, the debate on the Sanskrit adjective class is a paramount case of inconsistent category assignment. On the basis of the same empirical data, Sanskrit has been classified as having an adjectival category almost identical to that in Latin, as a language with quality nouns but no adjectives (or with noun-like adjectives) and as a language with verb-like adjectives. The radical difference between the results and the absence of any objective criterion to prefer one result over the others confirm that the method whereby these results are obtained is simply inconsistent. Both DCs and portable CCs are bundles of unweighted features and when the base of comparison – the *tertium comparationis* – is itself a bundle of unweighted features there is no logical method to establish what to do when the various features that compose the bundle are in contrast. In other words, if the Latin-based DC "adjective" is employed to classify Sanskrit adjectival typology, or if a portable CC abstracted from the Latin-based category "adjective" is employed for the same task, the only basis of comparison is the alleged existence of the Latin-based category "adjective", although the existence of this category has never been demonstrated but has rather been presupposed on the basis of misleading Eurocentric questions such as: "what are the adjectives of language X?" or "does language X have adjectives?". It is as if, in a juridical study, instead of asking "how does the Italian constitution work?" or "what are the most salient roles in the Italian constitution?" we asked "who is the king of Italy?" and went on to discuss whether the Prime Minister or the President (who have distinct roles in Italy) is the best candidate for being the king of Italy, ignoring the possibility that Italy might not have a king and that our typology of social roles should not include the role "king" as a primitive.[26] Therefore, the only possible way to overcome the paradox of inconsistent category assignment is to develop a cross-linguistically consistent method to descend from the study of LANGUAGE to the functioning of single languages in the field of PoS. This is what we will try to do in the next section.

---

26. See Dryer (1997: 116–119), Croft (2000, 2001: 29ff., 63ff., 2005), Croft & van Lier (2012), Haspelmath (2007, 2010, 2012) and Cristofaro (2009) for a similar conclusion.

4. A relatively new PoS theory

The PoS theory below is the result of a partly original elaboration based mainly on two previous sources, namely Hengeveld's PoS theory (1992: 47ff.) and Croft's definition of PoS (2001: 29ff., 63ff.). More precisely, it is a re-definition of the "Amsterdam Typology", and specifically of the lexical inventories [N, A, V] and [N (AV)], in the light of the criticism raised by the advocates of a radical distinction between CCs and DCs (see fn. 26).[27] Its goal is to show that, in contrast to the claims of the supporters of a radical division between DCs and CCs, a principled way to pass from CCs to DCs in the field of PoS can be obtained, at least as for IE languages.

The idea on which the theory is based is simple. Lexemes cannot be defined, if not starting from the constructions that define them, and constructions cannot be compared, if not on the basis of their function defined on a conceptual map. Therefore, if we develop a conceptual map on which the pure CCs of PoS are defined; a cross-linguistically valid method to classify the single language constructions on a conceptual map; and a cross-linguistically valid method to extract the lexemes from the constructions on the map, then a cross-linguistically consistent method to descend from the study of LANGUAGE to the description of the PoS in single languages is obtained. In other words, we are proposing to divide the continuum that goes from LANGUAGE to individual languages into three layers, which roughly correspond to the three types of CCs defined in Section 2 and to the three meanings in which the traditional notion of PoS can be understood.

4.1 PoS-concepts

The first and highest layer of analysis in the continuum is that of pure CCs. At this level, PoS are not single language DCs, but language-external universal concepts

---

27. For an overview on contemporary PoS theory, see Plank (1997), Anward, Moravcsik & Stassen (1997), Evans (2000), Comrie & Vogel (2000), Sasse (2001), Rijkhoff (2007) and Bisang (2013). On the Amsterdam Typology, see Anward (2000), van Lier (2009), Ansaldo et al. (2010), Hengeveld (2013), Alfieri (2013a). For a criticism, see Croft (2001: 65ff.) and Cristofaro (2009: 453ff.). The criticisms are serious, but they did not prevent the achievement of important results (Bisang 2013: 291ff.), such as the definition of different lexical inventories across languages (Hengeveld 1992: 69ff.; Beck 2002), the implicational hierarchy of PoS: verbs > nouns > adjectives (Hengeveld 1992: 68ff.), the discovery of correlations between PoS systems and word order (Hengeveld, Rijkhoff & Siewierska 2004), and the notion of flexibility (Rijkhoff & van Lier 2013, van Lier 2009, 2017).

defined on a conceptual map. The map can be purely semantic or "hybrid".[28] In this case, as in Croft (2001), the map is "hybrid", since it combines two prototypically correlated universal parameters, a semantic concept (Object, Quality and Action) and a discourse-pragmatic function (Referent, Modifier and Predicate). See Table 1 (Croft 2001: 92):

Table 1. PoS as pure comparative concepts

	Referent	Modifier	Predicate
Object	**Object Referent**	Object Modifier	Object Predicate
Quality	Quality Referent	**Quality Modifier**	Quality Predicate
Action	Action Referent	Action Modifier	**Action Predicate**

Each slot in the table represents a zone of conceptual space defined in terms of semantic notions and discourse functions. All the slots are relevant for establishing the PoS system of a language, but three slots have a special status. The Object Referent is the NOUN, the Action Predicate is the VERB and the Quality Modifier is the ADJECTIVE: these categories are not the formal categories of any language, they are the zones of conceptual-functional space that are the most typical intersection between a discourse function and a semantic notion (thus, they are termed as "unmarked correlations" by Croft 2001: 89). More specifically, they are the zones of conceptual-universal space arbitrarily identified by the researcher whose coding in single language is the subject of the typology.

4.2 PoS-constructions

The second and more particular layer in the continuum is that of "hybrid" CCs or constructions in Croft's terms (2016). PoS-constructions are the single-language constructions that code the various slots in Table 1. PoS-constructions are found in all languages, since each language in some way codes each slot in the table, but the specific features that define the construction that codes each slot in each

---

28. Both types of maps (thus, both types of definitions of PoS) have been proposed in the literature. PoS are basically semantic notions in Thompson (1988), Dixon (2004) and Haspelmath (2012: 122–4), discourse-based, pragmatic categories in Hengeveld (1992: 51ff.) and Hopper & Thompson (1984), and discourse-based categories further specified in terms of their prototypical semantics in Croft (2001: 87).

language are language-particular.[29] Nonetheless, constructions can be compared in terms of their function, that is, on the space that they occupy on the map.

Clearly, comparison cannot be immediate. In each language, several constructions can code the same slot, having overlapping functions, and several slots can be coded through a single construction. In Latin, the Quality Predicate can be coded through a verb-like or a noun-like construction: *aquae tepent* vs. *aquae tepidae (sunt)* 'the waters are warm'. The Quality Predicate slot, therefore, is split between two constructions with similar (though not identical) meanings, the latter of which is more frequent than the former. On the other hand, in Latin the Verb construction typically codes only the Action Predicate slot, but in the so-called omnipredicative languages (e.g., Classical Nahuatl, Launey 1994) a single construction codes the Action, the Quality and the Object Predicate slot, taking over three different slots (see Stassen 1997: 29 for the notion of takeover). However, for the sake of argument we establish that a single construction can take over several slots, but each slot has to be linked only to a single construction in each language.

The method whereby each slot is linked to a single construction is typicality, which is measured objectively as text frequency. If two constructions code the same slot in Table 1, a corpus of text is gathered, the relative frequency of each construction is measured and only the more frequent construction is projected on the map. Thanks to this method, the most typical (i.e., most frequent) construction that codes say, the NOUN slot (i.e., the Object Referent) in language X is considered *the* Noun construction of that language and it is the only construction mapped onto the NOUN slot, even if rigorously speaking it is not *only the* Noun construction that codes the NOUN slot in that language. Thanks to this method, the problem of distinguishing major word classes and minor word-classes or sub-classes can be overcome in a principled way, since minor classes and sub-classes are those that are defined by less frequent constructions or by constructions that code only a part of a slot (see fn. 22).[30]

Text frequency supplies an objective method to anchor a single construction to each slot in Table 1. Still, the single-language constructions so identified do not

---

29. PoS-constructions are termed differently depending on the approach of the research and of the level of language analysis at which the construction is fixed. They can be labelled as *token classes* (Broschart 1997; Vogel 2000), *phrasal categories* (Gil 2016; Mosel 2017) or, in the inflectional IE languages, simply *word classes* (Haspelmath 1996). In the following, we will confine ourselves to using the labels *construction classes* or *word classes*.

30. Clearly, minor constructions shall not be ignored, but they are looked at secondarily, only after the major word classes are defined thanks to the major constructions.

necessarily code exactly the same space in Table 1, therefore they do not share exactly the same function. The Latin Verb (i.e., the Action Predicate) construction codes a single slot in Table 1 (the Action Predicate), but the Classical Nahuatl Verb construction typically codes all three slots in the Predicate row (the Action, Quality and Object Predicate). However, comparability is always partial, or it is identity (Moravcsik 2016). If two constructions code the same slot in Table 1, they are comparable in relation to that slot, although the overall space that they code in the table is different in absolute terms. In fact, the ultimate purpose of typologies based on pure CCs is to discover how a given zone of conceptual space is coded across languages, not to discover how the typological space coded by a given single-language construction is coded across languages, which is the ultimate objective of the studies based on portable CCs.

4.3 PoS-lexemes

The third and most particular layer in the continuum is the level of portable CCs or "strategies" in Croft's term (2016). At this layer, PoS are the classes of simple lexical units (or *lexemes*) that enter the constructions.

Also, PoS-lexemes are universal from a certain point of view, but their universality differs both from that of PoS-concepts and of PoS-constructions. If PoS-concepts are the same in all languages and PoS-constructions are found in all languages with the same function but different forms, PoS-lexemes are found in all languages, but they have different forms and also different functions from language to language. A given class of lexemes can enter only one PoS-construction or may enter more, as the case may be: even if all languages define classes of lexemes, only some languages define a specific class of lexemes that enters only the Adjective (i.e., Quality Modifier) construction, as it is the case in Latin and in all languages with "true adjectives" (or with lexical inventory of type [N, A, V]); in other languages a single class of lexemes is the input form on which say, both Adjective and Verb constructions are built, as is the case in languages with verb-like adjectives (or with lexical inventory of type [N (AV)]).[31]

Once a single construction is anchored to each slot in Table 1 by means of text frequency, a principled way to extract lexemes from constructions must be defined, so as to stop splitting lexeme classes *ad infinitum*. Also, in this case, the

---

31. PoS-constructions and PoS-lexemes differ also in single language grammar (Haspelmath 1996). The IE *nomina actionis* (Skt. *vardʰ-ana-* 'growing') and the Semitic *maṣdar* (Ar. *dars* 'studying') are nouns in terms of their word or construction class, but they are productively derived from verbal roots, so they fall into the class of verbal roots in terms of their lexeme class (Skt. *vardʰ-* 'to grow', Ar. *d.r.s.* 'to study').

method is simple and is based on pure distributional reasoning. Only the constructions projected on the table are used to define lexeme classes. That is to say, we do not require that the lexemes falling into a single class be totally identical from a distributional point of view, which is clearly impossible (see the references in fn. 8, 9 and 14 for discussion). We confine ourselves to saying that the constructions mapped in Table 1 are the only distributional environments employed to define lexeme classes and that items which show the same behaviour with respect to these constructions are equated for the purposes of our typology (that is, they are grouped into one class). Also, in this case, the units compared are similar rather than identical; but if the similarity is defined in an objective manner, the comparison is consistent and any methodological opportunism (as Croft puts it, 2001: 70ff.) is avoided. In this way, the major lexeme classes in each language are objectively defined on their distributional privileges relative to the major constructions, avoiding heterogeneous and non-hierarchical criteria.

Obviously, we may discuss how many constructions are necessary to define the PoS system of a language. A different PoS theory emerges if we consider only the unmarked correlations or all the constructions in Table 1: the lower the number of slots (and thus of constructions) considered, the greater the possibility of lumping two or more lexeme classes into one; conversely, the higher the number of slots, the greater the possibility of splitting one lexeme class into two. However, in either case, the number of lexeme classes to be accepted in each language depends on the distribution of lexical units in the constructions projected on the table, and the number of constructions on the table is determined in an objective manner, through text frequency. The PoS theory proposed so far, therefore, is a "lumping" theory in Croft's terms, but it supplies a consistent method to define different lexical inventories across languages.

In sum, PoS-concepts, PoS-constructions and PoS-lexemes represent three types of CCs, each of which relates to a different layer of generality in the descent that goes from LANGUAGE to single languages, but scholars usually fail to distinguish them clearly.[32] The three meanings of the notion of PoS are summed up in the following table (Table 2):

---

32. Dryer (1997), Croft (2001) and Haspelmath (2012) accept PoS-concepts, but do not clearly divide PoS-constructions and PoS-lexemes, and consider both only as DCs. Hopper and Thompson (1984) focus on PoS-constructions, but disregard PoS-lexemes, while Dixon (2004: 2) defines PoS as lexemes but considers lexemes as primitive notions, although lexemes are the result of the work of speakers (or linguists) who extract them from the constructions in which they appear. Finally, Hengeveld defines PoS both as constructions (1992: 51) and as lexemes (1992: 61), but does not clearly distinguish between the two plans.

Chapter 9. Parts of speech, comparative concepts and Indo-European linguistics

Table 2. The three meanings of the traditional notion of PoS

Type of CC	Level of analysis	Type of classes	Graphic symbolization
Pure	Concepts	PoS-concepts	NOUN, VERB, ADJECTIVE…
Hybrid	Discourse	PoS-constructions	Noun, Verb, Adjective…
Portable	Lexicon	PoS-lexemes	noun, verb, adjective…

In the following, the PoS theory sketched above is used to compare the PoS system of Latin and RV Sanskrit. For reasons of space, only unmarked correlations are considered. However, Alfieri (forth.) has shown that the same result is also obtained if the analysis is enlarged to all the slots in Table 1.

5. The Latin PoS system

The PoS system in Latin is well known. The distinction between PoS concepts, constructions and lexemes is thus expected to confirm what is already common knowledge, rather than bring in substantial novelties.

The most typical Latin construction that codes the NOUN (Object Referent) slot in Table 1 is a "noun" in the most canonic sense: a word-form marked by case, number and gender, or simply: […]-Case.[33] The […]-Case construction can be filled by different types of stems: a simple noun stem (*milit-* in *miles* 'soldier'), a derived verb stem (*amant-* 'lover' from *amo* 'I love') and a simple or derived adjective stem (*album* 'list' from *albus* 'white'), etc. However, there is little doubt that simple noun stems are the most typical (i.e., the most frequent) fillers of the […]-Case constructions. The most typical Latin Noun construction, therefore, is [noun]-Case (Example 1):

(12) *arm-a*   *viru-m=que*   *can-o*
      weapon(NT)-ACC.PL man(M)-ACC.SG=and   sing-PRS.1SG
      'I sing the weapons and the man'   (Verg., *Aen.* I.1)

Similarly, the most typical construction that codes the ADJECTIVE (Quality Modifier) slot in Table 1 is the Latin Adjective construction. This construction is a word-form marked by agreement (and case, gender, number), or simply: […]-Agr. The […]-Agr construction can be filled by a simple adjective stem (*magn-* in *magnus*

---

33. The label […]-Case is a summary label that includes all the inflectional features defined in Section 3 (for Latin) and Section 4 (for Sanskrit), and the same holds for the labels […]-Agr and […]-Pers.

'big'), a participle (*notus* 'known' from *nosco* 'know') or a noun joined to an adjectival suffix (*gloriosus* 'proud' from *gloria* 'glory'). However, the most typical filler of the Adjective construction is a simple adjective stem, so the most typical Adjective construction in Latin is [adjective]-Agr (Example 13):

(13) tibi   ne   **tener-as**   glacie-s   sec-e-t
you.DAT not soft-F.ACC.PL ice(F)-NOM.SG cut-SBJ-3SG

asper-a   planta-s
rough-F.NOM.SG palm(F)-ACC.PL

'Ah, might the jagged ice not cut your tender feet'   (Verg., *Ec.* X.49)

In the same way, the most typical construction that codes the VERB (Action Predicate) slot in Table 1 is the Latin Verb construction, which is a word-form marked by person, tense, mood and diathesis: schematically […]-Pers. The […]-Pers construction can be filled by a verb stem (*cad-* in *cado* 'fall'), an adjective stem joined to a verbalizing affix (*albesco* 'become white' from *albus* 'white') a noun stem joined to an empty verbalizing affix (*maculare* 'to stain' from *macula* 'stain'), etc. However, the most typical filler of this construction is a simple verb stem and the most typical Latin Verb construction is [verb]-Pers (Example 14):

(14) miser   Catull-e   **desina-s**   inepti-re
miserable.M.VOC.SG Catullus(M)-VOC.SG cease-PRS.2SG be_a_fool-INF

et   quod   **vide-s**   peri-sse
and that.NT.ACC.SG see-PRS.2SG be_lost-INF.PST

perd-itum   duc-as
lose-PTC.NT.ACC.SG consider-SBJ.PRS.2PL

'Miserable Catullus, cease to be a fool, and that which you see to have been lost may you consider lost'   (Cat., *Car.* VIII.1)

Obviously, those exemplified above are the most frequent constructions that code the unmarked correlation defined in Section 3, but not the only constructions possible for those functions. For instance, in the first 40 chapters of Sallust's *De coniuratione Catilinae*, 393 Adjective constructions (i.e., Quality Modifiers) are found: 334 (85.0%) are (prefixed) simple adjectives (e.g., *bonus* 'good', *obscurus* 'obscure'), 30 (7.6%) are (prefixed) deverbal adjectives (*adulescens* 'young', *invisus* 'hateful'), and 29 (7.4%) are (prefixed) denominal adjectives (*urbanus* 'urban', *egregius* 'illustrious'). If all the constructions found in the corpus are gathered, the following table is obtained (Table 3):[34]

---

34. The appositions (e.g., *consul* 'consul', *senator* 'senator', *eques* 'knight', etc.) are not included, since they are considered as non-typical Object Modifiers.

Table 3. Latin Adjective constructions table (the number before the schema of the construction refers to frequency)

Adjectives	Number	Percent
1. [adjective]-Agr	334	83.7%
1. [adjective]-Agr	307	78.1%
2. Pre-[adjective]-Agr	27	6.9%
2. [...]$_V$-Agr	30	7.5%
4. [verb-NM]-Agr	16	4.1%
5. Pre-[verb-NM]-Agr	14	3.6%
2. [...]$_N$-Agr	29	7.4%
3. [noun-ADJ]-Agr	25	6.6%
7. Pre-[noun-ADJ]-Agr	4	1.0%
Total	393	100%

If only the most frequent constructions that code the Noun, the Verb and the Adjective function in Latin are mapped in Table 1, Table 4 is obtained:

Table 4. Latin constructions table (only unmarked correlations are reported)

	Referent	Modifier	Predicate
Object	[noun]-Case	----	----
Quality	----	[adjective]-Agr	----
Action	----	----	[verb]-Pers

The constructions [...]-Case, [...]-Agr and [...]-Pers define three classes of simple lexemes: nouns, adjectives and verbs. Each class has a specific and exclusive distribution: the nouns enter only the Noun construction without further measures being taken (as Hengeveld says, 1992: 58), the verbs enter only the Verb construction without further measures and the adjectives typically enter only the Adjective construction, but they can also enter the Noun construction without further measures.[35] Nouns and adjectives, therefore, represent two different classes of lexemes, the nouns being marked as [+ gender] and the adjectives as [+ agreement], but their difference is neutralized in all the slots on the Referent row, where the feature [+ agreement]

[35.] Hengeveld's wording refers to the absence of trans-categorization devices, be they coded overtly through an affix, or covertly through syntactic conversion (see also Croft 1991: 58, 2001: 66).

is not pertinent (see fn. 12). The threefold division of the lexicon is mirrored in derivation. Each Latin suffix attaches to a single class of lexemes and produces items belonging to a single class of derived stems, as seen in the case of adjectival-forming and adjectival-selecting affixes (see Section 3). Finally, syntax mirrors the threefold division established on the lower levels and defines three classes of constructions with exclusive inflectional features. If Table 4 is projected orthogonally dividing the lexeme and the word layer, the PoS system in Latin is obtained (Table 5):[36]

Table 5. Latin PoS table (only the primary categorization is reported; the arrows refer to grammatical processing)

	NOUN	ADJECTIVE	VERB
Phrase			
Derived stem			
Simple stem	[noun]-Case	[adjective]-Agr	[verb]-Pers
Lexeme	noun	adjective	verb

Traditional Latin grammars, which conflate all levels of language structure in a single word layer, conclude – quite simplistically – that Latin has three different PoS, although adjectives are similar to nouns. And modern scholars conclude that the PoS are defined by different criteria that do not overlap totally (Lyons 1979: 42), since the same threefold division found at the level of the lexicon holds also in derivation and in syntax, although it is manifested through different features at each level.

6. The RV Sanskrit PoS system

The same constructions that are found in Latin are also found in Vedic. In both cases, the most typical Noun construction is a word marked by case and the most typical filler of the [...]-Case construction is a simple noun (Example 15):[37]

---

36. Items can be re-categorized several times in IE languages (Simone 2007; Ježek & Ramat 2009) and they often increase (and stiffen) their categorization passing from a lower to an upper level (Lehmann 2008): *purificatio* 'purification' is an adjective in its lexeme class (*purus* 'pure'), a verb in its derived (or rather compound) stem1 class (*purifico* 'purify') and a noun in its derived stem2 or word class (*purificatio*). However, only the primary (or lexical) categorization and the final (or discourse) categorization of the most typical constructions will be discussed in this case.

37. If not otherwise specified, the translations follow those supplied by Brereton and Jamison (2014).

(15) pác-ya-te   yáva-ḥ
    cook-PRS4-3SG.MD grain(M)-NOM.SG
    'the grain ripens'   (1.135.8ᵈ)

However, in the RV derived nouns are so frequent that one may doubt whether the most typical Noun construction is indeed [noun]-Case. But a frequency count made on a small sample of 20 RV hymns (the first 20 listed in fn. 41) shows that the simple noun construction outnumbers the derived noun construction by about 60% to 40%.[38] Derived nouns, therefore, may be more frequent in the RV than in Latin, but in both cases the most typical Noun is [noun]-Case.

A slightly more complex situation is found with the VERB. In the RV the most typical Verb construction is a word-form marked by person, as in Latin (Example 16):

(16) táp-a-nti   śátru-m   svàr
    make_hot-PRS1-3PL   rival(M)-ACC.SG   sun(M).NOM.SG
    ná   bʰūmā
    as   earth(NT).ACC.PL
    '[the Gods] scorch the rival, like the sun [scorches] the worlds'   (7.34.19ᵃ)

However, two interpretations of Skt. tápanti are possible. The simplest segmentation is [root-AFF]-Pers. The affix can be a discontinuous morph if the template-and-pattern morphology is accepted: t.p- + -á.a- + -nti → tápanti, but it can also be a suffix, as the Indian grammarians said: tap- + -a- + -nti → tápanti.[39] In either case, while in Latin the most typical Verb construction is a simple verbal lexeme marked by person, in Sanskrit it is a 'verbal' lexeme marked by an affix and person.[40]

---

38. More specifically, 677 Noun constructions are found in the sample: 399 (58.9%) are simple nouns (i.e., [noun]-Case, e.g., mātár- 'mother'), 223 (32.9%) derived nouns built from verbal roots (i.e., [root-NM]-Case, e.g., pṛthivī́- 'earth', lit. 'the wide' from prath- 'to stretch, extend'), 45 (6.6%) are derived nouns built from primary nouns (i.e., [noun-ADJ]-Case, e.g., rathín- 'charioteer' from rátha- 'chariot') and 10 (1.4%) are miscellaneous construction types. On the whole, noun-based constructions total 445 (65.7%), while root-based constructions number 235 (34.3%).

39. The template-and-pattern morphology was proposed by Saussure (1878), implicitly, Meillet (1903: 116) and Benveniste (1962: 147ff.) for the IE family. For a discussion on the topic, see Alfieri (2016: 132, fn. 10; 157ff.).

40. If Aronoff's analysis of Latin verb inflection (1994: 33ff., 39ff., 45ff.) was applied also to RV Sanskrit, the vowel -a- should be considered a stem vowel and the typical Verb construction in the RV should appear as [verb]-Pers. But in the RV 10 classes of presents are found, similar to the Semitic binyanim: 6 classes are formed through affixes with or without ablaut; 2 classes with the -a- but no ablaut (class I, that of tapati, which is the most frequent, and class

As in Latin, in Vedic the most typical Adjective is a word marked by agreement: [...]-Agr. But Brugmann already knew that primary adjectives are scanty in the Veda (1904: 329) and many of the words usually classified as adjectives are, in fact, nominalizations built on verbal roots of stative or nearly stative meanings: *tap-ú-* 'hot' from *tap-* 'make or become hot, heat', *raṇ-vá-* 'pleasant' from *raṇ-* 'be pleasant, delight', *bṛh-ánt-* 'high, big, lofty' from *bṛh-* 'make big, strong'. It may thus be asked whether the simple adjective stem is really the most typical filler of Adjective construction in Vedic as it is in Latin.

To answer this question, a sample of 51 hymns of the RV was collected, all the Adjective constructions in the sample were gathered and a frequency count was made.[41] In the sample 892 Adjective constructions are found. As in Latin, all constructions are marked by agreement: [...]-Agr. However, below syntactic level, these constructions can be divided into five broadly different types. The most frequent filler of the [...]-Agr construction is a nominalized root, that is a root joined to one of the primary suffixes called *kṛt* in traditional Indian grammars: [root]-NM-Agr.[42] This construction is attested in 425 cases out of 892 (47.6% of the sample). The nominalizer is a standard *kṛt* suffix in Example 17 and a participial suffix in Example 18:

(17) kṛṣṇádʰvā   táp-ū   raṇ-vá-ś
of_black_path.M.NOM.SG   be_hot-NM.M.NOM.SG   rejoice-NM-M.NOM.SG

ci~ket-a   dyaú-r   iva
PF~observe-3SG   sky(M)-NOM.SG   as

smáya-mān-o   nábʰo-bʰiḥ
smile-PTC-M.NOM.SG   cloud(NT)-INS.PL

'[Agni], having a black road, red-hot, he appears bringing delight, smiling like heaven with its clouds' (2.4.6ᶜᵈ)

VI); 1 class with reduplication, which plays the same role as an affix from the structural point of view; 1 class with ablaut but no suffixes. Most Sanskrit roots build several present stems with different meanings: *tapati* 'burns' vs. *tápyate* 'becomes hot'. Aronoff's analysis is thus not plausible if applied to Sanskrit.

41. The sample includes the following hymns. Book 1: 1, 35, 61, 85, 135, 154, 160; book 2: 2, 4, 12, 24, 33, 35; book 3: 7, 49, 59; book 4: 49, 50, 51; book 5: 36, 83; book 6: 5, 16, 47, 54; book 7: 49, 55, 61, 63, 70, 71, 86, 103; book 8: 2, 4, 29, 33, 48; book 9: 1, 2; book 10: 14, 15, 30, 34, 87, 90, 127, 129, 130, 135, 168. The appositions (e.g., *deva...agne* 'God Agni', 6.16.12ᶜ) are not included, since they are considered as non-typical Object Modifiers.

42. *Kṛt* suffixes are glossed as NM since they usually build derived nouns, but they can also build derived adjectives, which are often considered as a special type of agent noun built on roots that do not have an action-centred meaning (MacDonell 1975: 113 on the *-as-* suffix).

(18)   prá   nā́ka-m   r̥ṣ-vá-m̐
       away vault_of_heaven(M)-ACC.SG elevate-NM-M.ACC.SG
       nu~nund-e   br̥h-ánt-am̐
       PF~push-3SG make_big-PTC-M.ACC.SG
       '[Varua] pushed forth the vault of heaven to be high and lofty'   (7.86.1ᶜ)

The second most frequent construction is a possessive compound, called the *bahuvrīhi* type by Indian grammarians. This construction is schematized as [...]_N-[...]_N-Agr and is found in 184 cases out of 892 (20.6%). Below its very general schema, however, different constructions are found. In 118 cases (13.2%), the second member of the compound (its "head", inasmuch as such a notion applies to an exocentric compound) is a derived noun taken from a verbal root: [...]_N-[root-NM]_N-Agr (Example 19), but in 52 cases (5.8%) it is a primary noun: [...]-[noun]-Agr (Example 20):

(19)   ví   suparó   antárikṣāṇi   a-kʰya-d
       away eagle(M).NOM.SG midspace(NT).ACC.PL PST-watch-AOR.3SG
       gabʰīrá-vepā   *ásura-ḥ*   *su-nītʰá-ḥ*
       deep-inspiration.M.NOM.PL[43] lord(M)-NOM.PL good-guidance-M.NOM.PL
       'the eagle has surveyed the midspaces – the lord possessing profound inspiration who gives good guidance'   (I.35.7ᵃ)

(20)   *híraṇya-pāṇi-ḥ*   *savitā*   *ví-carṣaṇi-r*
       gold-hand-M.NOM.SG Savitar(M).NOM.SG PRE-boundary-M.NOM.SG[44]
       ubʰé   *dyā́vā-p̥rthiv-ī́*   antár   īyate
       both.F.ACC.DU heaven-earth-F.ACC.DU between go.3SG.MD
       'Golden-palmed Savitar, whose boundaries are distant, shuttles between both, both heaven and earth'   (1.35.9ᵃᵇ)

The third most frequent construction coding the Adjective function is a noun joined to one of the prefixes *su-, dus-, nis-, sa-, a-*. This construction is schematized as Pre-[...]_N-Agr and is found in 133 cases out of 892 (14.9%).[45] In 103 cases

---

43. The word *vépas-* 'inspiration' is a regular action noun in *-as-* taken from the root *vip-* 'tremble'.

44. The adjective *vícarṣaṇi-* is of unclear meaning, although it is usually traced to *karṣ-* 'to drag, plough' with the suffix *-ani-* (Thieme 1967: 236ff.).

45. From the Indian point of view, this construction is a compound. However, unlike the nouns that build compounds, prefixes cannot stand alone in a sentence (a partial exception being represented by *su-*, which can also be found as an independent adverb, although it is much more frequent if prefixed to a noun).

(11.5%) the noun filling the construction is a derived noun taken from a verbal root: Pre-[root-NM]-Agr (Example 21), whereas in 23 cases (2.6%) it is a simple noun: Pre-[noun]-Agr (Example 22):

(21) huv-é vaḥ su-dyót-mān-am
invoke-1SG.MD you.PL.DAT good-brighten-NM-M.ACC.SG

su-vr̥k-tí-m viś-ā́m agní-m
well-twist-NM-M.ACC.SG clan(F)-GEN.PL Agni(M)-ACC.SG

átit^{h}i-m su-pray-ás-am
guest(M)-ACC.SG good-please-NM-M.ACC.SG

'I call for you the one of good brilliance, on Agni, the guest of the clans, who receives well-woven [hymns], who receives very pleasurable offerings'
(2.4.1^{ab})

(22) bab^{h}rú-r éko víṣuṇa-ḥ
brown-M.NOM.SG one.M.NOM.SG changing-M.NOM.SG

sūnáro yúvā
well.spirit.M.NOM.SG youth(M).NOM.SG

'brown, this one [the Soma] is changeable, a spirited youth' (8.29.1^a)

The fourth most typical Adjective construction is any (simple or derived) noun stem joined to one of the secondary suffixes that are termed as tadd^{h}ita suffixes by Indian grammarians: [..]$_N$-ADJ-Agr.[46] This construction is found in 94 cases out of 892 (10.5%). In 54 cases (6.1%) the nominal stem filling the construction is a simple noun: [noun]-ADJ-Agr (Example 23), whereas in 40 cases (4.4%) it is a derived noun built on a verbal root: [root-NM]-ADJ-Agr (Example 24):

(23) iṣ-iréṇa te mánas-ā su-tá-sya
incite-NM.NT.INS.SG you.GEN.M.SG mind(NT)-INS.SG press-PTC-M.GEN.SG

b^{h}akṣ-īmáhi pítr-iya-syeva rāy-áḥ
partake-PRS.OPT.1SG father-ADJ-M.GEN.SG.as wealth(M)-GEN.SG

'With a vigorous mind we would take a share of you when pressed, as of ancestral wealth' (8.48.7^{ab})

(24) sah-ā́-vā pr̥tsú tar-áṇi-r ná
prevail-NM-ADJ.M.NOM.SG battle(F).LOC.PL pass-NM-M.NOM.SG as

árvā vi-ā-naś-í
steed(M).NOM.SG PRE-PRE-traverse-NM.M.NOM.SG

---

46. Tadd^{h}ita suffixes are glossed as ADJ (adjectivalizer), since their typical function is that of building relational adjectives from nouns, although they can also build diminutives or other types of nouns.

ródasī   meh-ánā-vān
world_half(NT)-ACC.DU   urinate-NM-ADJ.M.NOM.SG

'[Indra] victorious in battles like an overtaking steed, traversing the two
world-halves, streaming abundance'   (3.49.3^{ab})

The fifth most typical filler of the Adjective construction is a simple adjective stem marked by agreement, which is exactly the same construction as in Latin. The construction [adjective]-Agr is found in 56 cases (6.3%), see Example 25:

(25)   āmād-aḥ   kṣvíṅkās   tám
       raw_meat.eat-NM.F.NOM.PL   spirit(F).NOM.PL   3SG.ACC

       ad-antv   énī-ḥ
       eat-IPT.3PL   colourful-F.NOM.PL

'let the *Kṣvíṅkā*-spirits, eaters of raw meat, of variegated colour, eat him [sc. the sorcerer]'   (10.87.7^d)

From a merely factual point of view, almost the same constructions that are found in the RV are found also in Latin: the deverbal adjective (*fervens* 'hot'), the compound adjective (*frugi-ferens* 'fruitful, which brings harvest'), the prefixed adjective (*obscurus* 'obscure'), and so on. However, the statistical distribution of these constructions is different in the two languages. If all the constructions found in the RV are gathered, the following table is obtained (Table 6):[47]

Table 6. RV Adjective construction table (the number before the schema of the construction refers to frequency)

Adjectives	Number	Percent
1. [...-NM]$_A$-Agr	425	47.6%
1. [root-NM]$_A$-Agr	425	47.6%
2. [...]$_N$-[...]$_N$-Agr	184	20.6%
2. [...]$_N$-[root-NM]$_N$-Agr	118	13.2%
6. [...]$_N$-[noun]$_N$-Agr	52	5.8%

(*Continued*)

---

47. Constructions with a frequency below 1% are not exemplified. Comparative and superlative suffixes are treated differently depending on the construction in which they appear: the suffix *-tama-* is glossed as NM if attached to a root and as ADJ if attached to a derived stem. Moreover, in order not to multiply the construction types, comparative and superlative suffixes are disregarded if attached to simple adjectives or to adjectives already attached to *taddʰita* suffixes: this means that *návīyasā* 'newer' (6.16.21^a) is included in the [adjective]-Agr pattern, but *vīrávattamam* 'the richest in heroes' (1.1.3^c) is counted as an instance of the [noun]-ADJ-Agr pattern.

Table 6. (*Continued*)

Adjectives	Number	Percent
9. [...]_N-[root]_N-Agr	7	0.8%
10. [...]_N-[noun-ADJ]_N-Agr	6	0.7%
14. [...]_N-[root-NM-ADJ]_N-Agr	1	0.1%
3. Pre-[...]_N-Agr	133	14.9%
3. Pre-[root-NM]_N-Agr	103	11.5%
8. Pre-[noun]_N-Agr	23	2.6%
11. Pre-[...]-[root-NM]_N-Agr	3	0.3%
12. Pre-[root]-Agr	3	0.3%
13. Pre-[...]-[root]-Agr	1	0.1%
4. [...]_N-ADJ-Agr	94	10.5%
5. [noun]_N-ADJ-Agr	54	6.1%
7. [root-NM]_N-ADJ-Agr	40	4.5%
5. [...]_A-Agr	56	6.3%
4. [adjective]_A-Agr	56	6.3%
Total	**892**	**100%**

If the constructions are grouped under the class of the lexical items they are constructed upon, it comes out that in the RV the most typical lexeme class used to build the Adjective construction is not the class of simple adjectives, as in Latin, but rather the class of verbal roots and, specifically, verbal roots of quality meaning. See Table 7:

Table 7. RV Adjective constructions table (version 2)

Adjectives	Number	Percent
1. root	**701**	**78.4%**
1. [root-NM]_A-	425	47.6%
1. [root-NM]_A-Agr	425	47.6%
2. [root-NM]_N-	265	33.6%
2. [...]_N-[root-NM]_N-Agr	118	13.2%
3. Pre-[root-NM]_N-Agr	103	11.5%
7. [root-NM]_N-ADJ-Agr	40	4.5%
13. [...]_N-[root-NM-ADJ]_N-Agr	1	0.1%
11. Pre-[...]-[root-NM]_N-Agr	3	0.3%

(*Continued*)

Table 7. (*Continued*)

Adjectives	Number	Percent
3. [root]-	11	9.8%
9. [...]$_N$-[root]$_N$-Agr	7	0.8%
12. Pre-[root]-Agr	3	0.3%
14. Pre-[...]-[root]-Agr	1	0.1%
2. noun	134	15.2%
5. [noun]-ADJ-Agr	53	6.1%
6. [...]$_N$-[noun]-Agr	52	5.8%
8. Pre-[noun]$_N$-Agr	23	2.6%
10. [...]$_N$-[noun-ADJ]$_N$-Agr	6	0.7%
3. adjective	56	6.3%
4. [adjective]-Agr	56	6.3%
Total	892	100%

If these constructions are mapped on the PoS table in Table 1, the following construction table is obtained (Table 8):

Table 8. RV construction table (the root-and-pattern analysis of the verb is accepted)

	Referent	Modifier	Predicate
Object	[noun]-Case	----	----
Quality	----	[root-NM]-Agr	----
Action	----	----	[root-AFF]-Pers

As distinct from Latin, constructions [...]-Case, [...]-Agr and [...]-Pers define only two major classes of lexemes in the RV, since the root, joined to different affixes, is the most typical filler both of the [...]-Agr and of the [...]-Pers constructions.

Saying that only two classes of lexemes are found in the RV is an oversimplification. A class of primary adjectives is found, but the class is notably small. In Grassmann's dictionary (1976[5]), bar function words, 1007 primary lexemes are listed: 565 roots (56%); 410 primary nouns (40%); 38 primary adjectives (4%), as shown in Table 9:[48]

---

48. Strictly speaking, Grassmann lists 34 primary adjectives, to which 4 further cases have been added by Alfieri (2016). The list is the following: *aghá-* 'bad', *ánūna-* 'complete', *árbʰa-* 'little', *ásita-* 'black', *āmá-* 'raw', *āhanás-* 'swollen', *āśú-* 'fast', *írya-* 'active', *udumbalá-* 'reddish',

Table 9. RV lexicon (1 = roots, 2 = nouns, 3 = adjectives)

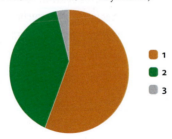

In the RV, therefore, a small class of adjectives is found. But languages with small classes of adjectives (usually 10–20 members, see Dixon 2004: 10) are often merged with languages "without adjectives", since in both cases the most typical Adjective construction is not coded by a dedicated class of adjectival lexemes stored in the lexicon. Instead, it is coded by a complex construction built by the noun-like or the verb-like lexemes that refer to quality meanings.

Moreover, simple adjectives are not only scanty in number in the RV. If those continuing a PIE adjective are excluded (āmá-, nagná-, mádʰu-, etc.), Vedic adjectives are etymologically derived from verbal roots and underwent a lexicalization process at some intermediate stage between PIE, Indo-Iranian and the RV. Skt. gurú- 'heavy' is etymologically traceable to *gr̯̄- 'be tired, onerous' (VIA 403), from PIE *gʷerh₂- (see Lat. gravis 'heavy', Gk. βαρύς 'id.'); the root *gr̯̄- is found in a handful of derivatives such as gárīyas- 'heavier', gariṣṭʰa- 'heaviest', grávan- 'a (heavy) stone for pressing the soma' (EWAia 490), but the word-formation rules needed to build them are not synchronically productive in the RV. Therefore, gurú- cannot be productively (that is, synchronically) derived from *gr̯̄-, but the relation between the two forms is etymologically (that is, diachronically) clear.[49]

To sum up, in the RV a different organization is found on the lexeme and on the construction or word layer. On the lexeme layer, only two major word classes

---

éni- and éta- 'dappled, rushing', kalmalīkín 'brown', kalyá- 'lovely, beautiful', kr̥ṣṇá- 'black', gurú- 'heavy', tílvila- 'rich', tīvrá- 'sharp', dīná- 'weak', dīrgʰá- 'long', nagná- 'naked', náva- 'new', nīla-° 'dark', palitá- 'grey', purú- 'many', pū́rva- 'former', babʰrú- 'brown', bradʰná- 'pale red', mádʰu- 'sweet', mádʰya- 'middle', yaśás- 'glorious', pāpá- 'bad', pŕ̥śni- 'spotted', róhita- 'red', śabála 'dappled', sána- 'old', stʰūrá- 'dense, thick'. These adjectives do not fall exactly in Dixon's list of basic adjectival meanings.

49. For an analysis of all of the RV primary adjectives, see Alfieri (2016: 152–4). The theoretical basis of that analysis is laid down by the group of Natural Morphology (Mayerthaler 1981; Dressler 1987; Panagl 1987), which investigated how semantic and formal opacity interact to determine the autonomous storage of formerly derived items. On the topic, see also Bertram, Schreuder & Baayen (2000).

are found – primary nouns and roots – in addition to a small set of primary adjectives that, as a rule, are historically derived from verbal roots. Derivation mirrors the twofold division of the lexicon: primary or *kṛt* suffixes attach only to roots and build derived nominal stems, whereas and secondary or *taddʰita* suffixes attach to simple or derived nominal stems and build secondarily derived nominal stems (see Section 3). Some (primary and secondary) derived nominals are more readily used as nouns, some others are more readily used as adjectives, but many of them can be either nouns or adjectives, depending on the context. At the levels of syntax, the sum of simple adjectives and derived adjectives determines the birth of a third major class of constructions, the Adjective. The three classes of construction are defined through almost the same inflectional features that are found in Latin, although some of the criteria that distinguish the Adjective and the Noun construction in Latin do not hold in Sanskrit. Therefore, while in Latin the 'adjective' is a class of simple lexemes, a class of derived stems and a class of words, in the RV it is a class of words, but is not or is only limitedly a class of simple lexemes and a class of derived stems (Table 10):

Table 10. RV PoS table (the arrow signalling the processing of derived nouns is dotted, since it does not represent the most common strategy for coding the Noun)

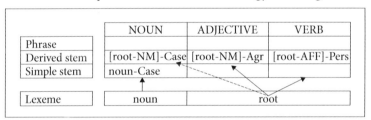

In sum, the difference between the PoS systems in Latin and in RV Sanskrit does not lie in the features that define the classes of words, it rather lies in three facts: i) the number of major classes of lexemes (three major classes in Latin, only two in the RV); ii) the level at which the most typical Adjective construction is grammaticalized, that is to say fixed (the simple stem in Latin, the derived stem in the RV); iii) the categoriality (that is, the function) of the verbal lexeme (a monocategorial unit that typically enters only the Verb construction in addition to some Noun and Adjective constructions in Latin, a pre-categorial or poly-categorial unit that typically codes the Verb and the Adjective constructions in addition to quite a few Noun constructions in RV Sanskrit).[50] Traditional Sanskrit grammars, which tend

---

50. On the notion of pre-categoriality, see Bisang (2008) and below Section 7.

to conflate all the levels of language structures into a single word layer, just as Latin grammars do, usually disregard these differences (or describe them only indirectly and in a very limited manner) by saying – again, quite simplistically – that the PoS system in Latin and in RV Sanskrit are almost identical, although in Sanskrit the adjective is not as clearly distinguished from the noun as it is in Latin (see Section 3).

7. Discussion and conclusion

PoS theory has always swung between the extreme poles of language universalism and language particularism – the two positions of the pendulum described by Bossong (1992, see Introduction). Scholars working in Generative Grammar consider the noun-verb-adjective distinction as universal.[51] Consistently with this view, they developed a morphological theory based on that universality, that is, they consider that lexical morphemes are by nature equivalent to stems and to word-forms, that word-forms (thus also stems and lexemes) are universally divided into the three traditional classes of nouns, verbs and adjectives and that each affix necessarily attaches to a single class of words (noun, verb or adjective) and produces derived words necessarily cast in one of these classes (noun, verb or adjective).[52] Therefore, in their view the term *root* by nature refers to the same type of linguistic unit to which the label 'simple verb stem' is also referred, and the PoS system in Latin is almost identical to that in Sanskrit – a conclusion that is not very different from that reached by traditional Sanskrit philologists, who in practice describe the Sanskrit PoS system through the lens of Latin-based grammar.

On the other hand, many other scholars working in typology think that linguistic forms can be considered as "lacking categoriality completely

---

51. This idea can be traced to Chomsky (1970), and has become the standard in Generative Grammar (see, e.g., Haegeman 1994: 36ff.), but has never been tested empirically, bar Baker's work (2003: 11ff.). However, Baker defines the noun, the verb and the adjective as unweighted bundles of features, so his definition of PoS has the same problems as Dixon's definition of the adjective (see Section 3.1.2).

52. Reference is made to the *Lexicalist Hypothesis*, that is the idea that input-forms for word-formation rules are always words, divided into the universal classes of noun, verb and adjective (Chomsky 1970; Halle 1973: 10; Aronoff 1976: 46), and to the *Unitary Base Hypothesis*, that is the idea that input forms and output forms of word-formation rules must be words – nouns, verbs or adjectives (Aronoff 1974: 47–8; Scalise 1984: 137). Both ideas are at the basis of any version of Generative morphology (see Bauer 2003: 9; Lieber 2010: 3; Aronoff 2012: 29–30), but they have spread also among different frameworks, such as word-based morphology (Matthews 1972: 163 fn. 3, 1974: 40; Booij 2007: 28, 321) and typology (Lehmann 2008).

unless nounhood or verbhood is forced on them by their discourse functions" (Hopper & Thompson 1984: 747, but see also Maranz 1997) or that "languages differ without limits and in unpredictable ways" (Joos 1957: 96) in their lexeme class division. In this latter view, each language defines its own classes, so that the PoS system in Sanskrit can be different from that in Latin, but a consistent typology of lexical inventories across languages cannot be obtained (or at least has not yet been obtained).

The data discussed so far show that both positions are excessive. Languages do not always define the same classes, nor do they avoid defining any class: the number of lexeme classes defined in each single language is a cross-linguistic variable, but a PoS theory that orders such variability can be developed, at least for the IE languages. If the continuum that goes from LANGUAGE to the IE languages is divided into three layers (PoS-concepts, PoS-constructions, PoS-lexemes), an objective method to anchor PoS-constructions to PoS-concepts and an objective method to extract PoS-lexemes from PoS constructions are found, at least two different PoS systems can be defined: type [N, A, V], which is found in Latin and, more generally, in Hengeveld's *specialized* languages (1992: 47ff.), and type [N (AV)], which is found in all of Dixon's verb-adjectival languages (2004) and in the non-specialized languages defined by Hengeveld (1992: 74ff.), be they *flexible* such as Lao or *rigid* such as RV Sanskrit.[53] The PoS system in Sanskrit, therefore, is different from that in Latin and the root is a different unit from the simple verb stem. Both are simple verbal lexemes, but only the Latin verbal lexeme is also a stem (thus, a word-form from which inflections have been subtracted), while the root is the verbal lexeme of a language in which only two major classes of lexemes are found and adjectives are coded verbally. It is a precategorial unit, or a lexeme that assumes stem- or word-form only when it attaches to the derivational morphemes (affixes and ablaut) that specify its categorial status as a noun, a verb or an adjective.[54]

---

53. In both flexible and rigid languages one or more lexical classes are 'lacking' (if compared with the specialized type [N, A, V]). The difference between the two types lies in the strategy used to code the function typically associated with the 'lacking' lexeme class: flexible languages use a single class of lexemes in different functions without any formal change, while in rigid languages a lexeme class is lacking and its function is coded through a periphrasis built on one of the extant lexeme classes (Hengeveld 1992: 65ff.). However, if flexible languages represent a coherent group, whose discovery has led to important generalizations (see fn. 27), rigid languages do not seem to share much among one another, bar their being non-specialized and non-flexible (Alfieri 2013).

54. The formal coding of linguistic functions is arbitrary in principle (Sapir 1921: 59). However, the template and pattern morphology (fn. 39) has an iconic function in IE (and in

If this view is accepted, the universality of the noun-verb-adjective distinction implicitly assumed by Sanskrit scholars and explicitly claimed by Generativists must be abandoned, alongside all of its corollaries, starting from the substantial identity of the PoS systems in Latin and Sanskrit, the structural equivalence between lexemes, stems and word-forms (apart from inflections), and more specifically the functional equivalence between the Sanskrit root and the Latin simple verb stem, on which Generative morphology is based. At the same time, if the method whereby Latin and Sanskrit have been compared is consistent, there is no reason to deny that it can be applied to other languages as well, so as to develop a consistent typology of the lexeme class inventories across languages, just as proposed in the Amsterdam Typology.

Clearly, these conclusions are not right nor wrong absolutely, they are simply consistent with the PoS theory proposed. Nor is the PoS theory right or wrong absolutely, it is arbitrary; one of many possible PoS theories. However, this theory and the results that descend from it can be (simplistically) considered "right" inasmuch as it is useful, that is, inasmuch it leads to relevant insights in language description and comparison. The insights that can be arrived at in Sanskrit descriptive grammar have been described in Section 6. In the following, therefore, the utility of the PoS theory proposed in historical and general-typological linguistics will be discussed.

7.1 Historical IE linguistics

Given the genetic relation between Sanskrit and Latin, the difference between the PoS systems in the two languages must be the result of a diachronic change. Theoretically the change can be either [N (AV)] → [N, A, V] or [N, A, V] → [N (AV)]. However, there are good reasons to think that the direction of the change is [N (AV)] → [N, A, V].

Most of the 38 primary adjective stems in the RV are the result of the autonomous storage of formerly derived items (see Section 6). Moreover, only 9 primary adjective stems are listed in Pokorny's *Indogermanisches etymologisches Wörterbuch* (1956) and only 17 primary adjective stems are found in *Nomina im Indogermanischen Lexikon* by Wodtko et al. (2008): in both cases RV Sanskrit shows more primary adjectives than those that are reconstructed for PIE,

---

Semitic, see Section 7.2): the stems, which are functionally equivalent to word-forms (fn. 10), are fully specified stems also phonetically, but the roots, which are consonantal templates, cannot be uttered nor be attached to endings if they are not endowed with the vowel patterns that specify their categorial and phonological status.

supporting the idea of a progressive lexicalization of a major class of primary adjectival stems through time.

Moreover, Ancient Greek is intermediate between RV Sanskrit and Latin, as Hittite may also be, while Avestan patterns rather with Vedic. A large class of simple adjectives is found in Greek: βαρύς 'heavy', ἀγαθός 'good', μέλας 'black', etc., but the first adjective in the extant Greek literature is a participle: μῆνιν... οὐλομένην "[Achilleus'] destructive wrath" (A.1–2), and deverbal adjectives are frequent and are formed productively in the Homeric language (κλυτός 'famous', Skt. śrutá-). The idea of a typological change is therefore consistent not only with the situation in Sanskrit and Latin, but also in Ancient Greek, Avestan and probably Hittite.

In addition, it is well known that the history of the IE family has been characterized by a progressive decrease in the index of gross complexity (the average number of morphemes per word) over time. This decrease is mainly due to the blurring of intra-word morpheme boundaries, especially those between the root and word-formation suffixes (including the stem vowel). In turn, this blurring triggered the change from the root-based word-formation typical of early Vedic, Hittite and Homeric Greek to the stem- or word-based word-formation typical of Latin, Old High German, English and Persian.[55] The blurring affected all types of derived words in the same way: nouns, verbs and adjectives. And probably the lexicalization of derived nouns and of derived verb stems was more evident than the autonomous storage of derived adjectives, given the larger number of nouns and verbs in the lexicon. However, from the typological point of view, the lexicalization of adjectives represented the most important part of the change, since it caused the lexicalization of a third major class of lexemes and the subsequent change from the rigid to the specialized PoS system (that is, [N (AV)] → [N, A, V]).

As a consequence, lexemes that are intermediate between true verb stems, precategorial verbal lexemes (i.e., synchronic roots) and diachronic roots (see fn. 4) are common in the history of IE languages. Coming from the same antecedent (i.e., PIE *tep-), the Latin root *tep- in tepeo 'I warm', tepor 'heat' and tepidus 'warm' and the Sanskrit root tap- in tápati 'he warms, burns', tápas- 'heat', tapú- 'hot' may

---

55. The evidence of this blurring is discussed by Belardi (1985, 1990, 1993) and Cipriano (1988) for derived nouns; by Cipriano (2001, 2007) and Di Giovine, Flamini & Pozza (2007) for derived verbs; by Alfieri (2016, 2018) for derived adjectives; by Belardi (2002a, 2002b) and Di Giovine (2001) for their general methodological consequences. See Cowgill (1963) on the decrease of the index of gross complexity and Panagl (1982, 1987, 2006) on the decrease in the productivity of nominalizations. On the change from root-based athematic morphology to the stem-, or later word-based, thematic morphology, especially in Germanic languages, see Kastovsky (1992, 1996).

easily seem to be the same type of unit. However, Skt. *tápati, tápas-* and *tapú-* are the result of productive word-formation rules, so *tap-* is a synchronic and precategorial unit. On the contrary, Lat. **tep-* is not the input form for productive word-formation rules in Latin. Only the stems *tepe-, tepid-*, and *tepor-* play such a role: *tepe-faci-o* 'I make hot', *tepid-arium* 'heated room in Roman baths' and *tepor-us* 'hot'. The form **tep-*, therefore, was a precategorial unit at some intermediate stage between PIE and Latin, but when Caesar crossed the Rubicon, say, it was already a semi-frozen lexeme or a diachronic unit (a diachronic root), just like the English 'root' [-sijv] in *de-ceive, con-ceive, per-ceive* quoted by Bloomfield (1933: 240), which English speakers can perceive but do not process to build new words.[56]

The IE family therefore attests a deep typological change in the PoS system, namely the change from type [N (AV)], which is still well preserved in the Rig-Veda, to type [N, A, V], which is found in Latin and in almost all the other, especially modern and Western IE, languages. The factual evidence of the change is well known to specialists in IE study, but it has never been interpreted in a coherent typological framework and many scholars, consciously or otherwise, still tend to equate the root with the simple verb stem, or with a diachronic unit, as if the change in PoS typology, as well as the difference between root- and stem-based word-formation, was the result only of a diachronic change, rather than being the result of both a typological and a diachronic change.[57]

7.2 Linguistic terminology

As clearly pointed out in the CC debate, labelling a category (that is, assigning a label to a distributional set of regularities) and identifying a category (that is, selecting a specific set of distributional regularities among the almost infinite sets of distributional regularities that can be defined across languages) are totally different things.[58] Both operations are arbitrary, though in a different sense. The CCs used in research trigger the identification of certain categories among the almost infinite categories that can be defined across languages: the categories identified, therefore, are indirectly arbitrary, since they logically descend from arbitrary CCs.

---

56. Units such as Engl. -[sijv] are 'quasi-morphemes' (Aronoff 1976: 11ff.). They are less transparent and less productive than 'blocked morphemes' (e.g., *cran-* in *cranberry*, see Mel'čuk 1982). They therefore represent the boundary between synchrony and diachrony (or between word-formation and etymology), but are already cast on the diachronic side of the boundary.

57. On the confusion between the diachronic and the typological value of the notion of 'root' in IE linguistics, see at least Belardi (1990, 1993, 2002: I, 256ff., 2008), Alfieri (2014c) and the references in Alfieri (2016: 133–6).

58. See LaPolla (2016: 365ff.) and Croft (2016: 387ff.) on this point.

On the other hand, the labels that refer to the categories are totally arbitrary: the same category can be labelled *verb, X_1, Jack* or *Ciro* without any consequence for the descriptive adequacy of the theory, as long as the labels selected avoid ambiguity. Any discourse on terminology, therefore, has to start from categories and discuss category labels subsequently.

If PoS-concepts are excluded, 8 categories have been defined in the paper: 3 construction classes (*Noun, Adjective, Verb*); 4 lexeme classes (*noun, adjective, verb, root*); 1 default category referring to any simple lexical unit (*lexical morph(eme)* or *lexeme*). All these categories have been defined on the basis of what Haspelmath (this volume) terms *retro-definitions* that is, definitions that "assign a precise meaning to an existing term that does not have a widely recognized precise meaning yet". Indeed, they comply with the adequacy criterion proposed by Hasplemath: "an established term should not be defined in such a way that its definition is at variance with its traditional use. It should cover the core of the phenomena designated by the term (as generally understood), it should cover at least 80% of the cases where the term has been applied, and it should not include too many cases which would not be included traditionally". However, not all these categories comply with Haspelmath's criterion in the same way, so they will be analysed individually.

The categories of *noun, verb* and *adjective* defined in Latin, and Western grammar generally, are the product of a "lexicalist" approach, which neutralizes (or, more precisely, fails to distinguish) the difference between PoS-constructions and PoS-lexemes (or, more precisely, between stem classes and morpheme classes) in the classical, inflectional notion of *word*, which can be simple or derived with no difference.[59] In the paper, therefore, we have confined ourselves to dividing the two levels and identifying the prototypical function of the traditional notions of *noun, verb* and *adjective*, with little change in the canonical reference of these labels. The sum of the noun lexemes and the Noun constructions in Latin, therefore, covers most of the phenomena designated through the label of *noun* in traditional grammars, probably about 80%, as Haspelmath's criterion requires (only non-prototypical nouns meaning Actions and Quality being excluded from the comparative definitions of Noun/noun). And the same holds true for the traditional labels of *adjective* and *verb*.

---

59. Saying that the Latin-based PoS theory and, generally, all the linguistic theory up to the 19th century is strictly lexicalist is a commonplace (see the literature in Alfieri 2013b, 2014c): before Bopp the word was not only the most important unit of language, it was also its minimum unit, and was divided into the universal classes of nouns, verbs and adjectives.

Slightly more complex is the use of the label of *root*. We have already said (see fn. 4), that the term *root* can refer to both a synchronic and a diachronic unit. The synchronic use of the term *root* is traced to Indian native grammar and to the Western grammars of Sanskrit from the 17th century onwards, where it refers to Sanskrit simple verbal units, which – as we showed – are synchronic and precategorial. Moreover, the term *root* is common in Arabic and Hebrew grammar (Ar. *aṣl-* 'root, trunk') and in Western grammars of the Semitic languages from the 16th century onwards, where it refers to a simple verbal unit. However, Arabic grammars usually admit that the adjective is a class of derived stems (Wright 1979: 106): the adjectives *kabīr* 'big', *ṣādiq* 'true', *saʿb* 'hard', etc. are formed with the same vowel patterns found in derived nouns (*raʾīs* 'chief', *kātib* 'writer', *dars* 'studying') and the roots *k.b.r.* 'become big, grow up', *s.d.q.* 'tell the truth', and *sʿ.b.* 'be hard' can be used verbally, just like the verbal roots *d.r.s.* 'to study' and *k.t.b.* 'to write', at least in the classical language (Ar. *huwa kabura* 'he grew old [3SG.M big<PST>3SG.M]', lit. 'he became big', from *k.b.r.* '(to be) big').[60] Therefore Arabic and, more generally, Semitic roots can be considered precategorial, like Sanskrit roots, and Arabic – especially Classical Arabic – can easily fall into the same PoS type [N (AV)] as RV Sanskrit. In this case, we simply redefined the unit traditionally termed as *root* in Indian and Arabic grammar from a functional-typological point of view, without any change in its original reference. My label of *root* thus covers almost 100% of the phenomena where the term has been applied in Indian and Arabic native grammar, as well as in Indian and Arabic grammars written by western scholars.

Much more complex is the case of the label used to refer to the 'simple lexical unit'. Dictionaries of linguistics and manuals of morphology usually define the *root* as "that part of a word-form which remains when all inflectional [...] and derivational [...] affixes have been removed" (Bauer 2003: 340, following Bopp 1824: 126) or "the simplest possible form of a lexical morpheme" (Trask 1993: 224). On this basis, Haspelmath (2012), following Dixon (2004: 2), proposed the use of the term *root* to refer to 'any simple lexical unit', rather than the labels of *lexeme* or *lexical morpheme*, as we have done in this paper. On the one hand, Haspelmath's proposal is natural, since the ambiguity of the terms *morph(eme)* and *lexeme* are

---

60. See Stassen (1997: 158) on the verbal coding of the Arabic quality predicate; Jelinek & Deemers (1994: 710ff.) on the precategoriality of Semitic roots; the references in Alfieri (2016: 130, fn. 1) for the psycholinguistic reality of the root in Semitics; Troupeau (1984), Rousseau (1989) and Alfieri (2017) on the history of the notion of root in Semitic studies; Alfieri (2014c) on the history of this notion in Sanskrit philology. Harris (1946: 166) noticed that stems are units of lexical storage in Latin, though not in Sanskrit and in Arabic, where they are only secondarily derived units, bar the existence of a few primary noun stems.

well known (see fn. 2), speaking of *lexical roots* meaning 'lexical morph(eme)s' is common, and in many languages with rich morphology distinguishing the inflectional stem from the root (i.e., the stem without the stem forming affix) is useful, although the root so defined is not always a completely synchronic unit (see Section 7.1). On the other hand, such a proposal is highly ambiguous, since it does not comply, or complies only partly, with the general adequacy criterion for retro-definitions proposed by Haspelmath himself.

The standard definition of the term *root* in dictionaries is unquestionable in practice, because it refers to any lexical simple unit, and the theory of general linguistics so far has included such a unit. However, this use contrasts with the traditional use of the term *root* in Sanskrit and Arabic grammar, where only verbal items are defined as *roots*, simple nouns, pronouns, adjectives and particles being labelled with different terms. On the other hand, it is very ambiguous from a theoretical point of view, since it hides the difference between a diachronic unit reconstructed by the linguist, e.g., Engl. -[sijv] and Lat. *tep- (or Lat. *am- in *amāre*, which is the paramount example of the notion of *root* in dictionaries), and a synchronic unit used by speakers as an input form for productive word-formation rules, e.g., Lat. *tepē-* or Engl. *sing-*. Moreover, in Sanskrit and Arabic, roots are synchronic and precategorial, so they differ both from the Latin verbal units such as *tepē-*, which are monocategorial, and from the Proto-Latin or English roots such as *tep- or -[sijv] which are diachronic units. If the term *root* was used to refer to any simple lexical unit, in other words, it would hide the difference between a diachronic unit (Proto-Lat. *tep-, Engl. -[sijv]), a synchronic monocategorial unit (Lat. *tepē-*, Engl. *sing-*), and a synchronic precategorial unit (Skt. *tap-*, Ar. *d.r.s.*), triggering the unwarranted inference that Proto-Lat. *tep-, Engl. -[sijv], Lat. *tepē-*, Engl. *sing-*, Skt. *tap-* and Ar. *d.r.s.* represent the same type of unit, since they are referred to with the same label, which is clearly not the case.[61] Haspelmath's use of the label of *root*, therefore, assumes the dictionary definition of the term *root* as the "traditional use", but he does not realize that this traditional use is intrinsically biased by the same confusion between single language grammar, diachrony and typology on which Bopp's original definition of the notion of root was based, a confusion that can be avoided if (and only if) our CC of root is retro-defined starting from the "traditional use" of such term in Indian and Arabic grammar.[62]

---

61. A part of this ambiguity was acknowledged by Mugdan (2015: 257), who noticed that many definitions of the term *root*, especially those cast in a Generative framework, are in fact definitions of what is commonly considered a *stem*.

62. On the confusion between synchrony, diachrony and typology in the definition of the *root* in 19th century IE linguistics, see Alfieri (2013b, 2014c).

7.3 Further research prospects

The PoS theory proposed in Section 4 was applied only to two genetically related languages. Still, if the method employed to classify the lexeme class system in Latin and in Sanskrit is consistent, it can be applied to other cases as well. In fact, even if we confine ourselves to unmarked correlations (Noun, Adjective and Verb), at least five different types of lexical inventories can be defined consistently.

If these three constructions define three different classes of simple lexemes, the lexical structure is [N, A, V] and the simple lexemes typically associated with Noun, Adjective and Verb constructions are termed as *nouns, adjectives* and *verbs* respectively. This is the situation in Latin and English, but also in Amele, Bukip and Dyirbal.[63] On the other hand, if the three constructions projected on the map are prototypically filled with only two classes of lexemes, then the lexical structure can be [N (AV)] if a single class of lexemes enters both Verb and Adjective constructions, as in RV Sanskrit, Garo, Lao and Yimas, or [(NA) V] if a single class of lexemes enters both Noun and Adjective constructions, as in Quechua.[64] In the latter case, precategorial lexemes can be called *nominals* rather than nouns, while in the latter they are called *verbal roots* or verbal *types* rather than *verbs*, because in both cases these lexemes are distributionally different from standard nouns and verbs.[65] If the three environments Noun, Verb and Adjective define a single class of lexemes, which can enter each of these constructions without differences, then a single class of lexical items is found, as may be the case in Late Archaic Chinese, Riau Indonesian and Kharia.[66] In this case, the lexical structure is [(NAV)] and the single class of lexemes is termed as *contentive*. To these, also type [(NA) (AV)] may

---

63. See Croft (2001: 88–9) on English and Alfieri (2014a) on the other cases.

64. See Alfieri (2014a) on Garo, Lao and Yimas and Quechua. Floyd (2011) showed that nominals meaning qualities and nominals meaning actions are distributionally different in Quechua. But none of their differences concern the prototypical Noun and Adjective constructions, so Quechua nominals are interchangeable in these two environments. On this point, see also Haspelmath (2012: 116ff.).

65. The term *type* was used by Broschart (1997) and Vogel (2000) with reference to the precategorial verbal units that are found in the analytic languages of South-east Asia, while *root* is limited to the Sanskrit and Semitic languages. However, from the functional point of view *types* are *roots* are the same type of precategorial unit, and the term root has often been used also with reference to the analytic and precategorial verbal morphemes in Chinese (e.g., Gabelentz 1811: 90).

66. The first candidates for this type were Salish, Tongan and Mundari (see Hengeveld, Rijkhoff & Siewierska 2004 and Hengeveld & Rijkhoff 2005), but the monocategorial interpretation of these languages has been rejected in recent years (see the references in fn. 11 for Salish and Mundari and Völkel 2017 for Tongan). However, Late Archaic Chinese (Bisang

be added, if the ADJECTIVE slot is split between two constructions with almost the same frequency and the lexemes are divided in two classes, roots and nominals, as in Japanese and Wari'.[67] The lexical inventories discussed so far are summed up in the following table (Table 11):

Table 11. The major lexeme inventories across languages

Lexical inventories	Languages
[N, A, V]	English, Amele, Bukip, Dyirbal
[N (AV)]	Lao, Garo, Yimas
[(NA) V]	Quechua
[(NAV)]	Kharia, Late Archaic Chinese, Riau Indonesian
[(NA) (AV)]	Japanese, Wari'

At present, not all these inventories are equally agreed: types [N, A, V], [N (AV)] and [(NA) V] are often accepted in the literature on adjectival typology, while type [(NA) (AV)] is rarely found and type [(NAV)] is looked at suspiciously outside the Amsterdam Typology. On a future occasion, I will try to show that all the types are acceptable on the cross-linguistic level. However, at present we can confine ourselves to saying that if the PoS theory proposed in Section 4 is accepted, a similar typology of lexical inventories across languages is possible in principle.

In turn, if a similar typology is accepted, at least in its application in IE languages, a better understanding of the relation between DCs and CCs can be obtained. If the theory of LANGUAGE really aims to be general, it must have a space for all the units that are found in single languages. This does not mean that the categories in the two domains coincide. Quite the contrary. All the concepts required to descend from the study of the LANGUAGE to the study of groups of languages defined by some kind of coding similarities are CCs, rather than DCs. But CCs can refer to different levels of generality, and at the lowest level a CC is not very different from a DC shared by two or more languages. Therefore, any DC must have its own space in (the lowest level of) the general theory of language, although at this level it has a space not as an individual, with all the idiosyncratic features of individuals, but rather as a member of a group of units that function alike with respect to some abstract, functional feature arbitrarily identified by the researcher.

2008), Kharia (Peterson 2005, 2011, 2013) and Riau Indonesian (Gil 2000, 2013) are still good candidates.

67. On Wari', see Everett & Kern (1997); on Japanese, see Uehara (1998), Lombardi Vallauri (2000) and Backhouse (2004).

If this view is accepted, CCs are not unrelated to DCs, rather they may also act as a tool for clarifying aspects of single language grammar (e.g., the structure of Sanskrit lexeme class system, the secondary nature of its adjective class, the functional difference between the Sanskrit root and the Latin verb stem, the neutralization of simple and derived stems in Latin grammar, the different functions and different productivity of word-formation in Latin and in Sanskrit, etc.), for studying the dynamics of language change, which is necessarily a history of individuals (Saussure 1922: 134), and for arriving at a better understanding of contemporary linguistic terminology.

In sum, at present we do not know which functional features are needed to describe the DCs in single languages consistently, nor which type of CCs should be used in each case. We may presume that each linguistic phenomenon should be described through a different system of CCs in terms of number, type and level of generality, but an agreed method to operationalize such idea has yet to be found. However, if the interaction of PoS-concepts, PoS-constructions and PoS-lexemes is accepted as a consistent method to analyse the continuum that goes from LANGUAGE to individual languages in the field of PoS, the above PoS theory or, more precisely, the above theory of lexeme class division may play a pivotal role in the general theory of language (that is, in the empirical-typological version of UG defined in the Introduction), just it played a pivotal role in the foundations of single language grammar in Greek-Latin times.[68]

List of abbreviations

ABL	ablative	ADJ	adjectivalizer
ACC	accusative	AFF	affix
AG	Ragreement	AOR	aorist

---

68. I prefer the label *General Grammar* (GG) to *Universal Grammar* (UG), so as to stress that the theory of LANGUAGE is general, though not universal, as it is based on arbitrary CCs and on historically determined empirical generalizations, which may change if the CCs used to detect them are changed or improved with the enlargement of the data. Moreover, the labels *PoS theory* and *theory of lexical inventories* are not equivalent. PoS theory is the sum of two theories, a theory of lexeme class division and a theory of the levels of language analysis at which constructions are fixed (Lazard 1999; Alfieri 2014a). Iroquoian languages have been said to lack nouns, but also to define the noun above the lexicon, thanks to the cooperation of various morphological and syntactic constructions (Mithun 2000). However, the morphology-syntax divide, which is the only theory of the levels of language analysis available at present, is inconsistent across languages (Haspelmath 2011, but already Saussure 1922: 186ff.), so also this aspect of PoS theory has not arrived at any consensus.

CC	comparative concept	OPT	optative
COMP	comparative	PERS	person
SBJ	subjunctive	(P)IE	(Proto)-Indo-European
GEN	genitive	PF	perfect
DC	descriptive categories	PL	plural
DAT	dative	POS	parts of speech
DU	dual	PRS	present
F	feminine	PRE	prefix
INS	instrumental	PRS	present
IPT	imperative	PST	past
LOC	locative	PTC	participle
M	masculine	RV	Rg-Veda
MD	middle	SG	singular
NM	nominalizer	INS	instrumental
NOM	nominative	SUP	superlative
NT	neuter	VOC	vocative

References

Alfieri, Luca. Forthcoming. The lexicalization of the adjective as an innovative feature in the Indo-European Family. *Poznań Studies in Contemporary Linguistics* 36(3): 379–412.

Alfieri, Luca. 2018. La definizione tipologica della radice e la teoria del segno lessicale. In *Linguistica filologia e storia culturale. In ricordo di Palmira Cipriano*, Alfieri Luca, Benvenuto Maria Carmela, Ciancaglini Claudia Angela, De Angelis Alessandro, Milizia Paolo & Pompeo Flavia (eds), 25–44. Roma: Il Calamo.

Alfieri, Luca. 2017. A proposito di Thomas Lindner, *200 Jahre Indogermanistik* (Salzburg-Wien 2016), ovvero la rilevanza della *Grammer* di Ravio (1648) per la storia della linguistica indoeuropea. *Archivio Glottologico Italiano* 102(2): 225–237.

Alfieri, Luca. 2016. The typological definition of the (apparently historical) notion of root. *Archivio Glottologico Italiano* 102(1): 129–169.

Alfieri, Luca. 2014a. Qualifying modifier encoding and adjectival typology. In Simone & Masini (eds), 119–139.

Alfieri, Luca. 2014b. The birth of a grammatical category: The case of the adjective class. *Studi e Saggi Linguistici* 52(1): 141–175.

Alfieri, Luca. 2014c. The arrival of the Indian notion of root into Western linguistics. *Rivista degli Studi Orientali* 87(2): 59–84.

Alfieri, Luca. 2013a. Review of: Ansaldo, Umberto, Don, Jan & Pfau, Roland (eds.). 2010. *Parts of Speech: Empirical and Theoretical Advances. Special issue of Studies in Language* 37(2): 425–434.

Alfieri, Luca. 2013b. L'ipotesi indoeuropea di Bopp e il problema del contatto tra grammatiche. In *Le lingue del Mediterraneo antico. Culture, mutamenti, contatti*, Mancini Marco & Lorenzetti Luca (eds), 15–35. Roma: Carocci.

Alfieri, Luca. 2009. La categoria dell'aggettivo in vedico. *Archivio Glottologico Italiano* 94(1): 3–41.

Anslado, Umberto & Don, Jan & Pfau, Roland (eds). 2010. *Parts of Speech. Empirical and Theoretical Advances. Special issue of Studies in Language* 32(3), 2008. See Alfieri (2013) for review.

Anward, Jan. 2000. A dynamic model of part-of-speech differentiation. In Vogel & Comrie (eds), 3–45.

Anward, Jan & Moravcsik, Edith & Stassen, Leon. 1997. Parts of speech: A challenge for typology. *Linguistic Typology* 1(2): 167–183. https://doi.org/10.1515/lity.1997.1.2.167

Aronoff, Mark. 2012. Morphological stems: What William of Ockham really said. *Word Structure* 5: 28–51. https://doi.org/10.3366/word.2012.0018

Aronoff, Mark. 1994. *Morphology by Itself. Stem and Inflectional Classes.* Cambridge MA: The MIT Press.

Aronoff, Mark. 1976. *Word-Formation in Generative Grammar.* Cambridge MA: The MIT Press.

Backhouse, Anthony E. 2004. Inflected and uninflected adjectives in Japanese. In Dixon & Aikhenvald (eds), 50–73.

Baker, Mark C. 2003. *Lexical Categories. Verbs, Nouns, and Adjectives.* Oxford: OUP. https://doi.org/10.1017/CBO9780511615047

Bauer, Laurie. 2003. *Introducing Linguistic Morphology.* Washington DC: Georgetown University Press.

Beck, David. 2016. Some language-particular terms are comparative concepts. *Linguistic Typology* 20(2): 995–402. https://doi.org/10.1515/lingty-2016-0013

Beck, David. 2013. Unidirectional flexibility and the noun-verb distinction in Lushootseed. In Rijkhoff & van Lier (eds), 185–220.

Beck, David. 2002. *The Typology of Parts of Speech Systems: The Markedness of Adjectives.* London: Routledge.

Belardi, Walter. 2008. Le "unità di lingua concrete", la parola e la frase. *Incontri Linguistici* 31: 11–39.

Belardi, Walter. 2002a. *L'etimologia nella storia della cultura occidentale*, 2 vols. Roma: Il Calamo.

Belardi, Walter. 2002b. *Il tema del segno lessicale nella diacronia linguistica.* Roma: Il Calamo.

Belardi, Walter. 1993. Sulla tipologia della struttura formale della parola nelle lingue indoeuropee. *Rendiconti dell'Accademia Nazionale dei Lincei, s. 9, v. 4, f.* 4: 525–570.

Belardi, Walter. 1990. Genealogia, tipologia, ricostruzione, leggi fonetiche. In *Linguistica, filologia e critica dell'espressione*, Walter Belardi (ed.), 155–218. Roma: Il Calamo.

Belardi, Walter. 1985. Considerazioni sulla ricostruzione dell'indoeuropeo. In *Tra linguistica storica e linguistica generale. Scritti in onore di Tristano Bolelli*, Ambrosini Roberto (ed.), 39–66. Pisa: Giardini.

Benedetti, Marina (ed.). 2001. *Fare etimologia. Passato, presente e future nella ricerca etimologica. Atti del convegno tenutosi presso l'Università per Stranieri di Siena, 2–3 ottobre 1998.* Roma: il Calamo.

Benveniste, Émile. 1962³[1936¹]. *Origines de la formation des noms en indo-européen.* Paris: Adrienne-Maisonneuve.

Bertram, Raymond & Schreuder, Robert & Baayen, Harald R. 2000. The balance of storage and computation in morphological processing: The role of word formation type, affixal homonymy and productivity. *Journal of Experimental Psychology: Learning, Memory and Cognition* 26(2): 489–511.

Bhat, Darbhe Narayana Shankara. 2000. Word classes and sentential function. In Vogel & Comrie (eds), 47–64.

Bhat, Darbhe Narayana Shankara. 1994. *The Adjectival Category. Criteria for Differentiation and Identification* [Studies in Language Companion Series 24]. Amsterdam: John Benjamins. https://doi.org/10.1075/slcs.24

Bisang, Walter. 2013. Word-classes. In *The Oxford Handbook of Linguistic Typology*, Song Jae Jung (ed.), 280–302. Oxford: OUP.

Bisang, Walter. 2008. Precategoriality and syntax based parts of speech: The case of Late Archaic Chinese. *Studies in Language* 32(3): 65–86. https://doi.org/10.1075/sl.32.3.05bis

Bloomfield, Leonard. 1933. *Language*. New York NY: Henry Holt.

Blevins, James P. 2016. *Word and Paradigm Morphology*. Oxford: OUP. https://doi.org/10.1093/acprof:oso/9780199593545.001.0001

Booij, Gert. 2007 [2015]¹. *The Grammar of Words. An Introduction to Linguistic Morphology*. Oxford: OUP. https://doi.org/10.1093/acprof:oso/9780199226245.001.0001

Booij, Gert, Lehman, Christian & Mugdan, Joachim (eds). 2000-2004. *Morphology. An International Handbook on Inflection and Word-formation*, Vol. 1 (2000); Vol. 2 (2004). Berlin: Mouton de Gruyter.

Bopp, Franz. 1827. *Ausführliches Lehrgebäude der Sanscrita-Sprache*. Berlin: Dümmler.

Bopp, Franz. 1824. Vergleichende Zergliederung des Sanskrits und der mit ihr verwandten Sprachen. *Abhandlungen der Königlichen Akademie der Wissenschaften zu Berlin, philosophische-historische Klasse* 1824: 117–148 (Repr. 1972. *Kleine Schriften zur vergleichende Sprachwissenschaft*, 1–33. Leipzig: Zentralantiquariat der deutschen demokratischen Republik).

Bossong, Georg. 1992. Reflections on the history of the study of universals. The case of the *partes orationis*. In *Meaning and Grammar. Cross-linguistic Perspectives*, Michel Kefer & Johan van der Auwera (eds). *Belgian Journal of Linguistics* 4: 27–51.

Bozzone, Chiara. 2016. The origin of the Caland system and the typology of adjectives. *Indo-European Linguistics* 4: 15–52. https://doi.org/10.1163/22125892-00401003

Broschart, Jürgen. 1997. Why Tongan does it differently: Categorial distinctions in a language without nouns and verbs. *Linguistic Typology* 1: 123–165. https://doi.org/10.1515/lity.1997.1.2.123

Brereton, Joel P. & Jamison, Stephanie W. 2014. *The Rig-Veda. The Earliest Religious Poetry of India*. Oxford: OUP.

Brugmann, Karl. 1904. *Kurze vergleichende Grammatik der indogermanischen Sprachen*. Straßburg: Trubner. https://doi.org/10.1515/9783111556857

Burrow, Thomas. 1955. *The Sanskrit Language*. London: Faber & Faber.

Cardona, George. 1997a[1988]¹. *Pāini. His Work and its Tradition*. Delhi: Motilal Banarsidass.

Cardona, George. 1997b[1976]¹. *Pāini. A Survey of Research*. Delhi: Motilal Banarsidass.

Chomsky, Noam. 1970. Remarks on nominalizations. In *Readings in English Transformational Grammar*, Roderick A. Jacobs & Peter S. Rosenbaum (eds), 184–221. Waltham MA: Ginn.

Cipriano, Palmira. 2007. Evoluzione tipologica e mutamento fonologico nell'area del persiano. *Rendiconti dell'Accademia Nazionale dei Lincei. Classe di Scienze Morali, Storiche e Filologiche s. 9, v. 18, f. 1*: 21–80.

Cipriano, Palmira. 2001. Il ruolo delle etimologie iraniche nello studio dell'indoeuropeo preistorico. In Benedetti (ed.), 107–120.

Cipriano, Palmira. 1988. Le implicazioni metodologiche e fattuali della teoria di W. Belardi sull'indoeuropeo. *Studi e Saggi Linguistici* 28: 101–126.

Corbett, Greville G. 2006. *Agreement*. Cambridge: CUP.

Coseriu, Eugenio. 2001. Les universaux linguistiques (et les autres). In *L'Homme et son langage*, Hiltraud Dupuy-Engelhardt, Jean-Pierre Durafour & Françoise Rastier (eds), 69–107. Louvain: Peeters.

Cowgill, Warren. 1963. A search for universals in Indo-European diachronic morphology. In *Universals of Language*, Joseph H. Greenberg (ed.), 114–141. Cambridge MA: The MIT Press.

Cristofaro, Sonia. 2009. Grammatical categories and relations: Language-universality vs. language-specificity and construction-specificity. *Language and Linguistic Compass* 3(1): 441–479. https://doi.org/10.1111/j.1749-818X.2008.00111.x

Croft, William. 2016. Comparative concepts and language-specific categories: Theory and practice. *Linguistic Typology* 20(2): 377–393. https://doi.org/10.1515/lingty-2016-0012

Croft, William. 2005. Word-classes, parts of speech and syntactic argumentation. *Linguistic Typology* 9: 431–441.

Croft, William. 2001. *Radical Construction Grammar*. Oxford: OUP. https://doi.org/10.1093/acprof:oso/9780198299554.001.0001

Croft, William. 2000. Parts of speech as language universals and language-particular categories. In Vogel & Comrie (eds), 65–102.

Croft, William. 1991. *Syntactic Categories and Grammatical Relations*. Chicago IL: University of Chicago Press.

Croft, William & van Lier, Eva. 2012. Language universals without universal categories. *Theoretical Linguistics* 38(1): 57–72.

Crystal, David. 1967. English word classes. *Lingua* 17: 24–56. https://doi.org/10.1016/0024-3841(66)90003-9

Dahl, Östen. 2016. Thoughts on language-specific and cross-linguistic entities. *Linguistic Typology* 20(2): 427–437. https://doi.org/10.1515/lingty-2016-0016

Dahl, Eynsten. 2010. *Time, Tense and Aspect in Early Vedic Grammar: Exploring Inflectional Semantics in the Rigveda*. Leiden: Brill. https://doi.org/10.1163/ej.9789004178144.i-475

Delbrück, Bertold. 1888. *Altindische Syntax*. Halle an der Saale: Waisenhause.

Demirdache, Hamida & Matthewson, Lisa. 1995. On the universality of syntactic categories. *Proceedings of the North-West Linguistic Society* 25: 70–93.

Di Giovine, Paolo. 2001. Etimologia indoeuropea ed etimologia romanza: Due metodi a confronto. In Benedetti (ed.), 285–293.

Di Giovine, Paolo & Flamini, Sara & Pozza, Marianna. 2007. Internal structure of verbal stems in the Germanic languages. In *Europe and the Mediterranean as a Linguistic Area. Convergencies from a Historical and Typological Perspective* [Studies in Language Companion Series 88], Paolo Ramat & Elisa Roma (eds), 49–62. Amsterdam: John Benjamins. https://doi.org/10.1075/slcs.88.05gio

Dixon, Robert M.W. 2004. Adjective classes in typological perspective. In Dixon & Aikhenvald (eds), 1–50.

Dixon, Robert M.W. 1977. Where have all adjectives gone? *Studies in Languages* 1: 19–77. (Repr. 1982. Berlin: Mouton De Gruyter).

Dixon, Robert M.W. & Aikhenvald, Alexandra Y. (eds). 2004. *Adjective Classes: A Cross-linguistic Typology*. Oxford: OUP.

Dressler, Wolfgang U. 1987. Word-formation as a part of natural morphology. In Dressler et al. (eds), 99–126.

Dressler, Wolfgang U. & Mayerthaler, Willi & Panagl, Oswald & Wurzel, Wolfgang U. (eds). 1987. *Leitmotivs in Natural Morphology* [Studies in Language Companion Series 10]. Amsterdam: John Benjamins. https://doi.org/10.1075/slcs.10

Dryer, Matthew S. 2016. Cross-linguistic categories, comparative concepts, and the Walman diminutive. *Linguistic Typology* 20(2): 305–331. https://doi.org/10.1515/lingty-2016-0009

Dryer, Matthew S. 1997. Are grammatical relations universal? *Essays on Language Function and Language Type Dedicated to T. Givón*, Joan L. Bybee, John Haiman, SandraA. & Thompson (eds), 115–144. Amsterdam: John Benjamins. https://doi.org/10.1075/z.82.09dry

Evans, Nicholas. 2000. Word classes in the world's languages. In Booij et al. (eds), Vol. I, 708–731.

Everett, Daniel L. & Kern, Barbara. 1997. *Wari: The Pacaas Novos Language of Western Brazil*. London: Routledge.

EWAia = Mayrhofer, Manfred. 1986–1996. *Etymologisches Wörterbuch des Altindoarischen*. Heidelberg: Carl Winter.

Floyd, Simeon. 2011. Re-discovering the Quechua adjective. *Linguistic Typology* 15: 25–63. https://doi.org/10.1515/lity.2011.003

von der Gabelentz, Georg. 1881. *Chinesische Grammatik*. Leipzig: T.O. Weigel.

Gil, David. 2016. Describing languoids: When incommensurability meets the language-dialect continuum. *Linguistic Typology* 20(2): 439–462. https://doi.org/10.1515/lingty-2016-0017

Gil, David. 2013. Riau Indonesian: A language without nouns and verbs. In Rijkhoff & van Lier (eds), 89–130.

Gil, David. 2000. Syntactic categories, cross-linguistic variation and Universal Grammar. In Vogel & Comrie (eds), 173–216.

Grassmann, Hermann. 1976[5]. *Wörterbuch zum Rig-Veda*. Wiesbaden: Otto Harrassowitz.

Gren-Eklund, Gunilla. 1978. *A Study of Nominal Sentences in the Oldest Upaniad*. Uppsala: Almqvist & Wiksell International.

Gross, Maurice. 1979. On the failure of generative grammar. *Language* 55(4): 859–885. https://doi.org/10.2307/412748

Haegeman, Liliane. 1994[2]. *Introduction to Government and Binding Theory*. Oxford: Blackwell.

Halle, Morris. 1973. Prolegomena to a theory of word formation. *Linguistic Inquiry* 4: 3–16.

Harris, Zelig. 1946. From morpheme to utterance. *Language* 22: 161–183. https://doi.org/10.2307/410205

Haspelmath, Martin. Forthcoming. *The morph as a minimum linguistic form*. Draft, May 2019.

Haspelmath, Martin. 2021. Toward standardization of morphosyntactic terminology for general linguistics. (This volume) https://doi.org/10.1075/tsl.132.02has

Haspelmath, Martin. 2014[2003][1]. The geometry of grammatical meanings: Semantic maps and cross-linguistic comparison. In *The New Psychology of Language. Cognitive and Functional Approaches to Language Structure*, vol. 2, Michael Tomasello (ed.), 211–242. New York NY: Psychology Press.

Haspelmath, Martin. 2012. How to compare major word-classes across languages. In *Theories of Everything in honor of Edward Keenan* [UCLA Working Papers in Linguistics 17, Article 16], Thomas Graf, Denis Paperno, Anna Szabolcsi & Jos Tellings (eds), 109–130. Los Angeles CA: UCLA. <http://phonetics.linguistics.ucla.edu/wpl/issues/wpl17/wpl17.html> (11 November 2020).

Haspelmath, Martin. 2011. The indeterminacy of word segmentation and the nature of morphology and syntax. *Folia Linguistica* 45(1): 31–80. https://doi.org/10.1515/flin.2011.002

Haspelmath, Martin. 2010. Comparative concepts and descriptive categories in cross-linguistic studies. *Language* 86(3): 663–687. https://doi.org/10.1353/lan.2010.0021

Haspelmath, Martin. 2007. Pre-established categories don't exist: Consequences for language description and typology. *Linguistic Typology* 11: 119–132. https://doi.org/10.1515/LINGTY.2007.011

Haspelmath, Martin. 1996. Word-class-changing-inflection and morphological theory. In *Yearbook of Morphology 1995*, Geert Booij & Jaap van Marle (eds), 43–67. Dordrecht: Kluwer. https://doi.org/10.1007/978-94-017-3716-6_3

Hengeveld, Kees. 2013. Parts-of-speech systems and typology. In Rijkhoff & van Lier (eds), 31–55.

Hengeveld, Kees. 1992. *Non-verbal Predication: Theory, Typology, Diachrony*. Berlin: Mouton de Gruyter. https://doi.org/10.1515/9783110883282

Hengeveld, Kees & Rijkhoff, Jan & Siewierska, Anna. 2004. Parts-of-speech and word-order. *Journal of Linguistics* 40(3): 527–570. https://doi.org/10.1017/S0022226704002762

Hengeveld, Kees & Rijkhoff, Jan. 2005. Mundari as a flexible language. *Linguistic Typology* 9(3): 406–431.

Hopper, Paul J. & Thompson, Sandra A. 1984. The discourse basis for lexical categories in Universal Grammar. *Language* 60(4): 703–752. https://doi.org/10.1353/lan.1984.0020

Janda, Richard D. & Joseph, Brian D. 2003. On language, change and language change – Or of history, linguistics and historical linguistics. In *Handbook of Historical Linguistics*, Richard D. Janda & Brian D. Joseph (eds), 4–113. London: Blackwell. https://doi.org/10.1002/9780470756393.ch

Jelinek, Eloise & Deemers, Richard. 1994. Predicates and pronominal arguments in Strait Salish. *Language* 70(4): 697–737. https://doi.org/10.2307/416325

Ježek, Elisabetta & Ramat, Paolo. 2009. On parts-of-speech transcategorization. *Folia Linguistica* 43: 391–416. https://doi.org/10.1515/FLIN.2009.011

Joos, Martin (ed.). 1957. *Readings in Linguistics I*. Chicago IL: University of Chicago Press.

Joshi, Shivaram D. 1967. Adjectives and substantives as a single class in the parts of speech. *Journal of the University of Poona, Humanities Section* 25: 19–30.

Kastovsky, Dieter. 1996. Verbal derivation in English: A historical survey. Or much ado about nothing. In *English Historical Linguistics 1994* [Current Issues in Linguistic Theory 135], Derek Britton (ed.), 93–117. Amsterdam: John Benjamins. https://doi.org/10.1075/cilt.135.09kas

Kastovsky, Dieter. 1992. Typological reorientation as a result of level interaction: The case of English morphology. In *Diachrony within Synchrony: Language History and Cognition*, Günter Kellermann & Michael D. Morrissey (eds), 411–428. Frankfurt: Peter Lang.

Lander, Yury & Arkadiev, Peter. 2016. On the right of being a comparative concept. *Linguistic Typology* 20(2): 403–416. https://doi.org/10.1515/lingty-2016-0014

LaPolla, Randy J. 2016. On categorization: Stick to the facts of the languages. *Linguistic Typology* 20(2): 365–375. https://doi.org/10.1515/lingty-2016-0011

Launey, Michel. 1994. *Une grammaire omnipredicative: Essai sur la morphosyntaxe du nahuatl classique*. Paris: CNRS Editions.

Lazard, Gilbert. 2001a. On the grammaticalization of evidentiality. *Journal of Pragmatics* 33: 359–367. https://doi.org/10.1016/S0378-2166(00)00008-4

Lazard, Gilbert. 2001b. Transitivity revisited as an example of a more strict approach in typological research. *Folia linguistica* 36: 141–200.
Lazard, Gilbert. 1999. La question de la distinction entre nom et verbe. *Folia Linguistica* 33(2): 389–418.
Lazard, Gilbert. 1997. Pour une terminologie rigoureuse: Quelques principes et propositions. *Mémoires de la Société de Linguistique de Paris (nouvelle série)* 6: 111–133.
Lazard, Gilbert. 1992. Y a-t-il des catégories interlanguagières? In *Texte, Sätze, Wörter und Moneme. Festschrift für Klaus Heger zum 65. Geburtstag*, Susanne R. Anschüz (ed.), 427–434. Heidelberger Orientverlag.
Lazzeroni, Romano. 2013. Divagazioni sul comparativo indoeuropeo. Ἀλεξάνδρεια – *Alessandria Rivista di Glottologia* 6–7: 265–276.
Lazzeroni, Romano. 2008. Il vedico tra varianti e standardizzazione. In *Standard e non standard tra scelta e norma. Atti del XXX convegno della Società Italiana di Glottologia, Bergamo 20–22 ottobre 2005*, Molinelli Piera (ed.), 109–116. Roma: Il Calamo.
Lazzeroni, Romano. 2005. Fra mondo indiano e mondo mediterraneo: Categorie scalari e gradi di comparazione. *Archivio Glottologico Italiano* 95: 1–18.
Law, Vivien. 1993. Process of assimilation. European grammars of Sanskrit in the early decades of the nineteenth century. In *La linguistique entre mythe et histoire*, Daniel Droixhe & Chantal Grell (eds), 237–261. Münster: Nodus.
Lehmann, Christian. 2008. Roots, stems and word classes. *Studies in Language* 32(3): 546–567. (Reprint: Ansaldo et al. 2010, 43–64). https://doi.org/10.1075/sl.32.3.04leh
Lieber, Rocher. 2010. *Introducing Morphology*. Cambridge: CUP.
Lombardi Vallauri, Edoardo. 2000. Gli aggettivi giapponesi fra nome e verbo. *Studi Italiani di Linguistica Teorica e Applicata* 29(2): 311–345.
Lyons, John. 1977–1979. *Semantics*, Vol. 1 (1977), Vol. 2 (1979). Cambridge: CUP.
Marantz, Alec. 1997. No escape from syntax: Don't try morphological analysis in the privacy of your own lexicon. *Penn Working Papers in Linguistics 4.2. Proceedings of the 21st Annual Penn Linguistics Colloquium*, Alexis Dimitriadis, Laura Siegel, Clarissa Surek-Clark & Alexander Williams (eds), 201–225. Philadelphia PA: University of Pennsylvania.
Martinet, André. 1980[1960][1]. *Éléments de linguistique générale*. Paris: Armand Colin.
MacDonell, Arthur A. 1975[1910][1]. *Vedic Grammar*. Delhi-Varanasi: Bhartiya Publishing House.
Matthews, Peter H. 1974. *Morphology. An Introduction to the Theory of Word-Structure*. Cambridge: CUP.
Matthews, Peter H. 1972. *Inflectional Morphology: A Theoretical Study Based on Aspects of Latin Verb Conjugation*. Cambridge: CUP.
Matthews, Peter H. 1967. Latin. *Lingua* 17:153–181. https://doi.org/10.1016/0024-3841(66)90008-8
Mayerthaler, Willi. 1981. *Morphologisches Natürlichkeit*. Wiesbaden: Akademische Verlagsgesellschaft Athenaion.
Meillet, Antoine. 1903[1934][7]. *Introduction à l'étude comparative des langues indo-européennes*. Paris: Hachette.
Mel'čuk, Igor. 1982. *Towards a Language of Linguistics. A System of Formal Notions for Theoretical Morphology*, Philip A. Luelsdorf (ed.). München: Fink.
Mithun, Marianne. 2000. Noun and verb in Iroquoian. In Vogel & Comrie (eds), 397–415.
Moravcsik, Edith A. 2016. On linguistic categories. *Linguistic Typology* 20(2): 417–425. https://doi.org/10.1515/lingty-2016-0015

Morgenroth, Wolfgang. 1977². *Lehrbuch des Sanskrit. Grammatik – Lektionen – Glossar*. Leipzig: Max Hueber.
Mosel, Ulrike. 2017. Teop – An Oceanic language with multifunctional nouns, verbs and adjectives. *Studies in Language* 41(2): 255–293. https://doi.org/10.1075/sl.41.2.02mos
Mugdan, Joachim. 2015. Units of word-formation. In *Word Formation: An International Handbook of the Languages of Europe*, Vol. I, Peter O. Müller, Ingeborg Ohnheiser, Susan Olsen & Franz Rainer (eds), 235–300. Berlin: Mouton De Gruyter.
Mugdan, Joachim. 1986. Was ist eigentlich ein Morphem? *Zeitschrift für Phonetik, Sprachwissenschaft und Kommunikationsforschung* 39(1): 29–43.
Panagl, Oswald. 2006. Zur verbale Konstruktion deverbativer Nomina. In *Word-Classes and Related Topics in Ancient Greek*, Emilio Crespo, Jesus de la Villa & Antonio R. Revuelta (eds), 47–57. Louvain la Neuve: Peeters.
Panagl, Oswald. 1987. Productivity and diachronic change in morphology. In Dressler et al. (eds), 127–152.
Panagl, Oswald. 1982. Produktivität in der Wortbildung. *Folia Linguistica* 16: 224–240.
Peterson, John. 2013. Parts of Speech in Kharia: A formal account. In Rijkhoff & van Lier (eds), 131–168.
Peterson, John. 2011. *A Grammar of Kharia*, 2 Vols. Leiden: Brill. https://doi.org/10.1163/ej.9789004187207.i-474
Peterson, John. 2005. There's a grain of truth in every "myth", or, Why the discussion on Mundari isn't quite over yet. *Linguistic Typology* 9: 351–390.
Plank, Franz. 1997. Word classes in typology: Recommended readings (a bibliography). *Linguistic Typology* 1(2): 185–192. https://doi.org/10.1515/lity.1997.1.2.185
Pokorny, Julius. 1959. *Indogermanisches etymologisches Wörterbuch*. Bern: Francke.
Pontillo, Tiziana & Candotti, Maria P. 2011. Discriminare tra aggettivo e sostantivo: Appunti sulla tradizione pāṇiniana. *Atti del Sodalizio Glottologico Milanese (n.s.)* 6: 66–84.
Radicchi, Anna. 1973–1974. Le parti del discorso nella tradizione grammaticale indiana. In *Materiali dell'Istituto di Glottologia dell'Università di Cagliari*, 1–64. Cagliari: Pubblicazioni dell'istituto di glottologia.
Ramat, Paolo. 2014. Categories, features and values in the definition of word-classes. *Studi e Saggi Linguistici* 52(2): 9–24.
Ramat, Paolo. 1999. Linguistic categorization and linguists' categories. *Linguistics* 37(1): 157–180. https://doi.org/10.1515/ling.1999.002
Renou, Louis. 1965. Remarques générales sur la phrase védique. In *Symbolae linguisticae in honorem Georgii Kuryłowicz*, Drewniak Stanisław (ed.), 230–234. Wrocław, Warszawa & Kraków: Zakład Narodowy Imienia Ossolińskich.
Renou, Louis. 1952. *Grammaire de la langue védique*. Lyon: Centre National de la Recherche Scientifique.
Rijkhoff, Jan. 2016. Crosslinguistic categories in morphosyntactic typology: Problems and prospects. *Linguistic Typology* 20(2): 333–363. https://doi.org/10.1515/lingty-2016-0010
Rijkhoff, Jan. 2007. Word classes. *Language and Linguistic Compass* 1(6): 709–726. https://doi.org/10.1111/j.1749-818X.2007.00030.x
Rijkhoff, Jan & van Lier, Eva. 2013. Flexible word classes in linguistic typology and grammatical theory. In Rijkhoff & van Lier (eds), 1–30.
Rijkhoff, Jan. 2013. (ed.). *Flexible Word-Classes. Typological Studies of Underspecified Parts of Speech*. Oxford: OUP. https://doi.org/10.1093/acprof:oso/9780199668441.001.0001
Robins, Robert H. 1964. *General Linguistics. An Introductory Survey*. Bloomington IN: Indiana University Press.

Roth, Heinrich. 1660–1668. *Grammatica linguae sanscretanae bracmanum Indiae orientalis*. Facsimile edition Arnulf Camp & Jean Claude Muller. 1988. *The Sanskrit Grammar and Manuscripts of Father Heinrich Roth S.J. (1620–1668)*. Biblioteca Nazionale, Roma, Mss. Or. 171 e 172. Leiden: Brill.

Rousseau, Jean. 1984. La racine arabe et son traitement par les grammairiens européens (1505–1810). *Bulletin de la Société de Linguistique de Paris* 79(1): 285–321.

Sapir, Eduard. 1921. *Language. An Introduction to the Study of Speech*. New York NY: Harcourt, Brace and Company.

Sasse, Hans-Jürgen. 2001. Scales of nouniness and verbiness. In *Language Typology and Linguistic Universals: An International Handbook*, Vol. 2, Martin Haspelmath, Ekkehard König, Wulf Österreicher & Wolfgang Raible (eds), 495–509. Berlin: De Gruyter.

Sasse, Hans-Jürgen. 1993a. Das Nomen – Eine universale Kategorie? *Sprachtypologie und Universalienforschung* 46(3): 187–221.

Sasse, Hans-Jürgen. 1993b. Syntactic categories and sub-categories. In *Syntax: An International Handbook of Contemporary Research*, 2 Vols, Joachim Jacobs, Arnim von Stechow, Wolfgang Sternefeld & Theo Vennemann (eds), 646–686. Berlin: De Gruyter.

de Saussure, Ferdinand. 1922[1916][1]. *Cours de linguistique générale*. Paris: Payot. [Italian translation: T. De Mauro (eds.). 1999. *Corso di linguistica generale*, Roma-Bari: Laterza].

de Saussure, Ferdinand. 1878. *Mémoire sur le système primitif des voyelles dans les langues indo-européennes*. Leipzig: Teubner.

Scalise, Sergio. 1984. *Generative Morphology*. Dordrecht: Foris. https://doi.org/10.1515/9783112328040

Schachter, Paul & Shopen, Timothy. 2007[2][1985][1]. Parts of speech systems. In *Linguistic Typology and Syntactic Description, Vol. 1: Clause Structure*, Timothy Shopen (ed.), 1–60. Cambridge: CUP. https://doi.org/10.1017/CBO9780511619427.001

Simone, Raffaele. 2007. Constructions and categories in verbal and signed languages. In *Verbal and Signed Languages. Comparing Structures, Constructs, and Methodologies*, Elena Pizzuto, Paola Pietrandrea & Raffaele Simone (eds), 198–252. Berlin: Mouton de Gruyter.

Simone, Raffaele & Masini, Francesca (eds). 2014. *Word Classes. Nature, Typology and Representations* [Current Issues in Linguistic Theory 332]. Amsterdam: John Benjamins. https://doi.org/10.1075/cilt.332

Speijer [alias Speyer], Jakob S. 1998[1886][1]. *Sanskrit Syntax*. Delhi: Motilal Banarsidass.

Speijer [alias Speyer], Jakob S. 1974[1896][1]. *Vedische und sanskrit Syntax*. Graz: Akademische Druck.

Stassen, Leon. 1997. *Intransitive Predication*. Oxford: OUP.

Thieme, Paul. 1967. Kṛṣṭí und carṣaṇí. *Zeitschrift für vergleichende Sprachforschung* 81: 233–244. (Reprint: Thieme Paul. 1971. *Kleine Schriften*, 2 Vols, G. Buddruss (ed.), Vol. 1, 247–258. Wiesbaden: Franz Steiner).

Thompson, Sandra A. 1988. A discourse approach to the cross-linguistic category 'adjective'. In *Explaining Language Universals*, John Hawkins (ed.), 167–185. Oxford: Blackwell.

Touratier, Christian. 2009. Questions surrounding the basic notions of word, *lexie*, morpheme and lexeme. In *Form and Function in Language Research. Papers in Honor of Christian Lehmann, Trends in Linguistics*. [Studies and Monographs 210], Johannes Helmbrecht (ed.), 157–166. Berlin: De Gruyter.

Trask, Robert L. 1993. *A Dictionary of Grammatical Terms in Linguistics*. London: Routledge.

Troupeau, Gérard. 1984. La notion de 'racine' chez les grammairiennes arabes ancien. In *History of Language Science. An International Handbook of the Evolution of the Study of Language from the Beginnings to the Present*, Vol. I, Sylvain Auroux, E.F. Konrad Koerner, Hans-Josef Niederehe & Kees Versteegh (ed.), 239–246. Berlin: De Gruyter.

Uehara, Satoshi. 1998. *Syntactic Categories in Japanese: A Cognitive and Typological Introduction*. Tokyo: Kurosio.

VIA = Werba, Chlodwig H. 1997. *Verba Indoarica. Die primären und sekundären Wurzeln der Sanskrit Sprache, Pars I: Radices Primariae*. Wien: Verlag der Österreichischen.

van Lier, Eva (ed.). 2017 Lexical flexibility in Oceanic Languages. *Studies in Language* 41(2): 241–254 (monographic issue on *Lexical Flexibility in Oceanic Languages*). https://doi.org/10.1075/sl.41.2.01van

van Lier, Eva. 2009. *Parts of Speech and Dependent Clause*. Utrecht: LOT.

Vogel, Petra M. 2000. Grammaticalization and part of speech systems. In Vogel & Comrie (eds), 259–284.

Vogel, Petra M. & Comrie, Bernard. 2000. *Approaches to the Typology of Word Classes*. Berlin: Walter De Gruyter. https://doi.org/10.1515/9783110806120

Völkel, Svenja. 2017. Word classes and the scope of lexical flexibility in Tongan. *Studies in Language* 41(2): 445–495. https://doi.org/10.1075/sl.41.2.06vol

Wakernagel, Jakob. 1905. *Altindische Grammatik, Vol. II.1: Einleitung zur Wortlehre. Nominalkomposition*. Göttingen: Vandenhoek & Ruprecht.

Wetzer, Harrie. 1996. *The Typology of Adjectival Predication*. Berlin: De Gruyter. https://doi.org/10.1515/9783110813586

Whitney, William D. 2000[1979][1]. *Sanskrit Grammar*. Delhi: Motilal Banarsidass.

Wodtko, Dagmar S. & Irslinger, Britta & Schneider, Carolin (eds). 2008. *Nomina im Indogermanischen Lexikon*. Heidelberg: Winter.

Wright, William. 1979[1896][1]. *A Grammar of the Arabic Language*, translated from the German of Caspari and edited with numerous additions and corrections by W. Wright, LL.D. 3rd ed. revised by W. Robertson Smith & M.J. de Goeje. Cambridge: CUP.

CHAPTER 10

Verbal vs. nominal reflexive constructions
A categorial opposition?

Nicoletta Puddu
University of Cagliari

Reflexives have been extensively studied from different approaches and perspectives, but no clear consensus has been established on the criteria for their definition. From a morphological point of view, a distinction between nominal reflexives and verbal reflexives has been generally accepted in both functional and generative approaches. However, it is ultimately hard to make a precise distinction between verbal and nominal reflexives which should possibly be viewed as a continuum rather than as a discrete partition. In this paper, I will discuss the opportunity of a categorial distinction between verbal and nominal reflexive constructions, identifying some general principles which allow us to classify a form as "verbal" or "nominal".

1. Introduction

Reflexives have been extensively studied from different approaches and perspectives in both typological and descriptive studies. In this paper, after reviewing what different scholars mean by "reflexives" and "reflexivity" (Section 2), I will mainly concentrate on the understudied topic of the morphological form of "reflexive markers" (Section 3). The focus of the discussion will be on the opposition between verbal and nominal reflexives, which is widely used in the studies on "reflexives". On the one hand, such an opposition rests on the distinction between "nominal" and "verbal" features which is not universally accepted, and, on the other, shows many difficulties when confronted with languages where traditional parts of speech do not apply or with languages presenting a highly complex verbal morphology (Section 4). In the conclusions, I will propose some more general principles which could be used in a cross-linguistic perspective, in order to characterise a form as (more) "nominal" or (more) "verbal", suggesting that a scalar classification is more suitable than a categorial one (Section 5.).

2. The debate on "reflexives"

2.1 The vagueness of "reflexives"

The marking of reflexivity is so widespread in languages that Heine and Miyashita (2008: 172), in their survey on reflexive and reciprocals in 150 languages, state that "reflexivity and reciprocity are universal concepts insofar as all languages can be expected to have some grammaticalized expression for both". Due to their diffusion, "reflexives" have been widely studied from both a comparative perspective (especially from a syntactic and a semantic point of view), and from a language-specific perspective in both formal and functional terms.

They are usually present in descriptive grammars and have also been the object of investigation from a diachronic point of view. "Reflexivity" is then expected to be a good field to discuss the relationship between "comparative concepts" and "language-particular categories".

According to Frajzyngier (2000a), the interest in reflexive constructions, in addition to their widespread distribution, is linked to the "apparent" multitude of functions coded by these forms and the potential interrelationship among them. Consequently, many studies have been devoted to reflexives either as a "category" (see Faltz 1985; Geniušienė 1987) or compared to other "categories" (for an overview of the studies on reflexives and related domains, see Puddu & Janic (2021) in preparation). The many different functions of reflexive markers are often subsumed under the definition of "middle voice" or "middle domain" (see Kemmer 1993), and Kulikov (2013: 261) points out that the notion of "reflexive", together with "middle voice" is "one of the most important and most intricate parts of the verbal grammar".

However, as Frajzyngier (2000a) has highlighted, the term "reflexive" alone is quite vague. In the introduction to his well-known volume on *Reflexives*, he admits that the term "reflexive" has such a wide formal and functional scope that "it is not very useful in linguistic analysis and it should be replaced by other terms, depending on what one actually finds in a given language or on the scope of a cross-linguistic study" (Frajzyngier 2000a: vii). In actual fact, as he points out, scholars usually use this term with (at least) two main senses: "one referring to the function of marking two arguments of a verb as co-referential, and the second referring to morphological markers of co-referentiality" (*ibidem*). Moreover, the use of a non-standardised terminology for defining "reflexive constructions" makes a cross-linguistic comparison difficult. The need for a clear definition of what is meant by "reflexives" and, more specifically, by "reflexive construction" has also been pointed out by Haspelmath (this volume, forthcoming in 2021). Here we will review some of the major positions on reflexive constructions, concentrating especially on studies in a functional-typological perspective. In discussing the different positions, we will sometimes use the vague term "reflexives" in order to maintain a certain level of neutrality with respect to different definitions.

2.2 Reflexive constructions in a typological perspective

2.2.1 Faltz's definition

One of the most widely used definitions in typological studies on reflexive constructions (see, for instance, König 2007; Moyse-Faurie 2008, 2017) is Faltz's (1985) who makes a first fundamental distinction between "reflexive context" and "reflexive strategy".

> Given any language, we can isolate a class of simple clauses expressing a two-argument predication, the argument being a human agent or experiencer on the one hand and a patient on the other. Such clauses will consist of a verb, denoting the predicate, two noun phrases, referring to the arguments, and any tense-aspect, modal, agreement, or other grammatical material required by the syntax. […] If the language has a grammatical device which specifically indicates that the agent/experiencer and the patient in such clauses are in fact the same referent, then the grammatical device will be called the primary reflexive strategy of that language. (Faltz 1985: 3–4)

In addition to this, he states that primary reflexive strategies should be detected "with verbs which take human or nonhuman objects indifferently, whose use with human objects is not semantically (socially? culturally?) distinguished from its use with nonhuman objects, and whose reflexive use is likewise not specially distinguished from its non-reflexive use" (Faltz 1985: 7).

Example (1) can then be considered an instance of a "primary reflexive strategy" where the "reflexive marker" *himself* is used.

(1) *John sees himself in the mirror*

We can highlight two main points in Faltz's definition:

1. it explicitly considers coreference not only at the semantic level (i.e., between agent and patient), but also at the syntactic level (i.e., between the two NPs) in a two-argument predication;
2. it defines a primary reflexive strategy as appearing in prototypical contexts and with a specific class of verbs.

These two points are also the base for the definition of reflexive constructions proposed by many other scholars. However, different approaches diverge in that they focus more on semantic or syntactic constraints and on the "tightness" of these constraints.

We will discuss some of these definitions in the framework of the more general discussion on "comparative concepts" in the following paragraphs.

2.2.2 *"Reflexives" as markers of coreference*

As stated in the previous paragraph, the marking of coreference for Faltz (1985) is the fundamental function of reflexive constructions, and scholars usually agree in identifying coreference marking as the core property of reflexive markers. However, it should be noted that in several studies Frajzyngier maintains that many of the functions of the so-called "reflexive markers" have no relationship to the domain of reference. In his (2000b) work focusing on the Polish "reflexive marker" *się*, he assumes that the fundamental function of reflexive forms in a number of languages is to code the point of view of the subject rather than to code coreferentiality.

Even among scholars who view coreference as the main function of reflexive markers, there are differences in the kind of coreference. On the one hand, reflexives are usually defined in functional-typological studies as expressing coreference between two semantic roles (Geniušienė 1987), actants (Lazard 2007) or participants (Haspelmath this volume; 2021, forthcom.) without any specification of the nature of their semantic roles. In other cases, it is explicitly stated that the two semantic roles must be an Agent and a Patient (Kemmer 1993; Zúñiga & Kittilä 2019).

On the other hand, in the generative framework, reflexives are generally considered as a particular case of binding expressing an identity relation between two co-arguments (Reinhart & Reuland 1991, 1993; Reuland 2018), without any specification of their semantic roles (see Everaert 2013). Schladt (2000) explicitly quotes the notion of subject, saying that "a reflexive marker typically denotes a referent that is identical with the one of the subject noun phrase".

Obviously, the choice of the definition is strictly related with the chosen approach to language study. In a broadly comparative perspective, the use of purely semantic notions, with no reference to the syntactic notions of 'subject' and 'object', allows a less disputable comparison between languages, and, as Croft (2016: 378) notes, "is relatively uncontroversial, but by no means entirely so". In the case of reflexives, the risk of such a purely semantic approach is, however, that the definition covers too large a range of cases. Kulikov (2013: 278), for instance, discusses Geniušienė's definition of "reflexives", who explicitly suggests that many more semantic roles than "Agent" and "Patient" are relevant to the analysis of reflexive verbs. He considers this definition too wide, since it also covers many examples usually inserted in the "so-called" middle domain in other studies.

Moreover, several universals of reflexive constructions rely on the notion of 'subject' and 'object': see for instance the "chief universals" on NP-reflexive strategies (Faltz 1985: 107–108), Comrie's (1999) universals of reflexives and local domain, and universal 3 of reflexives and adnominal possessor in Haspelmath (2008: 50–53).

Obviously, applying such universals to languages which do not have clear instantiations of 'subject' raises the question of the appropriateness of such a procedure, as already discussed by the editors in the *Introduction* to this work.

As is evident from the discussion, reflexives are defined by different scholars either as a "functional comparative concept", based on purely semantic notions or as a "hybrid comparative concept" (see Croft 2016), which combines both functional and formal concepts. While the former type of comparative concept has a simpler cross-linguistic applicability, the latter captures some widespread properties of reflexives (but does not necessarily apply to all languages).

Since comparative concepts are not considered as pre-existing categories, but, rather, as linguists' constructs (see *Introduction*), we may assume that we can have different comparative concepts in order to answer different research questions. This is particularly true in the case of reflexive constructions, which, as we have seen, are a very broad and complex area of research.

2.2.3 *"Canonical" or "prototypical" reflexives*

Another point shared by many definitions of "reflexives" is that, due to the aforementioned polyfunctionality of reflexive markers, many scholars presuppose that there is a "prototypical" or "canonical" reflexive construction. König and Gast (2008) propose an approach to the study of reflexive constructions in which notional characterisations are taken as a categorial prototype and the category also includes examples with similar meanings. Below I give some of the definitions of "reflexives" in a prototypical perspective:

> The most important type of reflexive, canonical reflexive, is the one where the Subject is co-referential with the direct object   (Kulikov 2013: 268)

> The canonical construction involves a transitive verb, with A and O arguments coreferential   (Dixon 2012: 146)

> The prototypical reflexive domain mostly concerns actions performed on oneself that one usually does to others, and it involves an agent and a patient which happen to refer to the same person; they presuppose intentionality and often draw attention to the unexpected nature of the event described"
> (Moyse-Faurie 2017: 111)

As can easily be seen, different definitions highlight different features of a "prototypical reflexive": on the one hand, the coreference of subject and object at the syntactic level and the coreference of agent and patient at the semantic level; on the other, the "unexpected nature of event", i.e., the fact that one performs on oneself an action usually performed on others. According to this approach, prototypical reflexive constructions have to be detected with typically hetero-directed verbs (or extroverted verbs according to Haiman's 1983 definition).

In this perspective, grooming verbs are considered typically auto-directed, and this explains why in several languages, such as English, a reflexive marker is not needed with these verbs to express the coreferentiality of subject and object (see Kemmer 1993: 53).

As Corbett (2013: 49) says, the canonical instances "are simply those that match the canon: they are the best, the clearest, the indisputable ones. Given that they have to match up to a logically determined standard, they are unlikely to be frequent. They are likely to be rare and may even be non-existent."

So, a corollary to the decision to use a prototypical or canonical definition of reflexive constructions is that the occurrences of the construction are rare.

Everaert (2013) explains the apparent paradox of this definition by commenting on the two following examples.

(2)   *Mary deceived herself*

(3)   *John washed*

While (2) is an instance of canonical reflexivization even if the frequency of this construction is rare, (3) is quite common cross-linguistically, but non-canonical.

A prototypical approach to linguistic categories can certainly be questioned (see for instance Cristofaro 2009 in more general terms, and, with special reference to reflexives, Frajzyngier 2000b, this volume; Haspelmath, this volume; 2021, forthcom.).

First of all, as Everaert (201: 191) points out, despite the huge body of studies on reflexives, "it is still not an easy task to define what a canonical case of reflexivization is".

Secondly, as noted by Frajzyngier and Shay (2003, 2016), a prototypical approach is often based on some "perceived semantic similarity" between forms, but it is impossible to determine whether this "semantic overlap represents the central function of these forms or whether it is only marginal" (Frajzyngier & Shay 2003: 33). Moreover, such an approach can lead to some important facts being ignored or underestimated because they do not meet the preconceived parameters. In place of a prototypical approach to language study, Frajzyngier and Shay suggest determining which functional domains exist across languages and then comparing the internal structure of such domains across languages. As for "reflexives", Frajzyngier (2000b) proposes that, in their wider sense, they include three functional domains: affectedness of the subject, coreferentiality and stativity.

In favour of a prototypical approach to the study of reflexive constructions, we could however recall the variety of the domains to which reflexives can be ascribed. Given that different functional domains have been identified, one could be interested in examining all (or many) of them or only in comparing forms which code coreference, or, even more strictly, in cases of coreference between subject and object in typically hetero-directed situations (the "prototypical" or "canonical" reflexive). Clearly, in this latter approach, the focus is only on one of the possible functions of the reflexive form, and one must remember that it is only a partial description. Again, we could imagine having different comparative concepts in order to answer different research questions.

To sum up, the different positions on the definition of "reflexives" reflect the debate recalled in the editors' *Introduction*, i.e., on the one hand, the need for concepts which allow comparison between very different languages, and, on the other, the necessity to compare categories which are relevant to the languages compared.

3. The morphology of reflexives

In Section 2 we have seen how the notion of "reflexives" and "reflexivity" has itself been extensively studied in order to define its categorial status. Moreover, a large body of studies have been dedicated to the semantics and syntax of reflexive constructions, leading to the formulation of several universals (for an overview on the universals of reflexive marking see Haspelmath 2008; 2021, forthcom.) In a generative framework, since Chomsky (1981), the syntax of reflexives construction has been widely studied.

Far less attention has been devoted to the morphological properties of reflexives, even if morphological features have been invoked in order to explain some syntactic or semantic properties of reflexives. As Zúñiga and Kittilä (2019) point out, the only systematic classification of the morphology of reflexives is in Faltz (1985).

Faltz establishes a morphological classification of reflexive strategies dividing them primarily into "nominal" and "verbal" strategies. In nominal reflexives, coreference is marked in the subject and/or object NPs, while, in verbal reflexives, marking appears on the verb.

Faltz further articulates the classification in the following way:

1. Verbal reflexives, like the Lakhota affix *ic'i*

    (4) *John   ayeo<ic'i>kas'in*   Lakhota (Faltz 1985:5)
         John   peek.at<REFL>
         'John peeked at himself'

2. Nominal reflexives, divided into:
a. Head reflexives, where a special nominal morpheme acts as the head of a reflexive NP. An example is Japanese *zibun*.

(5) *Taroo wa zibun o mamotta*
Taroo TOP REFL ACC defend.PST
'Taroo defended himself' Japanese (Faltz 1985: 29)

b. Adjunct reflexives, where a special reflexive morpheme is added to a pronoun head, like Irish *é féin*.

(6) *ghortaigh Seán é féin*
hurt.PST Seán PRO.3SG.M REFL
'Seán hit himself.' Irish (Faltz 1985: 34)

c. Reflexive pronouns, where a special reflexive pronoun is used like German *sich*.

(7) *Hans sah sich*
Hans saw REFL
'Hans saw himself' German (Faltz 1985: 42)

The distinction between nominal reflexives and verbal reflexives is considered by Faltz (1985: 15) as "fundamental to the typology of reflexive grammar".

Departing from this definition, Zúñiga and Kittilä (2019: 155) discuss four parameters of morphological variation of reflexives:

1. in terms of their locus of appearance, they can be nominal (argumental) or verbal.
2. in terms of their morphological complexity, they can be simplex or complex.
3. in terms of their person and number, they can be variable or invariable.
4. in terms of their multifunctionality, they can be syncretic either with intensifiers or with valency-reduction operators.

Some of these points have been treated in more detail in the literature. In particular, great attention has been devoted to both the morphological complexity of reflexives in relation to the "introverted" *vs.* "extroverted" nature of the verb (see Haiman 1983; Haspelmath 2008) and also to the syncretism between both reflexive and other valency reduction operators and between reflexives and intensifiers (see König & Siemund 2000; König & Siemund 2013).

Far less attention has been devoted to the opposition between variable and invariant reflexives (see for instance Benincà & Poletto 2005; Puddu 2010; de Benito Moreno 2015), and to the distinction between verbal and nominal reflexives. In the following section we shall concentrate on the latter point, i.e., on the nominal *vs.* verbal nature of reflexives.

4. Verbal *vs.* nominal reflexives

4.1 Definitions of "verbal" and "nominal" reflexives

While, as summarised in Section 2, the definition of reflexives has been the object of much discussion, the distinction between nominal and verbal reflexives has been generally accepted, even though the opposition between verb and noun has been questioned from a typological perspective (see, among others, Hengeveld 1992; Croft 2000; Haspelmath 2012). Such a distinction has been accepted in both functional and generative approaches (see for instance Geniušienė 1987; Kemmer 1993; Kazenin 2001; Lidz 2001; Gast 2006).

As we will see in the following subsection, the criteria used to distinguish nominal from verbal reflexives are not always clear. Dik even puts the existence of verbal reflexives in doubt, saying that:

> it is to be doubted whether there are any truly 'verbal' reflexives: verbally marked constructions which are only used for indicating reflexive relationships. […] The basic dichotomy is not between nominal and verbal reflexives, but between nominal and verbal middles which can also be used for reflexive purposes.
>
> (Dik 1983: 233)

While he admits the existence of verbal reflexives, Kazenin (2001) confirms that: "the consistently separated treatment of the two types of reflexives is misleading because a historical relation between them is obvious in a large number of cases". He points out that verbal reflexives deriving from reflexive pronouns are far more common than non-derived ones and a "pure" verbal reflexive is very rare across languages. By contrast, we do not have evidence of nominal reflexives derived from verbal reflexives.

A first discrepancy in treating verbal and nominal reflexives can be seen in their relationship with voice.

According to Faltz, since reflexivity "ties together" the agent and patient of a transitive predicate, it renders that predicate a function of one argument only, and hence equivalent to an intransitive.

On the contrary, in other approaches, the two kinds of reflexives are also formally distinguished in terms of voice. For instance, Zúñiga and Kittilä (2019: 154) distinguish two prototypical reflexives with respect to voice. On the one hand, they identify an "active reflexive", i.e., an agent-patient voice, where the syntactic valency of the verb is two, which denotes reflexivity through means unrelated to voice, expressed with nominal strategies. At the same time, they identify a "duplex voice" which has reflexivity as one of its possible readings, where two roles are assigned to a single syntactic argument at the thematic tier, so that the valency of the verb is one, expressed with verbal morphology.

Along the same lines, in a generative-canonical perspective, Everaert (2013) states that, when reflexivity is encoded on the predicate, it holds at a lexical level, but is not syntactically encoded. He also suggests that reflexives that are morpho-syntactically encoded on the argument are "more canonical" than those encoded on the predicate.

Moreover, even if the majority of the scholars agree on the distinction between verbal and nominal, they do not agree on how to classify different strategies. We will review some of the positions here, also summarised in Table (1).

Dimitriadis & Everaert (2004) identify 22 strategies for reflexivization which they divide between argumental and non-argumental, largely corresponding to the opposition between verbal *vs.* nominal reflexives. A similar distinction has been proposed by Dixon (2012) who then distinguishes the "pronoun technique" from "the verbal derivation technique", which again approximately corresponds to Faltz's subdivision between nominal and verbal strategies. Haspelmath (2021, forthcom.) adds a further third category, distinguishing between "reflexive nominals", "reflexive voice markers", and "reflexive argument markers" (the latter not considered as either argumental or voice markers).

If we look at more fine-grained classifications, we can find several differences. While Dimitriadis and Everaert (2004), for instance, classify zero reflexivization as "non argumental, affixal", Dixon (2012) classifies it as "others" while for Haspelmath (this volume; 2021, forthcom.), reflexive constructions are necessarily coded by a form.

Clitics, as we will see in the next paragraph, pose several problems. Faltz (1985), albeit with some doubts, considers them as an instance of verbal reflexives (calling them "pronominal verbal reflexives"), while Dimitriadis and Everaert (2004) classify them as a pronominal strategy, and Haspelmath (2021, forthcom.) treats them in a separate category (the aforementioned "reflexive argument markers").

Clearly, this variety in classification is linked to the different criteria chosen in order to classify a form as an instance of nominal or verbal reflexive. These will be discussed in the following paragraph.

4.2 Criteria for distinguishing nominal from verbal reflexives

Several studies have pointed out the different properties of verbal and nominal reflexives.

With respect to the form, verbal reflexives are typically "lighter" than nominal reflexives and show a higher degree of grammaticalization (Kazenin 2001; König 2007). According to Kazenin (2001: 918), while nominal reflexives can encode both direct and indirect reflexivity, verbal reflexives typically only encode direct reflexivity. Finally, while verbal reflexives are often syncretic with valency-reduction operators, nominal reflexives are often syncretic with intensifiers (Zúñiga & Kittilä 2019: 157).

Table 1. The opposition between nominal and verbal reflexives according to various scholars

	Faltz (1985)	Dimitriadis & Everaert (2004)	Dixon (2012)	Haspelmath (*forthcoming in 2021*)
Verbal	Affixal reflexives	Non-argumental Affixal: – inflectional – derivational – zero reflexivization Periphrastic constructions	Derivation technique	Reflexive voice markers
Nominal	Head reflexives	Argumental Nominal: – Possessive pronoun + body noun/self – Possessive body noun/self +body noun/self – Body noun/self	Pronominal technique	Reflexive nominals – Nouns with possessive person forms – Noun-like forms without possessive indexes – Self-intensified anaphoric pronouns – Anaphoric pronouns with other reinforcements – Reflexive pronominoids
	Adjunct reflexives Reflexive pronouns	Pronominal: – personal pronouns – doubled personal pronoun; – objective pronoun + intensifier; – objective pronoun + body noun /self; – underspecified reflexive clitic; – underspecified reflexive pronoun – phonologically weak underspecified reflexive pronoun; – phonologically strong underspecified reflexive pronoun + intensifier		Reflexive argument markers
			Other strategies	Other strategies

The main criterion proposed by Faltz (1985) in order to distinguish nominal from verbal reflexives is the fact that the reflexive marker may appear in non-object position alone or after a preposition. Moreover, verbal reflexives typically obey the subject-antecedent condition and do not permit long-distance coreference.

On the basis of these criteria, German *sich* is thus considered as a nominal reflexive, since it is needed to express coreference both in object (8) and non-object (9) position.

(8)   *Hans siet sich*
      'Hans sees himself'

(9)   *Hans sah eine Schlange neben sich*
      'Hans saw a snake near himself'   German (Faltz 1985: 115).

The criteria proposed by Faltz presuppose that reflexive constructions are defined on the basis of coreference between subject and object, with all the problems already mentioned in Section 2.2.1. However, even in languages where the identification of the two syntactic roles is unproblematic, the aforementioned criteria do not suffice to draw a neat distinction between verbal and nominal reflexives. We will discuss some of these cases in the following section.

4.3   Problematic cases for the distinction between verbal and nominal reflexives

French *se*, as a derivative of the Latin *se*, and, going back to the Indo-European, of the "reflexive" **se-s(e)we*, is usually considered by traditional grammarians as a pronoun, just like the German *sich*. This interpretation is supported by the fact that it occurs in the same position as non-reflexive pronouns (see the opposition between (10) and (11)) and it varies according to the person of the subject (Creissels 2007).

(10) *Jean se voit*
      'Jean sees himself'

(11) *Jean le voit*
      'Jean sees him'   French

However, since *se* cannot appear in non-object position (in (12) *lui-même* must be used) and cannot be used as a long-distance reflexive, Faltz (1985) considers it as a verbal reflexive.

(12) *Jean parle à Marie de lui-même*
      'Jean talks to Marie about himself'   French

Several other arguments based on language-specific parameters in favour of its interpretation as a verbal reflexive are discussed in detail by Creissels (2007: 90–91). In particular: *se* determines the presence of the auxiliary *être* instead of *avoir* in the accompanying verb (see the opposition between (13) and (14); it can be used with an impersonal value as in (15); it can be causativized as in (16). Moreover, it is impossible to manipulate the possible referents for a reflexive in object position (17).

(13) *Il l'a défendu*
'He defended him'

(14) *Il s'est défendu*
'He defended himself'

(15) *Ce jour-là il s'est dénoncé vingt personnes*
'On that day twenty persons were denounced'

(16) *Je l'ai fait se dénoncer*
'I made him denounce himself'

(17) *Jean se défend mieux que Pierre*
'John defends himself better than Peter'
'*John defends himself better than Peter defends him'
'*John defends himself better than he defends Peter'
French (Creissels 2007: 90-91)

As a matter of fact, there is much debate about the status of French *se* in the literature (see also Reinhart & Siloni 2005 and Haspelmath 2021, forthcom.).

Similar difficulties can be found in determining the nature of Bantu reflexives. In Tswana, pronouns are prefixed to the verb together with tense markers: subject pronouns precede, and object pronouns follow tense markers (18).

(18) ke-tla-mo-thusa
1SG.NOM-FUT-3SG.OC1-help
'I will help him.' Tswana (Faltz 1985: 58)

The primary reflexive strategy is the suffix -*i*, which, like an object pronoun, follows tense markers (19).

(19) ke-tla-i   thêk-êla selêpê
1SG.NOM-FUT-REFL buy-BEN axe
'I shall buy an axe for myself' Tswana (Faltz 1985: 58)

As Creissels (2002) notes, -*i*- has the same tonal properties as object indexes. Moreover, the reflexive can be separated from the verb stem by a first person singular object index (compare (20) and (21)) and this should point to a pronominal, rather than verbal nature of -*i*-.

(20) *Ba   tlaa mo   i-tshwar-el-a*
SC2 FUT OC1 REFL-hold-APPL-FIN
'They will forgive him'

(21) *Ba   tlaa i-n-tshwar-el-a*
SC2 FUT REFL-O1S-hold-APPL-FIN
'to forgive me' (lit. 'to hold me for oneself')   Tswana (Creissels 2002: 401)

Interestingly, this separation may also take place when -*i*- is lexicalized as in *itswarela*, since 'forgive' cannot be considered a "reflexive" form of *tswarela* 'hold'.

However, -*i*- cannot appear alone in non-object position or after a preposition, so, according to the criterion proposed by Faltz, it should be considered a verbal strategy.

As in French, the nature of Bantu affixal reflexives is still much debated and their definition as an "intransitivizing device" or as a "pronominal" depends much on the criteria chosen and is ultimately related to the nature of object prefixes.

Nduku Kioko (1999), for instance, in her discussion of the invariable Kikamba reflexive -*i*-, classifies it as a pronoun on the bases of three tests: it occupies the same position as object markers (immediately preceding the root); it changes the final vowel of the imperative from *e* to *a* like pronominal affixes, and it co-occurs with a full emphatic pronoun.

On the contrary, Marlo (2015) identifies the numerous exceptional morphosyntactic and phonological properties of Bantu reflexives compared to other object prefixes, as their phonological shape, their position with respect to other OPs, their (in)ability to co-occur with other OPs, and patterns of final vowel allomorphy in the imperative.

In both the French and Bantu cases, one could argue that the form should be classified as verbal if we adopt a broader typological perspective and only consider its appearance in non-object position, rather than any language-particular features. However, other languages show even more complicated examples that are not so easily dealt with, especially in cases where "traditional" word classes do not apply.

A case in point, already discussed by Faltz, is Vietnamese *mình*, which appears after the verb and which could be interpreted as either an NP or as a verbal suffix.

(22) tôi trong tháy anh áy
 I in see PRN DEM
 'I saw him.'

(23) tôi trong tháy mình
 I in see REFL
 'I saw myself.' Vietnamese (Faltz 1985: 61)

As mentioned before, Faltz (1985) states that nominal reflexives must be able to appear in non-object position after a preposition. However, the use of this criterion is problematic in languages like Vietnamese where prepositions are not clearly distinguished from verbs. According to Faltz (1985: 62) the constructions from (24) to (26) can be interpreted either as verb+ prepositional phrases or as serial verb constructions.

(24) cô Tám nói vê̂ mình.
 miss Tam talk about/return REFL
 'Miss Tam talked about herself'

(25) cô   Tám mua   xe   cho   mình
      miss Tam bought car for/give REFL
      'Miss Tam bought herself a car.'

(26) cô   Tám chơi cờ   tướng với   mình
      miss Tam play flag chess with/join REFL
      'Miss Tam played chess with herself.'   Vietnamese (Faltz 1985: 62)

Another case that shows how difficult it is to trace a neat border between verbal and nominal reflexives is Nivkh.

Gruzdeva (1998: 32) states that the reflexive-determinative pronoun *pʻi* in Nivkh cliticizes to the verb as a prefix, so that, for instance, the stem *lyv-*, 'to hide (something)', becomes *pʻ-lyv* 'to hide oneself'. Notice that *pʻi* occurs in the direct object position, where personal pronouns also cliticize, so it would seem to be a case of a nominal reflexive.

According to Nedjalkov and Otaina (2013: 108), the variant *pʻ-* is prefixed if a verb does not have two initial consonants and always occurs as a prefix, while *pʻi* can occur alone as in (27).

(27) ətək   pʻi   za+ñivkx+hīm-ḍ
      father self strike+man+know-IND
      'Father knew the man whom he had beaten.'
                                    Nivkh (Nedjalkov & Otaina 2013: 108)

Consequently, since the variant *pʻ-* does not occur as a separate unit, they suggest that it could be considered as an intransitivizing device.

Thus, Nivkh, at first sight, seems similar to the Romance languages, with a clitic form more similar to a verbal reflexive and a non-clitic form categorizable as a nominal reflexive.

However, it must be noted that *pʻ-* can appear prefixed in non-object position: in (28), it is a reflexive possessive referring to the subject

(28) ətək   pʻ-ōla+ḍu-ḍ
      father REFL-child+washes-IND
      'Father washes his son'   Nivkh (Nedjalkov & Otaina 2013: 194)

Even more interestingly, in (29) it is used as a long-distance reflexive referring to the subject of the following clause: it thus shows a "long-distance" use which is absolutely not typical of verbal reflexives.

(29) Imn   pʻ-siŋru-doχ   qʻau-ḍ   ha-gu-r
      They REFL-deceive-SUP not_be-IND   be_so-CAUS-CONV.NAR.3SG
      kəmlə-d   if
      think-IND   s/he
      'He thought (that) they did not deceive him (lit. 'himself')'
                                    Nivkh (Nedjalkov & Otaina 2013: 194)

In languages with very complex verb morphology, the criteria for the classification of reflexive constructions as verbal or nominal become even fuzzier (see also Janic & Puddu 2021). In Athabaskan languages, a reflexive prefix is used in order to mark coreference, but this determines, at the same time, a change in the verb stem which undergoes a "classifier change" as already noticed by Faltz (1985). See for instance example (31).

(30) sh-oo-į́
1SG.ACC-3SG.NOM-see
'He sees me'

(31) 'ád-oo-t'į́
REFL-3SG.NOM-Cl-see
'He sees himself'   Navajo (Faltz 1985: 125)

We could affirm that two strategies are applied at the same time: the "reflexive prefix", which could be considered as a "nominal strategy" and the classifier, which modifies the verbal root. However, the interaction between reflexive prefixes and classifiers as detransitivizing markers in Athabaskan languages is extremely complex, as Givón and Bommelyn (2000) pointed out. For reasons of space, we limit ourselves to noticing here again, that, in languages with a complex and opaque verbal morphology, deciding *a priori* on a criterion for considering a reflexive marker as a verbal or a nominal strategy can prove impossible, and we must also rely on language-specific features.

A final controversial case is constituted by reflexive markers in San Andrés Yaá Zapotec, as discussed by Galant (2015). San Andrés Yaá Zapotec is a VSO language as is shown in example (32).

(32) Yell=a'   ch-ge'el=be'   Kwann=a'
Miguel=DEM HAB-hate=3INF Juan=DEM
'Miguel hates Juan'   San Andrés Yaá Zapotec (Galant 2015: 232)

In (32) the subject is a pronominal clitic which is attached to the verb,[1] and the object follows the subject. This sentence has two possible reflexive forms: (33) and (34).

(33) Yell=a'   ch-ge'el=be'   kwimm=be'
Miguel=DEM HAB-hate=3INF REFL=3INF
'Miguel hates himself'

(34) Yell=a'   ch-ge'el-kwimm=be'
Miguel=DEM HAB-hate-REFL=3INF
'Miguel hates himself'   San Andrés Yaá Zapotec (Galant 2015: 232)

---

1. As Galant (2015: 232) points out "the lexical noun phrase preceding the verb in each of these cases is coreferential with the pronominal clitic following the verb but is not the true syntactic subject – such preverbal noun phrases appear to be topics"

In (33) the REFL *kwinn* plus the pronominal clitic which is coreferential with the subject of the sentence appears in the same position as the direct object in (32). In (34) it appears between the verb and the clitic subject, suggesting that it has undergone incorporation and, consequently, has made the verb intransitive.

In this case, the reflexive morpheme *kwinn* may appear either as an instance of "nominal" reflexive and of "verbal" reflexive. As Galant (2015) points out, there are also other possible interpretations of the phenomenon, determined by the existence of "covert subject constructions" in Zapotec languages, but it seems that these constructions are not possible in San Andrés Yaá Zapotec.

5. Conclusions

In this paper, after discussing the notion of "reflexive construction" in the light of the debate between "comparative concepts" and "language-specific categories", I have concentrated on the morphology of reflexive markers, and, especially, on the distinction between "nominal" and "verbal" reflexives. Although this distinction is widely accepted in the literature, I hope to have shown that it poses several issues at both a general and at a language specific level. At the general level, we are forced to rely on traditional parts of speech in languages where they do not apply, while, at the language-specific level, in languages with a complex verbal morphology it can be quite difficult to define a clear border between a "verbal" and a "nominal" strategy.

It may be possible to identify some general criteria to classify a form as "more verbal" or "more nominal". The possibility of a form appearing in non-object position is perhaps one of the most valid in a cross-linguistic perspective, even if, as we have shown, it could not be applied in some languages. On the basis of the relevant literature discussed in Section 4.2, Table 2 summarises some more general criteria which can be used in a cross-linguistic perspective, in order to characterise a form as more nominal or more verbal.

Table 2. Criteria for the classification of verbal and nominal reflexives

VERBAL	NOMINAL
cannot appear in non-object position	can appear in non-object position
does not permit long-distance reference	can permit long-distance reference
syncretic with other valency reduction operators	syncretic with intensifiers
encodes direct reflexivity	can encode also indirect reflexivity
morphologically 'light'	morphologically 'complex'

At a formal level, according to König (2007), the verbal vs. nominal opposition could be replaced with the grammaticalization hierarchy in (35). The elements on the left are more grammaticalized, have a lower morphological complexity and a higher referential dependency. At the same time, they show a higher range of uses in the so called "middle domain".

(35) formal properties of reflexive markers (König 2007: 111)
affix > clitic > weak pronoun > strong pronoun > noun > NP

Moreover, as is evident from the cases discussed in Section 4.3, the criteria proposed in Table 2 should be completed for each language with language specific features. In other words, it seems that many of the criteria which allow a reflexive to be classified as "more nominal" or "more verbal" should be language-specific, such as for instance the selection of the auxiliary form *être* in French, the interaction with the final vowel of the imperative in the Bantu languages or the relative position of the reflexive marker in San Andrés Yaá Zapotec.

To sum up, the reason why we cannot trace a neat border between verbal and nominal reflexives is ultimately due to their twofold nature. On the one hand, reflexive constructions operate on the referential level, since they indicate that two arguments are coreferential. But, at the same time, they operate at the predication level, since they modify a transitive verb. Consequently, as Faltz (1985) and Kazenin (2001) already noticed, positing a categorial opposition between nominal and verbal reflexives could be quite misleading and such a distinction should rather be viewed as a continuum.

Abbreviations

ACC	accusative	NAR	narrative
APPL	applicative	NOM	nominative
BEN	benefactive	O	object index
CAUS	causative	OCX	object index of class X
CL	classifier	PRO	pronoun
CONV	converb(al)	PRN	pronominal
DEM	demonstrative	PST	past
FIN	verbal ending	REFL	reflexive
FUT	future	SCX	subject index of class X
HAB	habitual aspect	SUP	supine
IND	indicative	TOP	topic
INF	informal		

References

Benincà, Paola & Poletto, Cecilia. 2005. The third dimension of person features. In *Syntax and Variation. Reconciling the Biological and the Social* [Current Issues in Linguistic Theory 265], Leonie Cornips & Karen P. Corrigan (eds), 265–299. Amsterdam: John Benjamins. https://doi.org/10.1075/cilt.265.15ben

Comrie, Bernard. 1999. Reference-tracking: Description and explanation. *Sprachtypologie und Universalienforschung* 52: 335–346.
Corbett, Greville C. 2013. Canonical morphosyntactic features. In *Canonical Morphology and Syntax*, Dunstan Brown, Marina Chumakina & Greville G. Corbett (eds.), 48–65. Oxford: OUP.
Creissels, Denis. 2002. Valence verbale et voix en tswana. *Bulletin de la Société de Linguistique de Paris* 97(1): 371–426. https://doi.org/10.2143/BSL.97.1.503765
Creissels, Denis. 2007. Réflexivisation, transitivité et agent affecté. In *L'énoncé réfléchi*, André Rousseau, Didier Bottineau & Daniel Roulland (eds), 83–106. Rennes: Presses Universitaires de Rennes.
Cristofaro, Sonia. 2009. Grammatical categories and relations: Universality vs. language-specificity and construction-specificity. *Language and Linguistics Compass* 3(1): 441–479. https://doi.org/10.1111/j.1749-818X.2008.00111.x
Croft, William. 2000. Parts of speech as language universals and as language-particular categories. In *Approaches to the Typology of Word classes*, Petra M. Vogel & Bernard Comrie (eds), 65–102. Berlin: Mouton de Gruyter. https://doi.org/10.1515/9783110806120.65
Croft, William. 2016. Comparative concepts and language-specific categories: Theory and practice, *Linguistic Typology* 20(2): 377–393. https://doi.org/10.1515/lingty-2016-0012
De Benito Moreno, Carlota. 2015. *Pero se escondiamos como las ratas*: Syncretism in the reflexive paradigm in Spanish and Catalan. *Isogloss* 1(1): 95–127. https://doi.org/10.5565/rev/isogloss.1
Dik, Simon C. 1983. On the status of verbal reflexives. In *Problems in Syntax. Studies in Language*, Tasmowski Liliane & Willems Dominique (eds), 231–255. Dordrecht: Springer. https://doi.org/10.1007/978-1-4613-2727-1_10
Dimitriadis, Alexis & Everaert, Martin. 2004. Typological perspectives on anaphora. In *Proceedings of the International Symposium on Deictic Systems and Quantification in Languages Spoken in Europe and North and Central Asia*, Bernard Comrie, Pirkko M. Suihkonen & Valentin Kelmakov (eds), 51–67. Iževsk: The Udmurt State University.
Dixon, Robert M.W. 2012. *Basic Linguistic Theory, Vol. 3: Further Grammatical Topics*. Oxford: OUP.
Everaert, Martin. 2013. The criteria for reflexivization. In *Canonical Morphology and Syntax*, Dunstan Brown, Marina Chumakina & Greville G. Corbett (eds), 190–206. Oxford: OUP.
Faltz, Leonard M. 1985. *Reflexivization: A Study in Universal Syntax*. New York NY: Garland.
Frajzyngier, Zygmunt. 2000a. Introduction. In *Reflexives: Forms and Functions* [Typological Studies in Language 40–41], Zygmunt Frajzyngier & Traci Curl (eds), vii–xv. Amsterdam: John Benjamins. https://doi.org/10.1075/tsl.40.01fra
Frajzyngier, Zygmunt. 2000b. Domains of point of view and coreferentiality: System interaction approach to the study of reflexives. In *Reflexives: Forms and Functions* [Typological Studies in Language 40], Zygmunt Frajzyngier & Traci Curl (eds), 125–152. Amsterdam: John Benjamins. https://doi.org/10.1075/tsl.40.06fra
Frajzyngier, Zygmunt & Shay, Erin. 2003. *Explaining Language Structure through Systems Interaction* [Typological Studies in Language 55]. Amsterdam: John Benjamins. https://doi.org/10.1075/tsl.55
Frajzyngier, Zygmunt & Shay, Erin. 2016. *The Role of Functions in Syntax: A Unified Approach to Language Theory, Description, and Typology* [Typological Studies in Language 111]. Amsterdam: John Benjamins. https://doi.org/10.1075/tsl.111
Galant, Michael. 2015. Changes in valence in San Andrés Yaá Zapotec. In *Valence Changes in Zapotec. Synchrony, Diachrony, Typology* [Typological Studies in Language 110], Natalie

Operstein & Aaron Huey Sonnenschein (eds), 213–236. Amsterdam: John Benjamins. https://doi.org/10.1075/tsl.110.11gal

Gast, Volker. 2006. *The Grammar of Identity: Intensifiers and Reflexives in Germanic Languages*. London: Routledge

Geniušienė, Emma. 1987. *The Typology of Reflexives*. Berlin: Mouton de Gruyter. https://doi.org/10.1515/9783110859119

Givón, Talmy & Bommelyn, Loren. 2000. The evolution of de-transitive voice in Tolowa Athabaskan. *Studies in Language* 24(1): 41–76. https://doi.org/10.1075/sl.24.1.03giv

Gruzdeva, Ekaterina. 1998. *Nivkh*. Munich: Lincom.

Haiman, John. 1983. Iconic and economic motivation. *Language* 59: 781–819. https://doi.org/10.2307/413373

Haspelmath, Martin. 2008. A frequentist explanation of some universals of reflexive marking. *Linguistic Discovery* 6(1): 40–63. https://doi.org/10.1349/PS1.1537-0852.A.331

Haspelmath, Martin. 2012. How to compare major word-classes across the world's languages. *UCLA Working Papers in Linguistics, Theories of Everything* 17: 109–130.

Haspelmath, Martin. 2021, forthcom. Comparing reflexive constructions in the world's languages. In *Reflexive constructions in the world's languages*, Katarzyna Janic, Nicoletta Puddu & Martin Haspelmath (eds). Berlin: Language Science Press.

Heine, Bernd & Miyashita, Hiroyuki. 2008. The intersection between reflexives and reciprocals: A grammaticalization perspective. In *Reciprocals and Reflexives: Theoretical and Typological Explorations*, Ekkehard König & Volker Gast (eds), 169–224. Berlin: Mouton de Gruyter.

Hengeveld, Kees. 1992. *Non-verbal Predication*. Berlin: Mouton de Gruyter. https://doi.org/10.1515/9783110883282

Janic, Katarzyna & Puddu, Nicoletta. 2021. The landscape of reflexive constructions: Form and function. In *Reflexive constructions in the world's languages*, Katarzyna Janic, Nicoletta Puddu & Martin Haspelmath (eds). Berlin: Language Science Press.

Kazenin, Konstantin. 2001. Verbal reflexives and the middle voice. In *Language Typology and Language Universals. An International Handbook*, Martin Haspelmath, Ekkehard König, Wulf Oesterreicher & Wolfgang Raible (eds), 916–927. Berlin: Mouton de Gruyter.

Kemmer, Susanne. 1993. *The Middle Voice. A Typological and Diachronic Study* [Typological Studies in Language 23]. Amsterdam: John Benjamins. https://doi.org/10.1075/tsl.23

König, Ekkehard. 2007. Vers une nouvelle typologie des marques réfléchies. In *L'énoncé réfléchi*, André Rousseau, Didier Bottineau & Daniel Roulland (eds), 107–130. Rennes: Presses Universitaires de Rennes.

König, Ekkehard & Gast, Volker. 2008. Reciprocity and reflexivity – Description, typology and theory. In *Reciprocals and Reflexives: Theoretical and Typological Explorations*, Ekkehard König & Volker Gast (eds), 1–32, Berlin: Mouton de Gruyter.

König, Ekkehard & Siemund, Peter. 2000. Intensifiers and reflexives: A typological perspective. In *Reflexives: Forms and Functions* [Typological Studies in Language 40], Zygmunt Frajzyngier, Traci S. Curl (eds.), 41–74. Amsterdam: Benjamins. https://doi.org/10.1075/tsl.40.03kon

König, Ekkehard & Siemund, Peter (with Stephan Töpper). 2013. Intensifiers and reflexive pronouns. In *The World Atlas of Language Structures Online*, Matthews S. Dryer & Martin Haspelmath (eds), Leipzig: Max Planck Institute for Evolutionary Anthropology. <http://wals.info/chapter/47> (20 February 2020).

Kulikov, Leonid. 2013. Middle and reflexive. In *The Bloomsbury Companion to Syntax*, Silvia Luraghi & Claudia Parodi (eds), 261–280. London: Bloomsbury.

Lazard, Gilbert. 2007. Le réfléchi est-il une voix? In *L'énoncé réfléchi*, André Rousseau, Didier Bottineau & Daniel Roulland (eds), 35–46. Rennes: Presses Universitaires de Rennes.

Lidz, Jeffrey. 2001. The argument structure of verbal reflexives. *Natural Language & Linguistic Theory* 19(2): 311–353. https://doi.org/10.1023/A:1010676623092

Marlo, Michael R. 2015. Exceptional properties of the reflexive in the Bantu languages. *Nordic Journal of African Studies* 24(1): 1–22.

Moyse Faurie, Claire. 2008. Constructions expressing middle, reflexive and reciprocal situations in some Oceanic languages. In *Reciprocals and Reflexives: Theoretical and Typological Explorations*, Ekkehard König & Volker Gast (eds), 169–224. Berlin: Mouton de Gruyter.

Moyse Faurie, Claire. 2017. Reflexive markers in Oceanic languages. *Studia linguistica* 71(1–2): 107–135. https://doi.org/10.1111/stul.12065

Nduku Kioko, Angelina. 1999. The syntactic status of the reciprocal and the reflexive affixes in Bantu. *South African journal of African languages* 19: 110–116. https://doi.org/10.1080/02572117.1999.10587387

Nedjalkov, Vladimir P. & Otaina, Galina A. 2013. *A Syntax of the Nivkh Language. The Amur Dialect* [Studies in Language Companion Series 139] Amsterdam: John Benjamins. https://doi.org/10.1075/slcs.139

Puddu, Nicoletta. 2010. Considerazioni di tipologia morfologica sul pronome riflessivo in greco. In *La morfologia del greco tra tipologia e diacronia*, Ignazio Putzu, Paulis Giulio, Nieddu Gian Franco & Cuzzolin Pierluigi (eds), 385–405. Milano: FrancoAngeli.

Puddu, Nicoletta & Janic, Katarzyna. 2021. Introduction. In *Reflexive constructions in the world's languages*, Katarzyna Janic, Nicoletta Puddu & Martin Haspelmath (eds). Berlin: Language Science Press.

Reinhart, Tanya & Reuland, Eric. 1991. Anaphors and logophors: An argument structure perspective. In *Long Distance Anaphora*, Jan Koster & Eric Reuland (eds), 283–321. Cambridge: CUP. https://doi.org/10.1017/CBO9780511627835.015

Reinhart, Tanya & Reuland, Eric. 1993. Reflexivity. *Linguistic Inquiry* 24(4): 657–720.

Reinhart, Tanya & Siloni, Tal. 2005. The lexicon-syntax parameter: Reflexivization and other arity operations. *Linguistic Inquiry* 36(3): 389–436. https://doi.org/10.1162/0024389054396881

Reuland, Eric. 2018. Reflexives and reflexivity. *Annual Review of Linguistics* 4: 81–107. https://doi.org/10.1146/annurev-linguistics-011817-045500

Schladt, Mathias. 2000. The typology and grammaticalization of reflexives. In *Reflexives: Forms and Functions* [Typological Studies in Language 40], Zygmunt Frajzyngier & Traci S. Curl (eds), 103–124, Amsterdam: John Benjamins. https://doi.org/10.1075/tsl.40.05sch

Zúñiga, Fernando & Kittilä, Seppo. 2019. *Grammatical Voice*. Cambridge: CUP. https://doi.org/10.1017/9781316671399

CHAPTER 11

The category 'pronoun' in East and Southeast Asian languages, with a focus on Japanese

Federica Da Milano
Università di Milano-Bicocca

The topic of the paper is an analysis of the debated notion of the category 'pronoun' in East and Southeast Asian languages, with a special focus on Japanese. After a description of the main aspects of the notion of 'person' as a grammatical category, the focus is devoted to personal pronouns in general and then to personal pronouns in East and Southeast Asian languages. Special attention is devoted to Japanese personal pronouns, taking into account the Emancipatory Pragmatics approach.

1. Introduction

The aim of this paper is to contribute to the discussion of the notion of 'descriptive categories' in linguistics, through the analysis of a case study, namely the debated notion of 'pronoun' in East and Southeast Asian languages, with a special focus on Japanese.

The question of the status of linguistic categories implies first of all a reflection on categorization from a cognitive point of view. One of the most basic human cognitive processes is the ability to categorize: categorization is essential to humans because it allows us to recognize familiar information, to assimilate new information and to distinguish among properties, objects and events.

In the typological community and in linguistic literature there is a heated discussion about the status and the epistemological value of the notion of 'category' and around the question whether grammatical categories can be considered universally valid entities or rather as language-specific phenomena. One of the last examples of this debate is witnessed by the discussion on the LingTyp mailing list on 2016, partly published in a special issue of Linguistic Typology and, of course, the papers of this volume.

https://doi.org/10.1075/tsl.132.11dam
© 2021 John Benjamins Publishing Company

2. Person as a grammatical category

It is often stated that the grammatical category of person covers the expression of the distinction between the speaker of an utterance, the addressee of that utterance and the party talked about that is neither the speaker nor the addressee.
According to Siewierska:

> In principle, there is no limit to the nature of the lexical expressions that a speaker may use to refer to herself. By contrast, it would be disfunctional for languages to have a wide range of expressions to denote the discourse role of speaker, addressee and third party. And indeed they tend not to. The vast majority of the languages of the world have a closed set of expressions for the identification of the three discourse roles embracing the category of person. The special expressions in question are typically called personal pronouns, or even just pronouns.
> (Siewierska 2004: 2)

Is the category of person universal? The question is strictly related to the notion of personal pronouns. Siewierska (2004: 8) states "[…] the universality of person as a grammatical category is sometimes called into question. The issue of whether all languages display the grammatical category of person is inherently tied to the issue of whether they have the category of personal pronoun".
So, next question could be: are personal pronouns universal?

3. Personal pronouns

Before starting with an attempt to analyze the possible categorical status of personal pronouns, some considerations are due with regard to the relation between the paradigmatic organization of personal pronouns (semantic side) and their usage in discourse (pragmatic side). Without this premise, the dynamics of usage of personal pronouns as well as their historical changes in pronominal paradigms cannot be understood. Personal pronouns are linguistic signs having conventionalized meaning and they are interpreted on the basis of a conventional rule. On the other side, peripheral uses of personal pronouns are functionally (pragmatically) motivated. As clearly stated by Helmbrecht:

> […] a functional study of personal pronouns, which intends to account for the dynamics of pronominal paradigms (grammaticalization of personal pronouns, historical changes in paradigms) need to distinguish between conventional meaning encoded in the paradigm and peripheral meanings of personal pronouns in actual usages, which can be explained only in terms of communicative intentions of the speaker and more or less inferences on the side of the hearer to recognize these intentions.
> (Helmbrecht 2004: 32)

Traditionally, pronouns are defined as words that 'stand for nouns' but most linguists consider this definition unsatisfactory. This is mainly because personal pronouns do not stand for any nouns as such. Another question concerns whether the distinction between personal pronouns and proforms constitutes a distinction between two different categories or whether the two only form part of a continuum of nominals.

Another relevant point is related to the status of third person forms in relation to first and second person forms, underlined by Benveniste: first and second person are deictic, referring to the actors of the speech event, whereas third person is anaphoric, because the individual or the thing referred to need not to be present in the speech event.

Again Benveniste noted:

> It is a remarkable fact – but who would notice it, since it is so familiar? – that the 'personal pronouns' are never missing from among the signs of a language, no matter what its type, epoch or region may be. A language without the expression of person cannot be imagined. It can only happen that in certain languages, under certain circumstances, these 'pronouns' are deliberately omitted: this is the case in most of the Far Eastern societies, in which a convention of politeness imposes the use of periphrases or of special forms between certain group of individuals, in order to replace the direct personal references. But these usages only serve to underline the value of avoided forms: it is the implicit existence of these pronouns that gives social and cultural value to the substitutes imposed by class relationships. (Benveniste 1971[1958]: 225–226)

As Bhat (2004) has pointed out in his monograph on pronouns in crosslinguistic perspective, a question has been raised as to whether some of the East and Southeast Asian languages like Burmese, Thai and Japanese can be regarded as not possessing any personal pronoun at all. Some linguists consider these languages as not possessing any pronouns as such, whereas others regard the nominal forms that are used in place of pronouns to be functioning as first or second person pronouns (Diller 1994).

According to Siewierska (2004), in the functional literature pronouns in the main continue to be viewed as a morphosyntactic category, but often the distinction between pronouns and nouns is considered to be not discrete but scalar, with some pronouns exhibiting less prototypically pronoun and more nominal characteristics than others.

Sugamoto (1989) posits seven characteristics as representing the pronominal extreme of what she calls the pronominality scale: (a) closed class membership; (b) lack of morphological constancy; (c) lack of specific semantic content; (d) lack of stylistic and sociolinguistic implicative properties; (e) expression of grammatical person; (f) inhability to take modifiers; (g) restrictions on reference interpetation.

Haspelmath (2010) assumes that universal or crosslinguistic categories do not exist and each language has its own categories; in order to describe a language, a linguist must create a set of descriptive categories for it. It was one of the major insights of structural linguistics of 20th century that languages are best described in their own terms rather than in terms of a set of pre-established categories that are assumed to be universal, although in fact they are merely taken from an influential grammatical tradition (e.g., Greek and Latin traditions).

As far as pronouns are concerned, it will not be a coincidence that Lehmann has chosen the personal pronoun as an example of linguistic concept and Japanese personal pronouns as less prototypical members of the concept:

> [...] the Latin personal pronoun is completely different from the Ancient Greek personal pronoun, but this has never impeded anybody, starting with the Roman grammarians, to cover the Latin variety by the same concept that the Greek grammarians had used for this variety. Nor was this scientifically inappropriate. Interlingual concepts like 'personal pronoun' are sufficiently abstract to comprise this kind of variation. [...] Thus, the personal pronoun of one language – say English – may represent the focal instance of the prototype, while the personal pronoun of another language – say Japanese – is only marginally comprised by this concept. (Lehmann 2018: 28–29)

Personal pronouns are generally considered among the most stable elements in language: however, they can undergo linguistic change (cf. Heine & Song 2010).

The main sources, especially in East-Asian languages, are nominal forms: in such languages, first person forms derive from nouns lowering the self: i.e., Viet. *tôi* 'slave', Kor. *so.in* 'little man', Thai *khâa* 'slave', etc., whereas second person forms derive from nouns exalting the addressee, such as 'master', 'lord', 'king'. This behavior is not restricted to East-Asian languages: in Persian (Teheran) a first person form is *bande* (lit. 'slave').

Another source for person form is represented by spatial deictic elements:

> The affinity between corporeality in spatial deixis and self-reference in participant deixis is not accidental. The participants in talk are the occupants of the corporeal field itself, the source points of the intersecting perspectives that it entails, the ones who have the reflexive *prise de conscience* that distinguishes coengagement from mere contiguity. In making reference to themselves, they project themselves and their perceptual, cognitive and affective engagements from the actual face-to-face situation onto the plane of discourse; they project themselves from the current context into a narrated one (the event line in which the referent of 'I' was, is, or will be a player). (Hanks 1990: 137)

An example from Korean (Song 2002: 14):

(1)   I   jjog-eun   gwaenchan-eunde   geu   jjog-eun   eotteo-seyo?
       This side-NOM   good-CONN   that   side-NOM   how-END
       'I am fine, and you?'

An example from Japanese (Ebi 2015: 605):

(2) Kotchi   mo   ureshii
     This.direction too   happy
     'I am happy, too'

Also Cassirer stressed the strict relationship between personal and spatial pronouns:

> "In nearly all langauges, spatial demonstratives provided the foundation for the personal pronouns. Historically, the link between the two classes of words is so close that it is hard to decide which to regard as earlier or later, original or derived. [...] Humboldt attempted to prove that the personal pronoun in general go back to words of local signification and origin; many modern linguists, on the other hand, tend to reverse the relation, tracing the characteristic trichotomy of the demonstratives found in most languages, to the natural trichotomy of the persons [...]. However this genetic question may ultimately be decided, it is evident that the personal and demonstrative pronouns, the original designations of persons and of space, are closely related in their whole structure amd belong as it were to the same stratum of linguistic thought."   (Cassirer 1953 [1923]: 213)

4. Pronouns in East and Southeast Asian languages

East and Southeast Asian languages are considered languages with particularly complex address systems: perhaps, the most extensive system of person honorifics is the one found in Thai, as presented in Cooke (1968). Some forms used for first and second persons are listed in Siewierska (2004: 228) and presented here.

Thai first person forms:

khâa'1phraphúd'thacâaw"2 (lit. 'Lord Buddha's servant' or '(your) Majesty's servant') – used by ordinary citizen, addressing the king and highest ranks of royalty;
klâaw1kraphŏm' (lit. 'hair of the head') – a highly deferential term used by males when addressing high-ranking non-royalty;
phŏm' (lit. 'hair') – a general polite term used by males speaking to equals and superiors;
dichăn' – a non-intimate deferential term used by females speaking to superiors or formally to equals;
chăn' – used by adult or adolescent male speaking to inferior or to female intimate;
khăw' – used by child or young women speaking to intimate; often endearing.

Thai second person forms:

tâajltàa'2la?ɔɔŋ'3phrá4bàad'5 (lit. 'dust underneath sole of royal foot') – used speaking to high royalty (though not the king);
tâaj 1thàaw'2 (lit. 'underneath foot') – used when addressing high-ranking superiors;
tua' (lit. 'body, self') – affectionate or intimate, used when speaking to equal or inferior not older than the speaker, especially between female friends or to one's spouse;
khun' (probably related to noun meaning 'virtue, merit') – general polite term used chiefly to equals and superiors

Many of the first-person forms literally refer to the hair or the head, whereas the deferential second-person forms refer to the 'sole of the foot' or 'underneath the foot'. According to Cooke, these expressions originate from a situation in which the inferior person places the sole of the superior person's foot on a par with his head or hair, the head being the highest and most respected part of the body. In Thai, as in Japanese (see Section 5), as already noted by Benveniste, most speakers prefer the use of ellipsis rather than one of the many first- or second-person forms when interacting with high-ranking royalty.

A more typical-sized system is found in Malay, which offers its speakers essentially two choices each for first and second person pronouns. As in Thai, the choice ultimately depends on one's attitude to the person one is speaking to, but this is strongly conditioned by factors such as social standing and relative age. One would not normally use the plain forms *aku* 'I' and *kau* 'you' unless one is on rather casual or intimate terms with the addressee. A good description of pronominal variants and usages can be found in Koh (1990: 140–146). She describes *aku* 'I' and *kau* 'you' as non-polite rather than impolite; because Malay society is extremely conscious of verbal politeness, however, the more formal pronouns such as *saya* 'I' and *awak/kamu* 'you' are required in a wide range of social situations.

It is interesting to note that the languages which are geographically in-between these regions, namely the Sinitic languages, do not have elaborate pronoun forms (though they use various other means of expressing respect and deference in speech).

A very complex system is found in Nepali, where different person forms are used depending on caste and age of speaker and addressee.

However, we can find complex address systems also in other languages: in many Romance languages, for example, using the third person singular form, the speaker does not address the interlocutor directly, but talks in a way which is conventionalized for referring to the absent third person. In so doing, the speaker does not force the interlocutor to behave in a certain way, but leaves it to the interlocutor to decide whether to interact at all, and if so, how (Da Milano & Jungbluth, to appear).

In Portuguese, for example, a nominal form addressing the hearer is *o senhor* 'lord' /*a senhora* 'lady'; Romanian developed an extraordinary rich system of address forms. In addition to the basic, informal, familiar address pronouns *tu* (2nd singular) and *voi* (2nd plural), with corresponding verb forms, most of the forms are based on the Latin *dominus* 'lord', *domina* 'lady', which resulted in Romanian *domn* 'sir' and *doamnă* 'lady' and in the derived form *domnie* 'lordship', the basis of address forms *dumneata* (originally 'thy lordship'), *dumnealui* (3rd masculine, originally 'his lordship'), *dumneaei* (3rd feminine, originally 'her lordship'), *dumneavoastră* (singular 'your lordship', historically plural, plural reference still possible), *dumnealor* (plural, originally 'their (masc.) lordships'). The second person form *usted*, in Spanish, was originally a nominal form, *Vuestra Merced* ('your grace'), which underwent a grammaticalization process; this development was paralleled in Portuguese with *Vossa Mercê* > *você*.

4.1 A focus on Japanese pronouns

In Japanese 'personal pronouns' are called *ninjō daimeishi*, a definition introduced in Japanese only in the XVIIIth century for the translation of Dutch grammars. In Japanese, pronouns do not differ morphologically from nouns. According to Hinds (1986) personal pronouns in Japanese differ from the pronouns of other languages like English in several respects: (i) in having nominal origins (*watashi* 'I', lit. 'private matters'; *boku* 'I', lit. 'slave'); (ii) in being terms of occupation or status titles; (iii) in being very large in number, with different forms being dependent upon sex, age, perceived social status, and emotional correlation; (iv) in showing most of the nominal characteristics like occurring after demonstratives (ex. *kono watashi*, lit. 'this I') and being modified by adjectives (ex. *yasashii anata*, lit. 'kind you').

Arguments over whether the category 'pronoun' applies to Japanese focus primarily on the existence of formal features that might distinguish personal pronouns from other nouns in the language. Kuroda (1967) concludes that items such as *watakushi* and *anata* are not to be termed pronouns, based on the fact that they do not have characteristic declensions. Kuroda also notes that the Japanese forms can be modified in the same way as other nouns, that the distribution of nouns and pronouns is identical in Japanese:

(3) Engl. *The short man*
    *the short he

(4) Jap. *Chiisai hito*   'little person'
    Chiisai kare   lit. 'little he'

Hinds (1971) argues, in contrast, that Japanese does indeed manifest a separate class of personal pronouns. A distinguishing feature of this class, he argues, is that it is obligatory that all its members add a suffix such as *-ra* or *-tachi* in the plural. For all other [+ human] nouns this is optional. Hinds fails to observe, however, that proper names in Japanese follow the same pluralization pattern as pronouns. Hinds also claims that the personal pronouns cannot be modified by demonstratives such as *kono* 'this' and *sono* 'that' as other nouns can. Martin (1975) provides evidence to the contrary: *kono watashi mo* 'even this person who I am' and *sono kare wa* 'that he'. Thus, there are no morphological or distributional criteria that warrant recognizing an independent class of pronouns in Japanese.

Diachronically, nouns are one of the sources of development of pronouns in Japanese. *Watakushi* is attested as a noun since stage Heian period (800–1200) and is used to describe things of personal and private nature. It is often contrasted with the notion of 'public': when there is such an opposition, there is a good chance for 'private' to be equated with 'personal', which has a strong connection with the speaker. *Watakushi* continues to be used as a noun in Kamakura/Muromachi period (1200–1600) but its usage is extended from private matters so as to include the notion of individual or self, thus invoking the first person interpretation. Although whether *watakushi* has semanticized as a person marker is not clear, its association started shifting from the described event to the speech event. In Meiji period (1870–Present) we find also the phonological reduction from *watakushi* to *watashi*. As a noun, *watakushi* tends to be phonetically unreduced, whereas there are a number of phonetic variants of *watakushi* in the first person sense: *watakushi* > *watashi* > *atashi* > *atai*. The difference in phonetic size between nouns and pronouns is consistent with the tendency that grammatical items such as personal pronouns generally have reduced phonological size relative to nouns. The case of *watakushi* exemplifies the natural and gradual development from a noun into a personal pronoun in that its change is primarily internal (the change is not motivated by a change in the social structure).

A different story is represented by the pronoun *boku*: its birth as a first person pronoun is largely due to extra-linguistic forces (i.e., loss of its literal meaning, 'servant', due to the abolition of feudalism, drastic restructuring of Japanese society and its subsequent adoption by students as a first person form). According to Traugott and Dasher (2002), linguistic change involving nouns is more susceptible than verbs to extra-linguistic and socio-cultural factors such as a change in the social structure.

As for the second person forms, *kimi* as a noun referring to the emperor or a person of very high social rank is attested since the earliest recorded history of the language; the use of *kimi* is extended even further as time progresses so that it can refer not only to the emperor/imperial family, but also to someone who is socially higher than the speaker in general. The use of *kimi* clearly changed in Meiji period:

it can now be used for any addressee of equal or lower social status: phrases such as *kimi to kimi* 'you and you' where each *kimi* refers to different entities (low semantic integrity) is possible. This change in the use of *kimi* seems to coincide with the drastic change of the social structure of Japan at that time: the meaning of 'lord' has become socially irrelevant with the abolishment of the feudal system.

Kisama was originally used as a term of address in formal letters of the Samurai class and rarely found in colloquial language. The etymology of *kisama* is somewhat controversial; three possible sources are considered: (i) shortened form of *kimisama* < *kimi* 'lord' + *sama*, a respectful suffix that originally meant 'appearence'; (ii) shortened form of *kishosama* < *kisho* 'your honorable residence' + *sama*; (iii) combination of *ki* 'graceful' + *sama*. According to Ishiyama (2018), the possibility in (iii) is the most plausible explanation.

Beginning with Edo period (1600–1870), *kisama* started being used frequently in the colloquial language; the loss of politeness toward the addressee becomes clearer and clearer in the second half of Edo period, and *kisama* is predominantly used for someone of equal or lower social status. In Meiji period its politeness is completely lost, and it is used derogatorily and carries the sense of contempt. This trend is even clearer in Present-Day Japanese, where the term is no longer used in a normal conversation because of the strong contemptuous sense that it carries. According to Ishiyama (2019) in these cases, in addition to semantic bleaching in the traditional sense (grammaticalization theory), what he calls 'pragmatic depreciation' is involved. Pragmatic depreciation refers to the decrease in politeness value toward the addressee.

However, most Japanese grammars and linguistic textbooks (e.g., Hasegawa 2015; Hinds 1986; Iwasaki 2013; Kuno 1973; Martin 1975; Shibatani 1990; Tsujimura 1996), regardless of their theoretical orientation, agree that there are elements of grammar that should be called personal pronouns.

The expressions used to refer to discourse participants in Thai are even more noun-like than in Japanese.

Just to have an idea of the polymorphy of first person forms in the history of Japanese (from Shibasaki 2005: 21):

Old Japanese: *a, (na), are, ware, wake, ōno, ōnore, maro*
Late Old Japanese: *a, wa, ware*
Early Middle Japanese: *ware, wanami, maro, maru, orera* (pl.), *warawa* (pl.)
Late Middle Japanese: *mi, midomo, wagami, soregashi, watakushi, kochi, konata, kono hō, wanami, ore* (masc.fem.), *warawa* (fem.), *sessha* (masc.)
Pre-modern Japanese: *kochi, kochito(ra)*(pl.), *soregashi* (masc.), *watakushi, watashi, washi* (fem.), *watai, watchi, midomo, ore* (masc.fem.), *orera* (pl.), *oira, oiratachi* (pl.), *temae, temaedomo* (pl.), *sessha* (masc.)
Modern Japanese: *watakushi, watashi, washi* (masc.), *washi* (masc.), *atakushi, atassia temae, wagahai, boku* (masc.), *ore* (masc.), *ora, oira, oiratachi* (pl.)

In addition to the distinction between male and female forms, the various forms belong to different stylistic registers, such as:

watakushi very formal; *watashi* formal for men, both formal and informal for women; *atashi* informal, mainly used by women; *ore* informal, mainly used by men; *boku* neutral, mainly used by men. This table (taken from Ishiyama 2019: 5) summarizes the pronominal inventory of Modern Japanese:

Table 1.

	Formal	Neutral	Informal	Derogatory
1st person				
Male speaker	*watakushi/watashi*	*boku*	*ore*	
Female speaker	*watakushi*	*watashi*		
2nd person				
Male speaker	*anata*	*kimi*	*omae*	*temee/kisama*
Female speaker	*anata*		*kimi*	*omae*
3rd person		*kare* 'he'		
		kanojo 'she'		

The differences between Japanese personal pronouns and Indo-European personal pronouns are significant: Japanese pronouns are relatively young, unlike the situation in Indo-European languages. In Japanese personal forms are relatively long, contrary to what happens crosslinguistically; moreover, the original meanings of Japanese pronouns are still traceable (see Table 2, taken from Ishiyama 2019: 8):

Table 2.

	Form	Literal meaning	Original		Current	
			Category	Pragmatic use	Category	Pragmatic use
i	*watakushi*	private	1st	formal	1st	Formal
ii	*boku*	servant	1st	humble	1st	Neutral
iii	*ore*	self?	2nd	contemptuous	1st	Informal
iv	*kimi*	lord	2nd	respectful	2nd	neutral/informal
v	*kisama*	nobility	2nd	respectful	2nd	Derogatory
vi	*omae*	honorable front	2nd	respectful	2nd	informal/derogatory
vii	*temae*	in front of (hand)	1st	respectful	2nd	Derogatory
viii	*anata*	that direction	3rd	neutral	2nd	Formal
ix	*kare*	that	3rd	neutral	3rd	Neutral
x	*kanojo*	that woman	3rd	neutral	3rd	Neutral

Another source of development for Japanese pronouns are demonstratives: from a cross-linguistic point of view, it is well known that demonstratives are a common source of third-person forms due to their functional similarity (Diessel 1999; Bhat 2004; Siewierska 2004): both of them can be used anaphorically and their use will result in a search for information either in the speeh situation or in the discourse context. In many languages, they are morphologically related to or formally indistinguishable from one another. This is not the case for first and second person pronouns, which typically have historical sources other than demonstratives (Lehmann 1995).

The third-person form *kare* 'he' originally was a distal demonstrative in Japanese: demonstratives *ka*-series was used exophorically on a limited scale for speaker-distal referents in Nara period (700–800) Although the *a*-series appears in Heian period and functions as speaker-distal forms, *ka*- is the dominant speaker-distal form. However, starting in Kamakura/Muromachi period, the *a*-series begins to take over the speaker-distal function of the *ka*-series, and eventually the *a*-series becomes dominant by the end of Edo period.

It is generally assumed that the birth of *kare* as a dedicated third-person masculine pronoun independent of the demonstrative system is due to the influence from third person pronouns in English and European languages.

As for the third person feminine form, *kanojo*, it is a combination of the speaker-distal demonstrative adjective *kano* and the noun meaning 'woman' (*jo*). The adaptation of *kanojo* as a third person feminine form seems to be similar to that of *kare*.

Demonstratives can refer to the speaker/addressee productively via metonymy without becoming independent personal pronouns (i.e., reference to a particular location/direction interpreted as reference to a person in that location/direction). According to Ishiyama (2019), although both demonstratives and first/second person pronouns are deictics, they are crucially different in terms of the nature of the referent that they designate. The main function of demonstratives is to direct the addressee's focus to entities in the surrounding situation and crucially to something or someone previously uninactivated in the addressee's cognitive state. The referent of first/second person pronouns (i.e., speaker and addressee), on the other hand, is in most instances presupposed in the speech situation.

However, there is a clear case in Modern Japanese of a second person pronoun developed from a demonstrative, namely *anata* (lit. 'that way'). The *a*-series in Japanese spatial deixis is speaker and addressee distal: according to Ishiyama its use as a second person pronoun is an instance of a distancing politeness strategy. *Anata* involves distancing in terms of space in that a speaker-and-addressee distal form is used for the addressee. At the first half of Edo period (around 1750), *anata* was used for the third person; its use for the second person became increasingly popular in the second half of Edo period. However, the status of *anata* as a second person becomes clear in Meiji period, when its original demonstrative function has died out.

Still referring to space, other person forms in Japanese can be traced back to location nouns. This is the case, for example, of *omae* attested since Heian period. Its use is generally reserved for a socially prestigious physical location such as in front of the altar or someone of a high social rank. Morphologically, it is composed of the honorific prefix *o-* and a spatial noun *mae* 'front'.

Another example is represented by *temae* which consists of *te* 'hand' and *mae* 'front'. In a literal sense, it was used as with the meaning of 'in front of the speaker' or 'the area that is close to the speaker'. Its use for person referents is not found until Edo period. The metonymic use of *temae* for a person referent, particularly for the speaker, is not surprising in that it refers to the areas around the speaker. In Meiji period, the form is used derogatorily for the addressee and is usually pronounced as *temee* with some phonological weakening.

Another interesting property that distinguishes Japanese personal pronouns from Indo-European personal pronouns is this: "A striking fact about the history of Japanese is the frequency with which pronouns shift over time to designate different speech act participants" (Whitman 1999: 358).

Some examples:

(5) Genji Monogatari (Whitman 1999: 381)
   Ware hito   wo   okos-a-mu
   I   person ACC   waken-MZ-PRESUMP
   'I will waken somebody'

(6) Kyōgen (Whitman 1999: 381)
   Itu   **ware** ga   ore ni sake o   kure-ta zo
   When you NOM   me to wine ACC   give-PFV EMPH
   'When have you given me wine?'

Whitman comments:

> I am unaware of shifts of the intrapersonal type in Indo-European languages. What we commonly encounter in the histories of many languages is personalization; shift of a non-person indicator (a 3rd person pronoun as conventionally labelled, or an epithet, title, or common noun) into a speaker – or hearer – designating role. (Whitman 1999: 360)

It is particularly interesting that Humboldt, in his *Notice sur la grammaire japonaise du P. Oyanguren* (1826) underlined:

> On doit regretter que ce chapitre, dans lequel nos deux grammairiens traitent du pronom, soit précisément un des plus imparfaits et des plus embrouillés. *Ware* est assigné à la première personne par Rodriguez, et à la deuxième par Oyanguren;

waga à la deuxième par Rodriguez, et à la première par Oyanguren; *konata* à la deuxième par les deux grammairiens, et en même tems à la troisième par Rodriguez, et à la première par Oyanguren.

J'ai peine à croire qu'une pareille confusion puisse réellement exister dans une langue quelconque. Si malgré cela, les deux auteurs avaient raison, la cause de cette confusion apparente pourrait se trouver dans les distinctions que l'étiquette établit entre les pronoms japonais   (Humboldt 1926: 8).

Personalization is found in a wide array of language families, but Whitman (1999) suggests that it is particularly common in Asian languages (Japanese, Korean, Thai) because they lack morphological person agreement on the verb. A shift of person categories that is especially common in the languages of the world is one where third person forms have come to be used as second person forms for the purpose of politeness. For example, German uses third person plural *Sie* as a polite second person form. Similarly, the Spanish polite second person pronoun *usted* comes from the nominal form *Vuestra Merced* 'your Grace', which is formally a third person form. The same type of development is observed in other languages such as Portuguese *você* and Italian *Lei*.

Other examples from Fujii (2012: 659):

(7) **Sonata** wa   omoi yora-zu   tomo,   **konata** wa   omoi yori
     You   TOP think.of-NEG if.not   I   TOP think.of
     te   sōrō
     GR   be.HMBL
     'If you do not think of (it), I think of it'
                                    (Otogizōshi, Benkei Monogatari, XIV–XVI cent.)

(8) **Konata**-no (kataru) Heike-wa   hito-ga   homema-ra-suru   hodoni
     You-GEN   (tell)   Keike-TOP person-NOM   praise-AUX-POL   more
     watashi-mo   ureshi   gozaru
     I-too   pleased   HMBL
     'The more people praise Heike story you tell, I am pleased as well'
                                    (Kyōgen, Muromachi period XIV–XVI cent.)

As for the shift from the first to second person forms, different approaches have been proposed. Whitman (1999) suggests what Suzuki (1978) calls 'empathetic identification' as a possible explanation for the shift. Empathetic identification refers to the change of perspective in the use of kinship terms where an older member of the family takes the perspective of the youngest member of the family. Empathetic identification is somewhat akin to the so-called 'medical *we*' in English, where doctors and nurses address patients with the first person plural as in *How we are doing today?*. Brown and Levinson (1987) call this use positive politeness. Although its potential explanatory power, Ishiyama agrees with Withman that, given the limited contexts in which it occurs, empathetic identification does not seem to account for the wide range of shifts observed in Japanese.

Withman (1999) then discusses an explanation based on the notion of empathy and direct discourse perspectives formulated by Kuno (1972, 1987, 2004). Intrapersonal pronoun shift would be motivated by the reflexive function in the so-called logophoric context. Whitman argues that this line of explanation may extend beyond the logophoric context and argues for the directionality of shift from pronouns to reflexives as well as from reflexives to pronouns.

Another hypothesis is presented in Shibasaki (2005): the shift of person categories can be accounted for by extending and reinterpreting Traugott and Dasher's (2002) intersubjectification. For Shibasaki (2005: 181) intersubjectification is the process by which "the first person is involved in either assimilating other-reference to the first person" or "accomodating first person reference to other- reference".

Ishiyama (2019: 89) explains the development of many personal pronouns that arose from nouns by the notion of 'extravagant politeness', recalling the notion of 'extravagance' used by Haspelmath (1999), who considered extravagance as speaker's use of unusually explicit information in order to attract attention. Ishiyama considers extravagant politeness as 'a politeness strategy that actively appeals to the addressee in order to achieve social success, usually by highlighting his/her positive social attributes, e.g., the use of unusually polite terms for someone whose social position does not necessitate it' (2019: 189). According to Ishiyama, the development of personal pronouns of nominal origins involves extravagant politeness in that extension of the original usage (e.g., members of the imperial family to someone who does not hold such a position) is almost certainly motivated by politeness to attract the addressee's attention and be socially successful in communication.

Again, Ishiyama stresses the need to distinguish between pragmatic and semanticized shift. The latter is the case where the post-shift usage has become a part of the semantic meaning of an item, e.g., Japanese *kimi* 'emperor' as a second person form and German *Sie* as a second person polite form. The former is restricted by the context of occurrence and used to yield a particular sociolinguistic effect in a given situation, e.g., Japanese *boku* 'I' used for a young boy with the meaning of 'you' and the so-called English medical-we. Pragmatic shift works on inferences, whereas semantic semanticized shift is coded in semantics.

Some researchers (Yamaguchi 1985; Vovin 2003) have pointed out that there is no need to treat the so-called personal pronouns and reflexives separately, at least in Pre-Modern Japanese.

4.2 Korean pronouns

Also Korean has a very complicated honorification system. In this language there are at least 138 first-person markers, according to a representative online Korean dictionary, namely *The Standard Dictionary of Korean*, published by the National Institute of Korean Language. Compared to the other attested Southeast and East Asian languages, Korean has even a greater number of first-person forms. In Korean linguistic literature, it is generally agreed that Korean has the category of personal pronouns; while the category appears to be open-ended, the most salient and representative personal pronouns are represented in the table 3:

Table 3. Personal pronouns in contemporary Korean (Sohn 2013: 287)

	1st person		2nd person		3rd person	
	Sing.	Pl.	Sing.	Pl.	Sing.	Pl.
Polite level	*Ce/cey*	*Ce-huy-(tul)*	*tayk*	*Tayk-(tul)*	D *pwun* D *elun*	D *pwun* D *elun*
Blunt level	*Na*	*Wuli-(tul)*	*Tangsin caki*	*Tangsin-tul*	D *i, ku, ku nye*	D *i-tul* D *tul* Kuney-tul
Familiar level	*Na/nay*	*Wuli-(tul)*	*Caney*	*Caney-tul*	D *salam, ku*	D *salam-tul* D *tul*
Plain level	*Na/nay*	*Wuli-(tul)*	*Ne/ney*	*Ne-huy-(tul)*	D *ai/ay*	D *ai/ay-tul*

5. Ellipsis

Another characteristic shown by Japanese and other Eastern languages, as already stressed by Benveniste (see Section 3) is the frequent use of ellipsis, or zero forms. The following examples are taken from Yamamoto (1999: 80):

(9) "... *asoko ja rokusuppo Ø   hanashi mo   deki nai shi, Ø*
      there   at property   (we) talk   ACC can   NEG and   (I)
      san-gai   no   ongaku kissa o   Ø   oshie-toita   no"
      third-floor CONN music   cafe   ACC (her) show-perf   CONN

'But it's too noisy to talk there and (I) told (her) about the coffee shop on the third floor instead.' (Yukio Mishima, *Hyaku-man Yen Senbei*, translated by Edward G. Seidensticker)

(10) "*Gomen-nasai, Ø   Hokkaidoo no   kata   desu-ka?*" "*Ø   Tookyoo*
       forgive.me   (you) Hokkaido CONN person COP-Q   (I) Tokyo

desu."	To	*boku*	*wa*	*it-ta*	"Ø	*Tookyoo*	*kara*	*o-tomodachi*	*o*
COP	that	I	NOM	say-PST	you	Tokyo	from	friend	ACC

sagashi-ni	*mie-tan*	*desu-ne*
to-search	come.up-PST	AUX-TAG

' "Forgive me. Are (you) from Hokkaido?" "(I'm) from Tokyo," I said. "Then (you)'re up here looking for a friend?" ' (Haruki Murakami, *Hitsuji o Megura Booken*, translated by Alfred Birnbaum)

Unlike in English, in Japanese the zero person forms occur regularly in declarative and interrogative clauses both finite and non-finite, main and subordinate and as subjects and non-subjects; moreover, the clauses in which they occur are not perceived as being evidently elliptical.

In Japanese, personal pronouns are omitted as often as possible, to the extent that frequent use of first-person pronouns is considered egocentric and unnatural (Hasegawa 2014), while the use of a second-person pronoun can be seen as contemptuous or even rude towards the addressee (Azuma 2000).

6. Towards an emancipatory pragmatics

The Emancipatory Pragmatics Project was featured in three special issues of *Journal of Pragmatics* in 2009 (vol. 41/1), 2012 (vol. 44/5) and 2014 (vol. 69):

> It is our shared conviction that pragmatics as analytic enterprise has been dominated by views of language derived from Euro-American languages and ways of speaking. In a sense, our project shares the classic Boasian aim of attempting to describe different languages in terms grounded in the cultures and societies to which they belong (Boas 1966) [...] we aim to integrate some of the cross-linguistic variations not only as objects, but also as part of the metalanguage of pragmatic description itself. (Hanks, Ide & Katagiri 2009)

In this framework, the behavior shown by Japanese personal pronouns has been explained through the concept of *ba* (Fujii 2012). *Ba* and *basho* are Japanese words meaning 'space, place, field' and they are commonly used in Japanese. *Basho* is a compound word made up of two morphemes, *ba* and *sho*, both normally translated as 'place'. *Sho* is used only in combination with other morphemes, as in *juu-sho* 'live-place' (a place where one lives = address) and *nan-sho* 'hard-place' (a place hard to pass).

Ba is the semantic space where the speech event takes place. The concept was developed by the Japanese biophysicist Shimizu and then applied to pragmatics; Shimizu claims that our way of situating self in the given *ba*/place of interaction is analogous with the relation between cells and organisms.

According to Otsuka:

> underlying ba theory are the Buddhist thought and the Japanese philosophy. In the West, subject and object are completely separated from one another, and the self and the other are understood as being opposed. However, in the East, subject and object are not considered separately, and the self and the other are not differentiated from one another. (Otsuka 2011: 5)

The interest of *ba* and *basho* for pragmatics is that it is a theory of contextual interdependence, alternative to our more familiar ones, and which speaks directly to what we commonly call 'situatedness, indexicality, co-presence and context'. The Kyoto School approach to *basho*, in fact, developed out of intensive dialogue with German phenomenology and, to a lesser extent, American Pragmatism.

As Hanks et al. recently noted, "In ordinary Japanese, *ba* is a semantically polyvalent noun. It figures in a large number of expressions, in which there are subtle shifts in its semantic focus. For heuristic purposes, we describe the semantic range of ordinary *ba* in terms of six broad (and overlapping) ideas:

1. A place for some activity
2. A scene (of a crime; in film or theatre)
3. An interaction (between two or more persons)
4. An occasion (as to schedule a meeting or get-together in the future)
5. An ambience (the feeling you have in a situation, relaxed, good, out of place, etc.)
6. Situational appropriateness (what is called for, what is out of bounds, propriety)" (2019: 64).

These aspects of *ba* push the concept in the direction of a deictic field: not just any setting, but a setting defined relative to co-participating people, implying perceptual fields and corporeality.

Neither *basho* nor the deictic field is a thing with a fixed degree of inclusiveness; both are relational spaces of variable extent. In this sense, *basho* is very similar to a 'field' of interaction:

> [...] the Japanese perspective on social life focuses on the relationship between what we in the West have most often perceived as dichotomies. But this significance will be lost if we try to perceive the Japanese through dichotomous lenses. Instead, the importance of Japanese society for us should lie in the possibility of reaching new perspectives on issues which have long perplexed us including the relation between the individual and the social order; variation and rule; flexibility and constraint; time and continuity; and particularity and general unity. (Bachnik 1998: 112)

7. Conclusion

Summing up, the fundamental difference between East-Asian and Indo-European personal pronouns is the following: while in Indo-European languages person forms are generally autonomous, context-independent, East-Asian person forms are more relational.

We can talk of 'person as evidential cline', following Quinn:

> It is sometimes said that there are no personal pronouns in Japanese or that there is no grammatical category of (first, second, third) person. This is true enough if one defines pronouns as morphologically related terms that come in paradigmatic sets, as in English (I, my, mine; you, your, yours, etc.), German, or the Romance languages. Nor there is there subject-verb agreement of person or number in the Japanese clause. But this hardly precludes expression of the same or similar functions in other ways. After all, deictic or indexical reference is the most basic kind of reference we humans practice. First, there is the highly developed set of deictic words in Japanese (which are, of course, also used anaphorically), the paradigm *ko-, so-, (k)a-* words [… that] correspond, and rather closely, to perspectives expressed grammatically by first, second, and third person in languages which have that category. Their proximal (*ko-*), mesial (*so-*), and distal ((*k*)*a-*) structure even matches the demonstrative paradigm in Romance languages. […] to define the cline of person only in terms of pronouns like 'I, you, he/she/it' and subject-verb agreement is to miss much about the way that cline can be structured. *While we have to be careful not to impose the categories of our language in the analysis of others, at the same time we must not assume that if we cannot find words like 'un(e)/le/la', 'a(n)/the', 's/he' and 'il/elle' in a language, it therefore 'does not have definite/indefinite', or that it does not 'have' person.* In charting a referential map for genuinely distant languages, it can be more revealing to begin by examining the expression of similar discourse functions than by looking for similar words or morphology, such as personal pronouns or person-number inflections.
> (Quinn 1994: 283–284)

As A.L. Becker and I. Gusti Ngurah Oka noted:

> While person appears to be a universal semantic dimension of language, structures of person and linguistic manifestations of persons – particularly personal pronouns – differ from language to language. Language students and linguists have to learn that I is not I, you is not you and we is not we from one language to the next. Within a language family, however, these differences may not be so great as across genetic boundaries. (Becker and Gusti Ngurah Oka 1974: 230)

And, as Quinn noted:

> The notion of a cline, a gradient range or field, is helpful in taking an evidential perspective on the category of person, which works particularly well when analyzing a language like Japanese. […] In mapping the cline of person in Japanese,

the trick is not to think of person as a collection of discrete words like *watashi* 'I', *anata* 'you' and *kanojo* 'she', but to conceive of it as an evidential cline, an indexical field (we can say, in other term, *ba* F.D.M.) extending out from a socially constituted *uchi*, the minimum instance of which is an individual speaker.

(Quinn 1994: 284–285)

Summing up, indexicality is strictly related to evidentiality (for a description about this strict relationship in Japanese, see Da Milano 2012, 2018).

In conclusion, I think that a prototype-oriented scalar approach à la Sugamoto (1989) and à la Lehmann (2018) could best describe the notion of 'pronoun': the difference between nouns and pronouns cross-linguistically can be considered a matter of degree, with conventionalized expressions of person deixis in Indo-European languages lying on the pronominal side of the scale, while Japanese and other East and Southeast Asian languages forms further towards the nominal side.

I agree with Mosby Irgens (2017: vi), according to which in Japanese (and I think that the same is true for other East and Southeast Asian languages) we can prefer the notion of 'empathetic deixis', instead of that of 'person deixis: 'the defining feature of empathetic deixis is not first, second and third person, but rather psychologically proximal versus distal: persons with whom the speaker identifies more or less closely'. In this view, Japanese and other East and Southeast Asian languages can be considered as empathy-prominent languages, whereas Indo-European languages as person-promiment languages. The concept of *ba*, the semantic space where the speech event takes place, can be thus considered as the field in which the relational features of pyschological proximity and distance are negotiated.

Abbreviations

ACC	accusative	NEG	negation
AUX	auxiliary	NOM	nominative
CONN	connective	PFV	perfective
COP	copula	POL	polite
EMPH	emphatic	PRESUM	presumptive
END	ending	PST	past
GEN	genitive	Q	question particle
HMBL	humble	TOP	topic
MZ	mizenkei		

References

Azuma, Shoji. 2000. Linguistic strategy of involvement: An emergence of new political speech in Japan. In *Beyond Public Speech and Symbols: Explorations in the Rethoric of Politicians and the Media*, Christ'l De Landtsheer & Ofer Feldman (eds), 69–85. Westport CT: Praeger.

Bachnik, Jane. 1998. Time, space and person in Japanese relationships. In *Interpreting Japanese Society*, Joy Hendry (ed.), 91–116. London: Routledge.
Becker, Alton & I Gusti Ngurah, Oka. 1974. Person in Kawi: Exploration of an elementary semantic dimension. *Oceanic Linguistics* 13: 229–255. https://doi.org/10.2307/3622745
Bhat, Darbhe Narayana Shankara. 2004. *Pronouns*. Oxford: OUP.
Brown, Penelope & Levinson, Stephen. 1987. *Politeness. Some Universals in Language Usage*. Cambridge: CUP. https://doi.org/10.1017/CBO9780511813085
Benveniste, Émile. 1971 [1958]. Subjectivity in language. In *Problens in General Linguistics*, 223–230. Coral Gables FL: University of Miami Press.
Cassirer, Ernst. 195 [1923]. *The Philosophy of Symbolic Forms, Vol.1: Language*. New Haven CT: Yale University Press.
Cooke, Joseph R. 1968. *Pronominal Reference in Thai, Burmese and Vietnamese*. Berkeley CA: University of California Press.
Da Milano, Federica. 2012. Classificazione tipologico-linguistica del giapponese in sincronia. In *Introduzione allo studio della lingua giapponese*, Andrea Maurizi (ed.), 43–84. Roma: Carocci Editore.
Da Milano, Federica. 2018. La soggettività linguistica: Un'analisi in prospettiva tipologica. In *Tipologia, acquisizione, grammaticalizzazione*, Marina Chini & Pierluigi Cuzzolin (eds), 51–62. Milano: Franco Angeli.
Da Milano, Federica & Jungbluth, Konstanze. To appear. Address systems and social markers. In *Cambridge Handbook of Romance Linguistics*, Adam Ledgeway & Martin Maiden (eds). Cambridge: CUP.
Diessel, Holger. 1999. *Demonstratives. Form, Function and Grammaticalization* [Typlogical Studies in Language 42]. Amsterdam: John Benjamins. https://doi.org/10.1075/tsl.42
Diller, Anthony. 1994. Thai. In *Semantic and Lexical Universals. Theory and Empirical Findings*, Cliff Goddard & Anna Wierzbicka (eds), 149–170. Amsterdam: John Benjamins. https://doi.org/10.1075/slcs.25.10dil
Ebi, Martina. 2015. Encoding deictic relations in Japanese. In *Manual of Deixis in Romance Languages*, Konstanze Jungbluth & Federica Da Milano (eds), 597–610. Berlin: De Gruyter. https://doi.org/10.1515/9783110317732-030
Fuji, Yoko. 2012. Differences of situating self in the place/ba of interaction between the Japanese and American English speakers. *Journal of Pragmatics* 44: 636–662. https://doi.org/10.1016/j.pragma.2011.09.007
Hanks, William. 1990. *Referential Practice. Language and Lived Space among the Maya*. Chicago IL: University of Chicago Press.
Hanks, William, Ide, Sachiko & Katagiri, Yasuhiro. 2009. Towards an emancipatory pragmatics. *Journal of Pragmatics* 41(1): 1–9. https://doi.org/10.1016/j.pragma.2008.02.014
Hanks, William, Ide, Sachiko, Katagiri, Yasuhiro, Saft, Scott, Fujii, Yoko & Ueno, Kishiko. 2019. Communicative interactions in terms of *ba* theory. Towards an innovative approach to language practice. *Journal of Pragmatics* 145: 63–71. https://doi.org/10.1016/j.pragma.2019.03.013
Hasegawa, Yoko. 2016. *Japanese. A Linguistic Introduction*. Cambridge: CUP.
Haspelmath, Martin. 1999. Why is grammaticalization irreversible? *Linguistics* 37: 1043–1068. https://doi.org/10.1515/ling.37.6.1043
Haspelmath, Martin. 2010. Comparative concepts and descriptive categories in crosslinguistic studies. *Language* 86: 663–687. https://doi.org/10.1353/lan.2010.0021

Heine, Bernd & Song, Kyung-An. 2010. On the genesis of personal pronouns: Some conceptual sources. *Language and Cognition* 2(1): 117–147. https://doi.org/10.1515/langcog.2010.005

Helmbrecht, Johannes. 2004. *Personal Pronouns. Form, Function, and Grammaticalization.* Habilitationschrift, Erfurt Universität.

Hinds, John. 1971. Personal pronouns in Japanese. *Glossa* 5(2): 146–155.

Hinds, John. 1986. *Japanese.* London: Croom Helm.

von Humboldt, Wilhelm. 1826. *Notice sur la grammaire japonaise du P. Oyanguren.* Paris: Librairie Orientale de Dondey-Dupré père et fils.

Ishiyama, Osamu. 2019. *Diachrony of Personal Pronouns in Japanese. A Functional and Cross-linguistic Perspective* [Current Issues in Linguistic Theory 344]. Amsterdam: John Benjamins. https://doi.org/10.1075/cilt.344

Iwasaki, Shoichi. 2013. *Japanese* [London Oriental and African Language Library 17]. Amsterdam: John Benjamins. https://doi.org/10.1075/loall.17

Koh, Ann Sweesun. 1990. Topics in Colloquial Malay. PhD dissertation, The University of Melbourne.

Kuno, Susumu. 1972. Pronominalization, reflexivization, and direct discourse. *Linguistic Inquiry* 3: 161–195.

Kuno, Susumu. 1973. *The Structure of the Japanese Language.* Cambridge MA: The MIT Press.

Kuno, Susumu. 1987. *Functional Syntax. Anaphora, Discourse, and Empathy.* Chicago IL: Chicago University Press.

Kuno, Susumu. 2004. Empathy and direct discourse perspectives. In *The Handbook of Pragmatics*, Laurence R. Horn & Gregory L. Ward (eds), 315–343. Malden MA: Blackwell.

Kuroda, Sige-Yuki. 1967. *Generative Grammatical Studies in the Japanese Language.* New York NY: Garland.

Lehmann, Christian. 1995. *Thoughts on Grammaticalization.* Munich: Lincom.

Lehmann, Christian. 2018. Linguistic concepts and categories in language description. In *Tipologia, acquisizione, grammaticalizzazione. Typology, Acquisition, Grammaticalization Studies*, Marina Chini & Pierluigi Cuzzolin (eds), 27–50. Milano: Franco Angeli.

Martin, Samuel Elmo. 1975. *A Reference Grammar of Japanese.* New Haven CT: Yale University Press.

Mosby Irgens, Benedicte. 2017. Person Deixis in Japanese and English. A Constrastive Functional Analysis. PhD dissertation, University of Bergen.

Otsuka, Masayuki. 2011. On ba theory. Paper presented for the lecture on ba theory at the 2011 Tokyo Workshop on Emancipatory Pragmatics. Ms.

Quinn, Charles J. 1994. Uchi/soto: Tip of a semiotic iceberg? 'Inside' and 'outside' knowledge in the grammar of Japanese. In *Situated Meaning. Inside and Outside in Japanese Self, Society and Language*, Jane M. Bachnik & Charles J. Quinn Jr. (eds), 247–294. Princeton NJ: Princeton University Press.

Shibatani, Masayoshi. 1990. *The Languages of Japan.* Cambridge: CUP.

Shibasaki, Reijirou. 2005. Personal Pronouns and Argument Structure in Japanese: Discourse Frequency, Diachrony and Typology. PhD dissertation, University of California, Santa Barbara.

Siewierska, Anna. 2004. *Person.* Cambridge: CUP. https://doi.org/10.1017/CBO9780511812729

Song, Kyung-An. 2002. Korean reflexives and grammaticalization: A speaker-hearer dynamic approach. *Sprachtypologie und Universalienforschung* 55(4): 340–353.

Sohn, Ho-Min. 2013. *Korean.* Seoul: Korea University Press.

Sugamoto, Nobuko. 1989. Pronominality: A noun-pronoun continuum. In *Linguistic Categorization* [Current Issues in Linguistic Theory 61], Roberta Corrigan, Fred Eckman & Michael Noonan (eds), 267–291. Amsterdam: John Benjamins. https://doi.org/10.1075/cilt.61.17sug

Suzuki, Takao. 1978. *Words in Context. A Japanese Perspective on Language and Culture*. Tokyo: Kodansha International.

Traugott, Elizabeth Closs & Dasher, Richard B. 2002. *Regularity in Semantic Change*. Cambridge: CUP.

Tsujimura, Natsuko. 1996. *An Introduction to JapaneseLlinguistics*. Cambridge: Blackwell.

Vovin, Alexander. 2003. *A Reference Grammar of Classical Japanese Prose*. London: Routledge Curzon.

Whitman, John. 1999. Personal pronoun shift in Japanese. A case study in lexical change and point of view. In *Function and Structure*. In *Honour of Susumu Kuno* [Pragmatics & Beyond New Series 59], Akio Kamio & Ken-Ichi Takami (eds.), 357–386. Amsterdam: John Benjamins. https://doi.org/10.1075/pbns.59.16whi

Yamaguchi, Yoshinori. 1985. *Kodai nihongo bumpoo no seiritsu no kenkyuu* [Studies in the birth of old Japanese grammar]. Tokyo: Yuseido.

Yamamoto, Mutsumi. 1999. *Animacy and Reference. A Cognitive Approaxh to Corpus Linguistics* [Studies in Language Companion Series 46]. Amsterdam: John Benjamins. https://doi.org/10.1075/slcs.46

Subject index

A
A-argument 42, 44–46, 48
abduction 259
abductive method 249, 258
accusative 8, 36, 119–121, 176, 230, 236–237, 244, 260, 262–263, 269, 304, 316, 356, 384, 407
achrony 23
action 41, 44, 53, 98, 104, 106, 109, 125, 254, 260, 263–265, 267, 281, 299, 329–331, 334–335, 338–339, 343, 371
actionality 27, 298
active reflexive 375
actor 194, 260, 266
address system 393–394
addressee 79–81, 83–88, 90, 127, 266, 268, 304, 390, 392, 394, 397, 399–400, 402, 404
adjectivalizer 340, 356
adjective 6–8, 11–13, 18–20, 28, 43, 47–48, 55, 65, 176, 215, 227–229, 237, 239, 242–243, 304, 313–321, 323–327, 329, 331, 333–336, 338–349, 351–352, 354–356, 360, 399
adposition 36, 109, 124, 256
affecting 104, 259–260, 264, 268, 299
affective. *See under* usage
affix 41–42, 46, 68, 334–335, 337–338, 346, 353, 356, 373, 384
affixation 27, 282, 292, 294
Agent (abbrev. A) 2, 10, 104, 170–171, 184, 230, 232, 264, 281, 317, 322, 338, 369–371, 375
agreement 9, 12, 44, 82, 154, 168, 173, 177, 185, 201, 212, 231, 249, 270, 272, 304–305, 318–321, 325–326, 333, 335, 338, 341, 359, 369, 401, 406
Aktionsart 298
alignment 11, 13, 316
ambiguity 36, 140, 148, 152–153, 172, 181, 185, 351–353
anaphora 387, 409
antipassive 116, 288
aorist 17, 304, 356
applicability 12, 35, 39, 54, 66–67, 73, 152, 163–164, 179–182, 202, 217, 219, 242, 300; *See also* 'universal applicability'
argument coding 42
article 2, 5–6, 25, 27–29, 43, 151, 153, 181, 183, 186–192, 194–195, 200, 232, 254–255, 257–258
aspect 26–27, 29, 47, 53–54, 64–65, 72, 75, 78, 90, 101–102, 107–109, 131, 194, 202, 258, 270, 272, 289, 297, 299, 302, 305, 321, 356, 360, 369, 384
  grammatical aspect 299
  imperfective aspect 74, 286, 289, 291, 300
  intensive aspect 281, 286, 288, 291, 300–302
  verbal aspect. *See under* verbal

B
basic standard category term 192
benefactive 114, 124–129, 304, 384
binding 54, 164, 361, 370
bivalent verb. *See under* verb
bound form 41, 44, 46

C
canon 67, 372
cartography 64, 67, 77
case 7–8, 11, 16–22, 24, 27, 29, 36, 41–45, 47–48, 61, 64, 68, 71, 74–75, 79, 82, 84, 89, 91, 94, 106, 108–109, 119–121, 125, 132, 134, 145, 147, 156, 161–163, 165, 168, 170, 176–178, 180, 184–185, 188, 190, 194, 197, 203–205, 213–214, 216, 218–221, 227, 230–232, 234, 237, 240–244, 248, 258, 260–264, 266, 273, 275, 280, 282–287, 291, 293, 297, 304–305, 315, 317–318, 320–322, 326–327, 329, 331–333, 335–337, 343, 352–354, 356, 370–372, 380–383, 389, 391, 396, 399–400, 402
case construction 18, 333, 336
categorial particularism 20, 66, 73
categorization / categorisation 20, 57, 61, 65, 68–69, 72, 75, 77, 94, 147, 262, 318–319, 335–336, 389, 410
category 2, 7–11, 15–16, 18–21, 24–29, 37–39, 44, 47, 49, 51, 60–65, 67–70, 74, 76–77, 79–80, 92, 94–95, 102, 106, 109, 115, 117, 119, 122, 137, 139–141, 146–148, 152, 154, 172, 174, 177–179, 183–200, 203–206, 212–213, 215, 217–221, 223–225, 228–234, 236–237, 239–240, 242, 244–245, 254–255, 270–273, 280–281, 299, 302–303, 315, 317–318, 323–325, 327, 350–351, 359, 368, 371, 376, 389–391, 395, 398, 403, 406
category general 20, 186, 198–200, 224
category labels 15, 25–26, 195, 351

category terms 137, 147–148,
    184, 186–193, 195–196,
    203–206
definition of category
    terms 147
derived standard category
    term 192
descriptive categories 182
notions of category 146–147
standard category term
    191–192, 194, 196, 205
typological category 10
universal category 19, 28,
    62, 67, 74, 215
causative 51, 103–104, 130, 262,
    264, 290, 304, 326, 384
causativity 290
characteristica universalis 3–4
characterization 144, 160, 196,
    206, 256–257
classificatory concepts 140
classifier 56, 270–273, 382, 384
clause 12–13, 18, 37–38, 41–45,
    53, 61, 70–72, 79, 96–97,
    99, 104–106, 111, 114, 117,
    119–122, 126, 128, 194,
    228, 246, 259, 261–262,
    272–273, 296, 317, 365–366,
    381, 406
cline 140, 406–407
clitic 46, 49–50, 304, 377,
    381–384
comparative concepts (abbrev.
    CC)
  CC as properties of
    construction/language
    pairs
  CC as properties of item/
    language pairs
  CC as properties of
    language/function
    pairs 177
  CC as 'pure' 27
  comparative-concept
    (functional) term 18,
    20–21, 171, 176, 189–192,
    200, 204, 206
  functional comparative
    concept 18, 20, 371
  hybrid comparative
    concept 18, 371
comparative grammar 4, 205,
    249, 252, 254–255, 270

comparative linguistics 2, 22,
    62, 94, 137, 141–142, 170,
    198, 201–202, 204, 206
comparative statement 170
comparativism 5, 32
comparison philosophical 4
concept 4, 8, 12–16, 18–21, 24,
    27–28, 37–39, 41, 43–44,
    47–49, 51–53, 63, 66, 68,
    104, 137, 140–141, 143, 145,
    147–148, 150–154, 163,
    165–169, 171–182, 185,
    187–197, 199–200,
    203–206, 213, 216–222,
    224–225, 227–233, 239,
    242, 244, 250–252,
    257–260, 268, 270–273,
    275, 281, 303, 315–316, 329,
    357, 371, 392, 404–405, 407
  universal functional
    concept 14
concept term 143, 153, 166,
    168–169, 171–172, 174, 176,
    187–192, 200, 203–204,
    206
conceptual framework 13, 56
conditional clause 53
constituent order 10, 135
construction 6, 8, 13, 15,
    18–20, 29, 38, 42–44, 51,
    59, 61, 73–75, 94, 96, 106,
    110, 126, 128–129, 134, 137,
    141–143, 148, 150–176, 179,
    182, 189–192, 194, 196–197,
    199, 203–204, 207–208,
    215–216, 245, 247, 266,
    271–272, 280, 289–290,
    303, 305, 314, 316–317,
    319–320, 325, 329–331,
    333–345, 351, 360, 368,
    371–373, 383
continua of techniques 250
continuativity 27, 285, 291
coreference 28, 43, 369–371,
    373, 378, 382
coreferentiality 115–118, 370,
    372
crosslinguistic categories 51,
    211, 213–217, 219–220, 232,
    237–238, 242, 244–245,
    260, 392
  inheritance hierarchies 212,
    235, 240, 245

monotonic, multiple
    inheritance 233–236, 238,
    241, 244
instantiation 8, 19, 211–212,
    217–224, 226–227, 229,
    232–234, 242

D

dative 8, 16, 48, 116, 124–125,
    131, 176, 213–214, 216,
    218–220, 232, 234, 236–237,
    244, 260, 264, 266,
    268–269, 271, 304, 357
dative case 48, 125, 176,
    213–214, 216, 218–220, 232,
    237, 304
dativus ethicus 266
dativus judicantis 266
deduction 253, 258
definition 8, 13–14, 16, 18–19,
    24, 26–29, 35, 38–39, 41,
    43–47, 49–50, 104, 108,
    114, 137, 141–143, 147–168,
    170–171, 173–176, 178–179,
    181, 185–192, 197, 199–200,
    203–204, 211, 216–217, 219,
    227, 229–230, 234, 243, 251,
    280, 282–284, 303, 313–314,
    316–317, 321, 325–326, 328,
    346, 351, 353, 367–370,
    372–375, 380, 391, 395
degrees of generality 182
deixis 74, 255, 257–258, 392,
    399, 407–408
demonstrative 13, 59, 65–66,
    131, 295, 384, 393, 399–400,
    406
description of a function 111
descriptive grammar 22, 348
descriptive linguistics 98, 137,
    141–142, 166, 175, 206
diachrony 23, 29, 247, 315, 350,
    353, 362, 385, 409
differentia linguarum 3–5, 21
dimension 23, 49, 69, 252,
    254–256, 258, 268–270,
    276, 406
direct object 36, 79, 126–128,
    269, 284, 304, 371, 381, 383
discourse roles 390
distal demonstrative 399
distributed morphology 65
distributivity 284, 291, 305

ditransitive verb. *See under*
    verb
documentary linguistics 5
double object construction 8

E
economics 39–40
effective verb. *See under* 'usage'
ellipsis 71, 394, 403
emancipatory pragmatics 389,
    404
enérgeia 250
ergative 18, 42, 44, 46, 221, 227,
    230–232, 237, 244, 260,
    304, 316
    ergative case 221, 227,
        230–232, 237
    ergative construction 18,
        42, 44
érgon 250
ethnopsychology 5
event 71, 74, 76, 85, 90,
    104–107, 115–117, 120, 125,
    127–128, 219, 223, 241,
    282–283, 285, 289, 291,
    299, 303, 371, 391–392, 396,
    404, 407
event-internal plural 285
events 27, 74, 90, 104, 109,
    112–113, 124, 169, 217, 233,
    239–240, 242, 285, 288,
    295, 299, 301, 389
evolutionary linguistics 22–23
experiencer 369
explicandum 150–151
explication 149–151, 154, 165,
    175, 255
explicative definition 150–151,
    154
explicatum 149–151, 154–156
exprimendum 270
extension 47–48, 80, 95, 148,
    152–153, 165–167, 169,
    171–172, 175–177, 189, 191,
    194, 200, 205, 273, 402
extroverted verb. *See under*
    verb

F
flag 41–42, 44, 381
formal definition 24, 164–165,
    167
formal logic 140

formal means of coding 108,
    124
frequentative 131, 285–288,
    293, 296–297, 304
frequentativity 28, 283, 285,
    291, 296, 298–299
function 12–13, 18–19, 28, 30,
    38, 56, 65, 74, 77–78, 80,
    82, 84–85, 89–94, 97, 99,
    102, 105–112, 114–117, 119–
    121, 124–127, 129, 143–145,
    150, 158–159, 162, 165, 172,
    175, 177–179, 182, 191–192,
    194, 197, 199–200, 219,
    228, 237, 241, 248, 251–252,
    272–273, 280, 282, 285,
    287, 289–291, 294–296,
    306, 315–317, 328–331, 335,
    339–340, 343, 345, 347,
    351, 355, 361, 365, 368, 370,
    372, 375, 399–400, 402,
    408–410
    discovery of functions 108
    function category terms 191
functional denominator 250,
    270
functional domain 26, 108, 111,
    113–114, 281, 290, 303
functional role 257

G
gender 43–46, 48–49, 56,
    101–102, 127, 131, 269–270,
    272, 277, 304–305, 318–321,
    324–325, 333, 335
General Comparative
    Grammar (GCG) 252
general linguistics 22–23,
    35–38, 51, 96, 137, 141–142,
    166, 202, 204, 206, 235, 315,
    353, 364, 408
generalization 102, 156,
    169–170, 176, 252, 267,
    291, 317
generative grammar 22, 25,
    202, 215–216, 346, 358
generative syntax 15, 98
generative tradition 59, 62–64,
    67, 69, 73, 77, 79
glosses 15–16, 53, 60, 66, 105,
    192, 227, 271, 282, 286
    interlinear glossing 53,
        254–255, 271

Leipzig Glossing Rules 15,
    52, 66, 173, 192, 282, 304
goal orientation 114, 119,
    121–122
gradience 239, 265–267
gram type 19
grammaire générale 4–5, 22, 31
grammar 1, 4–5, 10, 14–17, 22,
    25–26, 29–30, 33, 37–39,
    50, 54, 59–60, 62–63, 75,
    77–78, 85, 95–96, 98–99,
    110, 131–134, 155–156, 161,
    171, 173–176, 186–187,
    189–197, 202–206, 209–211,
    213, 215–216, 243, 245–249,
    252, 254–255, 258, 262,
    270, 275–277, 280, 299,
    305–308, 313, 315–316,
    319–320, 324, 331, 346,
    348, 351–353, 356, 358–360,
    363–366, 368, 374, 386, 397,
    409–410
grammatica universalis 3, 21
grammatical description 137–
    138, 201, 204–206, 282
grammaticalization 7, 22,
    31–32, 65, 69, 98, 131–134,
    208–209, 247, 275, 295,
    376, 383, 390, 395, 397,
    408–409
grammaticalization theory 397

H
habituality 27, 229, 285, 288,
    291, 298–299
head-final order 7
hearer 266, 390, 395, 400
Heaviness Serialization
    Principle 8
historical linguistics 22–23,
    362
honorifics 393

I
identification 142, 171–172,
    185–186, 193, 205, 241,
    249–250, 254–256, 258,
    350, 359, 378, 390, 401–402
identification statement 171,
    172, 193
identification vs.
    definition 186
identity of marking 27

ideophones 26, 55, 59, 91
idiolect 20, 162
imperfectivity 286, 291, 299
implicational relation 6
inclusiveness condition 64
incommensurability 16, 186, 313
indexicality 405, 407
indicativity 250–251, 255, 257, 268
indirect object 79, 108, 114, 122, 124–129, 264, 267, 269
induction 252–253, 258
infixation 292
inflection 337
informal definition 156, 160–164, 166, 173, 176
inheritance hierarchy 212, 235, 238, 240, 245
instantiation 8, 19, 211–212, 217–224, 226–227, 229, 232–234, 242
intension 165, 167–168, 172, 174–175, 179, 189, 197
intension-based concept types 175
intensity 286, 301
interlinear glossing *See under* glosses
International Phonetic Alphabet (abbrev. IPA) 9–10, 35–36, 44, 52, 213, 221–224, 237, 239
interrogative clause 404
intersubjectification 402
Intransitive 42, 104, 115–117, 128, 230–232, 261–265, 284, 295, 304, 365, 375, 383
introverted verb. *See under* verb
intuition 46, 252, 273
invariant 250–253, 273, 374
iterative 285–290, 296, 298, 304
iterativity 289

L
lambda calculus 144, 146
lambda expressions 159
language 1–33, 35–39, 45, 47–49, 51–57, 59–68, 73–82, 88, 91–99, 102, 104–108, 110–114, 118–119, 123–125, 129–130, 132–135, 137–139, 142–148, 150–152, 154–160, 162–164, 166–183, 185–195, 197, 199–210, 212–215, 219–220, 223–225, 227–229, 233, 236–237, 239–240, 242–243, 245–255, 257–260, 265, 267, 269–271, 274–276, 279–283, 290, 294, 296–297, 299, 302–303, 305–318, 321, 324–325, 327–332, 336, 346–349, 351–353, 355–366, 368–370, 372, 378, 380, 382–387, 389, 391–392, 395–397, 401, 403–404, 406, 408–410
language classification 5, 283
language comparison 24, 38, 61, 66, 68, 137–138, 143, 201–204, 212–213, 237
language faculty 5, 21–23, 63
language of logic 143, 148, 156, 160, 167, 172, 180
language particularism 24, 346
language reconstruction 5
language universals 5–6, 23, 27, 29, 60, 63, 78, 96, 204, 206, 249, 252–253, 274–276, 365, 386
language-specific category 74, 148, 178, 255, 270
language-specific criteria 61, 205, 220
languoid 21, 282
Leipzig Glossing Rules *See under* glosses
lexeme 28, 176, 214, 227–228, 242, 293, 313–314, 325, 331–332, 336–337, 342, 344–345, 347–348, 350–352, 354–356
lexical alternation 27, 292–294, 301–302
lexical categories 65, 68–69, 109–110, 225, 297, 358
lexicalism. *See under* lexicalist approach
lexicalist approach 346, 351
Lexicalist Hypothesis. *See under* lexicalist approach

lexicalization 344, 349
linearisation 11
LINGTYP 1–3, 5–8, 17, 22, 280, 389
linguistic sign 390
Linguistic Typology 1–3, 5–6, 17, 27, 29–33, 55–56, 96–98, 101, 119, 132, 134, 138, 207–211, 245–249, 275, 280, 306–308, 314, 318, 358–365, 385, 389
localization 256–257
location noun 400
locative predication 114, 123–124
logic 26, 69, 95, 137–138, 140–146, 148, 156, 160, 167, 172, 174, 180, 189–190, 201, 207, 210
logical form 159, 162

M
malefactive 112, 114, 124–126, 128–129
marker 8, 28, 37–38, 41–42, 44–46, 61–62, 70, 82, 105, 110–113, 115–118, 120–122, 127, 130–131, 176, 213, 216, 218–219, 229–232, 234, 259, 261–262, 266, 272, 285, 287, 295, 297, 302, 305, 369–370, 372, 378, 382, 384, 396
mental invariant 252
mental map 252
mental movement 251
metonymy 399
middle domain 368, 370, 384
middle voice 18–19, 317, 368, 386
minimalism 64
monotransitive verb. *See under* verb
morph 41–42, 44–45, 314, 337, 351–353, 361
morpheme 13, 16, 59, 110, 285–286, 314, 349, 351–352, 374, 383

N
nature of concepts clarified 173
neuro-biology 22
No Base Hypothesis 26
nomifier system 43–44

Subject index   415

nominal 6, 28, 41–42, 45, 70, 73, 75, 117, 121, 127–128, 148–149, 151–154, 215, 236–237, 241, 256, 263, 268–269, 271, 273, 289, 293, 295, 298, 305, 307, 322, 326, 340, 345, 361, 367, 373–378, 380–384, 391–392, 395, 401–402, 407
  nominal definition 149, 153–154
  nominal reflexive 367, 378, 381
nominalization 313, 314
nominalizer 131, 338, 357
nominative 36, 227, 230–231, 236–237, 244, 254, 260, 304, 357, 384, 407
nominative case 36
notational convention 194–195
noun 6, 10, 12–13, 18, 26, 28, 32, 39, 41, 43, 47, 49–50, 55, 61, 65, 70, 101, 105, 108–109, 111, 114, 117–119, 121, 124–125, 127, 130–131, 176, 189, 215, 227–228, 235–236, 239–240, 242, 260–267, 271–273, 298–299, 313, 315, 317–319, 321, 323–327, 329–330, 333–348, 351–352, 354, 356, 369–370, 375, 377, 382, 384, 394, 396–397, 399–400, 405
noun incorporation 50
number 6, 43–45, 47, 65–66, 69–70, 101–102, 107–110, 113, 125, 127–128, 130–131, 146, 153–155, 160–161, 163, 165, 168, 182, 205, 207, 249–250, 257, 269–273, 282, 292–293, 295, 299, 302, 305, 318–320, 322, 326, 332–333, 335, 337, 341–342, 344–345, 347, 349, 356, 370, 374–375, 395–396, 403, 405–406
numeral classification 269–272

O
Object (abbrev. O) 1–2, 8–10, 19, 21–22, 36, 41, 64, 79, 104–105, 108, 113–116, 118–119, 122, 124–129, 131, 152, 230, 232, 248–250, 259–269, 272–274, 276, 284, 295, 304–305, 329–331, 333–335, 338, 343, 368, 370–373, 375, 378–384, 405
oblique 36, 42, 44, 131, 305
occasion 67, 283, 355, 405
onomasiological approach 15, 258
ontological relationship 193
operation 269, 272, 320

P
P(atient)
panchrony 23
paradigm 43, 87, 216, 270–271, 293, 359, 390, 406
parameter 268, 291
participant deixis 392
participant plurality 284, 288, 291, 294, 301
particles 59, 85–89, 110, 243, 353
particularism 20, 24, 66, 73, 346
parts of speech 28, 214–215, 313–367, 383; see also word classes
past tense 17, 66, 111, 305
patient 2, 10, 104, 170–171, 266, 284, 369–371, 375
perfective 74, 127, 131, 194, 289, 300, 305, 407
periphrasis 347
person 41–43, 52, 65–66, 74, 101–102, 105, 110, 118, 128, 131, 135, 184, 230, 241, 265–266, 272, 289, 304, 318, 320–321, 334, 337, 357, 371, 374, 377–379, 389–404, 406–407, 409
  person agreement 401
personal pronoun 29, 377, 390–393, 396
personalization 400–401
phases 20, 285
phonological reduction 396
phonological weakening 400
pluractionality 27–28, 279, 281–284, 298, 302–303
politeness 29, 391, 394, 397, 399, 401–402, 408
portable terms 19, 195

pragmatics 32, 81, 96, 243–244, 362, 389, 404–405, 408–409
predicate 26, 41–42, 79, 108–109, 111, 114, 119–123, 125–126, 130, 144–145, 151–152, 158–168, 171–172, 178–179, 181, 228, 271, 273, 317, 325, 329–331, 334–335, 343, 352, 369, 375–376
predicate logic 26, 144
predicativity 250–251, 255, 257, 268
predictive value 6
prefixation 292
prepositional phrase 266
Principle of Head Proximity 13
problem of the hidden variable 142, 162, 173
problem of type-token relations 197
problem-solving system 250, 270
proform 391
pronoun 28–29, 44, 66, 118, 127–128, 131, 305, 320, 374, 376–381, 384, 389–396, 399–402, 404, 407
  pronoun shift 402
proper definition 151, 160, 164–165, 189
proper name 323
property 6, 12–13, 18, 41, 43, 47–49, 74, 89, 91, 115, 144–146, 165, 167–172, 174–176, 178–182, 188–189, 194, 199, 201, 217, 219–221, 224, 227–228, 230, 232–233, 239, 241–242, 251, 272–273, 286, 316, 370, 400, 403
prototype 29, 38–39, 49, 51, 147, 169, 260, 280, 371, 392, 407
prototype theory 147
prototypical action 104
prototypical property
prototypical reflexive 371
Proto-World 22

Q
quantification 164, 255, 257, 269–270, 385
quantitative concepts 140
questionnaire 14

R
real definition 149
reciprocal 287, 305
reciprocity 27, 287–288, 291, 368
reduplication 27, 131, 281–282, 286–292, 294, 300–301, 303, 305, 338
reference to languages made explicit 173
reflexive 28, 43, 50, 56, 103–104, 112, 115–117, 120–121, 192, 305, 367–384, 386–387, 392, 402
verbal reflexive 375–376, 378, 381
reflexive argument marker 376–377
reflexive construction 43, 368, 371, 383
reflexive content
reflexive marker 28, 116–117, 120–121, 369–370, 372, 378, 382, 384
reflexive nominal 376–377
reflexive strategy 369, 379
reflexivity 28, 50, 367–368, 373, 375–376, 383
relative clause 12–13, 18, 43, 45, 194, 228, 317
repraesentandum 251, 270, 273
revision 166, 172–179, 182–184, 188, 191–192
root 28, 41–42, 45–47, 65, 90, 94, 234, 239–241, 262, 313–315, 320, 322–323, 326, 337–344, 346–354, 356, 380, 382
root-and-pattern 343

S
semantic bleaching 397
semasiological approach 15
sentence 170, 178, 190, 339
serial verb construction 42, 137, 141–143, 148, 151–176, 182, 190–192, 194, 196, 199, 203–204, 207
sign language 39
simple descriptive statement
singular 70, 107, 110, 131, 153, 227, 236–237, 254, 271–273,
285, 290–293, 305, 357, 379, 394–395
Societas Linguistica Europaea (abbrev. SLE) 3, 101
spatial deixis 392, 399
spatial demonstrative 393
spatial distributivity 284, 291
speaker 51, 71–72, 79–80, 82–88, 90, 92, 110–113, 122, 215, 314, 390, 394, 396, 398–400, 402, 407
speech event 223, 391, 396, 404, 407
Standard Average European (abbrev. SAE) 273
standard comparative concept 197
standard descriptive category 194
state of affairs 86
stativity 372
stem 288, 333–334, 347
stimulus 19, 37
stipulative definition 149, 157, 187–188
strategy 12, 18, 20, 92, 283–285, 288, 290, 292–294, 301, 324, 345, 347, 369, 376, 379–380, 382–383, 399, 402
structural linguistics 392
structuralism 25
sub-dimension 252, 270
subject 2–3, 6, 9–11, 22, 35–36, 42, 45–46, 48, 54, 79, 103–106, 108, 112, 114–119, 121–122, 126, 131, 177–178, 184–185, 191–192, 194, 198, 200–201, 212, 230, 243, 248, 268, 273, 284, 295, 304–305, 321, 329, 370–373, 378–379, 381–384, 405–406
subordinate clause
suffix 38, 70, 105, 121, 126–128, 271, 288–289, 296–300, 302–304, 320, 322, 334, 336–339, 341, 379–380, 396–397
suffixation 292
SVO 2, 9–12, 104, 316
synchrony 23, 29, 315, 350, 353, 362, 385

T
technique 252, 255, 257–258, 270, 272, 376–377
telic verb. *See under* verb
template and pattern morphology
terminology 337
tertia comparationis 11–12, 270
theme 8, 213, 216, 232, 263, 268
theory of language 4, 22–26, 33, 155–156, 171, 174, 177, 182, 201–206, 315, 355–356
token 10, 197–200, 209, 330
transitive clause 42
transitivity 104, 106, 116, 260, 263, 269, 325
translation 7, 12, 15, 86, 123, 143, 160–161, 241, 270, 288, 395
transnumerality 273
transnumeral form 271
transnumeral noun 272
trivalent verb. *See under* verb
type 17–20, 25, 30, 37, 65–66, 72, 74, 77, 79–81, 86, 89–90, 95, 97, 128, 139–141, 143–144, 148–149, 151–152, 155–156, 158, 161–162, 164, 170, 174–179, 190, 192, 194, 196–200, 209, 261, 266–267, 271, 288, 299, 306, 315–317, 331, 333, 338–339, 346–347, 350, 352–356, 361, 371, 391, 400–401
typology 1–3, 5–8, 10, 14–18, 20, 22, 24, 27, 29–33, 39, 54–56, 62, 67, 77, 94, 96–99, 101, 103–104, 113–114, 119, 124, 129–130, 132–134, 138, 140, 170, 196, 198, 201, 203, 206–211, 245–249, 252–253, 275–276, 280, 306–308, 313–316, 318, 325, 327–329, 332, 346–348, 350, 353, 355, 358–366, 374, 385–386, 389, 409
aims of typology 101
multivariate typology 67, 77

U
undergoer 260

Unit of Language (abbrev. UoL) 60, 314, 351
Unitary Base Hypothesis 346
UNITYP project 6, 27, 140, 249–274
universal applicability 66, 169, 179, 182, 242
universal coding asymmetries 270
Universal Grammar (abbrev. UG)
Universal Spine 26, 59, 73–74, 76, 78–80, 82–83, 93–95
Universal Spine Hypothesis (abbrev. USH)
universality statement 170
usage 10, 14–15, 22–23, 29, 33, 45–47, 149, 155, 190, 218, 224, 262–263, 299, 390, 396, 402, 408
    affective 260, 262
    effective 260, 262
utterance 71–72, 74, 76, 79–83, 85–86, 88, 93, 106–107, 109–110, 112, 122, 130, 390

V
valency 49, 259–260, 262, 264–265, 267, 269, 275, 374–376, 383
Valency Classes Project (abbrev. ValPaL)
Verb (abbrev. V)
    bivalent 260–262, 265
    ditransitive 269, 304
    extroverted 374
    introverted 374
    telic 265
VO 9–10, 269

W
weak constructivism 183–184
word 2, 6–11, 14–15, 18, 20, 27–29, 31, 36, 38, 41, 46, 49–50, 53, 59, 64, 68, 78, 92, 102, 106, 109, 132, 142, 147–148, 172, 178, 181, 186–187, 189–190, 192, 224, 228, 238, 243, 245–248, 251, 257, 307, 314, 316, 318–321, 324, 328, 330–331, 333–334, 336–339, 344, 346–353, 356, 358–359, 363–366, 380, 385, 404
word classes 8, 28, 64, 142, 246–248, 307, 318, 320, 330, 344, 365–366, 380, 385; *see also* parts of speech
word order (abbrev. WO)
    basic WO 2, 15, 18, 316
World Atlas of Language Structure (abbrev. WALS)

Z
zero form 403

Language index

ǂHoan 284, 310

A
Akawaio 279, 299–300, 302
Amele 311, 354–355
Ancient Greek 36, 349, 364, 392
Arabic 48, 130, 309, 352–353, 366; *See also* Classical Arabic
Avestan 349

B
Bambara 225
Barasano 284, 307, 312
Basque 4, 312
Beja 279, 288, 299–303, 309
Bukip 354–355
Burmese 311, 391, 408
Burushaski 292, 312

C
Cantonese 2, 11, 311
Cayuga 297–298
Cha'palaa 93
Chadic 104–105, 112, 117–118, 121, 123–124, 126, 132, 135, 281, 292, 294–295, 307
Chai 225
Chamorro 19–20, 309, 318
Chechen 285
Chickasaw 293, 311
Chinese 4, 6, 12, 49, 85, 97–98, 270–272, 311, 354–355; *See also* Late Archaic Chinese, Late Middle Chinese, Mandarin Chinese
Chukchi 298, 310
Cilubà 288–289
Classical Arabic 352
Czech 21, 224

D
Dutch 115, 214, 221, 224, 395
Dyirbal 230, 354–355

E
Early Middle Japanese 397
Eastern Ojibwa 227–228, 240, 242
Edo 170–171, 397, 399–400
English 4, 8, 11, 29, 36–38, 40, 45, 48–49, 51–52, 55, 61–62, 65, 69–70, 76, 81, 84, 86, 88, 90–91, 97–98, 106, 108, 110–113, 117, 120–126, 128, 130–131, 143, 148, 155, 160, 181–182, 185–192, 194–195, 200, 209, 222–223, 225, 228, 238, 242, 259–260, 263, 268, 271, 273, 280, 310, 317, 349–350, 353–355, 359, 362, 372, 392, 395, 399, 401–402, 404, 406; *See also* Old English
Eton 294–296, 304, 308–309

F
Finnish 216, 218–219, 247, 312
French 11–12, 36–37, 52, 111, 115, 131, 310, 378–380, 384

G
Garo 18, 311, 317, 354–355
German 4, 25, 37–38, 48–49, 52, 55, 115, 143, 177, 187, 214, 221, 224, 254–255, 259–260, 263–264, 266, 268–269, 271, 310, 320, 349, 374, 378, 401–402, 405–406; *See also* Old High German
Gidar 126–128, 133
Greek 4, 20, 36, 270, 310, 317, 349, 356, 364, 392
Gurma 225

H
Hausa 123, 133–134, 292, 294, 307, 309
Hawaiian 233, 246
Hdi 105–106, 118, 121–122, 133
Hebrew 4, 6, 309, 352

Hittite 349
Hona 112–113, 134
Hungarian 214, 271–273, 312

I
Icelandic 93, 185
Indo-European 5, 28, 45, 103, 105, 112, 114, 116, 128, 281, 310, 313–314, 357, 359, 378, 398, 400, 406–407
Indonesian 225, 240–241, 308–309, 354–355
Irish 4, 310, 374
Iroquoian 297–298, 310, 318, 356
Italian 4, 11–12, 38, 45, 49, 115, 327, 401

J
Japhug 289–290, 297
Japanese 28–29, 45, 88, 90–91, 215, 259–260, 262–263, 268, 270, 272, 275, 310, 355, 366, 374, 389, 391–410; *See also* Late Middle Japanese, Late Old Japanese
Jicarilla Apache 225
Jóola Karon 287, 309

K
Kadazan 225
Karo Batak 287–288, 308–309
Kaytetye 223
Kharia 354–355, 364
Khwe 284, 290, 296, 307, 310
Kikamba 380
Kiribati 7
Koasati 292, 307, 311
Konso 281–282, 302
Korean 8, 70, 72, 216, 219, 247, 310, 392, 401, 403, 409
Korean 8, 70, 72, 216, 219, 247, 310, 392, 401, 403, 409
Krongo 293, 308, 310
Kutenai 194, 312

L
Lakhota 311, 373
Lango 215, 296, 307, 311
Lao 170–172, 190–192, 194, 199, 317, 347, 354–355
Lappish 4
Late Archaic Chinese 354–355
Late Middle Japanese 397
Late Old Japanese 397
Latin 4, 8, 18, 20–21, 28, 37–38, 40, 44, 49, 52, 177–178, 191–192, 194, 200, 273, 280, 313–315, 317–325, 327, 330–331, 333–338, 341–343, 345–354, 356, 363, 378, 392, 395
Lele 118, 124, 132, 294, 306, 309
Lezgian 17, 229, 311
Lonwolwol 225

M
Maa 279, 299, 301–303
Malay 225, 394
Mandarin Chinese 6, 85, 311
Maori 222–223, 309
Mapuche/Mapudungun 286, 309
Masa 294, 309
Mina 104–106, 133–134
Mojave 293, 310
Mundari 309, 318, 354
Mupun Polish

N
Nahuatl 330–331, 362
Navajo 309, 382
Nepali 394
Ngawun 225
Nivkh 312, 381, 386–387

O
Old English 51
Old High German 349
Old Japanese 397

P
Pero 309, 385
Persian 310, 349, 392
Polish 105, 110, 116, 119–122, 125, 370
Portuguese 395, 401

Q
Quechua 4, 292, 308, 311, 354–355

R
Rapanui 296, 306, 309
Riau Indonesian 240–241, 354–355
Romance languages 21, 49, 381, 394, 406, 408
Romanian 395
Russian 8, 47–48, 52–53, 121, 181, 192, 194, 216, 218–219, 232, 235–236, 248, 310
RgVeda Sanskrit (abbrev. RV) 313–314, 321, 326, 333, 336–337, 345–349, 352, 354

S
Salish 283, 318, 354
Sandawe 285–286, 312
Sanskrit 20, 28, 313–315, 318, 320–327, 333, 336–338, 345–349, 352–354, 356, 359, 364–366; *See also* RgVeda Sanskrit
Semai 225
Semitic 5, 331, 337, 348, 352, 354
Sinhalese 240–241, 246
Sinitic languages 394
Skwxwú7mesh 283, 311
Spanish 4, 105, 115, 194, 229, 310, 395, 401
Stau 292, 311
Swedish 4

T
Tagalog 114, 134, 194, 214, 248, 309, 318
Thai 312, 391–394, 397, 401, 408
Tima 294, 305, 310
Tongan 354
Tswana 379
Turkana 287
Turkish 49, 51, 213, 216, 219, 232, 247, 312

V
Vedic Sanskrit
Vietnamese 51, 309, 380–381, 408

W
Wambaya 51
Wandala 105, 117, 133, 294, 306, 309
Wari' 293, 306, 309, 355
Weining Ahmao 213
Welsh 4
West Chadic 123

Y
Yaá Zapotec 382–384
Yankunytjatjara 230–232, 246
Yimas 286, 306, 310, 354–355
Yukaghir Kolyma

Author index

A
Adelung, J. C. 4
Aikhenvald, A. Y. 141, 154
Alama, J. 144, 146
Alamin, S. 294
Alfieri, L. 1, 3, 28, 220, 313, 314, 317, 319–323, 325, 326, 328, 333, 337, 343, 344, 347, 349–354, 356
Ambar, M. 79
Anderson, S. 79
Ansaldo, U. 328
Anward, Jan 328
Arkadiev, P. 9, 16, 18, 20, 220, 315
Armstrong, D. M. 217
Aronoff, M. 314, 319, 337, 338, 346, 350
Austin, J. 79, 80
Austin, P. K. 128
Auwera, J. van der 24, 110, 146, 147, 183, 187, 211, 217, 218
Azuma, S. 404

B
Baayen, H. R. 344
Bachnik, J. 405
Backhouse, A.E. 355
Baker, M. 346
Baker, M.C. 39
Bakker, M. 102
Bar-el, L. 283, 284
Bauer, L. 346, 352
Beauzée, N. 4
Beck, D. 12, 16, 19–21, 138, 193, 195, 196, 314, 315, 318, 328
Becker, A. 406
Belardi, W. 23, 349, 350
Benincà, P. 374
Benveniste, É. 337, 391, 394, 403
Berthould-Papandropoulou. I. 269
Bertram, R. 344
Bhat, D. N. S. 66, 324–326, 391, 399

Bickel, B. 12, 67
Biermann, A. 273
Biggs, B. 222
Bird, A. 183, 184
Bisang, W. 213, 328, 345, 354
Blevins, J. P. 314
Bloomfield, L. 146, 350
Boas, F. 66, 279, 280, 404
Bommelyn, L. 382
Booij, G. E. 45, 346
Bopp, F. 4, 320, 351–353
Bossong, G. 24, 346
Bostoen, K. 288, 289
Botha, R. 22
Bozzone, Ch. 314
Brentari, D. 39
Brereton, J.P. 336
Broschart, J. 330, 354
Brown, C. H. 218, 224–226, 235, 236, 244
Brown, D. 37
Brown, P. 402
Brugmann, K. 338
Bubenik, V. 107
Burrow, Th. 322
Butters, M. 101, 102, 107, 109
Bybee, J. 2, 7, 22, 194, 291, 299
Bynon, Th. 5

C
Cabredo-Hofherr, P. 282
Candotti, M. 324
Cardona, G. 324
Carnap, R. 140, 143–146, 149–151, 159, 160, 165, 167, 168, 172, 178, 188, 189
Cassirer, E. 393
Ceong, H. H. 70–72
Chafe, W. 108
Chomsky, N. A. 46, 63, 221, 346, 373
Chumakina, M. 37
Cinque, G. 79
Cipriano, P. 349
Clements, G. N. 39, 235
Cohen, D. 102

Collins, Ch. 284
Comrie, B. 2, 6, 38, 42, 63, 101, 194, 259, 260, 267, 269, 282, 299, 328, 370
Coniglio, M. 79
Cooke, J. R. 393, 394
Coquand, Th. 144
Corbett, G. G. 43, 44, 48, 63, 67, 102, 103, 299, 319, 372
Cordes, M. 151
Coseriu, E. 267, 316
Cowgill, W. 349
Creissels, D. 378, 379
Cristofaro, S. 23, 46, 279, 280, 318, 327, 328, 372
Croft, W. 2, 6, 8, 13, 15, 17–20, 22, 24, 28, 37, 48, 66, 69, 147, 177, 194, 213–215, 221, 241, 280, 290, 313, 315, 316, 318, 324, 325, 327–329, 331, 332, 335, 350, 354, 370, 374, 375
Crystal, D. 319
Culicover, P. W. 212–216, 223
Cusic, D. 298
Cuyckens, H. 102
Cysouw, M. 21, 102

D
Da Milano, F. 3, 28, 29, 140, 389, 395, 407
Daelemans, W. 234, 235
Dahl, E. 314
Dahl, Ö. 15, 17, 19–21, 211, 315
Daneš, F. 250–252
Dasher, R. B. 396, 402
Davidse, K. 102
De Benito Moreno, C. 374
Deemers, R. 352
Delbrück, B. 323
Demirdache, H. 318
Di Giovine, P. 349
Diessel, H. 399
Dik, S. 375
Diller, A. 391
Dimitriadis, A. 376, 377
Dimmendaal, G. 287

Dingemanse, M. 38, 49, 77, 78, 91–93
Dixon, R. M. W. 2, 114, 230, 232, 318, 325, 326, 329, 332, 344, 346, 347, 352, 371, 376, 377
Dom, S. 288, 289
Dowty, D. 263
Dressler, W. U. 268, 344
Dryer, M.S. 7, 9, 10, 13–15, 18–20, 24, 37, 66, 102, 103, 227, 228, 280, 282, 313, 318, 327, 332
Du Feu, V. 296
Duchier, D. 205
Dunn, M. J. 298
Durie, M. 293

E
Ebi, M. 393
Edwards, A. 105, 123
Elbert, S. H. 233
Etxepare, R. 79
Evans, N. J. 8, 22, 62, 77, 109, 328
Everaert, M. 370, 372, 376, 377
Everett, D. L. 9, 10, 16, 293, 355

F
Faltz, L. M. 368–370, 373–382, 384
Fenk, A. 102
Fenk-Oczlon, G. 102
Fillmore, Ch. 107
Finck 5
Fitting, M. 145, 146
Fitzgerald, C. M. 293
Flamini, S. 349
Floyd, S. 354
Foley, W. A. 286
Fortescue, M. 109
Frajzyngier, Z. 12, 26, 101, 102, 104, 105, 107, 109–111, 113, 114, 116–118, 121 123–126, 129, 130, 203, 294, 295, 368, 370, 372
François, J. 250
Fraser, B. 79
Fujii, Y. 401, 404
Fujimori, A. 90, 91

G
Gabelentz, G. von der 5, 6, 21, 146, 258, 354

Gair, J. W. 241
Galant, M. 382, 383
García García, L. 51
Garrigue-Cresswell, M. 118
Gast, V. 146, 147, 371, 375
Gates, J. 293
Geniušenė, E. 368, 370, 375
Georgakopoulos, Th. 290
Gerner, M. 213
Gil, D. 6, 7, 11, 15, 16, 20, 21, 24, 240, 315, 330, 355
Gildea, S. 279, 299
Givón, T. 2, 279, 382
Goddard, C. 227, 230–232
Gold, E. 84
Goldberg, A. 110, 125
Good, J. 21
Graffi, G. 5, 21
Granger, G. G. 103
Grassmann, H. 343
Greenberg, J. H. 2, 5, 6, 102, 273
Gren-Eklund, G. 326
Grewendorf, G. 46
Gross, M. 242, 319
Grossman, E. 54
Gruzdeva, E. 381
Guillaume, A. 109
Gupta, A. 141, 148–150, 157, 158, 187

H
Hacking, I. 184
Haegeman, L. 79, 346
Haiman, J. 372, 374
Halle, M. 221, 346
Hammarström, H. 283, 309
Hanks, W. 392, 404, 405
Harley, H. 235
Harris, Z. 352
Hasegawa, Y. 397, 404
Haspelmath, M. 2, 3, 5–9, 12, 15–18, 20, 22–27, 35, 37, 38, 39, 41–43, 45, 46, 48, 52, 66, 67, 69, 73, 76, 103, 137–143, 145, 147, 148, 151–159, 162–174, 176–180, 182–188, 191, 192, 194, 195, 197–199, 202–206, 211–224, 227–230, 232, 234, 237, 239, 242–245, 260, 264, 267, 270, 271, 273, 280–282, 290, 303, 313, 314, 316, 318, 324, 327, 329–332, 351–354,

356, 368, 370–377, 379, 392, 402
Hawkins, J. A. 7, 8
Heim, J. 79, 80, 81, 83, 90, 91
Heine, B. 102, 368, 392
Helmbrecht, J. 390
Hempel, C. G. 140
Hengeveld, K. 228, 239–241, 328, 329, 332, 335, 347, 354, 375
Hennig, M. 37
Herder, J. H. 4
Heritage, J. 82
Hewson, 107
Hill, V. 79
Hinds, J. 395–397
Hippisley, A. 218, 235, 236, 244
Hirschberg, J. 88
Hjelmslev, L. 5, 23
Holmes, J. 84
Hopper, P. J. 63, 329, 332, 347
Hurford, J. R.

I
I Gusti Ngurah, O.
Ishiyama, O. 22
Iwasaki, S. 327

J
Jacques, G. 289, 290, 297
Jaggar, Ph. 294
Jamison, S. 336
Janda, R. D. 315
Janic, K. 368, 382
Jelinek, E. 352
Jespersen, O. 146
Ježek, E. 336
Johnston, E. 104, 105, 123
Jones, P. 284
Jones, W. 284
Joos, M. 25, 66, 347
Joseph, B. D. 315
Joshi, Sh. D. 324, 325
Jungbluth, K. 395

K
Kaplan, R. M. 234, 235
Karlsson, F. 218
Kastovsky, D. 349
Kazenin, K. 375, 376, 384
Keenan, E. L. 2
Kemmer, S. 368, 370, 372, 375
Kern, B. 293, 355

Keyser, S. J. 39
Kibort, A. 46
Kilian-Hatz, Ch. 284, 290, 296
Kim, J.-B. 219
Kimball, G. D. 292
Kishimoto, H. 260–262, 265
Kittilä, S. 125, 370, 373–376
Klein, W. 108, 238
Koch, H. 223
Koh, A. S. 394
König, E. 11, 257, 369, 371, 374, 376, 383, 384
Korbmacher, J. 144, 146
Kornfilt, J. 213, 219
Kulikov, L. 368, 370, 371
Kuno, S. 397, 402
Kuroda, S.-Y. 395
Kuteva, T. 7, 22, 102, 110

L
Laca, B. 282
Ladd, D. R. 52
Lakoff, G. 51
Lander, Y. 18, 20, 220, 315
Langacker, R. W. 63, 250
LaPolla, R. J. 8–10, 19, 20, 243, 350
Launey, M. 330
Laurence, S. 147, 169, 173
Law, V. 320
Lazard, G. 2, 13, 15, 24, 42, 102–104, 313, 356, 370
Lazzeroni, R. 321, 323
Lee, Q. 219
Leech, G. 79, 193
Lehmann, C. 24, 46, 138, 139, 197, 201, 218, 233, 250, 254, 274, 336, 346, 392, 399, 407
Leibniz, G. 3, 4
Levinson, S.C. 8, 22, 62, 93, 402
Li, C.N. 85
Lidz, J. 375
Lieb, H.-H. 26, 137–140, 147, 163, 169, 173, 184, 186, 188, 196, 201–203, 205, 220, 233
Lieber, R. 50, 346
Lier, E. van 24, 241, 313, 318, 319, 327, 328
Lindström, E. 292
List, J. M. 37
Liu, M. 130
Löbel, E. 273

Lombardi Vallauri, E. 355
Luís, A. 50
Lyons, J. 314, 319, 336

M
MacDonell, A. A. 323, 338
Maddieson, I. 24, 211
Maiden, M. 243
Malchukov, A. 259, 269
Maranz, A. 347
Margetts, A. 128
Margolis, E. 147, 169, 173
Marlo, M. R. 380
Martin, S. E. 396, 397
Martinet, A. 314
Massam, D. 50
Mathesius, V. 252
Matthews, P. H. 319, 346
Matthewson, L. 318
Mattiola, S. 3, 27, 28, 279, 280, 288, 290, 299, 301
Mayerthaler, W. 344
McCloy, D. 44
McGinn, C. 217
Meillet, A. 337
Mel'čuk, I. 350
Melis, A. 294
Michaelis, S. 6
Milewski, T. 102
Mithun, M. 108, 109, 293, 298, 318, 356
Mittwoch, A. 79
Miyagawa, Sh. 262
Miyashita, H. 368
Moran, S. 44
Moravcsik, E. A. 11, 20, 181, 197, 201, 217, 218, 233, 328, 331
Morgenroth, W.
Morpurgo Davies, A. 4
Mosby Irgens, B. 407
Mosel, U. 330
Mous, M. 302
Moyse Faurie, C. 369, 371
Mugdan, J. 314, 353
Munkaila, M. 123
Munro, P. 293
Munshi, S. 292
Mycielski, J. 129

N
Narrog, H. 102
Nduku Kioko, A. 380
Nedjalkov, V. 381

Nefdt, R. 184
Newman, P. 123, 281, 294
Newmeyer, F. J. 20, 24, 51, 211, 216
Nichols, J. 16, 17, 36
Noonan, M. 296
Nordhoff, S. 16
Nordlinger, R. 51, 62

O
Orilia, F. 145, 146, 169
Orkaydo, O. O. 282, 302
Otaina, G. 381
Otanes, F. T. 114
Otsuka, M. 405
Oyanguren, P. 400, 401

P
Pagliuca, W. 291, 299
Panagl, O. 344, 349
Parmentier, Y. 205
Paul, W. 79
Payne, D. L. 279, 302
Perdue, C. 108
Perkins, R. 291, 299
Peterson, J. 255
Plank, F. 7, 23, 328
Pokorny, J. 348
Poletto, C. 374
Polis, S. 290
Pomerantz, A. 93
Pontillo, T. 324
Poole, K. 69
Pozza, M. 349
Premper, W. 6, 27, 249, 251, 267, 268
Puddu, N. 3, 28, 140, 327, 368, 374, 382
Pukui, M. K. 233

Q
Quine, W. v. O. 150, 228
Quinn, C. J. 406, 407

R
Radetzky, P. 126, 129
Radicchi, A. 324
Ramat, P. 1, 4, 5, 12, 18, 318, 336
Reh, M. 293
Reiner, T. 27, 197, 198, 201, 211, 239, 240
Reinhart, T. 370, 379
Renou, L. 323

Reuland, E. 50, 370
Riemer, N. 227
Rijkhoff, J. 7, 13, 18–20, 211, 215, 217, 241, 316, 319, 328, 354
Ritter, E. 74, 98
Rizzi, G. 79
Roberts, I. 69, 202
Robins, R. H. 319
Ross, J. R. 79–81
Roth, H. 320
Round, E. 54
Rousseau, A. 69
Rousseau, J. 352
Rumsey, A. 7

S
Sadler, L. 62
Sahoo, K. 24, 183, 187, 211, 217, 218
Sambou, P. 287
Sapir, E. 5, 347
Sasse, H.-J. 318, 324, 328
Saussure, F. de 23, 258, 337, 356
Scalise, S. 346
Schachter, P. 114, 214
Schladt, M. 370
Schreuder, R. 344
Schuh, R. 105
Schwabauer, M. 101
Segerer, G. 288, 289
Seiler, H. 6, 27, 140, 249–259, 263, 266–274
Shay, E. 101, 105, 107, 110, 121, 126, 130, 372
Shibasaki, R. 397, 402
Shibatani, M. 5, 397
Shimizu, H. 404
Shopen, T. 318, 324
Siegwart, G. 151
Siemund, P. 374
Siewierska, A. 102, 328, 354, 390, 391, 393, 399
Siloni, T. 379
Simone, R. 27, 279, 336
Skirgård, H. 16
Smeets, I. 286
Smith, T. 50, 126, 129
Sohn, H.-M. 403
Sommerfelt, A. 23

Song, K.-A. 392
Součková, K. 292
Speas, P. 79, 80
Speijer, J. S. 324, 325
Spencer, A. 47, 48, 50, 54, 214
Stassen, L. 2, 241, 317, 318, 324, 325, 328, 330, 352
Steeman, S. 285, 286
Stefanini, J. 115
Steinthal, 5
Stock, M. 217
Stock, W. 217
Stivers, T. 93
Sugamoto, N. 391, 407
Suppes, P. 141, 151, 158, 178
Suzuki, T. 401
Swadesh, M. 11
Swoyer, Ch. 145, 146, 169
Sybesma, R. 271

T
Tatevosov, S. 299
Taylor, J. R. 51
Tenny, C. 79, 80
Thieme, P. 339
Thoma, S. C. 83
Thomasson, A. 146, 201
Thompson, S. A. 63, 329, 332, 347
Tobin, E. 182, 184
Tomasello, M. 22
Tonhauser, J. 62
Torreira, F. 93
Touratier, Ch. 314
Trask, L. 352
Traugott, E. C. 396, 402
Tremblay, M. 84
Troupeau, G. 352
Truckenbrodt, H. 89, 92
Tsujimura, N. 397

U
Uehara, S. 355
Unterbeck, B. 273

V
van de Velde, M. 294–296
van der Auwera, J. 24, 110, 146, 147, 211, 217, 218

van Lier, E. 24, 241, 313, 318, 319, 327, 328
Van Valin Jr., R. D. 243
Vanhove, M. 279, 288, 301
Vater, J. S. 4
Verstraete, J-Ch. 102
Veselinova, L. N. 282
Vogel, P. M. 328, 330, 354
Völkel, S. 354
von Humboldt, W. 250
Vovin, A. 402

W
Wade, T. 218
Wakefield, J. 88
Wakernagel, J. 323
Ward, G. L. 88
Weber, B. 233
Weber, D. J. 292
Weibegué, Ch. 118
Wetzel, L. 198
Wetzer, H. 317
Whitman, J. 400–402
Whitney, W. D. 323
Wierzbicka, A. 227
Wiltschko, M. 2, 3, 8, 26, 59, 61–63, 67–69, 72–75, 77, 79, 80, 83, 84, 94
Windischmann, K. J. 4
Wittgenstein, L. 106
Wodtko, D. 348
Wohlgemuth, J. 102
Wood, E. 285
Woollams, G. 287, 288
Wright, W. 352
Wundt, W. 5

Y
Yamaguchi, Y. 402
Yamamoto, M. 403
Ye, Y. 130

Z
Zaefferer, D. 239
Zegraen, I. 79
Zhang, B. 85
Zu, V. 79
Zúñiga, F. 370, 373–376